THE BLACK BERET

THE HISTORY OF SOUTH AFRICA'S ARMOURED FORCES

Volume 1: Beginnings to the Invasion of Madagascar 1942

Willem Steenkamp

Helion

Helion & Company Limited
26 Willow Road
Solihull
West Midlands
B91 1UE
England
Tel. 0121 705 3393
Fax 0121 711 4075
Email: info@helion.co.uk
Website: www.helion.co.uk
Twitter: @helionbooks
Visit our blog http://blog.helion.co.uk/

Published by Helion & Company 2016
Designed and typeset by Kerrin Cocks, SA Publishing Services
Cover designed by Paul Hewitt, Battlefield Design (www.battlefield-design.co.uk)
Printed by Gutenberg Press Limited, Tarxien, Malta

Text © SA Armour Association 2016
Photographs courtesy of the SANDF Archives
Maps drawn by George Anderson © Helion & Company 2016

ISBN 978-1-910294-68-0

British Library Cataloguing-in-Publication Data.
A catalogue record for this book is available from the British Library.

For details of other military history titles published by Helion & Company Limited contact the above address, or visit our website: http://www.helion.co.uk.

We always welcome receiving book proposals from prospective authors.

This book is dedicated to the men and women that wear the Black Beret of the Armour, past, present and future.
Lest we forget.

Contents

Foreword (Crew Commander) — 6
Foreword (National President of the South African Armour Association) — 6
Author's note — 6
List of maps — 8
List of photographs — 19

PART I: THE FORERUNNERS
1. Armour comes to the battlefield — 26
2. Horse versus armoured car: the German South West Africa Campaign — 35
3. The invasion begins at last — 43
4. Armoured cars in North Africa — 54
5. France … and South Africa's first acquaintance with tanks — 63
6. Armoured cars in East Africa — 69
7. First steps to mechanization — 78
8. The Pirow years — 90

PART II: THE EAST AFRICAN CAMPAIGN
9. The South African Tank Corps is born — 98
10. Preparation for Abyssinia — 111
11. First blood at El Wak — 122
12. Three days at El Yibo — 132
13. Invasion — 143
14. Problems at Banya Fort, victory at Mega — 152
15. Somaliland: Glory for the Armour — 161
16. Breakthrough at Yonte — 166
17. The great race to Addis Ababa — 174
18. The fall of Amba Alagi — 181
19. The southern battle for the lakes — 186
20. The northern battle for the lakes — 197

PART III: THE WAR IN THE DESERT
21. The South African Tank Corps takes shape as disaster strikes — 206
22. 4 South African Armoured Car Regiment is blooded — 218
23. Operation Crusader: test of fire — 235
24. War in the north and south — 245
25. South African disaster, and triumph — 251
26. The tide begins to turn — 265
27. Push to Benghazi — 276
28. Rommel strikes again — 289
29. The Gazala Gallop — 298
30. Retreat to the east — 306
31. Standing firm at El Alamein — 313
32. Under new management — 324
33. Breakout, victory and pursuit — 334

PART IV: THE MADAGASCAR INVASION
34. The invasion of Madagascar — 344

Epilogue — 354
Acknowledgements — 355
Index — 356
List of donors — 366

Foreword
(Crew Commander)

This is the story of men, fighting men, who served their country in the South African Armoured Corps. These men in their black berets have earned the respect of many, friend and foe alike. That black beret remains the symbol of their discipline, their efficiency and their dedication.

Their story starts in 1946 when just after the end of the Second World War the South African Armoured Corps was first established. Before this many regiments existed with long and illustrious histories of service even before the advent of the first armoured fighting vehicles, service as mounted units, the predecessors of today's mechanized forces. The stories of these mounted units have been recorded in several fine regimental histories and are not repeated here; however, they serve as the background to this book.

In 1993 when the Armour Association came into being, one of the goals set was to have the history of our corps recorded before too many aspects of that history was lost to time itself. This goal was a major one, sources of information had to be identified, an author had to be found and funds had to be raised.

May this book serve as motivation to all of the South African Armoured Corps members of the future.

*First Crew Commander and Honorary Life President of the South African Armour Association, the late Lieutenant-General John Raymond Dutton SSA, SD, SM, MMM

Foreword
(National President of the South African Armour Association)

It gives me great pleasure to be able to write the foreword of this first volume of The Black Beret, the story of South Africa's Armour. Through the efforts of countless contributors, with stops and starts over a period of 23 years, this opening volume can finally be shared with a very patient armour community and military historians the world over. The story is a fascinating one, made up of brave and interesting characters and equally importantly the solid core of men and women of the S.A.A.C. The narrative by Willem Steenkamp, a master storyteller brings them to life.

Yours in Armour,
Lieutenant-Colonel Heinrich Janzen
National President South African Armour Association
South Africa, 2016

Author's notes

This first volume of the South African Armoured Corps history has been a long a-borning. One might wonder why, given the fact that the SAAC itself is of comparatively recent vintage as these things go. But the SAAC of today is the latest stage in a long evolutionary process from which grew not only the development of its weaponry but, more important still, an institutional and doctrinal memory which extended over many decades, in spite of the fact that at several times defence funding was so skimpy and the armed forces so neglected that it was enough to daunt the stoutest heart.

Yet through all the bad times a core of dedicated men – not all of them armour – persisted with their dreams and managed to turn them into something more concrete, never forgetting the experience of the past but not letting it dictate the future. Oftentimes their ideas went against their seniors' conventional wisdom, much of which was still solidly rooted in the World War II experience (this, of course, is not unique: as General Heinz Guderian once ruefully noted, "It is sometimes tougher to fight my superiors than the French.") but they did not let go of the institutional memory.

In *Patton the Commander*, on the life of General George Patton, probably the greatest Allied armour leader of World War II, Major-General Hubert Essame wrote: "Little-minded men live entirely in the present; the minds of big men with historical imagination … range not only into the future but into the past." And so it was here. The lessons learnt in previous campaigns were developed and elements were transmuted into policy for the future, and so in this volume those early lessons and the experience from which they sprang have been described in appropriate detail.

It is my belief that one reason for the South African Defence Force's victories against huge odds during the fierce Angolan fighting of 1987 and 1988 was the fact that its officers were steeped in the tail-end of a doctrinal development process whose roots went back to before they were born, an advantage that their opponents did not have.

To an extent, of the course, the first volume is also a brief history of the Special Service Battalion, a unique unit which began as a social experiment but ended up becoming a premier armoured regiment of the Defence Force and a veritable breeding ground of future generals. Several of them were involved in the launch of the history project, and, to the great sadness of all, two died before the project yielded its first fruits, Lieutenant-General Jack Dutton and Brigadier-General O. J. 'Schalkie' Schalkwyk.

Another, Brigadier-General M. B. Anderson, compiled a great amount of historical material, and valuable further contributions of material, technical and otherwise, were made by a large number of armour men of the younger generation, too numerous to all be mentioned here, but among them Brigadier-General H. B. 'Fido' Smit, Colonel John French and Lieutenant-Colonel William Marshall, the country's leading expert on the renowned Marmon-Herrington armoured cars of World War II.

A great deal of the post-World War II material will only be seen in a later volume, at the correct points of the SAAC chronology, but it is worth waiting for.

Speaking for myself, it was a great honour to be asked to write this book, since I am not an armour man – although, as a mechanised infantryman, there is obviously a close association, and I like to think I have something of a special feel for the earlier campaigns of World War II as my father served in both Abyssinia and the Western Desert.

Later in the series Helmoed-Römer Heitman, an acknowledged expert on armoured matters, will be drawn in for his contribution to the fighting in Angola in the late 1980s and developments in armour of that period. His encyclopaedic knowledge will doubtless provide for a great enhancement of the armour story.

And at the end of it, we all hope, there will be a record of the South African Armoured Corps which will stand the test of time and be read far into the future by generations yet unborn.

List of maps

German South West Africa Campaign, September 1914–July 1915   9

East Africa Campaign, October 1940–February 1941   10

East Africa Campaign, Italian Somaliland, February 1941   11

Abyssinian Campaign: Battle for the Lakes, March–May 1941   12

Abyssinian Campaign: Allied Thrust through Addis Ababa to Asmara, March–November 1941   13

Western Desert Area of Operations, 1941–1942   14

Relief of Tobruk: Operation Crusader, 18 November–31 December 1941   15

Allied Collapse at Sidi Rezegh: Operation Crusader, 18 November–31 December 1941   16

Eighth Army Retreat from Gazala, 26 May–21 June 1942   17

Allied Invasion of Madagascar, 5 May 1942–6 November 1942   18

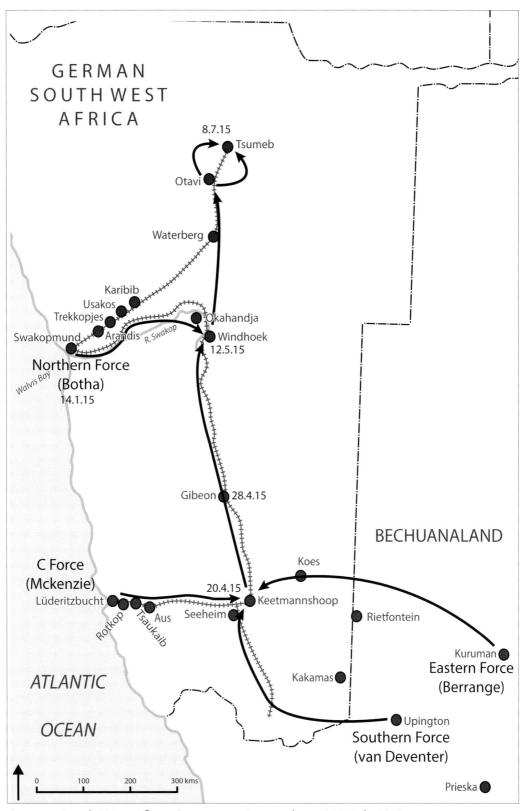

German South West Africa Campaign, September 1914–July 1915

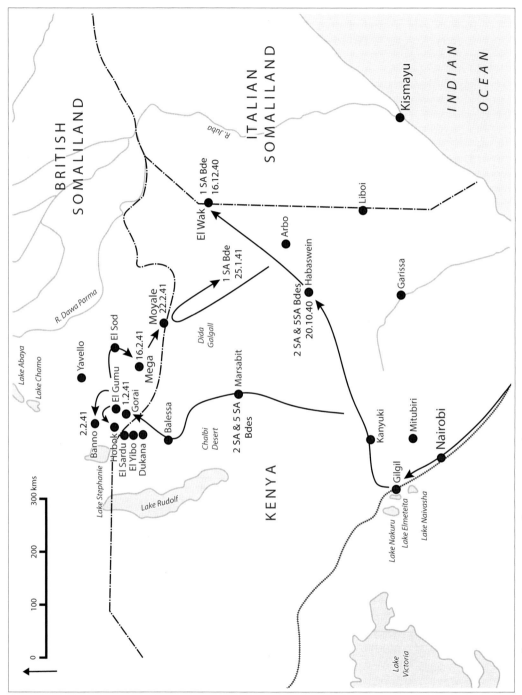

East Africa Campaign, October 1940–February 1941

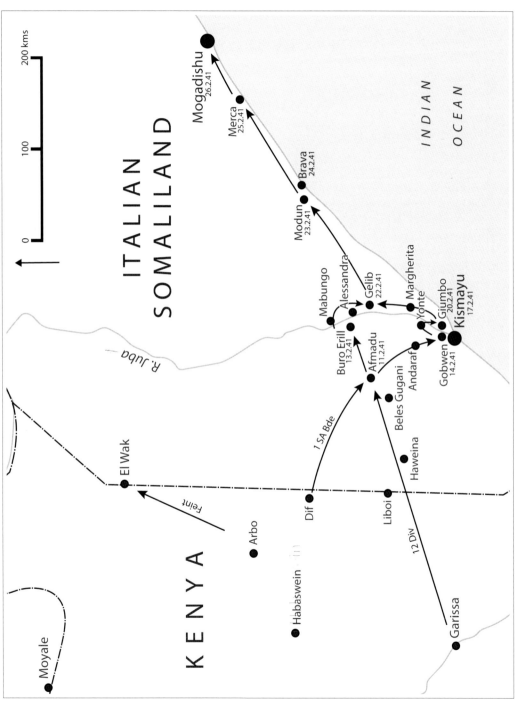

East Africa Campaign, Italian Somaliland, February 1941

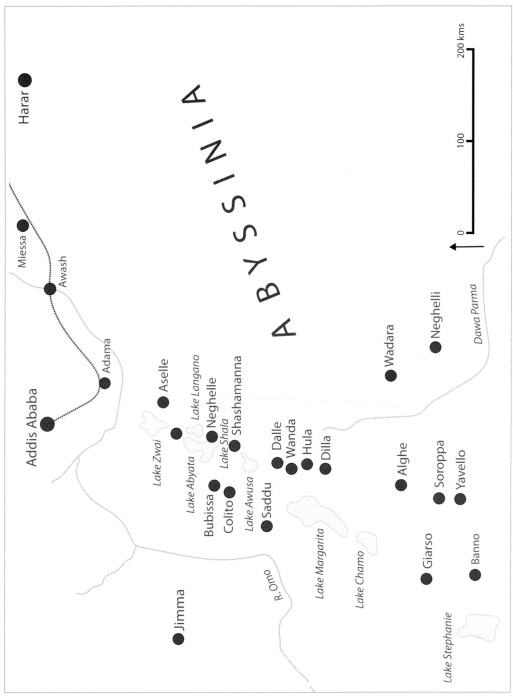

Abyssinian Campaign: Battle for the Lakes, March–May 1941

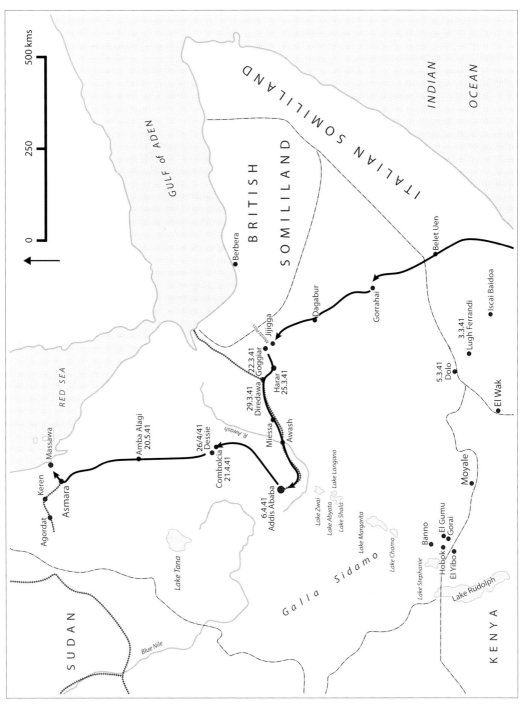

Abyssinian Campaign: Allied Thrust through Addis Ababa to Asmara, March–November 1941

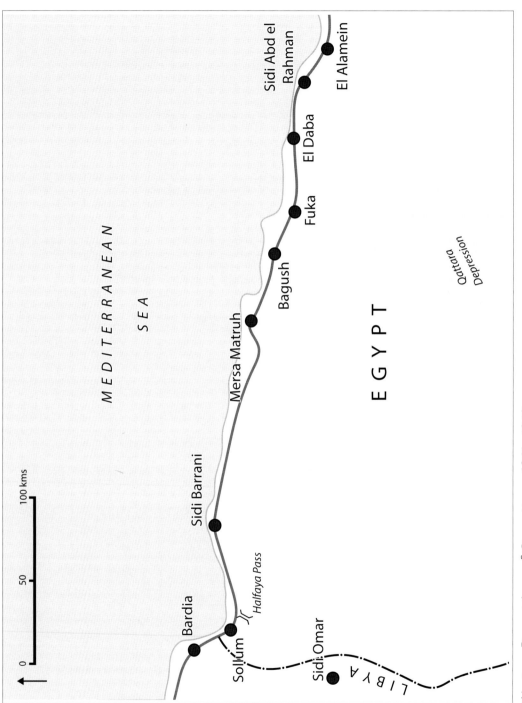

Western Desert Area of Operations, 1941–1942

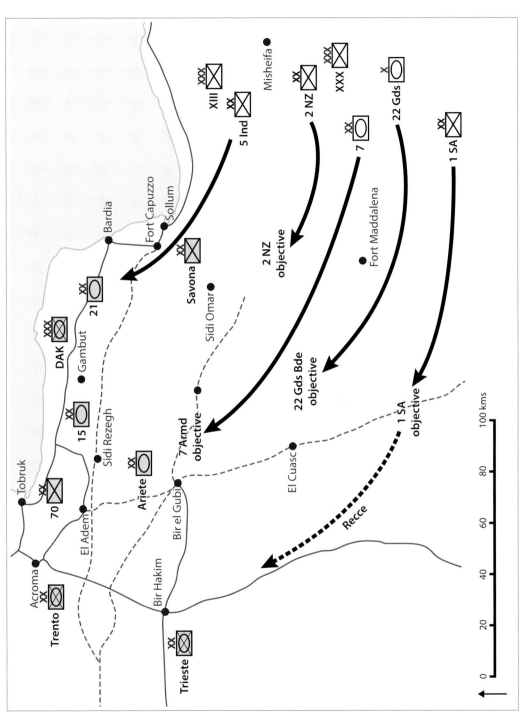

Relief of Tobruk: Operation Crusader, 18 November–31 December 1941

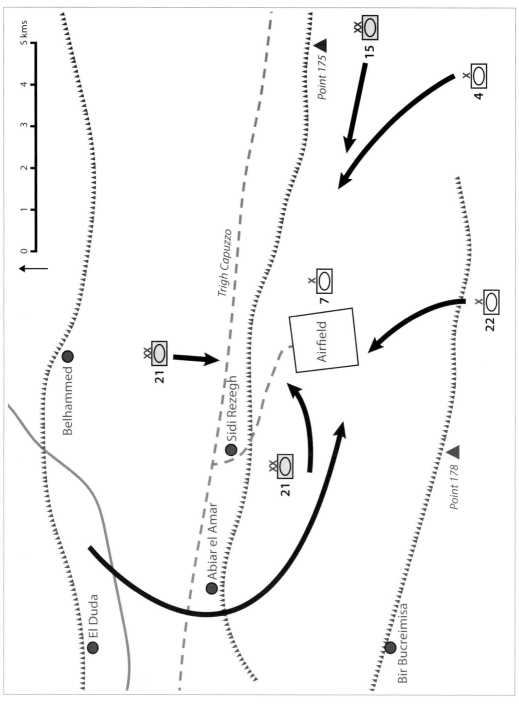

Allied Collapse at Sidi Rezegh: Operation Crusader, 18 November–31 December 1941

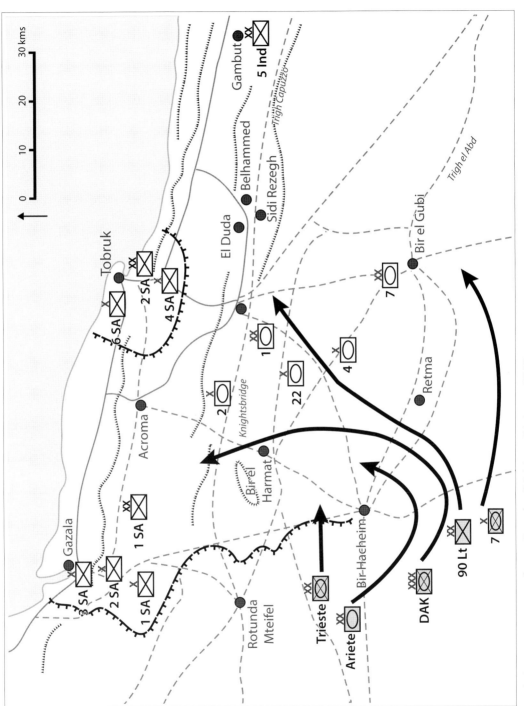

Eighth Army Retreat from Gazala, 26 May–21 June 1942

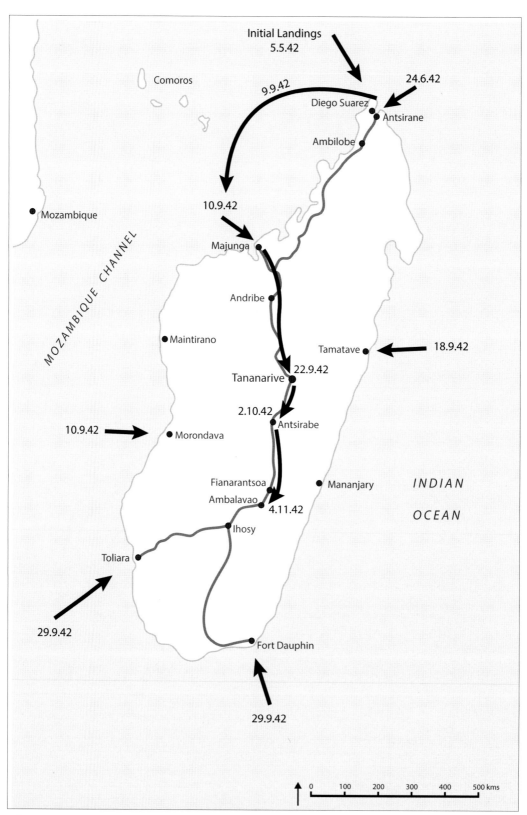

Allied Invasion of Madagascar, 5 May 1942–6 November 1942

List of photographs

Not all armoured trains relied on armour plating. The 'Hairy Mary' was draped in heavy ropes to protect its vulnerable boiler from rifle fire. 29

The British armoured ox wagons which served as a mobile pillbox during the Boer war. 29

A British armoured train ambushed at Kraaipan, October 1899. 31

General French's cavalry near Bloemfontein during the Anglo–Boer War. 33

Lieutenant Alexander Von Scheele used an Aviatik P14 to bomb the South African forces. 37

An airborne Aviatik. 37

Two British BE2C biplanes (left) and some French-built Henri Farman Shorthorns (right) served during the campaign. 39

German forces made use of camels for transporting man and equipment. 40

RNAS Rolls Royce ACs at Walvis Bay during the First World War. 40

Motor car commandos returning after a patrol. 41

RNAS Rolls Royce armoured car doing its first water crossing in the arid German South West Africa. 41

General Louis Botha. 45

Eight Rolls Royce ACs in German South West Africa, RNAS. 45

RNAS Rolls Royce GSWA, 1915. 47

Rolls Royce armoured cars used during the campaign. 47

RNAS Rolls Royce Armoured Cars in German South West Africa. 49

RNAS Rolls Royce armoured cars that participated in the battles at Trekkopjes, the first use of mechanized armour in southern Africa. 49

Armoured cars were brought ashore with considerable difficulty; they had to be ferried and manhandled with great care on to the beach. 51

RNAS Rolls Royce in German South West Africa. 51

Brigadier-General Lukin. 58

Seabrook armoured cars in the desert. 59

The Duke's cars were none other than the Rolls-Royce Admiralty 1914 Pattern type. 59

'Big Willie' Mk3 Male 'Iron Duke' France, First World War. 66

'Big Willie' Male at Flers, First World War. 67

Mk1 Female tank, France, First World War. 67

RNAS AC Rolls Royce in German East Africa, 1917. 71

Leyland Armoured car in German East Africa. 71

General J. L. van Deventer GOC RSA Forces GEA. 75

RNAS AC Rolls Royce in GEA 1917. 75

Armored Leyland Truck, HLMS *Nemesis*, used during the Rand Rebellion of 1922 by the SAP. 79

A white-topped Crossley armoured in South West Africa during the Mpumbo Rebellion. 79

Crossley armoured car near rifle stacks at the Indaba held at *Knobkierie* pan during the Ipumbu Revolt in Owamboland, South West Africa. 81

Demonstration of Whippet tank HMLS *Union* in Cape Town, 1920s. 81

Demonstration of Whippet tank HMLS *Union* in Cape Town, 1920s. 83

Home-built armoured car based on the Leyland Truck used by the UDF during 1922 Rand Rebellion. 83

Line up of the UDF armour in 1930s, two Crossleys, two Vickers Mk1s and the Whippet. 84

Rand Strike 1922, Leyland Armoured Truck 'HOT AZELL' and the Whippet. 85

The Whippet HMLS *Union* during the 1922 Rand Rebellion with some men of the
    Transvaal Scottish. 85
Vickers Mk1A gives a demonstration to the SSB. 87
A South African Vickers tank in base camp. 8
Oswald Pirow, minister of defense. 93
Pirows Bush Carts on parade in Pretoria. 93
Pirow's Bush Carts in action during the East African Campaign. 95
SA MaHe Mk 1 2 wheel drive. 95
Camouflaged SA Marmon Herrington Mk1 cars (U601 & U602) alongside truck convoy. 101
MaHe experimental during sand trails circa 1944. 101
MaHe1 on the way to Komatipoort to stop an invasion from Portuguese East Africa. 103
MaHe1 in field trials near Barberton. 103
Crossley upgrade with heavy duty desert tyres with white dome to reduce heat. 105
MaHe Mk1 AC with Vickers protruding from the left hull. 105
Production of MaHe ACs in South Africa. 107
The production of an MaHe Mk1 in a South African factory. 107
SA MaHe Mk2 on training near Barberton. 109
Badge of the South African Tank Corps during the Second World War. 109
Crew of aHe Mk2 maintain one of the Vickers MGs, East Africa. 113
Vickers Light Tank being loaded onto a portee, East Africa. 113
Vickers Light Tank with crew. 115
Vickers Light Tank with crew giving good indication of size. 115
Harley Davidson Motorcycle Company. 117
Harley Davidson and sidecar as used by the motorcycle companies. 117
1 SA Light Tank Company Vickers Light Tank on a Tank Portee truck. 123
Crew members of No. 1 South African Armoured Car Company, carrying out First Parades
    on their Marmon Herrington armoured cars. 123
Crew discussion. Marmon Herrington Mk 2 in the Abyssinian bush. 125
The driver of a Vickers Mk6 of 1 SA Light Tank Company. 125
Vickers Mk6 light tank being off loaded from a Portee truck. 127
A Vickers Mk3 and its crew in Abyssinia, East Africa. 127
Lieutenant Wensley in his Vickers 3 tank in Abyssinia, 1940. 128
South African Light Tank Company Vickers 3 being loaded onto a Portee truck. 129
A Vickers Mk3 of 1 SA Light Tank Company. 129
A convoy of Marmon Herrington Mk2s and trucks from 1 Armoured Car Company travelling
    through East Africa. 136
Marmon Herrington Mk2 1941, with crew and local. 137
A Marmon Herrington Mk2 at El Gumu, where the South Africans captured an enemy
    outpost. 137
Vickers Light Tank. 145
South African Engineers R2D to the rescue and pulling out a stuck Marmon Herrington
    Mk 2, Abyssinia. 145
Captured Italian cannon displayed in front of Fort Mega, Abyssinia. 157
Italian Fort Mega, Abyssinia. 157
South African Marmon Herrington Mk2 crossing the Union Bridge over the Juba River. 162
Marmon Herrington Mk2 cars in the field during the Abyssinian campaign. 163
South African troops, with Marmon Herrington Mk2 U23207, rest behind cover during the
    East African campaign. 163
Marmon Herrington Mk2 crossing a pontoon bridge at Bole, East Africa. 177
MaHe Mk2 on a pontoon bridge in East Africa during the Second World War. 177

Marmon Herrington Mk2 and a truck of 1 Armoured Car Company stuck in the mud after heavy rains in East Africa. 198

Natal Mounted Riflemen at the outbreak of the Second Word War carrying out 3-inch Mortar drills. 199

NMR Company wading through a swollen Dandada river, Abyssinia. 199

Marmon Herrington Mk 2. 209

Marmon Herrington Mk 5 trials. 209

Marmon Herringtons on patrol on Robben Island during the Second World War. 213

Marmon Herrington undergoing river crossing trails. 213

Marmon Herrington Mk2 during training the South African Lowveld. 214

MaHe Mk2 on training manoeuvres in the South African Eastern Transvaal (now Mpumalanga). 215

MaHe Mk3 armoured cars on coastal patrol on Robben Island stop at the Light House. 215

4th Armoured Car Regiment members with their Marmon Herrington Mk3. They were part of the 7th Armour Division, the Desert Rats and were entitled to wear the red Jerboa emblem. 219

4th Armoured Car Regiment Marmon Herrington Mk3 crew, Klerck, White Wittenberg, Wright. 219

4th Armoured Car Regiment Marmon Herrington Mk 3, named *Jakhals* II. 221

4th Armoured Car Regiment Marmon Herrington Mk 3 named *Rooikat* II. 221

4th Armoured Car Regiment officers. 223

4th Armoured Car Regiment other ranks. 223

4th Armoured Car Regiment officers. 223

4th Armoured Car Regiment other ranks. 223

4th Armoured Car Regiment_troopers on a training device. 224

Marmon Herrington Mk2 used for Anti-Aircraft purposes in Libya. 225

Marmon Herrington Mk 3 crew busy with a tyre change in North Africa. 225

Mamon Herrington Mk 3 upgunned with an Italian 47mm gun. 227

Marmon Herrington Mk2s and 3s cover a mountain pass in North Africa. 227

Marmon Herrington Mk2 bogged down in sand. 229

Members of Regiment President Steyn, unfortunately only their first names are known: Fish, Percy, Tim, James and Gordon. 229

South African troops in Marmon Herrington Mk 2s and Mk3s in Maddalena, Western Desert. 231

South African troops in Marmon Herrington Mk2 in Derna, Libya. 231

South African troops in Marmon Herrington Mk2s liaise with locals in Derna, Libya. 233

South African troops in Marmon Herrington Mk2s liaise with locals in Derna, Libya. 233

4th Armoured Car Regiment Marmon Herrington Mk2, *Jakhals* II. 239

Marmon Herrington Mk 2 at the occupation of Derna airport North Africa. 239

A Marmon Herrington Mk 2 observe destroyed German Ju52s at Derna Airfield, Libya. 241

A Marmon Herrington Mk 2 observe destroyed German JU52s at Derna Airfield, Libya. 241

An armoured wireless transmission car with a Lewis MG in the Western Desert. 247

A crew tent set up on the side of a Marmon Herrington Mk 3 U40654, with the Vickers gun protruding from the top. 247

Marmon Herrington Mk 3 under shell fire in North Africa. 258

Marmon Herrington Mk 3 used by C Squadron, Kings Dragoon Guards. 259

Post delivered by motorcycle U99326 to Marmon Herrington Mk 2 'Peggy', North Africa. 259

Marmon Herrington Mk 3 'Dairy' in North Africa. 267

Marmon Herrington Mk 3 in North Africa. 267

Marmon Herrington Mk 3 observes a German Ju-87 Stuka destroyed at Knightsbridge. 269

South African Marmon Herrington Mk 3 crew look out over the Mediterranean Sea. 269

South African Marmon Herrington Mk 3 crew look out over the Mediterranean Sea. 271

South African troops, in front of a Marmon Herrington Mk3, enjoying chicken in the streets of Cairo. 271

South African troops in Marmon Herrington Mk 2s and Mk 3s in Benghazi, Libya. 273

South African troops with their Marmon Herrington Mk 2 turret replaced by an Italian Breda 47mm gun. 273

Upgunned Marmon Herrington Mk 2, North Africa. 275

Upgunned Marmon Herrington Mk 2 with the 47mm Italian Breda gun, North Africa. 275

7 Field Regiment Marmon Herrington Mk 3, North Africa. 291

After the Gazala Gallop. 291

Marmon Herrington Mk 3 and crew. 295

The Marmon Herrington Mk 3 "Moon" and its crew at Gazala 1942. 295

44 Tank Repair Workshop, Alexandria, Egypt. 314

Marmon Herrington Mk 3 U38396 named 'Glamour Wagon' prepares for a patrol. 315

South African troops with a Ford Truck and a Marmon Herrington Mk 3 in the Egyptian Western Desert. 315

Lt Col Newton King, Natal Carbineers, Officer Commanding 4/6 Armoured Car Regiment. 326

Marmon Herrington Mk 2 and Mk3. 327

Sherman Mk V, Khatatba, Egypt, 1943. 327

Marmon Herrington Mk 2 in the streets of Benghazi. 335

Marmon Herrington Mk3s in North Africa. 335

Lieutenant-Colonel Reeves Moore, Imperial Light Horse, Officer Commanding 4th Armoured Car Regiment. 337

South African troops in a Marmon Herron Mk 2 and Mk3 in Benghazi, Libya. 337

South African troops in a Marmon Herrington Mk 3 pass Sikh troops. 339

Allied parade in Cairo, two Marmon Herrington Mk 3s. 341

Allied parade in Cairo, a SA MaHe Mk3 can be seen. 341

Marmon Herrington Mk 3 named 'Jeneuro' during the Madagascar invasion. 347

A South African Marmon Herrington Mk 3 at a roadblock on Madagascar. 347

PART ONE

THE FORERUNNERS

1

Armour Comes to the Battlefield

It is said that the first mention of armoured vehicles in recorded history can be found in the bible, in the Book of Judges: "And the Lord was with Judah; and he drave out the inhabitants of the mountain, but he could not drive out the inhabitants of the valley, because they had chariots of iron."

There is no indication that the chariots were actually armoured, but the principle of a soldier riding on or in an armoured conveyance appeared many centuries before the mechanized age. In fact clues within the Book of Judges suggest this may well have taken place prior to 1004 BC. The armoured soldier, mounted on an armoured steed, certainly made an appearance in the 50-year protracted Peloponnesian War when the ancient Greek cities of Athens and Sparta fought as allies against Persia, ending in 449 BC.

The Greek hoplites were the best heavy infantry of the era and could easily overcome the lightly armed Persians in a set-piece battle. But the Persians were masters of mobile warfare and surprise attacks, making good use of the terrain. Two lessons emerged from the Peloponnesian War.

The first was the importance of man-portable distance weapons, in this case the sling, the javelin and above all, the bow. The second was the need for heavily armoured cavalry to support the light horsemen – already a feature of most armies at the time. The equipment and weapons of the armoured horseman varied as concepts developed in the ensuing years; ancient depictions provide a good picture of at least one, the Persian heavy cavalryman of that era.

The Persian light cavalryman typically wore a cloth headdress, long trousers and a quilted cloth cuirass under a tunic. His offensive weapons consisted of two javelins, and he carried a light sword or single-handed battle axe for personal defence. He and his comrades were not shock troops, they were scouts and mobile raiders who could dash within range of the close-packed enemy infantry ranks, throw their javelins and pull back to rearm for another foray.

The Persian heavy cavalryman, on the other hand, wore a bronze helmet, a linen corselet with metal protective bands over his shoulders and bronze scales on his torso and legs. He carried two javelins and a short sword. There was nothing unusual about body armour *per sé*, but his horse, larger and heavier than that of the light cavalryman's, also wore armour – around its neck hung a leather-and-cloth apron covered in bronze scales and its forehead and nose were protected by a spoon-shaped piece of bronze plate armour. In a very real sense this was the first armoured 'vehicle'.

As time went by the concept of what became known as the cataphract – a soldier in full armour, on an armoured horse, carrying a lance and often working in cooperation with unarmoured, light-mounted archers – was adopted by many armies.

Later, in the 5th century, we find references to specialized cavalrymen of the Byzantine armies called the *Equites Sagittarii Clibanarii* – heavy-armoured archers on armoured horses. This meant that the 'tank' of antiquity now had a true distance weapon, the bow and arrow.

The cavalryman did not come completely into his own until the 6th century when the armies of Europe and Persia began to use solid tree saddles with cantles and stirrups. This was such a vital technological innovation that it has been regarded with the same significance for the conduct of warfare as the printing press was for civil society.

A solid-frame saddle reduced friction along the centreline of a horse's back, increasing its endurance and making it easier for a rider to control his mount, the stirrups gave him balance and support which helped him use his sword more effectively and the cantle increased his lethality with a lance.

By this time the basic pattern for mobile warfare had long been established. The fast-moving, daring light cavalry on small, nimble horses, trained, armed and organized for scouting and swift cut-and-thrust attacks were supported by the heavy cavalry, armoured men on large horses tasked with smashing into the enemy infantry, throwing it into confusion and then cutting it down, and of course fighting other heavily armoured men.

That basic pattern endures, although the light horseman now rides in an armoured vehicle or light tank and the heavy cavalryman in a main battle tank.

The greatest proponent of cavalry in ancient times was undoubtedly the Mongols' Genghis Khan, whose horsemen overran and conquered huge swathes of eastern Russia and today's Middle East. On one occasion, when a Mongol caravan and its envoys were massacred in the Khwarezmian city of Otrar in the early 13th century he invaded with 200,000 horsemen – undoubtedly the largest cavalry army in history.

The Mongols, incidentally, were fierce yet unsophisticated warriors from the plains. They made use of various siege techniques when reducing an enemy city; their horses were divided into light and heavy types. What made them such an exceptionally lethal enemy was their combat leadership and, above all, their mobility.

However, the ultimate 'tank' of antiquity was the elephant, whose role was to charge through the enemy infantry. Hannibal, the Carthaginian general, is famed for his use of trained elephants against the Romans after invading the Italian peninsula in 218 BC, but they were used by Indian rulers hundreds of years before Hannibal's time.

Alexander the Great encountered them for the first time at the Battle of Gaugamela in 331 BC when fighting the Persians, who had copied the idea from the Indians, and was so taken with the idea that after thrashing the Persians he incorporated their captured pachyderms into his own army. The Indians however finely tuned the use of these beasts of battle by armouring their elephants and eventually mounting light guns on them after the advent of artillery.

Now, fast forward three centuries and travel south to the Cape of Good Hope. On 28 February 1510 three Portuguese ships arrived in Table Bay, one of them carrying the outgoing governor of Portuguese India, Dom Francisco d'Almeida. A landing party went ashore and made contact with a local Khoi.

The initial cordiality turned sour and the Portuguese landed a punitive expedition of about 150 men, commanded by the viceroy himself. The Khoi evaded them and then ambushed the intruders as they passed through an area of thick bush on their way back to the beach, now in flight.

If a modern analyst were to examine this action he would be surprised by how closely that Khoi commander had adhered to the accepted principles of warfare. Relevant here is that the Khoi had a secret weapon – trained fighting oxen that could be controlled by whistles or shouts.

If ever there was an example of the philosopher Pliny's dictum that "there is always something new out of Africa", this was it. The stunned Portuguese found themselves facing a phalanx of charging oxen which not only promised imminent bodily harm but also protected the Khoi spearmen, running behind and between them, from the intruders' crossbow bolts, like modern battle tanks advancing with infantrymen following close behind.

This tactic worked so well that by the time the Portuguese were rescued by their ships' boats about a third of their number was dead, including D'Almeida. That small clash altered the course of southern African history because the Portuguese, the most daring mariners of the era, shunned the Cape of Good Hope.

Fast forward once more to 1652. Jan van Riebeeck arrived at the Cape to establish the equivalent of a modern truck stop to service the Dutch East India Company's ships on their voyages to and from the Far East. Under strict orders not to establish a colony, he maintained generally amicable trading relations with the various livestock-owning local Khoi clans, but came to blows with one of them, the so-called Peninsulars, the main *casus belli* being the latter's wish to force the Dutch to give them a monopoly on livestock trading.

It was not much of a conflict, but van Riebeeck learned a few valuable lessons from it. The first was that he needed more *snaphaans* – early flintlock muskets – to replace the cumbersome and unreliable matchlock arquebuses most of his soldiers carried. The second was that he must have more horses to provide his soldiers with the range and mobility they needed.

Van Riebeeck imported tough little Javanese mounts from the company's Far Eastern headquarters and built up a breeding herd, giving rise to the first South African light horseman. Van Riebeeck's soldiers and their indigenous allies served side by side in what started as *ad hoc* irregular mounted units; before long the fighting doctrines of both were being absorbed by one another.

By the late 17th century there had emerged the ancestors of the mobile, far-ranging and fast-moving Boer commandos of later years, "the most formidable mounted warriors since the Mongols," as Sir Winston Churchill would call them, almost three centuries after van Riebeeck's time.

In the years that followed the new doctrine spread beyond the confines of the Company's little outpost. The Griquas took it to the northwest Cape and then eastward, the Basotho picked it up from the Griquas, it travelled with the Oorlams Basters over the Orange river into what is now Namibia, the Xhosas along the Fish river adapted their tactics to it, to the detriment of many British (and not a few Boer) soldiers and settlers for most of the 19th century. The light horseman – part infantryman, part cavalryman – dominated South Africa's battlefields.

From the cavalry of bygone days – the heavy shock troops and the nimble light dragoons – mounted troops had now, the world over, evolved into something akin to their final form.

There was no place in the Cape for heavy cavalry, but there certainly was room for the light dragoons. From the 1680s onward companies of light horsemen began to be organized. Unlike their equivalents in European armies, the Cape light dragoons did not stray from their original shape or purpose. They might have looked like cavalrymen on parade, but they were primarily mounted infantrymen whose weapons of choice were long-barrelled muskets, frequently their own, since most of them were citizen soldiers of the Burgher militia; they had two functions.

They could be deployed at short notice as irregulars in commandos, for example as a rapid-response force in the event of cattle theft; but they were also trained to fight as uniformed companies of regular mounted infantry in the event of the Cape outpost being attacked by its French and English commercial rivals. This was a distinct departure from European practice but it suited local needs; during the two British invasions of 1795 and 1806 the light dragoons proved how effective they were in battle, both on foot and on horseback.

The earliest recorded battlefield use of an armoured vehicle in South African history was at the Battle of Muizenberg during the first British invasion. The Dutch East India Company's armed forces deployed a mobile magazine to support its field artillery, consisting of a wagon whose sides and sloping roof were covered with iron plates. During the second invasion in January 1806 the Batavian Republic's army, commanded by Lieutenant-General Jan Willem Janssens did likewise at the Battle of Blaauwberg. One might regard these armoured magazines

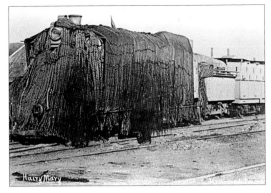

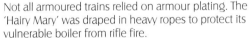

Not all armoured trains relied on armour plating. The 'Hairy Mary' was draped in heavy ropes to protect its vulnerable boiler from rifle fire.

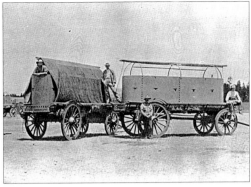

The British armoured ox wagons which served as a mobile pillbox during the Boer war.

as the distant ancestors of the mine-hardened 10-ton Kwêvoël logistics carriers of the South West Africa/Namibia Border War era, more than 150 years later.

The Cape's light dragoons were the progenitors of two ground-force elements in the modern South African Army, the mechanized riflemen with their infantry-combat vehicle as opposed to the horse as their battle taxi, the armoured troops, the ultra-mobile armoured cars descended from the light horsemen of old, and the tank regiments, representing the heavy cavalry.

Following the final British conquest of the Cape in 1806 armoured ground warfare – whether relating to the individual soldier or his means of locomotion – was not a significant factor during most of that conflict-beset century, although it was very much the age of the light horseman.

But the age of armoured vehicles had begun, as increasingly sophisticated technology allowed for the realization of a concept that had been around for at least a millennium.

The ancient Romans had evolved the arrow-proof *testudo*, or tortoise; a body of infantrymen in close order with their shields held aloft or to the front, sides or rear, depending on their placement within the order. Landships had been used by the Assyrians in 870 BC, Leonardo da Vinci even produced designs for a mobile fort powered by hand cranks – a replica built by the Royal Engineers in the 21st century proved to be workable – and in 1599 the Dutchman Simon Stevin turned his attention from his main interest of hydrostatics to construct two sail-driven, wheeled landships.

The first steps to full realization, however, were seen in the world's navies. The traditional 'wooden walls' of the sail era first acquired partial armour plating and then in time gave way to steel, steam-driven ships with varying degrees of protection against ever-more powerful and effective guns. As a result the early armoured corps, foremostly the British Empire and then the commonwealth, retained visible naval links for many years, thanks to the First World War-era Landships Committee established by the Royal Navy when Winston Churchill was First Lord of the Admiralty, and the Royal Naval Air Service's armoured cars. The first tanks featured time-honoured naval terms like hull and sponson, and as tank doctrine developed in the years leading up to the Second World War the tactical tasks allocated to armoured vehicles were often compared with naval requirements.

However, later events were to prove that armoured and naval tactics could not be regarded as close counterpart. In his book *In the Wake of the Tank*, the armoured-vehicle pioneer Lieutenant-Colonel Giffard le Quesne Martel later commented:

It is often suggested that a modern army which makes full use of fighting vehicles should be

modelled on the navy. There are, of course, points of similarity between a navy and a mechanized army, but the parallel does not go very far.
It is by the use of speed and mobility and a reasonable use of armour that we shall succeed on the land, and our work of development is not very greatly assisted by a comparison with the navy in this direction.

On land, though, one vital factor for the development of fighting armour was missing throughout the century: a practical means of self-propulsion. Horses and mules were too vulnerable to enemy fire, while oxen were not only vulnerable but slow as well. Steam was not the answer either, except for railways, because steam engines were too bulky, too heavy, too difficult to keep supplied and above all too vulnerable.

That some forward-looking military men were beginning to think ahead is clear; one such is the Zuid-Afrikaansche Republiek's negotiations with the Maxim-Nordenfeldt Company several years prior to the Second Anglo-Boer War (1899–1902) about the possibility of supplying 37mm quick firers – the renowned pom-poms – mounted on armoured ox-wagons. These talks did not come to fruition because without a practical built-in propulsion system the armoured vehicle could not be anything but a gun-carrier, and a vulnerable one at that.

Nevertheless, armoured vehicles of a fashion played a significant role after the start of the Second Anglo-Boer War. Just before the outbreak of war, four armoured trains were produced by the Cape government railway workshops in the Colony. Each consisted of lightly armoured freight trucks pulled by locomotives that had been covered with 9mm-thick boilerplate and fitted with steel doors and cabs.

The armoured trains were designed for a very specific role. The British were well aware that they would be fighting in the hinterland, many hundreds of kilometres from their main logistic bases at the seaports, and that they would therefore be totally dependent on the existing rail network to keep them supplied.

Thus the armoured trains, whose main task was to patrol and protect both the lines and the trains using them from attacks by Boer commandos came into being. A secondary task was to provide fire support.

Of course it was not an ideal solution because an armoured train had several weaknesses. It was confined to a set route, it could easily be derailed and it was unlikely that the Boers would be rash enough to venture into the range of its armament, rendering the troops on board redundant. In addition – at least at the beginning of the war – it would be unaccompanied during long patrols as the modest British garrisons in the Cape and Natal colonies could spare no troops to support such ventures. Under the circumstances, however, it presented the only solution to an otherwise impossible problem.

Its weaknesses were demonstrated from the outset, in fact on the evening of 12 October 1899 – just one day after the declaration of war. The victim was an armoured train called the Mosquito, armed with two artillery pieces and a machine gun, which was on its way from Vryburg to Mafeking (now Mafikeng) to deliver two 7-pdr guns to the garrison there.

The Mosquito ran into trouble when it steamed up to a dot on the map called Kraaipan, about 45 kilometres from its destination, where a commando under General Koos de la Rey had just spent considerable time and energy tearing up the line. As a result the train jumped the rails and juddered to a listing halt, the locomotive vented clouds of steam while its occupants sprayed their surroundings with shells and bullets.

De la Rey had no intention of wasting lives in a frontal assault on the Mosquito. Instead he sent for a detachment of guns from the Zuid-Afrikaansche Staatsartillerie and told his men to hold their fire and lie low for the time being.

At daybreak two Krupp guns duly made their appearance and after taking just three shells the train surrendered. These were the first shots fired in anger and the man who unleashed

A British armoured train ambushed at Kraaipan, October 1899.

them was a hulking *staatsartillerie* officer named Jacob 'Jaap' Louis van Deventer, who later became one of South Africa's greatest exponents of mobile warfare.

The incident was naturally a considerable propaganda coup for the Boers, but the best-remembered attack on an armoured train took place a month later when another train, travelling between Chieveley and Frere in the Natal colony, was derailed by a Boer commando and then shot up and captured.

Winston Churchill was among the prisoners taken; he was covering the war for London's *Morning Post* newspaper. Churchill's vivid account of his capture and subsequent successful escape from Pretoria made him a household name in Britain, launching him on a political career that would arguably lead to him becoming one of the greatest statesmen of the 20th century.

He had such admiration for the Boers' style of warfare that when he raised his special forces at the start of the Second World War four decades later he called them commandos, which has now become part of the international military lexicon as a generic name for mobile, hard-hitting raiding troops.

In spite of their flaws, armoured trains went on to play an important part in the war; by the end of hostilities more than 20 trains of all sizes had been armoured and armed with a variety of weapons, anything and everything from .303mm Maxim machine guns and light field artillery to 6-inch naval guns, and in one case even a hefty 9.2-incher. One famous armoured train, covered in heavy rope matting, was immediately christened 'Hairy Mary'.

Supporting them was the Railway Pioneer Regiment, commanded by Major J. E. Capper of the Royal Engineers, established to protect the railways – *inter alia* by manning the armoured trains – and repair bridges, culverts and rails damaged by the Boers, mainly on the Cape Town–Pretoria route.

The armoured trains and the Railway Pioneer Regiment kept the rail network clear and the supplies flowing, and they averted a great deal of potential damage; the Boers entertained a healthy respect for them, although it did not stop them from derailing the trains, damaging the lines or otherwise disrupting rail traffic whenever an opportunity presented itself.

As the war ground on the armoured railway trucks were also used as mobile blockhouses; and another armoured vehicle saw service alongside the trains. The British had realized early on that they would face a major logistic problem once their forces had moved beyond the rail network and would have to rely on animal-drawn transport between the railheads and the field forces. However, this would entail the large-scale importation of horses to a country that had been devastated by a rinderpest epidemic only three years earlier, not to mention the enormity of the implications regarding the amount of fodder and water that would be necessary.

The War Office's solution was to deploy some of the big steam-traction engines that were in common use for heavy hauling in Britain at the time. In early October 1899, 11 Fowler traction engines, complete with specially manufactured freight trucks and accommodation, were sent to South Africa.

Their first operational task was a fiasco. Three were deployed with a column that set out from Kimberley to Boshoff in the Orange Free State on 10 March 1900; they encountered unexpectedly heavy sand conditions and eventually came to a halt because their supplies of coal and water had run out.

No doubt this delighted various die-hards who did not believe that such contraptions had a place in any decent war, but the engines' value was soon recognized and they rendered much valuable service. The Boers obviously heeded their value as well, because they attacked the engines to such an extent that early in 1900 the British commander-in-chief, Field Marshal Lord Roberts of Kandahar, personally telegraphed the War Office to demand armoured versions.

Six armoured tractors, as they were officially designated, were constructed by the Cammell Laird shipbuilding firm – great boxy, open-topped vehicles with steel wheels and loopholes for rifles and a 7.5kw Fowler B5 engine with long copper fireboxes and brass smoke tubes that provided a working pressure of 12.41bar.

Each consisted of four separate vehicles, an armoured engine and three armoured wagons, capable of moving two 6-inch howitzers complete with crew and ammunition. The driver was completely boxed in with a number of vision slits and a mirror to give him a forward view on the left side of the engine.

The first four arrived in South Africa in July 1900 and soon proved their worth as haulers, if not as armoured vehicles. They were excessively heavy, weighing 22 tons, of which four-and-a half was the armour alone; 8mm vertical plates and 6mm for the rest. The huge rear wheels, 2.1m in diameter and 6mm wide, were shod with iron strakes that did much damage to the few tarmacked roads. This was solved by sending them straight to Bloemfontein to work in the Orange Free State and Zuid-Afrikaansche Republiek, where tar-surfaced roads were not an issue. To reduce the engines' weight the armour plating was removed and given to the military railway system for use on their armoured trains.

Only two more Fowlers were built for South Africa and both were delivered without armour, while the original armoured wagons were used as blockhouses in the later stages of the war. After the war, the armoured engines went to the North West frontier in India as mobile workshops.

The Second Anglo-Boer War provided the British Army with a great deal of food for thought about such things as mobility, reconnaissance, concentrated fire power, the futility of frontal attacks against magazine-fed rifles, proper entrenchments and the destruction of supplylines, all of which would pay dividends in wars yet to be fought.

Most important of all, however, although few realized it at the time, was that the war marked the start of the era of mechanization and the beginning of the end for the horse's long reign as the fighting soldier's primary mode of transport and locomotion.

Practical armoured vehicles were still a few years off but the war had produced the necessary components: the armed and armoured trains, the armoured traction engines with their off-road capability and at least two steam-powered cars that were able to withstand the rigours of campaigning against the Boers.

Very soon all these elements would be brought together; in Europe and elsewhere the age of combat armour would be ushered in. Internal-combustion engines were now being built that promised power and robustness for warfare, not only in Europe but – this being the age of empire – in less developed countries and territories.

From the beginning of the 20th century combat-orientated armoured cars of all shapes and

General French's cavalry near Bloemfontein during the Anglo–Boer War.

sizes began to appear in Britain, Austria, France, Germany, Italy, Russia, Belgium and the United States of America. Most were little more than civilian cars or lorries with steel plating bolted on to the most vulnerable areas and armed with a variety of weapons, from machine guns to light anti-aircraft pieces.

Generally speaking, their primary role was not reconnaissance. At this stage the average armoured car, slow and road bound, was no substitute for the light cavalry that most of the world's armies possessed in abundance. They were seen as being useful for tasks such as shooting down observation balloons – which had been used to great effect in the Second Anglo-Boer War – transporting raiding parties, rescuing pilots who had crash landed behind enemy lines and mounting security patrols around military installations such as airfields.

Some were distinctly odd looking; a very early model called the Simms Motor War Car, featuring a tub-shaped body, had been completed in 1898 and taken up by Vickers, Sons & Maxim Ltd, which manufactured the 6mm steel armour and provided the armament. The engine was a 12kw four-cylinder Daimler that was able to run on petrol or oil – the first example of a multi-fuel engine. A four-speed gearbox gave it a top speed of 15kph and its steel-tyred wheels meant it could only be used on hard roads. The car mounted a 1-pdr pom-pom, two .303mm Maxim machine guns and could be pressed into service as an armoured personnel carrier.

It was showcased in London in April 1902 just before hostilities in South Africa ended, arousing a great deal of public interest. The War Office was unimpressed; it was felt that the smell from its engine would upset the cavalry's horses, and the Simms was thrown onto history's scrap heap.

But development was taking place by leaps and bounds. Just three years later Austria unveiled the 1905 Daimler Panzerwagen, which represented something of a quantum leap in armoured car design. According to armour expert George Forty, the Panzerwagen's design illustrated "the basic ingredients that made up the true armoured car. It had good mobility, which enhanced it over its civilian counterparts by having four-wheel drive, thus enabling it to motor with some success across relatively poor going [*sic*], so that it was not confined to metalled roads. It had an armour-plated hull to protect the crew, although it was not very thick [3mm]. Finally, it had a fully traversing turret in which was mounted the main vehicle armament – in this case one or two Maxim machine guns – so it had respectable firepower … It thus had mobility, protection and firepower, the essential basic ingredients and in the correct order of priority."

The Panzerwagen's speed and endurance was very acceptable for the time. A 26kw engine gave it a top speed of 40kph and the car had a 230km range. However, the first true armoured car was still not advanced enough compete with the enormous sway held by the cavalry. When an improved model was demonstrated to the Germans at the 1905 Austro-Hungarian military manoeuvres, neither army adopted it.

Nevertheless, the armoured car was taking shape and in 1912 saw its first active service when Italy used its Isotta-Fraschini Tipo RM1911 with some success against the Turks during a clash over the possession of Tripoli. The Isotta-Fraschini, with its fully revolving turret and completely armoured hull had a top speed of 55kph and featured double rear wheels with solid rubber tyres and steel-flanged ones in front for better cross-country performance.

The Isotta-Fraschinis were "quite effective," Forty says, "but not spectacularly so, and their first appearance did not have quite the same emotive appeal to the world's press as did the first tank action. Nevertheless, it was clear that [armoured cars] future was now assured and that they would prove a valuable addition to all armies, especially as the speed of mechanization increased and the horsed soldier began to fade from the battlefield."

By the time the First World War broke out in August 1914 a variety of armoured cars were in service or development in Europe and America, and South African soldiers were soon to make the acquaintance of one of the best of the war, the 1914 Rolls-Royce Admiralty Pattern, which went into service in December that year.

Although steel-shod traction engines and the steam-powered cars of the Second Anglo-Boer War had passed into obscurity by 1914, the armoured trains were pressed into service again in later conflicts. One was employed against the insurgents of the South African 1914 Rebellion (*see* Chapter 2), and four: the *Trafalgar*, *Karoo*, *Scott* and *Schrikmaker*, were earmarked for service in the German South West Africa Campaign of 1915, although there is no evidence that they were actually deployed.

Two armoured trains were still operational when the Second World War broke out. Each mounting one 18-pdr gun, they were used as mobile coast defence batteries, although there was never a need for them in this role and their greatest service was in propaganda stunts and recruitment drives. But the concept did not die completely and in the 1980s was revived in a unique form.

The modern version of the armoured train appeared in South Africa during the 1980s, the then South African Railways and Harbours Administration became concerned about the safety of the huge numbers of passengers and equally huge quantities of goods in its trains and fleet of buses during those violent, tumultuous years. The South African Railways was worried about the violence spilling over onto its property. The result of their concern was *Kobus* and *Chris*, two prototype armoured personnel carriers with which the Railways and Harbours Police could patrol key points.

Designed by railway engineer Chris van der Merwe and built at the Langlaagte workshops, each 12½-ton armoured personnel carrier could survive landmines and small-arms fire and had a double set of wheels so that it could use road and rail. Converting from one method of travel to the other was simple, a personnel carrier in road mode would be parked over a railway line and the rail wheels would be lowered until they touched the tracks.

The armoured personnel carriers had a range of 750km by road and 1,000km by rail and possessed a unique propulsion system. Each of the four wheels had its own six-cylinder hydraulic engine, with a six-cylinder Magirus-Deutz diesel engine supplying all four with oil under high pressure.

The police drivers had to obtain special heavy-duty licences. To qualify they were trained on the South African Railways luxury Eagle passenger buses. Their effectiveness will never be known, however, because they did not go into production and the prototypes saw little, if any, field use. Both prototypes survive, one at the Windhoek (Namibia) railway station and the other is on static display at Elandsfontein in South Africa.

Horse vs Armoured car: the German South West Africa Campaign

South African forces fought in four campaigns during the First World War. The first was the invasion and conquest of Germany's South West Africa colony (1914–15), the only one that was solely a South African operation. The South West Africa Campaign is little discussed these days and generally regarded as a sideshow – even by South Africans – but apart from the fact that it was the allied nations' first successful campaign of the war, it was an extraordinary episode for a number of reasons.

Not least of them the fact that the South African field forces were commanded by the country's prime minister, a phenomenon not seen for at least a century. This gave rise to another uncommon occurrence: well after hostilities had commenced the campaign was abruptly placed on hold for several months while a pressing domestic issue was resolved, after which its protagonists picked up where they had left off.

Tactically this is interesting because it is the point where southern Africa abandoned its traditional methods of warfare in favour of modern ones.

In many ways it was a classic 19th century African campaign, conducted by foot-slogging infantry, wide-ranging light horsemen and animal-drawn artillery and transport, many of participating soldiers had honed their craft while fighting against the British during the Second Anglo-Boer War. At the same time it featured all sorts of 20th century innovations such as radio communications, combat aircraft, motor transport and the first truly battle-worthy armoured cars.

Most importantly, however, it was a classic example of a deliberate war of rapid manoeuvre that had not developed as a reaction to enemy tactics, but was planned and conducted as such from the outset.

The First World War broke out at the worst possible time for South Africa. The Second Anglo-Boer War had visited enormous devastation and misery on the two former Boer republics. Wounds were still raw, tempers easily flared and there was dissatisfaction that only a measure of autonomy had been granted instead of independence.

Now the British empire was at war with Germany, and was calling on its colonies, protectorates and the dominions within its to join king and country and fight. South Africa, now a British dominion, was immediately divided into two camps. On one side was the Prime Minister, General Louis Botha, and his lieutenant, General Jan Smuts – at the time Minister of Defence in Botha's Cabinet – who believed that they were bound, both contractually in terms of the 1902 Treaty of Vereeniging and ethically by the Boer signatories' formal acceptance of British nationality, to support Britain.

Botha and Smuts also saw the broader strategic picture: although the four imperial dominions (the others being Australia, Canada and New Zealand) were theoretically free to participate actively or not, the reality was that South Africa was located at the mid-point of the British–India sea-route, linking Britain to the greater part of its empire. It was also the conduit along which many of its imports and exports flowed.

This meant that South Africa would be in danger of being invaded and conquered. What it came down to was that the war in Europe was clearly going to be an all-encompassing struggle that would sooner or later suck in all countries and territories linked to either of the belligerents in one way or the other. They also believed (as Smuts stated on more than one occasion) that British-style governance was to be preferred over the totalitarian rule of Germany's Kaiser. They were vehemently opposed by General J. B. M. Hertzog and his newly established National Party.

The country was very nearly plunged into a civil war over the issue of whether or not to take an active part in the war. It is possible that if Botha's government had opted to play a supportive but passive role – for instance, by adopting General Hertzog's suggestion of a policy of armed neutrality – the political situation might have cooled down. In fact that was what Botha had suggested to the British government when war was declared on 4 August 1914, that the British garrison in South Africa be withdrawn and used elsewhere, while the Union would defended itself if necessary. But the stakes were too high.

To the average European in August 1914, the German colony of South West Africa must have seemed unimportant compared with what was happening closer to home. But it was of great importance to Britain because of the threat it posed to its sea-route to India.

Although the colony's two seaports of Lüderitzbucht (now Lüderitz) and Swakopmund lacked facilities for handling large vessels, they could be used for re-fuelling, re-supplying and re-fitting any German warships sent to operate in the southern oceans.

Even more important was that in the capital of Windhoek (or Windhuk as the Germans spelt it) stood the 100m-high masts of the second-most powerful radio station in the world. It was so powerful that it could communicate with Berlin – directly when the weather was good, or otherwise via a relay station in the German colony of Togo farther up the west coast of Africa. In addition, there were smaller stations at Lüderitzbucht and Swakopmund. Between them the radio stations posed a threat to Britain's domination of the high seas, a vital factor for her survival as a nation.

The powerful German East Asiatic Squadron commanded by Admiral Maximilian von Spee, with two large, heavily armed and armoured new cruisers, the *Gneisenau* and *Scharnhorst*, and three lighter ones, was prowling the southern reaches of the Atlantic Ocean, far from the main British naval strength in the North Sea.

When Botha cabled his suggestion, therefore, the British government not only accepted it but asked for more: would he be willing to invade and occupy South West Africa? It was a request that Botha felt he could not refuse, although he was perfectly aware of the likely political consequences. On 10 August 1914 the cabinet approved the invasion.

This decision would eventually result in what became known as the 1914 Rebellion. The rebellion did not break out immediately, however – at that stage it was by no means a foregone conclusion, and many of the later rebels were still thinking in terms of an armed protest at worst, a time-honoured but now outdated custom in the old republics which was meant not as an act of war but as a precursor to peaceful negotiations.

Botha appointed himself commander-in-chief for the invasion and began formulating a plan. It was his way of accepting responsibility for whatever might happen, and it was a fact that although the war of 1899–1902 had produced a number of fine Boer generals, Botha and Smuts were the only ones who had emerged as a strong commanders as well as military strategists. The fighting that followed would prove that he had not lost his tactical edge.

His invasion plan envisaged the destruction of Swakopmund's wireless station via a naval bombardment and a three-pronged invasion which would simultaneously threaten the Germans' southwestern, southern and southeastern flanks by means of three separate forces comprising a total of about 5,000 men.

In the southwest, C Force under Colonel (later Brigadier-General) P. S. Beves with 1,824 men would land and capture Lüderitzbucht. Further down the coast A Force, 2,420 strong and commanded by Brigadier-General Henry Timson Lukin, Inspector-General of the

Lieutenant Alexander Von Scheele used an Aviatik P14 to bomb the South African forces.

An airborne Aviatik.

Permanent Force, would go ashore at Port Nolloth on the upper Namaqualand coast, march inland and capture Ramansdrift and the other crossings over the Orange river. To the east, B Force under Lieutenant-Colonel S. G. Maritz, another former Boer War general, who was now commanding the Upington military base with about 1,000 men at his disposal, would reinforce Lukin.

When these forces were ready they would advance northward, pushing the Germans back to Windhoek and beyond, unless they surrendered first. Given Botha's military expertise and strategic vision, it is obvious that this plan was not his first choice, but had been forced on him by von Spee's presence in the southern Atlantic.

Ideally there should have been a substantial landing force at Swakopmund, only about 250km from Windhoek by rail, but the risk of a catastrophic German naval attack on his troopships and transports was too great. The approach from the south would ensure that only Lüderitzbucht would potentially be under threat from the sea.

Its main disadvantage was that it would entail a long, hard slog up the backbone of South West Africa: "a formidable natural fortress," as Gerald L'Ange correctly notes in his account of the campaign, *Urgent Imperial Service*, in the face of a mobile enemy who would have the initiative at all times.

On paper the figures strongly favoured Botha. He would have about 30,000 men available and more in reserve, and a safe conduit for the flow of war materiél from the Union, while the troops under German South West Africa commander-in-chief, Colonel Joachim von Heydebreck, numbered perhaps 7,000 – roughly 2,000 regulars of the Schutztruppe, about 4,000 reservists, various volunteers, 600-plus police and some field artillery.

But von Heydebreck's force would be no pushover if the Germans decided to fight. Nearly all the German troops were mounted, the Schutztruppe were tough, wily professionals led by first-class officers, the majority of his reservists would be men who had been thoroughly trained during their conscript service in Germany and he had a considerable number of artillery pieces and machine guns with ample stocks of ammunition.

Just as important, the campaign would be conducted over huge stretches of hard and often waterless terrain which made the Germans' narrow-gauge railway network a vital factor for both commanders' operations.

It started at Tsumeb in the north and ran down to Swakopmund, branching east near Karibib connecting it to Windhoek. From Windhoek it headed straight down to the arid south through Mariental and Seeheim, where one branch headed due west to Lüderitzbucht and the other farther south to Kalkfontein (today Karasburg), a mere 70km north of the Orange river.

If the Germans decided to fight, von Heydebreck would be able to ferry troops, guns and supplies to wherever they were needed with a speed Botha's army could not match. The South Africans would need to make heavy use of the railway – which the Germans were sure to sabotage – to traverse the vast distances that lay ahead.

Botha knew they would fight. These were the early days of the First World War, and so far things had gone well for them in Europe. The Germans in South West Africa believed, not without justification, that their armies would soon defeat the allied nations, which would automatically remove the South African threat.

Until that happened, a protracted delaying action would tie down thousands of South African troops who might otherwise be used elsewhere. Botha, on the other hand, needed to neutralize the radio stations as soon as possible.

Von Heydebreck also had two aircraft, an Aviatik P14 flown by Lieutenant Alexander von Scheele and maintained by its owner, Willie Truck, and a Roland Taube piloted by Lieutenant Paul Fiedler. No doubt Botha was aware of this embryonic air arm, because in 1913 South Africa had formed an Aviation Corps of its own. Its first graduates had received some very basic flight training in South Africa and had just completed their advanced training with the Royal Flying Corps in Britain when war broke out; the five who had qualified had immediately volunteered for active service with the Royal Flying Corps.

They were posted to two of the first four squadrons to be mobilized and sent to France, where they carried out some of the earliest aerial reconnaissance and artillery-spotting missions of the war. At this stage aircraft were not regarded as actual combat assets, a view that von Scheele and Fiedler were soon to change.

But Botha was not only one of the finest practitioners of mobile warfare, he had a host of battle-hardened, blooded veterans at his disposal. Men like Colonel Manie Botha, Colonel Jaap van Deventer, Brigadier-General M. W. Myburgh, Colonel Coen Brits, Brigadier-General Lukin – one of the few men to defeat General Christiaan de Wet and Brigadier-General Beves – one of Lukin's colleagues from 1899-1902.

All of them were thoroughly practised in the tactics Botha planned to use against the Germans: hard-riding light horsemen on tough Boer ponies descended from van Riebeeck's sinewy Javanese horses, would range far and wide over territory which would be the death of most European cavalry soldiers and their mounts, carrying out continuous outflanking manoeuvres, forcing the Germans to fight from fixed positions. At the same time his infantry would secure, and if necessary, restore the vital lines of communication. It was a classic example of commando fighting, tailored to the circumstances and the terrain, and designed to achieve the greatest effect with the least losses.

He would also command some of South Africa's best soldiers – infantrymen, artillerymen and light horsemen of the active citizen force, thousands of battle-hardened commando veterans and the five regiments of South African Mounted Riflemen, the efficient military *gendarmerie* which then constituted virtually the entire permanent force, each with its own artillery troop.

On 16 August 1914 the Germans unwittingly provided the South African government with a pretext – albeit a flimsy one – for invading South West Africa when they sent a modest detachment of troops to dig themselves in on a *kopje* overlooking a waterhole at Nakop, due west of Upington and just inside their border.

Some of the occupiers were German, while others were members of a free corps led by Andries de Wet, a former Boer commander and now commander of Afrikaners who had exiled themselves to South West Africa in 1902 rather than swear loyalty to Britain.

It so happened that while the waterhole was in South West African territory the kopje was not. The Germans later claimed they had not known this, but it made no difference. They had provided some justification for the invasion, and on 21 August 1914 inadvertently provided

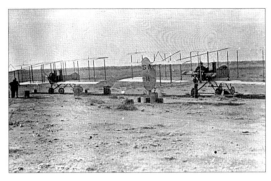
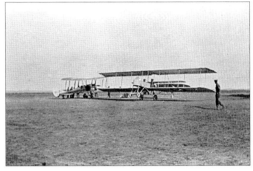

Two British BE2C biplanes (left) and some French-built Henri Farman Shorthorns (right) served during the campaign.

more by way of another minor incident.

A group of South African farmers just across the river were told to move their livestock to Keetmanshoop. They refused and headed south. German soldiers tried to stop them, but the farmers shot one soldier dead and got away. This caused considerable ire in South Africa, which naturally suited the government's purposes very well.

The first steps in the invasion came almost immediately. On 1 September 1914 General Lukin landed at Port Nolloth with A Force, an active citizen force infantry battalion, the Witwatersrand Rifles, an active citizen force artillery battery (the Transvaal Horse Artillery), all five South African mounted rifle regiments, two mounted field batteries (although one was later withdrawn) and various support troops.

Lukin immediately deployed the Witwatersrand Rifles on securing the northern part of the railway line between Port Nolloth and the copper mines at Okiep, and sent two squadrons of mounted riflemen to the Steinkopf mission station, halfway to Ramansdrift, where he would establish his headquarters.

Other mounted patrols headed east to occupy the crossings at Gudous (now Goodhouse) and Homsdrift (now Houmsdrift), then reconnoitre Ramansdrift. Then he got down to the business of disembarking the bulk of his draught animals and supplies.

As soon as he received the green light from Pretoria he would cross the river and advance northward from Ramansdrift. His immediate objective would be Warmbad, about 75km from Ramansdrift, from where he would attack the Germans' southern railhead at Kalkfontein (now Karasburg). At Kalkfontein he would be reinforced by Maritz's B Force which would cross the river at Schuitdrift, just south of Nakop, and head northwest to link up with him.

What no one realized (although Botha and Smuts suspected something was afoot) was that Maritz not only had no intention of taking part in the invasion but had already concluded a secret agreement with the Germans to defect to them with as many of his men as were willing to go with him.

While Lukin was busy getting ready for the invasion the *Armadale Castle*, an auxiliary cruiser or armed merchantman, steamed up the coast and on 12 September 1914 shelled Swakopmund. Although the bombardment damaged the radio station it did not knock it out, so a return visit had to be made to complete its job.

That same day Lukin received authority to cross into German territory. He immediately ordered 4 South African Mounted Riflemen to capture Ramansdrift and 5 South African Mounted Riflemen to take Homsdrift, which they did without difficulty as both were nearly deserted.

This done, he sent a scouting party to reconnoitre the German waterpoint at Sandfontein,

German forces made use of camels for transporting man and equipment.

RNAS Rolls Royce ACs at Walvis Bay during the First World War.

about 30km up the road from Ramansdrift. In order to advance on Warmbad he would need its wells to provide water for his horses and men. His scouts reported that Sandfontein was held by only 30 or 40 Germans and Lukin sent 200 mounted riflemen to occupy it.

On 18 September another piece of the invasion plan fell into place when Brigadier-General Beves and C Force landed (not without some difficulty due to rough seas) at Lüderitzbucht with one squadron of the Imperial Light Horse, a Natal Field Artillery battery, two active citizen force battalions, 1 Transvaal Scottish and the Rand Light Infantry, as well as a section of engineers.

Beves found the port deserted. The railway line had, however, been blown up as the Germans withdrew 16km to Kolmanskop, then another 3km to Grasplatz, where they left a small rearguard and pulled even further back to Rotkop. Many of the civilian population had left as well – though not the inhabitants of the local brothel. C Force set to work digging in for a possible counter-attack. But it did not come.

Meanwhile Lukin's 200 riflemen reached Sandfontein on the 19th, occupying it without difficult. The Germans had evacuated it after destroying the waterpump and poisoning the wells with dead animals. The 2nd South African Mounted Riflemen Regiment set about clearing the wells and building defensive *skanses* or breastworks out of loose stones – a wise precaution, as it turned out.

Still there was no reaction from the German side. The reason was that von Heydebreck had no intention of trying to recapture Lüderitzbucht; his aim was to hit the South Africans at Sandfontein as hard as possible and deny Lukin his water. If he could take and hold the wells the South African advance might be delayed by several months. To this end he was busy mustering all his available troops and guns from as far as Keetmanshoop – a total of about 2,000 men, four artillery batteries and a number of machine guns – and moving them down to the railhead at Kalkfontein.

At Ramansdrift Lukin got word on 25 September that German troops were being railed south. Conscious of the ease with which Sandfontein could be invested – the wells were surrounded on three sides by a chain of kopjes – he hastily sent 230 reinforcements, consisting of a squadron from 1 South African Mounted Riflemen, commanded by Lieutenant-Colonel R. C. Grant, and two guns of the Transvaal Horse Artillery. He could ill afford to detach Grant's force, having fewer than 400 men available at Homsdrift and Ramansdrift, but he had little choice.

Grant made for Sandfontein at top speed, leaving his supply wagons to follow at their best pace. He and his troops arrived at 0730 the next morning, not realizing that they were riding straight into a trap. During the night von Heydebreck had quietly deployed his force so close

Motor car commandos returning after a patrol.

RNAS Rolls Royce armoured car doing its first water crossing in the arid German South West Africa.

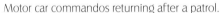

to Sandfontein that they spotted Grant's force long before it had even reached the wells and had even outflanked him and had a detachment to Grant's rear.

They let him enter, then closed the trap. The unsuspecting Grant had barely assumed formal command of Sandfontein when the telephone line to Ramansdrift went dead, some distant rifle fire was heard and a mounted rifle patrol came galloping back as a large number of von Heydebreck's mounted troops made their appearance.

Soon Sandfontein was being attacked from several directions and heavily bombarded by von Heydebreck's artillery. Hopelessly outnumbered and outgunned, Grant's men fought through that long, hot day, with von Heydebreck becoming increasingly concerned that they were buying enough time for Lukin to counter-attack from Ramansdrift.

Lukin could of course do nothing, and by late afternoon it was clear to Grant – who was still in command despite a serious wound to the leg – that further resistance would result in needless casualties. At 1800 he ordered a white flag be hoisted.

J. E. M. Attwell describes the scene just after the surrender: "There was little or no demonstration on the part of the enemy. The last rays of the setting sun showed both sides making one dash for the well at the foot of the kopje, where British and Germans mingled together to quench their terrible thirsts."

The surrender was a relief for von Heydebreck, who – not realizing how thin A Force was on the ground – had become more and more worried that the South Africans' stubborn defence would hold until relief arrived from Ramansdrift.

Maritz should have been well inside South West African territory by now, but he was still lying up at Upington and made no attempt to support Lukin, then or later.

According to an informant Botha had planted on Maritz's staff, he received a cable from Lukin requesting reinforcements but, "he subsequently … declared that he would see Lukin to blazes and would send him no reinforcements at all … Maritz said that Lukin could stew in his own juice … it was quite evident that Maritz knew about this business at Sandfontein before our own government did."

Sandfontein is an almost forgotten but significant incident for any modern armour soldier. Apart from being the start of the business end of the South West Africn Campaign it provides some interesting food for thought about the advantage of wheels over hoofs in the southern African soldier's centuries-old battle with the problems of time and distance.

If Lukin had motor transport he would have been in place much sooner and in fact would not have been so wholly dependent on Sandfontein's water for his horses and mules; he could have headed straight for Warmbad and perhaps even seized Kalkfontein before von Heydebreck had the chance to fortify it.

Sandfontein was such a disaster that not much notice was taken of a small yet successful action near Lüderitzbucht that same day, when two companies of the Rand Light Infantry and D Squadron Imperial Light Horse undertook a night march and at dawn fell on Grasplatz station, 20km east of Lüderitzbucht.

Eventually the South Africans overran Grasplatz station, capturing four Germans and 50 labourers, but losing four Imperial Light Horsemen, among them two brothers shot by the same German in one incident.

According to the personal diary of Lieutenant-Colonel James Donaldson of the Imperial Light Horse, a German non-commissioned officer had his horse shot from under him, pitching him hard forward and leading the South Africans to believe him dead. However, he recovered and started shooting, first killing Rex Winslow and then his brother Wilfred as he rushed forward to help. The other two Imperial Light Horsemen killed on 26 September were Trooper Clifford Gronau and Trooper Frank Croon, among the three wounded were Captain C. K. de Meillon, the C Force intelligence officer.

Less than a fortnight later Maritz made his move. He knew he was running out of time and opportunity. Smuts had despatched some infantry to the northern Cape – ostensibly to reinforce him in case of a German attack – appointed Coen Brits as overall commander of the region, and summoned him to Pretoria.

Maritz ignored the summons and on 2 October 1914 he took his men out for field training at Van Rooy's Vlei, halfway between Upington and the border. There, on the 9th, he called an assembly, read out the secret agreement he had made with the Germans, declared South Africa independent and at war with Britain, and called for volunteers to join him. About 500 agreed. Maritz handed most of those who had refused to a party of Germans and Andries de Wet's free corps members who happened upon this scene.

Regardless of the broader political circumstances, this was an outright act of high treason by a serving officer, and Botha took the only step he could to stop any further rot setting in – he declared a nationwide state of martial law. This effectively ignited the rebellion for which Botha placed the invasion on hold, went back to South Africa to command its quashing, using commandos either on horseback or crammed into civilian touring cars.

The last days of the insurrection saw old friends pitted against one another, Colonel Coen Brits chased down General de Wet on the Kalahari wastelands – from where he was hoping to make a dash to German South West Africa – with a combined force of horsemen and motor car 'commandos'. De Wet stayed out of Brits' grasp for a while, but the motorized commandos' stayed relentlessly on his spoor and on 1 December they caught up with him at a farm near the Bechuanaland border.

"It was the motor cars that beat me," de Wet remarked sadly as he and his men laid down their arms.

A prophecy of things to come.

While attending to the rebellion the situation in South West Africa had swung in Botha's favour. On 12 November 1914 Vice-Admiral F. Doveton Sturdee of the Royal Navy, commanding a powerful squadron that included the battle cruisers *Inflexible* and *Invincible*, fortuitously ran into von Spee at the Falkland Islands. A long, fierce battle followed in which Sturdee destroyed the entire German squadron except for one of the smaller cruisers.

This meant that Botha was now free to take his troopships up to Swakopmund 1,300km from Cape Town and strike directly at von Heydebreck's heartland.

3

The invasion begins at last

Botha now reorganized his forces into four components. At Lüderitzbucht Beves's C Force was absorbed into Central Force, commanded by Brigadier-General Sir Duncan McKenzie, former Officer Commanding 2 Imperial Light Horse during the Second Anglo-Boer War. Further troops arrived filling the C Force ranks to a robust 6,000 men, consisting of two mounted brigades of two regiments each (another mounted brigade was later added), two infantry brigades with seven battalions between them, two six-gun batteries of field artillery and two four-gun batteries of heavy artillery.

McKenzie was a renowned fire-eater, but his more tenacious enemy was the barren, waterless terrain of the Namib Desert, the Germans running a close second. His primary task was to get the railway line to Keetmanshoop working; providing Central Force with water was a major problem since Lüderitzbucht had barely enough for itself. Millions of litres, for his horses and men, had to be brought up by ship from Cape Town.

Mending the railway line was no simple matter either, L'Ange described it as, "rebuilding it at one end as fast as the retreating Germans destroyed it at the other." Without the railway line the desert was to all practical purposes impassable.

Botha had anticipated this and brought along a highly skilled team of engineers and operating staff presided over by Colonel (later Sir) William Hoy – who was the general manager of the South African Railways and Harbours in civilian life – as well as locomotives, rolling stock and civilian construction gangs.

Within two months the South Africans had laid 300km of track and had worked out the best way of using it. "What they [the Germans] had not bargained for," L'Ange continues, "was the speed with which the South Africans were able to rebuild it and their ability to march troops alongside it, using the line mainly for carrying water and supplies." At the same time the line from Prieska in the northern Cape was being extended to the border and beyond at an unprecedented four and a half kilometres a day.

Amid all this activity, Lieutenant Alexander von Scheele introduced Central Force to an unexpected new style of warfare on 21 November 1914 when he arrived in his Aviatik P14 from his base at Aus, 125km up the line. After flying over Lüderitzbucht to count the ships in the bay he headed inland to Rotkop where he dropped propaganda leaflets over the South African camp and followed them up with a few homemade bombs.

The soldiers fired back with rifles and the artillerymen with shrapnel; von Scheele returned to base with a large number of holes in his wings. Not much other harm was done, but it was a historic moment, L'Ange notes, "Von Scheele's flight … only three months after the outbreak of the First World War, appears to be the first recorded use of an aircraft for an offensive military purpose in the sub-continent."

Both von Scheele's and Fiedler's aircraft were small and under-powered, but they served their purpose. Their most remarkable task was naturally their bombing raids, for which they used artillery shells with cloth streamers attached to make them drop nose down. The raids did not accomplish much – aiming was of course a seat-of-their-pants affair and neither aircraft could lift more than four bombs at a time – but that was neither here nor there. The real value of the aircraft lay in the reconnaissance reports and beautifully clear photographs they brought back.

McKenzie's infantry started moving steadily up the line to protect it while it was being rebuilt. Tortured by heat, sand and flies, they set off to Tsaukaib on 13 December in dawn-to-dusk marches over 70km of virtually waterless desert. There they spent more than three months digging in, throwing up barbed wire and patrolling day and night. On 22 March 1915 McKenzie arrived, accompanied by the Governor-General of the Union, Lord Buxton, and ordered an advance on Aus on the 30th.

His troops were buoyed by the prospect of finally getting to grips with the Schutztruppe after months of boredom and hardship, but unbeknown to them Colonel Victor Franke (who had replaced von Heydebreck after his death in a grenade accident in mid-November 1914) had cabled the garrison at Aus on the 24th, ordering them to destroy the railway line and evacuate northward to Karibib with all their supplies and weapons.

The result was that when McKenzie sent in a combined infantry and mounted attack on 1 April 1915 Aus was deserted and mined. What was worse, its wells had been poisoned with sheep dip so that the water ration had to be reduced to just over two litres a day per man. In spite of its anti-climactic nature, however, Aus was a milestone in the war – from then on the mounted commandos would take the lead, rather than the infantry.

Lukin's A Force was replaced by Southern Force under Colonel Jaap van Deventer, operating from Upington and consisting of 29 commando units and a four-gun battery of field artillery, a total of about 5,000 men. Eastern Force, under Colonel C. A. L. Berrangé and based at Kuruman, was made up of four of the five regiments of South African Mounted Riflemen and a section of 12-pdr guns.

But the main component was Northern Force, commanded by Botha himself and operating from Swakopmund. Its foundation was laid on Christmas Day 1914, when Colonel P. C. B. Skinner's 3 Infantry Brigade (consisting of 1 Transvaal Scottish, the Kimberley Regiment and a squadron of the Imperial Light Horse) began to land at Walvis Bay, just 35km south of Swakopmund.

Eighteen days later he carried out a robust reconnaissance to Swakopmund, found it empty of German troops, although heavily mined, and occupied it. On 11 February 1915 Botha arrived to take command, by which time Northern Force was swelling to 6,000 men as ships from Cape Town disgorged a horde of combat and support troops at Walvis Bay and later Swakopmund.

His field troops were an infantry brigade comprising the South African Irish, the Rand Rifles, 2 Transvaal Scottish and 2 Kimberley Regiment, two commando brigades and two four-gun field batteries, as well as engineers and medical and communications troops. Skinner's brigade was tasked with protecting the reconstruction of the railway line; another two infantry battalions, 1 Rhodesia Regiment and 1 Transvaal Scottish, and a heavy artillery battery were deployed to secure the lines of communication. As time went on Northern Force would grow even larger.

A small army of civilians also arrived, including 170 post and telegraphs staff, 400 dock workers, 500 railway construction workers, even 50 labourers whose sole task was to keep the latrines functioning. With them came almost 900 horses, almost 700 mules and 200 oxen, and a vast range of equipment and supplies, including locomotives and rail trucks, sleepers, borehole drilling rigs, seawater condensing plants, steam cranes, motor vehicles and mountains of ammunition, food and fodder.

A fleet of Reo Speedwagon lorries grunted ashore, and at Walvis Bay and Swakopmund great stacks of 44-gallon (200-litre) drums arose in what were then called petrol yards – the forerunners of the dumps that dotted the Western Desert during the Second World War.

It was an impressive effort for a largely undeveloped and hardly industrialized nation which

General Louis Botha.

Eight Rolls Royce ACs in German South West Africa, RNAS.

had not only entered the war almost totally unprepared four months earlier but had to deal with an armed insurrection along the way; much of the credit belonged to a frustrated General Smuts, Botha's deputy and also minister of defence, who would have preferred to be in the field and by way of compensation poured all his energy and ruthless organizational ability into providing his old comrade with what was needed.

Botha was now ready to move forward on four separate but linked fronts. McKenzie's Central Force would advance up the railway line to Keetmanshoop. From Upington, Coen Brits' Southern Force would advance northward, seize Kalkfontein and then follow the railway line to Seeheim and Keetmanshoop. Berrangé's Eastern Force with its four SAMR regiments and its guns would cut across the Kalahari from Kuruman and head straight for Keetmanshoop. From Swakopmund Botha's Northern Force would head up the line to Karibib, Okahandja and finally to Windhoek.

The railway construction gangs immediately went to work, building a line to Walvis Bay and simultaneously tackling the thoroughly sabotaged narrow-gauge line inland, not repairing it but replacing it altogether with the broader standard South African gauge. For the infantry the next few months would mean repeated forced marches under terrible conditions and frequent clashes with the Schutztruppe.

Botha wasted no time in starting his advance along the Swakop river, leaving Colonel Hoy's men to continue building the new railway line in his wake. By mid-March 1915 the area had been cleared of Germans for a distance of 30km inland, and the first shots of the advance were about to be fired.

Botha's immediate objective was a German defensive line about 50km long that linked two waterholes along the railway line on the way to Usakos – Pforte and Jakkalswater – with a third a few kilometres south of Jakkalswater at Riet, on the Swakop river itself. He established a forward supply base at Husab on the Swakop, approximately northwest of Riet, secured the immediate area with his infantry and laid plans for a typical commando-style outflanking attack.

On 19 March 1915 the main force advanced, led by a column under the boisterous Coen Brits, with Botha riding at his side. Brits left Husab at 1900, carried out a 30km night march south of the river and fell on the German positions below the Riet mountain at dawn the next morning. With the Bloemfontein Commando attacking from the rear, Brits and his main body hit them from the front, broke the line and threw themselves at the left flank. A day-long battle ensued, after which the Germans retreated under cover of darkness.

Meanwhile Colonel J. J. Alberts with three commandos headed north and east, overran the German positions at the foot of the Pforte mountain and captured nine officers, 200 other ranks and two guns. Colonel W. R. Collins' column was engaged on an even more ambitious task – looping around north of Pforte by means of a gruelling 60km march to attack Jakkalswater, the northeastern-most German position and the location of their reserve. The idea was to prevent the Germans from reinforcing their positions at Pforte and Riet.

Collins reached his objective, but ran into problems when the Schutztruppe reserve fell on him and he was forced to retire temporarily, although eventually Jakkalswater was taken with the aid of artillery support.

It was a decisive series of actions that set the pattern for the rest of the campaign – after that the Germans would never again put up a solid line of resistance. The war had become the sort of cut-and-thrust affair that suited the burgher commandos down to the ground.

Now nature took a hand in determining the course of the war. The next leg of the advance would entail crossing a 100km-wide, totally dry stretch of desert, and Botha simply did not have enough water for the task. As it was, his troops had to operate for 36 hours on a single bottle of water per man, and they and their horses were desperately thirsty.

He was forced to withdraw to Swakopmund, garrisoning Riet with 600 infantrymen while it was stocked with supplies for the next leg. Of necessity it was a slow process, and for five weeks Northern Force's advance came to a halt.

The southern columns now came under new command. General Smuts had become convinced that they were not moving fast enough, so he shelved his other responsibilities *pro tem*, hastened to Lüderitzbucht and assumed overall command in the south. The campaign had become stranger than ever: not only was the prime minister in the field but so too was his deputy (and minister of defence). In his biography of Smuts, *Grey Steel*, F. C. Armstrong describes what happened then:

> He acted not so much as a general in command of a considerable force, but as he had acted when he was the leader of his three hundred men raiding full tilt across the Cape. He would take no excuses. The columns must hurry forward, supplies or no supplies, they must bustle.
>
> He sent McKenzie riding hard into the blue, from Aus across the desert to Gibeon to cut off the Germans retreating down the railway, and then sent messengers after him to urge him on.
>
> He pushed on with his tireless, fearless and unreasoning impetuosity, so rapidly that his staff and even his personal secretary could not keep up with him, would lose him, then find him again, stranded away out alone on the bleak plains. Once he was captured and brought in by his own patrols.
>
> Botha was somewhat troubled at these methods. He was afraid that Smuts might make some precipitous rash move that would lead to a defeat; and he tried to tone down his rampaging impetuosity. But within a month the Germans in the south were on the run.

Van Deventer's Southern Force saw considerably more action than Central Force during this period, fighting no fewer than six times. On 18 January 1915 a German force of about 800, including Maritz and Kemp, raided onto South African soil, attacked 400 Union Defence Force mounted riflemen 70km northwest of Upington and forced them to retreat. On 24 January 1915 Maritz, Kemp and their men attacked Upington itself, but van Deventer beat them off with considerable losses. Another raid, by Major von Ritter of the Schutztruppe, attacked Kakamas, but was also beaten off.

No doubt the soldiers and civilians toiling to set up Botha's big push did not have time to take much notice when the last tragic postscript to the long-dead *Huiloorlog* was written on 30 January, the surrender of Jan Kemp and his remaining 500 men near Upington.

The boot was on the other foot when van Deventer and his commandos started moving northward. On 8 March 1915, 270 commando members put to flight a German force at Nabas and captured all its supplies and transport. On 20 March the commandos routed another German force at Platbeen, capturing its supplies and transport as well.

RNAS Rolls Royce GSWA, 1915.

Rolls Royce armoured cars used during the campaign.

Eastern Force under Colonel Berrangé fought several times. On 19 March 1915, 100 burghers attacked a force of Germans double their number at the important well at Rietfontein and forced them to retreat, leaving behind their dead and wounded as well their transport and supplies. Then on 5 April Berrangé's men defeated the Germans at Koës and Kiries West. He then joined forces with van Deventer for the advance on Keetmanshoop.

On 16 April 1915 General McKenzie's Central Force marched northward with three mounted brigades and a battery of field artillery. En route McKenzie was informed that a Major von Kleist of the *Schutztruppe* was at Gibeon with 700 mounted riflemen, and decided to attack.

On 24 April McKenzie sent 9 Mounted Brigade under the officer commanding Natal Light Horse, Lieutenant-Colonel J. R. 'Galloping Jack' Royston (consisting of the Imperial Light Horse, the Natal Light Horse, the Umvoti Mounted Riflemen and 1 Royal Natal Carbineers) to outflank the Germans on the east and then lie in wait along their likely line of retreat, after which he would attack with the rest of the force.

The action at Gibeon got off to a bad start. On the approach to Gibeon station a train was spotted, as well as the dust of three approaching German columns. Royston blew the line, but the odds were in favour of Major von Kleist, who had earlier spurned reports of an approaching force but then reacted swiftly when he turned out to be wrong.

At 0200 on the 27th the Germans enfiladed Royston's position. The Natal Light Horse was now in a desperate situation. An hour later Lieutenant-Colonel W. T. F. Davies, the officer commanding Imperial Light Horse, ordered his regiment and the Natal Light Horse to retire to where their horses were tethered; Royston then ordered a general retreat.

By now Royston had 24 killed, 49 wounded, all from the Imperial Light Horse, and an entire 72-man squadron of the Natal Light Horse captured when the order to withdraw had not reached them, they had been surrounded and taken prisoner just before dawn.

The Germans were so jubilant, mistakenly assuming they had defeated the South Africans' main body. At first light McKenzie counter-attacked. Major von Kleist fought a stubborn rearguard action and by skilful handling of his troops avoided encirclement and made good his escape, leaving behind 11 dead, 30 wounded and 188 prisoners, including those of the Natal Light Horse, four machine guns, much ammunition, wagons and draught animals (the Imperial Light Horse was later awarded the battle honour 'Gibeon' for this action).

Berrangé and van Deventer defeated a 300-strong German force of mounted riflemen at Kubas; trapped between van Deventer's hammer and Botha's anvil, the Keetmanshoop garrison surrendered. This marked the end of the war in the south; now the commandos could head northward to join Botha for his push to Windhoek and, if necessary, beyond. His self-imposed task completed, Smuts returned to Pretoria as speedily as he had arrived.

On 24 April 1915 a new weapon of war threw its hat into the ring for the first time in sub-Saharan Africa; a squadron of 12 Rolls-Royce Admiralty Pattern 1914 armoured cars, crewed – of all people – by sailors of the Royal Naval Air Service under Lieutenant-Commander W. Whittall, was disembarked at Swakopmund to join Northern Force.

The Admiralty Pattern armoured car was undoubtedly the best vehicle of its type in service in any of the 1914-era armies. It was an elegant, long-snouted machine built on the famed Silver Ghost chassis, with a crew of three and a bevelled round turret mounting a water-cooled .303-calibre Vickers machine gun. Its 26kW Rolls-Royce engine gave it a top road speed of 75kph, resulting in remarkable ground-coverage ability for those days, and it was sturdy enough to fight just about anywhere. It was also amazingly quiet, which was to add to its effectiveness on several battlefronts of the war.

The fact that British sailors were manning armoured cars in an African bush-war campaign was just another oddity of the fighting in South West Africa. At the start of the war the British had two aerial forces, the Royal Flying Corps, which was part of the army, and the navy's Royal Naval Air Service.

In the frenzied early days of the war in Europe there was a serious lack of trained manpower in the army and Royal Flying Corps, so the task of guarding airfields was assigned to the Royal Navy, which had some spare resources. Apart from airfield protection, the Royal Naval Air Service used its vehicles to rescue the crews of downed aircraft. Early clashes with German cavalry led to a need for some sort of armour protection, whereupon the Royal Navy began to add mild steel to its cars.

Eventually the Admiralty Air Department designed and produced some vehicles which provided crews with fully enclosing armour protection and armament in revolving turrets. In *The Vickers Tanks: From Landships to Challenger*, Christopher Foss and Peter McKenzie speculate that the concept of a revolving turret was a familiar one that even diehard naval minds of the time could accept without difficulty.

The Royal Navy promptly formed the Royal Naval Armoured Car Division and equipped it with the hastily designed Admiralty Pattern cars and some others. The navy's lead in experience with armoured cars brought them into contact with the British Army when the latter took up the idea, and the Royal Naval Air Service units worked with the army in further developments.

The establishment of trench warfare in Europe led to the withdrawal of the Royal Naval Air Service's armoured cars from frontline operations and their redeployment to Gallipoli, Egypt, South West Africa, East Africa and the Middle East.

Commander Whittall's armoured cars were brought ashore with considerable difficulty – they had to be ferried to the surfline in lighters and then manhandled with great care and good timing on to the beach over planks that had been laid out to the lighters dancing about in the surf. With Whittall's cars safely on dry land, the next question was where and how they could be usefully employed.

It was generally agreed that the cars would not be able to keep up with Botha's mounted brigades, and so for want of alternative ideas, Whittall and his men were sent to join Colonel Skinner's 3 Infantry Brigade, which was providing protection for the railway construction gangs and by now had reached Trekkopjes, 70km from Swakopmund.

Unglamorous though the task was, it was essential to Botha's efforts because he needed the line for resupply for the push to Windhoek once he had reached Karibib. However, Trekkopjes was a long way from where his advance guard was heading northeastward along the Swakop river, which the higher command firmly believed would be the scene of the next bout of fighting.

They were so sure, in fact, that on the day nine of Whittall's cars were loaded onto railway

RNAS Rolls Royce Armoured Cars in German South West Africa.

RNAS Rolls Royce armoured cars that participated in the battles at Trekkopjes, the first use of mechanized armour in southern Africa.

trucks to travel to the railhead at Trekkopjes, Skinner's only field artillery assets – two 12-pdrs – were carted off on an open railway truck for delivery to Botha's forces. All he had left in the way of artillery was Botha's sole anti-aircraft defence weapon, an ungainly looking 15-pdr field piece irreverently nicknamed 'Skinny Liz', which had been modified so that its barrel could be cranked up to a 60° angle.

Skinner had protested in vain against the removal of his guns, believing that there was a very real danger that a Schutztruppe force under the able Major von Ritter of Kakamas fame would attack Trekkopjes at some stage.

He was also painfully aware of the fact that because of the necessity of guarding the line his men were concentrated in a tactically unsound position in a hollow, overlooked by a line of kopjes to their front and a ridge to their right, and surrounded by dense scrub that would allow an attacking force to get close without being discovered.

His pleas fell on deaf ears, but his unease was justified. Von Ritter was well informed about his deployment, because Lieutenant von Scheele with his Aviatik was now based only 65km away at Usakos, and paid regular visits to Trekkopjes to spy on the South Africans' progress and drop some of his homemade bombs on them.

Skinner's lone anti-aircraft gun, Skinny Liz, made sure the Aviatik kept its distance, but he must have guessed, as L'Ange notes, that von Scheele had observed the two 12-pdrs being taken away. Von Ritter certainly had noticed, and – thanks to von Scheele's photographs and notes – knew that Skinner now not only had no field artillery pieces left but had no more troops at his disposal than the Germans did. He passed this on to Colonel Franke, who immediately drew up a two-phase plan for attacking Trekkopjes.

In the first phase a demolition team would creep around to the south of Trekkopjes on the night of 25 April, while von Ritter and his troops with their two artillery batteries would use the broken terrain to get as close as possible. Next morning at dawn the demolition team would blow up the line so that Skinner would not be able to call for reinforcements from 1 Rhodesia Regiment at Arandis, 20km down the line.

Von Ritter would give Trekkopjes a thorough pasting with his artillery – his gunners knew the exact ranges to the South African camp – and then send in his Schutztruppe on foot with bayonets fixed. It was a simple but effective plan, and it nearly worked.

Skinner had become so uneasy that he had gone out with a squadron of the Imperial Light Horse to undertake a personal reconnaissance of the German lines. Fortunately his scouts detected von Ritter's advancing force without themselves being discovered and returned to tell Skinner, who then headed back to Trekkopjes in considerably greater haste than he had left it.

On arrival Skinner hastily sent his infantry into the shallow trenches they had managed to hack out of the flinty ground near the railway line, telephoned Arandis (which immediately dispatched the Rhodesians northward in a standby train) and then called general headquarters in Swakopmund, which likewise wasted no time sending off a train carrying two 4-inch guns.

Skinner split Whittall's armoured cars into three groups. Two were deployed at the junction of the Transvaal Scottish and Kimberley Regiment trenches, five others were sent forward to various places as far from the trenches as about 800m, and the remaining two were held in reserve with Skinner's transport in case of a hasty retreat.

Skinner might have been on a very sticky wicket indeed, except for three errors on the German side, two of them inexplicable when one considers the highly professional standards of the Kaiser's forces, and the third a misapprehension typical of the pre-mechanized era.

The first error was that von Ritter had advanced without a screen of scouts and was therefore unaware that Skinner had been alerted. The second was that the sappers sent to demolish the railway line as the opening gambit somehow managed to lose direction in spite of the mile posts along the line and planted their demolition charges *north* of Trekkopjes.

The third was that although von Scheele had spotted Whittall's armoured cars being brought up to Trekkopjes, they had been identified as water bowsers – a permissible error in an era still very much cavalry focussed.

As a result there were several unpleasant surprises awaiting von Ritter. The first was that, courtesy of the German sappers, the Rhodesians came rattling in from Arandis at dawn and occupied the trenches just before von Ritter's guns opened up. There they and their South African comrades crouched for three hours while von Ritter systematically blew their camp to bits, blissfully unaware of the fact that he was demolishing empty tents.

When von Ritter was satisfied that he had wreaked the maximum amount of havoc he sent in his infantry, his first objective was the ridge overlooking Trekkopjes. Here he encountered his second surprise. In the interim the ridge had been occupied by the Rhodesians and Whittall's forward armoured cars opened up on the Germans with devastating effect. Von Ritter ordered his gunners to fire shrapnel at the armoured cars, but it had no effect on them and the distinctive slow stammer of their Vickers guns never stopped.

When von Ritter realized he was getting nowhere he abandoned his attack and launched another one farther down the line to get around the armoured cars, but when this second attack advanced the same thing happened: the armoured cars were waiting, and once again stopped his advance in its tracks. Twice more he shifted position, but each time the armoured cars were in position to blunt his attack.

By this stage von Ritter had worked his way so far down the line that he was directly opposite the South African trenches. Here a series of stalemates ensued because the scrub was so thick that the South Africans' infantrymen could see little to fire at. The Imperial Light Horse troopers tried to outflank the German artillery, but failed when von Ritter guessed what they were about to do and put out a strong screen behind the guns.

The stalemate lasted until mid-morning when von Ritter gave the South African trenches another pounding and then sent his infantry in again. In spite of heavy rifle and machine-gun fire from the South Africans they kept advancing until they were within 50m of the trenches, only to be stopped again by the Vickers guns of the two armoured cars posted there earlier.

Von Ritter now gave up and ordered a withdrawal. Skinner immediately launched a counter-attack by his infantry and the Imperial Light Horse. It accomplished little due to heavy fire from the retreating German gunners, the cars' inability to get over the line's embankment and the South Africans' lack of any field artillery of their own to lay down counter-battery fire – although Skinny Liz's gunners did manage to crank their gun's high-angle barrel down to minimum elevation and fire two shells, one of which was seen to burst among the Germans.

L'Ange comments: "Whether (Skinny Liz) ever scored a hit (on an aircraft) is unknown.

Armoured cars were brought ashore with considerable difficulty; they had to be ferried and manhandled with great care on to the beach.

RNAS Rolls Royce in German South West Africa.

It certainly never brought an aeroplane down. Its most effective performance seems to have been when it was used as a straightforward artillery piece, firing horizontally."

Thus ended the Battle of Trekkopjes, an outright victory for the South Africans. It was not a massive bloodletting like the enormous conflicts being fought in France and Flanders. In spite of all the rifle, machine gun and artillery fire – L'Ange quotes an estimate of between 400 and 500 German shells on Trekkopjes – losses were small – 20 killed and 46 wounded in total – but not the implications a German victory would have had.

"Botha would, at the very least, have had to postpone his drive on Windhoek and divert substantial forces along the railway to chase the Germans back," L'Ange points out. "He might even have had to abandon the advance along the line of the Swakop river and take the slower alternative of the railway route. Von Ritter's failure now left Botha free to concentrate his attention on severing the German's railway spine."

The infantry regiments who fought there treasure the memory of Trekkopjes, they had endured a heavy artillery barrage without faltering and immediately afterward had kept up unflinching fire on the attackers. For some reason though, the armoured cars' contribution is almost forgotten, yet as L'Ange correctly comments, it "may have been pivotal. It was at least an important one, counter-balancing the Germans' exclusive possession of artillery."

In May 1915 the South Africans finally acquired some aircraft of their own. The South African Aviation Corps' pilots had been recalled from France to serve in South West Africa and arrived at Walvis Bay with two British B.E.2c biplanes and some French-built Henri Farman Shorthorns. The British aircraft never saw action – the harsh, dry South West African climate proved too severe for their wooden airframes – but after some refurbishment to offset the damage inflicted by the long sea journey the all-metal Henri Farmans were flight ready.

On 6 May Lieutenant K. R. van der Spuy flew the first reconnaissance sortie out of Walvis Bay. "Now I can see for hundreds of miles," Botha rejoiced. Botha himself went up for a sortie which nearly ended in disaster when the Farman developed engine trouble and Van der Spuy barely managed to land. Botha was undaunted and cracked a joke, but, as van der Spuy was to recall, "later General (J. J.) Collyer ticked me off for having suggested that the 'old man' should fly."

The aircraft's first operational base was Karibib, using the existing German airstrip and hangars. Reconnaisance and occasional bombing with artillery shells took place from here and other airstrips. A locomotive at Tsumeb was destroyed. They did not meet 'Fritz' though. Lieutenant Fiedler had written off his Taube in April 1915 and on 15 May the Aviatik was wrecked when Lieutenant von Scheele crash landed it.

Botha's final push started on 18 June; it had been delayed by a need for fresh horses and the time required to rebuild the sabotaged bridge at Usakos. A week before it started he visited Usakos for a brigade inspection, and Whittall's armoured cars led the march past at the end of the parade – which they did in fine naval style. Whittall later penned a graphic description:

> I think that everyone had expected this part of the affair to be rather humorous, and that the cars would rattle and bump their way past the saluting base, with much clanging of armour and machinery and in any sort of order.
> But, on the contrary, the cars, with their powerful engines turning slowly, simply stole silently past, four abreast and in perfect alignment, their grim outlines relieved by the flaunting White Ensigns which we flew on gala occasions. They made an impressive sight and, as one of the staff remarked afterward, no wonder the Huns don't like the look of them.

During the advance that followed Trekkopjes, the armoured cars' off-road mobility increased significantly as the crews worked out the best way to get them through the dry, sandy northern reaches. The engines generated so much power that the wheels made short work of matting, wooden poles and iron piping. The final solution was lengths of angle iron, the forerunner of the metal troughs that were standard fittings on their Second World War successors. The sailors accidentally discovered another technique that would see use in later wars, this time for crossing dry riverbeds – of which there are many in that part of what is now Namibia – when the driver of the lead vehicle mistook a signal and charged into the riverbed at full speed.

The result, Whittall later wrote, was that, "with a plunge that threw everything into the air that was not lashed or strapped fast, the leader took the dip, ploughed through the sand, throwing it up in front like the bow wave of a destroyer, and rocked and plunged herself up the opposite bank." This did not always work though, and on at least one occasion a bogged-down Rolls-Royce had to be hauled out by a team of oxen.

After some trial and error the sailors found that over difficult terrain they could move at least as fast as mounted troops, although it meant that each car used up five litres of petrol and five of water every 6½km. But it provided final proof that a strong, well-designed armoured car with skilled operators was not necessarily confined to roads.

Whittall's armoured sailors did not have much time left in South West Africa. From Otjiwarongo onward the terrain became so broken that not even they could operate off-road and it was decided that they had done their duty and must now go home so that, "they might be used to advantage in some theatre which would give them a fair opportunity for tactical action which local conditions now denied them," as Major-General Collyer put it.

And so Whittall and his tanned matelots embarked with their armoured cars and headed off to other military ventures, bearing both the thanks of the Union government and (at least as far as Whittall was concerned) fond memories of his late comrades in arms: "I have never seen better infantry anywhere than these five battalions of South Africans who moved out of Usakos on that June morning – and I have campaigned with many of the great military powers and with that of some of the smaller ones."

He was equally impressed by Botha's commandos, unorthodox in appearance, discipline and tactics they certainly were, but Whittall recalls them as, "… simply wonderful, those burghers. Why the Boers were able to keep the field for so long against overwhelming numbers in the Anglo-Boer War is no mystery to anyone who saw their work in German Southwest Africa."

There was no stopping or delaying Botha's juggernaut after Whittall's departure, although Franke's Germans fought to the bitter end. Botha adhered, as he had done up to then, to the old Boer belief that needlessly throwing a man's life away was equivalent to murdering him, so he avoided pitched battles and frontal attacks in favour of constant outflanking movements. It was a tactic perfectly suited to the terrain, and it wore the Germans out with a minimum cost in lives.

The end came at Otavi in the far north. Here the Germans dug in. It was a good position for a delaying action because even if they were forced out, as was inevitable, there was an almost trackless wilderness at their backs in which they could fight a protracted guerrilla campaign in anticipation of a victory in Europe.

Botha outwitted them. He held their attention by continuing to advance from the south while Coen Brits took his commandos on a wild ride through the desert and the marshes of the great Etosha Pan to attack from the rear. It was the end, and Franke knew it.

Commenting that "this is not war but a circus," he surrendered at 1000 on 9 July 1915 with 4,740 officers and men, 37 artillery pieces and 22 machine guns.

Botha returned home to vast acclaim and resumed his seat in parliament. He had fought a textbook campaign against a doughty enemy, in some of the most inhospitable terrain in the world, and secured the southern oceans for the allied nations – all this at a cost of 88 men killed in action, 25 mortally wounded and 153 dead as a result of illness or accidents. More South Africans had been killed during the short-lived 1914 rebellion (131 loyalists and 190 rebels).

The same would happen in Abyssinia in 1940-41, when Brigadier Dan Pienaar's 1st South African Brigade fought and won numerous large and small actions at such minimal cost in dead and wounded that in some British Army circles there were doubts about his eagerness for battle.

Likewise, Botha's losses were so low by the bloody standards of the European front that the South West Africa campaign has always been seen as something of a sideshow. Commander Whittall provides the last word on the matter: "To measure the success of a campaign by the size of the butcher's bill is to view it from an altogether wrong standpoint. As a matter of fact, the reverse may often be the case. It most certainly was so in South West Africa, where the loss of life was in inverse ratio to the results achieved."

As the German presence in southern Africa marched into obscurity so to did the traditional mounted soldiers. L'Ange writes:

> The campaign is seen by some authorities as the last great cavalry operation in history. While cavalry was used in other theatres of the First World War, nowhere else was its function so crucial, nowhere else in the war were there the wide-ranging movements by horsemen, extending over hundreds of miles, and nowhere else did strategy hinge on the mounted soldier as it did in South West.

Whether the South West Africa Campaign was, in fact, the "last great cavalry operation in history" is debatable. Just around the corner was the gruelling campaign in German East Africa, in which the war of movement was once again conducted by South African mounted brigades, and in the Middle East much use was made of Australian and British light horse later in the war. But the writing was certainly on the wall, and Commander Whittall's land-bound sailors had wielded the pen.

Much development, in structural strength, firepower and cross-country capability, would still be needed before the armoured car could reach its full potential. But it had proved its worth, and just over two decades later the sons of the hard-riding commando soldiers of 1915 would go to war, not on horseback, but in armoured fighting vehicles. And not just wheeled ones either.

At the time that Commander Whittall's fighting sailors were beating off Major von Ritter's Schutztruppe at Trekkopjes, a team led by a William Tritton, British engineer, was hard at work building a strange boxy all-terrain tracked vehicle known as 'Little Willie', which for reasons of security was described as a tank for transporting water.

There was no time for the South Africans to rest after the campaign in South West Africa.

4

Armoured cars in North Africa

Britain might control a vast empire and maintain the most powerful navy in the world, but her conventional land forces had always been surprisingly modest and, moreover, until halfway through the war were manned by full-time and part-time volunteers rather than the vast numbers of serving and reserve conscripts possessed by the other prominent nations.

The outbreak of the First World War had caught her short of even partially-trained soldiers for service on half a dozen fronts. The need for troops for the Western Front in Europe was particularly great, but there were also problems requiring urgent solutions in two other parts of the world which were far distant from France.

One such was East Africa. The German colony of Tanganyika (now Tanzania) threatened the southeastern oceans, but so far the British had achieved little against its defenders; doughty, locally recruited black troops with a handful of German officers who were led by a superb soldier and tactician, Colonel (later Major-General) Paul von Lettow-Vorbeck.

In the Middle East there was grave concern over a Turkish-sponsored threat to Egypt and thus the vitally important Suez Canal. Egypt was a strange political anomaly. Officially it was an autonomous province of the Turks' immense, loosely structured Ottoman Empire, which ruled vast stretches of the Middle East, and even had its own ruler, the Khedive. But it had been under *de facto* British control since the construction of the Suez Canal, a situation about which the weakened Ottoman Empire could do nothing.

The growing likelihood of hostilities between Britain and France on the one hand and the German-supporting Ottoman Empire on the other brought this into question and had strained Khedive's relationship with Britain. It was true that the Ottoman Empire was on its last legs, yet it was still a formidable entity with an army of renowned toughness and fighting spirit that was trained and properly equipped for European-style conventional warfare.

What had ratcheted up the tension was that on 11 November 1914 the Sultan of Turkey had declared a *jihad*, holy war, against France and Britain. This was potentially a very serious development because the sultan was nominally the religious head of most of the Islamic world. Theoretically, it meant that all Muslims were expected to take up arms against the French and British infidels. The only ones to heed the call had been a powerful, fiercely spirited Sanussi religious sect in neighbouring Libya, an unwilling Italian colony. The Sanussi had long been fighting their conquerors and now the rebellion threatened to spill over into Egypt. The Turks had gone to considerable effort to provide them with small arms, artillery and training, and had even sent a general, Gaafer Pasha, to lead them.

A successful Sanussi invasion of Egypt, particularly if it gained the support of its Egyptian co-religionists, would pose an immediate danger to the Suez Canal, Britain's military and commercial lifeline to the Far East. In addition, in the Middle East, respect was wedded to power, and such a blow to British prestige at its time of greatest weakness could not be permitted.

The immediate requirement, however, was for troops for the Western Front, and as early as April 1915, long before the South West Africa campaign had concluded, the South African and British governments began discussing the dispatch of a South African expeditionary force to Europe. Agreement was reached in July and recruiting began immediately. However, the 1912 Defence Act did not clearly define what constituted service in defence of South Africa; the invasion of South West Africa could be construed as having been in defence of the country, but service farther afield was another matter. This was circumvented by raising Imperial Service Units that would be locally recruited and trained but paid and equipped, by the British, once they sailed for Europe.

Volunteers streamed in for the 1st South African Brigade, made up of four battalions, of which many members were drawn from existing regiments. 1 South African Infantry (Lieutenant-Colonel F. S. Dawson) consisted of Cape men, 2 and 3 South African Infantry regiments (Lieutenant-Colonels W. E. C. Tanner and E. F. Thackeray) were manned from Natal, the Orange Free State, the Transvaal and Rhodesia, and Lieutenant-Colonel F. A. Jones's 4 South African Infantry (the South African Scottish) were mainly from the Cape Town Highlanders and Transvaal Scottish. Many other men joined artillery and other units for service in France.

Brigadier-General Tim Lukin was the natural choice as brigade commander. The Western Front was primarily an infantryman's war, unlike any of the freewheeling light cavalry wars of Africa, and he was by far the best qualified of South Africa's generals to handle it.

A great number of the volunteers were trained soldiers who had already seen active service in South West Africa. The brigade was assembled at Potchefstroom and organized and kitted out with remarkable speed. The first contingent set sail from Cape Town on 4 September 1915 and the last on 17 October 1915, a total of 160 officers and 5,648 other ranks. They started arriving in England on 23 September and immediately went into camp for three months' intense training.

Midway through their training the problems with the Sanusi boiled over. Things had been going badly for them and they were facing starvation. As a result incidents along the Libyan–Egyptian border escalated and finally their leader, the Grand Sanusi Sayyed Ahmed – egged on by the Turks and Germans – invaded Egyptian territory on 12 November 1915.

This caused an immediate crisis. The invaders were not a typical quarrelsome, organizationally unstable group of desert tribesmen raiding for plunder, but some 5,000 trained men united by their sect's beliefs. The only logical solution for the British was to rout the invaders as soon as possible and then chase them back across the Libyan border.

But here, as was the case elsewhere, the British were desperately short of troops. The Western Front's requirements were insatiable; simultaneously they were heavily engaged against the Turks in Mesopotamia, the vast and almost unmapped territory between the Tigris and Euphrates rivers that is today Iraq.

As a result they'd had to withdraw most of their regular garrison troops in Egypt and replace them with the Western Frontier Force under Major-General A. Wallace. The force's name was impressive, but in fact it was very much an *ad hoc* body with a hastily assembled staff which had not yet had time to settle in.

The rank and file consisted of an interesting mix of infantry, light cavalry and artillery from at least five different sources. There were two contingents of professional soldiers, a battalion of the Royal Scots and another borrowed from the Indian Army, the 15th Sikh Regiment, while the others were, almost to a man, citizen soldiers, some from existing part-time units and others hostilities-only volunteers.

There was a battalion of the New Zealand Rifle Brigade, and a composite light cavalry regiment of squadrons drawn from various units of the 5th Mounted Brigade in Mesopotamia – the Duke of Lancaster's Yeomanry, the Royal Buckinghamshire Hussars, the Hertfordshire Yeomanry, the Dorsetshire Yeomanry and the Australian Light Horse, and two troops of the Surrey Yeomanry.

Wallace's only support assets consisted of some reconnaissance aircraft, two citizen soldier artillery units – A Battery of the Honourable Artillery Company and the Nottinghamshire Battery Royal Horse Artillery – and a detachment of the Royal Naval Air Service's Seabrook heavy armoured cars. The cars were very much an unknown quantity. Although heavily armed with a 3-pdr artillery piece and four .303-calibre Vickers machine guns each, the Seabrooks were cumbersome vehicles, built on a 10-ton lorry chassis. Their mobility on poor roads and cross-country was in doubt.

The citizen soldiers were generally of good quality and highly motivated – in those days the part-time military system throughout the British Empire was not a type of job-creation scheme but an expression of patriotism which attracted volunteers of the best type – and in many cases had solid experience gained in other wars. But some were not yet fully trained in desert warfare, and Wallace had still been busy bringing them to up to scratch when the Sanusi invaded.

Wallace's task was an unenviable one. Not only had he not had time to run his less-than-formidable force with its scratch staff through the necessary shake-down process, but now he was expected to undertake a counter-attack on terrain which was as great an enemy of operations as South West Africa's had been for Botha's soldiers, and in some respects even less hospitable.

The sparse population of western Egypt lived mostly on the coastal strip which had some water but was hot and dusty in summer and a quagmire during the December–March rainy season. Beyond the coastal strip were ranges of rocky hills and beyond them lay several hundred thousand square kilometres of desert, waterless except for a few oases at Siwa and elsewhere and inhabited only by some nomadic bands of Bedouin Arabs.

The nearest jumping-off place to the border with Cyrenaica was the harbour of Sallum (which would become familiar to South African soldiers of a later war), nearly 450km west of Alexandria. Unlike Lüderitzbucht, however, it was eminently vulnerable to German U-boat attacks and the Royal Navy did not have enough anti-submarine vessels to protect convoys sailing to it. The next (and only) available option was the harbour of Mersa Matruh (or Marsa Matruh), 270km to the east, which had adequate water and facilities.

The reason why Sallum and Mersa Matruh were of such paramount importance was that western Egypt had virtually no landward lines of communication except camel-tracks. In South West Africa there had been a fairly comprehensive – if often sabotaged – railway network and some useable dirt roads of varying quality, but Egypt was another matter.

From Alexandria a poorly equipped railway line ran westward for 90km to El Daba. From there travellers to Mersa Matruh had to rely on the so-called Khedival Motor Road, which in spite of its imposing name was actually little more than a slightly improved camel-track. The Khedival Motor Road snaked along the coast to the small port of Sidi Barrani and then reverted to its real nature.

Under the circumstances the higher headquarters took the only possible decision: it ordered Wallace to withdraw to Mersa Matruh, 180km west of Alexandria, and wait for reinforcements. When they arrived Wallace was to advance westward and decisively defeat the invaders.

The choice for reinforcements fell to the 1st South African Brigade, possibly because its officers and men had recent battle experience and were old Africa hands. At the end of November they were told that they would not be leaving for France on 16 December 1915, as they had been informed, but would first be sent to Egypt to deal with the Sanusi. What they were heading for was not really an infantryman's milieu, but the experience they had picked up in the South West Africa Campaign would prove invaluable.

Meanwhile the Sanusi had not wasted any time moving eastward after the British withdrawal, and while waiting for the South Africans to arrive, Wallace went over to the offensive to slow them down and make sure that they did not build up enough prestige for themselves to attract members of the local population to their cause.

To this end he sent out columns that managed to disperse local Sanusi bands; by January 1916 he had inflicted some losses. But the Sanusi main body was untouched, and his men, particularly the infantry, were being worn down by the distances and harsh conditions of desert warfare.

From 10 January 1916 onward the first contingent of South Africans – 2 South African Infantry under Lieutenant-Colonel Tanner – started arriving at Alexandria and immediately went into desert training. They had barely started, however, when a British reconnaissance aircraft spotted the main Sanusi camp at Halazin, about 35km southwest of Mersa Matruh. Tanner's regiment was immediately dispatched by sea, since the railway line had no rolling stock available. After a gruelling voyage the regiment arrived at Mersa Matruh and the Frontier Force set off for Halazin.

The march to Halazin was gruelling; the pouring rain had turned the motor road into such a gluey morass that the armoured cars were left behind at Mersa Matruh, along with most of the other transport carrying the water and rations. Wallace had decided, probably correctly, that they would not be capable of keeping up with the infantry and light horse.

If it had been the dry season the situation might have been different, but the lumbering Seabrook cars had been built for the well-kept roads of Europe and not the glutinous mud of western Egypt in the rainy season.

Wallace arrived at Halazin on 23 January 1916 and went straight into the attack. Gaafer Pasha had done his work well; the Sanusi were properly dug in, in a concave semi-circle behind a long, low ridge with their flanks well forward; any attacking force would have to advance over a wide stretch of open ground under fire from three sides, not only from the Sanusi riflemen, but also from Gaafer Pasha's artillery and machine guns.

Wallace decided nevertheless on a frontal assault and at 1000 sent the Sikhs straight at the centre of the enemy line, backed up by Tanner's 2 South African Infantry and the New Zealanders, with support from the Nottinghamshire Battery's guns.

A long, fierce battle ensued, characterized by heavy fire – from the Sanusi side – and repeated flanking attacks all of which failed but the assault force continued its remorseless advance. By 1445 the Sikhs, South Africans and New Zealanders had overrun the Sanusi entrenchments and the invaders began to stream away in a disorganized mass.

This should have been the moment for a relentless follow up by the light horsemen to complete the destruction of the Sanusi as a coherent fighting force, but the long march to contact, followed by the battle, had rendered the Western Frontier Force's mounts incapable. The horses had not had water for the entire day and were exhausted by the manoeuvring during the Sanusi flank attacks.

The heavily armed Royal Naval Air Service armoured cars would now have been able to play a decisive part, but of course they were back at Mersa Matruh. Wallace had been frustrated by two of the three classic operational factors, the weather and the terrain.

This matter was soon rectified. Following Halazin, the Sikhs were posted home and replaced by the other three South African regiments, the rest of 2 Mounted Brigade arrived and the Royal Naval Air Service's Seabrooks were replaced by 17 lighter armoured cars, a Model T Ford mounting a machine gun and some motorcycles, all under the colourful command of Major the Duke of Westminster.

The Duke's cars were none other than the Rolls-Royce Admiralty 1914 Pattern type that had done so much to save the day at Trekkopjes in South West Africa, the only difference being that the tops and bevels of the turrets had been removed to provide some relief from the desert heat. Not only lighter, but stronger and more agile at cross-country than the Seabrooks, the Rolls-Royces were to play a valuable role in the rest of the campaign against the Sanusi.

By mid-February the Western Frontier Force was well on the way to acquiring enough transport and draught animals to operate independently and Major-General W. E. Peyton, the new force commander, prepared for a push to Sallum to deal a final blow to the invaders.

Brigadier-General Lukin.

At this stage Peyton's information was that the main Sanusi force was dug in at Agagia, near the so-called motor road about 16km southeast of Sidi Barrani, which itself was about 135km by march route from Mersa Matruh, with a smaller group at Bir Warr on the outskirts of Sallum, there was also said to be about 2,000 Sanusi at the distant Siwa oasis, but they appeared to be static.

This gave him two choices. He could advance along the coastal road and attack Sidi Barrani with part of his force while simultaneously landing at Sallum, or he could advance by land only, take Sidi Barrani and use it as a supply base for a landward attack on Sallum.

Both alternatives had major disadvantages. Sallum's harbour mouth was heavily mined, and was overlooked by the Haggag es Sallum, a high escarpment that would turn everything below it into a shooting gallery; a landing would be slow and laborious, without the element of surprise and costly in casualties. An overland advance from Sidi Barrani would require a journey through almost waterless terrain with many communications and supply problems, and quite likely, a heavy engagement at the port itself.

On the other hand, the Western Frontier Force now had 2,000 camels which could carry four times as much as horses, drink the most unpalatable water and require less rest. And so the decision was taken for a landward advance. Peyton envisaged a two-pronged approach. One prong would consist of a force under Tim Lukin, which would take on the Sanusi at Agagia, while the rest of the Frontier Force would hug the coast heading for Sidi Barrani.

For this purpose Peyton set up a forward supply base at Angeila, west of Mersa Matruh. The idea was that Lukin would march to Angeila with his brigade headquarters, Lieutenant-Colonel Thackeray's 3 South African Infantry, the Royal Scots, most of the Nottinghamshire Battery, the Dorsetshire Yeomanry under Lieutenant-Colonel H. M. W. Souter and an attached support and supply echelon. At Angeila he picked up 1 South African Infantry, which was 22 officers and 888 men strong.

Lukin left Mersa Matruh on 20 February 1916 and arrived two days later at Angeila where he left all but 300 of the Royal Scots as a guard force, along with the New Zealanders, Lieutenant-Colonel Dawson's 1 South African Infantry and the remainder of the Nottinghamshire Battery and carried straight on. His immediate destination was Wadi el Maktila about 40km away and about 3km north of Agagia.

He arrived there on 24 February 1916. He had pushed his infantry hard to maintain the element of surprise, and being wise in the ways of desert campaigning, he let them get their heads down as soon as they arrived. Here the Duke of Westminster with six of his armoured cars joined Lukin, having made use of the cars' superior speed to travel up from Mersa Matruh by night to preserve secrecy.

Lukin's intention was to let his men rest for all of 25 February's daylight hours, during which time an aerial reconnaissance flight would bring him the latest intelligence on the Sanusi defences and dispositions. That night he would set off on a march that would have him in position for a dawn attack.

But the Sanusi had become aware of him in spite of his precautions and late in the afternoon of 24 February they fired on the camp with machine guns and two artillery pieces. It seems to have been more of an intelligence-gathering probe rather than a serious attack; within half

Seabrook armoured cars in the desert.

The Duke's cars were none other than the Rolls-Royce Admiralty 1914 Pattern type.

an hour the Sanusi left having caused minimal loss among the South Africans (one killed and one wounded).

Never one to under-estimate an enemy, Lukin cancelled the rest day and set off for Agagia before dawn next morning, sending Souter and the Dorsetshire Yeomanry out ahead to occupy a small prominence near the objective. A little before 1100 Lukin had reached his objective with the infantry already deployed into extended line, bayonets fixed.

In the centre of Lukin's line, as it went into the attack, was 3 South African Infantry, with 1 South African Infantry following 500m behind. On their left was a squadron of the Dorsetshires and two armoured cars to beat off any out-flanking attempt by the Sanusi, while Souter and his main body of horsemen, with another two armoured cars, was stationed on Lukin's right to prevent the Sanusi from breaking away to the west.

Harried by rifle, machine gun and artillery fire, Souter took up position about half a mile from the enemy's left flank, dismounted and began to advance on foot to make sure the Sanusi stayed in place. Despite problems with the soft sand the two armoured cars accompanied them harrying the Sanusi in return with their machine guns.

At 1100 the attack proper started. Extended over a mile-long front 3 South African Infantry marched into a storm of fire with 1 South African Infantry following. Meanwhile the four flanking armoured cars opened up with their machine guns in support of the infantry and the Nottinghamshire Battery made all haste to get their guns into range, in classic horse artillery fashion, to lay down accurate fire on the Sanusi positions.

As Lukin had anticipated, Gaafer Pasha ordered a flanking movement aimed at his left. He ordered Lieutenant-Colonel Dawson to stretch out the flank with one company of 1 South African Infantry, which worked so well that Dawson stemmed the tide and ended up threatening the Sanusi flank instead. This allowed Lukin to send the detached squadron of Yeomanry and its armoured cars to join Souter on the opposite flank.

Thackeray's 3 South African Infantry pressed doggedly forward in spite of intense rifle and machine-gun fire, and by 1300 – augmented now by the other 1 South African Infantry companies and the two armoured cars – started overrunning the Sanusi lines, a laborious and distinctly life-threatening business because the desert warriors' positions were well situated and they were in no mood to give up.

In the meantime Lieutenant-Colonel Souter was awaiting his moment. It came at around 1300 when the infantry had occupied the Sanusi lines and the invaders were escaping. Souter waited until they were well clear of the trenches and barbed wire, then ordered what was, as Peter Digby says, "one of the last cavalry charges in modern warfare."

Covered by the armoured cars' machine-gun fire, Souter gave the order to charge. Swords sprang from scabbards and steel met steel; with a piercing battle cry the Dorsetshires galloped straight into the Sanusi. The mass of yelling horsemen thundering down on them was too much even for these resolute invaders, who broke and ran.

Souter featured bizarrely in this battle; his horse was shot dead from under him, pitching him forward to land at the feet of Gaafer Pasha himself. The Turk promptly drew his revolver to shoot Souter, but before he could fire Souter sabred him in the right arm and personally took him prisoner. (Souter was later admitted to the Distinguished Service Order for this exploit.)

While the Dorsetshire Yeomanry followed the fleeing Sanusi deeper into the desert, the South Africans mopped up. They had captured Gaafer Pasha's entire staff, all his artillery and machine guns, great numbers of Sanusi and a large amount of assorted supplies, including 50 camels laden with dates, which they discovered were the Sanusi rations for the next 10 days.

Agagia was the turning point of the invasion. After that the Sanusi did not fight from prepared positions again. But it had come at a cost; 1 and 3 South African Infantry Regiments had 17 killed and 98 wounded, while the Dorsetshires had lost 33 dead and 25 wounded, the yeomanry's sense of loss was made all the more bitter by the fact that the Sanusi had mutilated and killed some of their men who had been wounded during the final pursuit.

Lukin kept up the pressure. On 28 February he set off for Sidi Barrani and arrived after four hours of hard marching to find it abandoned and considerably knocked about after a shelling from the Royal Navy. The South Africans set up camp and reorganized for the final push through to Sallum 75km away.

Among other things an airstrip was cleared to allow a reconnaissance aircraft to land. The pilot was a young lieutenant of the South African Aviation Corps named Andreas Helperus van Ryneveld. He went on to distinguish himself on the Western Front, was instrumental in founding the South African Air Force after the war and ended his career as Sir Pierre van Ryneveld, Chief of the General Staff in the Second World War.

Supplies for the advance remained a problem. On 3 March 1916 the transport ship *Borulos* arrived with some stores. There was still not enough for the whole force, so when General Peyton and 2 South African Infantry arrived a few days later most of the mounted troops were sent back to Mersa Matruh. For the final showdown the Western Frontier Force would depend on its infantry, the remaining handful of light horsemen and the armoured cars.

Due to his aerial reconnaissance and local knowledge Peyton knew that Sallum would be a tough nut to crack. He considered his options and decided against a frontal attack. Instead he would send Lukin eastward to Buqbuq on the coast and then strike southeastward to Bir el Augerin, whose wells apparently had enough water. From there he would capture the Nagb Medean pass – little more than a rocky track about 32km south of the objective – to reach the top of the 180m-high Haggag es Sallum escarpment, where there was said to be water in two ancient Roman cisterns.

It would be a bare-bones operation, with every superfluous item and all wheeled transport left behind: baggage, equipment, ammunition, stores and above all water would be carried by a train of 600 camels. His only support weapons, apart from his machine guns, would be the armoured cars; because the Nagb Medean passes could not be negotiated by vehicles they would have to make a wide sweep to the southwest and climb the escarpment from the rear.

On 9 March Lukin set out with 1 and 4 South African Infantry Regiments, while the armoured cars headed off to the southwest. Four and a half hours of hard marching brought Lukin to Buqbuq, which indeed had a plentiful supply of water. He spent the night there and started off at 0400 next morning on a tough six-hour march to Bir el Augerin. There he encountered a serious problem – the wells were dry.

Digging during the one-hour rest period that Lukin allowed, his soldiers managed to find some water that not only smelled and tasted of sulphur but had animal parts floating in it.

The troops drank it anyway. Then they set off for the Nagb Medean pass about 8km away through incredibly difficult terrain. Tortured by heat and thirst the South Africans scrambled up the escarpment and found the pass undefended, except for a handful of Sanusi who were hastened on their way by nothing more than three rifle shots.

Meanwhile the Duke of Westminster and his Rolls-Royces were bashing their way over the untamed terrain of the plateau to rendezvous with Lukin, their overheated radiators boiling away the cars' water at such a rate – water that could not be replaced because the Sanusi had destroyed all the wells along the way – that he threatened to court martial any man that squandered water on the infantry, whether from the radiators or the bottles used for filling the cooling jackets of his Vickers guns.

The infantrymen were in such a parlous state, however, that the Duke's men gave them all they could. Some soldiers were so desperate that they drank their rifle oil or grubbed for roots; camel boys drank their animal's urine. Eventually more camels arrived from Bir el Augerin with some of the dreadful water found there, which now tasted even worse because it had been chlorinated. The infantrymen drank every drop – they were long past caring about such trivia.

At this stage plans changed. Peyton ordered Lukin to capture the Halfaya pass farther to the northwest so that the Western Frontier Force's mounted troops and guns could get through, on to the escarpment when they arrived. Lukin's flanking march made it impossible to defend the Halfaya pass, he arrived to find that the Sanusi had abandoned it, as well as their camp a few kilometres farther along the lip of the escarpment and were retreating toward the southwest, after destroying whatever ammunition and supplies they could not take with them.

The Duke of Westminster gave the Sanusi no rest. He set off in hot pursuit, caught up with them about 32km from the pass and hosed them with his machine guns. Two of the Sanusi camels, which had been loaded with ammunition, exploded and the remaining invaders scattered. Many surrendered or were captured, along with three Turkish officers, three 10-pdr artillery pieces and nine Maxim machine guns with 300,000 rounds of ammunition. For practical purposes the invasion was over, and the armoured cars had fired the campaign's final shots.

The South Africans picked their way down the escarpment to the deserted port and were personally welcomed by General Peyton who had arrived and occupied it in the meantime, then swallowed long draughts of tea that 2 South African Infantry had prepared for them.

1 South African Brigade remained at Sallum until the beginning of April, and among other things occupied its time by building a road up to the plateau that was still there a quarter century later and played an important role in South African and British operations during the Second World War. But it was diminishing almost by the day as one company after another was shipped back to Alexandria for reorganizing and re-equipping for France.

On 10 April 1916 it was inspected by General Sir Archibald Murray, general officer commanding British forces in Egypt, and on 13 April its regiments embarked for Marseille, having earned a great reputation; Lukin was not only made a Commander of the Order of the Bath by the King but was invested with the Order of the Nile by the Khedive of Egypt, who also gave him a beautiful Arabian charger.

The Duke of Westminster's armoured cars did not go with the South Africans. The fighting in Europe was an infantryman's war, and the Rolls-Royces still had much to do in the Middle East.

In retrospect, the campaign drove home the lessons learned from Commander Whittall's contingent during its short but meaningful time in South West Africa, because the Duke's cars had the opportunity to show what they could do, and because Lukin had understood their true potential and used them in combination with his infantry and light horsemen in such a way that the strengths of each arm was fully exploited.

This, too, was a lesson that, no doubt, stayed in the minds of many of the South Africans now sailing for Marseille to be flung into the horrors on the Western Front.

5

France ... and South Africa's first aquaintance with tanks

The 1st South African Brigade earned renown in the savage battles of the Western Front, among other things for its defence of Delville Wood. It did not again serve cheek by jowl with armoured cars, but it arrived at the front just a few months before the first British battle tanks made their appearance.

William Tritton's experimental 'Little Willie' had reached its final design in December 1915. In August 1916 a prototype battle tank nicknamed 'Mother' appeared; the first to employ the rhomboidal shape that was to be seen in most British tank designs, and the first copies of the Heavy Tank, Mark I were produced with remarkable speed.

It is commonly thought that battle tanks were first used at the Battle of Cambrai in November 1917, but this is not so. Tanks started seeing operational deployment more than a year earlier, at the tailend of the Battle of the Somme, which started in June 1916 and was so bloody the British alone suffered more than 60,000 casualties on the first day.

General Lukin's 1st South African Brigade, which captured and held Delville Wood against overwhelming odds for six days and five nights in mid-July 1916, suffered losses such as no South African unit or formation had ever experienced – from just over 3,000 officers and men, 647 were killed in action, died of wounds or were posted missing/presumed dead, 1,476 were wounded and 297 were taken prisoner.

The Somme dragged on (at its end it had cost about a million British, French and German lives without achieving anything significant). By September 1916 a deadly stalemate had settled over the battlefield, and the first offspring of Tritton's 'Mother', the Mark I heavy tanks, were brought up to break the deadlock.

The Mark I came in two versions: Male and Female, the former had a sponson on each side mounting a 57mm 6-pdr gun and a machine gun, whose primary task was demolishing enemy emplacements and wire entanglements. The Females only had machine guns in the sponsons to deal with the enemy's infantry after his line had been broken. The nicknames stuck and became part of the accepted nomenclature.

The Mark Is went into action for the first time on 15 September 1916 – 36 great clanking monsters with tail-wheels to help their steering and which shrugged off the storms of rifle and machine-gun fire directed at them by the understandably concerned enemy.

It is difficult for a modern armour soldier to appreciate the ordeals these early tank crews suffered as a matter of routine, both in and out of action. The Mark I needed a crew of eight men: the commander, who also operated the brakes, the driver, two gearsmen and four gunners. The driver's controls were limited to throttle and clutch. To change direction by the skid steering he had to signal his intentions to the gearsmen at the rear of the vehicle.

According to Foss and McKenzie, conditions inside the first tanks were uncomfortable and frequently highly dangerous – and not just when under fire from the enemy. The engine was noisy, so that communication was possible only through hand signals and it was located in the centre of the fighting compartment, where it produced a great deal of heat and fumes.

When under attack, molten lead, or splash, as the crews called it, from bullets which had penetrated the riveted joints and shed their jackets flew around the interior; to combat this the crews were issued with leather jerkins, goggles and special visors of chainmail, although it was so hot inside that they usually discarded much of the protective kit.

The Mark Is did not achieve anything really significant because the British did not yet understand how tanks should be used and diluted their potential by employing them in small groups. Nevertheless, they made such an impact that the British commander-in-chief, Field-Marshal Sir Douglas Haig – even though he was a dyed-in-the-wool cavalryman – ordered another 1,000.

A small batch of Mark IIs was manufactured which incorporated certain modifications; the tail-wheels were discarded – reputedly after one tank's wheels were shot away without any deterioration in the steering – the armour was 10mm thick in front and 8mm on the sides, and some trackshoes were wider than others to give better traction. They were followed by the Mark III, which was almost identical but had slightly thicker armour. Both were used for training only, the next operational model being the Mark IV which went into production in March and April of 1917.

The Mark IV incorporated a number of important modifications. Among other things, the frontal armour was now 12mm thick and the side-armour 8mm; its high-octane aviation petrol was in an external armoured 272-litre fuel tank located between the rear horns, instead of internally on either side of the driver – a virtual guarantee of a fiery death – and the gun sponsons were higher off the ground. The crew had improved escape facilities, and safety – and presumably morale and combat confidence – had been enhanced by moving the petrol tank to the rear.

A total of 1,220 Mark IVs were built, 205 of them tenders which had been adapted to follow the battle tanks into action. Others were modified to serve as logistic vehicles, wireless tanks, searchlight tanks and mine exploders – an early appearance of the 'family' concept of one basic model and a number of specialized variants.

It took some considerable time before the British realized that using the tanks in 'penny packets' diluted their potential, but by Cambrai in November 1917 they seemed to have learned the lessons of the Somme. This time they concentrated their available tanks (one source says 378, another 476) into three brigades which were flung at one of the most strongly defended German sectors of the Western Front, supported by a 1,000-gun bombardment and followed by six infantry divisions.

For the German defenders the attack was a horrible surprise because it came without the usual artillery ranging shots that were always a dead giveaway of an impending assault, and the rolling chalk downs were ideal tank country. Their lines were smashed wide open and the British infantry moved more than 11km forward in the first few hours, an unprecedented advance in Western Front trench warfare – all this without the appalling losses that had become such a ghastly part of earlier frontal attacks.

Much of the ground gained was later lost again because there had not been enough exploitation by the attackers, but the fact remains that Cambrai is generally regarded as the start of armoured warfare as we know it today, although it would take 25 years for its doctrines to develop to their full extent.

The machine guns of the Western Front had proved beyond doubt that the day of massed infantry attacks on well-defended static positions were passing; it had served well enough in the days when the foot soldier faced only grapeshot and muzzle-loading muskets, but now things had changed.

The lethality of the infantryman's personal weapons had increased exponentially and had been enhanced by such things as barbed wire entanglements, aerial attacks, man-portable trench mortars, mines and poison gas. The future tactics of choice were to be found in assaults combining armour and infantry whenever the circumstances allowed it. It would take years, however, for this quantum leap in doctrine to sink into the more reactionary military minds.

The same applied to cavalry attacks; the machine gun had made the heavy cavalry obsolete almost overnight, although light horsemen still had a vital role in places – like the Middle East and North Africa where the open spaces made it possible to outflank enemy trenches – at least until armoured cars had developed to the point where they did not merely act in coordination with the light horsemen, but could replace them altogether.

One of the observers at Cambrai was a forceful major, soon to be a temporary colonel, from the newly arrived American Expeditionary Force: Major George S. Patton. Patton commanded the two-battalion first brigade of his country's newly established tank corps, and what he saw there he never forgot.

"He came away," writes one of his biographers, Major-General Hubert Essame, "convinced that even the primitive tanks then available, acting in conjunction with the air, artillery and infantry arms, could restore mobility to the battle, and that the scale had at last been tipped in favour of the man against the machine gun."

Cambrai also provided considerable food for thought for the 1st South African Brigade, which did not take part in the battle but immediately afterward relieved some of the troops who had fought there and saw what the tanks had accomplished.

British and French tanks rapidly grew larger, heavier, more powerfully armed, more thickly armoured, longer ranging and easier to operate. The German response to the landship concept was surprisingly tardy, according to George Forty, the armoured concept lacked advocates at high level. Development did not start in earnest until October 1916, after the British deployment on the Somme, and sped up after Cambrai, but by then the Germans were so hard-pressed that they never came anywhere close to catching up with their opponents.

Just one German tank type ever became operational, the A7V Sturmpanzerwagen. The A7V was a very large 33-tonner that was top heavy, poor at trench crossing and so tall that it was easily seen by artillery spotters; the only really significant British anti-tank arm of the time. On the other hand it mounted a limited-traverse 57mm artillery piece in the nose and bristled with machine guns.

Only a handful ever went into action, but the Germans did not hesitate to use numbers of captured Mark IVs against their former owners, and concentrated on developing man-portable, anti-tank weapons – specifically flame throwers, armour-piercing ammunition for the standard infantry Mauser and a large 13mm-calibre rifle that had a notoriously violent recoil but could do serious damage.

The British and French tanks had many spin-offs that most of today's armour soldiers would probably think first appeared when Major-General Percy Hobart evolved his highly specialized 'funnies' for the invasion of France in 1944. There were tanks with 'tadpole tail' extensions to improve trench-crossing capability, tanks with pivoting tracks for better traction, support tanks for carrying infantry or supplies, bridging tanks, fascine tanks which rolled bundles of wood into ditches to make them passable and tanks fitted with rollers to explode mines.

There was also a tank with a trench mortar in an open hatch and a gun carrier mounting a 6-inch howitzer which could be fired from the tank itself, making it the world's first self-propelled artillery piece – the guns could also be dismounted and the carriers used for transporting ammunition. A famous photograph exists showing an early attempt at solving the communications problem – a Mark II Female with a large and cumbersome radio aerial.

Before very long the first light tanks were born. The heavy tanks' main role was supporting infantry operations in breaking through enemy lines, so they moved at hardly more than walking speed; but experience had shown that after a breakthrough the enemy could rush up more machine guns and bring them to bear on the infantry and cavalry. Clearly there was a requirement for a lighter, faster tank that could exploit any breakthrough of the heavies by swiftly penetrating into the area behind the enemy trenches.

The Tank Medium A 'Whippet' – originally dubbed Tritton's Light Machine, or the Tritton Chaser – resulted from a revised operational concept that started emerging in November 1916, just two months after the armour's first blooding at the Somme. In its final form the Whippet weighed only 14 tons compared to the battle tanks' 27-odd tons, so that although it had the same 14mm armour as the Mark IV's successor, the Mark V, it had a top speed of between 12 and 14kph, with a range of 130km, compared with 55km for the Mark IV and 70km for the Mark V.

'Big Willie' Mk3 Male 'Iron Duke' France, First World War.

In appearance it differed totally from the heavier tanks. Tritton had reverted to low tracks of the type used on Little Willie and given it a fixed turret situated well back and manned by two crew members and mounting four .303-calibre Hotchkiss machine guns. The driver was located behind two 33kW Taylor 4-cylinder engines of the type used in London buses – one for each track, with its own clutch.

This dual propulsion system made the Whippet fiendishly difficult to drive. Steering was by means of a small wheel; when the small steering wheel was turned to the left, it opened the throttle of the right engine. If a tighter turn was needed, the driver would depress the appropriate clutch and brake simultaneously.

With practice it was possible to handle Whippets with dash and skill and the type was eminently successful, particularly when the best ways of using them emerged – the original concept, which had envisaged the Whippets operating in conjunction with the cavalry during exploitation, turned out to be impracticable. They might have been fast in comparison to the heavy battle tanks, but on good going the horsemen outpaced them by a considerable margin.

This meant that in a fast-moving advance the Whippets would fall behind, and when the cavalrymen encountered machine guns they had to halt and wait for the light tanks to catch up and deal with the resistance. But, as Foss and McKenzie point out, the Whippets provided a foretaste of what could be achieved by deep penetration of armour behind enemy lines.

The French, who produced some advanced combat and specialist tanks, scored a particular design success with the Renault FT17, a 6½-tonner mounting an 8mm Hotchkiss machine gun – replaced in due course by a 37mm gun – in the first fully revolving turret ever fitted to a tank. It was "a remarkable little tank," according to George Forty, "a true milestone in design which lasted right up to the start of the Second World War and was adapted and produced by many countries all over the world."

Undoubtedly the most versatile light tank produced up to that time, it saw widespread use, not only by the French but by the Americans; the FT17 was the tank of choice for George Patton, a cavalryman imbued with the old French cavalry maxim of "attack, attack again," who used them to great effect in the Battle of the Meuse-Argonne, and was to become the best United States tank general of the Second World War. The British also made considerable use of FT17s, mainly for liaison and communications.

The FT17 served in many configurations besides the obvious: there was a bulldozer version and another mounting a 75mm gun, the largest ever fitted to the series, as well as a successful amphibious variant and a widely employed communications version with built-in wireless. The French were even experimenting with a modified FT17 mounting a massive long-barrelled 105mm gun when the war ended.

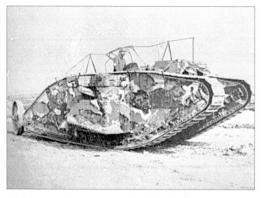

'Big Willie' Male at Flers, First World War.

Mk1 Female tank, France, First World War.

The Germans, on the other hand, were so far behind the Allies that they never managed to produce any equivalent to either the Whippet or the FT17. They did design a light tank they called the LK I, which weighed seven tons and mounted a machine gun in a revolving turret, but the war ended before the project had got beyond producing the original prototype and two improved developmental models: the LK II with thicker armour and a 57mm gun and the LK III which mounted a 20mm gun.

It was to be many years before the world's armies reluctantly accepted that tanks were anything more than an infantry support weapon, but seven months before the war ended the inevitable happened; on 24 April 1918, near Villers-Corterels, Mark IVs and A7Vs deliberately traded shots with one another instead of merely acting as the foot soldiers' strong right arm.

The protagonists were one Male and two Female Mark IVs – the British had learned by now that a team like this was good for knocking out heavily entrenched machine guns (the Male) and dealing with infantry and lightly protected automatic weapons (the Females) – and four A7Vs.

The resulting action was not of great consequence in itself but they heralded the shape of things to come, the tank-versus-tank combat of the Second World War.

The tank swiftly became an important weapon in the desperate and apparently never-ending struggle along the Western Front, and while the 1st South African Brigade remained what it was from beginning to end –a superb infantry formation – it forged links with the coming age of armour that were to stand the Union Defence Force in good stead.

When 'Little Willie' morphed into a fleet of real fighting vehicles, a number of South African soldiers serving in France volunteered to serve in them. Four are known to have died in action – Captain H. T. Trafford, second lieutenants A. H. Albertson and N. H. A. Ready and Gunner A. W. Benyon – while several were decorated for gallantry. One was a lieutenant named A. J. Kenyon who ended the war with a Military Cross for gallantry.

Another was Major Eric Deane Blackburn, educated at the Diocesan College and St Andrew's College, he was farming when the war broke out, promptly attested and served in both the 1914 Rebellion and the South West Africa Campaign. After that he went to England and was posted to what was then still the Heavy Branch, Machine Gun Corps and served in France from September 1916 to June 1919. He ended the war with both a Distinguished Service Order and a Military Cross.

When the Second World War broke out in 1939 both Kenyon and Blackburn joined the new South African Tank Corps, the forerunner of today's South African Armoured Corps, and applied the invaluable experience they had picked up while serving in these first landships.

The fighting on the Western Front – pre-dominantly an infantry and tank war – was a great contrast to the campaign simultaneously being waged in German East Africa. For some reason the East African Campaign – and for that matter the South West Africa Campaign – has never gripped the military or public imagination like the Western Front, although it featured some famous heroes and actions, involved a far greater number of men and served an important strategic purpose. Although more sparing of blood than the Western Front, it was certainly the most gruelling conventional war ever waged in the sub-continent.

It was also the last campaign in sub-Saharan Africa where the horse soldier and the traditional foot-slogging infantryman dominated the battlefield – although here too, as in South West Africa, they did so with the aid of such modern innovations as reconnaissance aircraft and wheeled transport where the terrain allowed.

6

Armoured cars in East Africa

Armoured cars played only a small role in East Africa during the First World War, but the story of South Africa's introduction to armour would not be complete without a brief description of the campaign, not only for the sake of context but because this was where the mechanization concept received its toughest early testing.

German East Africa (later Tanganyika and still later Tanzania) came into Kaiser Wilhelm's hands as a result of an Anglo-German agreement in 1885 that defined the two countries' spheres of influence in East Africa. It was an enormous, thinly populated area that was the size of Germany and France combined.

It was divided from British East Africa (later Kenya) and Uganda by an arbitrary border running from midway between the Indian Ocean ports of Mombasa (British) and Tanga (German) northwestward to Mount Kilimanjaro, where it skirted around to the British side, continued up to the middle of the eastern shore of Lake Victoria, then turned westward across the lake itself.

From the British point of view there were three compelling reasons to conquer German East Africa: It lay along the sea route to India, with well-developed ports at Dar es Salaam and Tanga from which German warships could operate, it was a threat to British East Africa, particularly the railway line that ran roughly parallel to the border, from Mombasa to Nairobi and thence to the borders of Uganda, and at the port of Dar es Salaam as well as at Bukoba on the western shore of Lake Victoria there were powerful radio transmitters capable of reaching Berlin.

In London the War Office believed that German East Africa could be conquered without great effort because of its great military disadvantages. The territory had a total Schutztruppe force of less than 5,000 all told, and the Germans were thousands of kilometres away from any sources of supply or reinforcement. A vigilant Royal Navy could patrol the coastline to keep them isolated – which it did with almost complete success– while British East Africa was conveniently close to provide own forces with access to all the accoutrement of war.

But the German military commander, Lieutenant-Colonel Paul Von Lettow-Vorbeck, intended to make a fight of it, for the same reasons as Colonel von Heydebreck in South West Africa: to divert British resources until the war in Europe had been won. He was far worse off in both weapons and manpower than von Heydebreck had been, but the Germans had several things in their favour.

One was German East Africa itself – a huge and mostly undeveloped territory, virtually bereft of any transport system except for a railway line from Dar es Salaam to Mwanza on the southern shore of Lake Victoria. This line bisected the country roughly southeast to its center, then west to Tabora where it split, north to Mwanza and west to Kigoma on the northern shore of Lake Tanganyika. Its terrain varied from cold, misty highlands to savannah-type grasslands to thick bush and dense jungle; much of it was prone to long periods of rain. It was abundantly stocked with game, including large numbers of predators and harboured all manner of debilitating diseases like malaria and sleeping sickness.

Another advantage for the Germans was that they would be fighting along internal lines of communication, while supplying the British forces as they advanced into the interior would be a logistic nightmare. But above all the Germans had von Lettow-Vorbeck himself, undoubtedly one of the finest generals to command a battlefield.

Von Lettow-Vorbeck looked like a typical Prussian officer, which he was, but in addition to possessing a keen mind and great charisma he was that rare combination of a professional soldier, trained in conventional European warfare, who was also well versed in African campaigning.

He had been attached to General Louis Botha's forces as an observer during the Second Anglo-Boer War, and had also served in China during the Boxer Rebellion of 1900 and in South West Africa in the war against the Herero tribe in 1904. His genius was that he had been able to digest what he had seen and apply it. It was a fearsome blend of skills, talent and intellect, although the British did not realize it when they set out to conquer Tanganyika.

At the start von Lettow-Vorbeck had only about 260 German leader group and 4,700 locally recruited *askari*, divided into 14 self-contained mobile field companies, each with its own supply and transport section, between two and four machine guns and about 250 civilian porters. He did not have much in the way of field artillery, his askari's standard weapon was still the efficient but antiquated Mauser Model 71 service rifle, firing black-powder cartridges, and they had no concept of modern conventional warfare or even the proper use of machine guns.

But he was to prove a master at improvisation and the art of living off his enemies, and once he had trained his askari to an acceptable standard, his tactics, including his masterful use of machine guns, would provide much grief for his opponents.

There was another factor in his favour, invisible but nonetheless vital, as Major R. J. Sibley points out:

> … substantial enlightened reforms applied by the liberal-minded Governor Heinrich Schnee after the harsh suppression of the Maji-Maji Rebellion at the turn of the century had changed attitudes among at least some of the local population, the proof of this being that between 1914 and 1918 there was not one tribal insurrection against the Germans in spite of the fact that Von Lettow-Vorbeck was totally occupied with fighting the British.

When the war started, the governors of the two territories, who had long had an amicable relationship, tried to keep out of the fighting. Governor Schnee ordered that no hostile action was to be taken, while Governor Sir Henry Conway Belfield on the British side of the border stated that "this colony has no interest in the present war." Both wished to adhere to the Congo Act of 1885, which called for overseas possessions to remain neutral in the event of a European war.

It was, needless to say, a hopelessly naïve desire under the circumstances, and no one knew that better than von Lettow-Vorbeck, who had spent much time travelling around to get the feel of the country and had done a thorough appreciation of his situation.

The most vital sector, he had concluded, was along the 200km-long stretch of the border with Kenya between the coast and Mount Kilimanjaro – the main area of German settlement – with the German railway line from the port of Tanga to the Kilimanjaro area running on one side of it, and on the other side the British line from Mombasa on the coast to Nairobi and then Uganda. The great hulk of Mount Kilimanjaro and adjoining mountain features covered much of the border's danger area, with three well-defined gaps that any invaders of Tanganyika would have to use.

This being the case, he decided that his best approach would be to immediately go on the offensive and threaten the British in their own territory by attacking the Uganda railway,

RNAS AC Rolls Royce in German East Africa, 1917.

Leyland Armoured car in German East Africa.

which was more vulnerable than its German equivalent because where it ran near the border it went through an uncultivated and uninhabited tract of bush land.

No doubt, given the Germans' efficient intelligence service, he was also perfectly aware of the fact that in real terms the available regular British force was weaker than it seemed. The British had 17 companies available from the three battalions of the King's African Rifles, but they were dispersed all over British East Africa and Uganda, and each had just one machine gun and no artillery of any kind. In addition, the British had some tribal unrest to deal with, and there was no provision for increasing their local force levels.

It needs hardly be said that neither the British nor the German governments had the least intention of honouring the Congo Act. For Commander Max Looff, captain of the Dar es Salaam-based German light cruiser SMS *Königsberg*, the war actually started before the official declaration of hostilities, when three cruisers of the Royal Navy's Cape Squadron – HMS *Astraea*, HMS *Hyacinth* and HMS *Pegasus* – set off to bottle up *Königsberg* at Dar es Salaam.

Looff forestalled them by sailing on 1 August 1914, gave them the slip and headed out into the Indian Ocean with the British cruisers in hot pursuit. Three days later the Germans marched into Belgium, and on 8 August 1914 a British warship opened hostilities in the East African theatre by steaming to Dar es Salaam and shelling the radio station into ruin.

On 15 August 1914, less than a fortnight after war had been declared, von Lettow-Vorbeck made his first move by sending a small force to capture the British border post at Taveta, just southeast of Kilimanjaro. The Germans then moved further inland to raid the railway line as well, but were beaten back by a company of the King's African Rifles.

The point had been made, though, and Sir Henry Belfield called urgently for reinforcements from India. The Indian government sent two hastily scraped-together contingents: Expeditionary Force B, under Brigadier-General J. M. Stewart and Expeditionary Force C, commanded by Major-General A. E. Aitken.

Stewart's 4,000-strong Force C, consisting of three infantry battalions, a battery of light mountain guns and a battery of machine guns, was to reinforce the King's African Rifles in the Kilimanjaro area, then advance on the German border post at Neu-Moshi, opposite Taveta, to secure the western terminus of the German railway. Force B was to land at Tanga, the Indian Ocean terminus of the railway, capture it and then bring the rest of Tanganyika under British control while Stewart's force pushed northwestward toward Moshi.

Force C landed at Mombasa on 1 September 1914 and elements of it were soon in the Kilimanjaro area, assisting the King's African Rifles with internal security and standing by to repel any German attacks. But at Tanga it was a different story altogether.

Von Lettow-Vorbeck had concluded that an attack there was likely and had prepared a hot reception, which Aitken duly walked into. His 8,000-strong Force B looked formidable but consisted mostly of second-rate Indian troops, and his attack on Tanga was badly planned and badly executed. The result was a decisive defeat by Von Lettow-Vorbeck's 1,000-odd Schutztruppe, with four machine guns and no artillery.

Force B suffered about 800 casualties and abandoned hundreds of rifles, 16 machine guns, half a million rounds of ammunition, enough field telephones for all of von Lettow-Vorbeck's purposes and so much clothing that he could kit out the whole of the *Schutztruppe* for an entire year in addition to re-equipping three full companies with modern .303-calibre magazine-loading Lee-Enfield rifles. The total cost of acquiring this vast windfall was 60 men.

Less than three weeks later there was another humiliating defeat for the British, this time at sea. When war broke out on 4 August 1914 Looff was 1,000 nautical miles into the Indian Ocean, still at large but now low on bunkers. Looff determined to get coal from whatever source, and to this end intercepted a British freighter called the *City of Winchester* off the coast of Oman; she turned out to be carrying coal of such poor quality that Looff sank her and moved on.

Later he managed to rendezvous with a collier named the *Somali* and obtained enough coal to get him to a hiding place suggested by the *Somali*'s knowledgeable young captain; the Rufiji river delta, 160km south of Dar es Salaam, the water of which was deep enough to float his ship. On 3 September 1914 *Königsberg* entered the Rufiji's mouth and made her way up to the little settlement of Salele.

In the next fortnight she was fully bunkered with lighters of coal towed down from Dar es Salaam, so that Looff was ready for action when he heard that a warship, which he guessed must be either HMS *Astraea* or HMS *Pegasus*, had entered Zanzibar harbour.

On 19 September 1914 he put to sea, and at dawn next day reached Zanzibar. There he found *Pegasus*, which had broken away from the cruiser squadron with engine problems, and mortally wounded her with 20 minutes of gunfire. Later that day Looff was back in the delta, leaving *Pegasus* capsized on the harbour's bottom, although six of her eight guns were salvaged and two would later be used on land against the Germans.

Looff's next target was the shipping lanes off the South African coast, but he could take no immediate action because urgent repairs were needed to *Königsberg's* boilers, parts of which had to be laboriously taken overland to the workshops at Dar es Salaam. In the meantime the Royal Navy squadron, which now included the old battleship HMS *Goliath* and the cruiser HMS *Chatham*, were scouring the seas for the German cruiser.

Chatham discovered *Königsberg* at the end of October; by now Looff had dug himself in, emplacing his secondary armament on shore to cover the approaches to the delta and deploying observers and some troops on shore. The repaired boilers eventually returned, but it was too late, two more British cruisers, HMS *Dartmouth* and HMS *Weymouth*, had arrived to reinforce the squadron.

The British ships drew too much water to get within effective range, and after some ineffectual shelling Looff moved *Königsberg* further up river. There the hunt stalled, and although the British made several attempts to get at *Königsberg* during the next few months, all of them failed.

Von Lettow-Vorbeck radically reorganized his fighting forces, training them for the campaigning that lay ahead, recruiting thousands more (at its peak his strength was to amount to about 3,000 Germans and 11,000 askari) and launching raids on the Uganda Railway. To ensure the most efficient running of his lines of communication he recruited a retired German general who had happened to be visiting the territory when war broke out.

The only noteworthy British successes during this period was the capture of the radio station at Bukoba and the destruction of *Königsberg* in July 1915. Using accurate coordinates supplied by a famed South African hunter and soldier, Major P. J. 'Piet' Pretorius, the British squadron sent two shallow-draft monitors – essentially heavily gunned self-propelled floating batteries – part of the way up the Rufiji.

When they were within range of the German ship they shelled her with the aid of a Royal Naval Air Service Farman spotter aircraft operating from Dar es Salaam – before it was shot down. After two days *Königsberg* was on fire below decks and so badly damaged that Looff scuttled her.

Neither victory really harmed von Lettow-Vorbeck, and he made the best of *Königsberg*'s loss by salvaging her 105mm guns, mounting some at Dar es Salaam and improvising field carriages for the others to give him heavy artillery support for the real war, the one he was waging on land. He mauled the British at a rather senseless little fight about 16km east of Taveta and followed that up by adding another threat to the Uganda railway with the capture of a British strongpoint at Kasigau.

The British government was so preoccupied with the fighting in Europe that the East African theatre was starved of both equipment and manpower, although it did acquire two batches of armoured cars in mid-1915; a light-armoured battery of four Rolls-Royce cars from No. 1 Squadron of the Royal Naval Air Service Armoured Car Division, and a peculiar outfit called No. 1 Willoughby's' Armoured Motor Battery, commanded by a colourful and very wealthy character called Sir John Willoughby.

Willoughby had been a close associate of Cecil John Rhodes and had seen service in Mashonaland and the Second Anglo-Boer War; deemed too old for active service in 1914, he had simply bought four armoured cars built on Leyland lorry chassis and offered them, and himself, to the Crown in February 1915.

Perhaps out of sheer desperation the British government accepted Willoughby's little private army into the military as 322 Company, Army Service Corps, and sent it to East Africa. He went out filled with martial spirit, although he did not forget to take a light hunting rifle along in case he could put up some game.

The Leylands were clumsy beasts, totally unsuited to East Africa: they had no mudguards, their centre of gravity was too high and their wheelbase too narrow. The Rolls-Royces were better, but none of the armoured cars made much of a contribution to the campaign, often being defeated – like the fleet of Model T pickups and other vehicles deployed in the area – by the horrendous terrain, although they were to see some action.

By the beginning of 1916, however, help was forthcoming from a source closer at hand – South Africa. With the South West Africa campaign out of the way, an East African expeditionary force was raised in the Union, consisting of some 20,000 foot and mounted troops, artillerymen and support services.

Among the South Africans was Jaap van Deventer, now a brigadier-general and commander of 1st South African Mounted Brigade. Another was Manie Botha and yet another was Coen Brits. With them came numerous other old sweats, most of whom were convinced that von Lettow-Vorbeck would be finished off as swiftly as were the Germans in South West Africa.

The troops poured into a huge tent city at Voi on the Uganda line, 96km from the border. While the South Africans and their British, Indian, East African and Rhodesian comrades went through their final training, army engineers hastily laid a railway line toward Taveta.

Command of all the forces in East Africa was to be given to General Sir Horace Smith-Dorrien, an Anglo-Boer War veteran who had fought at Ypres, but was then laid low by pneumonia and in his place the British government appointed General Smuts.

Smuts set off immediately to take up his new command, arriving just a week after another British defeat at Salaita Hill on the approaches to Taveta. Once again von Lettow-Vorbeck had been waiting in well-prepared positions, and in spite of a heavy softening-up bombardment won a decisive victory.

Smuts decided that the way to deal with von Lettow-Vorbeck was by a war of manoeuvre rather than British-style sledgehammer blows. He would burst through the Taveta Gap with his 2nd Division, while at the same time his 1st Division would break through at Longido in the north, swing left and march down the northern railway toward the town of Moshi. Von Lettow-Vorbeck would have to stand and fight or surrender.

Around this time the South Africans acquired an air arm in the form of No. 26 South Africa Squadron, that arrived at the end of February, equipped with BE2C aircraft, "throw-outs from the Western Front," according to James Ambrose Brown in his detailed history of the campaign, *They Fought for King and Kaiser*, which had been rigged for dropping small bombs, although in the next two months they would also receive some Henri Farmans.

The airmen were put to work almost immediately, flying photo-reconnaissance sorties, bombing troop concentrations, railways and bridges, and maintaining communications between the forces in the thick bush and mountains. It was exhausting work – fever took a heavy toll, while spares, fuel and bombs were perpetually in short supply, and both pilots and aircraft were lost through mechanical failure or enemy ground fire.

In one case a Captain A. T. O'Brien crashed after being hit by ground fire, evaded capture by the skin of his teeth and got back to base after a 80km march which took two and a half days, and in the course of which, he reported, "I swam across six streams or rivers and I was followed at one stage by a lion, which chased me up a tree despite my three broken ribs."

Early in March 1916 the simultaneous advances started. While 2nd Division headed for Taveta, Jaap van Deventer's horsemen swung around north of Taveta and skirted the approaches of Kilimanjaro – a diversionary movement laid on by Smuts to make the Taveta defenders feel insecure. It did, and 1st Mounted Brigade occupied Salaita Hill and then Taveta without firing a shot.

About 8km west of Taveta the Germans offered strong resistance at two hills: Latema and Reata. Brigadier-General Michael Tighe's brigade of Indians, Rhodesians and King's African Rifles nearly captured Reata, but were eventually driven back by von Lettow-Vorbeck's askari. Then van Deventer's brigade threatened the German flanks as it moved down toward Moshi, and Brigadier-General P. S. Beves, another of Smuts' South West Africa veterans, overran both positions with his brigade.

Von Lettow-Vorbeck managed to slip away and pulled back to the important railway town of Kahe, mainly because Brigadier-General Stewart was four days late advancing down the line from Longido. Smuts sacked him and got on with the war. He sent 1st Division – now commanded by Brigadier-General H. S Sheppard – to smash into the German main line of defence, while van Deventer hooked in on von Lettow-Vorbeck's flank from the south.

Van Deventer made heavy going through the thick bush, but the threat he posed was enough to persuade von Lettow-Vorbeck to retreat. Once again the elusive colonel had escaped, but the turning point of the campaign had been reached. Smuts had broken through into Tanganyika, neutralized the Germans' Northern railway and chased von Lettow-Vorbeck out of the best and richest part of the colony.

The only readily available recorded use of the armoured cars near the Lukiguru river during this period is to be found in James Ambrose Brown's history, at which stage it appears Willoughby was in command of the Rolls-Royces as well as his own cars:

Daylight saw Sheppard's column marching briskly along the motor road fringed with bush and forest. As the sky lightened the tramp of marching feet, the creak of wheels and clatter of hooves had ominous echoes to those with memories of the Boer War ...

The silence across the river seemed to deepen where the road took a right-angled turn to the left. A shot rang out. Among the leading horsemen scouting ahead a trooper of the 17th Indian Cavalry tumbled from his mount. At once the hidden machine guns began their deadly chatter. A quick-firer pumped over a stream of shells.

General J. L. van Deventer GOC RSA Forces GEA.

RNAS AC Rolls Royce in GEA 1917.

Major Sir John Willoughby waved forward his three armoured cars, their engines roaring and backfiring as noisily as the pom-poms' fire. The 50hp Rolls-Royce cars moved ponderously down the road and as abruptly pulled up. Willoughby looked from his car to see a four-foot trench.

"Back!" he ordered, and as the car ground into reverse a pom-pom shell hit it exactly in the space between the opened louvres of the radiator. The other cars gave covering fire as Willoughby's crew worked with shovels to fill in the trench. From the turret their Maxim engaged a machine gun across the river, and the car was got away.

Now the 29th Punjabis came trotting past, bent low, with bayonets fixed as they deployed and made for a tall hill rising from the luxuriant tropical growth. Orders were to seize it. The Germans had just realized its value and were scrambling up the rear side. There was a brisk fight, and the German force fell back, leaving its dead and wounded …

The pom-pom Brown refers to seems to have been a 1-pdr, similar to those used so effectively by the Boers between 1899 and 1902. In his book *Three Years of War in East Africa*, Captain Angus Buchanan relates that soon after this he tested the cars' armour plate, using a captured gun. His diary entry for 19 June relates:

I had some practice with a 1-inch Krupp gun which we had captured in the late engagement … I took part in some tests of armoured car armour plate, at the request of Major Sir John Willoughby. The armour plate withstood the blow of the Krupp gun shell at 100-yard range, and was merely dented.

We then tested the German made-up iron-plate shield on the Krupp gun. Our service rifle failed to penetrate the plate, but a .245 high-velocity sporting rifle of Sir John Willoughby's put a neat hole clean through it.

The ferocious spring rains now brought a lull to the fighting. Smuts used the time to reorganize. He rebuilt 1st Division as a British-Indian-Rhodesian-King's African Rifles formation under Major-General Reginald Hoskins, turned 2nd Division into an all-South African formation under the hard-riding van Deventer, who now became a major-general, and created a new formation, 3rd Division, under Coen Brits, now also a major-general. Each of the South African divisions consisted of two infantry brigades and a mounted brigade.

Now van Deventer embarked on one of his most famous exploits when Smuts ordered him to take his division on a far-ranging sweep westward and capture the fort of Kondoa Irangi (today Kondoa), just over 100km from the German Central railway which ran roughly westward from Dar es Salaam.

Smuts reasoned that von Lettow-Vorbeck would have to divert a considerable portion of his main force to counter this threat, which would facilitate a southward advance along the Northern railway by General Hoskins' 1st Division. It was an unseasonable time to undertake such a raid, but like all good commanders Smuts was willing to take a calculated risk, and he reasoned that it would be possible because according to information from various settlers, the rains were torrential only in the vicinity of Kilimanjaro and its associated mountains and rivers.

The risk backfired. Smuts' information turned out to be hopelessly wrong. It did not stop van Deventer, however, although his infantry suffered incredible hardship as they struggled though kilometre after kilometre of almost bottomless mud, plagued by malaria-bearing mosquitoes and endless torrents of rain. The mounted troopers suffered even more. Ranging far ahead of their scanty supplies, they were felled by malaria and dysentery, and were reduced to living on nuts, berries and raw mealies.

But their fighting spirit was undimmed, and when they came across a steep hill called Lolkisale where a company of askaris was well dug in, they stormed it on foot and captured it; it was the first time one of von Lettow-Vorbeck's units surrendered. On 18 April 1916 the mounted brigade reached Kondoa Irangi and overran it, its 400-strong garrison fleeing. Van Deventer's push was later described by one military writer as, "one of the outstanding cavalry feats of the First World War."

The capture of Kondoa Irangi persuaded von Lettow-Vorbeck to march there with about 4,000 men – more than half of his available force – to deal with van Deventer, his appreciation being that Smuts and Hoskins would not be likely to move southward along the Northern railway until the rains had ended.

Van Deventer found himself besieged in Kondoa Irangi under almost indescribable conditions, his division's effective strength shrinking daily under the onslaught of disease and starvation. On 9 May 1916 von Lettow-Vorbeck attacked, but at a point where the South Africans' defences were strong. Hours of savage fighting followed, after which von Lettow-Vorbeck withdrew.

Smuts' chief intelligence officer, a brilliant British captain named Richard Meinertzhagen, whose sharp-tongued comments remain to condemn almost every participant of any note in the East African campaign, jotted down a grudging compliment in his diary, "the first real knock Von Lettow has had... All credit to old van Deventer and his South Africans."

That same month Smuts started moving down the Northern railway, then swung south and kept going until he reached Morogoro on the Central railway. By the end of 1916 half of Tanganyika was in his hands, including both Tanga and Dar es Salaam.

At the end of 1916, No. 26 South Africa Squadron, now considerably smaller in both men and machines, was ordered back to Britain because the nature of the war had changed. Von Lettow-Vorbeck was on the run, and they were needed elsewhere. On arrival the squadron was disbanded and its personnel absorbed into other Royal Flying Corps units.

In January 1917 Smuts too departed for London, to represent the South African government at the Imperial War Cabinet which had been established by Prime Minister David Lloyd George to coordinate the British Empire's military policy.

He had succeeded in his primary task, to neutralize the threat to British East Africa, and his talents were now needed at a higher level. It was true that von Lettow-Vorbeck was still free somewhere south of the Rufiji river, but his ability to influence events in East Africa were finished.

Smuts handed over *pro tem* to General Hoskins and left, having enjoyed more success by this time than any of the other senior British generals. Hoskins reorganized, strengthened and re-equipped the badly weakened British East African forces. Then, when the rains ended in May, Hoskins was superseded by van Deventer, now a temporary lieutenant-general. He and his chief of staff, the British Brigadier-General Sheppard, were an unlikely but dynamic duo, and the writing was on the wall for von Lettow-Vorbeck.

Van Deventer slowly but surely pushed von Lettow-Vorbeck southward, and on 15 October 1917 forced him to fight toe-to-toe at Mahiwa-Nyangao. Four days of sanguinary battle followed; the result was inconclusive, but von Lettow-Vorbeck suffered heavy losses and was forced across the Rovuma river into Mozambique. Leaving a King's African Rifles contingent to guard the Tanganyika border, van Deventer followed and harried him with several independent columns.

At this stage the German High Command made an attempt to deliver supplies to von Lettow-Vorbeck by means of an incredible airship journey that remains an aviation landmark. The naval dirigible Zeppelin L59, nicknamed Das Afrika-Schiff, left Bulgaria on a 6,800km journey and was nearing its destination when von Lettow-Vorbeck managed to get a message through saying he had been forced out of the flat terrain where it was to have landed. The L59 was then recalled. There are two versions of the recall: one is that the German high command sent the message, while Meinertzhagen claims that it was a fake, sent by himself.

Its mission would have failed in any case, von Lettow-Vorbeck, the Prussian who thought like a Boer general, was long past holding either suitable or unsuitable ground. He and his increasingly tattered and disease-ridden soldiers had now been reduced to dodging around northern Mozambique, living off the land and capturing whatever Portuguese military posts they came across. The Schutztruppe's situation became so desperate that a 1,000-strong detachment was forced to surrender because it was out of both food and ammunition.

In August 1918 von Lettow-Vorbeck re-entered German East Africa and crossed into Northern Rhodesia (now Zambia). There he occupied Kasama on 13 November 1918 not knowing that the war had ended two days earlier. On 14 November news of the Armistice finally reached him, and on 25 November he 'surrendered' at Mbala, undefeated to the end.

Looking back, the East Africa campaign really was the last of the old-style African bush wars – although even there the era of modern warfare had begun to intrude, in the shape of the armoured cars and transport lorries, some use of aircraft and the pioneering airship flight – but it is of particular interest to the modern armour soldier because once again it gave indications of the shape of things to come.

For all his talent, von Lettow-Vorbeck only managed to hold out to the end because of the terrain and the level of technology, both on the ground and in the air. One generation later in Abyssinia the South Africans overcame much the same sort of conditions because they had good aerial support, tougher and more mobile four-wheel drive armoured cars and dedicated engineer units to improve road communications which facilitated the movement of troops and supplies.

It is interesting to speculatewhat might have happened if van Deventer had the benefit of suitable vehicles and road builders in his epochal dash to Kondoa Irangi. On the other hand, it is ironic but true that von Lettow-Vorbeck's lack of motor vehicles was the main reason why he was able to hold out to the end.

Because his troops marched on their feet in the traditional way of the infantryman, he did not need technical back-up like vehicle workshops or never-ending shipments of fuel; his only supply column consisted of porters and draught animals. If he'd had a mechanized force, his total isolation would have forced him to submit as early as the end of 1915 through sheer lack of fuel, spares and tyres.

The inevitable question is whether his indomitable stand achieved his primary purpose of diverting British troops from the Western front. The answer is "no." Although huge numbers of Allied troops were required to defeat him, the bulk of them from 1916 onward, they were Indians and South Africans who were not destined to serve in Europe anyway and the Royal Navy's deployments to the East African theatre in 1917/1918 were so modest that they did not result in any scaling down of the naval war elsewhere.

7

First steps to mechanization

"The war to end all wars." But there were those who harboured doubts. One of them seems to have been Marshal Foch, France's hero of the great conflict, who reportedly remarked: "This is not peace. It is an armistice for 20 years."

Vicious cutbacks in defence spending were the order of the day as all countries began to feel the bite of the inevitable post-war economic depression, coupled with an immense war weariness and justified, at least in the British Empire and its dominions, by the infamous Ten Year Rule of 1919.

The premise of this declaration was that no engagement in a major war could be expected for the following 10 years. The rule was accurate enough at that moment in time, but it encouraged a well-nigh fatal inertia among many governments that would ultimately have serious after effects.

The cutbacks in South Africa came close to completely destroying the Union Defence Force's ability to perform its fundamental task of defending the country. Cutting down the bulk of the war-swollen armed forces was not the problem, since the overwhelming majority consisted of citizen soldiers who could slip back into peacetime occupations. But the permanent force was hit hard and shrank to a shadow of its modest pre-1914 self, as one by one the five first-class regiments of South African Mounted Riflemen were disbanded.

The official purse strings were drawn so tight that in 1922 just one lieutenant was commissioned into the permanent force, and then only after a political squabble in parliament in which the appointment had to be personally justified by the minister of defence, Colonel Hendrik Mentz —the lieutenant in question was Dan Pienaar, probably the best artilleryman South Africa had produced, and an iconic South African general during the Second World War.

Circumstances did not encourage the development of the Union Defence Force's capability, especially as regards armoured fighting vehicles. This is not to say that the Union Defence Force was blind to the potential of armoured vehicles.

Many of its members had seen what they could do during the war years, but after an initial false boom the first priority in the post-war years was simple survival rather than development – although a determined struggle by Lieutenant-Colonel Sir Pierre van Ryneveld and others ensured that the South African Air Force became a separate service when it was established in 1920, rather than just another corps of the army.

At this time the Union Defence Force's armoured component consisted of a lone Medium A Whippet light tank.Whippet A387 (locally registered as U552), arrived at Simon's Town in September 1919 on the SS *Umvuma*, underwent trials at the naval dockyard and was then driven to the railway station amid great public interest. There it was railed to Pretoria, where it was taken by road to the mechanical transport section at Roberts Heights (later Voortrekkerhoogte, now Thaba Tshwane).

The South African Whippet was mobilized for active service of sorts during the very violent miners' strike of 1922 and was named HMLS (His Majesty's Land Ship) *Union* and was crewed by members of the South African Air Force.

Armored Leyland Truck, HLMS *Nemesis,* used during the Rand Rebellion of 1922 by the SAP.

A white-topped Crossley armoured in South West Africa during the Mpumbo Rebellion.

Its first foray into action was somewhat inglorious; it clanked off toward the miners' stronghold, accompanied by soldiers of the Transvaal Scottish in commandeered Leyland lorries which had been hastily bullet-proofed with steel sheets (one had HMLS *Otazell* emblazoned on its side and flew a skull-and-crossbones flag).

This foray ended in a fiasco, since the Whippet broke down in the Fordsburg Dip and never actually got to grips with the insurrectionists – in a later engagement, however, it did come under fire and the driver was killed by an accurately aimed bullet which went through his viewing port. But one could say that this was the first time the Union Defence Force deployed a tank with armoured infantry in support.

Financial stringency apart, there was still a great deal of muddled thinking in all of the world's armies about the future role of armoured vehicles, particularly tanks. Adherents of the horse cavalry and horse artillery, of whom many now populated the upper military hierarchies, spent years fighting tooth and nail against what the British army's armour enthusiasts were still calling 'mechanicalization'. Inevitably the dissension and confusion in the British army affected the Union Defence Force as well.

The cavalry adherents had no objection to armoured cars, whose role was seen as clear enough, namely to assist, but not replace, the light cavalry in reconnaissance and similar tasks. While more heated discussions arose about the future role of tanks, the British army was making extensive use of armoured cars for patrolling not only in Mesopotamia but also in India.

The Indian armoured cars were used for several purposes outside their official reconnaissance role, ranging from supporting the police in suppressing the frequent street riots to fighting semi-conventionally against the permanently turbulent mountain tribesmen on the northern and northwestern frontiers, who were opposed in principle to any sort of imposed authority, British or otherwise.

One of these cars was the Rolls-Royce India Pattern, a specially modified variant of the earlier 1914 Admiralty pattern. It retained the characteristic long-nosed look but had a slightly larger body and a dome-shaped turret with ports for mounting several water-cooled Vickers machine guns. The tyres were solid rubber and the interior of the hull was lined with woven asbestos to insulate it against India's notorious summer heat.

The Indian government also ordered some other armoured cars, built on the cheaper four-wheel drive Crossley chassis. These India pattern 1923 cars with their 4-cylinder 37kW engines bore a fair resemblance to the Rolls-Royce India pattern and used the same dome-shaped turret – intended to deflect rifle shots – with four machine gun ports for .303-calibre machine guns.

The turret was fitted with a 'clamshell' opening for the commander. The side doors opened opposite ways to provide cover for a crew member getting out while under fire. Solid tyres were fitted and the complete vehicle weighed around 7.5 tons. The crew area was lined with asbestos to keep the temperature down, in addition to which Forty notes that the hulls of some cars could be electrified on the outside to discourage rioters from laying hands on them.

The Crossley cars underwent various modifications– the 1925 models, for example, had more cooling louvres for the radiator and a different system for attaching the ditch-crossing channels to the sides – and were to serve for many years.

Proof that the Union Defence Force was not blind to the armour concept can be seen from the fact that in 1924 the general staff discussed the establishment of an armoured car section and asked the government about acquiring some suitable vehicles. This was the age of Imperial Gifts – surplus British equipment given to the dominions –and in February 1925 two India pattern Crossleys and numerous other vehicles were offloaded at East London.

The Crossleys were put through their paces on the artillery barracks square at Roberts Heights – top speed turned out to be about 24kph – and some minor modifications for local conditions were made with water-cooled Vickers machine guns mounted in the turrets.

The first steps toward manning them followed almost immediately in the shape of Permanent Force Order No. 2652, dated 21 March 1925, requiring the names of permanent force members who had served in an armoured unit during the First World War to be submitted to the chief of the general staff. A nil return was received – no doubt because only a handful of South Africans had actually served in armoured units and all or most had been citizen soldiers.

This clearly did not quench the Union Defence Force's enthusiasm.In April 1926 the chief of the general staff instructed the quartermaster general to take every opportunity to train his motor drivers on the armoured cars, and to keep the vehicles in good running order and ready for emergency action.

That year one of the Crossleys was handed over to the commandant of the South African Military College (now the South African Army College) for him to use for armoured car training and demonstrations. The only training manual available was one printed by the British War Office in 1921, which the college rewrote, and by 1930 all staff at the Small Arms Branch had been suitably trained.

While the Union Defence Force was taking these halting steps toward acquiring armour an enormous controversy about the future of the tank was raging in Britain, where the Royal Tank Corps not only had managed to avoid being abolished but actually achieved a little expansion. It was a wrangle which was to directly affect South Africa.

The upper hierarchy still believed firmly that the tank's main role was to support the infantry. But the opposite view was taken by a small group of middle-level officers – men like Percy Hobart, G. le Q Martel, Tim Pile, J. F. C. Fuller, Charles Broad and George Lindsay – who had seen the limitations of cavalry during the First World War and experienced the porridge-making artillery barrages of the Western Front which had led to both men and machines bogging down.

They risked their careers; a very real risk, since the British regular army was also being ruthlessly hacked down, to foster the concept of the tank as something more than a lumbering destroyer of trenches. Their reward for trying to discern the shape of things to come were sideways promotions, accusations that they were trying to destroy all cavalry and create an all-tank army, which they were not, and scoffing that in any future battle tanks would soon be useless because the enemy's anti-tank guns would take them out at the earliest opportunity.

The military commentator and writer Captain (later Sir) Basil Liddell Hart wholeheartedly supported them, and being a retired, rather than a serving officer, was free to speculate and warn about the future shape of things, a shape that envisaged all-armoured formations

Crossley armoured car near rifle stacks at the Indaba held at *Knobkierie* pan during the Ipumbu Revolt in Owamboland, South West Africa.

Demonstration of Whippet tank HMLS *Union* in Cape Town, 1920s.

and tactics, self-propelled armoured artillery, reliable radio communications and many other things that today's soldiers take for granted.

To illustrate the direction in which their minds were reaching it is worth quoting from two of the many letters Hobart and Lindsay wrote to each other in 1925 about their vision of the future, when Hobart was an instructor at the Indian Army Staff College at Quetta and Lindsay an instructor at a Royal Tank Corps training school in England.

In a remarkably prescient letter Hobart wrote:

Until we have the means of commanding and controlling tanks on the move, we cannot be a formation or force, but only an uncoordinated crowd of units in action … The other paramount need, I take it, is Accompanying Artillery. The Royal Tank Artillery. Extreme mobility – go for nerve centres. Live on the country. You'll only need petrol, oil and very little food, all of which are endemic in any (even semi-civilized) country these days...

We always preach the necessity of infantry following up to take over, at once, what tanks have captured. Is that the idea of war that Alexander, Hannibal, even Ziethen or Napoleon had? We were reduced to that by inadequate mobility... Why limit ourselves to a 3,000–4,000 yards advance? The distance gunners can reach without moving. This artillery obsession.

Given (a) efficient, fast tanks with good means of control; (b) accompanying artillery (i.e. The Royal Tank Artillery, designed for the support of tanks just as (the Royal Horse Artillery) was for the support of Cavalry) (c) suitable air force. Why piddle about with porridge-making of the Third Ypres type? When one is possessed of modern weapons one shoots a tiger in the brain, heart, or spine. One doesn't painfully hack off a foot at a time, "consolidating" as one goes.

In another letter, Lindsay addressed the questions of coordination, something the British were still struggling to master in the Western Desert 15 years later, and mobility: "Why fight for positions? If centres of command and supply, and communications, are overcome by the Mobile Force, the enemy cannot remain in their positions … no, the war will be won, or lost, as far as military operations go, by the Mechanical Force, in the air and on the ground, working in cooperation. The ground troops, present infantry and cavalry, will occupy, administer, and police, the areas conquered by the Mechanical Force."

It was radical and deeply unpopular thinking, but Hobart and the others stuck to their beliefs and evolved some principles that are as valid today as they were then. In his fine biography of Hobart, *Armoured Crusader*, Kenneth Macksey comments:

Hobart's lectures in 1926, his last full year at Quetta, crystallise the concept of the mobile force of the future and reach maturity in a long paper proposing an organization for a mechanized force. The arguments are beautifully balanced in that they consider every side of the problem, arising from a study of the lessons of history concerning the old mobile armies, linked with recent experience of mobile war, and then interwoven to form a tapestry of striking originality. From the ancient days of bow and arrow against armour, Hobart demonstrated how the varying relationships between fire power, protection and mobility impinged upon organization, tactics and strategy.

Applying these thoughts to recent events, he foresaw a quickening of the race between gun and armour on the tank – a race which had started with the very first tank action, when it was discovered that the Germans already possessed, by chance, a bullet that would penetrate the armour of the early machines. He sought to circumvent the gun/armour race by means of speed, concentration of effort joined with surprise, and the cooperation of all arms.

Thus at an early stage Hobart spoke of the need for other arms to work in cooperation with tanks, "the infantry to hold gains … artillery to protect by fire and smoke. Tanks cannot cover themselves with smoke. Great increase in tank casualties when beyond support of artillery."

But he was convinced that, unless the infantry stayed relatively close to the tanks in action, they would fail in their task, and that the artillery had to be capable of keeping up with the tanks to ensure the guns could maintain continuous fire support no matter how far the tanks travelled.

Here was the point at which vested interests came into contest, the cause of a host of misunderstandings and of bitterness in the years to come. With the old, slow-moving tanks it had been comparatively simple for the infantry and artillery to keep up with the speed of advance. Now, said Hobart, "the pace of the modern tank [the 1924 Vickers Medium Mark I] has rendered this method obsolete."

He agreed, with General Eric Ludendorff that, "the fact that the 'light' machine gun was now the true 'infantryman' had not yet sunk deep into the army," and that being so, the infantryman with his light machine gun needed to travel in a light armoured vehicle.

He enquired of the progress in artillery mechanization, of the 'Birch' gun, which was a field gun mounted on the chassis of a Vickers tank. Only a few of these machines were ever produced and held no attraction for horsed gunners – not least, one suspects, because they bore a strong resemblance to a tank.

Today it is taken for granted that infantry travel, if possible, in their own lightly armoured vehicles, and that artillery has to be self-propelled on tracked vehicles when fighting alongside tanks and motorized infantry. Moreover, one of the original staff of the Tank Corps, Major G. le Q. Martel, was at that moment designing and manufacturing a thinly armoured, one-man, track-cum-wheeled vehicle in collaboration with the motor manufacturer William Morris, from which was to descend the generations of light carriers that became the first armoured infantry carrier.

In 1926 this was a dream, but clearly visible to Hobart in his search for a technical solution to his demand for armoured mobility. He went even further, suggesting that the time might come when the general advent of cross-country vehicles would lead to the disappearance of the Tank Corps as a separate entity. But in the meantime he applied only what was immediately obtainable to his short-term proposals.

The tank was the only armoured vehicle available; it would dominate and therefore its destruction would be a matter of overriding importance. In Hobart's view, mines could impede tanks and field guns be a menace in the close battle, but once action became mobile, the tank with a 3-pdr or 6-pdr gun became the only viable anti-tank weapon.

By sheer persistence Hobart and his fellow heretics slowly began to make progress and gain some recognition from higher up. They managed to experiment with armoured tactics, radio communications and other things, and in 1931 formed the British army's first all-tank

Demonstration of Whippet tank HMLS *Union* in Cape Town, 1920s.

Home-built armoured car based on the Leyland Truck used by the UDF during 1922 Rand Rebellion.

brigade, in spite of the fact that Britain had been so badly wounded by the Great Depression that the government actually cut its already none-too-generous military service pay by 10 percent.

In spite of these adverse circumstances the British managed to produce a few good armoured fighting vehicles, some of which were to see long and varied service in several countries and a number of wars. One was the excellent 1924 Vickers Medium Mark I, which weighed nearly 12 tons and could reach a top speed of 26kph.It had a rotating turret, a radio and a 47mm 3-pdr gun as well as six mounted and dismounted machine guns. It was soon followed by the Mark II, which had thicker armour and had dispensed with the dismounted machine guns.

Another excellent design was the Carden-Lloyd Carrier of 1926 – inspired by a two-man 'tankette' co-designed by Martel and the Morris car company as a private venture – from which the Bren carrier of Second World War fame evolved, as well as the Light Tank Mark III of 1934, later the first tracked armoured fighting vehicle to see action in South African hands. Yet others included the Tetrarch of 1938, which became the first airborne tank, and the slow and inadequately armed but heavily armoured Matilda Mark II infantry tank that inflicted a decisive defeat on Rommel's armour at Arras in 1940 during the Battle of France and later rendered sterling service in the Western Desert.

At the same time though, they made a terrible mistake by settling on a 40mm 2-pdr gun as the main armament for their late-1930s cruiser tanks instead of the 47mm 3-pdrs and 57mm 6-pdrs of the previous decades. Circumstances later made it difficult to move quickly to a larger calibre, and no high explosive shells were developed for it – a lapse for which British and Commonwealth tank soldiers were to pay dearly during the first half of the Second World War.

In the United States, tank pioneers like George Patton and Adna Chaffee ran into the same sort of antiquated mindset about the appropriate employment of tanks. Patton in particular had come back from the First World War full of ideas for research, development, experimentation and training, only to be instantly slapped down as the United States army embarked on a drastic shrinking exercise that reduced it by 50 percent to a mere 120,000 all ranks, with funding for armour dwindling almost to nothing for the next 17 years.

As far as the United States army's upper hierarchy was concerned, tanks were useful only for facilitating infantry attacks by crashing through wire entanglements and flattening machine guns. Speed was not important; what counted was the ability to crush static enemy defences and ward off enemy anti-tank fire. So tanks were placed under command of the chief of infantry and the cavalry maintained its elevated position by virtue of its much-vaunted speed, manoeuvrability and shock value.

Line up of the UDF armour in 1930s, two Crossleys, two Vickers Mk1s and the Whippet.

Like their British counterparts, Patton, Chaffee and others stuck to their guns, but it was not until 1933 that Chaffee was allowed to start experimenting with a lone cavalry regiment which would eventually become the United States army's first tank brigade. It is possible that Hobart and the others fared better than Patton because even in peacetime the British army was frequently involved in internal security operations, particularly in India, that often involved light armour.

In France, too, some of the younger and more progressive-minded colonels like Charles de Gaulle were concerned about the tank doctrine that their elders were opposing.

The French were building some of the most formidably armed and armoured tanks in the world – like the 31-ton Char B1 of 1935, regarded as one of the most formidable heavy tanks in the world at that time, and the fast, reliable Char S35 Somua medium tank which according to George Forty was, "better armed and armoured than its German opponents in 1940." But the tactics the old-style generals favoured were identical to that of the horsed cavalry of their regimental days, and the excellence of their tanks did them no good when the war started.

The Polish army was no better, and not only still believed firmly in penny-packeting its substantial tank forces in support of the infantry but actually maintained no less than 11 full brigades of horsed lancers right up to the German invasion in 1939.

The only military thinkers who shrugged off the old prejudices and absorbed all discussion of the 1930s, particularly Liddell Hart's visionary writings, were the Germans, who had now discarded the restrictions imposed on them by the Treaty of Versailles and were busily building up their armoured forces while starting to evolve a new doctrine they would call the *blitzkrieg*.

A particular devotee of the revolutionary new thinking was a colonel named Heinz Guderian, later the finest of the panzer generals; on one occasion Guderian reportedly scoffed at the opinions of an anti-tank expert saying: "That is the old school and already old history. I put my faith in Hobart, the new man."

In his autobiography, *Panzer Leader*, Guderian freely acknowledges his intellectual debt to Liddell Hart and other British armoured thinkers. Like them, he had served through the First World War, also like them he was trying to develop insights into the unknown future of warfare and determine the right ways and means of handling the challenges that mechanization would bring:

> During (the First World War) there had been very many examples of the transport of troops by motorized vehicles. Such troop movements had always taken place behind a more or less static front line; they had never been used directly against the enemy in a war of movement.

Rand Strike 1922, Leyland Armoured Truck 'HOT AZELL' and the Whippet.

The Whippet HMLS *Union* during the 1922 Rand Rebellion with some men of the Transvaal Scottish.

Germany now was undefended, and it therefore seemed improbable that any new war would start in the form of positional warfare behind fixed fronts. We must rely on mobile defence in case of war.

The problem of the transport of motorized troops in mobile warfare soon raised the question of the protection of such transport. This could only be satisfactorily provided by armoured vehicles. I therefore looked for precedents from which I might learn about the experiments that had been made with armoured vehicles.

This brought me in touch with [a] Lieutenant Volckheim, who was then engaged in collating information concerning the very limited use of German armoured vehicles, and the incomparably greater employment of enemy tank forces during the war, as a staff study for our little army.

He provided me with a certain amount of literature on the subject; though weak in theory it gave me something to go on. The English and French had had far greater experience in this field and had written much more about it. I got hold of their books and I learned.

It was principally the books and articles of the Englishmen, Fuller, Liddell Hart and Martel, that excited my interest and gave me food for thought. These far-sighted soldiers were even then trying to make of the tank something more than just an infantry support weapon. They envisaged it in relationship to the growing motorisation of our age, and thus they became the pioneers of a new type of warfare on the largest scale.

I learned from them the concentration of armour, as employed in the battle of Cambrai. Further, it was Liddell Hart who emphasised the use of armoured forces for long-range strikes, operations against the opposing army's communications, and also proposed a type of armoured division combining panzer and panzer-infantry units.

Deeply impressed by these ideas I tried to develop them in a sense practicable for our own army. So I owe many suggestions of our further development to Captain Liddell Hart.

The deeper Guderian delved into future mechanized tactics, the more he became, if not a prophet crying in the wilderness, then certainly a member of a very small minority of truth-seekers, because as Liddell Hart writes in his foreword to Guderian's autobiography, it is not to be supposed that the German general staff was "a far-sighted and united body of planners ceaselessly seeking to get a march ahead in preparation for the next war."

The result was that Guderian found himself willy-nilly re-cast as a leading thinker on tank warfare, with few of his seniors taking him and his theories seriously: "In the country of the blind, the one-eyed man is king. Since nobody else busied himself with this material, I was soon by way of being an expert."

One of the few senior officers who did heed the young major's prophesies and speculations was a general named von Altrock, who happened to be editor of the *Militär-Wochenblatt* (Military Weekly) and, "a few small articles that I contributed ... served to enhance my reputation … General von Altrock, visited me frequently and encouraged me to write more on the subject. He was a first-class soldier and was anxious that his paper should publish material dealing with contemporary problems."

In 1929 Guderian had become convinced, as he later wrote in his autobiography that "tanks working on their own or in conjunction with infantry could never achieve decisive importance … until the other weapons on whose support they must inevitably rely were brought up to their standard of speed and of cross-country performance. In such a formation of all arms, the tanks must play the primary role."

For that year's summer tactical exercises without troops Guderian wrote one for such an (imaginary) armoured division. It was a success, but the Inspector of Transport Troops, General Otto von Stulpnagel, forbade theoretical use of tanks in greater than regimental-strength units in future exercises because "it was his opinion that panzer divisions were a Utopian dream."

He did not change his mind; when von Stulpnagel was forced into retirement in 1931, his parting words to Guderian were: "You're too impetuous. Believe me, neither of us will ever see German tanks in operation in our lifetime." But von Stulpnagel's was a voice from the past and by 1933 – Guderian was now a colonel and chief of staff for motorized troops – the Germans were hard at work creating an armoured force, Guderian continues:

The year 1933 was one of considerable progress. A series of experimental and training exercises with dummy tanks did much to clarify the relationship between various weapons and served to strengthen me in my convictions that tanks would only be able to play their full part within the framework of a modem army when they were treated as that army's principal weapon and were supplied with fully motorized supporting arms.

If the tactical developments were not unsatisfactory, the equipment side was by contrast all the more worrying. One of the results of our disarmament after the Versailles Treaty was that for many years our industry had produced no war materials; consequently it lacked not only the skilled labour but also the very machines with which to turn our intentions into facts. In particular the production of a sufficiently tough armour plating proved very difficult. The first sheets delivered splintered like glass.

It similarly took a considerable time before our requirements in the wireless and optical field, which, it must be admitted, were technically very advanced, could be filled. However, I have never regretted my insistence at that time on our tanks being equipped with first-class visual and command facilities. So far as the latter is concerned, we were at all times superior to our enemies and this was to compensate for many other subsequent inferiorities that necessarily arose.

That year General Freiherr von Fritsch became commander-in-chief of the army: "he had not a great deal of technical knowledge, but he was always ready to try out new ideas without prejudice and, if they seemed to him good, to adopt them. As a result of this my official dealings with him concerning the development of the armoured force were easier and more agreeable than with any of the other members the of army high command … He had devoted a period of detached service to the study of the Panzer Division [and] he continued to show the same interest in our doings."

But many generals had yet to be convinced. Guderian recalls that "the Chief of the General Army Office, General Fromm, ordered that the 14th (anti-tank) company of all infantry regiments be motorized. When I maintained that these companies, since they would be working with foot soldiers, would do better to remain horse-drawn, he replied: "The infantry's got to have a few cars too." My request that, instead of the 14th company, the heavy artillery battalions be motorized was turned down. The heavy guns remained horse-drawn, with unfortunate results during the war, particularly in Russia."

Vickers Mk1A gives a demonstration to the SSB.

A South African Vickers tank in base camp.

There can be no doubt that if the Second World War had broken out a few years later than it did the German mechanized forces would have been even more formidable than they were, to judge by the following comment from Guderian: "The development of tracked vehicles for the tank supporting arms never went as fast as we wished. It was clear that the effectiveness of the tanks would gain in proportion to the ability of the infantry, artillery and other divisional arms to follow them in an advance across-country. We wanted lightly armoured half-tracks for the riflemen, combat engineers and medical services, armoured self-propelled guns for the artillery and the anti-tank battalions, and various types of tank for the reconnaissance and signals battalions."

The equipment of the divisions with these vehicles was never fully completed. Despite all increases in productivity the limited facilities of German industry never succeeded in catching up with the vastly expanded requirements of the motorized Wehrmacht and Waffen-SS formations, and of industry itself.

One reason for Guderian's professional survival and the advances he and his fellow enthusiasts made was undoubtedly the fact that Adolf Hitler "manifested a liking for new military ideas, and the tank idea in particular," as Liddell Hart writes in the his foreword: "Hitler showed an inclination to back that revolutionary idea."

As a result, Guderian, filled with "the passion of pure craftsmanship," was more favourably disposed toward Hitler than most of the professional military hierarchy because both men were in conflict with the general staff and with established conventions, "until disillusioned by what he saw for himself when he eventually came into close contact with the Führer," Liddell Hart writes.

The moment of disillusionment came at the end of 1941 when Guderian – unlike many of his colleagues – spurned some of Hitler's wilder plans and was effectively sacked by being transferred to the army reserve commanders' pool. There he stayed until March 1943 when he was yanked out of what amounted to semi-retirement and made inspector-general of armoured troops.

Among other things this new appointment entailed frequent conferences with Hitler, and to the first of these took an aide-memoire which was typical of his blunt approach and must surely have carried some risk of professional censure, if not worse.

The thrust of Guderian's submission was that a panzer division could only attain complete combat efficiency if the number of tanks was in the correct proportion to the other vehicles and weapons; if that condition was not reached, "then the land battles will be long and drawn-out and will cause us heavy casualties." And in the aide-memoire is a note to himself: "Read out article by Liddell Hart – on the organization of armoured forces, past and future."

Presumably Germany's need was too great for Hitler to hold Guderian's forthright views against him for a second time, because in June 1944 he was appointed chief of the army general staff. It was of course far too late; unwittingly Hitler had done the Free World a great favour by sidelining his greatest armour field commander at precisely the time when the Germans were still winning, instead of letting him loose on the Allied armies.

In the meantime the Union Defence Force's movement toward battlefield mechanization took another modest step forward in 1930 when a further Imperial Gift resulted in the acquisition of two Vickers Medium Tank Mark Is and eight light Dragon Mark IID tracked mechanical haulers. They were promptly put into use for technical and operational training.The technical training was carried out at the South African Air Force Mechanical Transport Section at Roberts Heights, which had a virtual monopoly on such matters in those technologically unsophisticated days.

The Vickers Mark I, the first British battle tank to have all-round traverse for the turret and geared elevation for the main armament, was an ageing but still very successful and useful vehicle. Its spring bogey suspension contributed to its high speed – 48kph in practice, as opposed to the design speed of 28kph.

Its standard main armament was a 60-calibre 47mm (3-pdr) quick-firing gun – although one of the South African imports had a 12-calibre 3.7-inch howitzer – with four .303-calibre Hotchkiss machine guns mounted in the turret and two water-cooled .303-calibre Vickers machine guns in the hull. Weighing 11.75 tons, the Mark I was powered by an air-cooled 70kW Armstrong-Siddeley engine and featured 8mm-thick armour. The crew numbered five men, and it had an operational range of 195km.

The Dragon derived its existence from the development of a variety of specialized tracked vehicles for use as artillery gun tractors which could also accommodate an artillery gun detachment and ammunition; its name was a corruption of 'Drag-Gun'. The first Dragon, the Mark I, was used for towing the 18-pdr field gun and was based on the Vickers Medium Tank Mark I. The Mark IIDs the Union Defence Force received had more powerful engines, better armour protection and better accommodation for crew and passengers.

In 1931 the Union Defence Force decided to put both Crossleys into commission and form an armoured car section under command of Lieutenant (later Brigadier) J. B. Kriegler at the South African Military College; the section had barely been established when the Crossleys were hastily mobilized in August 1932 for a punitive expedition to South West Africa's Ovamboland region which turned into a somewhat farcical but nevertheless educational episode.

A chief called Ipumbu had defied the jurisdiction of the South West African administration, and it had been decided that Kriegler's armoured cars and a flight of the South African Air Force's old Westland Wapitis must beard him in his den and show him a demonstration of force.

The plan was that Kriegler and his cars would travel to Ondangwa in northern South West Africa – which half a century later would become a major air base during the border war – link up with the five Wapitis under Lieutenant-Colonel Sir Pierre van Ryneveld and then jointly deal with Ipumbu.

Kriegler duly joined hands with van Ryneveld, although by the time he got to Ondangwa his two-car force had been reduced by 50 percent because one of the Crossleys had suffered a breakdown while battling the inhospitable terrain between Windhoek and the Etosha Pan.

The surviving car and Van Ryneveld's Wapitis then carried out a combined air and ground attack on Ipumbu's kraal, a bloodless exercise because he had thoughtfully vacated it in the interim. It ended on a rather comical note when a swarm of angry bees that had been disturbed by the bombardment invaded the Crossley's turret, at which the car's occupants beat a hasty and presumably disorderly retreat.

Some good practical experience about African bush operations was gained during the expedition, however. The 'Popham Panel' system of air-ground communication was successfully tried out for the first time, while it was noted that the cars had good engines but weak springs, and that their solid tyres resulted in poor mobility, this problem was solved by fitting them with pneumatic tyres.

Early in May 1940 both Crossleys' engines were replaced with 63kW Ford V8 Flathead engines, and the original chassis by a standard 3-ton Ford lorry chassis. The Ford chassis was shorter than its predecessor, but this problem was easily overcome by applying the national talent for improvisation. What was done about the weak springs is not known, but it is interesting to note that when locally-built armoured cars were first deployed in Abyssinia in 1940, they too suffered from continual problems with their springs.

In the meantime training on the two Vickers tanks continued. But the times were very bad for the introduction of anything new. The worldwide depression now had South Africa in its grip; there was widespread bankruptcy and deprivation. Amid all this the Ten Year Rule was renewed, although it would not have made any difference if it had not, considering the parlous state of the national fiscus.

The Pirow years

In 1933 the South African and National Parties formed a coalition with General J. B. M. Hertzog as prime minister and General Jan Smuts as his deputy. The coalition was designed primarily to drag the country out of the Depression without wasting energy on party-political disputes and manoeuvrings, and it succeeded.

It was a potentially unstable combination, however, because the new United Party contained too many sharply divergent undercurrents. But it served its purpose for the next six years, and it brought to power a dynamic new minister of defence, Oswald Pirow.

Pirow soon showed that he was not afraid of lateral thinking or of making proposals of a scope which were positively shocking to the governors of a nation which had been traumatized by years of economic hardship; although most of his more ambitious schemes failed to materialize, he nevertheless achieved certain things that turned out to be essential to the nation's military survival in a few years' time.

Pirow soon tabled a five-year plan for the reorganization and strengthening of the country's defences, including its coastal batteries. It was a good scheme that addressed some very real weaknesses, but very little of it could be brought to fruition. The South African government was disinclined to spend a penny more than was absolutely necessary as it struggled to keep the economy's head above water, and no funding was forthcoming from Britain, whose immediate preoccupation amid its own economic devastation was the strengthening of the defences of Singapore in the face of a newly resurgent and aggressive Japan.

Yet the defence machine was in a truly shocking state. By 1934 the permanent force consisted of just 1,791 all ranks. The active citizen force with its 24 infantry battalions, its artillery and support components – supposedly the backbone of the land defences – numbered a mere 8,143 men, not all of whom had been adequately trained. Money was so tight that in 1934 no continuous training at all took place. No modern light machine guns or mortars were to be had, while the available field and coastal artillery pieces dated back to the First World War and in some cases to the Second Anglo-Boer War.

A less visible but equally serious defect was the fact that, as in Britain, some senior members of the Union Defence Force recalled the past with nostalgia and regarded the petrol-driven future with scarcely concealed disdain. An additional problem was that others were very turf conscious, partly one supposes because of the post-First World War permanent force reductions and the realization that with the disbandment of the regiments of the South African Mounted Riflemen the army would have to rely almost totally on the citizen soldiers of the active citizen force.

Thus although a number of active citizen force brigades were formed, they existed only on paper except for the headquarters staffs, and the higher command level would not permit staff courses to be run for the part-timers. The active citizen force brigade staff officers, most of them youngish but experienced veterans of the Great War, compensated for this lack by holding regular meetings to debate the strategic and tactical implications of a possible outbreak of war.

This was even though, as Brigadier E. P. 'Scrubbs' Hartshorn recalls in his book *Avenge*

Tobruk, they were "aware of the sterile fate that awaited our recommendations … Definite staff course training was denied until after the war had started. By then of course, there was insufficient time for anything resembling effective training. South Africa was to pay a heavy price for this wilful act".

As evidence of some senior regulars' struggle to digest the concept of armoured warfare, Hartshorn recalls the evening he and other senior active citizen force officers held a discussion meeting, the subject of which was: "The supply and maintenance of an armoured brigade in southern Africa".

The guest of honour was then commanding officer of the Witwatersrand area, and when he was asked to make a closing comment he said: "Gentlemen, what you have been discussing is beyond me. I'm glad I shall be retired before this next war. You're in for a bad time. When I started soldiering we moved on horses, with trek carts and oxen. When supplies failed we killed the oxen and cooked them on the trek carts. You are going to find tanks tough eating."

The South African Air Force was technically proficient but desperately short of operational and training aircraft; those it had were all obsolescent at best, "for years," as Major-General George E. Brink later wrote, "[it] had existed as a glorified flying club." The South African Air Force was also short of pilots, and the country's civilian flying clubs, a potential manpower source for rapid wartime expansion, had mostly succumbed to the Depression.

The bomber force consisted of a few Junkers 86 civil passenger aircraft which were capable of being converted to wartime use, albeit at a significant cost in airspeed when bomb-racks were fitted. The South African Naval Service had no ships and, other than the part-time volunteers of the South African division of the Royal Naval Volunteer Reserve, consisted of a total of three officers and three ratings.

The litany of problems was almost endless, and in 1934 Major-General Andries Brink, general officer commanding the Union Defence Force and secretary for defence, spoke no less than the truth when he reported that since the end of the First World War the country's defence machine, "has languished for lack of necessary financial support … the Defence Vote has shown progressive decreases until finally it [has] reached a figure at which it was almost impossible to carry on."

Yet the Union Defence Force did somehow carry on. Plans were in hand to set up an artillery training depot at Roberts Heights, which would have several kinds of field pieces and one of the two old armoured trains left over from the First World War, each of which mounted a single 18-pdr field gun.

More officer-cadets for the permanent force were recruited and 18 were selected for the first of a new series of 18-month 'amphigarious' courses in which they would be trained as staff officers, gunners and pilots – and which, according to Neil Orpen, eventually played a major role in "the extraordinarily close cooperation between the South African ground and air forces" during the Abyssinian campaign.

Two other steps that Pirow did manage to implement left a lasting imprint on the Union Defence Force. He established eight new active citizen force infantry battalions in the platteland (rural farming areas), of which Regiment President Steyn – established on 1 April 1934 – still exists as one of South Africa's tank regiments; and on 1 April 1933 he created a unit called the Special Service Battalion, partly as a social scheme to assist unemployed youths and partly to act as a feeder for the permanent force.

Its founder and first commanding officer was Lieutenant-Colonel George Brink, who established the unit at Roberts Heights and in due course handed over to Major W. H. Evered Poole, a brilliant young officer who became a major-general and commander of the country's first armoured formation, 6 South African Armoured Division, during the Italian campaign of the Second World War.

Between them they turned the Special Service Battalion, which also had a 100-man company in Durban and another of 150 members in Cape Town, into something quite unique in South Africa's military annals. Recruits joined for a year and were drilled, instructed in basic military subjects and given strenuous physical training. Soon they had gained an enviable reputation for discipline and smartness, so that graduates were sought after not only by the permanent force but also by other government departments as well as civilian employers.

But the Special Service Battalion, although no one knew it yet, had another important role waiting for it, as a building block of today's South African Armoured Corps.

By 1936 the output of the Special Service Battalion totalled about 2,000 youths a year; in 1937 the South African Railways and Harbours Administration established a special school at Roberts Heights to prepare entrants to its ranks. In 1937 3,788 youths passed through the ranks of the Special Service Battalion, a total of 882 joined the permanent force, and with the expansion of the South African Air Force now in progress at last, 248 were taken on for special training as air apprentices.

Many of Pirow's schemes were later derided by his political opponents, but in retrospect he was struggling with an impossible situation. Although he had a very clear conception of the sort of force South Africa would need to defend itself during a future world war, he was stymied at every turn by lack of funding and his inability to obtain certain essential items from Britain.

Pirow's vision of what the Union Defence Force required was based on his belief that in a future conflict South Africa would face either or both of two scenarios: an amphibious landing on its shores, and a bush war fought under typical African conditions. It went without saying that in either case the Union Defence Force would most probably be outnumbered as well.

To this end, he believed, it would have to have a chain of fortified harbours, mounting heavy guns and backed up by a least a third of the ground forces, plus a field army which was not a clone of any elaborate European combat force but was trained, organized and equipped to operate in mobile self-contained raiding columns.

This vision would later be heavily attacked, particularly his proposal that such columns use animal-drawn bush carts for logistic transport. According to Orpen, Pirow dreamed up the idea of adopting an adapted form of the traditional 'Indian Transport Cart' after consulting none other than Major-General Paul von Lettow-Vorbeck.

The so-called bush carts, as they were popularly known, had a very old-fashioned look about them and excited much contemptuous mirth when they were tried out experimentally in 1938. But the scoffers did not take into account that at the time the Union Defence Force had almost no battle-worthy motor transport, and few immediate prospects of obtaining any:

As H. J. Martin and Orpen point out in Volume 7 of *South Africa at War*, "since 1919 the defence department had bought virtually no motor vehicles, and … it was a miracle that its solid-tyred old lorries could run at all."

In a situation like that, especially in a bush war context, the animal-drawn transport of pre-mechanized days was infinitely better than no transport at all; it should also be noted that at that time even the highly mechanized German army still made large-scale use of horse-drawn heavy artillery and transport, and continued to do so well into the Second World War.

Nor did they grasp the basic accuracy of Pirow's vision of the future. In the early years of the Second World War there was grave concern about the possibility of an amphibious assault by the Japanese – one reason why Madagascar was invaded in mid-1942.

South African forces' first deployment was in 1940 in a war of manoeuvre in the almost trackless interior of Abyssinia, where they were far more self-contained and mobile than either their British equivalents or their Italian foes. A major reason was that they had efficient motor transport, which had been an unattainable dream in the bush cart era. It should also be pointed out that an important reason why South Africa could build a large and effective

Oswald Pirow, minister of defense.

Pirows Bush Carts on parade in Pretoria.

war machine so quickly after 1939 was because on Pirow's watch certain preparations were initiated which would stand General Smuts in good stead a few years later, when he had to create both a defensive and an offensive capability out of almost nothing.

In late 1937, Colonel George Brink – soon to be promoted to brigadier-general – was appointed director-general of army organization and training, and in addition to various onerous tasks was also responsible for developing Pirow's concept of an as-yet non-existent bush war army.

Brink had served in the South West Africa and East African campaigns during the First World War and was one of only four South African officers to have passed the gruelling staff course at Camberley, the breeding ground of British generals. He had much valuable hands-on experience of staff work and as a roving military attaché had gained an in-depth knowledge of the British, German, French and Italian armies. He was also a thinker, who unlike so many of his contemporaries in South Africa and further afield, was not mired in the past; he was steeped in the type of fast-moving mobile warfare that the country's soldiers had made their own in previous wars.

Although seriously hampered by an almost total lack of resources, Brink immediately started organizing tactical exercises with troops, and evolving structures and doctrines, mixing in the knowledge of the Wehrmacht he had gained while serving as a military attaché – his conclusion then, even though the German armed forces were not nearly as awesome as they would become, was that they would thrash the French in a future war.

Now Brink concluded that the best structure for the future would be the brigade group, an all-arms formation capable of operating independently for considerable periods, instead of being tied to the traditional cumbersome, vulnerable and often time-wasting supply columns which would usually be based far back at the divisional headquarters.

It was exactly the right approach, as was to be proved time and again in Abyssinia and the Western Desert; during the Abyssinian campaign some British staff officers entertained deep suspicions that the South Africans, who usually seemed to have enough petrol, habitually falsified their fuel returns. In fact the figures were due to economies of scale.

All this set off a type of peristaltic movement in Union Defence Force planning. For the brigade group concept to work, it was imperative to mechanize, so that infantry "would have to motor virtually into battle," as Carel Birkby puts it in *Uncle George*, his fine biography of Brink. That meant the army needed a variety of different vehicles: troop carriers, command vehicles, signals vans, and in particular, armoured cars which were designed to operate in African conditions.

Another of Pirow's innovations was the establishment in May 1937 of a War Supplies Board under the Union Defence Force's director of technical services, which began to hatch plans for local production of certain munitions and items such as 4.5-inch howitzer barrels. At the same time a structure for improved wartime medical services was established which was to prove invaluable in the near future.

The South African Air Force, too, benefitted from Pirow's far-sightedness. At bargain-basement prices he bought up numbers of the only combat aircraft to be had – obsolescent or obsolete surplus ex-Royal Air Force aircraft like Hawker Harts or Hartbeeste as the South African called them, Gloster Gladiators and Hawker Furies. His belief was that the wars in China and Spain had shown that even somewhat outdated combat aircraft could still be of value if expertly piloted.

The fighting in Abyssinia a few years hence proved him right; the South African Air Force pilots performed small miracles with their biplanes before the trickle of modern fighters like the Hurricane and Spitfire turned into a steady flow. A pool of men to fly the new acquisitions was building up as well. In four years the number of pupil pilots had jumped from 24 to 432, and there were 150 fully trained reserve pilots and more than 2,000 reserve air mechanics.

The same expansion was taking place in the ground forces; there were 20,000 men under training in the active citizen force, and the Union Defence Force now had 12 batteries of, admittedly obsolescent, artillery. There were still huge gaps to be filled of course, a major one being the lack of armoured fighting vehicles of any kind.

Pirow's War Supplies Board approached local companies as early as 1937 about building a locally designed armoured reconnaissance vehicle, and was informed that there would be no real technical difficulties involved in doing so, even though the country's automotive industry was still in its infancy.

Early in 1938 the Union Defence Force produced some preliminary designs, but a lack of technical staff in the military stalled the project, in addition the Iron and Steel Corporation, which had undertaken to develop suitable armour plating, had also run into technical difficulties. Near the end of the year the project began to move again, however, with a review of the earlier designs.

While Oswald Pirow was trying to drag the Union Defence Force out of its post-Depression financial paralysis, Percy Hobart's untiring and often abrasive efforts to establish mechanicalization as the backbone of the future British army lurched a step forward when he was promoted to major-general and sent out to the Middle East in 1938 to establish and train what was called Mobile Force (Egypt).

In spite of all obstacles – principal among them a lack of equipment and constant sniping by his numerous nay-sayers in the upper military and civilian hierarchy, one senior general reportedly welcomed him to Egypt by barking: "I don't know why the hell you're here, Hobart, but I don't want you!" He built up a modestly sized but superbly trained and highly motivated mechanized force which was to play a crucially important role in the near future and directly affect the growth of South Africa's armoured forces.

It embodied all of the thoroughly mechanized 'lightning war' features Hobart had been promoting for so long without any notice being taken by any of the world's military hierarchies … except of course, Adolf Hitler's.

By April 1939 it seemed clear that the armoured-vehicle project was progressing far too slowly. Europe was moving inexorably toward war; without so much as a by-your-leave the Germans had re-occupied the Rhineland in spite of the 1919 peace treaty, swallowed a large chunk of Czechoslovakia and taken control of Austria.

Meanwhile the Union Defence Force could not satisfy even its very modest requirement of 22 light tanks and 67 armoured cars. The problem now was not money so much as time, and an order was placed for 22 of the United States Army's M1 armoured cars, a fast – 88kph cruising speed – 6 x 4 vehicle first produced in 1932 and mounting .50-calibre and .30-calibre

Pirow's Bush Carts in action during the East African Campaign.

SA Marmon Herrington Mk 1 2 wheel drive.

Browning machine guns in its turret.

For one reason or another this was found not to be practicable and in August 1939 the order was cancelled. By now it was also clear that no armoured cars would be forthcoming from Britain either, and there was only one logical conclusion: if South Africans wanted armoured cars they would have to build their own.

This left only a mild-steel local prototype that had been developed in the interim by Germiston-based Dorman Long (Africa), based on a locally designed hull with a cylindrical turret mated to a 3-ton 4 × 2 lorry chassis manufactured by the Ford Motor Company of Canada and powered by a Ford V8 engine. Its armament consisted of two .303-calibre Vickers water-cooled medium machine guns, one in the turret and the other in a ball mount in the left rear of the hull.

Initial testing had shown promise, according to Harry Klein in *Springboks in Armour*, and the Union Defence Force's war supplies section was told to see to the manufacture of seven of the same type; then another 22 were added, so that an experimental armoured car company could be equipped. The vehicles were to be available by the end of July 1939 for further testing by the Military College, with a demonstration company of the Special Service Battalion providing the manning.

Under the press of circumstances, however, neither of these plans came to fruition. The two-wheel drive vehicle, a combination of local, imported and existing parts and equipment, was delivered in August 1939, but had yet to be evaluated on 6 September, when parliament voted in favour of active participation in the war rather than a state of armed neutrality. The long-awaited other boot had dropped in no uncertain fashion.

The prime minister, General J. B. M. Hertzog resigned, and the coalition that had governed South Africa since 1933 fell apart. General Hertzog was replaced by his deputy, General Smuts, who also assumed Mr Pirow's defence portfolio. Now the rush was on to build up a viable South African war machine from the ruins of two decades of neglect.

It was an awesome task; the first was a lack of trained manpower. The entire permanent force consisted of about 352 officers and just over 3,000 other ranks, the only other full timers being 1,722 one-year volunteers in the Special Service Battalion. The active citizen force numbered 918 officers and 12,572 other ranks.

There were also about 122,000 members in the Defence Rifle Associations, the descendants of the commandos of earlier days, but only about 18,000 were suitably armed and many of these were not properly trained for any type of modern warfare.

In addition, the bitter political dissension caused by the decision to take part in the war made it likely that a substantial proportion of the first- and second-line armed forces, both full-time and part-time, might refuse to volunteer for war service; the operative word being 'volunteer', since the grey area in the Defence Act that had led to the formation of the "imperial service units" during the First World War was still in force.

Smuts believed – correctly, as it turned out – that Mussolini's Italy, which had very large forces deployed in its colonies of Libya, Eritrea and Abyssinia, would soon throw in its lot with Germany. As a result, "Smuts … regarded Kenya and Uganda as South Africa's strategic boundaries and was determined to deploy Union Defence Force units 'up north'," according to Professor André Wessels of the University of the Orange Free State in his incisive Military History Journal article entitled *The First Two Years of War*.

But "in the light of the prevailing tense political climate, and because the act could be interpreted as not making provision for active service by Union Defence Force units beyond the Union's borders, Smuts announced that he would not press a single man to go beyond the country's geographic borders, and would create a fighting force of volunteers."

A further complication was that full use of the Union's black, coloured and Asian citizens was hampered by the extremely delicate political situation, which had an unlikely and unwitting ally in the person of Lieutenant-General Sir Pierre van Ryneveld, who was now chief of the general staff.

According to Martin and Orpen he was a micro-manager whose "forceful personality dominated all about him, while his monumental memory for detail enabled him to dictate at levels not usually associated with his exalted position." Among other things this would lead to "ill-considered decisions" which resulted in the official limitation of people of colour to non-combatant roles, "even against the intentions of Field Marshal Smuts and Major-General [Evered] Poole."

This was "in sharp contrast," Wessels comments, "to the situation during the First World War, when 'non-whites' were actively involved not only as auxiliary troops but also as soldiers in German South West Africa … German East Africa … Palestine and France."

The key word here is "official." As the war progressed and manpower needs increased, men of colour became employed in all manner of combatant roles, both officially and unofficially, a fact of which the famously eagle-eyed van Ryneveld was obviously aware – although it seems largely to have escaped the notice of the parliamentary opposition.

The armaments situation was even worse. At the outbreak of war there were just 16 field artillery batteries with only 87 guns between them and only eight 3-inch anti-aircraft guns, while the total inventory of artillery ammunition was a scant 28,941 rounds; the infantry battalions had a mere 23 3-inch mortars. Coastal defences remained both inadequate and, where they existed, obsolete in spite of attempts to improve them that dated back to the early Oswald Pirow years.

In spite of Herculean efforts, including those of van Ryneveld, the South African Air Force still consisted of only 173 officers and 1,664 other ranks, one operational and two training squadrons and six modern aircraft – four Hawker Hurricanes, a twin-engined Blenheim light bomber and an obsolescent single-engined Fairey Battle light bomber. Backing them up were 63 obsolete Hawker Hartbeeste fighter-bombers, six equally obsolete Hawker Fury fighters and an assortment of other bits and pieces.

But now everything changed. The department of defence and the Union Defence Force rushed to make up the deficiencies that had plagued them during the Pirow era in a burst of hard work and improvisation which is unique in South African history for its sheer scope and achievements. And that included the matter of armoured vehicle production, which was tackled within three weeks of the declaration of war.

PART TWO

THE EAST AFRICAN CAMPAIGN

9

The South African Tank Corps is born

On 18 September 1939, just 12 days after the outbreak of war with Germany, the 4 x 2 prototype armoured car was delivered to the Union Defence Force and immediately put through intensive testing by a production committee consisting of Lieutenant-Colonel Evered Poole, Lieutenant-Colonel J. B. Kriegler, Captain G. N. Nauhaus and Lieutenant I. M. L. Kat-Ferreira.

According to Harry Klein, writing in 1967, the test car had a four-wheel-drive drive train provided by the Marmon-Herrington company of Indianapolis, in the United States, but it is now clear that the Marmon-Herrington conversion kit was only fitted on the later Mark II armoured car.

At the end of the tests the committee concluded that while the car was definitely superior to the Crossleys in every way, it still required many modifications: the chassis needed to be shortened to a 3.4m wheelbase and strengthened. These modifications were carried out, and in November the car was put through another series of strenuous tests which took it from Pretoria and back via Sabie, Kowyn's Pass, Schoemanskloof and Machadodorp.

Although its performance was now much improved, the car's cooling system and springs were still inadequate and on wet roads, requiring much low-gear driving, when its petrol consumption dropped to only 7–7.9 miles per gallon (2.5–2.8km/litre). Still more modifications followed, and in January 1940 the car was put through another test, in which it covered 1,800km.

This time it passed the requirements and the 190 cars by Dorman Long went into production (although only 113 appear to have actually been manufactured). It was the first of a stream of constantly evolving armoured fighting vehicles, large and small weapons, munitions of all kinds and many other items from boots to steel helmets that would flow from South Africa's industries for the duration of the war.

It has now been largely forgotten that in addition to supplying fighting men, South Africa also produced large quantities of other war matériel, not just for itself but for the other Allied nations, not to mention training thousands of pilots from Commonwealth nations.

A variety of industrial assets were inspanned to build South Africa's first locally made armoured car, with the tempo drastically increased after the fall of France in 1940, when the initial order was increased to 1,000, with a delivery requirement of 50 per week.

Dorman Long not only supplied drawings for all South African armoured car designs during the war but also undertook final assembly at its Germiston plant in a facility which was specially erected for the purpose. Some 70 other sub-contracted companies acted in support, often designing and building special tools and jigs to produce the required components.

The core of the armoured car project, however, was the South African Railways and Harbours Administration, the single largest industrial organization in the country, with 20 major workshops which employed a plethora of skilled and semi-skilled artisans whose abilities encompassed a wide range of mechanical trades.

Clustered around the South African Railways were hundreds of separately controlled factories in all parts of the country whose work was coordinated by the War Supplies Board. This included the Ford and General Motors subsidiaries which assembled imported North

American chassis as well as some bodies, others being built in South Africa.

The steel industry, whose main consumer so far had been the mines, naturally played a vital role in the process. The Iron and Steel Industrial Corporation, having overcome its earlier technical problems, was now producing suitable medium manganese steel armour plating, each piece of which was individually tested before being cut to shape and size by acetylene profile-cutting machines.

The plating was sent to the South African Railways workshops, which worked around the clock to rivet or weld the plates together to form the turrets and bodies. The Mark I and Mark II hulls were constructed by riveting the plating on to mild steel frames; it was soon discovered that welded hulls were much better, and the older method was abandoned. The turrets and bodies were then despatched to Dorman Long for final assembly, where they were mated to their adapted commercial chassis.

The interior of the armoured car was roomy and unobstructed, with adequate space for the crew of four men. The armament, as originally fitted, consisted of one water-cooled .303-calibre Vickers machine gun in a ball mounting in the circular turret and another in the left-hand side of the hull. The last was an archaic concept, apparently derived from early British medium tank armament, and was soon discarded.

The official designation of the first 1,000 armoured cars was 'South African Reconnaissance Car Marks I and II', abbreviated to 'SARC Mark I and II', by which name it was known in all South African military manuals and inventory lists.

The South Africans' success in getting effective armoured cars into quantity production was followed with interest by the War Office in Britain, which had none under manufacture, and the Union government was asked to supply some of the vehicles for use in the Middle East.

As a first step 400 of the four-wheel drive Mark IIs out of the 887 built or being built for the Union Defence Force went 'up North' to the British forces, long before any South African soldier set foot in the desert. These cars – designated Armoured Car, Marmon-Herrington, Mark II, by the War Office – were mainly of the later welded-hull type. Based on this nomenclature the entire series soon became popularly known as Marmon-Herringtons – strictly speaking this name refers only to the four-wheel drive drivetrain – which in any case was only fitted from the Mark II onward.

The cars rolling out of Dorman Long's assembly plant were, of course, far from perfect. As Klein comments: "In the light of theoretical knowledge available to the production committee on prospective armoured car operations in African theatres of war, the car was a good product, but it was unfortunate that greater emphasis was not placed at the time on the comparatively weak suspension system, which proved to be such a bugbear during operations in East Africa, where the high rate of broken springs caused untold difficulties."

Klein might have added that the problem with broken springs was alleviated in due course but never completely resolved, not even in later models in the Western Desert, and that this car and its successors had two other defects that only became apparent later on, when the South Africans were deployed there.

The first was the inadequate armour. The South African cars' armour was designed to repel small-arms ammunition and hand grenades, which proved to be the case during the Abyssinian campaign, but the Western Desert was another story – according to the writer/historian John Sandars the armour was even thinner than that of the old Rolls Royce cars deployed in the Western Desert during the First World War and the early years of the Second World War.

The second was the inadequate armament. At that stage of the war several countries, including France, Italy and Germany, had armoured cars mounting guns ranging from 20mm to 47mm, but in the British sphere they still carried nothing more potent than one or two rifle-calibre medium machine guns and/or the .55-calibre Boys anti-tank rifle, and this would not start changing – officially anyway – until late in 1941.

It would be easy to accuse the production committee of short sightedness, but the prototype was in line with the requirements laid down in the early Union Defence Force training instructions derived from the 1921-vintage vision of an armoured car's function.

Klein quotes the early Union Defence Force training instructions, which stipulated that "armoured cars act either as mobile troops or as advance-guard mobile troops declaring bounds clear as indicated in operations order. Tasks still recce. Armoured cars will not fight except to gain information and even then this will seldom happen … Armoured cars will not be used in the role of tanks for frontal attacks. They must make use of their mobility and circuit of action."

Later, of course, it was realized that mounting a more powerful weapon than a machine gun on a "light" car increased its scope beyond mere reconnaissance, but the South African armoured cars only achieved their full potential in the Western Desert when they began replacing their automatic weapons – involving the removal of the entire turret – with captured German and Italian anti-aircraft and anti-tank guns and, when they could get them, British 40mm 2-pdrs. But that still lay many months and a number of battles in the future.

There was also the question of mobility on bad roads or altogether off road. When the first Mark I armoured cars were deployed in East Africa in 1940 it soon became clear that a two-wheel drive configuration was not adequate for the very rough terrain encountered there. This was not a design fault, however, but a case of happenstance because the two-wheel drive version of the "reconnaissance car" was ready first, and the Union Defence Force could not wait for a four-wheel drive prototype.

As it transpired, the Mark II armoured cars with the four-wheel drive Marmon-Herrington drivetrains went into production in the first half of 1940 and were issued well in time for the principal fighting in Abyssinia, and in several versions were to serve in their thousands in half a dozen armies.

In the 1940 context, the choices made by the committee were entirely logical. The fact that the battlefield has its own imperatives, and that what was good for the European goose was not necessarily good for the African gander, is neither here nor there.

What was important was that the Union Defence Force now had a viable armoured car design: somewhat rough and ready by European standards, perhaps, but a real bushveld beast in spite of its flaws, whose successors would serve until long after the war.

Although the South African Army now possessed a prototype armoured car it did not, however, have any armour-trained personnel. This was addressed on 31 January 1940 when authority was given for the establishment of No. 1 South African Armoured Car Company which was to be located at the Military College and consist of 22 cars, six officers and 161 other ranks when these became available.

The founder members of its command group deserve being mentioned by name, given their pioneer status as the first three officers to be appointed to the South African Tank Corps, although its official birth was still four months away: Lieutenant I. M. L. Kat-Ferreira (commanding officer), Lieutenant Craig Anderson (second-in-command) and Second Lieutenant Harry Klein (adjutant and intelligence officer).

Finding the first batch of suitable other ranks proved more difficult. At that stage South Africa was still making use of the phoney war that had followed the outbreak of hostilities in Europe to get its ramshackle military house in order, and the active citizen force was on standby while it awaited the order to mobilize for active service.

As a result, 1 South African Armoured Car Company had recruited only 35 of its authorized strength of 161 other ranks by the end of February. Nevertheless, training commenced immediately at the depot, which was headquartered in an old corrugated-iron building in the

Camouflaged SA Marmon Herrington Mk1 cars (U601 & U602) alongside truck convoy.

MaHe experimental during sand trails circa 1944.

Small Arms Enclosure of the Military College.

Providing the trainees with the standard parade-ground drill and small-arms training was no problem, but more dedicated instruction was difficult because of a lack of equipment, particularly armoured cars. At this stage the only available cars were the two Crossleys, which had just returned from yet another jaunt to South West Africa. They were now definitely showing their age, and according to Klein were, "more often than not in the repair shop." In lieu of anything better, the instructors used the Dragon tracked haulers imported in 1930.

A distinctive working dress for all ranks soon began to emerge: a khaki one-piece overall, boots, webbing, anklets and a black beret like that of the Royal Tank Corps, a very visible quiff, since no other unit in the Union Defence Force wore a beret of any kind at that time.

Originally the Union Defence Force general service badge was worn with the beret, but before long a distinctive insigne was introduced which closely resembled that of the Royal Tank Corps, which had just been renamed the Royal Tank Regiment: a Mark IV Male tank, surrounded by a wreath, with a bilingual scroll bearing the initials SAAC-SAPM (South African Armoured Cars – *Suid-Afrikaanse Pantsermotors*).

As time went by the prospects began to improve. In April four more armoured car companies were authorized and the external-service problem was circumvented by an extraordinary stratagem that could only have originated from General Smuts' brilliant legal mind.

This ingenious solution lay buried in the military archives for more than 60 years before being unearthed in 2003 by Captain Peter Digby of the Transvaal Scottish – historian and author of the justly famed book *Pyramids and Poppies* about 1 South African Brigade's adventures in the First World War.

Two signals from Defence Headquarters, numbered DD.88.B and DD.88.B.O, ordered the creation not merely of Imperial Service Units as in the First World War but of an entire shadow Defence Force which existed in parallel with the existing one: in essence, units, corps and services were directed to form parallel volunteer equivalents of themselves.

All members volunteering for foreign service, as the chief of the general staff explained in a telex message dated 4 April 1940, "will then be posted to their parallel volunteer units, corps, etc for the duration of the war." At the end of hostilities each unit, corps or service would revert to its old persona – this is why one finds the repeated use in official histories of the puzzling phrase that after the end of hostilities one or other unit was re-established. What was actually meant by this was that the volunteer units were officially absorbed into their 'parent' units.

The first 22 South African Reconnaissance Car Mark Is were scheduled to be delivered in May 1940, a much-anticipated event at the Roberts Heights depot. But within a fortnight of the end of April the embryonic corps found itself caught up in a tidal wave of events, both overseas and nearer to home.

On 16 May 1940 the phoney war suddenly turned into the real thing when the German armies fell on Luxembourg, Belgium, the Netherlands and France. If they had been formidable before, they were twice as formidable now, thanks to the brief but fiercely fought invasion of Poland.

The German intervention in the Spanish Civil War a few years earlier had provided valuable lessons, and the Polish invasion supplied the final polish. It had helped the Germans perfect the technique of their 'lightning war' and they had learned some new ones – among other things that their tanks needed thicker armour, and that appropriately used anti-tank guns could cause losses out of all proportion to their numbers.

It was clear, as Smuts had long suspected, that the Germans would soon be joined by the Italians, and when this happened, the entire Allied war effort would be plunged into mortal danger. To understand why this is so it is necessary also to understand the political and strategic geography of the region in 1939–40.

At that time the Horn of Africa and its environs, along which ran the Red Sea route to the Suez Canal, consisted of a number of territories dominated by the British, French and Italians. On the Mediterranean littoral the Italians controlled Libya. East of Libya lay British-dominated Egypt with its Suez Canal. South of Egypt was the Sudan, a so-called 'condominium' jointly administered by Britain and France, with a port on the Red Sea.

South and east of the Sudan and facing on to the Red Sea was Eritrea, an Italian colony since 1890, with its port of Massawa, and west of it, Abyssinia, which the Italians had seized in 1936. Below it was French Somaliland, a small and inconsequential colony except for its Red Sea port of Djibouti which was linked to the Abyssinian capital of Addis Ababa by a railway line.

South of French Somaliland was British Somaliland, a territory of equally inconsequential size but which also possessed a strategically important port, Berbera. Even further south was Italian Somaliland, a colony since the 1880s and by far the largest of the three Somali territories.

Italian Somaliland extended over most of the actual Horn of Africa, with two large ports on the Indian Ocean, Mogadishu (the territorial capital) and Kismayu (or Kismaayo), the latter located just south of where the great Juba river runs into the sea. West of Italian Somaliland and south of Abyssinia was Britain's possessions of Kenya and Uganda.

Since Italian dictator Benito Mussolini had not been fettered by cost-conscious politicians during the post-Depression years – to the extreme detriment, it might be added, of his country's economy – the Italians had huge conventional, semi-conventional and irregular forces deployed in its possessions, particularly Libya, where Marshal Italo Balbo commanded over 150,000 men, and Abyssinia.

A successful Italian pincer attack on the numerically inferior British forces in the region would endanger not only the Suez Canal but would also effectively close off the Red Sea, the main southern supply route to the British forces in Egypt. Abyssinia could be a springboard for an invasion of Kenya and by extension Portuguese Mozambique as well, then South Africa itself. If South Africa fell into enemy hands, British supply routes, not just to the Middle East but also to the Far East, would be completely disrupted.

Control of the Horn of Africa was, therefore, crucial to the Allied war effort in both the Middle and Far East. Although the Abyssinian Campaign has been completely overshadowed by the later fighting in the Western Desert, it would not be going too far to say that in addition to being the first victorious Allied campaign of the Second World War it might well have been the key to the ultimate defeat of the Axis powers.

So there was a clear and immediate crisis building up in the Middle East and the Horn of

MaHe1 on the way to Komatipoort to stop an invasion from Portuguese East Africa.   Marmon Herrington in field trials near Barberton.

Africa and the British were disastrously ill prepared to do anything about it when it boiled over. And boil over it would. When that happened Marshal Balbo would attack into Egypt as soon as hostilities broke out between Italy and Britain, with the ports of Mersa Matruh and Alexandria as his first objectives.

Facing them was the only substantial British military force in all Africa – initially about 31,000 men under General Sir Archibald Wavell, commander-in-chief Middle East, and it was so outnumbered and thinly spread that very little could be spared to counter an Italian thrust along the Horn of Africa and down into British East Africa – certainly not any artillery or motor transport.

In a nutshell, the British military cupboard was almost bare, and everyone knew it, although in some cases Italian intelligence did not realize just how bare. The total military presence in the Sudan consisted of three British battalions, the small and lightly armed Sudanese gendarmerie and assorted police and irregulars, a total of about 9,000 men, although the Italians thought there were three times as many, to hold 1,800km of borderline.

British Somaliland had just 1,475 troops, once again lightly armed, although Italian intelligence estimated their number at almost 10,000. Kenya was just as vulnerable with only about 8,500 bayonets (combat effectives) – two under-strength East African brigades, an East African reconnaissance unit and two light artillery batteries – to defend a 1,200km border.

Some Royal Air Force fighter bombers were available, but no combat armour, anti-tank guns or field or medium artillery. None of the complicated logistic infrastructure required for modern conventional warfare existed except for eight reserve motor transport companies. East Africa Force would eventually become a fairly formidable fighting machine, but at this moment it was anything but.

Yet, with this laughably small army the new general officer commanding East Africa Force, Major-General D. P. Dickinson, was expected to defend Kenya in the event of war and contain any Italian advance as far as possible without compromising his primary defensive task.

The huge disparity between the opponents can be seen by comparing East Africa Force with the assets at the disposal of the Italian viceroy and commander-in-chief of Abyssinia, Duke Amadeo of Aosta.

According to accurate British intelligence estimates the Italians had 255,000 conventional or semi-conventional troops in Abyssinia, 160,000 of them locally enlisted, as well as more than 35,000 para-military *Carabinieri*, customs guards, police, naval and air force personnel. Aosta also had a large number of locally enlisted irregulars of various kinds, consisting of 1,500-strong groups which were divided into five subgroups; South Africans called all irregulars by the collective name of Banda.

He also had ample supplies of small arms, 39 light tanks and 126 wheeled armoured vehicles of various kinds, excellent mortars which outranged those of the South Africans, 800 artillery pieces of various calibres – although admittedly most of these were of pre-First World War vintage – and several hundred aircraft, ranging from fighters to light bombers to transports. Many of these were obsolescent, but then so were almost all the South African warplanes.

It was true that this immense force was not nearly as formidable as it appeared to be on paper. Aosta himself was a capable soldier and airman, and some of his Italian regiments were of a high standard – as the British later discovered when they assaulted the Abyssinian mountain stronghold of Keren. So were some of the colonial soldiers, such as his veteran Eritrean brigades and the well-led, war-like Somali irregulars.

Most of the Italian soldiers, however, were poorly trained and equipped and led by officers with no experience of modern conventional as opposed to colonial-style warfare. A large portion of the local irregulars were not only almost untrained and badly led but also less than trustworthy: the majority of Abyssinians were far from being reconciled to Italian rule.

Aosta's predecessor, Marshal Rodolfo Graziani, had been one of the generals who had conquered Abyssinia, and he had done so with the utmost brutality; Aosta had taken pains to improve relations, but his efforts had borne little fruit in regions like the Gojjam (Amharaland in the federally-structured, present-day Ethiopia), whose famously fierce and congenitally unruly warriors had always been in a state of semi-permanent insurrection.

He was also beset by serious transport problems. Although he had large reserves of petrol, oil and lubricants, his motor transport was worn out and there was a great shortage of tyres in spite of his repeated requests for more. As Orpen says: "He found himself with a superabundance of manpower which was not only untrained but also immobile."

Aosta's projected role for the immediate future was to prepare to support the invasion of Egypt. As soon as Balbo invaded and started driving eastward to seize the ports of Mersa Matruh and Alexandria, Aosta was expected to strike northwestward into the Sudan and seize the capital of Khartoum or Port Sudan, or both. In Rome there was a belief that a German invasion of Britain was imminent, and that the war might well be over by October. With Britain out of the war and Italy firmly allied with the Germans, all of southern, central and eastern Africa would be there for the taking.

As an efficient military officer, Aosta knew the task given him was hopelessly unrealistic unless he received, he told Rome, 100 modern combat aircraft, 10,000 tons of fuel and 10,000 tyres. He was also uncomfortably aware, as Orpen points out that, "his sea communications could easily be cut [and] Eritrea, Ethiopia and Somalia could be neither reinforced nor reprovisioned from the homeland or North Africa. The air would be the only remaining link between the widely separated parts of the Italian empire."

But Aosta's urgent requests for help had not achieved a great deal. Before Benito Mussolini staked his claim to part of Germany's spoils by invading the south of France, Aosta received a few hundred officers and specialists, two tank companies and some field artillery, machine guns and mortars, but after that the supplies dried up as the Royal Navy intercepted some Italian ships and others were recalled by Rome.

As a result he concluded that the only way he could fulfil his primary mission, which was to maintain the political and territorial security of the Italians' East African empire, would be, as he later informed Rome, "to play a purely passive and defensive role, to avoid wasting our energy and to conserve our forces for as long as possible."

Since he did not have the transport assets to react in time to any Allied initiatives, he decentralized his forces and positioned them so that they would be in place and ready to fight wherever the British were likely to attack.

All that was cold comfort for the British, however. With such a disparity in numbers, even a less than completely efficient juggernaut could roll without difficulty over their paltry defences

Crossley upgrade with heavy duty desert tyres with white dome to reduce heat.

Marmon Herrington Mk1 AC with Vickers protruding from the left hull.

in East Africa. This being the situation, the only source of help was from elsewhere in Africa.

Two brigade groups from the west coast of Africa were mobilized, one from the Gold Coast (now Ghana) and the other from Nigeria, which after two changes of name would be deployed as 11 and 12 African Divisions, and in South Africa another brigade group – the now-famous 1 South African Brigade – was preparing to start training in the Transvaal at the Premier Mine at Cullinan.

South Africa's reaction had been unbelievably swift for a nation which had started the war just eight months earlier bereft of virtually everything it needed; it was a reprise of Louis Botha's effort at Lüderitzbucht and Swakopmund in late 1914, but on a much greater scale. 1 South African Brigade and the two others being raised for 1 South African Division would be the only formations in East Africa organized and equipped to fight a modern conventional war.

The British colonial units were typical of their kind, designed to spend more time on internal security duties and border protection than on conventional military tasks; they marched on foot, with animals and porters to carry or draw their supplies, guns and equipment, and were not geared to operate at anything higher than battalion level.

The nascent South African contribution was a different proposition altogether. For one thing it would be the first totally motorized brigade in sub-Saharan African history. South Africa's modest automotive industry was working flat out to provide suitable vehicles; the military absorbed the entire output of the Ford assembly plant – which assembled no less than 18,349 lorries during the first year of war – and as early as October 1939 the Chevrolet plant had already been turning out 24 1½- and 2-ton transport vehicles every day.

Then again, it would have to have everything it needed to be a self-sufficient combat formation geared for conventional warfare – infantry, field and anti-aircraft artillery, anti-tank guns, mortar platoons, engineers, signallers, medics, logistics units, staff components and, of course, armoured cars, as well as some light tanks, although this last was not generally known yet.

True, it would still suffer from some serious lacks in equipment, and many of its soldiers were recent ex-civilians rather than long-serving regulars. But it was sufficient for its immediate needs and a good number of its more senior officers and men had learned the art of leadership in the hard school of the Great War.

The South Africans would also contribute a range of specialist technical and other services that were essential to the campaign but were not available from any other source. Among them were technicians who manufactured missing or broken parts for artillery pieces from scratch, doctors and nurses providing medical services such as East Africa had never before seen, construction units to hack usable roads out of the unpromising terrain and – most important of all – well-drilling companies which laboured under back-breaking conditions to supply both men and vehicles with the many thousands of litres of the water they needed above all else.

From 21 May 1940 the first South African Air Force fighter and bomber squadrons also began to touch down at Nairobi, and within the next few days the main elements of 1 South African Brigade – actually a self-sufficient brigade group, a type of formation the Union Defence Force preferred – were in training at the Premier Mine at Cullinan.

At the armoured car section of the Military College, meanwhile, this new urgency brought two immediate drastic changes. One was when No. 1 South African Armoured Car Company's commanding officer, Major Kat-Ferreira, and almost all his trained personnel – 12 officers and 51 other ranks – found themselves abruptly transferred into a new unit called No. 1 South African Light Tank Company.

They were told that they would leave almost immediately for Kenya, where they would be equipped with Vickers Mark III light reconnaissance tanks and trained by instructors sent down from the Middle East. In due course reinforcements would arrive to bring the company up to strength.

At the same time soldiers in training at the Zonderwater camp near Pretoria, mostly from Cape Town, were asked to volunteer for service in "tanks in the North" to bring the new unit up to strength. The volunteers – six officers and 86 other ranks – were sent immediately to Roberts Heights for armour training, pending departure to Kenya.

The other change was that on 23 May 1940 the 1st Battalion, South African Tank Corps, officially came into being with seniority from 1 May 1940, and was placed under command of Lieutenant-Colonel V. C. B. O'Brian Short. The battalion had an authorized strength of 58 officers and 1,063 other ranks and was issued with a modified version of the existing headdress badge, whose scroll now read SATC-SATK (South African Tank Corps – *Suid-Afrikaanse Tenkkorps*).

It would consist of 1 South African Light Tank Company, 1 and 2 Armoured Car companies, and 1, 2 and 3 Motorcycle companies – the first to be supplied by the South African Police and the second and third would be raised from scratch as new active citizen force units.

At this stage an armoured car company consisted of 22 armoured cars, 14 motorcycles, seven motorcycle combinations, one staff car, 11 1-ton pickups and 10 3-tonners. A motorcycle company had an authorized inventory of 93 motorcycles, 30 combinations, two 1-tonners and eight 3-tonners.

On 1 June 1940 Kat-Ferreira and his advance party of light tankers set off for Mombasa on the SS *Inchanga*, the same day that the first South African ground unit to deploy in Kenya, 1 Anti-Aircraft Battery, started digging in at the Kenyan port – the forerunners of tens of thousands of South Africans of all arms and services who were to stream into East Africa in the next few months.

Behind them at Roberts Heights they left Captain Craig Anderson to rebuild 1 South African Armoured Car Company almost from scratch, and Colonel Short with a battalion numbering just 326, although more volunteers were beginning to come in, now that full-time active citizen force service had been authorized.

On 9 June 1940 Kat-Ferreira and his troops disembarked at Mombasa and were immediately hustled on to a train, which brought them to Nairobi two days later. They went straight into camp at Kabete on the town's outskirts and began to prepare for a shooting war that was no longer simply imminent; from one minute past midnight that morning Italy had been at war with Britain and South Africa. The struggle for East Africa was on.

At Mombasa the anti-aircraft gunners braced themselves for an immediate Italian air raid, as did the pilots of No. 1 Fighter Squadron with their four precious Hawker Hurricanes, the

Production of Marmon Herrington ACs in South Africa.   The production of an MaHe Mk1 in a South African factory.

only ones the South African Air Force had, and No. 11 Bomber Squadron with their Ju 86 militarized airliners.

But nothing happened. What they did not know was that the Italians had no intention of bombing the port because, Orpen says, "they had no desire to endure retaliatory bombing of Mogadishu or Addis Ababa … in the whole of Italian East Africa they themselves had only six heavy anti-aircraft batteries to cover an area six times the size of Italy, and four of those batteries consisted of guns which were antiquated."

Instead the South Africans struck the first blow of the campaign. Major (later Major-General) D. S. du Toit and four Ju 86s took off from Nairobi at dawn to bomb a large Banda camp on the Italian side of the Moyale border post. The raid set the tone for the Abyssinian Campaign: aggressiveness as a counter to the imbalance of forces.

And so the stage was set for what Klein aptly describes as "the last of the great border wars. It was a war of swift movement and manoeuvre, of surprise and ambush, fought in the southern bush and deserts and in the green northern highlands, in blistering heat, torrential rain and biting cold."

In other words, it would be very much the sort of war that Oswald Pirow had foreseen a decade earlier, when he was struggling to bring the Union Defence Force to some sort of readiness for the challenges of an unknown and uncertain future.

In 1967 Klein could not have predicted that within a few years of his writing there would be another conflict – this time in southern Angola, as an overspill from the drawn-out insurrection in South West Africa (now Namibia) – in which South African armoured cars and tanks would serve in ways which were sometimes very reminiscent of the Abyssinian campaign.

The four-wheel drive descendants of the original two-wheel drive South African Reconnaissance Car Mark I saw widespread service during and after the Second World War. The first, the Mark II, still based on the shortened Ford 3-ton lorry chassis (as was the Mark III) started its field service in November 1940, but by May 1941, after 887 had been manufactured, it was replaced on the production line by the improved Mark III – the most ubiquitous of all the South African armoured cars – which had passed its field tests in December 1940.

Re-designed by Captain D. R. Ryder in September 1940, the Mark III retained the familiar long-nosed, hump-backed external appearance of its predecessors, but incorporated various modifications, visible and invisible. At 2.97m the wheelbase was slightly shorter, there was better sloped armour protection, a greater power-to-weight ratio, an additional radiator, a strengthened front axle, and stronger suspension and steering components.

The Mark III was also slightly better armed. Instead of the circular turret it now had an eight-sided structure with a flat front, mounting not only a water-cooled .303-calibre Vickers machine gun but also a .55-calibre Boys anti-tank rifle.

The Boys rifle, incidentally, was not as inadequate as it has been made out to be, but it was an unpleasant weapon to fire as a result of its heavy recoil and it was ineffective against German main battle tanks during the Western Desert fighting – the result being *ad hoc* additions of a variety of scrounged and captured heavier armament.

More Mark IIIs were built before it went out of production in August 1942 than any other model – a total of 2,630.

The South African armoured cars were in a constant state of evolution. The 6.7-ton Mark IV, which went into production in 1943, was a new development altogether. Crewed by a commander, gunner and driver, it had a monocoque body instead of a separate hull and chassis.

A rear-engine configuration was adopted, causing a need for some special mechanical modifications and the provision of extra control linkages. In some of the early Mark IVs the engine was mounted facing forward with the gearbox behind it, and the radiator at the back of the car with air being drawn through the rear of the hull. Only 96 cars of this type were built; all the others had the engine facing the rear, so that the gearbox was in front and air was taken in from the fighting compartment through the radiator mounted in the dividing bulkhead.

Experiments were conducted with a 2-pdr tank gun mounting, but it was decided that the Mark IV's turret was too light for this type of mounting, and so a 2-pdr field mounting was adopted instead. At first no provision was made for a co-axial machine gun in the turret, but later a water-cooled Vickers was mounted, which was later replaced by an air-cooled .30-calibre Browning on a coupled mounting in most of the vehicles. An anti-aircraft machine gun was carried on the turret roof: a .50-calibre Browning in some early vehicles, but later a .30-calibre weapon.

The Mark IV was powered by a 71kW Ford 90° V8 water-cooled petrol engine, with a crash-type, high/low-range gearbox with four forward and one reverse gear, and selectable four-wheel drive. It had a maximum speed of 80kph (cross-country 30kph), and the 227-litre fuel tank provided a road range of 322km (cross-country 193km). It arrived too late for the Western Desert fighting, but a total of 840 were built, plus 96 of a variant called the Mark IVX, and 1,180 Mark IVFs, whose automotive components were slightly different because they were derived from the Canadian F60L lorry.

The delivery of Mark IV armoured cars was limited by the supply of automotive components from North America and 2-pdr guns from the United Kingdom. No doubt the difficulty in obtaining 2-pdrs was the reason why 626 Mark IVs supplied to the Union Defence Force for home use were equipped with only a .50-calibre Browning in a turret ball-mount instead of the 2-pdr.

Along the way several advanced prototypes were produced that did not go into production. The best-known of these is the hulking Mark VI, which was inspired by the German heavy armoured cars and intended to take full advantage of terrain conditions in North Africa. Known as the South African Heavy Armoured Car Mark VI – later changed to the South African Reconnaissance Car Mark VI, it had eight wheels, two sets of Marmon-Herrington four-wheel drive drivetrains, two Ford Mercury V8 engines mounted at the rear, and a 52-calibre 40mm 2-pdr (later a 50-calibre 57mm 6-pdr) gun. The first prototype weighed 16 tons, but after several modifications and the addition of more armour the weight grew to 23 tons.

The Mark IV was ready for production in 1942, with 750 on order, 500 for the Union Defence Force and 250 for the War Office, but due to a delay in the importation of certain

SA MaHe Mk2 on training near Barberton.

Badge of the South African Tank Corps during the Second World War.

automotive parts from the United States, manufacturing could only start in 1943, by which time it was no longer necessary. Five Mark VI prototypes were built, of which one is on display at the National Museum of Military History in Johannesburg, and the other at the Royal Armoured Corps Museum in Bovington.

Armoured car researcher William Marshall refers to a third that went to the Middle East for trials, after which it was cannibalized for its components, and two other prototypes that were used for research by the Union Defence Force, then also cannibalized.

Other South African experimental armoured cars were the Mark VII, which was very similar to the Mark IIIA but with a Vickers machine gun on an open ring mounting, and the Mark VIII, a front-engined car of broadly the same configuration as the earlier vehicles. It was, however, up-gunned and had a 2-pdr gun and co-axial 7.92mm Besa machine gun in an exceptionally long turret which followed the lines of the hull.

By the time quantity production ended in April 1944 a total of 5,746 cars of various marks had been manufactured, 4,466 for the Union Defence Force and 1,180 for the British government. A few Mark IIs and many Mark IIIs and IVs were operated – both during the war and afterward – by an astonishing variety of armed forces in many parts of the world.

These included Southern Rhodesia, India, Malaya, West Africa and the British-controlled parts of the Middle East, Transjordan, the Lebanon, Palestine and even the French Congo (now Republic of the Congo), where a small number was handed over to the Free French forces.

In the Western Desert alone Mark IIs and IIIs were used by the British, New Zealand, Indian, Free French, Free Greek and Free Polish forces. On occasion, too, the Germans pressed captured South African armoured cars into service, and these were not the only ones to serve under the Axis banner: In the Dutch East Indies a small number of Mark IIIs bought by the Netherlands government in 1941 were later taken over by the victorious Japanese, then 'liberated' by the Dutch when they returned in 1945 and put back into service.

Another batch of 175 arrived in Singapore in November 1941 in time for the fighting withdrawal following the Japanese invasion of northern Malaya; after the fall of Singapore on 15 February 1942 the Japanese made use of the surviving cars.

In the Western Desert, as in Abyssinia, the armoured cars were put to a wider variety of uses. In at least some cases infantry battalions' Vickers machine gun platoons used Mark IIIs, carrying the guns, tripods, ammunition and water cans inside the cars and dismounting them for use.

Although the Mark IVs were too late for the desert fighting and were not used in Italy, some served on, well past what should have been their sell-by date. Retro-fitted Mark IVs served in the Greek army until the early 1990s; they were used post-1948 by the new state of Israel and as late as the mid-1970s were still in service with the British South Africa Police in Rhodesia.

All in all, a remarkable record for a homemade armoured vehicle which had been designed and produced in haste by a relatively undeveloped country without any aid from any of the major powers.

*The author has been unable find an example of the first 1 South African Armoured Car Company badge described by Klein, although examples of the SATC-SATK ones exist and also many of the 1942-vintage badge – basically the same as its predecessors, but topped by a springbok head and with the initials on the scroll replaced by the motto *Ons Is* (translated as We Are, implying readiness for battle) – which was reportedly designed by Major-General George Brink in September 1941.The scarcity is probably due to the very small number made before it was superseded by the SATC-SATK badge; it is even possible that the founder members jumped the gun and paid for manufacture of the badge out of their own pockets before it was officially sanctioned.

10

Preparation for Abyssinia

Du Toit's raid on Moyale was the start of months of back-and-forth bombing sallies and aerial combat by the South African Air Force, the Royal Air Force and Italians which by February 1941 would reduce Aosta's air forces to impotence, but on the ground the shooting war did not commence for months to come. This was because of a fatal timidity by the Italian government that ultimately doomed its military forces in East Africa, and a marked reluctance by Marshal Rodolfo Graziani – now commanding in Libya after Balbo's death in a shooting accident – to invade Egypt.

In mid-1940 the Italians had the resources to attack in overwhelming strength in both regions, which would have forced the British with their scanty assets to fight simultaneously on several fronts, usually a recipe for military disaster. If Aosta had attacked immediately after the outbreak of war he could easily have overrun much of Kenya in spite of his transport problems, and in fact he had proposed launching a pre-emptive attack before the outbreak of war, only to be told to stay his hand.

In Libya, Graziani, like Balbo before him, was convinced that his water-supply system was inadequate, and believed that although he had a huge force at his disposal – 150,000 Italians and local enlistments, 600 tanks and 1,200 artillery pieces – it was almost totally unmotorized and therefore unfit for desert warfare.

He was so gloomy; he suspected he had been handed a poisoned chalice by Italy's military chief, Marshal Pietro Badoglio, and on 8 August 1940, five days before the invasion's scheduled start, he told the Italian foreign minister, Count Galeazzo Ciano: "We move toward a defeat which, in the desert, must inevitably develop into a rapid and total disaster."

Graziani's state of mind could be written off as simple defeatism, but it was surely the considered opinion of a man who – guilty though he undoubtedly was of ghastly war crimes in Abyssinia and Libya – was also a veteran career soldier of such ability that during the First World War he had become the youngest colonel in the Italian army while still in his middle 30s.

Before the year was out his predictions were proved accurate when his men ran into the Western Desert Force under Lieutenant-General Richard O'Connor and suffered a series of embarrassing defeats, although at full strength, O'Connor's force consisted of only 37,000 men with 275 – mainly obsolescent – tanks, 60 old armoured cars dating back to the First World War and 120 artillery pieces.

But O'Connor had three great assets that the Italians did not: a commander-in-chief who was eager to take the war to the enemy, an innate grasp of mobile warfare and, above all, the Desert Rats – 7 Armoured Division, the newly renamed descendant of the Mobile Force (Egypt) that Percy Hobart had painstakingly constructed out of next to nothing before being so brutally Stellenbosched, as the military slang of the time described an officer who had been totally sidelined.

The result of all this was that by the time the shooting started in East Africa the British and South African forces there had had several months of their own version of the phoney war to build themselves up and put some of the necessary infrastructure in place. And it is not often realized how immense an effort was made, particularly by the South Africans.

As Klein says: "It was, in many ways, the most striking and satisfying illustration of South Africa's military contribution to the Second World War. South African administrative services and engineers were the mainspring of the advance of the East Africa Force from Kenya; air support was almost entirely South African; and South African artillery, infantry and armoured cars played a vital role in the series of victories that highlighted the campaign."

A week later after its arrival at Kabete 1 South African Light Tank Company was shifted to a training camp in the Langate area, and on 17 June 1940 its light tanks arrived. The Vickers Mark III India Pattern Light Tank – although it was built by the Royal Ordnance factories – was not so much a tank as what was then often called a 'tankette'. Essentially the British had taken their very successful Carden-Lloyd tracked machine gun carrier – later famous as the Bren carrier – and given it a new superstructure with a rotating turret mounting a water-cooled .303-calibre Vickers machine gun.

Each was crewed by two men – a driver and a gunner/wireless operator – the little 4½-ton tanks' primary task was reconnaissance, and they had already seen active service in the Battle for France. The Mark III was powered by a 49kW Rolls-Royce engine, giving it a maximum speed of 48kph and a road range of 240km. Suspension was the 'slow-motion' Horstmann type, comprising pairs of wheels in bogies pivoted to the hull by leaf springs.

The Mark III differed from the earlier Mark I and II light tanks in that the suspension was modified to use inclined instead of level coil springs – the front one pointing forward and down, the rear one pointing backward and down – and the number of return rollers was reduced from three to two. The Mark III was the only series-production light tank to be built with a Rolls-Royce engine from the start.

By 1940 the light tanks were obsolete for their assigned role, which was more suited to armoured cars, and they were not meant to withstand the rigours of campaigning in Africa because they had been designed for a European war of the 1930s. But they were all that was available, and in the months to come the South Africans used them to good advantage.

On 17 June 1940, while the light tank crews were familiarizing themselves with their new vehicles, the broader strategic picture lurched when France surrendered to Germany. In terms of the subsequent peace treaty the southern part of the country was demilitarized and governed from the resort town of Vichy by what amounted to a puppet government. The immediate effect was that all French soldiers, sailors and airmen, as well as their war matériel, was no longer available to Britain, barring those who, like General Charles de Gaulle, had fled and were reconstituting themselves as a Free French force.

This was a serious blow to Allied strategy in East Africa. A strike westward toward Addis Ababa by Franco-British forces along the railway line from Djibouti had been on the cards for some time. But now French forces would not be available because French Somaliland had been neutralized, in terms of a separate treaty with Italy, which also meant that the railway line from Djibouti was unavailable. British Somaliland would have to stand alone against any Italian invaders.

According to Neil Orpen, however, the loss of Djibouti had an unintended side effect that actually advantaged the Allies. For all the blood-curdling threats uttered by Benito Mussolini the Italian government's stance had been timid and defensive in the immediate run-up to the declaration of war, as evidenced by its refusal to approve Aosta's proposal for pre-emptive action.

Now, as Orpen says:

...the neutralization of Djibouti also acted as a brake on the staff in Addis Ababa ... To virtually no one except the peoples of the Commonwealth and British Empire in June 1940, did anything but a crushing German victory seem even remotely possible... and Italy was now Germany's ally. With her numerical superiority of more than 10 to one in East Africa, and with the strategic threat

Crew of aHe Mk2 maintain one of the Vickers MGs, East Africa.

Vickers Light Tank being loaded onto a portee, East Africa.

from French Somaliland about to be removed by the Vichy government, it seemed pointless for the Italians to launch out into the Sudanese desert or the forbidding Northern Frontier District of Kenya with troops whose services were sorely needed as a guarantee for the lives of Italian colonists living among the predatory, if not actively vengeful, Abyssinians.

Particularly in the Gojjam, the chieftains nursed bitter memories of Graziani's cruelties and commanded willing support from a populace who – it must be granted – enjoyed a bit of brigandage, especially when it could be sanctified in the name of patriotism.

While Rome hesitated the South African tankers got down to training, solving problems as they made their appearance. For example, the 3-ton lorries which were to have been used as portées to transport the tanks over long distances turned out to be inadequate, and until more suitable vehicles could be prepared were replaced by 5-ton artillery portées converted from commercial Fords at the Kenya and Uganda Railways and Harbours workshops – one of many improvisations by British and South African engineers and technicians which enabled the wheels of war to roll unchecked.

The declaration of war with Italy had an electrifying effect on the Tank Corps depot at Roberts Heights. "The pace of recruitment and organization … was speeded up immediately," Klein recalls. "Hundreds of volunteers of the finest calibre poured in for attestation. New companies were formed in rapid succession, and the facilities of the depot were strained to the utmost limits."

The depot was renamed the Armoured Fighting Vehicle Training Centre, and that very A. J. Kenyon who had served with distinction in the Royal Tank Corps' Mark IVs in France was now appointed its commander in the rank of lieutenant-colonel. The training centre was organized into a headquarters, dealing with technical matters and controlling all companies which were equipped and organized, the Armoured Fighting Vehicle School conducted classes for officers and non-commissioned officers, and the Reservists' Training Depot put recruits through six weeks of infantry training before posting them to an armoured car company.

By the end of June 1940 the South African Tank Corps had formed a total of five armoured car and two motorcycle companies. At this stage motorcycle companies were seen as mounted riflemen, but it would later be discovered that they simply did not have the same performance level as armoured cars in Abyssinia with its harsh broken terrain and execrable roads, where roads existed at all.

As a result no more motorcycle companies were raised and the existing ones were put to other uses. Klein comments: "Although pride of place in the Tank Corps goes to the armoured cars, the contribution made by the motorcycle companies must not be under-estimated, even though their experiences in the field proved the limitations of motorcycle units in bush and desert conditions."

Initially the companies were mounted on BSAs and other civilian motorcycles bought from commercial dealers, commandeered or acquired from private owners, but in August 1940 the Union Defence Force placed an order for 156 olive-drab 1,200cm^3 Harley Davidsons with side-cars and 2,350 750cm^3 solo machines. The big, tough Milwaukee bikes suited the Union Defence Force very well, and by the end of the war South Africa had bought more than 4,500 Harleys for all sorts of uses.

On 15 July 1940 the South African Tank Corps took another evolutionary step when it was reorganized into 1 and 2 Armoured Fighting Vehicle Battalions, each consisting of three armoured car companies and one motorcycle company; the light tank company and 3 South African Motorcycle Company remained unattached. As it turned out, 3 Motorcycle Company was never more than one platoon strong and eventually became a reinforcement pool.

As each armoured car company was formed it was taken through a cycle of intensive training in vehicle maintenance, weapons' handling and reconnaissance tasks, but it was recognized that the companies' tactical training would not be complete until they had actually exercised with infantry brigades. Late in July 1940 therefore 2 South African Armoured Car Company and 2 Motorcycle Company went to Barberton in the then Eastern Transvaal for combined training with Brigadier B. F. Armstrong's 5 South African Infantry Brigade. This was successful, and in the next few weeks all the other armoured car companies, except 3 South African Armoured Car Company, underwent similar training.

At the same time 1 South African Light Tank Company's Zonderwater volunteers completed their training at the Armoured Fighting Vehicle Training Centre and were sent to Durban to take ship for Mombasa. They had barely arrived at the Langate training camp when the company – now under command of Major W. P. Clark – took receipt of 12 newly arrived Ford 10-ton trucks that had been converted into portées and was on the move again.

This time its destination was Gilgil, about 120km east of Nairobi, for a fortnight's joint tactical training with the newly arrived 1 South African Infantry Brigade under Brigadier (later Major-General) Dan Pienaar. It had just got there when the Italians finally made their first tentative offensive move by invading British Somaliland, where Major-General A. R. Godwin-Austen, general officer commanding-designate of 12 African Division, had been placed in temporary command.

One large force from Eritrea crossed the northern border through the French-held pass of Jirre, conveniently accessible now because the Vichy forces formerly securing it had withdrawn, while another crossed over from Abyssinia and advanced directly eastward toward Berbera by way of the town of Hergeisa, whose only defenders (a lone motorized company of the Somaliland Camel Corps), did the only sensible thing and retreated. Other Italian forces struck into the Sudan and occupied Kassala, Gallabat and Kurmuk. To Mussolini's rage, however, Graziani sat tight in Libya while his scheduled date for invading Egypt came and went.

In the meantime the tank men completed their tactical training with 1 South African Brigade and set off to an old waterhole called Arbo Wells, about 450km to the east, where they were to come under command of 12 Gold Coast Brigade and receive abbreviated but intensive training at the hands of Major Knox Peebles of the Royal Tank Regiment who had been sent from Egypt for this specific purpose.

The day they left, 14 August 1940, General Godwin-Austen accepted, after three days of trying to resist the Italian advance, that British Somaliland was a lost cause for the time being, and that his forces were now in danger of being cut off from Berbera, their only avenue of escape. Next day he carried out a covert night withdrawal to the port and began preparing to embark his troops.

Vickers Light Tank with crew.

Vickers Light Tank with crew giving good indication of size.

On 17 August 1940, the day Clark and his tankers arrived at Arbo Wells, having travelled by train to Nanyuki and then lurched over appallingly rough roads to get there, Godwin-Austen started embarking. By 19 August 1940, the embarkation was complete and he sailed away. With Berbera lost to the Italians, the evacuation put paid to any remaining hope of a British attack on Addis Ababa from the east.

Meanwhile the war was getting closer, and on 20 August 1940, 12 Gold Coast Brigade received a historic operations order, committing them to take action against the enemy in the Northern Frontier District, meaning specifically Banda elements operating in the outer regions of British Somaliland. The immediate consequence of this was that the next day the Light Tank Company got its first – albeit very mild – taste of action.

One of its tanks, manned by a Corporal Burns and a Private Wall, was sent along to provide extra firepower for a reconnaissance group from 24 Gold Coast Brigade which had been tasked to gather intelligence about enemy strengths in and around British El Wak, about 200km away. In that area the borderline – which was no more than a narrow cutting through the thick bush that was barely passable for vehicles – ran directly northward between Kenya and Italian Somaliland to a point where it abruptly dog's legged to the northeast.

Situated on either side of the border at the dog's leg lay two Somali villages, both called El Wak and "equally squalid and dirty," as Klein remembers. British El Wak was situated about 6,000m west of the border, with an airstrip about 10,000m to its south. Italian El Wak, which sported a small fort, lay immediately to the east of the border, with another village whose name is variously spelled El Buro Hachi and El Bura Haja, 1,500m to its northeast.

The reconnaissance group left Arbo Wells at 1400 on 21 August 1940, travelled until 1900, stopped for two hours and then carried on more slowly with headlights switched off. At 2345, according to the company's war diary:

> … the head of the Convoy encountered slight opposition by rifle fire. All vehicles reversed into bush in case withdrawal necessary and infantry brushed resistance aside.
> This took about 30 minutes, after which the group carried on, even more slowly than before and at approximately 2415 hours on 22 Aug 1940 encountered further resistance of a minor nature. This was again brushed aside and Convoy continued to El Wak Aerodrome where further opposition was encountered. Column debussed and took up a position near aerodrome – infantry proceeded to investigate area. At 0930 hours Convoy embussed and returned to Arbo.

The final conclusion was that the El Wak airstrip was lightly held by Banda but not yet established as a base.

None of the participants in this minor venture knew that within a matter of months El Wak would become several South African regiments' first battle honour of the war after an attack that would alter the expected course of the entire campaign.

At the end of August 1940, the light tanks were on the move again, this time back to Habaswein, 75km to the west, which was considered more suitable for training because it was feared that Banda groups that were known to be active in the Arbo Wells area would see them and report back on their presence. This might seem exaggeratedly cautious, but it has to be borne in mind that at that stage the Italian local forces had no idea that the East Africa Force possessed any armour at all.

In Libya, meanwhile, Graziani finally ran out of excuses for not invading Egypt. On 9 September 1940, after being threatened with demotion, he sent off most of his 10th Army. It recaptured Fort Capuzzo just inside the Libyan border, which Wavell's 11th Hussars and elements of 1 Royal Tank Regiment had occupied within a week of Italy's declaration of war, and then crossed the border, harassed by a mobile element of 7 Armoured Division, while the main body of the small British force stationed at Sallum withdrew to Wavell's main defensive positions to the east of Mersa Matruh.

Graziani's forces were not geared to mount a *blitzkrieg* and progress was slow. In the next three days they advanced about 95km into Egypt then stopped at Maktila, 16km east of the port of Sidi Barrani. There they constructed a chain of fortified positions running for 24km from Maktila to Sofafi on the slopes of the coastal escarpment to the southwest, then sat down to wait for supplies and reinforcements.

The captive Italian press lauded this cautious advance as the beginning of the end for Britain, but Wavell knew better, and began to prepare his counter-offensive, while Britain beefed up the Royal Navy presence in the Mediterranean to blockade the Italians' logistic routes. The man who would take the war to Graziani was Lieutenant-General Richard O'Connor, the brilliant and much-decorated soldier commanding the Western Desert Force.

The South African light tanks were still at Habaswein as the components of the Union Defence Force's field force – 1 South African Division under Major-General George Brink – started coming together. On 2 October 1940, 2 South African Brigade (Brigadier F. L. A. Buchanan) and 5 South African Brigade (Brigadier Armstrong) started arriving. 2 South African Brigade is of particular interest as regards South African armoured history because it had strong links with the Special Service Battalion.

When war broke out the Special Service Battalion was not itself mobilized for war service but became a reservoir of high-quality troops. Some of its members were posted out to active units that were under-strength, such as batteries of the coast artillery, and in February 1940 it had supplied reservist manpower for two newly established infantry units, 1 and 2 Field Force battalions, which were brigaded for the Abyssinian Campaign and went on to serve with distinction in the Western Desert as well.

By now the South African Tank Corps had bloomed to 122 officers, 2,265 combat personnel and 108 support personnel, a vast growth since it had set up shop with three officers and 35 other ranks just six months earlier, and it had so thoroughly outgrown its cramped quarters at Voortrekkerhoogte that the Armoured Fighting Vehicle Training Centre moved to a new base at Block 9 at the Premier Mine, Cullinan.

It was also under new management, in the shape of Lieutenant-Colonel (later brigadier) J. P. A. Furstenburg, Colonel Kenyon having been appointed deputy director of Armoured Fighting Vehicle Development, and had acquired a temporary roommate at the new location, 1 South African Division's Armoured Fighting Vehicle headquarters under Lieutenant-Colonel G. K. Roodt.

On 5 October 1940 the first armoured components of 1 South African Division arrived at Gilgil, having set sail from Durban to Mombasa on 26 September: 2 South African Armoured

Harley Davidson Motorcycle Company.

Harley Davidson and sidecar as used by the motorcycle companies.

Car Company under Major C. G. Walker, 3 South African Armoured Car Company (Major S. B. Gwillam) and 1 South African Motorcycle Company (Major R. D. Jenkins). Only two of its sabre units were still in South Africa – 1 South African Armoured Car Company (Major Harry Klein) and 2 South African Motorcycle Company (Major C. L. Stander) – and they were on standby to leave for East Africa as well.

The companies immediately got down to assembling their vehicles as they arrived, drawing stores and equipment and preparing for local training around Lake Naivasha and Lake Elementeita. It was beautiful soft countryside which the armoured men and motorcyclists would soon remember with nostalgia when they hit the badlands of Abyssinia and northern Kenya, "none who experienced those early weeks in Kenya," writes Harry Klein, "will forget the hustle and bustle of excitement of preparation for active service, and the loveliness of the gentle country in which they carried out their training."

This did not apply to Major Walker's 2 South African Armoured Car Company which had barely set foot in Gilgil before it was abruptly ordered to the Mitiburi camp at Thika, 45km from Nairobi. Although they did not know it yet, they were destined to fire the South African Tank Corps' opening shots of anger, and put its armoured cars through their first operational test.

2 South African Armoured Car Company set off by train, by a fortunate coincidence they managed to hook on the trucks bringing their armoured cars from Mombasa, and arrived at Thika on 8 October 1940, ready for action. Four days later 2 South African Armoured Car Company was dispatched to join the Nigerian brigade group at Garissa on the border with Italian Somaliland, and on arrival on 14 October 1940 was immediately set to patrolling between Liboi and the border itself.

No. 1 Platoon, led by Major Walker, left Garissa at 0800, scouted and temporarily occupied the Hagadera waterhole, and next day set off for Liboi, about 50km away. Liboi had been abandoned by the Italians, and Walker sent two sections of cars under lieutenants G. J. Labuschagne and G. T. Loser to see if they could make contact, but not to engage if they met a superior force. Along with one of the sections, were a dispatch rider and an anti-tank gunner on a motorcycle combination who were so keen to smell powder that they had attached themselves to the patrol, although as Major Walker later remarked, they "had no right to be there at all."

While forcing their way through thick bush, the cars drove into an ambush laid by a mixed force of Italians and Banda about 3km from the border. As they advanced down a narrow track bound on both sides by almost impenetrable bush they were suddenly assailed by a storm of rifle, mortar and machine-gun fire, and showers of the little red Italian 'moneybox' hand grenades.

Pumping bullets into the surrounding bush with their Vickers guns, the cars forced their way through the ambush without suffering any significant damage and carried on until they were out of immediate range. Then, prevented by the bush from spreading out or attempting a flanking movement, the cars turned around and went back along the road, fighting their way through another barrage of enemy fire. On the way Lieutenant Loser picked up the two motorcyclists, who were now lying lightly wounded by the roadside after being blown off their mount by a grenade, and took both them and their motorcycle back to Garissa.

The clash at Liboi had been a small one, but it provided Major Walker with some interesting feedback on the cars' performance when he reported to Colonel Kenyon a few days later. On the positive side was the fact that "the enemy grenades have absolutely no effect on the cars whatsoever. There is an explosion and a flash, and that is all. Their rifle bullets also have no effect." On the negative side, "one car tyre was punctured by a bullet. It went through the rim of a wheel. It would make a big difference if you could hurry up the supply of bulletproof tyres, as we work so far away from our base, and our tyres are frequently punctured by the bush."

Another was the suspension and engines: "The roads are very rough and sandy, in parts 12-inches deep, but cars can manage to get through. The main trouble with the roads is the numerous hidden furrows and the occasional soft spot which bumps hard if you drop into it. The springs of these cars must be strengthened to enable them to stand up to the strain. U-bolts are also breaking and are difficult to replace ... The engines are also wearing badly, two of them already using one gallon of oil in 200 miles. We are looking forward to the day when our four-wheel drive cars come up here. Our present cars will not last too many months."

Most important of all, though, was that this first inconsequential brush gave the South Africans a good indication of what their patrols could expect when they started making more serious contact.

As Major Palmer graphically described it to Colonel Kenyon:

The tactics adopted by the enemy up here are as follows: They select a dense, bushy part on the road where it is impossible to turn, and allow you to pass, and then suddenly ambush you on your return when you think you are clear. It apparently appears to be a general scheme which they adopt and it is impossible to see far into the bush. Then as you pass, they open on you with mortars.
The teaching of tactics in open country is quite useless as everywhere you go up here it is bush. I would strongly advise training in country like Pienaar's river [northeast of Pretoria] where conditions are nearly like these. The country is dead flat and no landmarks can be picked out. Another difficulty up here is the very short vision one has along the road. The roads in part twist and turn to such an extent that you cannot see a car in front of you over 30 yards away, and you will appreciate that sectional work is very difficult, especially in a fight when dust is flying about.

Klein comments:

Either the South African armoured car commanders in Abyssinia had not studied their tactics, or they had set out to write a new handbook of their own. From [that] very first clash with the enemy they revised the accepted tactical use of their vehicles in the light of what they were called on to meet, and took on the role they were obliged to undertake throughout the campaign – that of infantry tanks ...
This first brush with the enemy virtually set the tactical pattern for patrol action in bush country. Later, when the South African brigades took over the front line from East and West African troops, the most effective patrol formation was found to be a combination of motorized infantry and armoured cars.

The latter travelled in front, in the centre, and at the rear of the patrol, to protect the column against attack and ambush while on the move, and at the same time were on hand for immediate action when contact with the enemy was made, so giving the infantry time to debus and deploy …

This procedure proved most satisfactory and allowed extensive patrolling with the maximum degree of protection for the infantry. On a number of occasions the prompt action of the armoured cars in patrol clashes saved the infantry from serious casualties.

Here was born the legend of what the Banda called the Gharri Kifaru, the rhinoceros car, which smashed down the bush like a charging rhino and shrugged off both bullets and grenades.

2 South African Armoured Car Company's adventures were not yet over. On 19 and 25 October 1940 it was on the receiving end of Italian bombing raids, and when the entire company, except for No. 3 Platoon under Lieutenant G. M. Stegmann and Lieutenant J. B. Dunning was recalled to Mitiburi it made the acquaintance of yet another Abyssinian enemy, the main rainy season.

"Heavy rain was falling when the move started," Klein recalls. "The road was churned to a quagmire and all the vehicles bogged down almost immediately. Company Headquarters and No. 1 Platoon were stranded in the morass and had to remain where they were until pulled out one by one by a borrowed tractor." The rains did not stop 2 South African Armoured Car Company from further patrolling, however. No. 3 Platoon scouted Hagadera and Galma-Galla districts for the next three weeks.

While No. 3 Platoon battled the mud around the Hagadera and Galma-Galla districts, ominous events were afoot in the Middle East and Balkans whose consequences were to directly affect the South Africans in the not-too-distant future. Mussolini had seen an opportunity to add yet another possession to the already over-stretched Italian empire, and so while the Germans were busy fighting the British and French in Europe he overran the tiny, poorly defended country of Albania, then cast his eyes on Greece.

It was a bad time for such military adventures. Hundreds of thousands of his troops were engaged in the Western Desert and East Africa, he was still battling to get the distinctly bloody-minded Albanians under full control, his advisors had warned him that Italy was five or six years away from being fit to fight a conventional war and his nation's economy was staggering under the strain of sustaining his various campaigns.

No doubt Mussolini was encouraged by the German successes in Europe, and the question of Italian prestige was also involved. It was also true that General Ioannis Metaxas, the Greek Prime Minister, had made no secret of his hope to remain neutral – not because he thought his nation was unwilling to fight but because it was not prepared for war. But for Mussolini's imperial ambitions Metaxas might well have succeeded in maintaining his country's neutrality, because Greece was not strategically important enough for either side to justify an invasion.

Without informing Hitler of his intentions, Mussolini tried to intimidate Greece into his sphere of influence by a combination of strong-arm tactics and threats, which in hindsight, were perfectly calculated to get the Greeks fighting mad. First the Italians sank the Greek cruiser *Elli* in the harbour of Tinos, with great loss of life. Then on 28 October 1940 the Italian ambassador to Greece called on Metaxas and presented him with an ultimatum which basically demanded that the Greeks allow strategic parts of their country to be occupied by the Italian army, or face invasion.

General Metaxas, a tough-minded former professional soldier, bluntly rejected the ultimatum and showed the ambassador the door. A few hours later Italian troops began to pouring into northern Greece from Albania. The Greeks responded by immediately mobilizing their sizeable if rather ill-equipped army, and counter-attacking.

On 12 November 1940 2 South African Armoured Car Company's No. 3 Platoon was relieved by No. 2 Platoon under Lieutenant C. A. H. Heard, just before General Brink began setting up his divisional headquarters at Gilgil. The once-sleepy little outpost had become a veritable hive of activity as the various units of the Division congregated there. The only missing element was Dan Pienaar's 1 South African Brigade which had been withdrawn in September and attached to 2 African Division – later 12 African Division – its place being taken by 23 East African Brigade under Brigadier W. Owen – an under-strength new formation made up mainly of partly trained new local enlistments.

At the time there was much bitterness and suspicion about the reallocation of 1 South African Brigade, but in retrospect there was good reason for it. The two new African Divisions, expanded from the West African brigade groups, had great responsibilities, yet were anything but battle-ready.

1 African Division – soon to be renumbered 11 African Division under Major-General H. E. de R. Wetherall – was responsible for the coastal and Tana river sector but had only the Nigerian brigade group and the hastily established 1 East African Brigade under command. 2 African Division, under Major-General Godwin-Austen, had an even greater responsibility, namely securing the entire northern sector of the border with Abyssinia, but consisted of no more than 24 Gold Coast Brigade Group and the newly raised 22 East African Brigade.

Neither division had any immediate prospect of reaching full strength by acquiring a third brigade; suitable staff officers, always a fairly rare commodity during wartime, "had to be gathered from far and wide," as Orpen says, and neither had adequate divisional support troops, transport or artillery, which is why General Brink was also destined to temporarily lose two of his three field artillery units.

"It was obvious," Orpen notes, "that the only place these were likely to come from was South Africa, on whom the divisions were likewise to be almost wholly dependent for air support, and for the build-up of administrative, engineering, medical and supply services to make any worthwhile operations possible."

Although it was not widely realized at the time, 1 South African Brigade, like its companions, was not just fully motorized but had gone a step beyond placing everything it had on wheels: it was also organized on what would today be called a modular concept, from its battalions right down to individual vehicles. In its final form the concept meant that every 3-ton troop carrier with its section of troops carried enough petrol for 800km of road movement, as well as water and food for seven days, with a special emergency reserve food supply for another seven days.

As a result the South Africans could operate at all levels for extended periods without requiring constant and time-wasting resupply, providing them with a flexibility and mobility hitherto unknown in Africa. This was something of a revolutionary concept in those early days of mechanization – and some of the British higher command in East Africa never quite realized what an important success factor it would be in the fighting to come. Once again Oswald Pirow's 1933 vision of light-footed fighting columns tailored for an African bush war was vindicated.

The final allocations of the armour were now decided on. When 1 South African Armoured Car Company under Major Harry Klein arrived it would be attached to 5 South African Infantry Brigade, and 2 South African Armoured Car Company to 2 South African Infantry Brigade. Sid Gwillam's 3 South African Armoured Car Company would join Pienaar's 1 South African Infantry Brigade at 12 African Division, while 2 South African Motorcycle Company (Major C. L. Stander) would join 1 South African Motorcycle Company in General Brink's divisional troops when it arrived.

On 23 November 1940 Lieutenant Heard and 2 South African Armoured Car Company's No. 2 Platoon caused something of a flap when they were reported lost north of Garissa. It turned out that Heard was not lost but had been marooned when the rains had turned all tracks into impassable morasses. By the 30th however, he and his platoon were back at Mitiburi, where its main body was now engaged in swopping its two-wheel drive Mark I cars for the first of the long-awaited four-wheel drive Mark IIs with their Marmon-Herrington drivetrains and the equally long-awaited bulletproof tyres.

2 South African Armoured Car Company's No. 1 Platoon under Lieutenant G. J. Labuschagne had vanished by this time, ordered to Wajir to join 3 South African Armoured Car Company and 1 South African Brigade for the first deliberate South African operation of the war, an attack on the Italian airfield at El Wak.

Harry Klein's description of what awaited the eager South Africans on the eve of their first campaign is as vivid as only one who was there could paint it:

> The frontier between Kenya and Italian East Africa, where the first exchanges of the war in East Africa took place, stretches for 1,200 miles from Lake Rudolph [now Lake Turkana] on the west to the Indian Ocean on the east. In spite of its great extent, the border country does not vary greatly in topography. At almost every point it passes through the same area of bush, semi-desert and lava desert, although at Moyale it traverses a green and rocky escarpment on which there are some patches of cultivation.
>
> On the Kenya side of the frontier there is a barrier of desert stretching for nearly 300 miles from the frontier line to the rich farmlands of central Kenya. Inside the great barrier, known as the Northern Frontier District, there were, from the military point of view, certain focal points, of no great value in themselves, yet important because of the water supplies they commanded.
>
> Of these the most significant were Marsabit and Wajir – the former a mountain oasis, the latter consisting of a fort and Somali village. It was on these two points that, initially, the defence of Kenya was based, and they later became the springboards for the offensive. It was in this no-man's-land of the Northern Frontier District that the South African armoured cars performed outstanding service. It was a harsh and inhospitable battlefield; a waterless land of bush and scrub, of sand and lava deserts.
>
> There were no made roads when the South Africans moved into their front-line positions in November and December 1940. The sun burned down day after day from pitiless, cloudless skies; the daily temperature was over 100° F rising to over 120° in the lava belt. Blistering heat, skin rashes caused by insect bites, and intestinal troubles from the chemical content of the drinking water from some of the wells, added to the trials of the waiting troops.
>
> And the road into the Northern Frontier District! This was another never-to-be-forgotten memory for those who served in East Africa and Abyssinia. North from Gilgil to Nanyuki and Isiolo it ran; northeast from Isiolo to Garba Tula, Mado Gashi, Habaswein, Arbo Wells and Wajir; north-northeast from Isiolo to Archers Post, Laisamis, across the powder-fine Kaisut desert, to the green oasis of Marsabit.
>
> A road not easily to be forgotten. A road of heat, dust, dirt and flies; of body-wrenching potholes and skidding sand. A road along which plunging wheels and whining, overheated engines, grinding in low gear, wrote the marching song of the South African motorized forces moving into the forward areas.

11

First blood at El Wak

On 8 December 1940 General Wavell initiated Operation Compass, his offensive in the Western Desert, aimed at pushing the Italians out of Egypt and as far back into Libya as the port of Benghazi. Supported by the Royal Air Force, General O'Connor's Western Desert Force burst through a gap in the Italian defence line to launch a completely successful surprise infantry, artillery and armoured attack.

Within five hours they had destroyed a brigade-plus Italian force and over the next three days wiped out 237 Italian artillery pieces and 73 tanks, capturing 38,300 men in the process. This done, O'Connor climbed the Halfaya Pass and occupied Fort Capuzzo. No doubt to O'Connor's frustration, Wavell then temporarily halted the advance for five days so that he could withdraw 4 Indian Division for operations in the Sudan and replace it with the newly arrived 6 Australian Division.

While O'Connor awaited his Australians in the Western Desert, Major-General Godwin-Austen was busy planning an attack on El Wak, the South Africans' first conventional action in Abyssinia. El Wak was a curtain-raiser to a broader aim: to capture the port of Kismayu at the southeastern end of Italian Somaliland, only about 350km up the coast from Mombasa, and thereby deal with a number of actual and potential problems standing in the way of the eventual drive to conquer Italian East Africa.

Kismayu's occupation would remove a potential threat to Mombasa, a vital point of entry for the Allies, shorten the interior lines of communication during an Allied advance – a very important consideration given the vast areas of extreme desert to its west – and close a gap in the British blockade of Italian East Africa through which some supplies were being smuggled to Aosta in dhows by the Japanese and others.

Wavell had instructed Lieutenant-General Sir Alan Cunningham, the new general officer commanding East Africa Force, to examine the possibility of attacking Kismayu before the rainy season broke in March 1941, an all-important factor because of the havoc it invariably inflicted on such roads as existed, not to mention the hindrance it placed on cross-country movement.

Cunningham finally decided, however, that for various reasons an attack on Kismayu would not be possible until June 1941, after the mid-year rains. The Italian forces' morale was reported to be high after their initial easy victories in Somaliland, and his available force was far too small. He calculated he would need a minimum of six vehicle-transported brigades, at least one of them armoured, and before advancing on Kismayu he would have to solve the massive logistic problem of crossing the bleak, waterless desert between the Tana and Juba rivers.

At this stage, it would appear, the British high command's plans for dealing with the Italian threat in East Africa were mainly unformed, because the overriding British priority in Africa was to defeat Marshal Graziani in the Western Desert in order to safeguard Egypt and the Suez Canal, the key to British interests in the entire Middle East.

As far as East Africa was concerned, the ultimate aim was still to capture the Abyssinian

1 SA Light Tank Company Vickers Light Tank on a Tank Portee truck.

Crew members of No. 1 South African Armoured Car Company, carrying out First Parades on their Marmon Herrington armoured cars.

capital of Addis Ababa, but Wavell's appreciation was that the immediate need was to occupy Kismayu in order to protect Mombasa, and meanwhile to foster the existing insurrection in Abyssinia by helping the insurrectionists with arms, ammunition, money and propaganda – the idea being to make things as difficult as possible for the Italians, not just to hamper their southward movement but also to soften them up for an invasion at some point in the future.

The most favoured choice for an invasion route would, of course, have been a strike westward from Djibouti and Berbera, along the general line of the Djibouti-Addis Ababa railway, but this had become a dead letter after the effective loss of both French and British Somaliland. Wavell now favoured a thrust north or northwest of Kenya's Lake Turkana, toward the area of great lakes south of Addis Ababa and then up to the capital itself, although, Orpen says, "at no time were there cut-and-dried plans for any meticulously drafted scheme of conquest" – no doubt because at that stage there were more urgent fish to fry than East Africa.

Thus there were two options, both of which were obvious to the Italians. The first, the shortest route but the most difficult, was along the road northwestward from Wajir, up an escarpment to Italian Moyale, which enjoyed a commanding position and was heavily fortified, then to Mega and Neghelli (now Negele Borena), both of which were also heavily fortified. From there further use would be made of the Italians' existing road network to get through the extremely unfavourable mountainous terrain of the upper lakes region and then head for Addis Ababa.

Moyale could be taken in either one of two ways. The South Africans could advance directly from Marsabit in Kenya through the dreaded Dida Galgalla (Dida Galgalu), the 'Desert of the Night' in the local Boran language – which would obviously favour the defenders; or it could be outflanked along with Mega by looping around westward through the equally dreaded Chalbi Desert, then driving north by way of the remote Kenyan wells of El Yibo and El Sardu – the only bits of Kenyan soil still occupied by the Italians – and swinging eastward.

The second route was along the coast into Italian Somaliland via Kismayu to the port of Mogadishu, northwestward through the Ogaden Desert to Harar, and then westward to Addis Ababa, although at that stage, according to Orpen, Wavell's intelligence staff had not yet appreciated the advantages of the Ogaden route.

The Ogaden route was much longer, but had one great advantage: for part of the way through the desert the invading forces would have the benefit of the Italians' *Strada Imperiale* or Imperial Highway. Although the war had interrupted the highway's completion in places, Orpen notes that "this grim, almost waterless country, with its sparse bush maintaining a nomadic population, had none of the great mountain barriers and escarpments which barred [the way] to Addis Ababa from Kenya's Northern Frontier District."

To implement Wavell's interim vision of keeping up the pressure on the Italians, Cunningham planned to harass the Italians by aggressive patrolling and what he termed the "cutting out" of various fortified border outposts, while at the same time preparing for the attack on Kismayu by improving the horrendous roads or making new ones along his planned route of advance and developing water supply points between the Tana and Juba rivers.

The first of five defended localities to be selected for cutting out was El Wak, which according to Brigadier E. P. Hartshorn, "has the melodious English translation of 'The Wells of God'", about 165km northeast of Wajir. There were several good reasons for selecting El Wak: the villages had good wells, Italian El Wak was the base for the Banda crossborder forays and, of course, there was the airstrip, an asset in a territory in which such roads as existed were not to be relied on.

According to Cunningham's intelligence the Italian village with its little fort was occupied by 191 Colonial Infantry Regiment with 16 guns, plus the Banda who had been prowling around west of the border. As it later transpired, Aosta rated the garrison at the equivalent of three battalions, and there certainly was a brigade headquarters just to the east, down the road which led to the next border post at Mandera, about 200km away.

Commanded by General Godwin-Austen, who had taken up his appointment as general officer commanding 12 African Division by now, the assault force consisted of elements of Pienaar's 1 South African Brigade – including Major Gwillam's 3 South African Armoured Car Company – elements of 24 Gold Coast Brigade (Brigadier C. E. M. Richards), 1 South African Light Tank Company, No. 1 Platoon of 2 South African Armoured Car Company, a full regiment – or brigade, as artillery field regiments were then still called – of 4.5-inch howitzers, a squadron of the East African Armoured Car Regiment and various support troops.

Considering the relative strengths of the two sides, it might seem that this erred unnecessarily on the side of caution, but the thinking behind it was sound. Firstly, the need to remove the Italian armed presence from the area and control the various wells and the airstrip was tactically important. Secondly, most of Godwin-Austen's field commanders needed practical experience in moving and controlling large bodies of troops under local conditions. Thirdly, the Allied troops would be blooded at small cost, and an attack, particularly in such strength, would do serious damage to the Italians' morale.

There was another advantage to be gained, although neither Cunningham nor Godwin-Austen knew it at the time: El Wak would also yield an intelligence benefit of such importance that its capture had a significance out of all proportion to the scale of the operation.

Nor was the assault force – effectively not much more than a brigade and a half – excessive in size. The classic ratio in any attack was three attackers for every one defender, and given (as Godwin-Austen believed) that there was a full Italian regiment holding El Wak, the Allies were actually under strength.

Godwin-Austen proposed to advance as swiftly as the execrable road from Wajir allowed, occupy the landing strip south of British El Wak on the night of 15 December 1940 and from there launch a three-pronged dawn attack on the 16th. For this purpose he divided his assault force into three columns:

Column A under Brigadier Richards – otherwise known as Dickforce – was made up of 24 Gold Coast Brigade Headquarters, 3 Gold Coast Regiment and 1 South African Light Tank Company. Column B comprised the Duke of Edinburgh's Own Rifles under Lieutenant-Colonel G. T. Senescall, the East African Reconnaissance Regiment squadron and two howitzer batteries. Each column had its quota of engineers and other support troops.

'Pinforce' was provided by 1 South African Brigade, which had now been considerably diminished by the detachment of the Dukes, its light tanks and its howitzers to the other columns, and its anti-aircraft detachments, one platoon of 3 Armoured Car Company and

Vickers Light Tank.

The driver of a Vickers Mk6 of 1 SA
Light Tank Company.

other elements to the divisional headquarters which Godwin-Austen intended to establish at the airstrip.

This left Pinforce with 3 Armoured Car Company (headquarters and two platoons) 1 Transvaal Scottish, 1 Royal Natal Carbineers (less one company detached to the brigade reserve) 12 Field Battery South African Artillery and 1 Field Company South African Engineer Corps, plus other support troops.

Godwin-Austen's plan of attack provided for Senescall's Column B to head directly northward from the airstrip, occupy British El Wak and then turn eastward and take the wells at El Ghala. At the same time Dickforce and Pinforce would head through the bush in an approximately northeasterly direction, cross the international boundary, debus their infantry and strike due north.

Dickforce would attack Italian El Wak; Pinforce would send the Carbineers to hit El Beru Hagia, while the Transvaal Scottish would swing further eastward to block off any counter-attack from the direction of Mandera, overrun the reported Italian brigade headquarters, and capture any enemy forces retreating from Italian El Wak.

On the morning of 14 December 1940 the long convoys set off from Wajir amid the inevitable clouds of dust on the first stage of the 165km of thirstland that lay between them and El Wak, Dickforce leading. A detachment of 28 South African Road Construction Company had laboured to improve the first 105km of the track, but before long the heavy traffic had undone much of their work. Nevertheless, Klein says, "the excitement of impending action relieved the tedium of jolting through a dust haze under a blazing sun in a temperature of over 100°F."

They made fair speed as far as El Katulo, about 105km from Wajir, where they halted at about 1700 to wait for darkness because Godwin-Austen was concerned about the fact that Banda elements were known to be operating in the vicinity. After dark they set off again, but now the 'road' had ended and a struggle with the rough track leading to the airstrip commenced.

This was a saga in its own right. As the march went on the unspeakably wretched road conditions began to exact their toll. The springs of the light tanks' portées started to break and 3 Armoured Car Company, which had not yet received the four-wheel drive Mark II cars, made such heavy going of it that crews frequently had to dismount and call on the accompanying infantry to wrestle their cars through patches of deep sand. Somehow both the tanks and armoured cars managed to keep up.

At 0345 on 15 December 1940 the assault force halted in the hilly area south of Dimo to lie low under cover during the daylight hours – all but the engineers, who worked right through the scorching heat of the morning to bring some structure to the road ahead. The others spent the daylight hours 'resting' in the bivouac area," Klein says, "if scratching for shade in thorn scrub in a temperature of over 100° can be termed resting."

At 1715 Godwin-Austin restarted the advance. Many more hours of struggle passed, made worse by the fact that proper control was impossible because strict radio silence had been imposed, so that "the night was made miserable by lengthy and inexplicable halts which exhausted the troops and upset the time-table," Klein says.

"Fortunately, the enemy showed a hopeless lack of enterprise and, apart from some spasmodic shelling during the night, a few shots from Banda patrols and a futile bombing attack by a Caproni at dawn, nothing was done to impede the advance." 3 Gold Coast Regiment and its attached anti-aircraft and field artillery occupied the airstrip after chasing away some Banda, and in the small hours of 16 December Pinforce and the divisional headquarters started arriving.

Column B was now in place, but Dickforce and Pinforce had still to cross the border and reach their forming-up positions. Their advance started when the Transvaal Scottish under Lieutenant-Colonel E. P. Hartshorn reached the airstrip at 0200 to the accompaniment of desultory shell fire from Italian El Wak, and were immediately sent off on a course of 70° through the trackless bush, the 3 Armoured Car Company armoured cars bush-bashing open a road of sorts ahead of the infantry.

The going was so bad that at one stage, about 3km from the border, Brigadier Pienaar's headquarters staff actually had to leave their vehicles and proceed on foot. Pienaar now spread out the cars over a wide front, ordering the ones in the rear to smash open new tracks for themselves. The rhino cars did exactly that without loss, and at first light Hartshorn's Transvaal Scottish became the first South African unit of the war to enter enemy territory in full battle order.

The Scottish were still moving to their forming-up place when Brigadier Richards took position and sent Clark's light tanks northward with the Gold Coast infantry following. By 0605 the tanks were within 700m of the first barbed-wire entanglements, and beginning to pick up fire from machine guns as well as the Italian artillery deployed at El Beru Hagia. One of the tanks fell into a tank trap but was towed out.

The Transvaal Scottish and Gwillam's armoured cars were in their forming-up place by 0630. An hour later the Carbineers had also arrived and were moving into position, with the rest of Pinforce's combat and support elements following close behind. "The Italians had not believed it possible for tanks and mechanized transport to travel through the boulder-studded bush," Klein says, "yet tanks and mechanized transport were there in coordinated formation, ready to deliver the blow a few hours after dawn on 16 December 1940 … The South Africans and the men from the Gold Coast who were blooded there, rose to their hour with a fire and a fury which made light of a temperature of 106° and of the enemy's defences."

At 0825 Dickforce set off, the light tanks leading and, as Klein says, "the tanks moved forward [and] there were dramatic happenings aplenty in the next few minutes."

Crashing through the bush in two waves of six tanks each, No. 1 South African Light Tank Company smashed into the attack. Swerving right, the tanks swung parallel with the defences and, while under steady fire from artillery and machine guns, delivered devastating broadsides along the whole quarter mile of the wire from a range of 20 yards. One tank received a direct hit from a shell yet sustained only a cracked plate.

Under covering fire from the tanks, Gold Coast sappers dashed forward to blow gaps in the wire with Bangalore torpedoes. Second-Lieutenant Christopher Ballanden, only three weeks out from England with the Gold Coasters, seized a live Bangalore torpedo which had fallen short and, running through a hail of fire, placed it beneath the Italian wire – and lived to tell the tale.

With bayonets fixed, with the light tanks roaring at their side, the Gold Coast infantry

Vickers Mk6 light tank being off loaded from a Portee truck.

A Vickers Mk3 and its crew in Abyssinia, East Africa.

dashed through the gaps in the wire and routed the demoralized enemy. Rallying south of the fort after helping the mopping up, the light tanks were bombed by aircraft of No. 40 Army Cooperation Squadron of the South African Air Force.So quick had been the ground attack that the Air Force knew not whether friend or foe was in possession of the fort.

By 0900 all of Pinforce's combat and support elements were in place and Pienaar started his advance. The first to move were the Transvaal Scottish, followed by the Carbineers 10 minutes later. With the armoured cars giving fire support to protect the infantry's flanks and standing by in case of counter-attacks – although some cars had to be dug out several times in the process – the forward elements crashed through 3,000m of thick bush in just 50 minutes, the Transvaal Scottish peeling off northeastward toward the Mandera road.

By 1015 the Carbineers had captured Zariba, south of El Beru Hagia, and five minutes later the Transvaal Scottish arrived at its objective, the Italian headquarters. The leading company opened fire, then charged with bayonetsfixed, scattering the occupants without a shot being fired.

The Carbineers left their armoured cars behind at Zariba because of the incoming Italian artillery fire and continued to advance through bush so dense that Colonel McMenamin could not use his mortars because he did not know where his leading troops were. Less than an hour later they fell on the northernmost objective, El Beru Hagia, whose artillery was shelling both the Gold Coasters and Pinforce.

They shot it up very thoroughly with mortars and rifle fire, then charged with bayonets fixed. Orpen says, "routed the defenders, who abandoned their guns just as they had bracketed Pinforce Headquarters." Some Italian officers rallied about 100 of the colonial soldiers and mounted a counter-attack, but this was quickly annihilated with heavy losses by rifle, machine gun and mortar fire. That was the end of the resistance at El Beru Hagia.The Italians had lost 55 dead and the Carbineers none.

Column B's progress was no less spectacular: "In Column B, it would appear, there was some difference of opinion on tactics between the South African Infantry and the East African Armoured Cars," Orpen writes, "and the latter were not keen to move forward without an infantry screen ahead of them. Consequently, the Dukes sent forward Lieutenant J. C. Molteno with their own scouts in 3-tonners, which made a great din. With the enemy thrown in a state of bewildered shock by an eight-gun salvo from the 4.5-inch guns of 10 and 11 Field batteries, the Dukes made short work of El Wak and [the] El Ghala waterhole."

Barring a brief air raid next morning, which ended with a Caproni bomber being shot down by No. 40 Squadron South African Air Force, this was the end of resistance at El Wak. The Italians had suffered an estimated 123 dead, not counting an unconfirmed number killed by the armoured cars; nine field artillery pieces had been captured, as well and four machine guns, 109 rifles, large amounts of ammunition, three lorries, a touring car, numerous documents and the colours of both 191 Infantry Regiment and the fort.

Most of the captured weapons and equipment were older than and inferior to the South Africans', but one item was booty of the first order and much sought-after – the Italians' aluminium water bottles, which were infinitely preferred over the enamelled Union Defence Force issue.

Lieutenant Wensley in his Vickers 3 tank in Abyssinia, 1940.

Thus ended the attack on El Wak. In spite of the obstacles and delays it had gone so well that as Klein says, "the actual battle was an anti-climax to the pent-up emotions of the troops … The raid was entirely successful. When the forces withdrew to Wajir, there were not four walls standing in any part of El Wak or its adjoining villages … and the most important strategic outpost the Italians possessed in this sector had been razed to the ground."

Klein does not, however, mention a less obvious but immensely valuable intelligence bonanza that fell into South African hands at El Wak. Hartshorn relates:

Against the broader canvas of the whole war El Wak was undoubtedly an incident of only minor importance and yet it had results which to my knowledge have never before been officially acknowledged.

Dashing into a cave, which was obviously Italian headquarters, I found papers burning in among rows of neat steel filing cabinets and glass-topped desks. It seemed it was too late to find anything of value. A moment later, however, members of our Intelligence arrived with a Carabinieri major who was a border police officer and who spoke excellent English.

"Has everything been burned?" I asked him. "Oh no, sir," and then, with the obvious pride of one anxious to show off his office efficiency, he went down the lines of filing cabinets indicating what particular plans they held.

Poring over these documents later I was delighted to find among them a large volume full of folded blueprints, which not only gave the proposed disposition of all the Italian forces throughout the whole of their East African empire, but also the actual plans of every major fixed defence from the Sudan through Eritrea to Massawa, down the coast and right round the Somali coast to Kismayo.

Even the fortifications for such important points as Dessie, Gondar and Amba Alagi were shown. There were, however, no codes, which was, fortunately, a disappointment soon to be allayed.

A patrol of the Natal Carbineers, returning from helping repulse a counter-attack, noticed a mass of paper in some heavy thorn scrub. Major 'Jock' Flower, their second-in-command, ordered it to be retrieved and it proved to be none other than the complete volume of the Italian most secret codes, its pages lying open, fluttering in the desert wind.

All these vital documents were immediately flown in a special aircraft to Nairobi and were to play a vital part in the rest of the campaign. The code provided not only the key to all the Italian codes but was extremely valuable in breaking the German codes because they could now be read in conjunction with this Italian code.

The plans of the Italian fortifications, too, were invaluable and I was to derive great personal satisfaction from their capture later in the campaign. When we overran Dessie [April 1941] I placed before the astonished eyes of the captured Italian fortress commander a photostat copy of the plan of his fortifications … Why these valuable documents should have been in a frontier post it is hard to understand.

South African Light Tank Company Vickers 3 being loaded onto a Portee truck.

A Vickers Mk3 of 1 SA Light Tank Company.

The most immediate benefit of the raid, however, was the devastating blow it had dealt to Italian morale and conversely the boost it had given the Allied soldiery. It was a classic illustration of the old military axiom that battles are won or lost primarily in the minds of the protagonists, and that the best way to achieve or initiate the process of gaining spiritual ascendancy is to give your enemy a bloody nose at the very start.

"The most far-reaching and important result of this raid was the effect it had on the entire East African strategy," Hartshorn writes. "Hundreds of the enemy escaped to the north and carried the news to the Italian forces of a new terror that was loose, of large powerful white troops and equally large and belligerent native troops who came through heat and bush on the run and closed with the bayonet.

"Until then the Italians had considered their numbers and armament invincible. Now, as General Cunningham wrote, 'all the survivors became apostles of terror to their brethren'. The information from captured officers and later from Intelligence reports showed that Italian morale had been destroyed in a single day. It was even being asked by terrified Italians: 'Is it true that these South Africans are cannibals?'"

Klein says: "In the ultimate result, the success at El Wak … showed the ascendancy of Allied morale and the decline of the Italians'; it changed the whole course of the campaign in East Africa, and hastened the thrust northward by at least six months. After El Wak the Italian forces withdrew to the Jube Line, leaving only a screen of Banda west of the river, with some troops and guns at Afmadu in a strongly wired position.

"All this had been accomplished at the cost of two South Africans killed and a few South African and Gold Coast wounded. El Wak set the pattern for those almost bloodless victories which were to be a feature of the East African campaign."

Orpen, in turn, says: "General Cunningham had used an elephant gun to kill a hare, but the raid paid high dividends. The enemy who escaped proved to be more valuable to the Allied cause than those who had been captured, for they were emissaries of gloom and despondency. Even the Duke of Aosta had to do some lengthy explaining to Rome, especially as regards the behaviour of the commander of the El Wak sub-sector."

According to reports in British and South African newspapers this worthy had fled in a mule-cart, and on 21 December 1940 the Duke – presumably unaware of the fact that the Allied booty had included a touring car – signalled Marshal Pietro Badoglio, the chief of the Italian general staff: "Even if it were accepted that he took to flight, it would be absurd to believe that he had fled in a mule-cart when he could have done so in a car."

Orpen adds: "Such attempts to explain away (the report) did not satisfy Mussolini. He was keen to have details, from which it transpired that two Italian companies on the left had withdrawn to (Mandera) and left the artillery unprotected."

After a "fierce" battle lasting all day – according to reports from Addis Ababa – the Italian gunners retreated with the rest of the force northeast toward Lugh Ferrandi, since the road leading southeast to Bardera was in enemy hands. The alternative route to Lugh Ferrandi, strangely enough, appears to have been ignored by 12 African Division.

Admitted Italian losses were 8 Italians and 200 Colonial troops killed and 12 guns, 1 radio station, ammunition and food supplies lost. The reverse had shaken the enemy more than they cared to admit.

An official inquiry revealed that Lieutenant-General Gustavo Pesenti, governor of Italian Somaliland and commander of the Juba Sector, had never even visited El Wak. He was very soon replaced by Major-General Carlo de Simone, a First World War veteran, previously commanding the Harar and Jijiga area and hero of the conquest of British Somaliland, where he had led the main invading column which had advanced through Hargeisa in August.

Though the boundary cutting was not crossed in force, the Italian Commando Superiore appreciated the significance of the coordination achieved by 12th African Division. Such cooperation between tanks, motorized troops and aircraft was something quite unattainable by the poorly trained, ill-equipped and undisciplined mass of the Italian Colonial forces.

"This action," General Cunningham was to report on El Wak, "marked the start of the ascendancy of the morale of East Africa Force over that of the Italians."

General Wavell's sweeping successes along the Egyptian Frontier were extolled in pamphlets dropped on El Wak and duly reported back to Rome in a back-handed slap at Marshal Graziani. The [British] capture of Sollum on the same day as the El Wak raid, and the growing strength of the forces in Kenya and the Sudan, had once and for all robbed the Italians of the initiative in East Africa.

An advance on Kismayu no longer seemed so formidable an undertaking as General Cunningham had been led to believe.

As Hartshorn says after El Wak, "the phoney war was over."

El Wak also seems to have settled the lingering British doubts about the South Africans' capability. Hartshorn writes that prior to the raid he undertook a personal reconnaissance of the area and suggested that he take a column on "a long left-hand swing from Wajir through apparently impenetrable bush and synchronize an attack from the north with one from the south, thus completely bottling up the Italian forces in El Wak," but his proposal was "vetoed by General Godwin-Austen. "Too dangerous for inexperienced troops" was his infuriating decision.

El Wak changed all that. On 18 December 1940, Orpen says two days before Pinforce got back to base at Arbo, Godwin-Austen sent a special message to Pienaar which stated that "the raid … had given the enemy 'his first really sharp lesson' and … also confirmed the General's confidence in the South Africans, whose leadership, dash and enterprise he praised unstintingly."

Further evidence of his regard came a little later when Pienaar was admitted to the Distinguished Service Order, obviously at Godwin-Austin's recommendation – Pienaar in turn made mention in despatches to 12 African Division of a number of his officers, among them Major F. I. Gerrard, his brigade major, McMenamin and Hartshorn, Major H. Mill Colman of 1 Field Company South African Engineer Corps and Captain A. E. Coy, of 1 Mobile General Workshops.

The last word on the El Wak attack came from Godwin-Austen on 19 December 1940 when he wrote a letter filled with high praise to Major W. P. Clark on the departure of the light tanks:

Will you please accept my personal thanks and convey to all ranks under your command my deep appreciation of, and admiration for, their brilliant work in the El Wak operations. High efficiency was required to reach the battlefield over such bad roads, but this efficiency was surpassed in battle, and you have won the admiration of all.

Though I shall sorely miss you all, I am glad to know of your early departure for a well-deserved rest and refit ... You have done well throughout your period under my command, and I look forward eagerly to the day when I may be so lucky as to have you with me again.

In Greece, it had taken Metaxas's forces just six weeks to drive the invading Italians back into the inhospitable mountains of Albania, seriously humiliating not only Mussolini but by extension his partner in the much-vaunted Rome-Berlin axis, Adolf Hitler, by disproving the myth of Axis' forces invincibility. Hitler had been building up his forces for a sneak attack on the Soviet Union in spite of the fact that he and Stalin were signatories to a mutual non-aggression pact. Now, much against his will, he had to put these plans on hold so that he could send troops to pull Mussolini's Greek chestnuts out of the fire.

However, it was not merely a case of saving Axis face; the Italians had forced the Greeks into the Allied camp, which meant that the Germans now had to protect their southern flank against a new potential enemy threat. This meant in turn that they might have to tie down thousands of soldiers and hundreds of aircraft in the Balkans instead of using them against the Russians.

12

Three days at El Yibo

On 17 December 1940, just one day after the capture of El Wak, the last of 1 South African Division's armoured components appeared when 1 Armoured Car Company (Major Harry Klein) and 2 South African Motorcycle Company (Major C. L. Stander) arrived by train at Gilgil and went to their new 'homes', 5 South African Brigade and the divisional reserve respectively. Ten days later Lieutenant-Colonel G. K. Roodt, who had earlier established 1 South African Division's Armoured Fighting Vehicle headquarters near the Premier Mine, arrived as well to join the divisional staff as its Armoured Fighting Vehicle staff officer.

Soon afterward 2 Armoured Car Company, less its No. 2 Platoon at Garissa, joined 2 South African Brigade at Marsabit on the central Northern Frontier District front. Now, as Klein says: "With the preliminaries over and the main battles about to be joined, the armoured car and motorcycle companies, strung along the borders of the Northern Frontier, were to learn what tough campaigning really meant.

"The toughness was not due entirely to enemy action, although some worthy patrol skirmishes were recorded during this period, but to the harshness of the land, the pitiless heat, shortage of water, and the atrocious roads and tracks which played havoc with mechanized transport. Not to mention insect pests, jigger fleas, and vicious thorn scrub."

"Aggressive patrolling" meant just that as far as the armoured cars were concerned. While 2 South African Brigade probed northward from Dukana, 5 South African Brigade at Marsabit sent out a series of reconnaissance and fighting patrols northeastward through the Dida Galgalla desert in the direction of the Turbi hills near Moyale and the rest of the general area below the Moyale escarpment itself.

From the very start of January 1941 combined armoured and infantry patrols from General Brink's two remaining South African brigades probed relentlessly at the Italians' backyard. From Dukana, parties from Brigadier Buchanan's 2 South African Brigade roamed the areas to the north, while Brigadier Armstrong at Marsabit launched constant reconnaissance and fighting patrols to sniff around the Turbi Hills. There was nothing casual or routine about these patrols, which were designed to serve two specific purposes.

The first derived from General Brink's aim to keep the Italians guessing about 1 South African Division's true intentions, and the active patrolling along the road to the strongly fortified and garrisoned Italian position at Moyale was intended to persuade Aosta's forces that he contemplated attacking the fortress, which he did not.

The second purpose was to gain as much detailed knowledge of the region as possible. Each patrol was accompanied by detachments of armoured cars, engineers, a field ambulance and signallers – the armoured cars being particularly useful because of their mobility – and as the patrols came back the information they had acquired was carefully added to the blank spaces on the situation maps: waterholes, potential landing grounds, alternative routes, helpful or hindersome terrain features and anything else of interest or possible use.

The Italian version of the phoney war had not only given the Allied forces enough time to build themselves up but had also provided the South Africans with a heaven-sent opportunity to 'debug' their armoured cars as painlessly as possible before the ground campaign really began. Through force of circumstance the cars had been rushed into production, and the harsh terrain and climate pitilessly exposed all unforeseen design and manufacturing flaws that would otherwise have been discovered at great cost during combat. Klein writes:

Broken springs were the principal mechanical defect in the armoured cars at this stage. Spring and U-bolt breakages were daily occurrences, and the constant repairs necessary imposed a severe strain on the units' light aid detachments … These troubles were not overcome until … a new type of spring was manufactured in the Union, based on field experience.

Another major mechanical difficulty was damaged steering-gear tie-rods, which were regularly bent by the scrub and boulders. Tyres caused yet more trouble. Even when bulletproof tyres were introduced, there were still many 'flats' due to the thorn scrub and sharp lava rock formations. Fortunately, enemy small-arms fire had no effect on tyres, and there is no recorded incident of tyre failure during action.

The workshop sections of the three armoured car companies performed yeoman service and contributed largely to the units' successes in keeping the cars mobile in the face of difficulties that might well have posed problems to motor mechanics in the Union.

The transport of reserve petrol and water was another major problem. Under normal operating conditions each armoured car had a self-contained petrol and water range of 200 miles, but in southern Abyssinia this range was reduced on average by more than half because of the amount of low-gear work necessitated by the rough going.

The Abyssinian campaign was undertaken before the advent of jerrican petrol containers, and petrol in the field was supplied in 4-gallon tins. Unfortunately these tins had not been tested in advance under field conditions, and wastage through leakage was as high as 50 percent.

Engine overheating, due to the excessive weight of the armoured cars in relation to the load specifications for which the engines had originally been designed, and constant low-gear running, resulted in abnormal water consumption. On the approach march from Hobok to Banno (later in the campaign), a distance of roughly 36 miles over rough country, 40 gallons of water per day were used by each of the 14 armoured cars engaged in the two-day operation.

Toward the end of 1940 the mobile radio receiving and transmitting sets with which the armoured cars were equipped were still in their infancy in comparison with the highly efficient sets supplied later in Egypt.

Those used in Abyssinia were likely as not to peter out at the crucial moment, as happened when the armoured cars of No. 1 Company came under their own artillery fire at Hobok and all the radio sets failed simultaneously; the company commander could not communicate with his leading platoon to get them out of the range of fire, much to the disgust of the battery commander, who complained most bitterly that the armoured cars had ruined his shoot by dashing into the field of fire and capturing the fort before his guns could demolish it.

In the original design of the armoured cars no thought had been given to anti-aircraft protection, and exterior turret mountings for Vickers machine guns were improvised in the field. It was this ability to improvise that carried the South Africans through many tight spots in Abyssinia and elsewhere.

During the Battle of the Lakes, when No. 1 South African Armoured Car Company was under command of the 24th Gold Coast Brigade, Brigadier C. E. M. Richards, the commander, repeatedly declared his admiration for South African improvisation, particularly that of the Road Engineering companies, which overcame almost insuperable obstacles in the flooding rains of that dramatic campaign in the central Abyssinian highlands.

Klein also highlights an all-important characteristic of the armoured car crews which was to play a major role in their later successes: the intense personal bonds that swiftly took hold.

In spite of, and possibly because of, all the physical trials and tribulations which came their way, a high camaraderie was born in the armoured car units. Under field conditions the car crews, each consisting of driver, turret gunner, hull gunner and wireless operator, lived and fought as self-contained units.

Officers, non-commissioned officers and men shared the same primitive living conditions, ate the same rations, cooked in communal mess kits, slept side by side on the ground at night next to their cars, shared the same discomforts of heat and rain, bodies bruised and sore from the jolting of their vehicles – and shared, too, the triumphs of the chase.

The two motorcycle companies fared less well than their armoured car comrades – not so much as a result of mechanical failures but because the terrain was totally unsuitable for them. As a result, Klein notes the companies "experienced every type of physical torture and mental strain in riding their bucking, skidding mounts across the rock-strewn, potholed tracks of the lava belt, and through the mud and sand of the southern deserts." He quotes an extract from the war diary of 1 South African Motorcycle Company from November 1940 which, as he says, "bears eloquent testimony to the hardships endured":

The journey from Nanyuki to Marsabit was terrible. Deep sand and rock had to be overcome, and on many a stretch a speed of less than two miles an hour was registered. Time and again those riding solo machines had to walk with the machines between their legs, with engines roaring and burns being suffered by the men as their machines fell on top of them.

In the Chalbi Desert, returning in the rain from North Horr to Kalacha Wells, the platoon started to move back on November 20, but their machines soon became bogged in the mud. They could only get one out. Ultimately they returned on foot to Kalacha, only to find their camp had been flooded. Wearily they moved to higher ground.

For three days they struggled unavailingly to pull the motorcycles out of the mud. On 24 November three machines were salvaged, and three more next day. On 27th November a reconnaissance of 25 miles was made into the Chalbi Desert. The mounted remnants of the company managed to travel 65 miles across the desert in 12 hours. The desert trip had been a great strain on the men and their machines.

The motorcyclists soon realized that in the circumstances their prospects of seeing action in their prescribed role were minimal, but their spirit remained undimmed and, as their war diary recorded on 31 January, "all the men are willing to join other units in order to have a chance of fighting." But in fact they were still to come in very useful later in the campaign and performed valuable service in a variety of roles until the end of the campaign.

If the terrain had tortured the South Africans and their vehicles before, it was as nothing compared to what they were about to face as they began to move nearer to the Italian defence line in the north and northwest.

The Italians were perfectly aware of the two likely approach routes from Kenya's Northern Frontier District – an advance on Moyale, and a westward flanking movement via the Chalbi Desert through El Yibo and El Sardu – and had fortified and garrisoned various parts of the border area accordingly.

Moyale and Mega in particular, which guarded the only roads into Abyssinia east of Kenya's Lake Turkana, had been "developed into veritable fortresses," as Orpen says. "Italian prestige throughout this area depended on retaining these two strongholds." West of Mega there were reported to be about 200 Banda at El Gumu and another 200 at Buluk, 100 each at El Yibo and El Sardu, and other detachments at Hobok, Gorai, El Dokolle and Buna. Not all of these garrisons consisted of Banda, however, some were reported to be conventional troops with artillery.

Once again though, the Italians' actual as opposed to their potential threat was mitigated by the fact that they were short of supplies and transport, while the headquarters of 21 Colonial

Division, the regional controlling body, had only recently been formed and had not had time to settle in. This meant that coordinated operations at divisional level were next to impossible.

The Allies' first priority, though, remained the matter of dealing with the lack of roads and water so that 11 and 12 African Divisions could advance along the Kismayu and Moyale routes. Union Defence Force road construction, water and bridging companies set to work almost immediately after El Wak, while combined armoured and infantry patrols from 1 South African Brigade ranged up and down the western border of Italian Somaliland and the southern border of Abyssinia, reconnoitring waterholes and occasionally clashing with elements of the enemy forces.

On one such occasion the reputation of the rhinoceros cars was reinforced when No. 2 Platoon of 2 Armoured Car Company was attached to a King's African Rifles company and some selected Abyssinian irregulars who were tasked to attack an enemy outpost at Liboi. About 1km from the objective the cars came under heavy rifle fire and grenades, neither of which could penetrate the armour "and in several cases grenades burst backward and disconcerted the Banda," according to Klein.

It was an extremely arduous business. The Dida Galgalla was a no-man's land consisting of a lava desert extending more than 150km between Marsabit in the south, Moyale in the east and the El Yibo area in the west. As Harry Klein describes it:

> When night hid the desert's secrets, cloaking its nakedness and frightfulness in the benevolent mantle of darkness, it did not appear to be such a grim proposition. But in the heat of the day, with the sun beating down from brazen skies on to the tumbled piles of black lava rock, the stoutest heart quailed in the face of the wasteland revealed to view.
>
> Burning rock, jagged stone that tore the stoutest boots and tyres, and the potholed, dust-blinding tracks made patrols a nightmare. Water and shade there was none – only sand and lava stretching through the haze to where the shadowy outlines of Garba Turbi and the Moyale escarpment in the north and the Huri Hills in the west broke the desert monotony.

Southwest of the Dida Galgalla was the Chalbi Desert, "a wide expanse of soda salt flats: gleaming, eye-blinding and dusty in dry weather, a morass in wet," Klein says, adding that they were "deeply etched in the memory of every member of the South African Tank Corps who served in southern Abyssinia … [the two deserts were] probably the two nearest approaches to hell on earth recorded in any history of war."

Small wonder, then, that the Italians with their inadequately motorized forces regarded their western flank as the least likely portal for an invasion and believed that the first moves would be along the Juba river front. But 1 South African Division's units, together with friendly Shifta (Abyssinian irregulars), were creeping ever nearer to the southern Abyssinian border, while 2 South African Brigade was already established at Dukana, just south of El Yibo.

5 South African Brigade's patrols ventured into the Dida Galgalla from Marsabit on an almost daily basis, but the Italians proved elusive. They had a well-established outpost in the Turbi hills that commanded all the approaches to it and invariably made themselves scarce when they spotted a patrol; then, after the patrols had returned to Marsabit, Verey lights arcing into the sky above Turbi would show that the Italians had returned.

The Dida Galgalla took a heavy toll on both men and machines.

2 South African Brigade's patrolling in the Chalbi Desert was equally taxing:

> Day after day … the sun blazed from cloudless skies, turning the bowl of the desert into a dazzling inferno of heat. The tracks of armoured cars wove crazy patterns as they criss-crossed the desert sand. Fantastic mirages distorted the convoys into weird pictures: lorries travelling through mirror-like lakes, armoured cars waltzing along upside down in the distant haze. The

choking dust and the fierce glare of the white desert light made heavy demands on the men of the Chalbi patrols.

It was a world of biblical scenes at the far-scattered water-holes of Kalacha Wells, Gamrah and North Horr, where the patrols rested. There fugitive Boran and Galla herdsmen, who had fled with their goats and camels from the Abyssinian hills, told of the marauding Habash and Somali Banda who had slaughtered their cattle and made off with their women, and who boastfully cried of the terrors they held for the advancing South Africans.

A convoy of Marmon Herrington Mk2s and trucks from 1 Armoured Car Company travelling through East Africa.

Very early in January 1941 there was a skirmish in the Turbi hills, featuring an infantry patrol supported by No. 1 Platoon of 2 Armoured Car Company. Scouting out ahead of the infantry, two cars made contact on the morning of 2 January but were recalled to their main body. There the patrol was given permission to take out the enemy force – later estimated to consist of one heavy and one light machine gun and 40 riflemen – and returned next morning. When contact was made again, the infantry debussed and attacked with the cars in support. After a short skirmish the Italian force hurriedly withdrew so far that the armoured cars advanced 10km up the road without making further contact.

General Brink, a veteran of the First World War who was not hobbled by nostalgia for the past, knew that neither the Dida Galgalla nor the Chalbi Desert was an insurmountable obstacle, and on 7 January presented General Cunningham with a plan for an encircling movement, to be carried out by 2 and 5 South African brigades on one flank and a 'loaned' 1 South African Brigade on the other.

General Cunningham turned this down for several reasons. He was still bound by General Wavell's tasking to encourage the loyalist Abyssinians to rise in rebellion and thereby keep up a continuous pressure on the Italians, his priority task remained the capture of Kismayu on the coast, he could not supply the substantial air support and munitions Brink would need, and 1 South African Brigade was needed for other operations.

On the other hand, Wavell's onslaught in the Western Desert and the Royal Navy's Mediterranean and Red Sea blockades had put paid to any remaining hopes Aosta might have had of supplies and reinforcements from the north, and as Orpen puts it, "any timidity in the formulation of plans in Kenya did not fit in with the formulation of plans by Mr Churchill or General Smuts for the building up of a general reserve in the Nile Valley."

In the interim General Brink sent elements of 2 South African Brigade on another cutting-out raid on 16 January 1941, this time an attack on the wells at El Yibo and El Sardu by elements of 2 South African Brigade. Capturing the wells would serve two purposes: their water was crucially important to a future advance into western Abyssinia, and there was serious propaganda value to be derived from expelling the Italians from their last holdings on Kenyan soil.

The assault force – the Natal Mounted Riflemen under Lieutenant-Colonel N. D. McMillan – less one rifle company held back at the brigade headquarters – a section of mortars and another of Vickers guns, two companies of Shifta and five of 2 South African Armoured Car Company's cars under Major Walker – was drawn up in three small groups in the brightly moonlit early hours of 16 January with ample supplies of food, water and petrol.

The plan called for Force A, one company of Shifta in Natal Mounted Riflemen's transport,

Marmon Herrington Mk2 1941, with crew and local.

A Marmon Herrington Mk2 at El Gumu, where the South Africans captured an enemy outpost.

to move 9km to the northwest of Dukana, debus and march on foot along some high ground to attack the Italians' right rear and cut off their withdrawal. Force B, B Company Natal Mounted Riflemen, Major Walker's five cars, a section of Vickers guns and a section of mortars, would attack El Yibo from the northeast. Force C, consisting of C Company Natal Mounted Riflemen – less one platoon – two of Walker's cars as well as Vickers and mortar sections, would follow Force B and attack simultaneously.

The available intelligence indicated that the wells were not strongly held – each had about 100 Banda under Italian officers – but detailed facts about them remained scanty. There were no accurate maps available, something which was to make the South Africans' lives difficult throughout the campaign, and as a result it was not even known exactly where El Yibo was located, except that it lay in a deep donga (locally a *lugga*) called the *Lugga* Bulat, about 15km north of Dukana. The *lugga* was dominated by a substantial lava mound, later dubbed Sugarloaf Hill by the South Africans, which had been fortified with walls of lava.

That much was known, since aircraft of the South African Air Force's No. 40 Army Cooperation Squadron under Major (later Major-General) Jimmy Durrant had earlier reconnoitred and photographed the position, but not much more. A further complication, which was not apparent during the planning, was, as Orpen notes, a "lack of experience in cooperation between infantry and armour [which] showed itself at once in the splitting of Major Walker's armoured cars without any really clear understanding as to just who was ultimately to control their movement and employment."

At 0410 the column moved off, B Company Natal Mounted Riflemen leading. But the wells proved to be a tough nut to crack. Apart from the lack of information, the defenders were to offer a stubborn resistance from very well-prepared and sited strongpoints, the going was very bad and the heat truly appalling: temperatures were almost always above 120° F, while inside the armoured cars it sometimes reached 150° F. There was also a shortage of water which was, as Klein says, "hell for the riflemen pinned down on the searing rock … in going down to firing position, [they] had their arms and chests scorched."

In the end it took three days to subdue El Yibo, by which time A Company Natal Mounted Riflemen had been brought up as well. Major Walker's armoured cars proved to be remarkably versatile in spite of the lack of topographical knowledge, the broken ground and intense heat. The cars were always well out in front as the South Africans pushed their way through a maze of *luggas* and thick bush.

On the first day Walker's cars overran the enemy outposts facing El Yibo, which was now seen to be situated at the head of a valley whose floor was covered in rocky outcrops and areas of dense bush, then went in ahead of the infantry and used their machine guns to force the enemy soldiers on Sugarloaf Hill to keep their heads down with accurate machine-gun fire, so that total infantry casualties were just two wounded.

Buchanan halted the attack at nightfall and resumed it at 0500 next day. As before, progress was slow, and the deep dongas in front of the valley prevented the armoured cars from getting to grips with the Italian troops, although early in the afternoon four cars repulsed a spirited counter-attack on the right flank with bursts of machine-gun fire.

By nightfall the South Africans were still entangled in the maze of *luggas*, but at 0830 on the third day No. 40 Squadron's aircraft bombed Sugarloaf Hill, the artillery let loose an eight-minute barrage and the infantry moved in – only to discover that during the night the enemy forces had retreated up a *lugga* that led to El Sardu, 6km away.

Six cars immediately roared up the watercourse to El Sardu, where they scattered a number of Banda with Vickers fire and took one prisoner. The wells had not been mined and equipment was lying about, an indication of a very hurried withdrawal in the direction of Hobok. The fight for the wells was over. It had cost the enemy three Italian officers and 20 Banda dead, while another 50 Banda were reportedly wounded; 2 South African Brigade's casualties were one Abyssinian irregular killed and two wounded.

It had not been a perfect operation by any means, and it was clear that better infantry-armour cooperation procedures (and mutual knowledge of one another's capabilities) were needed. It had taken place under very difficult circumstances, however, with broken terrain, a radio breakdown, almost non-existent topographical knowledge and inadequate intelligence – a prisoner later stated that the garrison had consisted of 400 Banda rather than 100 with nine machine guns.

At the end of the day, however, it had achieved its purpose. At the cost of almost no own casualties, it had expelled the Italians from the last part of Kenya they had held and, most of all, had captured the wells.

Orpen notes: "the Natal Mounted Riflemen … could hardly have dreamed that the 100 gallons of poor water a day would soon be increased to 18,500 gallons daily by the South African engineers, who were at work on the main position within half an hour of its occupation … The operation had been a stern reminder of the dependence of all troops on water, and the South Africans' water discipline had on the whole been good. The troops had been through a physical ordeal of heat and thirst and had stood up to it admirably. But it did not blind [the commanders] to shortcomings in the planning and execution of the operation."

Klein observes:

> The armoured cars learned several lessons at El Yibo, the principal of which was that infantry support was essential in bush country to obviate the danger of ambush. In this action Major Walker considered that cooperation between infantry and armour had been very unsatisfactory. His car commanders had been given orders, often conflicting, by sundry infantry officers.

He maintained that the cars should get their orders from the infantry force commander exclusively, through their own commanding officer. Armoured cars had been sent from the reserve group without his knowing the direction in which they had been sent, and too frequent use had been made by the infantry of armoured cars as escorts in the middle of the action. This had almost led to disaster on the right flank when the enemy counter-attacked.

"The armoured cars performed well over the varied country traversed in the action. The ground was very broken, and covered almost completely by masses of lava rock … No mechanical breakdowns were experienced, but the bulletproof front tyres of two cars were punctured by jagged sticks. The crews had come through in good shape in spite of the cars' very high interior temperatures, apart from suffering from heat fatigue."

When the dust of El Yibo and El Sardu had cleared, and the true value of the operation had been assessed, the armoured cars received high acclaim from 1 South African Division headquarters. General George Brink's report on the operations of 1 Division in East Africa paid special tribute to the work of Major Walker's platoon:

"The work performed by the armoured cars under Major C. G. Walker MC, 2 South African Armoured Car Company, merits special mention," Brink wrote. "The way in which these armoured cars moved across-country which, up to that time, had been considered impassable for any form of wheeled vehicle, and then worked round the enemy's flanks, undoubtedly contributed largely to the collapse of the defence, which had been exceptionally well sited and prepared by the enemy." In a signal to East Africa Force headquarters on 20 January, Brink said: "Armoured cars did splendid work and their handling and cooperation undoubtedly accounted for absence of casualties on our side."

Less than 10 days after the raid on El Yibo the phrase "aggressive patrolling" took on new meaning. Up to then the South African patrols had not seen much action, but all that changed on 24/25 January 1941 when Brigadier Armstrong dispatched a strong fighting patrol to scout out the Turbi Hills area and then advance to Sololo Hill, about 30km west of Moyale, to look for a combined force of colonial infantry and Banda irregulars which was reportedly in the vicinity.

The patrol, commanded by Major G. S. Sturgeon of 3 Transvaal Scottish, consisted of B Company 3 Transvaal Scottish, C Company 2 Regiment Botha (Captain E. A. Delaney), and No. 3 Platoon of 1 Armoured Car Company under Lieutenants Roy Irwin and W. H. Penny, with support troops. It bivouacked at the Turbi Hills and Penny was instructed to take four of the armoured cars and escort the Regiment Botha company on a probe toward Sololo.

The other cars were held back as a mobile protective element for the Transvaal Scottish – a serious error of judgment, no doubt stemming from the as yet imperfect understanding of combined infantry-armour tactics – which, as Klein says, "could well have cost the Regiment Botha patrol more dearly than it did."

The patrol left Turbi at 0500, two of Penny's cars leading and the other two bringing up the rear, through bush so thick on both sides of the road that there was no question of moving in any formation except single column. It was an ideal situation for an ambush, and the Italians – no doubt forewarned by some of their Banda scouts – were waiting for the South Africans.

Overlooking an S-bend about 32km from Turbi was an outcrop of rock, about 25m high and 1,700m long, next to the road along which the South African vehicles would have to pass. There the Italians lay in wait, and when the patrol entered the S-bend the armoured cars found themselves being pounded by rifle and machine gun bullets from the hill which was about 1,000m to their front at that point.

They immediately radioed back to Captain Delaney, who sent forward two sections of infantry, a Vickers machine gun section and the two rear armoured cars. While the infantry debussed two of Penny's cars smashed into the bush in true *Gharri Kifaru* style, firing on the move, to try and work their way around, behind the machine gun, while the other two advanced on the hill with the Regiment Botha men and gave them covering fire.

The infantry took the hill without firing a shot. The Banda fled leaving behind only a pool of blood at the machine gun post. Soon afterward the other two cars returned, having got into position too late to cut off the enemy line of retreat, so Delaney reformed the patrol and set off in the same formation as before.

Nothing happened for another 6km or so. Then, as the patrol was passing through a patch of heavy bush which made off-road deployment impossible, the Italians struck again. The commander of the leading armoured car saw a lone Banda sprint across the road and immediately afterward drove into a well-concealed tank trap – a metre-deep ditch which had been covered with a mat of brushwood and twigs, and dusted with sand and grass to blend into the surrounding road surface. It was also covered by a heavy machine gun to the left of the road and a light machine gun on the right.

The Italians seemed to have been taken by surprise – possibly because the patrol had moved faster than they had expected – and neither of the posts was manned. One of the Banda darted across the road in an attempt to reach his machine gun but was knocked down by two bursts of fire from the second armoured car. Evidently a brave and determined man, he kept on crawling toward the machine gun, "and the car crew reluctantly had to finish him off," Klein says.

Captain Delaney's reaction was to send his rear armoured cars forward and bring up the rest of his patrol. The cars deployed to the left and right of the road, while the third pulled the trapped car out with the help of the sappers, who then set about filling in the trap. Now they discovered that the trap also contained an electrically operated mine, but it could not be detonated because the plunger was in the area covered by the trapped car's hull gun, and therefore out of enemy reach.

Delaney ordered two of the armoured cars and a platoon of infantry to reconnoitre Sololo Hill about 3km ahead, deployed the rest of his force on either side of the road and sent another car up the road beyond the tank trap, keeping the fourth, commanded by Staff Sergeant A. Kahn, to provide fire support for the infantry.

At this moment of vulnerability a combined group of colonial infantry and Banda charged, yelling, out of the bush in the rear and on the left flank of the patrol, firing furiously and throwing strings of grenades which not only "burst with startling effect and flashes," Klein records, "[but] immediately set the bush alight. Before cohesive counter-action could be taken the infantry wireless truck was riddled by fire, putting the set out of action; a blazing 3-ton troop carrier blocked the road; and all was pandemonium."

The loss of the radio vehicle meant that Delaney could not contact the two armoured cars he had sent toward Sololo Hill, and they were unaware of the fighting at the tank trap because they were busy shooting up a Banda outpost they had found near the hill. Delaney managed to get to the car he had sent to patrol ahead of the tank trap, only to find that its radio could not contact the two leading cars, so he climbed in and went to fetch them himself.

In the meantime Staff Sergeant Kahn in the fourth armoured car was heavily engaged. He was unable to turn around on the narrow track and wanted to keep his hull gun aimed at the main body of attackers, so he reversed down the track and then charged forward again with both of his guns firing at the attackers.

Klein continues, "sensing the kill, they surged forward and at one time were within 10 yards of the armoured car, yelling frenziedly and splattering it with hand grenades. Blinded by the flash of two grenades which burst simultaneously, one on the engine bonnet and the other beneath the turret gun, the driver momentarily lost control and the car and crashed headlong into a tree. A damaged radiator and a jammed gun put it temporarily out of action."

Fortunately, returning at this stage from recalling the other two cars, the third raced into the fray. With both guns firing, it helped to beat the enemy off, who by now were taking heavy punishment from the Regiment Botha men.

When the other two cars returned to the scene they found the bush on fire on both sides of the road and the road itself blocked by the blazing lorry. Crashing through the burning bush they lent their fire in the few remaining moments of the action before the badly shaken Banda and colonial infantry retreated into the Burrolli Hills. The bush was too dense for the cars to follow up, and the surviving enemy got away.

That was the end of the action. Two of the three remaining operational armoured cars retrieved the Regiment Botha platoon and at 1245 the patrol – now distinctly short of transport – set off back to the Turbi bivouac with the armoured cars providing the rearguard, one carrying five wounded infantrymen and another towing the tank-trap casualty – which by nightfall was functional again.

Surprisingly, the armoured cars had suffered no casualties, but the fiercely fought little clash had cost the Regiment Botha dearly, with one officer killed and ten other ranks wounded. Enemy casualties were difficult to estimate, but reports gathered later from friendly Boran tribesmen put them at between 40 and 50 killed and wounded. Lieutenant Penny and Staff Sergeant Kahn were highly commended for the part they played at the height of this action in saving the infantry from greater punishment.

Klein writes in *Springboks in Armour* that in this, their first taste of real combat, 1 Armoured Car Company's cars had "performed a wide variety of roles: they were used for reconnaissance, to provide covering fire for infantry at long range, for a direct attack up a hill, for close fighting in attack and defence, to make an outflanking move to cut the enemy's line of retreat, and for the ferrying of wounded infantrymen."

There were valuable lessons in this action which were learned without too great an expenditure of blood, painful though Regiment Botha's casualties were. Harry Klein, then 1 Armoured Car Company's commanding officer and more than two decades away from writing his history of the South African Tank Corps, made some pointed comments and suggestions in the immediate aftermath of the Sololo Hill affray.

The section – the tactical unit in armoured car operations – should be kept intact and not split up, he said: "by being instructed to use small numbers of his cars in patrols of this nature, the armoured car commander was prevented from carrying out the correct tactical employment of his command because he did not have the strength to cover the front of a column while simultaneously defending its rear."

This, he said, "had been shown clearly at Sololo when the two armoured cars from the rear were sent forward. In their absence, the enemy had attacked the left flank and rear of the column, but had withdrawn when they had raced back to their original position. No doubt, too, notice was taken of the fact that for the first time the cars had come across a well-designed, anti-armour defensive work which had proved effective, even though by a stroke of good fortune, its full destructive potential had not been realized."

While General Brink's armoured cars were eating dust up and down the border, General Wavell's strategy of fostering the insurrection in Abyssinia was taking shape as well, and a new word was now firmly ensconced in the South African military lexicon: Shifta, the catchall term for Abyssinians fighting on the Allied side.

The Shifta were lean, tough warriors who had been fighting the Italians for five years. Originally Shifta had meant an outlaw or brigand. But after Abyssinians who refused to submit to Italian rule fled into the mountains to continue fighting it came to be applied to them. Klein writes:

> In the Gojjam, in the wild Lake Tana area, in the Galla Sidamo and in the Gundile mountains, chieftains gathered their clansmen together. Swooping down from their lairs, the men of Dejasmath Abeba, Blatha Thakale, Fitaurauri Tesfai Wolde, Ras Abeba Aregai, Haile Degaga and the lesser chieftains made the name of Shifta one of terror to the harassed Italian garrisons. For five years the Shifta lived in exile. They raided Italian convoys, pillaged outlying posts, sniped at unwary patrols; perfecting their savagery and cunning during their time of waiting. Italian punitive expeditions failed to drive them from their mountain strongholds.

Death, hardship and a scarcity of arms and ammunition had thinned out the Shifta by 1940. Now the outbreak of war had lifted the spirits of these *bitterenders*, and they were amenable to Wavell's encouragement for a revolt in the area south of Lake Tana. Fostering that revolt was 1 South African Division's responsibility, and in January 1941 Brink's representatives met in the forest at Marsabit with emissaries from Haile Degaga, the most influential of the Shifta leaders in the south.

At first the Abyssinians, led by one Robi, were wary about committing themselves, they were sceptical about the South Africans' capability and whether they really meant to invade Abyssinia. What persuaded them that the South Africans would be potent allies were 1 Armoured Car Company's armoured cars. Klein describes that dramatic moment:

> It was to No. 1 Armoured Car Company that Robi – grizzled, aquiline-featured leader of the Shifta emissaries – was brought to examine the strength of South African arms. Appreciatively he stroked the plating of an armoured car, nodding wisely as the turret was rotated and the power of the machine gun, spitting forth its belt of 250 rounds in a flash, was demonstrated. Volubly Robi and his companions talked after the display, their Semitic features lighting with excitement ... planning a new war while they stood in the forest of Marsabit. Through their interpreter, they made known their decision, 'Give us ammunition,' they said, 'and we will fight when you call us.'"
> "Kwaheri," Robi saluted in departure, "we shall meet again."

A few days later a South African Air Force bomber visited Hadu mountain, Haile Degaga's headquarters in the Gundile range at the western edge of the Yavelo Plain, and dropped cases of captured Italian ammunition for the Shiftas' rifles, thereby putting a match to the fuse of the new Abyssinian revolt. Soon the armoured cars would tell Haile Degaga that it was time to rise against the Italians.

13

Invasion

The invasion of southwestern Abyssinia was now only a few days away. For weeks General Brink had been accumulating the necessary elements of bush warfare: 114,000 litres of petrol and 15 days' worth of reserve supplies for 5,000 men at North Horr, 160,000 litres and another 15 days' supplies at Dukana, and 30 days' supplies and 227,000 litres of petrol for the under-strength 25 East African Brigade at Kalin and Lokitaung.

More artillery had been brought forward, ample supplies of small arms and artillery ammunition had been stockpiled, and transport, communications and the myriad other details had been adequately seen to. Major Jimmy Durrant's No. 40 Squadron was standing by to provide air support and reconnaissance.

On 28 January 1941 columns of troop carriers, armoured cars, guns and support vehicles bumped over the southern tail of the lava-strewn Dida Galgalla and then over the sterile, achingly hot white flats of the Chalbi Desert as the main body of 5 South African Brigade under Brigadier Armstrong began moving out of Marsabit to join hands with Brigadier Buchanan's 2 South African Brigade at Dukana. 2 Regiment Botha under Lieutenant-Colonel J. C. du Preez, along with a detachment of 1 Armoured Car Company, stayed in place at Marsabit.

In a nutshell, 1 South African Division was ready to go. All that was now needed was approval from the higher headquarters. That came on 29 January 1941, when generals Wavell and Cunningham flew in to Marsabit, where Brink met them and took them to the divisional headquarters at Dukana. There they discussed Brink's plan for invading Abyssinia from the southwest and approved a somewhat less ambitious undertaking than the one he had originally laid before Cunningham.

Essentially Brink's battle plan was typically South African in its approach. Instead of frontally assaulting either Moyale or the other frontier fortress at Mega, probably resulting in a needless loss of lives, he would simply go around the 300km-long escarpment on which they stood and attack them from the flank.

In the first phase 2 South African Brigade would hit the Gorai Crater, about 60km east of the Division's axis of advance, while 5 South African Brigade would simultaneously attack the fortified Italian outpost of El Gumu, which was located at the junction of the Yavelo – Gianciaro – Hobok roads, a few kilometres north of the Gorai Crater.

As a result Mega and Moyale would be marooned on their escarpment, their defences pointing the wrong way and powerless to do anything significant to halt the advance. In the unlikely event of the Italians at Moyale deciding to attack the Division's rear, it was the task of 2 Regiment Botha and its attached armoured cars at Marsabit to stop them, and if necessary also to support the division when it finally attacked Moyale.

There had been some unconfirmed information that the Italians intended to withdraw from the Moyale escarpment and fall back on the Juba river line, and if this happened, Cunningham told Brink, they were to be vigorously pursued in spite of any administrative difficulties that might arise. Pienaar's 1 South African Brigade might be placed temporarily under 1 South African Division for this purpose, and Brink would be allowed to leave 25 East African Brigade behind if it hampered his swiftness of movement.

During this period 1 South African Brigade was busy with reconnoitring of its own, on behalf of its temporary parent formation, 12 African Division. On 25 January 1941 a strong fighting patrol consisting of a company of the Duke of Edinburgh's Own Rifles, a detachment of anti-aircraft guns, a platoon of Major Gwillam's 3 Armoured Car Company and a platoon of Somali irregulars headed up the Moyale road from Wajir. The patrol's task was to prepare the way for a subsequent reconnaissance in force. To this end they were to occupy and establish bases at Buna, about halfway from Wajir, and Debel, about 50km northwest of Buna. After that the remainder of the base force would keep moving northward to reconnoitre beyond British Moyale but must not become involved in fighting.

The initial patrol duly took place, and the following day the main body followed – the Royal Natal Carbineers, the Dukes (less two companies), 3 Armoured Car Company (less one platoon), two field artillery batteries, a section of anti-aircraft guns, engineers and other support elements. The main aim was to find out more about the enemy situation on the Moyale escarpment and his intentions. Little was achieved, although considerable fighting took place and the armoured cars scouted up to the vicinity of Moyale, and by 29 January the 1 South African Brigade force withdrew.

All three of East Africa Force's under-strength but highly motivated divisions were now coiling themselves for the attack on Abyssinia. Southeast of 1 South African Division, Major-General Godwin-Austin's 12 African Division was lying up close to the border, ready to force the Italian defence line along the Juba river. South of 12 African Division, Major-General Dickinson's 11 African Division was preparing to advance on and capture Kismayu – five months in advance of Cunningham's original time estimate, due to El Wak. Unseen but definitely not to be ignored was the simmering revolt within Abyssinia, where the loyalist Shifta were waiting for the right moment.

On 30 January 1941 Brink issued his operational order, the immediate intention of which was the occupation of the line Gorai–El Gumu–Hobok. The order "marked the real beginning of offensive operations from Kenya," Orpen says, "in what was to be the Allies' first fully successful campaign in the Second World War." Ahead lay, as Klein remarks, "one of the greatest adventures ever undertaken by South African arms."

On 31 January 1941 the wheels began to turn, both figuratively and literally, and Klein writes that during the following month, both on 1 South African Division's front and a few weeks later when 12 African Division advanced on the Jube Line, "the South African armoured cars rose to one of their greatest heights of achievement during the entire war, even including their better-known exploits in the Western Desert.

"For it was largely through the dash and daring of the armoured cars that the Italian forces were routed with such comparative ease in southern Abyssinia and Italian Somaliland."

Just how far they had migrated from the cautious teachings of the Union Defence Force instructions could be seen from what happened as the Allies thrust remorselessly into Abyssinia. As Klein writes:

"It was the seeming abandon with which the armoured cars were thrown into battle, and the ease with which they overcame serious natural obstacles and crashed through the defences, that bred the story of the invincibility of the advancing South African and British forces, which swept through Italian-held Abyssinia and struck terror into the hearts of the defenders.

"Wherever the Italians stood they saw armoured cars, skilfully and daringly used in cavalry fashion, coming at them from all sides. And if this threat in itself was not enough to chill the defence with fear, the long columns of motorized infantry following behind the armoured car screens put finish to their enthusiasm to stand and fight it out.

"The armoured cars not only paved the way for the success of the attack, but were also in

South African Engineers R2D to the rescue and pulling out a stuck Marmon Herrington Mk 2, Abyssinia.

Crew discussion. Marmon Herrington Mk 2 in the Abyssinian bush.

large measure responsible for keeping down infantry casualties. This important point has often been omitted in the final analysis of the Abyssinian campaign. Heavy Italian fire was always encountered in the initial approach to any defended locality. By their crash tactics the armoured cars took this fire and subsequently pressed home the attack, with the infantry moving into position behind.

"The tactical employment of the armoured cars in the role of infantry tanks was made possible by the Italian troops' dread of them, and because of their extreme manoeuvrability in the comparatively flat country in the south. These tactics had to be modified when the Italian mountain defences were reached in the north and the armoured cars were mostly confined to the roads. Then the infantry had to bare the brunt of reconnaissance and attack.

"No one who served in Kenya and Abyssinia will forget the sight of the armoured cars crashing through the bush, with wireless masts whipping back and forth, smashing their way to where the defences lay. Little wonder they were called *Gharri Kifaru* by the demoralized Italian (colonial) troops, who melted away before them."

In spite of this boldness the armoured car crews had a negligible casualty rate: "Practically always in the van of battle," Klein says, "they bore charmed lives, though they did observe their basic training in not allowing themselves to be caught as sitting targets for Italian artillery – as did an unfortunate troop of the East African Armoured Car Regiment, which was wiped out to a car and every man by Italian pack guns in the battle at Uaddara [May 1941]."

"And be it not thought that the South African armoured cars did not endure more than their fair share of artillery, heavy and light machine gun, and concentrated small-arms fire in the course of their service in Kenya and Abyssinia."

On the afternoon of 31 January 1941 Brink's motorized brigades rolled over the border in two parallel groups, and under strict radio silence advanced northward at speed through pleasantly open grassland. In their vehicles travelled the most highly motivated fighting men in East Africa, confident in their weapons and their leaders, "knowing full well the nature of the risks ahead," Klein says, "the 1st South African Division moved out on the 400-mile march in high spirits. Every man knew he had to fight from waterhole to waterhole and succeed in every battle if the venture was to be a success and the bid for the Mega and Moyale escarpments was to be won."

The brigades spent their first night on Abyssinian soil bivouacked between Dibbandibba kopje and Mount Murdur, very near to Gorai. In "a vast plain of sun-bleached grass the long lines of troop carriers, artillery portées, transport and service vehicles were marshalled into defensive leaguers for the night," Klein writes. "Armoured cars, the outriders of modern bush warfare, kept watch on the perimeter and guarded the sleeping brigades from surprise attack."

Then in the grey dawn of 1 February 1941, the two brigades formed up into battle order. Hundreds of troop carriers were strung out in box formation in splendid array. Artillery, anti-aircraft units, staff cars and wireless vans filled the plain.

Ahead and on the flanks of the great force armoured cars of No. 1 and No. 2 (Armoured Car) companies took up their positions, like protective destroyers guarding the main battle fleet. The allotted task of the armoured cars that day was to scout ahead and to guard the flanks and rear of the columns – but what a different role became theirs as the day advanced …

At zero hour the brigades moved north toward their objectives. The troops, with rifles loaded and ready for action, were tense, for none knew what lay ahead. Above the roaring mechanized force, army cooperation with aircraft of the South African Air Force ranged the skies. Armoured cars swept ahead in arrow formation.

For two hours the brigades headed north as fast as they could manage. Then the seemingly unstoppable juggernaut was halted in its tracks – not by enemy action but by a belt of almost impassable bush that had not been marked on the inadequate maps by which the South Africans had to navigate.

"One moment the vehicles were bounding along in good formation," Klein says. "The next the columns were crashing through thorn scrub in a sorry mess of straggling transport. Apart from the vehicle ahead everything was lost to view in that indescribable maze. On all sides the sound of rending trees and ripping troop carrier canvas covers was heard. To take a motorized division through that network of intertwined thorn bush and dense scrub seemed an impossibility."

A halt was called and the command group went into a quick huddle. From it emerged a solution that would have amazed and horrified any remaining adherents of the Union Defence Force instructions. Each brigade's leading armoured car screen would be reshuffled so that every column was led by a Marmon-Herrington whose role was to act as a combination of steamroller and battering ram, smashing open a viable path for the infantry vehicles following it. Like the other Abyssinian unorthodoxies, it worked, although it was an arduous business that inflicted considerable damage on the cars.

"Moving in parallel lanes," Klein writes, "the armoured cars plunged ahead on compass bearings, carving new trails into Abyssinia. Hour after hour the bush and scrub tore at men and vehicles as the columns ploughed forward.

Frequent halts were called so that compass courses could be checked and rechecked. Standing on top of their vehicles, officers and non-commissioned officers tried to maintain contact with their platoons and companies as the plunging troop carriers followed the pennants, by this time sadly tattered, fluttering from the armoured cars' wireless masts.

Above the crackling bush a pall of brown dust, rising high in the still air, marked the passage of the South African cavalcade. Throughout the day aircraft of No. 40 Army Cooperation Squadron, South African Air Force, commanded by Major Durrant, circled overhead and checked the course of the bush-blinded ground forces."

Klein believes that the Italian regional command passed up a golden opportunity to wreak serious damage on the brigades during this stretch of the advance. The Italians had strong air bases at Neghelli and Yavelo, both less than 100km by air from the advance route. If they had dropped incendiary bombs into the dry bush most of the transport vehicles would almost certainly have burnt out, probably with heavy loss of life, and the advance would definitely have been crippled.

But they did not, for the simple reason that they did not know what was heading their way. Klein comments that "subsequent events tend to prove the belief held at the time that the Italian high command and the district commanders were completely unaware of the South African attack, and had no idea of its strength until some days after the first successes had been registered."

The result was that early in the afternoon the brigades' leading elements emerged from the scrub belt and laid rough hands on Gorai and El Gumu, to the complete surprise of the garrisons at both posts.

At Gorai 2 Armoured Car Company was the first of 2 South African Brigade's units to go into action. At first glance Gorai must have looked like a difficult proposition. Its stone fort was well situated on the southern rim of a low crater, about 2½km across, which was high enough to provide it with a 360° field of fire. South of it the ground was so broken that no mechanical transport could cross it. The fort was surrounded by barbed wire, with a number of machine gun emplacements among the boulders around it.

But this did not stop the attackers, because Brink's men were fighting a South African-style war of manoeuvre that made nonsense of direction-orientated static defences. Instead of coming up the road, 2 South African Brigade looped around to its left and then turned eastward. Armoured cars under Captain C. A. C. Saunders, 2 Armoured Car Company's second-in-command, led 2 Field Force Battalion (Lieutenant-Colonel C. L. Engelbrecht) down the El Gumu road, having outflanked both the Gorai fort and its impassable terrain. About 12km north of the fort the column ran into an enemy outpost. They were dealt with quickly; its occupants fled leaving their stores and camels behind, and kept going at full speed.

About 1,200m north of the fort itself the South Africans ran into an immovable roadblock which was covered by rifle fire. Once again the defenders were quickly subdued, and some hasty reconnoitring showed that the armoured cars would be able to bypass the roadblock by picking their way down a donga on the right of the road.

Colonel Engelbrecht sent A Company of 2 Field Force Battalion with six armoured cars down the donga to set up a stop line to the left and rear of the fort, while he led the main attack from the right with B and C companies of 2 Field Force Battalion and the four remaining cars under Captain Saunders. At 1600 both forces were in position. The Field Force Battalion's Vickers machine guns and mortars laid down a blanket of fire on the fort, while No. 40 Squadron's Hartbeeste bombed it. Klein records that, "the infantry fire was extremely accurate and one mortar bomb decapitated the Italian commander, who was sheltering in a sangar."

The defenders were in no mood to give in, though, and poured machine-gun fire at 2 Field Force Battalion, killing two soldiers. Then Saunders and his four armoured cars went into action. They burst through the barbed wire, the infantrymen close behind, taking out one machine gun after another with bursts from their Vickers guns while the 2 Field Force Battalion men mopped up behind them. The defenders fled in all directions with the armoured cars hot on their heels.

Harried by the Hartbeeste's machine guns and bombs, the fleeing Banda ran into the Field Force Battalion's A Company and its six accompanying armoured cars. They had not been able to block off the whole enemy line of retreat due to the broken ground, but nonetheless inflicted heavy casualties on the fleeing Banda.

Soon the action was over. Gorai had been taken at the cost of two South Africans dead and seven wounded, while the Italians lost two officers and 26 Banda killed, and one officer and 48 Banda wounded or captured. A number of others managedto avoid capture because of the very rough terrain – something that would happen again and again during the course of the campaign.

A little way up the road, 5 South African Brigade was also making quick work of subduing El Gumu. Just before 1600, "with a crashing and rending of timber and the roar of open exhausts," the armoured cars of 1 Armoured Car Company's No. 1 Platoon under Lieutenant L. G. Williamson charged out of the bush and on to a grassy clearing in front of the position. Close behind them were the troop carriers of 1 South African Irish under Lieutenant-Colonel John Dobbs.

Almost immediately the leading cars ran into an impassable roadblock constructed of felled trees, and Banda infantrymen covering the blockage opened fire with their rifles. A few bursts from the cars' Vickers guns persuaded the Banda to decamp, after which two sections of cars formed up in line abreast and poured into El Gumu "in a charge that would have delighted the heart of any old-time cavalryman."

Machine-gun fire from trenches in front of El Gumu village peppered the cars, which replied with their Vickers guns. This proved too much for the Banda manning the trenches, and within minutes they also abandoned their positions and scattered into the bush, leaving behind 13 dead and five wounded. Six cars under Staff Sergeant C. W. Hallowes roared through the village in hot pursuit.

Some of the Banda headed for Hobok to the west and others to Gianciaro in the east. Major Klein had foreseen this and had already radioed Williamson to send three cars out into the bush on a wide flanking move intended to cut the enemy line of retreat. Two of the cars broke down, but the third managed to get into a suitable position and fired on the Banda, who then scattered into the bush.

That was the end of the action. The Irish had little left to do except occupy the village and take a handful of prisoners. From start to finish it had lasted just one hour at no cost to the attackers – Lieutenant Williamson was subsequently decorated with the Military Cross for gallantry and Staff Sergeant Hallowes was highly commended.

The armoured car companies were applauded both for their spirited attacks and for the vital work they had done in bashing a way through the belt of bush that had almost sabotaged the two brigades' advance on Gorai and El Gumu. In his dispatch to Wavell, General Cunningham gave it as his opinion that the armoured cars' resolute actions had undoubtedly prevented many casualties.

But the plaudits came later. 1 South African Division's work was far from finished. The bush bashing had cost 1 Armoured Car Company's cars dearly, and its workshop section laboured deep into the night to replace or repair broken or damaged springs, radiators and steering gear in time for the advance to the next objective, the fort at Hobok, 32km west of El Gumu.

The Italians had been taken so much by surprise – or their intelligence gathering was so disorganized – that at about 0200 on 2 February a farcical episode took place when an anti-tank detachment at El Gumu, which was securing the road from Gianciaro, saw headlights approaching.

The anti-tank gunners, no doubt delighted to be able to fire their first angry shot at long last, promptly loosed a shell at the headlights, which turned out to belong to a 10-ton Italian lorry bringing rations to El Gumu in blissful ignorance of its capture about nine hours earlier. The shell smashed the lorry's engine and its occupants – one understandably bewildered Italian soldier and 10 equally bewildered colonial troops – tumbled out of the wreck and surrendered.

Next morning early 5 South African Brigade set off westward toward Hobok. The light aid detachments' strenuous efforts had been successful, so that all of 1 Armoured Car Company's cars were battleworthy again and ready for more mobile-warfare adventures. The leading element was 3 Transvaal Scottish under Lieutenant-Colonel W. H. Kirby, supported by Lieutenant Ray Irwin's No. 2 Platoon of 1 Armoured Car Company and Major Klein with his three-car headquarters group. The rest of 1 Armoured Car Company's sabre cars provided flank and rearguards for the brigade's main body, with Klein controlling them while also maintaining close contact with the brigade headquarters.

By all accounts the cars' radios functioned well this time, with a constant flow of information about conditions and tactical features lying ahead being promptly relayed back to Brigadier Armstrong. For the armoured cars, Klein recalls, "the Hobok action was a near-perfect text-book exercise."

The first part of the approach march was through open country, with good visibility along the road. The leading armoured car section, Irwin's platoon headquarters and the 3 Transvaal Scottish soft skins advanced along the road, while Irwin's remaining two sections scouted to left and right. Klein's headquarters group moved with 3 Transvaal Scottish headquarters.

Progress was unhindered until about 1400, by which time the leading element was only about 4½km from Hobok. The element of surprise had been well and truly lost by now, and when the terrain changed abruptly to a badly broken ground surface covered with thick bush, the Italians made intelligent use of it by setting fire to the vegetation on the South Africans' southern flank. The flames progressed swiftly in the tinder-dry bush, and Irwin's flanking armoured cars were pulled back to the road.

About a mile further Irwin's leading section ran into a roadblock and came under rifle fire. The cars drove off the riflemen so that the brigade's engineers could start clearing the roadblock and Irwin sent his other two sections to outflank the obstruction by way of a shallow donga, from which they would roll up the defended outposts.

All three sections now came under heavy machine gun and rifle fire from Hobok fort, an adjacent stone blockhouse and various *luggas* in the vicinity. The cars took cover in some dead ground between the fort and one of the *luggas*, from where they radioed accurate information about the enemy dispositions back to Irwin. In turn he relayed the information to Colonel Kirby, who had gone over to Klein's command vehicle in the interim.

Hobok's fort was located on high ground at the edge of the Lak Bulal, with a garrison estimated at 800 Banda led by Italian officers and it looked, as Gorai had, like a difficult target. But Klein says, in reality the enemy "proved less determined than on the previous day … Actually, if the armoured cars had pressed home their initial attack, it is probable that the Banda would have taken to their heels then and there, as did their Italian officers. But the lull that followed the first brush, while the full machinery of a planned attack came into action, must have reassured the defenders, of whom some hundreds stayed to fight it out."

The Scottish started deploying for the attack, and meanwhile the armoured cars lay up in some *luggas* to the south and east of the fort. From there they saw a column of dust heading northward, which indicated that at least some of Hobok's defenders were making themselves scarce. Irwin thereupon detailed a section of three cars to sweep around the fort's right flank as fast as possible to cut off the road and disrupt the movement. This proved to be easier said than done, because the cars were faced with very broken terrain, criss-crossed by deep *luggas*.

The ground was so difficult in fact, that the flanking movement was called off after one of the cars capsized The Light Aid Detachment under Lieutenant S. Chiappini promptly winched the car out of the *lugga* in spite of fire from the fort and got it on to its wheels again. Its crew members, who had suffered nothing worse than a shaking up, got back inside and returned to the fray.

Kirby planned a coordinated attack by the armoured cars and his infantry under cover of fire from his support weapons and the brigade's artillery, while one of No. 40 Squadron's Hartebeest two-seaters distracted the defenders by dropping 25-pound, anti-personnel bombs on them.

Five armoured cars under Irwin and three under Lieutenant A. W. Thompson would work along a *lugga* to a position to the right of the fort, and then wait in concealment until the infantry were ready. Three other cars under Staff Sergeant R. M. Brodigan would also use the *lugga* to get to the left of the fort. When the Scottish started to advance, Irwin and Thompson would give support by charging the fort and then work around behind it to cut off the expected enemy withdrawal. On the left of the fort, Brodigan would coordinate his attack with the movement of the infantry. Major Klein with his company headquarters group, meanwhile, would speed down the road and head straight for the fort.

The attack was timed for 1630 and by 1615 all the armoured cars were in place. At this stage Murphy's Law stepped in: "At the psychological moment," Klein writes, "due to battery wear, four out of the five sets in use failed simultaneously. There was just sufficient strength in the batteries to give the word of command to move forward before the W/T went off the air … when the cars were in danger of coming under our own artillery fire and could not be warned."

There was nothing to be done about it, however, and when the artillery barrage started at 1630 Irwin's and Thompson's cars charged out of the *lugga*, straight into a frightening storm of close-quarter fire from the defenders' machine guns and rifles. Irwin knew better than to sit and take punishment, and so on his own initiative ordered his cars to attack without waiting for the infantry to close in, and in spite of the very real danger of being blown to bits by his own artillery bombardment.

Unseen amid all the turmoil on the ground were Lieutenant J. D. W. Human of No. 40 Squadron and his gunner, Air-Sergeant J. Jackson, who were circling low over the fort in their Hartebeest. Irwin's car was under such concentrated fire from one group of machine guns that to Human it looked as if it was about to be knocked out, so he dived on the machine guns to allow Jackson to spray them with bullets.

But the machine gunners fired first and damaged his engine which started losing power so rapidly that Human found he could not gain altitude. In spite of this he made another low pass over the fort so that Jackson could fire another burst at Irwin's tormentors. But now the Hartebeest's engine seized up altogether. Human banked and glided away to crash land in the bush near the forward elements of the Transvaal Scottish, the only injury being a cut above one of Jackson's eyes.

Back at the fort, in the meantime, Irwin's detachment rumbled forward as fast as possible, guns blazing, while 1 Armoured Car Company's headquarters cars stormed up the road – all this, Klein writes, "to the considerable annoyance of the battery commander, who perforce had to call off his shoot [when] the armoured cars moved into the field of artillery fire. The Banda broke cover now, and momentarily seemed to intend closing in on the cars, but the rattling Vickers guns dissuaded them."

Irwin went bald-headed at the fort, circled it and burst inside. Thompson and his three cars worked their way around to the right to cut off the defenders, who were now streaming out of the fort, while Brodigan charged in from the left and the headquarters group headed straight up the centre.

It took only a few minutes to clear the fort itself. But the action was not yet over. The Banda might have abandoned the fort but they were still full of fight and regrouped in a *lugga* below the fort on high ground to its left. Klein sent three of his cars to swing around to the right of the fort and three to the left, then bring their combined fire to bear on the Banda.

This was the decisive moment. The Banda broke away into a deep valley behind the fort, and from there kept on firing at the fort area. Two cars took up a hull-down position on a ridge overlooking the valley, but the Banda filtered away to join their comrades on the high ground and kept firing until repeated sweeps had cleared the area. The armoured cars were then posted out to strategic points to wait for the infantry to take over.

Some Banda were then seen retreating down the valley and a section of armoured cars set off after them, but eventually abandoned the pursuit because it was getting dark and there was too much danger of an ambush. Instead the cars pulled back to protect the engineers who were already busy cleaning the wells below the fort.

The fight for Hobok was over. The Transvaal Scottish had lost one man killed in action and two armoured car troopers had been wounded; it took a while to determine enemy casualties, because surprisingly few enemy dead and wounded were found. Much later, after the capture of Yavelo, an Italian officer reported that more than 300 had been killed or wounded in the actions at El Yibo, El Gumu, Gorai, Hobok and Banno.

Four South Africans were decorated for gallantry after this action. Lieutenant Irwin received an immediate Military Cross and Staff Sergeant Brodigan an immediate Military Medal, while Irwin's unseen good Samaritans, Lieutenant Human and Air-Sergeant Jackson, were later awarded the Distinguished Flying Cross and the Distinguished Flying Medal respectively – the latter was the first DFM to be awarded to a South African Air Force air gunner.

Major Klein's report on the action of the armoured cars at Hobok commended "the courage and dash shown by all officers and men … and the outstanding manner in which all ranks fulfilled their tasks in accordance with their training."The report emphasized the value of ground–air cooperation, and suggested that the experiment be tried of linking aircraft to the leading armoured cars by radio.

In Libya, too, the British were sweeping all before them. The Australians captured Bardia on 5 January 1941, Tobruk on 22 January and Derna (now Darnah) on 3 February. Graziani, seeing that it was impossible to halt O'Connor's momentum, ordered his Tenth Army to abandon the entire region of Cyrenaica and fall back through Beda Fomm (now Bayda Fumm). When this came to O'Connor's ears he immediately revised his battle plan. Leaving the Australians to keep pushing the Italians back along the coast, he ordered Major-General Michael O'Moore Creagh's 7 Armoured Division to turn inland and rush across the desert to capture Beda Fomm before the Italians got there.

Creagh found the desert terrain such tough going that he began to fall behind his schedule, so he sent Lieutenant-Colonel John Combe ahead with a 2,000-strong flying column of infantry and field artillery, supported by light and cruiser tanks, to take Beda Fomm. Combe did so on 4 February, then constructed north-facing defensive propositions.

Next day about 20,000 Italians with more than 100 tanks started launching repeated attacks on Beda Fomm. Combe held them off all that day and the next. On 7 February 20 Italian tanks managed to break through his lines, but were destroyed or driven back by Combe's field artillery. That was the Italians' swansong. With 7 Armoured Division and the Australians now breathing down its neck, Graziani's Tenth Army disintegrated and its troops began to surrender in great numbers.

14

Problems at Banya Fort, victory at Mega

With Hobok in his hands, the next phase of General Brink's plan was to secure his western flank by capturing the strongly held Italian position at Banno (or Banya), about 50km to the north, so that he could outflank Moyale. Then he would be in place to attack his next major objective, the fortress at Mega. At the same time he intended to ignite the Shifta rebellion in the Galla Sidamo area. To this end Brink sent composite armoured car and infantry patrols, drawn from his two South African brigades, to probe more deeply north and west from Hobok and north and east from El Gumu, where 2 South African Brigade was now headquartered.

The patrols roamed over a wide area without finding any sign of an Italian presence except some abandoned fortified posts whose former occupiers had retreated to Mega and the other mountain fortress at Yavelo, about 180km to its north. Linking up with the Shifta, however, was proving difficult. Nothing had been seen or heard of Haile Degaga's representative, Robi, since the meeting at Marsabit in January 1941, and the exact location of Hadu mountain was a mystery.

Brink was under no illusions about the fact that taking Banno might turn out to be difficult. For one thing, it was reportedly held by at least two battalions of colonial infantry, with a strong contingent of Italian officers who presumably had a good grasp of conventional warfare. For another, the only viable approach route was along the road from El Gumu that ran eastward to where it linked up with the one between Mega and Meti, both of them strongly held. To make it worse, the Mega–Meti road passed within 32km of Yavelo, so that there was a distinct danger of reinforcement from one of several directions.

Then there was the question of water, of which, as far as was known, there was none between Hobok and Banno. Another problem was, of course, that the assault force would have to operate with what Klein describes as "patchwork maps and air reconnaissance reports which sketchily filled in possible cross-country routes." All in all, the Banno attack looked as if it might be the Division's most hazardous task so far (which in fact proved to be the case).

Brink's solution was to attack Banno with an all-arms column he called Dobbs Force, consisting of 1 South African Irish under Lieutenant-Colonel John Dobbs, 1 Armoured Car Company's No. 1 Platoon and company headquarters, a section of artillery, engineer and medical detachments, and a company of local irregulars. Dobbs Force would travel across-country almost due north from Hobok by way of a route plotted from the air – not a good substitute for ground reconnaissance, but all that was available.

Dobbs' primary task was to capture Banno, but he was also ordered to reconnoitre likely approach-routes to the Yavelo stronghold and, by hook or by crook, make contact with Haile Degaga. It was a heavy burden to lay on what was, after all, not a very large force. To prevent any counter-attack which might be launched from Yavelo, a fighting patrol made up of a company from 1 Field Force Battalion and a section of 2 Armoured Car Company, all commanded by Major (later Brigadier) Jack Bester, would patrol the road north of Gianciaro; aircraft from No. 40 Squadron would coordinate the two forces' movement.

At 0600 on 8 February 1941 Dobbs Force set off from Hobok, with two sections of armoured cars from Lieutenant L. G. Williamson's No. 1 Platoon scouting well forward, while Major Klein's headquarters group and a platoon of the South African Irish were deployed as advance mobile troops a few hundred metres ahead of the main body. A third section of armoured cars hung back a few hundred metres from the rest of the column to prevent possible enemy infiltration from the flanks or rear.

In the leading armoured car with Lieutenant Williamson was an Abyssinian guide who had volunteered to lead them to Banno – it seems that the South Africans did not have much faith in his abilities, which turned out to be fully justified. All went well at first, with Dobbs Force moving in good order along a camel track marked on its maps. Then, while it was crossing a bush-studded plain, the track abruptly faded out.

"The Abyssinian guide was then called to indicate the way to Banno," Klein writes. "The less recorded about his efforts the better, for after a number of fruitless attempts to locate a route he finally admitted he had last been to Banno when he was a boy, and the tracks must have changed since then!" Dobbs could do nothing except struggle on in the mid-morning heat that raised temperatures to nearly 100° F in the shade and made the interiors of the armoured cars almost unbearable, across terrain that turned out to be unspeakably rough. The "open plain," part of the air report, was alright from the airman's point of view, but soaring comfortably aloft the pilot who wrote it did not know that the ground surface was stubbly bush, covering a basin of dry, knobbly cotton soil that just about broke every spring on the armoured cars and troop carriers, racked the joints of the riflemen, and cut down the speed of the column to 3 miles in an hour.

To increase the difficulties, a light tail wind caused excessive overheating of the armoured car engines as the vehicles crashed along in extra low gear. Fortunately this possibility had also been foreseen, and a plentiful supply of reserve radiator water was carried by B Echelon.

After the action it was calculated that the 14 armoured cars which made the gruelling march to Banno each used 40 gallons of water per day – over 1,000 gallons collectively for the two-day march. During the day six cars blew their cylinder-head gaskets due to overheating. The workshop mechanics slaved tirelessly in effecting running repairs and keeping the struggling vehicles going.

Dobbs Force struggled on for hour after hour, while along the Gianciaro road Jack Bester's fighting patrol waited for them, no doubt impatiently. But at 1600 Colonel Dobbs called it a day, after what Klein later said "must be accepted as one of the toughest approach marches ever made by a South African force." The column had been able to cover only 47km in 10 hours and was not even within sight of the objective yet, but a night march was out of the question in the circumstances. Dobbs passed his decision on to Bester and both forces lay up for the night, each of them now about 10km from Banno.

Soon after first light Dobbs was on the move again, and when he reached the mouth of the Gochi Valley at 1015, after several more hours of punishment, he had Banno in sight for the first time: a stone fort on top of a ridge about 5km away, overlooked to the northwest by the slopes of the Gundile mountains.

Dobbs radioed this news to Bester, who said that he, too, had the fort visual. Dobbs then ordered Bester to coordinate with him and refrain from moving forward on his own, since the valley was a ready-made ambush site – a narrow defile, choked with thick bush and crossed by several *luggas*. But there was no sight or sound of the Italians, and a little before noon Bester's cars cautiously approached the fort. One of No. 40 Squadron's aircraft strafed the fort and dropped some anti-personnel bombs on it, but there was still no reaction. It was, as Klein notes "ominously and unhealthily quiet."

Dobbs ordered Bester to send his cars as far as possible along the ridge to the left and right of the fort. Bester complied and then reported that they had not encountered any enemy or been fired on. Dobbs then sent Klein ahead with one section of cars to enter the fort itself. At

1230 Klein radioed back to say that he was now inside, that his patrols to the left and right of it had failed to draw any fire, and that he would not be able to advance over the ridge because the northwestern side's reverse slope was too steep. He added that he could see Bester's patrol approaching the fort from the northeast, and the leading vehicles of 1 South African Irish's advance guard, which were entering the clearing below the fort from the southeast.

The South Africans were tensed for trouble, so the leading Irish vehicles made short work of crossing the clearing and heading for the shelter of the ridge. It was as well that they did so. The Italians had laid a carefully prepared ambush, which was why the armoured cars had drawn no fire: the defenders, quite correctly, had identified the motorized infantry as the primary target.

The two battalions of colonial infantry were concealed on high ground between 600 and 800m northwest of Banno, waiting for the right moment to spring the trap. But they sprang it too late. "A veritable wall of machine gun and rifle fire," Klein's words in 1967, fell on the clearing, but the leading vehicles had already reached safety. Dobbs immediately halted his main body out of range, debussed his troops and ordered them to advance on the fort under cover of the bush. Now started the heaviest firefight of the campaign up to that time.

From hull-down positions on the ridge the armoured cars pinned down the ambushers until the infantry were in position. Then the Irish advance guard scaled the ridge while the main body attacked through the valley. The South Africans pounded the Italian position with everything they had at their disposal – machine guns, mortars and artillery. The Italians fired back. This went on for several hours until late in the afternoon, when the Italian force was seen withdrawing to the west into the ridges.

Dobbs now broke off contact because darkness was approaching and the armoured cars were generally in poor shape after the battering they had taken on the approach march. This action had an unfortunate result: the colonial infantry returned to their positions during the night, so that the next day they had to be driven out again by long-range fire – a pattern that was to be repeated for several days.

That night the mechanics laboured mightily and managed to get enough of the armoured cars in condition for a long-range reconnaissance of the ground between the Orbatte Hills and Yavelo itself in order to update the inadequate available maps. In addition they had to discover the exact location of Hadu Mountain, so as to find a way of contacting Haile Degaga. This last task proved easier than expected, Klein writes, because "quite casually, after a hard morning's work, an Abyssinian guide in the leading armoured car pointed out the direction of Hadu Mountain!"

The burning question that night was how to actually contact the Shifta. That problem, at least, solved itself at dawn next morning (11 February 1941), when Haile Degaga's representative, Robi, arrived out of the blue with five of his comrades, explaining that heavy Italian patrolling had cut off his party until that very day. But now, he added, if the armoured cars saw their way clear to breaking through the enemy's patrol area, he would personally convey word to Haile Degaga that the time had arrived.

Dobbs immediately sent Klein with four armoured cars and a section of the Irish to take Robi and his companions to the mountain, which lay an estimated 145km away on the other side of the Yavelo Plain. Radio silence was only to be broken if they ran into difficulties, Dobbs told Klein, and he must be back by 1800, failing which a relief column would be sent out to find him. Klein assented, loaded Robi and his followers into the vehicles and set off, accompanied by farewell shots from the colonial infantrymen. Klein describes the trip as follows:

> Four silvery Caproni bombers picked up the patrol a few hours later on the Yavello [sic] plain, without a vestige of cover in sight. The armoured cars and troop carrier scattered, but the

aircraft after circling overhead flew off in the direction of Yavello without attempting either to bomb or machine gun them.

Moving round the foot of the Gundile range, into a vast and lovely plain of golden yellowing grass, the patrol proceeded steadily on a northwesterly course. Large herds of startled gemsbok, their long horns slashing the air, galloped away before the vehicles. In the distance the Yavelo mountains rose clear and blue above the edge of the plain.

After the Italian air reconnaissance earlier in the morning, enemy interference was expected when the patrol approached the Yavello Giarso road shortly before noon. But the road was deserted as far as the eye could see in either direction.

From rubber-sandalled footprints and mule spoor on the sandy road, Robi indicated that enemy troops with pack transport had passed that way in the direction of Banno some few hours before. His reading of the tracks proved to be correct, for by the next afternoon Italian mountain pack-guns were brought into action against the South Africans at Banno.

A short while later Robi indicated a change of direction. Gradually the patrol closed in on a range of high peaks on the left. Fifty-two miles and four hours after leaving camp, Robi called a halt and he and his Shifta dismounted. He pointed to a high peak "Hadu," he cried. "Haile Degaga." There was quiet drama in the moment. With arm upraised, rifle slung across his shoulder, Robi saluted in farewell:

"Kwaheri – we shall meet again."

Without a backward glance he marched away with his companions into the grim recesses of the mountains.

Klein set off back to Banno at all possible speed, his eye on the threat posed by gathering rain clouds, although he felt there was enough time to collect some fresh meat from the abundant game on the plain – on foot and with rifles, Klein emphasizes, "and not in their armoured cars or with machine guns, as some of the more envious claimed later."

On reaching Banno just before 1800 they were somewhat taken aback by a distinctly chilly greeting from Colonel Dobbs and his officers, "who had spent a weary day being sniped at by colonial infantry and were just then busy organizing a relief column to go in search of the 'lost' patrol, [but] much was forgiven when grilled game steaks appeared at mess that night."

While Colonel Dobbs and his officers were enjoying Klein's gemsbok steaks, Wavell's intelligence officers in the Western Desert were counting the spoils of Operation Compass, which had ended three days earlier. In just ten weeks General O'Connor had succeeded in not only expelling Graziani's Tenth Army from Egypt and chasing it deep into Libya, but had destroyed it as a coherent fighting force.

The Italians had lost about 3,000 killed and 130,000 captured, as well as about 400 tanks and 1,292 artillery pieces, for a cost to the British of 494 dead and 1,225 wounded. Quite clearly the way was open to keep advancing and destroy the entire Italian army in Libya.

But Wavell's hopes of achieving complete victory evaporated when new orders came from Whitehall: The advance was to be stopped at El Agheila because of the crisis in Greece. As an experienced soldier General Metaxas knew very well that the Greek army, no matter how resolute, would be no match for the numerous, well-equipped Germans if they came to the Italians' rescue, and so he called for help from the only nation capable of aiding him, Britain.

As a result Wavell was ordered to send the Greeks a substantial part of his forces and great quantities of supplies – assets he could ill spare and would not be able to replace if they came to grief. Operations in Cyrenaica came to a halt for the time being and General O'Connor returned to Cairo after handing over to Lieutenant-General Philip Neame.

On 12 February 1941 2 South African Motorcycle Company under Major Stander arrived to take over the Banno fort so that Dobbs Force could join 5 South African Brigade for the assault on Mega. Next morning Dobbs Force departed, leaving behind a section of 1 Armoured Car Company under Lieutenant Williamson to provide protection, a platoon of

Abyssinian irregulars and a detachment of engineers. On 14 February 1941 Major Stander got some modest but welcome reinforcements in the shape of a platoon and a mortar section from 1 Natal Mounted Riflemen.

They had a warm time of it, weather aside. The Italians had again returned during the night and still had considerable fight left in them. As a result 2 South African Motorcycle Company became the first motorcycle unit to see action – and plenty of it. For the next three days the motorcyclists were shelled intermittently and repulsed a number of enemy sorties; Williamson's three armoured cars were almost lured into a trap set by the Italian artillery, but withdrew rapidly as the shells started falling and got away without loss.

The South Africans fought back with regular aerial bombing and resolute patrol action by Stander's men, and on 18 February 1941 the attackers gave up and withdrew completely from the Banno area. Next day Stander handed over the fort to two companies of Abyssinian irregulars; 2 South African Motorcycle Company went back to the divisional reserve and the other elements of his little garrison rejoined their units.

Within a week the long-awaited Shifta revolt had broken out in southern Abyssinia, with a horde of irregulars attacking the Italian rear and flanks in the mountains west and north of Yavelo. The result was chaos and bloodshed on a large scale, and months were to pass before the Allies could exert some sort of control over the Shifta so that they could be used effectively. In the meantime, however, their very existence strongly curtailed Italian movement between fortified positions, and when such movements had to be made the Italians did not stray far from the roads.

The Banno attack had achieved its aims, but it provided more lessons for the South Africans because it was "unsatisfactory from many angles," Klein writes:

Both the 1st South African Irish and No 1 South African Armoured Car Company reports emphasised the difficulties and dangers of cross-country operations, in unknown terrain without reliable guides, accurate maps, or aerial photographs. Cooperation between air and ground was unsatisfactory, as was coordination between the two converging forces in the initial phase of the first day's fighting.

"We spared the enemy many casualties for fear of hitting the Field Force Battalion," the South African Irish report complained. Acknowledging the importance of mopping-up operations and explaining why such operations were not carried out, the report revealed that Dobbs Force, burdened in advance by the long-distance patrol duties expected of it, had not sufficient strength to execute this function as well as drive out the enemy, and consequently left the Italian colonial infantry free to reorganize and return to fight the next day.

A disquieting feature from the armoured car reconnaissance point of view was the way in which the defence had allowed the cars to enter the main position without firing on them. If the Italians had timed their ambush better they would undoubtedly have inflicted serious casualties on the infantry after the false impression created by the ease of the armoured car occupation of the fort. Fortunately, however, the Italians bungled their plan, and only one South African Irish infantryman was killed in the ambush.

Now it was the turn of Mega, which dominated the southern Abyssinian defence line. "A picturesque Beau Geste fort set on a high mountain plateau," as Klein describes it, "ringed by an outer bastion of precipitous hills which stood out sharply above the surrounding plain, equipped with heavy artillery, its approaches protected by wired-in minefields."

Mega was undoubtedly the most difficult objective 1 South African Division had tackled so far. Apart from its strong defences, it was manned not by lightly armed Banda who were geared for irregular warfare but by well-trained Blackshirts – roughly equivalent to Germany's Waffen SS – and selected battalions of the Italians' colonial infantry, some of which were known to be of good quality. The state of the Blackshirts' morale was an unknown quantity,

Captured Italian cannon displayed in front of Fort Mega, Abyssinia.

Italian Fort Mega, Abyssinia.

but until evidence to the contrary was gained it was presumed high.

General Brink envisaged a two-pronged attack on the Mega plateau by 2 and 5 South African brigades, the intention being to cut off the Italians' lines of retreat and to prevent reinforcements from being sent to Mega from Yavelo and Neghelli in the north or Moyale in the south. This done, Mega itself would be stormed.

In the first phase, 2 South African Brigade plus Dobbs Force was to move from Gianciaro along the road to Mega and then, north of the fortress, swing eastward to block the Mega–Neghelli road at El Sod. 1 South African Irish would then head south and occupy Madaccio, which overlooked the junction of the Mega–Yavelo and Mega–Gianciaro roads; the brigade would put a holding force in place at El Sod and move further east and south to block the Mega–Moyale road.

5 South African Brigade, meanwhile, would advance from El Gumu and head for Mega. The fortress would then be cut off from all hope of help or reinforcement and Brink would be ready for the second phase, the combined assault on it by the two brigades.

At 1745 on the night of 13 February 1941 a covering party of four of 2 Armoured Car Company's cars under Lieutenant John Dunning and A Company 1 Field Force Battalion left Gianciaro. They moved cross-country as far as El Dokelle, just west of the Mega–Yavelo road, where they spent a quiet night. Next morning 2 South African Brigade and the South African Irish moved out as scheduled, first along the Gianciaro–Mega road and then across through scattered bushland until they reached the Mega–Yavelo road.

The movement of 2 South African Brigade and the Irish on 14 February 1941 proceeded smoothly. After following the Gianciaro--Mega road for 16km the columns struck across-country through light, scattered bush and reached the road without incident. The Irish and some 1 Armoured Car Company cars duly peeled off to occupy Madaccio without meeting anyone except sublimely indifferent Boran tribespeople and one magnificent lion.

At this stage 2 South African Brigade's Brigadier Buchanan deviated from Brink's plan by detaching C Company of 2 Field Force Battalion and leaving it astride the Mega–Yavelo road with two cars of 2 Armoured Car Company under Second-Lieutenant D. A. Wood to protect the brigade's rear, an unscheduled change which was to have unexpected consequences and give the South Africans – who were somewhat over confident at this stage – a sharp reality check.

What Brigadier Buchanan did not know was that a very large convoy was coming down the road from Yavelo to reinforce Mega – at least 100 supply and transport vehicles, along with three companies of motorized colonial infantry and 15 light tanks which had been specially sent down from Addis Ababa for the purpose; on the other hand, the Italians did not know that General Brink was already preparing to attack Mega.

It would appear that the South Africans made the mistake of under estimating the situation and that as a result the normal defensive measures were not taken, so that no sentries or listening posts were set out. The result was that at 0345 the two forward 10-ton lorries of the Italian convoy with their escort of about 20 Banda drove unchallenged and undetected into the middle of the company position without either side realizing it.

The alarm was given by Lieutenant Wood, who was awoken by the lorries' engine noise when they were just 15m from him. Mutual recognition soon followed and, "while the startled South Africans struggled to their feet, the Banda dropped to the ground, took cover beneath the lorries and opened fire with rifles and a machine gun," Klein recounts.

Silhouetted against the skyline, Lieutenant Wood's armoured car made an excellent target, and the crew endured a couple of nasty moments while scrambling aboard. Quickly moving his car into position where he would avoid hitting his own troops, Lieutenant Wood raked the Banda beneath the lorries with well-aimed bursts of machine-gun fire, killing and wounding a number. The Banda ceased firing after about 10 minutes.

In the calm that followed, Lieutenant Wood collected his other car and, acting on the infantry company commander's instructions, drove forward a couple of hundred yards. In the case of a tank attack he was to retire with his two armoured cars behind an anti-tank rifle to protect its crew while they engaged the tanks.

The Italian reaction was swift. At 0515 the position was attacked by the light tanks and supporting infantry. The light tanks roared out of the pre-dawn darkness, almost surrounded the South Africans and poured machine-gun fire at them. Then the tanks burst into the position itself, scattering the 2 Field Force Battalion men. One tried to ram Wood's car, but due to the bad light achieved nothing more than a near miss.

Wood tried to fall back to protect the anti-tank rifle as per instructions, but amid the general confusion could not find it. A general retreat followed, Wood's cars trying to protect the shaken infantrymen as they fell back on foot toward El Sod, having suffered two dead and four wounded, with another 10 taken prisoner. Fortunately for the South Africans the Italians did not pursue them but turned around to head back to Yavelo, since it was obvious that the road to Mega was blocked.

At El Sod, Brigadier Buchanan immediately ordered Colonel Engelbrecht of 2 Field Force Battalion to pursue and destroy the Italian column. Engelbrecht set off along the Mega road with his A Company, six of 2 Armoured Car Company's cars under Major C. G. Walker and a section of anti-tank guns. They seized a straggling lorry, recovered some of the Field Force Battalion prisoners and captured six colonial soldiers and an Italian mechanic, then pushed on.

The South Africans had no idea what they were up against until No. 40 Squadron aircraft reported back on the size of the Italian force when it was about 7km south of Yavelo, at which stage Engelbrecht's pugnacious but outnumbered team was only about a kilometre and a half behind them. General Brink immediately ordered No. 40 Squadron to delay the Italian convoy so that Walker's armoured cars could catch up.

For the next four hours relays of Hartebeests bombed and strafed the convoy, damaging some of the tanks and lorries. The delaying stratagem worked, because whenever Durrant's aircraft appeared overhead the Italian vehicles scattered into the bush. But Engelbrecht did not get an opportunity to avenge the C Company fiasco. Brigadier Buchanan eventually called him back because so little was known about the convoy and he was concerned that the pursuers would be ambushed.

This decision frustrated Major Walker who was convinced that he could have captured all the light tanks, but in retrospect Buchanan's decision was quite correct. Engelbrecht's team would have been outnumbered three to one and could not have been reinforced in time.

Mega was essentially an infantry action, but two armoured cars were involved in a number of roles, and in fact the first shots were fired by a section of 1 Armoured Car Company cars under Second-Lieutenant D. Hellen in what Klein describes as a "strange episode [which] was the opening sally of the first major battle of the campaign." Hellen was leading a 1 South African Irish patrol toward Mega when "… about 2 miles from the first of the foothill ridges, when moving across-country about 350 yards from the road, the crew of the leading armoured car saw two motor-cyclists in dark uniforms and peaked caps, with rifles slung across their backs, travelling slowly toward them along the road from Mega.

It was a strange performance, because the armoured cars were in full view of an Italian artillery observation post on a hill ahead. Italian spotters could actually be seen with the naked eye – and yet the two motor-cyclists rode on, apparently oblivious of the armoured cars a few hundred yards away. Reluctantly, Lieutenant Hellen ordered fire to be opened on them. While the machine gun in his car was being loaded, the leading rider disappeared into dead ground, but the second was knocked over by the first burst of fire.

When the other reappeared, now retreating toward Mega, he too was shot down. Immediate reaction was forthcoming from the Italians who opened artillery fire on the armoured cars, without securing a shellburst closer than 50 yards from any of the three.

The battle that followed had the South Africans fighting two enemies simultaneously – the Italians and the weather. By this time the South Africans had become used to the terrible heat, and when 1 South African Irish and 3 Transvaal Scottish went into battle on the morning of 16 February 1941, they wore the typical East African campaign garb of shorts and shirts, which was reasonable enough, considering that the temperature was more than 100° F, and arrangements were made to send forward one blanket per man toward nightfall. But huge black clouds began building up around noon, and at 1600 torrential rain began to fall.

It rained right through the night, and with the raindrops fell hundreds of accurately aimed Italian artillery shells that fell not only on the infantry but also on the brigade transport echelon as it forced its way forward through blackest night. The temperature dropped precipitately, torturing the ill-clad infantrymen to the point where Klein records, they "stripped at midnight and beat each other's bodies to restore circulation. Cases of exposure and collapse were frequent." To make their existence even more miserable, footpaths and tracks had been thoroughly mined and caused a number of casualties.

Although badly hampered by the weather and terrain, the armoured cars were kept busy with a variety of support and patrol tasks. On 2 South African Brigade's front southeast of Mega, 2 Armoured Car Company cars prowled to El Sod and further east, dispelling reports of supposed advancing enemy columns, and went far south toward Moyale to stop any possible intervention from that direction, although aerial reconnaissance reports now indicated that the Italians had abandoned Moyale and withdrawn to Neghelli via a long detour.

A section of 1 Armoured Car Company under Lieutenant E. J. W. Rees meanwhile was directly involved with the right flank of the assault on Mega, supporting 3 Transvaal Scottish. In this role Rees had a number of adventures, not always through enemy action.

At the end of the first day Rees and his cars were with 3 Transvaal Scottish on a feature that the Scottish had dubbed Kirby Hill. On the second day Rees struggled forward to another important feature, Two Tree Hill, avoiding the road to the fortress, which was being shelled. This was easier said than done, because the rain had turned the black clay soil into a fearful mess. Rees sent two cars forward to reconnoitre, and it was only by dint of great effort that they managed to struggle back to Kirby Hill, where they then bogged down so thoroughly that they could not be dragged out until 2100 the following day.

Rees obviously could go no further, so he stationed his cars in positions from which they could lay down supporting fire for the Transvaal Scottish as it went into the attack. The going in the South African Irish sector was even worse, but a section of cars under Lieutenant

Thompson provided supporting fire whenever they could bring their machine guns to bear.

Under these intolerable conditions the infantry persevered with their advance, Klein writes:

> It is difficult to envisage worse physical conditions than those which confronted the two South African brigades during the three-day operation at Mega. Yet on the third day men of the 2nd Field Force Battalion … led by Lieutenant-Colonel Engelbrecht, manhandled their mortars up a precipitous cliff, which native guides had previously declared to be unscalable, to capture the main Italian gun positions.
>
> This rendered the enemy's position hopeless. At 1745 hours, when the two infantry battalions of the 5th Brigade had fought their way forward and when bayonets had been fixed for the final attack, there came the dramatic moment when, through a rift in the mist clouds, a white flag was seen flying from the fort. Mega had surrendered.

Large numbers of prisoners and great quantities of equipment and supplies fell into the triumphant South Africans' hands: 26 officers, 598 Blackshirts and 500 colonial infantry, seven field artillery pieces, 80 heavy and light machine guns, anti-aircraft guns, transport vehicles, petrol and other supplies, including considerable quantities of food. There were still loose ends to be tied up, however, so on 22 February 1941 1 and 2 South African Motorcycle companies, under Major Jenkins, were sent south to Moyale.

Getting there took longer than they had anticipated, thanks to the very heavy rain and the resultant unspeakable surface conditions, and when they eventually arrived they were greeted by a patrol of Abyssinian irregulars under a Lieutenant Brookbanks, who informed them that the fortress had been abandoned after the fall of Mega – thanks, at least in part, to an ingenious deception scheme which had been mounted earlier by a South African–East African team.

In the next two weeks far-ranging armoured car patrols failed to find an Italian military presence anywhere in that part of southern Abyssinia, and just a fortnight after Major Klein had transported Robi the Shifta representative to Hadu Mountain, 25 East African Brigade signalled 1 South African Division Headquarters that the fortress of Yavelo had been abandoned by the Italians and was now occupied by Haile Degaga's men.

With the conquest of the escarpment, 1 South African Division's task in southern Abyssinia was over – although not its detached 1 South African Brigade, whose work had barely begun. Brink had done what he had set out to do, which was to open up a portal for an advance via Yavelo and Neghelli into central Abyssinia's region of lakes, beyond which lay the main prize, Addis Ababa. Arguably he could have kept on going, as Klein writes: "Even though the first rains had fallen and the wooded mountain country to the north abounded in strong defensive positions, in all probability by rapid exploitation of the situation the 1st South African Division could have achieved the conquest of Abyssinia earlier than was accomplished by the attack through Italian Somaliland. There was still a spell of good weather ahead, the Division was well equipped, its morale was high, and in hitting power it was far superior to any Italian division that stood between it and Addis Ababa."

But the emphasis had now swung around to the south. Cunningham's main aim was still to attack eastward over the border into Italian Somaliland and take Kismayu as soon as possible. As a result 1 South African Division was recalled to Kenya and went into reserve at Nanyuki, where it was to stand by to rapidly reinforce Cunningham in his assault on Kismayu if this proved necessary. What actually happened to it, however, was something else altogether, and came about as the result of events far away.

15

Somaliland: glory for the armour

2 South African Brigade was held back to support General Cunningham's upcoming Somaliland offensive, in which Brigadier Pienaar's 1 South African Brigade was, of course, already involved as part of 12 African Division. Now he was to come so spectacularly into his own that to this day General Brink's achievement of taking the war to the Italians and breaking their grip in the south has never been fully appreciated. 2 South African Brigade, too, was to render tremendous service during the fighting around the great lakes in central Abyssinia.

"The glory of the attack – for military glory there was in that magnificent burst through Italian Somaliland to Addis Ababa from the over-all South African aspect – passed to the 1st South African Brigade, the South African Air Force, No 3 South African Armoured Car Company and No 1 South African Light Tank Company," Klein writes, adding "Although the limelight was now to be centred on these two South African Tank Corps units, great work was done as well by No 1 and No 2 South African Armoured Car Companies in the high mountains, rains, mud and slush of the Battle of the Lakes."

Cunningham's attack on Italian Somaliland was conceived by General Wavell as a limited operation, the aims of which were to capture Kismayu and establish a bridgehead over the Juba river at Giumbo before the rainy season began; if this was accomplished, an immediate attempt was to be made to cut the road between Mogadishu and Addis Ababa. The actual advance on Addis Ababa, however, would not take place until after the rains had ended in mid-1941.

Cunningham proposed to use both 11 African Division (Major-General Wetherall) and 12 African Division (Major-General Godwin-Austen) for the attack on Italian Somaliland. Of the two, 11 African Division was the weaker, with only two brigades (21 East African and 23 Nigerian). 12 African Division, on the other hand, was not only at full strength, with 1 South African Brigade, 22 East African Brigade (Brigadier C. C. Fowkes) and 24 Gold Coast Brigade (Brigadier C. E. M. Richards), but of course, possessed a large, fully-motorized element in the shape of Dan Pienaar's men.

The South Africans would also supply virtually all the support which was vital to the operation: aerial attack assets, artillery, well drilling, road construction, motor transport, a plethora of engineering services, medical services and various others.

It was clear that the operation would be no push over. After the capture of El Wak in December 1940 the Italians had been digging in along the Juba river, the only noteworthy natural obstacle in that harsh stretch of thirstland plains. To defend the Juba Line they had deployed six full conventionally-trained Italian brigades and six Banda *gruppos* of wily, pugnacious local irregulars whose duties included patrolling the borderline.

Intelligence indicated that there were two particularly tough objectives to be taken along the Juba Line. The first was Kismayu itself, which was held by a large number of Italian and colonial troops and was well-defended – to seaward by coastal artillery and on land by minefields, artillery, barbed wire and anti-tank ditches. The second was Afmadu, located northwest of Kismayu at the junction of the important roads to Kismayu and to Gelib on the eastern bank of the Juba. The most important road junction in the region, Afmadu was garrisoned by an infantry battalion with supporting artillery, also well dug in.

Cunningham's battle plan was a combination of simplicity, straightforwardness and daring. His jumping-off place would be Garissa, a daunting 345km from the railhead. Then from Garissa he was going to make a 420km dash straight at Kismayu over the well-nigh waterless plain east of the Juba river.

It was an ambitious undertaking, fraught with potential difficulties. One of the most important was the requirement for speed. The offensive had to move fast at all stages; lagging behind Cunningham's tight schedule would mean, at the very least, a humiliating withdrawal to Kenya

South African Marmon Herrington Mk2 crossing the Union Bridge over the Juba River.

because of a lack of water and supplies. But the plan was to pay huge dividends because, as Klein writes, "by his bold advance to Kismayu he threw the Italians off balance, which they never again recovered."

His plan of attack was equally simple. The Italians would be distracted by a mock attack near El Wak. While this was taking place, 12 African Division would leave from Garissa, head for Afmadu and capture it. One column, consisting of 24 Gold Coast Brigade, would then carry on directly eastward, capture Bulo Erillo and threaten Gelib on the eastern bank of the Juba.

At the same time 1 South African Brigade would set out from the border post at Dif, about halfway between Afmadu and Wajir, swing south to dash down to the coast on the Kenyan side of the Juba and capture the village of Gobwen. Gobwen lay on the western bank of the river's last bend before it ran into the sea, just north of Kismayu and was connected to the village of Giumbo on the other bank of the Juba by a 200m-long pontoon bridge. With the southern approach secured, the brigade would go slightly north again and force its way across the river to cut off the Kismayu garrison's escape route.

While all this was taking place Wetherall's 11 African Division, reinforced by 2 South African Brigade, would make use of the confusion caused by 1 South African Brigade's threat to Gobwen to advance on and capture Kismayu itself with off-shore support from the Royal Navy.

The greatest test had now arrived for 3 South African Armoured Car Company and 1 South African Light Tank Company. In the weeks after the offensive started they would be employed everywhere on a myriad different duties. As Klein writes, they found themselves "operating … as brigade, divisional and force troops, [and] performed extremely valuable services – particularly the armoured cars which, being less prone to mechanical failure than were the light tanks, went here, there and everywhere on escort duties, reconnaissance patrols, attack and pursuit."

Major Gwillam's 3 Armoured Car Company was at its operational peak at this time. Since the capture of El Wak in December 1940 it had been busy supporting numerous infantry patrols northwestward to Moyale and eastward toward the Somaliland border from its base at Wajir and "these operations," Klein writes, "had built up the efficiency, bush-lore and self-confidence of the car crews to a high degree." Small wonder, then, that 3 South African Armoured Car Company in particular would later be commended for its exceptional services.

Marmon Herrington Mk2 cars in the field during the Abyssinian campaign.

South African troops, with Marmon Herrington Mk2 U23207, rest behind cover during the East African campaign.

In its summary of the Somaliland operations, 1 South African Brigade reported as follows under the heading 'Services of Units or Individuals Deserving of Special Mention':

> 3 (SA) Armoured Car Coy. Maj S B Gwillam Comd. for the readiness with which they met constant and unending demands made on them from the time of leaving Wajir until the time of leaving Brava to assist 24 Gold Coast Brigade. These demands were, literally, constant and unending. Every other unit in any sort of difficulty turned to 3 (SA) Armoured Car Coy for assistance. This assistance was cheerfully given and without hesitation or exception.

All this in spite of the fact that although 3 Armoured Car Company had finally swopped its well-worn, two-wheel drive Mark I cars for Mark IIs with the four-wheel drive Marmon-Herrington drivetrain, it had the bare minimum available for field use. For the Somaliland campaign No. 3 Platoon was allocated to Godwin-Austen's divisional troops, so that all 1 South African Brigade had were 15 Mark IIs left for field tasks, four Mark Is with the infantry to act as machine-gun carriers and two Mark Is for mobile artillery observation posts.

1 South African Light Tank Company was also in good shape, well-rested and with vehicles in sound mechanical shape: after El Wak they had been sent back to Nanyuki for refitting and further training, moving forward only in February 1941 to join 1 South African Brigade.

For Lieutenant Heard, commanding 2 Armoured Car Company's No. 2 Platoon (attached to 22 East African Brigade) the offensive started early. On 24 January 1941 Heard's platoon led elements of the brigade in their successful attack on Liboi, the site of that first quick engagement in 1940. During the fighting Heard's armoured car fell into a tank trap and set off a mine. About a dozen Banda immediately attacked it with rifles, grenades and petrol bombs until one of the other cars chased them away and took Heard in tow.

Three days later it was the turn of Hauina, a little under 40km northeast of Liboi. The defenders were softened up by mortar fire, after which Heard and his platoon charged in from the west, silenced their fire and forced them to capitulate. At the beginning of February, Heard's cars and East African infantry patrolled in the vicinity of the waterhole at Beles Gugani west of Hauina and almost within sight of the border where the Italians had a skilfully prepared defensive position, meant to cover the approach to Afmadu.

For Heard the month started with a bang. On 1 February 1941 some of his cars were covering a King's African Rifles' patrol when one of them set off a landmine which damaged it so severely that it had to be towed back to base. Three days later Heard's platoon was deeply involved in 22 East African Brigade's attack on Beles Gugani itself, among other things coming under a mortar bombardment during the advance. The actual attack was something of a non-starter.

"The King's African Rifles were ready to assault the position… when, almost to their chagrin, they saw the enemy withdrawing," writes Carel Birkby in his famed early account of the campaign, *It's a Long Way to Addis*. The King's African Rifles "wasted no more time but went in with bayonets fixed and the East African war cry of *Sokoli, Sokola* ringing in the air, laid many of the enemy low and captured the machine guns that were waiting for them at the far end of a cunning clearing."

After a last scouting trip near Afmadu, during which the cars were fired on by Italian artillery, Heard went home to Wajir, only to become part of 21 East African Brigade's deception plan.

Afmadu was already being shelled by the South African artillery, and on 10 February 1941 the South African Air Force dropped 7½ tons of high explosive on it in two hours. After that Afmadu fell without a fight. "No sooner had the bombing ceased than the Banda in Afmadu took to the bush," Birkby says, "and that night the 94th Italian Colonial Infantry battalion defending the village, which was such an important administrative and trading centre, set off eastward in an effort to reach the Juba river.

"The fate of that lost battalion has never been entirely cleared up, but many of them never emerged from that waterless wilderness alive. They set off in a panic, without food and water, and soon they had broken up into wandering bands … Their priest was found dying of thirst. When the King's African Rifles went into Afmadu on February 11, only a few half-hearted defenders remained at their posts, and soon the village with its white-walled buildings and its barbed-wire defences was in our hands."

"Among the equipment captured at Afmadu," Birkby says, "were five Italian armoured cars made of steel so soft that a Bren-gun burst pierced them easily." This last is an interesting remark which might partly explain the Banda's and colonial infantry's dismay at the seeming invulnerability of the South African cars in the face of small-arms fire and grenades.

24 Gold Coast Brigade then moved as per schedule to attack Buro Erillo on 13 February 1941, capturing it in a bloody action in which the resolute Italian defenders exacted a heavy toll of attackers, while 1 South African Brigade – nicknamed 'Pincol' for this operation – spent the day bivouacked at Eyadera on the Afmadu–Kismayu road, preparatory to heading for Gobwen, and strictly forbidden by 12 African Division Headquarters from breaking radio silence or undertaking any patrolling or reconnaissance.

It was a frustrating and worrisome wait for Pienaar. He could hear explosions from the direction of Kismayu, and he suspected (correctly) that the Italians were destroying the port installations and evacuating the fortress. But Godwin-Austen's stringent ban on radio traffic prevented him from passing on this very valuable information.

It was the classic field commander's dilemma: should he stick to the greater plan, or use his own initiative, which might upset that plan? Although never one to hesitate about following his own nose, Pienaar decided to abide by his orders – perhaps because Godwin-Austen's plan was a very detailed and precise one, although he bent them a little by reconnoitring the area down to a satellite airstrip just west of Gobwen which had been identified as his jumping-off point.

"Perhaps it would have been better," Klein says, "if he had disregarded his orders altogether … as it was, the Italians abandoned Kismayu without a fight, extricated the garrison in its entirety and sabotaged the harbour and town."

One can see why he says so. Pincol was by far the most potent fighting formation in either of the two British divisions. It was a self-contained brigade group, fully motorized with 1,200 vehicles and included medium and light artillery batteries, 1 South African Light Tank Company and 3 Armoured Car Company (less its detached platoon). If ever there was a force capable of speeding to Kismayu, flattening everything in its path, this was it.That night Pincol started moving across country toward Gobwen, as per schedule. According to Klein it was: "… a most difficult night march … in which the light tanks bulldozed paths for the infantry through thick thorn bush … While the tanks were advancing on Gobwen, No.

3 (Armoured Car Company) armoured cars were busily occupied on escort duties and in supporting infantry patrols detailed to cut the Gobwen–Kismayu road."

One such armoured car detachment, under Lieutenant L. S. Steyn, operating with a company of the 1st Royal Natal Carbineers (Lieutenant-Colonel J. G. McMenamin), whose orders were to round up enemy escaping from Kismayu, encountered a strong Italian group along the road. In the ensuing action, three officers and four other ranks were captured, as well as a number of colonial infantry.

Gobwen, which was known to have been heavily fortified, lay in an area of thick thornbush and was overlooked by high sand dunes, just 200m or so away lay Giumbo, to which it had been connected in better days by a ferry service as well as the pontoon bridge. In spite of its fortifications and the protection offered by its natural defenses, Gobwen would have been no match for Pincol, but as Klein writes, "the attack … was somewhat of an anticlimax … the infantry swept down on the village on the morning of the 14th, only to find it deserted and abandoned by the enemy. Only a few lorries and some war material were left behind by the Italians, who had crossed the Juba to Giumbo."

The long-awaited occupation of Kismayu itself took place without any drama, six days ahead of schedule. 3 Armoured Car Company's No. 1 Platoon under Lieutenant P. E. B. Halliwell was detailed to support 22 East African Brigade during the entry, and for the last 16km his cars spearheaded the advance of the leading element, 5 King's African Rifles. They were met, Orpen relates, "by the populace out in the streets ululating to welcome the 5th King's African Rifles and mostly rolling drunk after looting all the wine stores."

By 1700 all of Kismayu had been occupied and it was found that three out of its eight 120mm coastal defence guns and 10 of 16 76mm anti-aircraft guns were still functional. That same evening a party of the South African Engineer Corps' ubiquitous sappers under Lieutenant E. W. Bibby alleviated the water shortage by finding a sound windmill and putting it back into running order.

Gobwen might have been abandoned, but not the Juba Line. The South African infantrymen came under heavy Italian artillery fire as they entered Gobwen; by the time B Company of the Duke of Edinburgh's Own Rifles reached the pontoon bridge it had been set on fire. The Dukes then found themselves on open ground, under heavy machine-gun and artillery fire from the eastern side – immediately several men were wounded.

Due to the heavy enemy fire they could not be evacuated, but the heroic Corporal H. R. Kent of 1 South African Light Tank Company went out and, ignoring the bullets and shells aimed at him, brought back a number of the wounded men. Kent, later a sergeant, was given a field award, the Military Medal. The infantry abandoned the attempt to take the pontoon bridge and took refuge in Gobwen and its surrounding dunes. The Italians continued to bombard the village until 1130, dropping an estimated 3,000 shells on it – one every second – from just 2,750m away.

Casualties from this storm of fire were very light, but when Godwin-Austen came to visit Pincol headquarters during the afternoon – Klein records that he had to wait for Pienaar, who had gone forward in an armoured car that hit a mine, without suffering significant damage – they concluded that forcing the river at Gobwen would be too costly. Godwin-Austen therefore told Pienaar to find another crossing north of Gobwen.

The hold up at Gobwen notwithstanding, Cunningham's advance had done extremely well: "Three days after the launching of the main attack, and six days ahead of time-table, objectives had been captured which two months before had seemed unattainable before the rains broke," Klein writes. "But the major battle for Italian Somaliland had yet to be fought – the crossing of the Juba at Yonte by the 1st South African Brigade on the night of 17 February – the battle in which the South African armoured cars were to play such a dashing role."

16

Breakthrough at Yonte

Godwin-Austen's and Pienaar's decision to force a crossing elsewhere was not lightly made. A river crossing is a hazardous affair at the best of times, and this was not the best of times. It is easy to see why the Italians chose the Juba as their principal line of defence. The plains, bushlands and deserts to the west provided the terrain for a war of manoeuvre for which their forces were not geared. But the greatest river in Italian Somaliland was something else altogether.

Heavily bushed on both banks, with many swamps and cultivated fields, it was, as Klein notes, "a natural defensive position which the Italians had strengthened by strong-points along the eastern bank. At the time of the attack the Juba was fast-flowing and 175m wide: all bridges had been destroyed, and Italian artillery, massed opposite the attacking forces, commanded the recognized approaches."

What was more, the Italians were determined to fight for it. They were determined to prevent Cunningham from getting his hands on the high-quality network of roads they had been building for the past five years which connected the eastern bank of the Juba to the port of Mogadishu and to Lugh Ferrandi, Doolow, Neghelli and the southern highlands of Abyssinia. What a prize.

Yet it had to be crossed. If the Jube Line fell, so would Italian Somaliland, and the way would be open for an advance on Addis Ababa. And there was no doubt about the force best equipped to do it: 1 South African Brigade. 24 Gold Coast Brigade would be in support, as would the South African Air Force, but the brunt of the crossing would be on Dan Pienaar and his men.

Pienaar started the ball rolling on the morning of 16 February 1941 with a personal aerial reconnaissance flight along the Juba to look for a suitable crossing point. He settled on Yonte, 22km upstream from Gobwen, which had once been used for a ferry service and whose remaining infrastructure would simplify the erection of a pontoon bridge, built in the engineering workshops of the Randfontein Estates mine, which was being held in dismantled form at Godwin-Austen's headquarters. He passed on this recommendation to 12 African Division Headquarters, Godwin-Austen told him to go ahead with reconnoitring the route to Yonte, but not to attempt a crossing without permission.

Pienaar sent off a reconnaissance patrol consisting of B Company 1 Royal Natal Carbineers, 3 Armoured Car Company's No. 2 Platoon (less one section) and a section of 1 Field Company, South African Engineer Corps. For backup he put together a strong fighting column consisting of the brigade's tactical headquarters, 1 Transvaal Scottish, three artillery batteries, 3 Armoured Car Company's headquarters and one platoon, anti-tank and anti-aircraft batteries, and medical and engineer detachments. Later that day he and Major Sid Gwillam of 3 Armoured Car Company went on another reconnaissance flight to ascertain the progress being made by the Yonte patrol and the fighting column following in its tracks.

Meanwhile 3 Armoured Car Company's No. 1 Platoon under Lieutenant P. E. B. Halliwell – which had led the King's African Rifles' advance into Kismayu as part of the divisional troops – was withdrawn from the port and at 0900 came under command of the Dukes at

Gobwen. Later in the morning the platoon, less one section, was instructed to reconnoitre the western bank of the Juba, opposite Giumbo, to ascertain the presence and whereabouts of the enemy.

This turned into something distinctly more lively at noon, when Halliwell's cars found themselves on the receiving end of a brisk shelling from Giumbo when they were only 300m from the river, followed a few minutes later by heavy small arms, machine-gun and anti-tank fire from across the river when they approached some barbed-wire entanglements.

Halliwell noticed that the fire was being directed from the wire and had all his Vickers guns open up on the entanglements and machine-gun emplacements, which substantially reduced the amount of shooting. He and his men also noted the localities of the enemy's automatic weapons for future reference. This done, he withdrew without having suffered any casualties.

Another reconnaissance later that day – this time to check the locations of enemy observation posts which had been spotted on a ridge overlooking the river – had more or less the same result, with the cars being shelled as soon as they came into sight. The cars fired back with all their guns as they withdrew in line astern along the river bank, stopping every 50m or so to fire an accurate broadside, and got back with some fragmentation damage but no casualties. Patrols like these carried on for the next few days, while Pienaar concentrated on massing Pincol at Yonte and preparing for the crossing.

Pienaar's fighting column made good progress toward Yonte. Many reports of enemy activities and movements were received, but no opposition was encountered, though handgrenades were thrown at the anti-tank battery in the column just after sunset on the 16th.

On the morning of 17 February 1941, C Company 1 Transvaal Scottish actually crossed at a drift, landed unopposed at a spot on the western bank called Mesandaro and established a bridgehead. But Pienaar kept to his original choice of the Yonte site, and a ground inspection confirmed it as more suitable for the pontoon bridge – at Mesandaro the river banks were high and steep, and there was a tidal rise and fall of several metres.

When the Brigade reconnaissance patrol arrived at Yonte it spotted some enemy soldiers on the eastern bank. The Carbineers company commander used his initiative and immediately sent two of his platoons across the 200m-wide river in collapsible canoes to establish a bridgehead, which they did after a short exchange of long-range fire with enemy machine guns. C Company 1 Transvaal Scottish now arrived after having been ordered back from Mesandaro and crossed to take over and expand the Carbineers' footing.

That night the bridgehead came under three fiercely courageous attacks by the Italian colonial infantry, who were beaten off with heavy casualties in each case by rifle, mortar and artillery fire and – during the second and third attacks – accurate bursts from 3 Armoured Car Company's armoured cars on the west bank.

Godwin-Austen now ordered Pienaar to make the main crossing at Yonte, establish a bridgehead, cut the Giumbo–Gelib road when Pincol was on the east bank and then clear the enemy out of the Giumbo area. Pienaar's sappers spent the next day, 18 February 1941, preparing the approaches for the pontoon bridge, while a 60-lorry convoy made all possible speed from 12 African Division Headquarters with 19 Field Park Company South African Engineer Corps and the components of the pontoon bridge.The convoy commander happened to be Lieutenant W. F. Faulds who had been decorated with the Victoria Cross for his gallantry at Delville Wood in 1916.

While waiting for Faulds to arrive, Klein says, the Pincol men "took advantage of the lull in operations to have their first real bath and wash for over three months. For a considerable portion of that period they had been limited to a water ration of one gallon per man per day for all purposes."

Faulds and his convoy appeared in the late afternoon, and construction of the bridge began immediately. The engineers worked right through the night and into the next day, and by noon on 19 February 1941 it was almost ready. Godwin-Austen, who had arrived to discuss the general situation with Pienaar, christened it Union Bridge.

By now a small South African force – A Company 1 Transvaal Scottish under Captain A. W. Briscoe – was already moving inland from the bridgehead to sit astride the Giumbo–Gelib road, which ran more or less parallel with the river and about 5,500m from it. Briscoe's company had nearly reached the road when it was subjected to heavy, accurate fire from 193 Colonial Infantry which had come down from Margherita, 29km to the north, with four light artillery pieces and two 20mm Breda anti-aircraft guns.

The Scottish fought back to the best of their ability but made little progress, since the enemy far outnumbered them and were thoroughly entrenched in broken ground. But at 1330 Union Bridge was finished, to the accompaniment of the battle sounds from a few thousand metres away as the Scottish and Italians traded bullets. Then Briscoe's situation improved very rapidly. Klein writes:

> The moment the last plank of the bridge was laid six armoured cars, led by Major Gwillam and Lieutenant H. H. Anderson, proceeded to cross. Following the sound of the fighting ahead, the armoured cars swung at top speed around the southern flank of the enemy and formed up, line abreast, for a fine 'cavalry' attack.
> With machine guns firing on the move, shrouded in the dust of their passing, Gharri Kifaru – the South African rhinoceros cars – fell on the enemy in a splendid charge. In the face of the armoured car attack, the enemy gunners and the colonial infantry broke and fled, leaving a number of dead and wounded, their guns and transport, in the hands of the victorious South Africans.

Over 40 dead and many wounded were found on the battlefield, and many more were carried away by the survivors of the shattered battalion who fell back in disorder through the bush. The 1st Transvaal Scottish had two wounded in the action, the armoured cars none.

The forcing of the Juba at Yonte broke the back of Italian resistance in the Giumbo–Gelib sector.

That same afternoon the Pincol elements which had not yet left Gobwen to move up to Yonte inflicted a telling long-range physical and psychological defeat on the Italian forces manning the other side of the river at Giumbo. As an opening move Lieutenant Halliwell and his platoon moved forward to the river's edge and poured murderous fire into the palm trees and bushes in which the enemy troops were positioned. Then, Klein writes: "At a pre-arranged signal the armoured cars withdrew, and the artillery put down 20 rounds of gun-fire on the same spot. Highly successful results were achieved. The Italian black troops suffered nearly 100 casualties, and they were so shattered by the experience that they evacuated their positions during the night after refusing to fight any longer. Their arms and equipment were subsequently found in their abandoned positions along the river bank."

Thereafter the end came quickly at Giumbo. On the morning of 20 February when the armoured cars, 1st Royal Natal Carbineers and 1st Transvaal Scottish closed in on Giumbo from the north, supported by artillery fire from Gobwen, the enemy had no heart for further resistance. As soon as the artillery opened fire white flags appeared all over the village and the Italian flag was hauled down from the fort.

A party from the Dukes succeeded in crossing the river and received the surrender of Giumbo. The greater part of the garrison was captured, together with 14 guns and much matériel.

At Gelib 1 South African Light Tank Company Headquarters under Captain R. C. J. Anderson was intimately involved in yet another action when it joined 1 and 3 Gold Coast regiments in an unopposed crossing of the Juba at Mabungo about 48km upstream from

Yonte. The expected counter-attack against the bridgehead duly took place, but it was late and lacked enthusiasm because Gelib had been so thoroughly bombarded by the South African artillery by then that the Italian commanders there were convinced that they faced a frontal assault themselves.

Godwin-Austen's plans for Gelib envisaged not a frontal assault, however, but a multi-pronged attack from several directions. 22 East African Brigade and the East African Armoured Car Regiment in its new four-wheel drive South African Mark II armoured cars crossed at dawn on 18 February 1941 and began to plough their way through the thick bush in a flanking movement aimed at cutting the Gelib–Mogadishu road 29km east of Gelib. At the same time 24 Gold Coast Brigade moved down to attack Gelib from the north, detaching one battalion for a simultaneous attack from the west, while Pienaar hit Gelib from the south with the whole of Pincol.

At 1400 on 20 February 1941, only a few hours after the surrender of Giumbo, Lieutenant Halliwell's No. 1 Platoon of 3 Armoured Car Company left Gobwen with the rest of Pincol's advance guard – the Dukes and the 4.5-inch howitzers of 10 and 11 Field Batteries – their immediate destination being the Italian defences at Margherita, halfway between Giumbo and Gelib. They crossed the newly laid pontoon bridge at Yonte an hour later and headed northward.

About 20km later a well-sited Italian position brought heavy machine-gun and artillery fire down on them, and since it was too late to bring up the two artillery batteries before nightfall, the column was ordered to lie over until morning. During the night 10 and 11 Field Batteries arrived, and at first light the advance continued with the guns well forward and ready to go into action.

Initially the column encountered nothing but desultory opposition, which was brushed off without it even being necessary to debus the infantry, but about 6½km from Margherita it ran into strong resistance from a substantial Italian force consisting of two battalions of colonial infantry and two artillery batteries.

The Italians' field pieces were served with "some skill and determination," Orpen says, and their artillery and machine-gun positions were well-prepared and skilfully camouflaged. An additional problem for the South Africans was that although their howitzers immediately came into action, they were hamstrung by the lack of observation points in the thick bush.

Halliwell and one section of his cars solved the problem by deploying into the bush, locating the Italian gun positions and radioing the coordinates back to the column. The South African gunners quickly ranged on the Italian positions and brought down a short but intensive counter-bombardment which soon silenced the enemy artillery and inflicted losses on the infantry.

Up to now B and C companies of the Dukes had been advancing at speed, but were being slowed down by the thick bush, the artillery fire and the machine guns of their well-trained opponents, so as soon as the Italian guns fell silent, Halliwell charged forward unsupported, shot up various machine-gun positions and burst through the enemy defence lines. By 1530 the village was cleared and half an hour later the Dukes occupied it, taking about 500 prisoners and capturing three artillery pieces, 16 machine guns and 20 vehicles of various kinds.

The Carbineers (commanded *pro tem* by Lieutenant-Colonel Gordon le Roux), now relieved the Dukes who were ordered to temporarily occupy an outpost 6½km north of Margherita. The battle plan now was that the Carbineers and Dukes would advance directly on Gelib, while 1 Transvaal Scottish under Colonel Hartshorn, with 1 Field Battery and 3 Armoured Car Company's No. 2 Platoon in support, would swing around and attack from the northeast, cross the road to Mogadishu and join hands with 22 East African Brigade.

At 0500, 22 February 1941, Halliwell and two of his sections set off again on the final leg to Gelib, this time in support of the Carbineers and an engineer party. Just 45 minutes later

Halliwell's armoured cars ran into a company of colonial infantry and opened fire, killing two officers and 20 troops and capturing another three officers and 200 troops. No further resistance was encountered until the column halted at 1000, 5km from Gelib itself. There the armoured cars scouted ahead and had another firefight which led to more enemy casualties and the capture of several machine guns, some prisoners and vehicles full of ammunition and supplies.

1 South African Medium Battery had been systematically pounding Gelib from the west bank and by 1100 an armoured car forward patrol reported that no enemy forces remained there. What remained of Gelib's garrison, 102 Colonial Division – three battalions and five artillery batteries – was in retreat. The bombardment went on until 1320 however – the advance had been so swift that at 12 African Division Headquarters it was believed that there must be some mistake.

The armoured cars now found themselves in yet another role, helping the Carbineers to deal with small groups of enemy soldiers who were roaming the countryside without any clear-cut aim. In one particularly nasty action a group of colonial soldiers under an Italian officer brandished a white flag, but when a platoon patrol of Carbineers came forward to take his surrender the enemy troops ambushed them, killing 13 and wounding seven.

For almost two hours the survivors managed to hold off their attackers, then, when it seemed as if the entire patrol would be wiped out, a section of armoured cars arrived and dispersed the Italian infantry with long bursts of machine-gun fire. One suspects that no prisoners were taken.

Halliwell and his cars got involved in yet another action, this time on the outskirts of Gelib, when they suddenly came under heavy artillery fire from concealed positions only 200m away. Halliwell decided to charge the guns, and with one other car zigzagged through the bush toward them, firing on the move. The gunners had no option but to throw in the towel at this aggressive response, and Halliwell found himself master of a battery of 15-pdr guns, three officers and 30 other ranks.

Halliwell was to be decorated with a field award, the Military Cross, for his gallantry at Gelib, but his spur-of-the-moment charge there also marked the end of his war in Abyssinia. Soon afterward a carefully camouflaged 20mm quick-firing Breda anti-tank gun put six shots into his car, seriously wounding him and one of his crew, a Private Heydenreich. The gun was so skilfully concealed that it was only detected later in the afternoon when another section of armoured cars in the vicinity fired a burst at a suspicious-looking emplacement, upon which the two Italians manning the Breda jumped up and surrendered.

Halliwell's cars were not the only ones to see *ad hoc* close-in action. Second-Lieutenant B. S. Mannion, commanding an old two-wheel drive Mark I car, which was Colonel le Roux's personal scout vehicle, took time off to put to flight a group of Italian troops which was attacking a numerically smaller South African infantry platoon. More action came the way of the No. 2 Platoon cars with 1 Transvaal Scottish, which was still forcing its way across country to cut the Gelib–Mogadishu road. The Scottish had spent the morning 1130 the three armoured cars in the vanguard caught up with the tail of the Italian 196 Colonial Battalion.

The colonial soldiers immediately responded – inaccurately – with small arms, heavy and light machine guns and artillery pieces. Unable to disperse, the cars stood fast and replied with their Vickers guns while a platoon of the Scottish moved forward and some of the other armoured cars gave flanking and overhead fire. This soon ended the resistance, albeit in unexpected fashion, when a chance shot detonated a box of shells in an Italian ammunition lorry full of artillery and rifle ammunition.

The lorry blew up in such spectacular fashion that the entire column had to stand by and wait for the conflagration to die down before it could move on, the Scottish captured four Italian officers, 80 other ranks, four light artillery pieces, four 10-ton lorries, a crawler tractor and some machine guns and rifles in the meantime.

When the impromptu fireworks display had subsided the column resumed its difficult trek and soon afterward laid hands on some distinctly unexpected spoils of war: two Italian officers in a safari car who "drove gaily into the armoured cars at the head of the column," according to Klein. "They had heard that the South Africans had been smashed up at Gelib, and they had received leave from Mogadishu to come to see the fun."

At 1320, when the artillery fire on Gelib finally ceased, the Carbineers entered the position from the south, just ahead of the Gold Coast column which had been advancing from the north. An hour later 1 Transvaal Scottish managed to reach the Gelib–Mogadishu road. Hartshorn and the armoured cars sped north for a few kilometres and made contact with Brigadier Fowkes's 22 East African Brigade.

11 African Division was now across the Juba at Mabunga, thanks to a bridge 35 Works Company South African Engineer Corps had built in terrain so difficult that the sappers first had to carve a 5km track through a veritable jungle just to get to the river bank. At 0600 the next day, 23 February 1941, it set off southward with 22 East African Brigade and 23 Nigerian Brigade under command, bound for Mogadishu.

It was victory, complete and utter. The door to Italian Somaliland – and everything beyond it – had been kicked open in no uncertain fashion. It was true that most of Gelib's garrison had got away – no doubt largely because of that unnecessarily long artillery barrage– but it did not really matter.The entire Italian military structure in the region had disintegrated and thousands of prisoners and great amounts of valuable war material, particularly stocks of precious petrol, had been taken.

"The crushing blows of the 12th African Division had left the enemy in a hopeless position … Whole units were dispersing in the bush," Klein writes, "and the orders and counter-orders of the Italian Command indicated the enemy's extreme confusion." By now, too, the Italian Air Force in Abyssinia had long since largely crumbled into ruin after a sustained campaign by the South African Air Force, and to some extent the Royal Air Force, which had started with that rapid-response raid on Moyale by Major D. S. du Toit within hours of the outbreak of war with Italy.

"The break-through on the Juba had been greatly assisted by the collapse of the Italian Air Force," Klein writes. "In the earlier stages of the battle it had been possible to move only by night and, in spite of all precautions, there had been losses from enemy bombing. But in a short time the South African Air Force had driven the Regia Aeronautica from the skies, enabling the East Africa Force to change its methods and move entirely by day."

Now the time had come to annihilate the wreck of the Italian military in Somaliland by ruthless hot pursuit. Which was precisely what General Cunningham planned to do, having received further orders from General Wavell to capture the port of Mogadishu 400km up the coast and the capital of Italian Somaliland, "provided it does not involve heavy commitment."

Orpen comments that "as operations in southern Abyssinia were now thought never likely to be decisive, General Cunningham was being asked if the South African division could be withdrawn … It was assumed that no major operation except possibly the capture of Mogadishu would be required after the fall of Kismayu. And already it was hoped that quick victory in East Africa might deter Japan from aggression."

But a decisive victory in Italian Somaliland was now very much on the cards. To Cunningham it was clear that the Italians had committed practically all their available forces to the defence of the river, leaving very few assets between the eastern bank of the Juba and Mogadishu. Kismayu was already being cleared and put into running order; if he now captured Mogadishu and the nearby smaller port of Merca (now Marka) as well, he would control all the developed portals to the interior south of Berbera in British Somaliland.

The possibilities were even greater however. "With a cut-and-dried plan, but ready to exploit success to the full," Orpen says, "he was confident that in view of the disorganized state of the enemy, East Africa Force would have to face little resistance between the coast and Harar once Mogadishu was in his hands, and he had time to bring up supplies by opening its port and that of Merca."

Accordingly he had already signalled General Wavell on 22 February 1941 to suggest that he be allowed to continue operations. The rains in Italian Somaliland arrived later than in Kenya, he pointed out, and he believed that by the end of April – six weeks hence – he could take Harar, almost on Addis Ababa's doorstep.

Harar was all of 1,200km away by road to the northwest, on the other side of the Ogaden Desert, but Cunningham calculated that by commandeering transport from units on the Kenyan front he would be able to dispatch three brigades immediately. In terms of speed and distance the advance would be unparalleled in European terms, but this was not Europe and Cunningham was not fighting with European troops. And he was right. On 24 February 1941 General Wavell, himself a great exponent of mobile warfare, authorized the plan, and the East Africa Force started girding its loins to roll northwestward.

Pincol, or 1 South African Brigade, now that the breakthrough was over, took no further part in the operations between the Juba and Mogadishu. Pienaar and his men had acquitted themselves very well indeed, but now the brigade, together with the rest of 12 African Division, was given a breathing space. On 23 February 1941, as Wetherall and his attached brigades sped southward toward Kismayu, Godwin-Austen personally signalled Pienaar: "You have done splendidly, and made far more brilliant progress than I had even anticipated. I hope your troops are heartened by this success … Remember that 11 Div must have their chance, so do not mind if they are chosen to press on to Mogadishu."

12 African Division was tasked to mop up along the Juba, while 1 South African Brigade went into force reserve and was concentrated in the Gelib and Margherita areas – all but 1 South African Light Tank Company, which originally formed part of 11 Division's advance guard, although not for long: "The pace was too hot for the tanks," Klein says, "and they gradually fell to the rear of the rapid advance."

In less than a fortnight the entire strategic picture had changed. Total victory in Abyssinia was no longer a prospect lurking in the middle distance but an immediate possibility, with all that it implied for Wavell's increasingly hard-pressed forces in the Western Desert. This would soon be the arena for desperate battles that had a direct effect on the outcome of the war: Wavell had already advised Cunningham that he wanted General Brink's 1 South African Division to be on standby to leave for Egypt at short notice.

The dominoes of the Italian empire in East Africa now began to topple in rapid succession, with negligible resistance offered to Cunningham's men as they raced up the coastal road. On the evening of 23 February 1941, 22 East African Brigade took Mudun, halfway to Mogadishu, and next morning the small nearby port of Brava. 23 Nigerian Brigade then leapfrogged into the lead and on 25 February 1941 seized the fort at Merca, 75km further.

On 25 February 1941 the Nigerians worked their way through to Afgooye, virtually on Mogadishu's outskirts, seizing what Orpen describes as "immense quantities" of enemy matériel. While they were taking care of this booty an attached East African Armoured Car Regiment patrol sped into Mogadishu itself, having not fired a single shot in anger in the past 32km.

There they dropped off three South African military policemen to secure the telephone exchange and other key points, preparatory to General Wetherall formally entering and taking the surrender next morning. Since leaving Mabungo at 0600 on 23 February 1941, 11 African Division had covered 440km in just 41 hours.

That same day Pienaar's Pincol moved to the Brava area, where it was ordered to block off the road junction at Tassin to prevent an enemy column escaping to the north. On 26

February 1941 Pienaar sent the Dukes to hold Tassin and also relieve 1/1 King's African Rifles at Mudun and Brava. Pincol then bivouacked in the Mudun area and, as Orpen says, "an enemy column south of Brava was gradually collected during the next few days."

Mogadishu declared itself an open city and was spared the destruction of a full-scale assault. The victors were not only spared casualties but were delighted to find that the Italians' withdrawal had been so hasty that they had lacked time to carry out any significant sabotage; there was an enormous amount of booty to be collected, including 1,600,000 litres of petrol, 364,000 litres of aviation fuel, 10,000 rifles and large quantities of war matériel and food.

Sabotage to the tugs and harbour installations was soon put to rights. The only major problem was that the retreating Italians had sown some magnetic mines in the harbour, so that for the time being Merca was used as a temporary base until they could be destroyed.

Just six weeks had passed since the first border crossing at Liboi, and just two weeks since Dan Pienaar's 1 South African Brigade had punched a hole in the Juba Line at Yonte. In that short space of time, as Klein says, "250,000 square miles of enemy territory had fallen to the East Africa Force. The Italian 102nd Division and nearly the whole of the 101st Division had been destroyed. Up to the fall of Mogadishu alone, more than 30,000 men of the Italian forces had been killed, captured or dispersed into the waterless bush."

It was an achievement which has never received its due because it was overshadowed by the great battles fought in the Western Desert a little later. Let Klein have the last word to put it into perspective: "Before the fall of Gelib … Cunningham's advance had been fast enough by any military standards. After the fall of the Jube Line it quickened and developed into a relentless pursuit of a stricken enemy: a pursuit that for speed and distance was unequalled during the war."

But there was no time for East Africa Force to rest on its laurels. The race to Addis Ababa had first to be run.

17

The great race to Addis Ababa

Thanks to the huge amounts of hidden petrol found at Mogadishu – the result of information General Wetherall had gained by paying small bribes to various avaricious Somalis – 11 African Division was now geared to push on boldly to Harar without further delay, "an enterprise," Orpen says, "which in the early days of the war with Italy would have been considered by Middle East Headquarters to be quite impossible without French support from [Djibouti] and a base at Berbera."

Godwin-Austen and 12 African Division, still retaining Major Gwillam's 3 Armoured Car Company, was already on the move, headed into southern Abyssinia by way of Bardera, Lugh Ferrandi, Mandera and Doolow to Neghelli, to the southeast of the lakes region, accompanied and supplied (as would be 11 African Division) by hard-bitten motor transport companies of South Africa's Cape Corps. In rapid succession the Gold Coast Brigade and Gwillam's cars cleared Bardera on 26 February 1941, Iscia Baidoia on the 28th, Lugh Ferrandi on 3 March, and Doolow on the 5th.

By the time Doolow was taken, 11 African Division, reinforced by the attachment of Pienaar's 1 South African Brigade, was already well on the way to Jijiga, Harar and Addis Ababa. Klein writes: "On 1 March [1941] the 23rd Nigerian Brigade and the East African Armoured Car Regiment began their spectacular chase along the Strada Imperiale toward Jijiga. Following Graziani's route of conquest in 1936, the Nigerians raced along the 30-foot wide road, passing abandoned and destroyed Italian transport vehicles, through Bulo Burti and Belet Wen, past the Scillave Wells, north, ever north, at top speed in the wake of the retreating enemy.

The Strada Imperiale faded out but, never pausing, the Nigerians crossed the white sand deserts leading to Fort Degeh Bur, and finally came out on the plains of Jijiga. It was an epic advance of 1,190km in 17 days, over good roads and bad, through minefields and desert sands, against sporadic resistance, but never ceasing and relentless in its determination not to allow the Italians to stand and offer organized resistance until the mountains were reached.

On 17 March advance elements of the Nigerian Brigade swept over the hills and round the wide loop of road leading into the fertile plains of Jijiga to where the Italians stood in fixed defences on the Marda Pass. This headlong advance from Mogadishu not only forced the Italians into the mountains but also brought about their evacuation of British Somaliland on 16 March, which opened up Berbera as the main supply port for Major-General Wetherall's division.

From here on the nature of the campaign changed radically as far as the armour was concerned. The armoured cars' freewheeling light cavalry days were over, at least for the time being. The terrain was quite different now and the East Africa Force was in infantry country. The bush and desert of the Somaliland coastal belt had given way to endless ranks of high mountains of the interior, so that the armoured fighting vehicles had little opportunity to move off the roads and tracks, and it was the infantry and artillerymen who bore the main burden of forcing the Italian defences – although this is not to say that the armoured cars and light tanks did not play a role in the fighting that followed.

The formidable Italian defence line lay along the craggy ramparts of the central Abyssinian plateau, a few kilometres beyond Jijiga. There was no question of outflanking them in this new Abyssinia, a place of steep mountains and narrow winding roads. The Marda Pass would have to be taken, and it would have to be done in the traditional way, with an artillery bombardment to soften up the defenders, followed by an old-style infantry attack.

1 South African Brigade had been following closely on the Nigerians' heels, but only 1 South African Field Battery, 7 South African Field Artillery Brigade and five sections of light tanks arrived in time to take part in the attack on 21 March. Supported by accurate fire from the South African guns, the Nigerians assaulted the Italian positions with bayonets fixed and took them one by one, as Klein says, "in a series of resolute actions fought through the heat of the day and into the cold of the night on the 7,000-foot ranges."

It took just one day's fighting "among the sternest of the campaign," Klein writes – to capture the pass. Although the South African infantry arrived just too late to see combat, C Company of 1 Transvaal Scottish and a detachment of light tanks under Lieutenant J. R. McHarry managed to get a slice of the action by mopping up a flanking position at Goggiar on 22 March 1941, taking 80 prisoners and four artillery pieces.

At this stage Major Gwillam's 3 Armoured Car Company – which was now at full strength, a first since the start of the invasion of Italian Somaliland– had come up from Brava and joined 1 South African Brigade at Jijiga, and as Klein says:

> The difficulties confronting armoured fighting vehicles in the mountains were illustrated by the extensive anti-tank defence at the top of the Marda Pass, which consisted of a huge tank trap cut right across the approaches to the summit, varying from 15 to four feet in depth and from six to eight feet in width.
> The trap was covered by machine guns and artillery and was protected in front by three rows of landmines and barbed-wire entanglements. Even if the armoured cars had arrived in time for the battle they could not have tackled the defences with any prospect of success.
> From now on, until the end of the Abyssinian campaign, the role of No. 3 South African Armoured Car Company was to be limited to road patrols, the provision of armoured cars as mobile machine-gun posts, and general reconnaissance and protective duties. Nevertheless, the mere presence of the armoured cars on a battlefield was of inestimable value because of the very healthy respect they had engendered in Italian minds by their activities farther south.

The Marda Pass was 1 South African Light Tank Company's last taste of action in the advance on Addis Ababa.On 25 March 1941, as the Allies approached Harar, the company became part of the divisional reserve once more, and was earmarked to be sent down to 22 East African Brigade to lend support in the northern part in the harrowing struggle which was to become known as the Battle of the Lakes.

Although Cunningham's advance into the bowels of Abyssinia was going well, the situation in the Western Desert was building up to a crisis in which Wavell's loss of resources to the Greek expedition would bring the Allied forces to the brink of defeat. To reinforce Graziani, Hitler had sent him a well-equipped, well-trained force called the Deutsches Afrikakorps under a general named Erwin Rommel, who had made his name during the Battle of France as a leading exponent of the blitzkrieg style of tank warfare.

Rommel's original orders were to remain on the defensive, but soon after his arrival in late March he went into the attack and unleashed the Deutsches Afrikakorps on the British line at El Agheila, pushing the weakened Western Desert Force back from its earlier gains. An early casualty of Rommel's push – and a telling blow for the Allies – was the loss of General O'Connor, Britain's best desert commander in the Middle East.

He had been recalled from Cairo to advise General Neame, who was commanding what was now called XIII Corps, but by evil mischance both of them ran into a German reconnaissance patrol near Martuba during the night of 7 April 1941 and were taken prisoner.

Harar was Abyssinia's second-most important city.It was defended by two strong positions at the Babilli Gap and the Bisidimo river, 16km east of Harar itself. The Babilli Gap appeared the more formidable of the two, but it was overcome with less difficulty than might have been the case because East Africa Force saw an opportunity for the sort of out-flanking movement that had worked so well further south.

The tactics at the Babilli Gap made use of a known weakness of the Italians that had often been exploited in the immediate past: resolute in defending against frontal attacks from fixed positions, they tended to crumble rapidly if threatened from a flank. There were two obvious approach routes: while the Nigerian Brigade attacked up one of them, supported by 7 South African Field Brigade, 1 South African Field Battery, 1 South African Medium Battery, 1 Royal Natal Carbineers and 11 armoured cars crept undetected up a disused road and then fell on the Italians' northern flank.

This effectively disrupted the Italians' defence planning.

"Although putting up a good defence against the Nigerians on their front," Klein says, "they were rattled into a rapid withdrawal when confronted with the sight of South African armoured cars and infantry coming in on their flank." Covered by accurate artillery fire, the defenders managed to fall back in reasonable order to the second position at the Bisidimo river, 24km east of Harar.

Bisidimo was overwhelmed as well, in spite of another resolute defence in very difficult terrain, and on the afternoon of 25 March 1941 Harar surrendered, yielding 1,000 prisoners and much else, including two batteries of 105mm guns, thousands of rifles and large quantities of war matériel.

At Harar 1 South African Brigade leapfrogged into the lead, leaving 23 Nigerian Brigade (Brigadier G. R. Smallwood) and the East African Armoured Car Regiment to rest briefly on their well-earned laurels, having covered about 1,500km in 30 days at an average rate of more than 50km a day – although the final 100km or so to Harar, through very difficult country in the face of considerable opposition, took three-and-a-half days.

The light tanks, however, did not leave Harar with their fellow countrymen. Petrol was now so scarce that before 1 South African Brigade went on to the next objective the tanks were withdrawn and left to make their way as best they could toward Addis Ababa.

1 South African Brigade's first objective was Diredawa (or Dire Dawa), just over 50km to the northwest through some of the wildest mountain country in Abyssinia. Harry Klein provides a graphic description of what awaited Pienaar's men: "For the first 20 miles the road traverses a well-watered high plateau of rugged hills. Some 25 miles west of Harar these hills fall away in a series of great escarpments, and here the motor road pours, as it were, over the edge of the 7,000-foot tableland and plunges down a 4,000-foot defile in 10 miles of nerve-racking, twisting spirals to Diredawa, hot and mosquito-ridden, at the foot of the hills on the Addis Ababa-Djibouti railway."

It was definitely not armoured car country. The road was perfect for demolitions, and the Italian engineers had made the most of it. They blew up several bridges on the Harar plateau itself, and further on they blasted the mountainside at five of the steepest places in the descent to Diredawa.

One of the craters was 70 yards long, and together the five blow outs formed such a serious obstacle that at first it was estimated that it would take eight days to fill them. However, the 1st South African and 54th East African Field companies (engineers) and the Nigeria Regiment, which was moved up to assist them, attacked the task with such energy that the working day and night they cleared the road in 36 hours.

The Italians might have used the demolitions to make the South Africans pay for every inch of the advance, but on only one occasion did they make an attempt to use the destruction for anything except a means of gaining time. The exception was at the top of the pass, where it

Marmon Herrington Mk2 crossing a pontoon bridge at Bole, East Africa.

MaHe Mk2 on a pontoon bridge in East Africa during the Second World War.

opened up on to the escarpment. There, on the evening of 27 March 1941, two companies of machine gunners which were manned largely by regular officers whose units had disintegrated put up "a really stout resistance for a few hours," Klein says, before 1 Transvaal Scottish forced them to retreat.

But this, too, was nothing more than a delaying action. The Italians had no intention of defending Diredawa; two companies of Transvaal Scottish set out on foot toward the town, while the sappers were still engaged in making the road passable, and when they arrived there on 29 March they entered unopposed.

The Italians retreated from Diredawa in two columns. One took the main route to the next town, Miesso, relentlessly harried all the way by 3 Armoured Car Company and the Carbineers. The other, dogged by the Dukes, took an old Abyssinian road which looped south of the highway through the hill country around Deder and Asba Littorio and then rejoined the main route at Miesso. The pursuers were convinced that they were now on the final leg of the dash to Addis Ababa, and indeed they had reason for their belief. Klein has left yet another graphic description of the situation: "Italian morale had now definitely cracked. Collapse was no longer confined to the colonial infantry: it had spread to the Blackshirt battalions. Evidence of disintegration was everywhere. Demolitions were sometimes deliberately left uncovered; road blocks were abandoned by the covering troops, or otherwise they stood their ground and surrendered. The Miesso–Asba Littorio Line [where the Dukes arrived on 2 April] was abandoned after a mere skirmish. Over 800 prisoners, with four 65mm guns and 43 machine guns, handed themselves over at Deder without a fight."

One major obstacle still lay ahead, though – the Awash river, which ran through a deep gorge, spanned by road and railway bridges, that Klein describes as "the last of the great natural obstacles in the advance on Addis Ababa. The river runs between tall precipitous cliffs, and it was here that the Italians had always planned to make their last stand in defence of the capital … a splendid defensive position."

The Italians had made the most of the natural advantages. On 3 April 1941 they blew up both bridges and constructed numerous machine gun positions on the side of the gorge facing the approach from Diredawa. 1 South African Brigade was not deterred, however, and looked forward to forcing its way over the river for the final advance into the capital. All it needed was fuel for their vehicles, something Pienaar had repeatedly complained about to General Wetherall.

But then Wetherall claimed that it was impossible to refuel the Brigade quickly enough to maintain the momentum of the advance, and ordered 22 East African Brigade into the lead. The South Africans, Klein says, "were justifiably sore at this cavalier treatment." The truth of the matter is now lost forever, but Scrubbs Hartshorn provides a possible clue in *Avenge Tobruk*. In the first 965km of the advance from Mogadishu he writes of 1 South African Brigade:

> ... did little or no actual fighting. Against the Italians, that is. We found ourselves doing plenty of fighting with General Wetherall, whom we soon found most unpleasant. His staff, too, did nothing to endear themselves to the South Africans. Without any attempt to investigate the position they assumed that our apparently large supplies of petrol and rations could have been obtained by only one method – the submission of false returns.
> What, in fact, was the case was that the South African units were so organized that each rifle, mortar or Vickers section had its own truck which carried the men and arms, its entire ammunition supply, its petrol, oil, water and rations, making it independent for long periods at a time.
> It was a system made possible by the large number of trucks with which the South African forces were equipped, but this could not be made clear to General Wetherall and his staff, who persisted in casting doubt on the honesty of our petrol and ration returns. This led to endless bitter quarrels between Dan [Pienaar] and General Wetherall, which lasted to the very end of the East Africa campaign.

Whatever the case, the fuming South Africans were held back while Brigadier Fowkes' 22 East African Brigade went forward on 4 April 1941 to cross the Awash, which they did with great élan. Undeterred by the wrecked bridge and strong opposition from the Italian machine guns, they forded the river at two places and attacked. A short but fierce fight followed, after which the Italians surrendered, having lost a considerable number killed and wounded.

South African sappers immediately started constructing a box-girder bridge over the Awash, which they did in record time, but the brigade did not wait. They found an old Abyssinian drift, manhandled six of the East African armoured cars over the river, hauled them up the precipitous slopes by dint of blocks, tackles and much old-fashioned elbow grease, and then sent them to reconnoitre the next 30km of the road to Addis Ababa.

Next morning 22 East African Brigade set off on the final dash amid great clouds of dust. Thousands of cheering, flag-waving Abyssinians lined the road in the last stretch to welcome them. The occupation did not take place immediately; although the Italian civil administration asked Fowkes to take over without delay because it feared that disorder would break out, but he was ordered to remain outside the town, and the brigade camped on its outskirts.

On 6 April 1941 East Africa Force formally occupied Addis Ababa, albeit without pomp or ceremony. Preceded by a lone East African armoured car flying a homemade Union Jack, Wetherall, Pienaar and Fowkes drove into the city to receive its official surrender from General Mambrini, the Italian chief of police. The Italian flag was struck and the Union Jack hoisted. One day later the South African infantry battalions marched proudly through the streets of the straggling capital.

"They and their comrades of the East Africa Force had made history by their 1,725-mile advance from Bura on the Kenyan frontier to Addis Ababa in 53 days," Klein writes, "against an enemy always numerically superior; the rigours of desert and mountain warfare; the discomforts of sweat and dust and bumping, backbreaking lorries, exhaustion and scanty, tepid water supplies."

Huge piles of arms and equipment were seized by the victors as they spread out through the city and the adjacent airport, where runways were littered with the remains of Italian aircraft destroyed on the ground by the South African Air Force, and lines of vehicles of all descriptions in the transport park.

Thousands of prisoners cluttered the streets and detention stockades. The Italian forces suffered tremendous losses from the time of the opening of the Somaliland advance to the fall of Addis Ababa. In addition to the many thousands killed, wounded and dispersed in the bush, 10,350 Italian and 11,372 African colonial infantry (a total of 22,082 men) had been made prisoners of war by the 11th African Division alone, bringing the total Italian casualties since the crossing of the Juba to well over 50,000. The 11th Division's own casualties for the period of the advance from Mogadishu were under 100 killed.

Busy mopping up on the outskirts of Addis Ababa, No. 3 South African Armoured Car Company did not share in the triumphant entry. Alone, the travel-stained armoured cars and dust-smothered transport lorries, with their happy, black-bereted fighting crews and second echelon personnel, passed slowly through the streets of the city on 8 April and made camp four miles beyond. Theirs was a story of high endeavour, of reconnaissance and patrol, of ambush and attack: the fleet-footed cavalry of the fighting brigade.

But the fall of Addis Ababa did not signal the end of the campaign. It was true that the city was the national capital, but the Italian resistance continued. Klein believes that "after the fall of the capital the Duke of Aosta would have preferred to have surrendered his remaining forces and save further bloodshed, but strict orders from Rome compelled him to continue the struggle and to hold up the transfer of British forces from East Africa to the Middle East for as long as he could."

There were good reasons for this intransigence. That same day, 6 April, a large, well-equipped German force with ample support from Luftwaffe fighters and bombers smashed into Greece.News of Rommel's early victories in the Western Desert had encouraged the Italians in Abyssinia to hold out for as long as possible in the belief that before long the Germans would conquer Egypt and come to their assistance. And so, as Klein writes, "the beleaguered Italian garrisons in Abyssinia took heart again and stood resolute, for a while, in their mountain strongholds."

After withdrawing from Addis Ababa the Italian Supreme Command set up its new headquarters at Jimma, about 250km southwest of Addis Ababa, from where it planned to direct the rest of the campaign. The Duke of Aosta joined his generals there, but was then ordered by Mussolini to fly to the formidable mountain fortress of Amba Alagi, about 525km north of Addis Ababa, and hold it to the end.

The Italian forces were now badly battered and under attack from all sides, both internally and externally. Cunningham's East Africa Force was operating in the central highlands. In the west the entire Gojjam region had risen in support of the Shifta, and Emperor Haile Selassie was marching on Addis Ababa to restore his rule. In the north, British and Indian troops had kicked in the door to Eritrea.

The turning point there had been the battle for the mountain fortress of Keren, an extremely bloody affair for the Allies "against as stubborn an enemy and as forbidding a position as had ever faced a British army." When Keren surrendered the Italians withdrew to the southeast, losing the ports of Asmara and Massawa in the process, and fell back on Dessie and Amba Alagi, where they were joined by the forces retreating northward from Addis Ababa.

Battered though they were, they were far from annihilated or ready to concede defeat. All of their substantial remaining forces were now concentrated in the western sector, with its forbidding mountain ranges and winding roads. In the south, in the lakes and mountains of the Galla Sidamo, the so-called Lakes District, were seven Italian divisions and an estimated 200 artillery pieces. North of Addis Ababa, at Dessie and Amba Alagi, were the substantial forces which had retreated there from Eritrea and Addis Ababa.

Given enough resolution, a drawn-out last stand could be mounted in expectation of the German conquest of Egypt, which seemed likelier by the day. From the British viewpoint, on the other hand, it was quite clear that the Italian presence in Abyssinia must be knocked out completely before all Allied efforts could be concentrated on the Western Desert. As a result, South African forces would find themselves fighting simultaneously on no less than three fronts in the next two months, with the prospect of being shipped to the Western Desert as soon as they were done.

For the officers and men of 1 and 2 South African Motorcycle companies the fall of Addis Ababa brought a variety of tasks far beyond what they had volunteered for. Up to then they had provided a number of different support services to 1 South African Division – such as patrolling its lines of communication during its advance in February and March and providing garrisons for garrisoning El Yibo, El Gumu, Gorai, Hobok and Banno after their capture – before rejoining the division at Nanyuki in mid-March.

It had been gruelling work without much opportunity to see action, but as Klein correctly states:

> Unspectacular though the roles of No. 1 and No. 2 South African Motor Cycle companies may have been in battle (through no fault of their own), there was nothing unspectacular in the feats of endurance performed by their long-suffering personnel in riding hundreds of miles, in intense heat and in torrential rain, over some of the worst roads and tracks imaginable.
> Their round journey of approximately 1,000 miles on the trail of the 1st South African Division, from Nanyuki in Kenya through southern Abyssinia and back to Nanyuki, must rank as one of the most outstanding performances ever registered by motorcyclists in any military operation.

On 19 March 1941, however, East Africa Force Headquarters detached part of 1 Motorcycle Company – three officers, 98 other ranks and 61 motorcycles, under Major R. D. Jenkins – to Addis Ababa for policing and garrison duties. They were to travel on their motorcycles to Mogadishu, and from there would be taken to the Abyssinian capital by lorry.

Major Jenkins' detachment arrived at Addis Ababa on 26 April 1941 after a predictably long and arduous trip, set up its headquarters under the aegis of the new British inspector-general and embarked on its new role, which was to patrol the town, maintain law and order and prevent loyalist Abyssinian patriots from murdering Italian civilians.

That they were crucially necessary could not be doubted. Addis Ababa, like the rest of the country, was awash with firearms, hand grenades and other weapons and munitions. Law and order, never a very powerful influence in Abyssinia, had vanished altogether and left the way open for the traditional national pastime of brigandage, while the generally free-and-easy atmosphere allowed for the settling of numerous old and new scores.

When Jenkins and his detachment rode into Addis Ababa the only law enforcement body was the Ethiopian state police, commanded by a British officer, only 15 days old and composed of completely untrained men. The arrival of Jenkins' men was a matter of life and death, but since most of them were career policemen who had volunteered for war service, they had a great deal of hard-won expertise to apply to their task.

To carry out the plethora of potentially life-threatening tasks 1 Motorcycle Company was re-equipped, the officers with little Fiat cars, and other ranks with Moto-Guzzi motorcycles acquired from the now-defunct Italian police force, plus four recycled Italian armoured cars armed with Breda machine guns. All ranks carried revolvers and Italian light automatic weapons.

One of Jenkins' first tasks was to train an escort for the Emperor Haile Selassie's triumphant return, which took place as scheduled. The detachment handled this historic event with remarkable *sang froid*, it would seem.The detachment's war diary entry for 6 May 1941 records the event such: "Haile Selassie enters city. City is orderly. Extra duty for us."

In the next four months the motorcyclists, although disgruntled by the scanty rations and lack of home mail, found plenty to do. They carried out continuous street patrols, investigated sporadic grenade explosions and gunshots, guarded the airfield, dealt with frequent disturbances and began training the Ethiopian police force's recruits, whose members became so enamoured of their mentors that as a tribute they adopted the black beret as their official headdress.

18

The fall of Amba Alagi

By now 11 and 12 African divisions were paying the price for their rapid penetration of the Abyssinian heartland. In wars throughout history it has always been the case that the farther and faster a victorious army advances, the more difficulty it has in sustaining itself because it outruns the lines of communication on which it depends for supplies and reinforcements. Conversely, its opponent benefits because his lines are greatly shortened.

Thanks to the East Africa Force's high degree of motorization this was less of a problem than it had been for the horse-drawn armies of yore, but the two African divisions were nevertheless in a difficult situation. They had become widely separated, to the point where they were now unable to provide mutual support, and "behind them lay long lines of communication that became even more precarious in the growing intensity of the rains, which started early in April," Klein writes. "There were shortages of everything, from rations to – most importantly – fuel for their thousands of vehicles."

But, shortages or not, they had to subdue the Galla Sidamo's lakes and mountains. And then yet another task was heaped on their shoulders. General Cunningham had envisaged a pincer movement to the Galla Sidamo. Godwin-Austen's 12 African Division and Major-General George Brink's 1 South African Division would advance from the southeast and Wetherall's 11 African Division from the north, with Jimma being attacked by Dan Pienaar's 1 South African Brigade.

This made perfect sense, particularly from the point of view of fuel, since the brigade was already at Abalti on the Omo river, only about 125km away. But the plan was scuppered by the increasingly desperate situation in the Western Desert. A signal from Cairo ordered Cunningham to clear the road northward to Massawa as soon as possible, so that South African troops could be rushed to Egypt as soon as the fighting in East Africa was over.

Cunningham gave this task to 1 South African Brigade, which was to travel northward at all possible speed, force the great Combolcia Pass, capture Dessie and then, in conjunction with 5 Indian Division under Major-General A. G. O. M. Mayne – which had earlier reduced Keren at enormous cost to itself – storm and capture the awesome fortress of Amba Alagi, where the Duke of Aosta was holed up. That done, it would keep on going until it reached Massawa.

It is likely that the news was welcomed by the 1 South African Brigade men, who were engaged in messy general clearing-up operations which were definitely not what they had volunteered for. All semblance of civil order had now disappeared, and groups of Shifta were wandering about everywhere "fighting where they could and looting where they could not fight," Klein writes, "and they were in little mood to differentiate too carefully between British and Italian forces; all white troops were fair game to them at the time – and later."

3 Armoured Car Company's cars in particular found themselves undertaking a variety of small operations to rescue both Italian and Abyssinian civilians from mutilation and massacre at the hands of the marauding Shifta bands.

1 South African Brigade pulled back to Addis Ababa and set off for the steep Combolcia

Pass, just south of Dessie, which was itself about 200km from Amba Alagi. As the long columns of vehicles climbed up into the mountains along the Italian-made roads, the finest Abyssinia had, it became increasingly clear to Sid Gwillam that what lay ahead was an infantryman's war *par excellence*.

It would be fought by way of winding mountain roads which had no space for vehicles to manoeuvre, interrupted by frequent demolitions or obstacles, and in endless hard rain and mist, because the wet weather had started in earnest after the brigade's departure from Addis Ababa. At most his armoured cars would be able to protect infantry reconnaissance patrols and engineer parties clearing the road, carry out forward road patrols and provide general fire support. It was an accurate assessment, although it still left 3 Armoured Car Company with enough scope to perform valuable service in the hard fighting that lay ahead.

On 13 April 1941, just two months after the capture of Afmadu so far to the south, 1 South African Brigade arrived at last light at the Mussolini Tunnel, the gateway to the Combolcia Pass. There it was forced to stop while its sappers cleared away concrete obstacles. While they did so the Duke of Edinburgh's Own Rifles scaled the steep slopes in search of the Italian left flank. The Dukes came under heavy, accurate Italian artillery fire and returned to report kilometres-long defensive positions on the mountains which were manned by thousands of Italian soldiers.

The narrow, twisting road up the pass was heavily mined and covered by artillery, and commanding it were four high, heavily fortified hills whose occupiers included some crack troops who were determined to mount an aggressive defence. Taking the pass promised to be an unpleasant task, and if General Wetherall had his way it would have been even more unpleasant.

According to Hartshorn, Pienaar and his commanders were in a planning session when General Wetherall appeared and demanded that the Brigade attack immediately up the road because he had accurate intelligence that there were no more than 1,769 Italians deployed above them. The South Africans were appalled: "The road ... was a death trap, narrow, winding, fully exposed to artillery fire from both flanks and in front, and with infantry defences running up mountains on both sides to nearly 3,000 feet, with every approach thickly mined."

Pienaar refused, firmly but politely, saying the number of defenders was far greater – it was later shown, Hartshorn said, that the pass was defended by a total of 2,500 Italians and 2,000 colonial infantry, with 800 more Italians in reserve as well as 41 artillery pieces and anti-aircraft guns.

"Wetherall threatened to relieve him of command. Pienaar responded that only General Smuts could do so. Wetherall replied that he would send a signal to Smuts immediately. 'Not on one of my bloody sets you won't,' said Dan in the confident knowledge that the only transmitting sets available were those of the South African Brigade. General Wetherall was speechless ... he swung around and strode to his car. The doors slammed and the car and its armoured escorts drove away. Dan made an unprintable comment and we went back to work."

The attack on the Combolcia Pass is fully described further in this narative. Suffice it to say that Pienaar planned to infiltrate his three infantry battalions into the mountains to his right "a task which imposed fearsome physical difficulties," as Hartshorn says, and involved running a serious risk that the assault force would exhaust its ammunition and then drive home a flanking attack.

For four days the men of 1 South African Brigade clawed their way up the steep slopes under unceasing shellfire, stockpiling supplies and ammunition, soaked by unending sheets of rain and chilled to the bone by the cold of the high mountain nights. On the fifth day the infantry attacked in an unstoppable wave, supported by the brigade artillery, and in spite of a furious counter-bombardment by the Italians, forced them to retreat.

It was a heroic episode which showed that South Africans, while preferring the bushwise way of fighting, would not hesitate to go in with bayonets fixed when the occasion demanded it.

"The enemy's positions were strong, well-sited, and constructed in great depth. Italian artillerymen resisted courageously, and the dominating note of the battle was the strength, accuracy and persistence of the enemy's artillery fire," Klein writes. "By grit and determination the three South African infantry battalions fought their way forward and upward, through valley and ravine, through blankets of machine gun and artillery fire, until they came to the enemy's mountain entrenchments. Combining all the wiles of fieldcraft and manoeuvre, the South African infantry outflanked the Italian defences and carried the heights of Combolcia."

After the pass had been captured "pursuit was impossible," Hartshorn writes. "[The road] was being blown up at every turn and culvert … In the concrete gun emplacements on the ridge Dan and I looked through the sights of naval 3.5-inch guns … Where we had previously stood on the road below we could recognize our men's faces. We wondered why we were still alive."

The victory at Combolcia was, as Klein writes, "particularly satisfying for 1 South African Brigade. It was an entirely South African effort – apart from the work of a small group of Abyssinian patriots under a British officer – in which South African artillerymen, infantry, engineers and signallers proved their superiority in conditions and against positions that favoured the defence.

"It had been a hard fight, but only 10 South Africans were killed and 30 wounded: the enemy lost upwards of 500 killed, and surrendered 8,024 prisoners (of whom 5,258 were Italian) 52 guns of various calibre, 236 machine guns, 40,151 rifles and between 200 and 300 motor vehicles."

No doubt to the relief of the battle-worn infantrymen, Dessie fell five days later on 26 April 1941 without a shot being fired, and on 16 May 1941 1 South African Brigade stood at the threshold of Amba Alagi, which it was to assault from the south in conjunction with an attack from the north by Major-General Mayne's 5 Indian Division.

In the Western Desert the situation had gone from bad to worse in the interim. By now Rommel had pushed Wavell's attenuated forces all the way back over the Egyptian border to Sallum. The only significant British position he had not managed to take was the heavily fortified port of Tobruk, 160km inside Libya.

Rommel was determined to capture Tobruk because its substantial British and Australian garrison constituted a major potential threat to his drawn-out line of communications and supplies. He was so determined that he withdrew most of his front-line strength to concentrate his forces around the port. But Tobruk's garrison maintained an obstinate defence, and each of several German attempts to breach its perimeter failed.

Churchill now addressed Wavell's lack of equipment by sending a convoy codenamed Tiger" to Alexandria, carrying 295 tanks and 53 Hawker Hurricanes; in view of the urgency of the situation he ordered Tiger to sail through the narrow Strait of Gibraltar rather than around the Cape of Good Hope because this would save 40 days of sailing time.

It was a risky decision, given the Axis domination of large parts of the Mediterranean coast, but a necessary one. The Royal Air Force was a vital factor in holding the Axis forces back; the wear and tear Operation Compass had inflicted on so many of 7 Armoured Division's hard-used tanks had many of its personnel deployed on other tasks. Fortunately for Wavell, Rommel had run short of fuel and ammunition as a result of his unexpectedly rapid advance and was in no position to keep moving eastward for the time being.

Amba Alagi was a truly daunting objective, far and away the most formidable yet encountered in the Abyssinian campaign. Essentially it consisted of two huge peaks, Amba Alagi itself and Mount Carassu (nicknamed The Triangle by the South Africans), surrounded by a long range of lesser mountains. In a telling phrase, Carel Birkby called it an "inland Gibraltar." As Klein graphically describes it:

> Towering 10,000 feet into the misty skies, the peak of Amba Alagi was the background setting for the final drama in the collapse of Mussolini's vaunted East African empire. Surrounded by a tumbled maze of mountains, with the Strada Imperiale coiling in fantastic layers of road through the passes, with defences cut through rock and into mountain faces, the fortress of Amba Alagi was all-dominating in that wild piece of country where the Duke of Aosta made his last stand.
> Buttressed by lesser peaks and pinnacles, isolated by abyss and ravine, swept by mist and rain, Amba Alagi was a natural fortress of rare strength and magnificence. Adding to its natural defences, Italian engineers had honeycombed the caves and gullies with gun emplacements and machine-gun nests.
> All road approaches had been prepared for demolition, and at the appointed time great slabs of mountainside were blown to impede the advance. Garrisoned by over 10,000 troops, ringed with machine guns and artillery, with nearly a year's supplies secreted in caves, the Duke of Aosta prepared for a long siege. All the advantages of a defensive battle were in his favour.

Yet it had to be taken. Quite apart from the physical blow it would strike at the remaining Italian presence in Abyssinia and the devastation the capture of the Duke of Aosta would visit on Italian morale, it commanded the Toselli Pass, a miracle of engineering along which ran the road to Asmara.

Pienaar, a veteran of the First World War's great slaughter, had been worrying all the way from Addis Ababa about the prospect that his beloved brigade would suffer massive casualties while taking Carassu, the objective assigned to him; he lost so much weight that at one stage his medical officers had feared he was suffering from stomach cancer.

But he was not, and in the end he applied the solution most obvious to this greatest of all South African artillerymen. "If I can't blow the Italians from the mountains," he said, "then I'll blow the mountains from under the Italians." Which is exactly what he did, and to this day Amba Alagi is among the proudest battle honour to be held by the regiments that took it. Klein describes it thus:

> From the north and south the pincer closed on the fortress. Ceaseless artillery pounding smashed the Italian defences, tore at and sapped Italian morale. By feint and stratagem, by cold courage and resource, Indian and South African soldiers crept ever closer to the enemy. The peaks and ravines echoed and re-echoed to the dull roar of shell and explosive, to the staccato rattle of machine guns, to the hoarse cries of attacker and defender.
> Slowly, remorselessly, valley by valley, peak by peak, the attack was pressed home; by South Africans from the south, Indians from the north, through mist and sleet, through a hail of shot and shell. Fifteen days after the Indians had started their attack in the north, five days after the South Africans had stormed the southern approaches, with his men beaten back into their last lines of defence, with casualties and despair mounting rapidly, the Duke of Aosta sued for an armistice on 16 May 1941.
> A white flag flickered to and fro on the heights. Cheers of victory were wafted in snatches from South Africans, Britons and Indians as they stood on the high mountains, fanned by the winds of Africa, and fanned by the elation of success in the knowledge that a great army and empire had crashed before them.
> On 18 May 1941 the Duke of Aosta accepted the terms of surrender proposed by his besiegers. The next day the defeated remnants of the Italian Army of Eritrea, Addis Ababa and Dessie, and all that was left of the Savoia Division, were accorded the honours of war and filed past a guard of honour to the music of the pipe band of the 1st Transvaal Scottish. They deposited their arms in neat heaps against the grey background of the mountain peaks which bore mute witness to their defeat.

On 20 May 1941 the Duke surrendered personally, and with his staff, marched into captivity.

1 South African Brigade's work in Abyssinia was done, after a "2,500-mile trail of victory through thornbush, desert and great mountain passes," as Klein puts it.

It set off up the road to Massawa that it had helped clear by dint of such great effort. Next stop: Egypt.

With it went Major Gwillam's 3 Armoured Car Company – soon to become 3 South African Armoured Car Reconnaissance Battalion – which had won a shining reputation during that long march, and would add to it in the life-and-death struggles that lay ahead in the Western Desert.

1 South African Divisional headquarters, the divisional troops and 5 South African Brigade had arrived at Suez on 3 May 1941 after an 11-day voyage from Mombasa. 2 South African Brigade sailed from Berbera and joined them on 8 June 1941, and on 12 June 1941 1 South African Brigade left from Massawa.

19

The southern battle for the lakes

The capture of Amba Alagi is so famous in South Africa's military annals that it overshadows the grim and hard-fought struggle which became known as the Battle of the Lakes which was waged by the rest of 1 South African Division in the central Abyssinian highlands, simultaneously with Dan Pienaar's advance on the Duke of Aosta's stronghold in the north.

"The real merit of the battles fought by 11 and 12 African divisions, in the northern and southern sectors of the lakes area respectively, has never been recognized," Klein correctly notes. "The British Broadcasting Corporation referred to them as "minor mopping-up operations," assuming that the occupation of Addis Ababa had virtually ended the East African campaign, [but they were] the most strenuous, the most difficult, and among the most creditable of any undertaken by the East Africa Force."

A chain of seven lakes separated General Cunningham's two divisions in the rugged central highlands. In the north, Ziway, Algato (or Abiata), Langano and Shala lay huddled close to one another. In the centre was Lake Awasa, and in the southwest were two large ones called Margherita (otherwise known as Abaya) and Chamo (otherwise known as Ruspoli).

Between the lakes the Italians had built a myriad strong defensive positions in the mountains and the valleys between them, and in the well-nigh impenetrable forests and along the rivers. Plentiful heavy artillery pieces, minefields, tank traps and demolitions had turned the area into one long potential killing ground, and the Italians' men and guns outnumbered those of the two African divisions by more than three to one. In addition the heavy rains had transformed roads into little more than bogs, and everywhere were bands of Shifta who answered to no law and preyed on all strangers without discrimination.

Short of rations and petrol, tired after months of campaigning, the two divisions were in for "a hard fight indeed, apart from enemy resistance, that was waged for four months in the high mountains, at altitudes of 3,000m and over, in intense cold and ceaseless rain," Klein says.

"Little did the outside world realize at the time the intensity of the Lakes campaign, fought by the Gold Coast, Nigerian and East African brigades and various South African units, including the 1st Natal Mounted Riflemen, 1 Field Force Battalion, No. 1 and No 2 (South African) Armoured Car companies, No. 1 South African Light Tank Company, artillery, engineers, transport and road construction companies, not to overlook the magnificent South African Air Force pilots who flew, mostly in bad weather, over the inhospitable ravines and forests of the battle areas in constant support of the waterlogged ground forces."

This, too, was mainly an infantryman's war, not only because of the terrain but also because the roads had become quagmires as a result of the rain. Nevertheless, 1 Armoured Car Company, which was attached to 12 African Division after 1 South African Division had gone into reserve following the fall of Mega and Moyale, and 2 Armoured Car Company and 1 South African Light Tank Company with 11 African Division, made a notable contribution.

1 Armoured Car Company (Major Klein), operating with 12 African Division, was spread out over a front of nearly 480km in the south, from Neghelli westward to Maji on the farther shores of Lake Turkana. 2 Armoured Car Company (Major Walker) and 1 South African

Light Tank Company (Major Clark), attached to 11 African Division, worked south from Addis Ababa on a concentrated front to Sciasciamana and Soddu, and then northwest to Jimma.

For clarity the movements and adventures of the three South African Tank corps units in the complex operations that followed will be told in two sections, starting in the south with 1 Armoured Car Company.

It will be remembered that after the fall of Mega and Moyale near the end of February 1 South African Division was ordered back to Nanyuki in Kenya and went into reserve, to act as a standby force for General Cunningham and also (although this was not yet official) to refit and reorganize for deployment in the Middle East. But 12 African Division's need for 1 Armoured Car Company's armoured cars was so great that eventually it would have sub-units spread out on detachment all over the divisional front.

The first detachment, in fact, took place before 1 Armoured Car Company had even reached Nanyuki, when No. 2 Platoon (minus one section) was detached en route to support 21 East African Brigade in its attack on Soroppa, a strongly defended mountain position north of Yavelo. Soroppa was garrisoned by the 1,000-strong 61 Colonial Infantry Regiment and protected by efficiently laid minefields that were covered by machine guns and artillery – although, with a remarkable lack of perspicacity in view of the recent experience of Allied tactics, the Italian commander was persuaded that there would be an armoured car attack and focussed his defence on the road to the position.

The result was that he was taken completely by surprise when Soroppa's left flank was overrun by a combined force of infantry and armoured cars. A short, sharp fight ended with 50 enemy killed and 18 Italians and 200 colonials taken prisoner, along with five light mountain guns and a considerable number of machine guns.

No doubt the haul would have been even greater if there had been a full-scale pursuit as the former defenders hastened north toward Alghe, but although the sappers had cleared away roadblocks, tank traps and mines, the off-road going was simply too rugged for the armoured cars to operate freely across country.

But the next action was "a failure which might well have ended in disaster had it not been for the South African Air Force and South African armoured cars." Reconnaissance aircraft located an enemy position in the hills at Giarso, about 80km west of Yavelo, which was reportedly garrisoned by a battalion and a half of infantry and some artillery pieces.

A column consisting of 1 Northern Rhodesia Regiment, a new unit which had not seen much action, 7 South African Field Battery and a section of 1 Armoured Car Company, together with a party of Abyssinian irregulars, set out to attack it on 4 April 1941. The column crossed the Sagan river, in pouring rain that made movement difficult, and spent two days looking more or less unsuccessfully for the Italians' forward positions.

By the early hours of 9 April 1941, however, the column was in place. The battalion commander decided against a flanking movement, and in darkness and rain launched a frontal infantry assault supported by his mortars and machine guns. The first objective was taken, and then a company of 1 Northern Rhodesia Regiment stormed a stone fort on high ground. But it was more heavily armed than anticipated. Under heavy fire for the first time, the Northern Rhodesia Regiment soldiers began to waver after their commander had been killed, and were called off at 1000.

Justifiably elated, the Italians got ready to mount a counter-attack which might well have succeeded, "but their ardour was somewhat cooled," Klein says, "by the appearance of the three South African armoured cars which struggled forward through the mud, and by a ground-strafing attack by South African Air Force Hartebeests."

Another section of 1 Armoured Car Company under Lieutenant A. W. Thompson reached Wajir, was then also temporarily detached for service with 21 East African Brigade, and went back, no doubt amid some grumbling, to Moyale. Meanwhile the rest of the 1 Armoured Car Company men, considerably bush-worn after five hard months, enjoyed a few weeks of relative luxury at Nanyuki which included leave in Nairobi while their cars were attended to; most were in such bad shape that they were simply scrapped and replaced by others, some new and others reconditioned.

By 16 March 1941 the unit's refit was complete, but plans had changed in the interim, instead of heading for the Western Desert, 1 Armoured Car Company would be detached from 1 South African Division and posted to 12 African Division for more service in Abyssinia.

On 22 March 1941 Lieutenant R. D. Meeser fetched five new cars at Nairobi and set off for Lokitaung in western Abyssinia on detachment to 25 East African Brigade, followed a few days later by Captain Guy de Marillac with two more cars. Major Klein struggled to Yavelo through the rain and mud with the remainder of his company and on arrival was immediately told to make ready for two new tasks: to support 21 East African Brigade's attack on an Italian position at Magado and then to join its advance to Alghe.

He was still preparing for the move when the situation changed because a squadron of the East African Armoured Car Regiment attached to 24 Gold Coast Brigade had suffered heavy losses at Uaddara (or Wadara). As a result he was ordered to report immediately to 12 African Division Headquarters at Neghelli with his company headquarters group and 17 other cars. The rest of the company – 12 cars under Captain E. H. Torr, his second-in-command, and Captain R. J. T. Irwin – remained with 21 East African Brigade for the advance to Magado and Alghe.

21 East African Brigade's attack on the well-prepared Italian position on a ridge at Magado on 6 and 7 May 1941 was carried out amid typical rain, mud and mountainous terrain, and taxed the detachment's determination and ingenuity to the utmost. The rain was so exceptionally heavy that although 1/4 King's African Rifles were in position by 30 April 1941 and ready for action as soon as the rest of the brigade arrived, the attack had to be postponed for a week because parts of the road turned into such lethal morasses that vehicles frequently had to be abandoned where they were bogged down.

The intention was that 1/4 King's African Rifles would threaten the Italian left, which held a feature called Brown Hut Hill, while 1/2 King's African Rifles went on a flank march to capture Path Hill, the position's western end. At the same time the brigade's Abyssinian irregulars would make a wide loop to the east around Magado and cut the road to Alghe. Weather and road conditions permitting, three cars under Irwin would give close fire support to the assault on Path Hill and Torr, with three more helping to take Brown Hut Hill.

The chances that the armoured cars would be able to make any sort of contribution seemed slim, but a sceptical Brigadier A. McD. Ritchie nonetheless wrote them into his plan, outlining two alternate roles. If they could manage it, they would advance across country in support of the infantry. If they could not, they were to lend support from the road.

Torr undertook some forward reconnaissance of likely approach routes because he was determined to take part in the attack, but during the night of 5 May 1941 it rained so heavily that it was agreed the armoured cars should not try any cross-country movement.

At first light A Company 1/4 King's African Rifles attacked Brown Hut Hill in spite of a torrential downpour and by 0900 had captured it, but the Italians simply fell back to another prepared position on a ridge to the north, from which they mounted an obstinate resistance. Around 1000 Torr was asked if, the rain having stopped earlier, he could try to reach Brown Hut Hill with some barbed wire for the King's African Rifles and thereafter provide fire support.

Torr set out with three cars, fighting his way through the thick mud and crossing one deep kloof by means of ditching-boards, ropes and sheer hard labour, then detoured around a second and even worse one by enlisting the help of a King's African' section to hack a path through the dense undergrowth and trees. By the afternoon, looking and feeling considerably the worse for wear, he and his cars finally reached Brown Hut Hill.

The King's African Rifles' company commander's immediate concern was the possibility that the Italians would counter-attack during the night.He and Torr worked out a contingency plan: if the Italians did attack, the cars would emerge and sweep the area with their spotlights. Torr reconnoitred a suitable route and then stood down.At 0230 the company commander's fears were realized when bursts of small-arms fire broke out.

As prearranged, Torr's cars emerged, drove off the attackers with their Vickers guns and withdrew again. A little later there was another attack, which the cars drove off as well. This time the cars lost their way in the dark when returning to the King's African Rifles' position, and the company commander braved the continuing machine-gun fire to lead them back on foot.

Nothing further happened at Brown Hut Hill, but at first light Irwin – who had meanwhile struggled forward on the road – was called in to give supporting fire for a successful attack on the Italians' left flank, although roadblocks and mines prevented his cars from anything more mobile. The King's African Rifles then proceeded to take Magado as planned, and Torr provided escorts and patrols as the brigade continued up the road to Alghe and Giabassire.

21 East African Brigade advanced no further, however, due to petrol shortages and supply difficulties, except for a small infantry group which occupied Dilla on 17 May 1941, and then withdrew to Yavelo. Torr was then attached to 25 East African Brigade at Mega, but his detachment had a quiet time of it and eventually returned to Nairobi, where his detachment handed in the cars and equipment before going on leave, pending departure to the Middle East.

Klein's group had an equally difficult time fighting with the mud along the 230km trek north of Yavelo to Neghelli, although he'd had the foresight to lay hands on a small lorry-transported crawler tractor which eased his lot somewhat. The road had been wrecked to such an extent by the unceasing rain that the wheels of supply columns, without his scrounged tractor "would not have got through before the dry season.

"All went comparatively well on the first day of the move, during which 77 miles were covered. On the second day every vehicle in the long convoy, armoured cars and lorries, had to be dragged individually by the tractor through long stretches of mud, in some places over three feet deep. A cold, wet and cheerless group of armoured car men rested uncomfortably that night on the roadside, after covering only 45 miles. An equally gruelling third day, in which 31 miles were covered, brought the detachment to Neghelli."

General Godwin-Austen immediately sent Klein with his headquarters and one platoon on to Uaddara, 45km further north, where 24 Gold Coast Brigade, under Brigadier Richards, was engaged in a long, grim struggle with a tenacious Italian defending force. Uaddara was a natural stronghold, famed in recent local history as the place where a lightly armed Abyssinian Shifta force under the renowned Ras Desta had held off a large Italian force for 11 months in 1936.

Now the Italians had the advantage of those same natural strengths that had foiled them five years earlier, and had garrisoned Uaddara with a battalion of Blackshirts, five battalions of colonial infantry which had been strengthened by an infusion of some of their veteran Eritrean troops, and 12 field pieces.

"The precipitous slopes of Uaddara [lay] beyond a great ravine through which ran the road from Neghelli to the north," Klein wrote. "The Italians held a three-mile front to the depth of four miles, based on mountain ridges and dense forest. This forest dominated the battle of Uaddara: it hid the dispositions of the Italian forces and limited the use of aircraft, artillery and armoured cars.

"Many desperate encounters were fought out in the confusion of its depths and in the even greater peril of its occasional open glades. By the end of the operation the forest of Uaddara was a charnel-house of death. It reeked with the stench of decaying bodies – human and animal – which lay, bloated and unburied in its tangled web. The battle of Uaddara lasted for three weeks, and was the most prolonged and stubborn of the whole campaign in southern Abyssinia, for the most part fought in driving rain and bitter cold."

In the initial phase of the struggle, which ended in the third week of April, 3 Gold Coast Regiment, supported by artillery and a squadron of the East African Armoured Car Regiment, managed to drive the Italians from their outposts and back to their main defence line. The second phase consisted of 10 days of constant patrolling through the kloofs and almost impenetrable forest to plot the flank positions and strength of the garrison.

It was during this phase that the Italians scored their only major success against the Allied armoured cars in East Africa, the reason why 1 Armoured Car Company's orders were changed so drastically on Klein's arrival at 12 African Division. The direct cause of it was that the East African armoured cars had not yet learned how fundamentally the nature of the campaign had changed and had committed the literally fatal military mistake of under estimating their adversaries.

Emboldened by the success of their carefree tactics to date, a troop of East African armoured cars deployed in a glade opposite an Italian strongpoint. Not taking the precaution of finding hull-down positions from which they could cover the infantry advance in fair safety, the three armoured cars stood their ground in the open and brought their fire to bear on the enemy to their front.

Within a few minutes the three cars, and all their crews within, had been destroyed by artillery firing at point-blank range over open sights. When captured by the South African armoured cars a few weeks later, the Italian artillery officer who had been responsible for the disaster to the East Africans at Uaddara apologized with genuine regret for what he described (in good English) as "shooting sitting ducks."

1 Armoured Car Company arrived in time for the last phase of the struggle for Uaddara, which started on 3 May 1941 and ended on the 10th. This phase saw the opening of the attack, a frontal assault with simultaneous flanking thrusts on either side. Due to the terrain there was little work for Klein's cars during the central assault, but the two sections he deployed for the flanking attacks – under Staff Sergeant C. W. Hallowes on the right and Staff Sergeant E. H. Hangar on the left – provided covering fire for the infantrymen advancing through the jungle.

The Italians fought hard for seven days, but by the morning of 10 May 1941 they had evacuated Uaddara and withdrawn in the direction of Adola. Such rapid pursuit followed that 1 Gold Coast Regiment caught up with the Italian rearguard and attacked it. The Blackshirts fixed bayonets and counter-attacked, but lost and suffered many casualties.

The Italians resumed their withdrawal with the brigade still hot on their heels, heading up the winding road of the 3,350m-high Afrara escarpment toward Hula. Brigadier Richards knew that a strong Italian force was dug in at Hula and hoped that by keeping up the pursuit he would be able to avoid another drawn-out pitched battle, although he was painfully aware that there were difficult road conditions ahead and that transport difficulties to his rear had left him short of petrol and supplies.

But the commander of his company-strong advance guard, a Captain Styles, shrugged off these fears and set out at a rapid clip, his column led by four of 1 Armoured Car Company's armoured cars under Lieutenant E. J. W. Rees. No doubt Rees was imbued with the same gung-ho spirit. Rees was actually 1 Armoured Car Company's adjutant but had long yearned to command a platoon in action and had finally achieved his ambition when he was posted to the advance guard.

"For three days the convoy of open lorries, packed with cheerful Gold Coast troops, was led on its tortuous course, up hill and down dale, through dense, rain-drenched jungle, through swamp and morass, by the four South African armoured cars.

"Road blocks, blown causeways and bridges were encountered and quickly dealt with. The road was strewn with evidence of the hasty Italian retreat. Dead donkeys, mules, horses and camels, and overturned trucks blocked the way. Every conceivable item of Italian equipment, including personal kit, rifles, guns, thousands of rounds of ammunition and mortar bombs had been cast aside by the demoralized enemy.

"The constant hauling, towing, pushing and pulling of bogged vehicles was accelerated and forgotten when the column came upon a convoy of thirty-three Italian 10-ton lorries, abandoned in axle-deep mud, on a section of the road passing through treacherous marshland. The road was completely blocked for nearly a quarter of a mile, and the retreating Italians must have thought with satisfaction that this obstacle would hold up the pursuit for days.

"How badly they had miscalculated the calibre of the men chasing them was proved by the fact that the armoured cars and Gold Coast lorries were bumping their way across the morass within four hours, over a runway made of the stout wooden bodies of the abandoned Italian trucks.

"Not a single man-made road block was encountered the whole of the next day, further evidence of the Italians' mistaken faith in the pursuit-retarding efficacy of the natural mud traps."

On the third night the advance guard's soldiers slept in the rain at the foot of another escarpment while Styles and Rees considered what to do next. They had not yet caught up with the Italians and now petrol was running very low. They decided on a solution which was radical, not to say daring to the threshold of foolhardiness.

They would leave the bulk of the advance guard where it was until the petrol supplies caught up with it, and in the meantime press ahead with just Rees' armoured cars and three lorries carrying 60 infantrymen; the 17 armoured car crew members brought the total of Styles' little force to seventy-seven.

"Then followed," Klein writes, "the most remarkable exploit of any in which South African armoured cars participated during the entire Abyssinian campaign."

"At first light next day the now reduced column set off again, the convoy ploughing through the mud. After an hour of sunshine a mist descended, and the column groped its way forward into the gloom of a forest. Suddenly the mist lifted, to reveal to the astonished pursuers that they were in the middle of a group of 500 Italian colonial infantry, squatting alongside the road having their breakfast.

"The enemy troops gave only a casual glance at the armoured cars and trucks and continued with their meal, not crediting for a moment that their pursuers had caught up with them. Taking in the situation at a glance, Captain Styles dismounted from the armoured car in which he was travelling, strode over to a group of Italian officers, and informed them they were his prisoners.

"Startled, but not quite sure of the turn of events, the Italians started a heated argument with Captain Styles, demanding to know where the rest of his troops were. Pointing airily into the mist behind him the young Gold Coast officer assured them of the very strong support he had coming up behind.

"While this altercation was taking place, Lieutenant Rees noticed some mounted Italian cavalry officers dashing up a hill to his right. Without hesitation he followed them quickly with three armoured cars, and arrived on the hilltop in time to see them galloping after a troop of mules loaded with mountain pack-guns, being driven over a rise a few hundred yards ahead.

"It was a race between the armoured cars and the horsemen. Would the armoured cars be in time to prevent the mules being unloaded and the guns brought into action? This was the burning question in Lieutenant Rees' mind as he urged his driver forward. A hundred yards from the crest his car stuck on the muddy road. It was reversed, and with a roar of the engine and madly spinning wheels it reached the top on the second attempt, to find the mules being unloaded.

"The pack-guns and shells were already on the ground, but the armoured car had arrived just in time. Without further ado the battery commander surrendered his guns. This was the same officer who had destroyed the three East African armoured cars in the forest glade at Uaddara."

Styles and Rees now set off on the next phase of their lone assault on Hula. Leaving one car to watch over the artillery pieces, Styles, Rees and the latter's four cars headed for the Italian brigade headquarters, where they presented themselves to some understandably bemused staff officers.

"The Italian officers … blinked unbelievingly, turned away and looked again. They could not credit the reality of the situation. Were the armoured cars not German? They asked. When assured to the contrary, they tried again: Were the South Africans not trying to give themselves up?

"On being informed that this was not the case and that further argument was useless, pandemonium broke loose. A little bearded major jumped up and down, gesticulating wildly and screaming imprecations at all and sundry.

"Leaving one of his cars to guard this group, Lieutenant Rees drove forward to find the brigade commander, a bewildered colonel, who climbed into the car and drove down the hill with him to where the Italian infantry were already stacking their arms under cover of the armoured car which had remained behind with Captain Styles.

"When Captain Styles came forward to accept the colonel's surrender the latter realized what had happened, and that his rearguard officers had been taken in by a colossal bluff. The almost demented Italian colonel raved and swore, shaking his fist at his officers.

"The situation was tense. An itchy trigger finger could have sparked off the massacre of the Gold Coasters and the South Africans. But within an hour the tension lessened, as company after company of Italian troops marched out of the forest to lay down their arms. In all 1,400 Italian troops surrendered, with their pack artillery, without a shot being fired, to Captain Styles' 77 men."

Styles and Rees were still in a ticklish situation, but while they had been engaged in their colossal bluff, petrol supplies from the brigade headquarters finally reached 1 Gold Coast Regiment's main body, and now the West Africans caught up and took over the advance guard's prisoners. After refuelling the advance guard's vehicles and Lieutenant Rees' four armoured cars, Captain Styles set off without delay for Hula, before the estimated 2,000 enemy troops there received warning of the débâcle in their rear.

"The sun was sinking when Hula came into sight. The slow pull up the long hill leading to the fortress was another test of nerves for the men of the Gold Coast detachment. Unchallenged by enemy fire, the four armoured cars halted midway between two hills whose fortified crests were not 200 yards apart. With great aplomb, Captain Styles dismounted from the leading car and strode over to a puzzled group of Italian officers.

"If the first Italian force had been astonished by the events of the morning, the Italians at Hula were dumbfounded. The air was electric with suspense. Italian officers crowded around Captain Styles. After a while he left the hysterical group and walked back to the armoured cars, coolly telling Lieutenant Rees that the Italian commander had said it was beneath his dignity to lay down his arms to such a junior officer, and in any case, before doing so, he wanted an order in writing from his brigade commander – the incoherent colonel who had surrendered to Captain Styles earlier in the day.

"Captain Styles said he had told the Italian commander that it was not his habit to carry bits of paper about with him, and that if the Italians did not surrender within 10 minutes the armoured cars would be ordered to open fire and over-run them. Almost interminably those ten minutes dragged by. Captain Styles walked forward again, under cover of the armoured car guns, to receive the reply to his ultimatum."

"It was almost dark. But it was still light enough to see the enemy swarming from the defences on all sides to pile their rifles, machine guns and ammunition in front of the armoured cars. Over 3,000 prisoners had been taken that day, without a shot being fired. But the finale of this extraordinary adventure was yet to come." Lieutenant-Colonel Bruce [officer commanding 1 Gold Coast Regiment and the column commander] ordered Rees and 1 Gold Coast Regiment to head at all possible speed for Uondo (or Wondo), a few kilometres up the road, and force the Italians there to surrender while they were still off-balance.

At 0700 1 Gold Coast Regiment, with Styles and Rees in the lead, set off for Uondo. According to the Brigade intelligence section they would be coming up against a famous Italian cavalry regiment which could be expected to make a fight for the town, but for a few hours they made steady progress with no sign of the enemy except small bodies of soldiers coming down … waving white flags.

They climbed to the top of the Rift Valley escarpment, took in the view and then began the descent, looping downward through one hairpin bend after another as the road followed the contours of the escarpment's slopes, 915m down to Uondo – ideal ambush country. The standard tactic for a situation like this was to exercise maximum caution, but that luxury was thrown to the wind in the interests of maximum speed.

"With tension mounting, particularly in the forward car in which Lieutenant Rees led the way, the four armoured cars nosed their way round each bend, increasing speed on the open sections of the descent. The crews expected to be fired upon at any moment. A clash had to come, and all knew it.

"Swinging around a corner, without warning of anything ahead, Lieutenant Rees almost collided with the rear of an Italian armoured car, one of two, travelling slowly downhill toward Uondo. The Italian vehicles mounted wicked-looking anti-tank guns in their turrets – subsequently found to be Vickers 37mm cannon.

"Fortunately, the Italians had not heard the approach of the South African armoured cars in their rear and their guns were pointing downhill. With frantic but belated efforts the Italian crews attempted to swing their turrets. But, before they had a chance to do so, Lieutenant Rees ran his car alongside the rear Italian car, blocking the traverse of its turret with his own, at the same time bringing his turret gun to bear on the second car in front of him. Without pretence of resistance the Italian crews thereupon leaped to the road and surrendered, in spite of their superior armament.

"Pausing only long enough for an infantry guard to be mounted on the Italian vehicles, the South Africans continued on their way. A little farther on they drove into a company of colonial infantry supposedly guarding the outskirts of Uondo. The Italian company commander was so surprised at being overrun that he surrendered without a fight, although his anti-tank guns were manned and ready for action.

"He explained that he had expected to receive warning of an enemy advance from the two Italian armoured cars he had sent out on patrol along the mountain road. At first he thought Lieutenant Rees' cars were his own returning … Lieutenant-Colonel Bruce then ordered the armoured cars, closely supported by Captain Styles' company, to dash into Uondo and force the Italian surrender.

"The streets of the straggling town were crowded with a milling mob of Italian troops, who gaped in amazement at the South African armoured cars which suddenly appeared in their midst. They offered no resistance and waited patiently to be told where to stack their arms."

Uondo yielded 600 Italian troops, a battalion of colonial infantry, seven armoured cars, 100 lorries, a complete hospital, large stocks of food and some medical and ordnance stores – a rich haul, particularly considering that not a shot had been fired in anger or otherwise.

The headlong advance continued that same day, only to come to a reluctant halt 5km north of Uondo, when the column reached the Falla river and found that the bridge over it had been demolished. There they met up with the leading elements of 11 African Division's 22 East African Brigade, a platoon of 2 Armoured Car Company's reconnaissance cars and B Company of Lieutenant-Colonel J. R. Wocke's 2 Field Force Battalion, which were reconnoitring in search of Italian strongpoints that now no longer existed.

It was a historic moment. 11 African Division's main body was only about 10km north of the Falla; after months of fighting on separate fronts the two African divisions had joined hands once again. Now, as Orpen says, "the road from Nairobi to Addis Ababa was open – rain permitting."

"The seemingly impossible task of attacking the southern Abyssinian highlands at the height of the rains had been accomplished," Klein writes. "The enemy, now a disorganized mass of men, mules and guns, was struggling and slithering away through the rain-soaked mountains toward the northwest, where the 22nd East African Brigade was moving to close the escape route through Soddu to Jimma (or Gimma) and the far west."

For all practical purposes the bloodless capture of Uondo had finished off the Allied task in the highlands. The Shifta revolt, which had started so inconspicuously months before when Klein had taken Robi to his home base at Hadu Mountain, was now bearing terrible fruit. At Hula, Klein and Brigadier Richards watched a veritable horde of Shifta marching down to Addis Ababa, pausing to slaughter hundreds of Abyssinian civilians who had cooperated with the enemy, and promising the same fate for any Italians they encountered.

Within a few days of Uondo's capture came the fall of Soddu, an important road-junction to the east on the road to Jimma "and the situation of the 21st and 24th Italian divisions struggling back toward Jimma became not only hopeless because of British pressure, but perilous because of Shifta ambushes, murder and pillage along the sodden roads," Klein writes. "Mass Italian surrenders were the order of the day, and the enemy front collapsed completely."

The collapse was so complete, in fact, that the Italians were reduced to begging their erstwhile enemies for protection: "Over the wireless waves there crackled an urgent appeal from General Pralorma, stuck fast in the mud west of Soddu, with his bedraggled troops desperately fighting to ward off horrible death and mutilation: an appeal to the British for succour from the Shifta, fast closing in, imbued with only one thought 'Kill!'"

For the time being there was an uneasy quiet in the Western Desert. The Tiger convoy had arrived at Alexandria on 12 May 1941 with 238 tanks and 43 Hurricanes, the others having been lost when one of its ships was sunk by a mine. Unloading the tanks took longer than expected and their first stop was at the base workshops to be overhauled and modified for desert warfare. In addition 7 Armoured Division had to be divested of its other tasks, re-equipped, reorganized and retrained. All of this meant that Wavell's full counter-attack, Operation Battleaxe, would not be possible until 10 June 1941.

This did not immediately affect the operational situation, because on the same day as Tiger's arrival Lieutenant-General Friedrich Paulus of the German general staff was present at one of Rommel's attempts to capture Tobruk and subsequently signalled the Oberkommando der Wehrmacht (the German forces high command), pointing out Rommel's critical shortages of both fuel and ammunition.

The Oberkommando der Wehrmacht was then gearing up for Operation Barbarossa, its invasion of the Soviet Union, and Rommel was told not to attack Tobruk again or launch a further advance; instead he must hold his position and conserve his forces for the time being.

Since the British Ultra deciphering programme had broken the German codes, Paulus' report landed on Prime Minister Winston Churchill's desk as well, and so firmly convinced him that an immediate advance in strength would dislodge Rommel from his gains that he ordered Wavell to do the necessary.

Wavell hastily prepared a limited operation, codenamed Brevity, to be commanded by Brigadier William 'Strafer' Gott of 22 Guards Brigade. Gott was tasked to recapture Sallum, the Halfaya Pass and Fort Capuzzo, thereafter advancing as far toward Tobruk as his supplies would permit and destroying as much Axis equipment as possible without going out on a limb. This would secure a foothold for Operation Battleaxe, which was to be launched when 7 Armoured Division had been re-equipped.

Brevity began on 15 May 1941 and at first was on schedule. But without enough armour it was doomed to failure. When Fort Capuzzo and the Halfaya Pass had been captured, Gott pulled almost his entire force back to the Halfaya Pass because he had become concerned that 22 Guards Brigade faced annihilation if the German tanks attacked it out in the open. On this unsatisfactory note Brevity ended on 17 May 1941 with only the pass solidly in British hands – but not for long, on 27 May the Germans took it back.

The last days of May brought more bad news: Crete fell to the Germans and Italians after a ferocious struggle, including a parachute attack which resulted in such heavy casualties that the Wehrmacht never again dropped its airborne troops directly into battle. But that was small consolation. Thousands of Allied troops were evacuated to Egypt to fight on, but thousands more were captured and thus lost forever to Wavell, along with great amounts of weapons, equipment and supplies.

Even worse, the Luftwaffe now had possession of more airfields from which to attack Allied shipping, protect the Germans' own convoys and support their forces in Cyrenaica. To the British imperial general staff there was only one solution: Battleaxe must be launched as soon as possible to recapture the area between Sallum and Derna so that the air force could operate from there.

1 Armoured Car Company was not quite done with the highlands after Amba Alagi. The Italians might have been defeated, but that part of Abyssinia had relapsed into total chaos, with bands of Shifta roaming around in "a blood-bath of primitive passions, unleashed in sordid looting and killing against friend and foe alike. British and South African supply convoys, road parties and isolated outposts became favourite targets for these rebel groups," Klein writes. So after the fall of Soddu the company sent out patrols almost on a daily basis from the provincial capital of Dalle (now Yirga Alem), the Gold Coast Brigade's headquarters, to protect service units from the robbers.

By mid-June 1941 the supply situation had deteriorated to such an extent because of the dreadful weather conditions and impassable roads that practically the entire Gold Coast Brigade was immobilized because its petrol supplies were exhausted and its troops subsisting on short rations.

1 Armoured Car Company's sojourn at Dalle was now almost at an end. On 20 June 1941 Harry Klein, with one armoured car and a 3-ton lorry, escorted Brigadier Richards back to 12 African Division Headquarters at Neghelli – where Godwin-Austen complimented him on the work the South African armoured cars had done while attached to the division – before carrying on to Nairobi.

There Klein was ordered to reassemble his unit from the various parts of Abyssinia where the war had taken them, and then head for Massawa to take ship for the Middle East. This was easier said than done, and several weeks passed before he could get them all together and undertake the long road trip to Massawa.

Captain Torr reported in at Nairobi with his detachment, lieutenants Penny and Rees brought in No. 1 Platoon from central Abyssinia and Neghelli, and Captain De Marillac and

Lieutenant Meeser arrived with their detachment from Lokitaung with harrowing tales of their attachment to Brigadier Owen's 25 East African Brigade in the far west of Abyssinia.

Brigadier Owen had been tasked to occupy Maji and combine forces with the Sudanese Equatorial Corps to close on Jimma from the south and cut it off. Thanks to the rains the brigade did not get to blockade the southern approach to Jimma but managed to clear southwestern Abyssinia of the enemy.

In spite of flooding that restricted the armoured cars from full use they succeeded in accompanying 2/4 King's African Rifles to Maji in spite of virtually impossible road conditions and occupied it on 21 April 1941, but were then hamstrung by lack of fuel, not to mention endless torrential rain that brought the entire force to a standstill for a month. After the force finally extricated itself, De Marillac spent some more time patrolling in the untamed countryside near Lake Rudolf; more than 60 percent of his men suffered from malaria while in the west.

But now, at last, 1 South African Armoured Car Company's work in East Africa was done. On 15 August 1941 the company sailed from Mombasa on board the troopship *President Doumier*, bound for Suez and the Western Desert.

20

The northern battle for the lakes

Much had happened to 2 South African Armoured Car Company and 1 South African Light Tank Company before 2 Armoured Car Company's forward platoon met up with its colleagues from 1 Armoured Car Company at the Falla river in mid-May 1941. As it turned out, the northern sector of the Battle for the Lakes was as arduous and eventful a campaign as 12 African Division's in the south had been.

After the fall of Addis Ababa the Italian high command assembled a powerful mobile column of infantry, tanks and artillery at Sciasciamana (Shashamana) near Neghelli, under command of a General Bertillo. Bertillo was tasked to recapture Adama on the Harar–Addis Ababa road, and General Cunningham took this threat very seriously.

If Adama fell into Italian hands, even if only temporarily, it would disrupt 11 African Division's tenuous line of communication with the south, on which it was entirely dependent for fuel and other supplies. This, in turn, would disrupt the vitally urgent task of clearing the road to the port of Massawa to allow the dispatch of troops to the Western Desert to help fill the gap left by the disastrous expedition to Greece.

The appearance of Bertillo, who was reputedly a resolute fighter, came at a bad time for 11 African Division. Already deprived of 1 South African Brigade, it had been weakened even more by the need to drop off contingents at various places it had captured, and its supply situation was none too healthy. In addition, there was also an urgent requirement to exert some sort of control over the large numbers of Italian troops still at large south of Addis Ababa.

The task of meeting and defeating Bertillo's column was given to Brigadier Fowkes' 22 East African Brigade although he was not only short of supplies but had less than 1,500 all ranks available. To swell his numbers, two of 2 South African Brigade's infantry battalions – 1 Natal Mounted Riflemen and 1 Field Force Battalion – were recalled from Berbera in British Somaliland, where they had been awaiting shipment to the Middle East.

These additions would eventually be a powerful boost to Fowkes' force (known as Fowcol for the purposes of the operation) but even at its maximum size it never exceeded 6,000, a fairly modest number for the task it had been given, and it would take time to gather all his support assets, which were scattered far and wide – time he could not afford. As it was, it was a small miracle that he had any armoured support at all, given the problems 2 Armoured Car Company and 1 Light Tank Company experienced simply in reaching him.

It will be remembered that due to a lack of petrol the light tanks had been dropped from 1 South African Brigade before the advance on Diredawa and told to get to Addis Ababa as best they could. In spite of Major Clark's efforts he could find no one willing to take on his tanks' fuel problems. Then salvation came from an unexpected source: General Wetherall, who personally intervened to see that Clark was given enough petrol to get to Adama, where Brigadier Fowkes was preparing to move to Aselle.

By 11 April 1941 the company had managed to reach Adama, and Wetherall gave Fowkes permission to take one section of tanks with him if he could find the necessary fuel. Fowkes agreed, and Major Clark went back to Wetherall and parlayed this small advantage into the attachment of the entire company to 22 East African Brigade at Aselle on 13 April 1941.

2 Armoured Car Company joined up with Fowcol by an even more roundabout route. After the capture of Mega in February the company had returned to Nanyuki for refitting, pending its departure to the Western Desert, but when this was complete Major Walker was ordered instead to take the company, minus Lieutenant J. B. Dunning's No. 3 Platoon, to British Somaliland with all possible speed to assist in recapturing the territory. Dunning, meanwhile, was sent to Mombasa to travel to British Somaliland via Berbera.

Marmon Herrington Mk2 and a truck of 1 Armoured Car Company stuck in the mud after heavy rains in East Africa.

After a trek of more than 2,200km Walker arrived in British Somaliland to find that the reoccupation was a *fait accompli*, and eventually he and his men ended up at Harar on 3 April 1941. Then, just two days later, he was ordered back to British Somaliland to be based at Hergeisa for mopping-up operations in the territory and along the eastern Abyssinian frontier – minus No. 1 Platoon and a three-car section under Captain C. A. C. Saunders, which were to stay behind at Harar. Saunders' section was the first 2 Armoured Car Company component to reach Fowcol, arriving there in the company of 1 Natal Mounted Riflemen; they were later relieved by Captain Heard and No. 2 Platoon.

Major Walker left immediately with the rest of the company and duly reached Hergeisa, *en passant* routing a Banda force 32km from Jijiga, while Dunning's No. 3 Platoon went off to Mombasa. After they got there it was discovered that Berbera did not have the facilities for off-loading heavy vehicles, so they were sent off on the long overland journey to Hergeisa, where they eventually arrived, as Klein puts it, "in dribs and drabs."

Fowkes had two potential routes of advance: by way of the Ponte Malcasa bridge to the east of Lake Ziway, or from Mojjo through Bole to the west of the lake. Ideally, of course, a simultaneous movement along both routes would have served best to disrupt General Bertillo's plans by forcing him to fight on two fronts, but Fowkes' paucity of troops and armour left him without that option.

His choice – necessarily a gamble in the absence of accurate maps – was to go east of Lake Ziway. On 9 April 1941 Fowcol crossed the Awash river south of Adama and reached Aselle later the same day with his section of light tanks. But then it became clear that through no fault of his own he had made the wrong choice. Unrelenting rain meant that the gravel surfaces of the road soon turned into one long swamp. The light tanks could get no further than a few kilometres south of Aselle, and by mid-April Fowcol's main body was stuck fast on the 3,660m-high passes of Mount Carra-Cacci, south of Bocoggi.

Fowkes realized it was hopeless, and by 24 April 1941 had pulled his entire force back to the main road and concentrated at Bole; reconnaissance had now indicated that the western route to Lake Ziway was more passable, so his intention was to rebuild the demolished bridge at Bole and go west. At this stage 1 Light Tank Company was temporarily withdrawn from Fowcol and went into Wetherall's divisional reserve at Addis Ababa.

While they were here, General Wetherall ordered Clark to send a detachment to Mombasa via Berbera to take over six light tanks which had been sent to Kenya for 12 African Division in the south. Clark duly sent off a detachment on what turned out to be a wild-goose chase: the tanks arrived too late to be of any use, and he did not lay eyes on his detachment again

Natal Mounted Riflemen at the outbreak of the Second Word War carrying out 3-inch Mortar drills.

NMR Company wading through a swollen Dandada river, Abyssinia

until it rejoined the tank company in the Middle East.

On 24 April 1941 Fowkes was ready to advance again, this time southward from Bole and around the western side of Lake Ziway in the direction of Adamitullo. By now Fowcol had received its reinforcements: 1 Natal Mounted Riflemen, 1 Field Force Battalion, No. 2 Platoon of 2 Armoured Car Company under Captain Heard and two sections of seven light tanks, commanded by Lieutenants L. F. Gallimore and J. G. Potts respectively.

But General Bertillo chose not to fight, and his column withdrew to Sciasciamana without firing a shot. After negotiating various demolished bridges and culverts, Fowcol's main body – 1 Natal Mounted Riflemen, 1 Field Force Battalion and 5 King's African Rifles – concentrated at the Didaba river. 5 King's African Rifles was told to attack a strong Italian position at Bubissa Hill, supported by two sections of Heard's armoured cars which had managed to struggle forward through the mud and swamps. It looked as if a fight was on the cards, since Bubissa Hill was defended by artillery.

By late that afternoon 5 King's African Rifles and the armoured cars were in position 450m from Bubissa Hill. Here they found track marks in the mud indicating that in addition to artillery the Italians also had an undisclosed number of medium tanks (presumably obsolescent Carro Armato 11/39s) which not only mounted 40-calibre 37mm guns but had a distinct mobility advantage in the appalling ground conditions.

During the night 5 King's African Rifles and a section of armoured cars under Lieutenant C. K. Brown moved closer to prepare for attack, while Heard and another section of cars went over to the Italians' left to create a diversion. At 0600 on the 11th Fowcol's artillery shelled the crest of Bubissa Hill, and an hour later 5 King's African Rifles started to advance – more slowly than planned because of the ground, which was so swampy that over on the Italians' left flank one of Heard's cars bogged down with such thoroughness that it had to be temporarily abandoned.

The infantry got through, however, and by 0900, 5 King's African Rifles had overrun the crest and taken 80 prisoners. But then the Italians brought forward seven medium and three light tanks, which made use of their better mobility to counter-attack. Lacking any sort of effective anti-tank weapons, 5 King's African Rifles was chased off the hill again.

When he sighted the tanks Captain Heard recalled his second car and went to the aid of the one that had bogged down earlier. But it was immoveable, so he did the only thing possible: he stripped out its guns and left it where it was. On the Italians' right, Lieutenant Brown decided on offensive action in spite of his inferior weaponry and the swampy ground, and took three cars forward to cover the withdrawal of 5 King's African Rifles and its haul of prisoners, by drawing off the tanks' fire.

What took place then was the first firefight against Italian tanks in the East African campaign. One of Brown's cars bogged down immediately, but the other two carried on and engaged the tanks with their Vickers guns at 400m. Then, however, Brown spotted three other tanks swinging around on his right to outflank him.

He ordered a retreat and tried to pull free the bogged-down car. It resisted all his attempts, so he removed its guns and set it on fire, then pulled back in all haste with the tanks in hot pursuit. Then a second car bogged down; Brown had time only to take out its guns before the sole survivor moved back to the cover of the artillery as fast as it could with the other two crews clinging on to it. Fortunately the tanks veered off before the artillery could fire on them.

The rain had now come back in full force; Fowkes called off the attack and set out by an alternate route to try again at Sciasciamana, on the Little Didaba river. This entailed crossing the Awasa and Didaba rivers, neither of which were defended, but the Italians had demolished the bridge over the Little Didaba and two days earlier had proved their willingness to resist when a section of light tanks under Lieutenant Potts reconnoitred the area to find out if it was being held in any strength.

They were within 500m of the river when they ran into heavy artillery and anti-tank fire, and Potts' tank suffered a direct hit by a shell which went right through the visor-flap and out through the rear, missing the engine in the process. The tank was a wreck and both Potts and his driver were wounded. On another reconnaissance patrol an East African armoured car was also hit and destroyed – later it transpired that the attackers had 18 guns and nine medium tanks.

Fowkes launched a straightforward assault with 1/6 King's African Rifles and 1/3 King's African Rifles, with artillery support, while the Natal Mounted Riflemen took to the bush in a wide looping approach and emerged to attack the Italian left. It was a complete surprise that destroyed the integrity of the Italian defences, since their guns and tanks were deployed to defend the river line. Nevertheless, the Italians put up a stiff resistance, as Klein writes:

> The enemy had some good Eritrean troops, supported by [the guns and tanks] ... the guns continued firing at point-blank range until overrun with the bayonet. During the final phase of the action, when the Italian tanks were trying to manoeuvre to meet the unexpected direction of the South African attack, Captain Blamey of the 1st Natal Mounted Riflemen jumped on to a tank and killed the driver with his revolver.
> This gallant action took the heart out of the rest of the tank crews, who surrendered without further fight. The 1st Natal Mounted Riflemen lost three killed and twelve wounded, but captured all the Italian tanks and guns and over 800 prisoners. The battle of the Little Didaba was one of the best actions fought by South African troops in East Africa.

Throughout the campaign the enemy made the mistake of massing its forces on the tops of hills and along banks of rivers. The battle of [the] Little Didaba was no exception. In addition, the enemy flanks were far too short and his patrol work ineffective. The Italians asked to be outflanked, and they were.

The temporary officer commanding 1 Natal Mounted Riflemen, Major L. M. Harris – Lieutenant-Colonel McMillan had taken ill and been evacuated a few days before the battle – was admitted to the Distinguished Service Order for his leadership in action at the Little Didaba.

1 Natal Mounted Riflemen was allowed to retain two of the tanks it had captured, which apparently proved useful later on for dragging vehicles out of the ever-present mud – the regiment's first but not last use of armoured vehicles since it was soon to be converted into an armoured reconnaissance regiment in 1943 for service in the Italian campaign.

Next day patrols of 1 South African Light Tank Company entered Sciasciamana without encountering any resistance, and the Natal Mounted Riflemen prepared to continue the pursuit southward through Dalle. This promised to be difficult, because according to information received – which turned out to be inaccurate – the main road south had been damaged and the bridges along it demolished, In consequence B Company 1 Natal Mounted Riflemen, supported by some armoured cars and Major Clark's light tanks, was sent to reconnoitre an alternative route to Dalle.

The force followed an old track which wended its way through woodland country and dropped down a steep escarpment into dense forests. Eventually, as Erich Goetzsche recounts in *The Natal Mounted Riflemen History*, they found themselves passing between patches of cultivated land with "standing wheat eight feet high [and] acre upon acre of scarlet tomatoes … in their prime." There was even a deserted tomato-canning factory the Italians had built. To their surprise, friendly locals ran alongside the troop carriers, filling helmets and empty boxes with the tomatoes.

Near Lake Awasa the Natal Mounted Riflemen' force rejoined the main road and hastened northward, the armoured cars probing ahead. After about 3km they came on a strong Italian force numbering more than 900 deployed astride the road, supported by a lone armoured car. One of the South African armoured cars shot at it and without further ado the Italian force surrendered – telling evidence of their degree of demoralization, or so it was assumed.

But there was more to it than that, as Clark discovered when he sent one of his little tanks south along the road in the direction of Sciasciamana. Eight kilometres south of where the B Company force had climbed back on to the main road, the tank ran into yet another Italian outpost, in which some 300 troops were entrenched in what turned out to be the forward defensive position of the 900-man force which had just surrendered. No doubt to the tank commander's surprise this outpost gave itself up with hardly a shot being fired.

The real reason for this astounding lack of fighting spirit was only revealed when the two batches of prisoners were brought together. The troops at the main outpost had surrendered because they had assumed that the forward position had been overrun. The men in the forward position, however, having been taken from the rear, had assumed that the main garrison had been overcome, and had seen no sense in what would have been a futile defence.

Such bitter rebukes passed between the two groups for not putting up a fight, Goetzsche notes that they came close to laying violent hands on one another. It was yet another illustration of the effects of the South Africans' reputation for outflanking movements followed by fierce attacks.

Dalle was occupied without difficulty. According to Goetzsche, the arrival of Clark's light tanks on the morning of 18 May 1941 was a complete surprise to its garrison of around 600 men of a renowned "death or glory" battalion, specially paid troops who had vowed to fight unto death, regardless of the circumstances. By this time, however, they had obviously concluded that fighting to the last man for a hopelessly lost cause was a contract-breaker, and surrendered without offering any resistance.

With Dalle occupied, Brigadier Fowkes sent reinforcements in the shape of 1 Natal Mounted Riflemen and 1 Field Force Battalion to hold the Sciasciamana–Dalle road, with catastrophic results for the Italians. Now two of their colonial divisions which were lying up east of Lake Margherita, the 21st and 24th, found themselves trapped between Fowcol and 24 Gold Coast Brigade, which was advancing up the road from Neghelli.

Brigadier Fowkes was now ordered to swing west with the remainder of his brigade and capture Soddu, about 50km from Dalle. On 17 May 1941 an advance party of 1/6 King's African Rifles, supported by Captain Heard with seven armoured cars, set out on the road to Soddu to find the whereabouts of the enemy and establish a battalion base. After advancing unopposed for about 27km the column halted, and while A Company 1/6 King's African Rifles set up camp, C Company under Captain R. M. Cresswell kept moving forward with

Heard's armoured cars.

Cresswell's company followed the road southwestward until it was within about 10km of the next village, Colito. There it spotted two Italian patrols.The infantry immediately debussed and advanced on foot, with one section of armoured cars on the left flank and Heard's headquarters section covering the infantry.

At 1500 the Italians opened fire at a range of about 400m. The patrol kept advancing in spite of the enemy fire. Then Cresswell saw what appeared to be a white flag on the right of his troops and went forward in an armoured car to find out for himself. Whether it was a white flag or not, he was hit and mortally wounded while standing next to the turret and looking through his binoculars.

The patrol then withdrew, but this was not the end of the fighting at Colito. Two days later 1/6 King's African Rifles avenged Cresswell's death: Fowcol's 1 South African Field Battery (Cape Field Artillery) bombarded the enemy guns on the other side of the Billate river while two King's African Rifles companies crossed over to the west bank in the face of accurate machine-gun and mortar fire – watched by Heard's cars, which could not accompany them because the bridge had been demolished – and then fell on the enemy positions.

The Italians resisted stubbornly for most of the day. But the King's African Rifles companies were unstoppable, and by 1600 the defenders began to pull back, with large numbers surrendering. From previous experience it seemed likely that for all practical purposes this was the end of the action, but the Italians had one more shot left in their locker. Six or seven medium tanks which had been lurking unseen in the riverside bush suddenly roared into view and advanced on the bridgehead.

Then, Orpen says, "South African gunners, manning two Italian anti-tank guns captured at Sciasciamana, immediately opened fire and forced the tanks to retire under cover of thick bush, where they were almost in the midst of the East African infantry. The field battery officers watched helplessly, as the telephone line to their guns had been cut. Re-establishing communication, 1st Field Battery Cape Field Artillery engaged, and the tanks began to fall back."

Then there took place a supreme act of gallantry by Sergeant Nigel Leakey of 1/6 King's African Rifles' mortar platoon, who had used up all his bombs and thrown in his lot with the infantry, as recorded by Klein:

As the leading tank approached he leapt upon it and shot one of the crew by firing his revolver through a crack in the badly fastened lid of the turret. Pulling the turret top open, Leakey poured four or five revolver shots into the tank, which immediately stopped. He then jumped off, opened the side door of the tank, and pulled out two bodies. One was the colonel commanding the squadron.

Leakey then crawled into the tank, and at pistol point forced the terrified Italian driver to move it to the side of the road, where he endeavoured to bring the turret gun into action against the other tanks.

Failing to get the gun to work, he jumped to the ground and raced after the remaining tanks. As they withdrew he was last seen attempting to open the top of another as it bore him away into the bush. Sergeant Leakey's subsequent fate has never been established and his body never found. His courageous exploit saved the day. [Leakey was decorated with a posthumous Victoria Cross.]

If the tanks had persevered the outcome might have been somewhat different, but their premature withdrawal spelled the end of resistance. Nearly 100 of the enemy had been killed and were buried where they fell – later many wounded from Colito were found at Soddu –and the King's African Rifles captured a total of 489 Italians and 300 colonial infantry together with 10 field artillery pieces, 38 machine guns, three tanks and 15 heavy diesel lorries.

Colito pretty much broke the back of organized Italian resistance in the lakes area. After that they streamed westward over the Omo river. On 22 May 1941 Fowcol's leading elements entered Soddu, in the shape of three South African light tanks, led by Lieutenant P. G. F. Shaw in one of the Italian medium tanks captured at Colito, with Gunner P. S. van der Westhuizen, on loan from 5 Field Battery (Natal Field Artillery), manning the 37mm gun.

About 9km from Soddu the tanks came up against an Italian artillery battery in the town's forward defence line. Van der Westhuizen dealt swiftly with the Italian guns, and by mid-afternoon the Allies – Shaw, another section of light tanks under Major Clark, two of 2 Armoured Car Company's armoured cars and a King's African Rifles' rifle company – occupied Soddu. At 1615 Clark formally struck the Italian flag. The war in that part of Abyssinia was over.

Soddu provided a rich haul of prisoners and equipment – General Liberati and the staff of 25 Italian Division, General Baccari with the staff of 101 Italian Division, 4,800 officers and men, six medium tanks, four light tanks, 100 machine guns and what was left of 21 Italian Division, which had been moving slowly around the northern end of Lake Abaya to escape 12 African Division as it advanced from the south.

"The taking of Soddu," Klein points out, "was a textbook example of relentless pursuit and surprise and the speedy use of armoured fighting vehicles. The fall of this bastion of Italian hopes marked the final phase of the northern Battle of the Lakes."

Now, at last, 2 Armoured Car Company could resume its interrupted journey to the Western Desert. Its armoured cars were ordered back to Hergeisa in British Somaliland to be reunited with Major Walker. Then, at full strength for the first time in months, it embarked at Berbera on 3 June 1941. The South African Tank Corps was not quite done with the Abyssinian campaign, however. 1 South African Light Tank Company remained with 11 African Division for the time being, and Major Clark's 'lost patrol' which had been sent south by General Wetherall would also be dragged into the final fighting in East Africa.

PART THREE

THE WAR IN THE DESERT

21

The South African Tank Corps takes shape as disaster strikes

The South African Tank Corps was now assuming its final shape. In less than a year it had expanded phenomenally from its original 40 all ranks. By October 1940 it had 150 officers and 2,326 other ranks on strength – by December 1941 it would reach 7,165 all ranks – with a corresponding growth in its recruitment, selection, training, development and administrative structures. The Abyssinian campaign had provided a steep learning curve and full advantage had been taken of its hard-won lessons.

The Armoured Fighting Vehicle Training Centre, established near the Premier Mine by Lieutenant-Colonel A. J. Kenyon in October 1940, now comprised South African Tank Corps Headquarters, the Armoured Fighting Vehicle School, a tactical training branch, a recruits depot, a manpower pool, a reservists' depot and a vehicles training and workshops depot.

It continued to grow as new armoured car companies were established, an important but not exclusive source of manpower being well-recruited regiments with surplus personnel or ones, which, for one reason or another, either could not recruit to full strength or could not proceed on active service.

Officers and men from the South African Railways and Harbours Brigade arrived to form the cores of two new companies, the second battalions of the Royal Natal Carbineers and Imperial Light Horse were similarly converted, and two rural regiments, Regiment Westelike Provinsie and Regiment Suidwestelike Distrikte, each formed an armoured car company.

Under Lieutenant-Colonel (later Brigadier) J. P. A. Furstenburg, who took over when Kenyon was appointed deputy director armoured fighting vehicle development in October 1940, the Armoured Fighting Vehicle Training Centre grew to such dimensions that within a year it was to have a staff of 48 training officers and 305 other ranks.

At the end of 1940 there was such a massive infusion of new personnel, when it was decided to convert 1 Mounted Brigade to armour, that in January 1941 a branch of the Armoured Fighting Vehicle Training Centre was established at Ladysmith in Natal under Major P. H. Grobbelaar, who was later to earn a brilliant reputation in the Western Desert and rise to high rank in the post-war years. Grobbelaar oversaw the conversion until April 1941, when he was posted to the Middle East as commanding officer of the new 7 South African Armoured Car Reconnaissance Battalion and was replaced by Lieutenant-Colonel F. M. Sykes, the Ladysmith branch was later amalgamated with its parent body.

Grobbelaar's posting, and later in the year Furstenburg's as well, resulted from a sweeping process of redesignation, amalgamation and restructuring that had been set in motion in March 1941 and was to continue until the end of 1942 as the South African Tank Corps evolved to keep pace with changing requirements. In mid-1941, however, the South African Tank Corps' operational units consisted of:

- 1 Armoured Fighting Vehicle Regiment, formed out of 1 Mounted Regiment in July 1940 (renamed 1 Armoured Car Commando in January 1942).
- 2 Armoured Fighting Vehicle Regiment, formed out of 2, 4 and 6 Mounted Regiments in January 1941 (renamed 2 Armoured Car Commando in April 1942).

- 3 Armoured Car Reconnaissance Battalion, formed by amalgamating all the armoured elements of the Abyssinian campaign – 1, 2 and 3 South African Armoured Car companies, elements of 1 and 2 South African Motorcycle companies and eventually the members of 1 South African Light Tank Company when they finally arrived from Abyssinia (renamed 3 Armoured Car Regiment in October 1942).
- 4 Armoured Car Regiment, formed from 4 and 5 Armoured Car companies in March 1941.
- 5 Armoured Car Regiment, formed by amalgamating 11 Armoured Car Company (Regiment Suidwestelike Distrikte) and 12 Armoured Car Company (Regiment Westelike Provinsie) in April 1941.
- 6 Armoured Car Regiment, formed in April 1941 by amalgamating 13 South African Armoured Car Company (converted from 2 Imperial Light Horse) and 14 South African Armoured Car Company (converted from 2 Royal Natal Carbineers).
- 7 Armoured Car Reconnaissance Battalion, formed from 21 (Railways and Harbours Brigade) Armoured Car Company and 22 (Railways and Harbours Brigade) Armoured Car Company in March 1941 as 7 Armoured Fighting Vehicle Regiment, then redesignated.
- 8 Armoured Fighting Vehicle Regiment, formed from 23 (Railways and Harbours Brigade) Armoured Car Company and 24 (Railways and Harbours Brigade) Armoured Car Company in March 1941 (renamed 8 Armoured Car Commando from March 1942).
- 9 Armoured Car Reconnaissance Battalion, formed from 31 (Special Service Battalion) Armoured Car Company and 34 (Cape Town Highlanders) Armoured Car Company in March 1941 as 9 Armoured Fighting Vehicle Regiment, then redesignated the following month (in January 1942 it would be renamed 9 Armoured Car Regiment, and then 9 Armoured Commando in April 1942).
- 10 Armoured Fighting Vehicle Regiment, formed from 3 Mounted Commando Regiment in April 1941 (renamed 10 Armoured Car Regiment in November 1941, and 10 Armoured Commando in April 1942).
- 2 Mounted Commando, formed from 4 and 5 Mounted Regiments in February 1941 (renamed 11 Armoured Car Commando from January 1942 and then 11 Armoured Commando in June 1942).
- 12 Armoured Fighting Vehicle Regiment, formed from 1, 2 and 3 Mounted Regiments in February 1941 as 1 Mounted Commando, then redesignated in April 1941 (12 Armoured Car Regiment in November 1941, 12 Armoured Car Commando in March 1942 and 12 Armoured Commando in June 1942).

In addition to these, there was 13 Armoured Car Regiment (Reserve), which was formed on 30 May 1941 and according to Klein was a test-bed "phantom" unit "which was at all times the make-or-break training and special duties regiment." Its three squadrons were drawn from 9 Reconnaissance Battalion, 2 Armoured Fighting Vehicle Regiment and 10 Armoured Fighting Vehicle Regiment respectively.

Each of the three types of operational units had its own role and characteristics. An armoured car unit now had a nominal strength of between 58 and 64 cars; a reconnaissance battalion's authorized strength, on the other hand, was 116 Mark III cars in three companies (36 in each company, each comprising three 12-car platoons and two cars allocated to the company headquarters) plus 4 cars in the regimental headquarters.

The armoured commandos also had 58 to 64 cars, but were dedicated to internal-security and home-defence duties of various kinds, and presumably absorbed designated 'key men' and others not available for external or full-time service – although 1 Armoured Car Commando took part in the 1942 invasion of Vichy-held Madagascar, an operation of short duration (about nine weeks) which was an out-and-out conventional-warfare interlude, and acquitted itself extremely well.

Most of these units did not see foreign service, but this does not mean they were not gainfully employed in the overall war effort. At that stage there was still great concern about a possible Japanese amphibious attack – the reason why Madagascar was to be invaded in late 1942 – which meant that a sizeable home army had to be maintained, and there were also certain concerns about a possible insurrection by anti-war elements.

As a result armoured cars were attached to the coastal defence commands at various ports – 41 Mark IIIs in Durban, 14 in East London, seven in Port Elizabeth and 55 in Cape Town – until late in 1942; according to Brigadier-General M. B. Anderson, while the South African Air Force had two armoured car companies of its own for airfield protection.

The army's commando cars were used for a variety of purposes: training, recruitment, patrolling the coastline for evidence of enemy incursions and protection of key points such as railways, dams, power stations and electrical infrastructure against sabotage by pro-German or anti-British elements.

No insurrection ever took place – at least partly because the parliamentary opposition, while not in favour of participation in the war, would have nothing to do with any such action – and sabotage was minimal. But the existence of such sentiments obviously demanded unceasing vigilance.

In retrospect, 9 Armoured Car Reconnaissance Battalion is of particular historical interest to today's armour soldiers, even though it did not see foreign service as a unit. It will be remembered that when war broke out the Special Service Battalion as such was not mobilized for active service, but was used as a feeder to bring several other units up to strength and also generated two full-sized infantry service battalions, 1 and 2 Field Force Battalions.

While 1 and 2 Field Force Battalions were campaigning in Abyssinia and later in the Western Desert, the Special Service Battalion itself was changing shape. The first phase of the transformation was the establishment of 31 Armoured Car Company, which was then amalgamated with 34 Armoured Car Company, formed from 200 officers and men of the Duke of Connaught and Strathearn's Own Cape Town Highlanders, which at that stage was very well recruited but had not yet seen active service.

In his history of the Cape Town Highlanders, Neil Orpen notes that "some of Support Company's best sergeants and Vickers gunners transferred to the armoured car company, and it was a great disappointment to them when they learned they would not carry the Highlanders' insignia into battle. However, when the Special Service Battalion became an armoured regiment, many of these men served with distinction in tanks" – possibly an indication that the Cape Town Highlanders had originally had ambitions of spawning a separate armoured unit in addition to its existing infantry battalion.

The result of these developments was that by late 1941 the Special Service Battalion had shed members under the age of 18, who were transferred to the new Youth Training Brigade, and now consisted of three separate components: the Special Service Battalion itself, which was basically a machine gun battalion; two infantry battalions (1 and 2 Field Force Battalion) and part of 9 Armoured Car Reconnaissance Battalion.

9 Reconnaissance Battalion (aka 9 Armoured Car Regiment and 9 Armoured Commando) was disbanded in December 1942 – just after 1/2 Field Force Battalion had returned from the Western Desert and been re-absorbed by the Special Service Battalion, and 6 South African Armoured Division was in the process of formation. Small wonder, then, that the Special Service Battalion was chosen for conversion to tanks for the Italian campaign.

Be all that as it may, of the six armoured units that did see service abroad, one never got to fire a shot in anger, one acquitted itself well in Madagascar and the other four went on to win renown in the Western Desert. But all that still lay in what promised to be a tumultuous near future.

The external-service units of the South African Tank Corps began concentrating in Egypt

Marmon Herrington Mk 2.

Marmon Herrington Mk 5 trials.

from mid-June onward. 4 Armoured Car Regiment (Lieutenant-Colonel D. S. Newton-King) and 6 Armoured Car Regiment (Lieutenant-Colonel V. C. G. O'B. Short) arrived straight from the Union; Lieutenant-Colonel Grobbelaar was already there with 7 South African Armoured Car Reconnaissance Battalion, while the veteran East Africa hands of 2 and 3 Armoured Car Companies were amalgamated with 2 South African Motorcycle Company to form the core of the new 3 South African Armoured Car Reconnaissance Battalion under Lieutenant-Colonel G. K. Roodt.

1 South African Armoured Car Company, 1 South African Motorcycle Company and 1 South African Light Tank Company were still involved in Abyssinia but were earmarked for Roodt's 3 Armoured Car Reconnaissance Battalion and were duly absorbed when they arrived in August and September respectively. An unfortunate fate was to befall 5 Armoured Car Regiment which was broken up as soon as it arrived in October 1941 so that its personnel and equipment could be distributed among the other units.

The only laggards were the handful of light tank men General Wetherall had sent off on what had turned out to be a wild-goose chase, and found themselves involved, together with elements of the South African Air Force, South African Artillery and South African Engineer Corps, in 11 African Division's final assault on the Italian forces in Abyssinia.

The Italians were now holed up west of the Omo river, a large and forbiddingly difficult watercourse that ran down to the sea through a long series of deep gorges. Sheltering behind the gorges of the Omo was Jimma, the last significant town in Abyssinia in Italian hands, although in the distant northwest they still held the ancient Portuguese forts around Gondar, and capturing it was the task of 22 East African Brigade and 23 Nigerian Brigade.

It was a formidable task indeed, which had to be executed "amid the rugged grandeur of the Omo gorge, where cliffs rise from the river to 1,525m in piled-up tiers, amid the mud, muck and slush of the rains, across minefields and through demolitions," as Klein describes it. But at the end of May 1941 the East Africans were advancing on Jimma from Soddu in the south, and the Nigerians from Abalti, 90km away to the north.

1 South African Light Tank Company, its own tanks augmented by a few 'liberated' Italian mediums, spearheaded 22 East African Brigade's advance from Soddu, clearing the road all the way to the river. They were prevented from taking part in the battle due to the actual river crossing, the deep *kloofs* (ravines), where most of the battle was fought, and the demolition of all the bridges.

But their role was not yet over. On 6 June 1941 Fowkes's 5 King's African Rifles' askari forced their way across the Omo in assault boats. Next day one section of light tanks under Lieutenant L. F. Gallimore was ferried over the river and joined hands with the waiting

King's African Rifles; the combined force set off after the retreating Italians' rearguard. By now the Nigerians were over the Omo as well, and between them the brigades relentlessly shrank the remaining enemy-held area.

The end-result of these "splendid passages of arms and of human endurance in forcing simultaneous crossings of the river … as desperate an account of grim adventure as anything in the East African campaign," as Klein describes the episode, came not long after. On 21 June 1941 Brigadier Fowkes took the surrender of Jimma, along with 12 generals, 8,000 troops, 500 vehicles, artillery pieces, tanks, armoured cars, large stocks of supplies and gold bullion worth £250,000.

The main body of South African armoured cars started arriving in Egypt at a time when an uneasy lull had broken out between the Allied and Axis forces after yet another failed British offensive that had been much more disastrous than Operation Brevity.

Operation Battleaxe was launched on 15 June 1941, one of its aims being the relief of Tobruk. For the first time since the start of the Second World War a German force of substantial size would be fighting a defensive battle, although this was from necessity rather than choice.

General Rommel later summed up the situation: "Unfortunately, our petrol stocks were badly depleted, and it was with some anxiety that we contemplated the coming British attack, for we knew that our moves would be decided more by the petrol gauge than by tactical requirements."

But Rommel proved to be as adept in defence as when masterminding the blitzkrieg. He had learned some valuable lessons in the recent fighting. Operation Brevity had shown how easily his defence lines could be breached, and his failed attacks on Tobruk had given him much food for thought.

Now he constructed a long line of strongly fortified positions stretching 30km from Halfaya to Sidi Azeiz, and installed anti-tank guns and anti-tank mines on the Halfaya Pass, on Point 206, south of Fort Capuzzo and on Point 208 on the Hafid Ridge west of the little fort.

The defence of this formidable line he entrusted to Major-General Walter Neumann-Silkow's 15 Panzer Division, a formation skilled in tank and anti-tank warfare, of whose presence the Allies appear to have been unaware. He also made good use of a lapse in 7 Armoured Division's signals security, which provided him with invaluable advance knowledge of such things as the division's dispositions and intentions.

Armed with this knowledge he shifted his 5 Light Division to a position south of Tobruk, from where he could use it either against the Sallum area or against Tobruk itself, as circumstances required. To prevent Tobruk's garrison from breaking out, he also laid on a heavy artillery bombardment of the port for the night before Battleaxe was scheduled to roll.

Battleaxe began as scheduled on 15 June 1941 and soon turned into a total disaster. Rommel's defence proved almost impregnable, and only one of three British thrusts penetrated his lines. By the end of 17 June 1941 the British had lost almost half their new tanks. Next day they repulsed a powerful German counter-attack on their centre but were then pushed back on their western flank and on the third day retreated just in time to avoid being encircled and cut off.

The final British toll was 91 out of 190 tanks, 969 men and 36 aircraft. The German losses were about 670 men, 12 tanks and 10 aircraft. It was also the end of the line for Wavell, who had achieved so much with so little for such a long time. Churchill transferred him to India as commander-in-chief and replaced him with his predecessor, General Sir Claude Auchinleck.

This was the situation in which the South African armoured car units found themselves when they started concentrating in Egypt. The German and Italian armies had consolidated west of the Egyptian border, from where they cast covetous eyes on Tobruk, while the Allied forces held the borderline while they regrouped, reorganized and built up their remaining strength at their bases farther back in Egypt.

Marmon Herringtons on patrol on Robben Island during the Second World War.

General Brink's 1 South African Division, fresh from its successes in Abyssinia and Eritrea, lay at Mersa Matruh, while the as-yet unblooded 2 South African Division under Major-General I. P. de Villiers was occupied in preparing the great defence line at El Alamein, virtually a stone's throw west of Cairo itself.

The stalemate gave the South African armoured units time to prepare for a new style of fighting under the tutelage of two veteran desert British regiments, the King's Dragoon Guards and the 11th Hussars, the famed 'Cherrypickers' of Napoleonic wars fame, which had acquired a particularly rich lode of desert lore.

In 1926 the 11th Hussars had been one of the first two British cavalry regiments to convert to armoured cars. From then until 1934 they had alternated with the 12th Lancers in serving in the Middle East, and from 1934 had been permanently stationed there. They were, as armoured-vehicle writer John Sandars says, "the acknowledged experts on armoured car matters in the desert, devising their own tactics and instructing other units in them when they arrived in the theatre."

The King's Dragoon Guards had been mechanized as a light tank unit in 1937, but converted to armoured cars when it arrived in Egypt in late December 1940, just in time for one squadron to join the Cherrypickers in defeating the Italians at Beda Fomm. At the time of the South Africans' arrival the King's Dragoon Guards' C Squadron was actually besieged in Tobruk, and would later lead the breakout from the embattled port.

By the time the South Africans arrived the British armoured cars had been making life difficult for the less mobile Italians for an entire year. The 11th Hussars had, in fact, crossed the 'Wire', the Libyan–Egyptian border fence, and fired the opening shots of the campaign on the day hostilities with Italy broke out.

The Hussars had been given *carte blanche* to raise as much hell behind enemy lines as possible, and in the next few months they had done just that. They raided over the border for long periods at a time, identifying enemy movements and dispositions, picking off unescorted soft-skinned vehicles, harassing supply convoys to the small border forts like Capuzzo and Maddalena and shooting up the forts themselves.

This being the case, they had much to teach the South Africans, for example about the terrain. The nature of the terrain in any theatre is all important in any war – and was even more so in the days before armies possessed such things as helicopters and aircraft capable of short take offs and landings – because it determines the nature of the tactics used and the resupply organization needed.

The desert terrain was vastly different from what the veterans had cut their teeth on in East Africa, or the bushveld plains in the Transvaal where the new armoured units had done their field training before deployment to the Middle East.

Many people labour under a misconception fostered by such films that the great battles in the Middle East took place in the enormous dune-ribbed wastes of the Sahara Desert. But it is just that: a misconception.

Small, specialized raiding and reconnaissance units such as the Long Range Desert Group, Popski's Private Army and the Special Air Service certainly ventured into the distant desert wastes, but the Western Desert campaign was waged mainly by conventional infantry and armoured formations whose principal theatre of operations was a comparatively small area in which mechanized armies could manoeuvre.

Their battleground was an arid coastal plain consisting, as Klein says, "of rocks and sand, few tracks, occasional wells, and 'going' that varies from good to impassable. Much of the area is covered with scrub, and this, together with the hills, depressions and ridges, gives variety – albeit monotonous – to the scenery." The southern margin of the plain was a high escarpment beyond which the actual desert began.

The depth of the plain varied from place to place. At its far eastern Egyptian end it was no more than about 70km wide at most, southwest of El Alamein lay the Qattara Depression, a huge basin 19,500km² in extent and 133m below sea level – a bleak expanse of saline marshes, saltpans and dry lakes, with hard crusts overlaying sticky mud and fine, almost powdery sand in which no humans lived except for a few nomadic Bedouin. Its only permanent water source was a brackish lake at the Moghra Oasis.

By its mere presence the Qattara Depression's vast and inhospitable expanse shaped the fighting during the Western Desert campaign because it was considered impassable for tanks and most other vehicles. Generally speaking, no one ventured into it except for the British Long Range Desert Group and occasional Deutsches Afrikakorps patrols. It had one great advantage though, of which General Bernard Montgomery would later take advantage: at its southern edge were the high cliffs of the Libyan escarpment, which meant that El Alamein could not be outflanked.

West of the Qattara Depression lay another and even more formidable obstacle, the Great Sand Sea – an unbroken 225,000km² wilderness of high sand dunes without any water sources whatsoever.

The distances involved might seem great to Europeans, but not to inhabitants of Africa. From El Alamein to Sallum is only about 375km; from Sallum to Tobruk about 210km; from Tobruk to Benghazi about 250km. But it did not go merely about distance. Mechanization had improved the general's lot since the agonizing struggles Lukin and the Duke of Westminster had experienced there just a quarter century before, but the terrain remained a significant obstacle. Klein notes: "The nature of the ground was such as to throw a great strain on most types of motor vehicles and on maintenance and repair facilities. In the earlier part of the campaign a railway line from Alexandria ran as far west as Mersa Matruh, 125 miles short of the frontier [although] as the war progressed the railway was extended to the frontier and beyond. Only one proper road served the troops from Alexandria to Mersa Matruh and the forward areas. It would be well for those who are critical of the conduct of the earlier desert campaigns to reflect on the immense difficulties – on the transport side alone – that faced commanders and troops."

The desert brought other privations as well, as the South Africans soon discovered. One was the severe temperature fluctuation, so that in summer it would be stunningly hot in the daylight hours but freezing cold that same night. Then there was the Khamsin, [a hot south wind that] whirls up huge clouds of dust and sand, fills every crevice, and makes life almost unbearable: when the Khamsin blows it is impossible to cook or carry on any other activity, and visibility is reduced to a few yards." According to Klein,

Marmon Herrington undergoing river crossing trails.

That was not to mention a myriad tirelessly persistent flies that plagued all desert camps, or the endless shortage of water, although the South African Mark III armoured car had a 39-litre internal water tank to help with this problem. Even so, in the field the South Africans were usually rationed to 4½-litres per man per day if they were lucky, sometimes it had to be cut in half, and now and then it was so tainted that it was almost undrinkable. In addition, part of each man's daily ration had to go toward washing, cooking and – most important of all – the cars' radiators. Not that cooking involved much finesse. Fresh food was a rarity. The staple desert ration was the ubiquitous bully beef and biscuits, tinned milk, tea and sugar, with tinned meat and vegetables when they were available. According to Sandars "delicacies such as jam, tinned butter, tinned fish, tinned bacon and soya link sausages [were] much sought after, but seldom available in any quantities.

Ailments included sandfly fever, jaundice and desert sores that developed even from small scratches, and dysentery was a constant companion. Anecdotal evidence is that the South Africans adapted relatively more easily to the desert than the Europeans. A British writer says that the British ignored the desert as much as possible, the Germans instinctively fought it with special equipment like foot powder, sun-glasses, lip-salves and the like, and the Italians tried to make it as much like home as they could. Quaintly put.

Another desert veteran, the journalist Brian Barrow, once told the author that once sand-goggles had been issued to the South Africans they managed to weather the Khamsin without too many morale problems, other than the normal irritation at the unspeakable discomfort, whereas some German and Italian prisoners he spoke to regarded the windstorms with instinctive fear and loathing.

But there was one great improvement over Abyssinia: better navigational aids. In East Africa, it will be remembered, the South Africans had encountered great problems with maps that were both inaccurate and lacking in detail, but here it was a different matter.

Before the outbreak of war the 11th Hussars and other units had thoroughly reconnoitred the entire desert west of the Cairo–Alexandria road, from the Siwa Oasis and the Libyan Sand Sea in the south to the coast in the north, all the way to Sallum and the western Egyptian border with Libya. One result was an invaluable 'going' map that showed the nature of the surface in each area and the type of vehicle for which it was suited.

The South African-manufactured armoured cars were a godsend to the British. They had at least two basically

Marmon Herrington Mk2 during training the South African Lowveld.

sound designs to hand, but at this time they were still struggling to cope with the enormous demands of war production, and a modern home-grown armoured car only started trickling in at the end of 1941.

Until then, all they had on hand were the old 1924 pattern Rolls-Royce cars which had been modernized by fitting them with special broad desert tyres, radios and a larger open-topped turret mounting a Boys anti-tank rifle, a Bren light machine gun and a smoke discharger, and some Morris 4 x 2 light scout cars which mounted nothing more potent than a Bren. The desert tyres had improved the Rolls-Royce cars' off-road performance, but their two-wheel drive configuration remained a handicap.

As a result the British armoured units were using the Marmon-Herrington Mark II long before the South African armoured units assembled in Egypt and they and the later Mark IIIs remained the mainstay of the Allied armoured car units throughout the desert fighting, for the very simple reason that they were the best cars available to do the job.

As early as January 1941, according to Sandars, the first Mark IIs were issued to the King's Dragoon Guards and soon after to the Royal Dragoons, "but the first batch were quickly removed from [the Royals] to re-equip the 11th Hussars during the flap caused by the Afrikakorps' first offensive."

In fact, Sandars says, a Mark II was involved in a strange incident in late February 1941 which was "one of the first indications that the Afrikakorps had arrived in the desert … [there was] a minor collision between a car of the King's Dragoon Guards and a German eight-wheeler on a desert track … it was dusk and both cars were so surprised that the only damage done was a bedroll torn off the Marmon-Herrington as it scraped past the German."

Judging by Sandars' comments the British were not overly impressed at first by the Mark II:

A large clumsy car with a four-man crew, built around a Ford chassis and engine … it had four-wheel drive, but suffered from easily broken springs and a tendency to overheat in a following wind, with thinner armour than the Rolls-Royce and Morris and no more armament except a Vickers gun on a anti-aircraft mount, it was not much of an improvement …
But its main redeeming feature was apparently the fact that it invariably started first go, which must have been comforting for crews faced with the more formidable German vehicles!

Be that as it may, the South African vehicles significantly out-performed the Rolls-Royces, and the British government eventually bought no fewer than 1,180 Mark IIs and Mark IIIs, the latter remaining a staple for British armoured car regiments in the Western Desert to the end of the campaign.

In November 1941 the 11th Hussars received a trickle of Mark II Humbers, armed with a 15mm Besa gun, "a distinct improvement on the Marmon-Herrington," Sandars says,

MaHe Mk2 on training manoeuvres in the South African Eastern Transvaal (now Mpumalanga).

Marmon Herrington Mk3 armoured cars on coastal patrol on Robben Island stop at the Light House.

"[although] rather under powered and only [with] an engine life of 3,000 hours." Another British regiment, the 12th Lancers, later arrived in the desert already equipped with Humbers.

The Hussars persevered with the Mark II Humbers despite of their lack of power and short engine life, but the Royal Dragoons and King's Dragoon Guards were reissued with South African Mark IIIs and retained them until mid-1942 when the improved Mark III Humber and the much better Daimler made their appearance.

The South African cars needed various modifications at the base workshops in Alexandria to make them desert-worthy. According to Klein the cars in the Western Desert "were subject to the same faults as were manifest in East Africa – steering, radiators, shutters, springs, tyres and engines. Trouble was also experienced with the gear ratio, and experiments were carried out with a lower front and back axle ratio to give the cars more speed.

"However, armoured car commanders in the desert considered armament and spare battery-carrying capacity to be of greater importance than speed ... The actual performance differed with the different marks, and depended on a number of factors such as power-to-weight ratio ... speeds of 50mph were possible under pressure, with cruising speeds of 30mph." According to Brigadier-General M. B. Anderson "the first Mark IIIs sent to Egypt were well received, but the crews requested the fitting of a rear escape door and better main and anti-aircraft armament."

The armament was a matter that obviously required urgent attention, and within months of the South African Tank Corps' unit's landing in Egypt steps were taken to improve their firepower. The Mark IIs' hull guns were removed and mounted on top of the turrets because, as Klein says, "anti-aircraft protection, only an academic point in Abyssinia, now became a vital issue ...

"Experiments were carried out in mounting heavier guns, and the car which was perhaps best known in the desert, the Mark III, usually carried one water-cooled Vickers machine gun in the turret, and a Bren gun or Vickers for anti-aircraft protection, later replaced by .30 or .50 Brownings."

One reason for the famously untidy appearance of the South African cars, according to Klein, was that the armour-piercing rounds used by the German Luftwaffe "easily penetrated the armour-plating, until it was found that these bullets mushroomed on striking any equipment fastened to the outside of the cars – even bedding rolls – and failed to go through.

"As a result of this knowledge, it was not uncommon to see the exteriors of armoured cars on reconnaissance covered with a motley array of bedding rolls, kitbags and other equipment as protection against armour-piercing bullets."

Other modifications of a strictly *ad hoc* and unauthorized nature took place at various times to address the question of armament, namely the replacement of the issue machine guns and Boys rifles with a variety of salvaged, looted or scrounged heavier main weapons of various types which would later become a feature of the South African cars.

When Mark II armoured cars were first issued to the King's Dragoon Guards in January 1941, according to Sandars, on the suggestion of the 11th Hussars some had the tops of the turrets removed and "captured Italian 20mm Breda light anti-aircraft guns [were] fitted to give them more punch; eventually most regiments had some of these 'Breda cars', usually in squadron headquarters."

This helped to some degree, although, as Sandars says, "air attacks were probably the greatest cause of casualties, and despite parking anything up to 400 yards apart in daylight and the use of Breda cars, the armoured regiments really had no effective answer to strafing and bombing."

Fitting a 'liberated' Italian light anti-aircraft gun to a turret was one thing, but during mid-1942 Sandars says, "the lack of heavy main armament became so acute that units took the drastic and definitely unauthorized step of actually removing the turrets altogether and mounting captured German 37mm or Italian 47mm guns, as well as the occasional 2-pdr or French Hotchkiss (72-calibre) 25mm."

Klein indicates, however, that the South Africans had started replacing their turrets and machine guns with various items of potluck main armament within months of their arrival in the Middle East almost a year earlier. Quoting an impeccable source, Lieutenant-Colonel Robert Reeves-Moore, who was then a major and B Company commander of 4 South African Armoured Car Regiment:

> It was claimed ... that the first South African armoured car to have an ordnance piece fitted to it was one of the 3rd Recce Battalion cars, from which the turret was removed and an Italian 37mm gun fitted to the frame.
> The 4th SAACR claimed to the contrary, however, that the first hard-hitting gun to be fitted on an armoured car was a 2-pdr anti-tank gun recovered from a knocked-out tank by B Squadron commander, 4th SAACR and two attached (Technical Services Corps) personnel. The mounting of the gun and testing were completed on 19 September 1941.
> The gun had been salvaged from a derelict tank in no man's land ... and those salvaging the gun were subjected to a 30-minute air attack by a Me 110. The squadron commander received a mild "rap" for removing the gun without proper authority. [But] the value of the gun to the troop to which it had been allocated was very soon proved and from then on our armoured cars lost no opportunity of fitting such guns as became available.

Immediately on arrival, personnel of the four armoured car units also set about learning the finer points of desert navigation, reconnaissance and radio procedure, in preparation for the duties that lay ahead, because it was a given that tactical employment of the armoured cars in the Western Desert would be completely different from what it had been in East Africa.

The freewheeling *Gharri Kifaru* days in which the cars had not hesitated to act as virtual infantry tanks if the occasion demanded, were now well and truly past. Instead of facing mainly lightly armed colonial troops, they would now be drinking of stronger waters altogether, and would have to fight 'by the book': reconnoitring, escorting, raiding and pursuit.

This became clear to Major Reeves-Moore of 4 South African Armoured Car Regiment when he spent eight days as an observer with B Squadron 11th Hussars in the forward area of the western Egyptian frontier. Reeves-Moore scrutinized all levels of the Cherrypickers' operation – the forward troops, squadron headquarters, regimental headquarters and squadron B Echelon – not only at rest but also under operational conditions when the regiment spearheaded a reconnaissance in force toward Fort Capuzzo.

To Reeves-Moore, Klein writes:

It became immediately apparent ... that the armoured car role in the desert was to be entirely different from that envisaged in the training programme carried out in the Union.

The 11th Hussars covered a frontage of 40 miles and more by the careful dispositions of their forward troops, whose role was essentially that of reporting any and all enemy movement back to their respective squadron headquarters, which were generally located from 1 to 3 miles in the rear of the forward observation line.

The squadron commander was in contact with his forward troops through the forward W/T [wireless] link; while contact to the rear was maintained by the squadron commander to regimental headquarters and also to the other squadron headquarters on the rear W/T link, operated on a different radio frequency.

Information passed by any one squadron to regimental headquarters was therefore picked up by all the squadrons, and the exact position prevailing along the entire front covered by the regiment was therefore known at all times to all the squadrons.

The forward armoured car troops were never called upon to patrol an area, but established a continuous observation line at sight distance, generally six miles apart on average, depending on suitable high ground. Normally an armoured car regiment covered a front of 40 miles with two squadrons forward, but could cover a 70-mile front when necessary by employing all three squadrons up forward.

Troop observation points were maintained daily from first to last light, and the troops stayed close to their day positions at night (moving only a few hundred yards at most) constantly listening for enemy movement.

Squadron headquarters were positioned to halve the wireless distance between the forward troops and regimental headquarters, sometimes employing a relay wireless set if the distance between the two headquarters was too great for clear communication on a direct link. Any other reconnaissance regiment operating with a division was on the same frequency, as were brigade commanders, so that everyone had a picture of the complete front line.

Although tremendously impressed by the Hussars' high level of efficiency, Reeves-Moore could not help but note one serious deficiency, the absence of more potent weapons than their rifle-calibre Vickers machine guns – no doubt his inspiration for the fitting of that first salvaged 2-pdr in September 1941.

All these and many other lessons were eagerly absorbed by the newcomers, and as Klein writes, "the South African armoured car regiments in the Western Desert soon earned a high reputation for their standard of operational efficiency and courage. Many officers of the 4th and 6th regiments and the 3rd South African Reconnaissance Battalion owed a great deal to their colleagues of the 11th Hussars from whom they received their desert training and who initiated them into the lore of desert operations."

The lessons learned were to be applied all over the Western Desert because the need for armoured cars was great in the second half of 1941 when a series of battles was soon to start. 4 South African Armoured Car Regiment would be attached to 7 Armoured Division; 3 South African Reconnaissance Battalion to 1 South African Division; 7 South African Reconnaissance Battalion to both 2 South African Division and a formation called the Oasis Group – an Indian brigade straddling the Libyan borderline and holding the important oases of Siwa and Jarabub at the edge of the Sand Sea – and 6 South African Armoured Car Regiment to the Eighth Army and the Oasis Group.

22

4 South African Armoured Car Regiment is blooded

The South African Tank Corps contingent was still gathering itself when 4 South African Armoured Car Regiment's B Squadron under Major Reeves-Moore became the first South African armoured unit in the Middle East to fire a shot in anger.

The regiment had spent the first weeks of July 1941 carrying out desert training in the Alem Shaltut-Burg el Arab areas and getting its cars and B Echelon transport into final shape, but on the 19th it was recalled and detached to the headquarters of what was then still called the Western Desert Force.

At the end of the month 4 South African Armoured Car Regiment was attached to 7 Armoured Division – the beginning of a long and mutually respectful relationship with the 'Desert Rats' – and sent to the forward observation line for training with the 11th Hussars. B Squadron went first and joined the Hussars in the Bir Dignaish area on 31 July 1941. Reeves-Moore's men systematically relieved B Squadron of the Hussars and remained in place until 4 South African Armoured Car Regimental Headquarters and the other squadrons arrived on 12 August 1941.

Now the armoured car men got their first taste of aerial attack. 4 South African Armoured Car Regimental Headquarters and A Squadron (Major R. Whitley) were strafed by enemy aircraft while moving up. The cars did not suffer any damage or casualties, but things were a little different when B Squadron's No. 3 Troop under Lieutenant G. Young was shot up on the same day in a low-level attack by three Me 110 fighter-bombers.

Young's car was hit eight times, four of the shots penetrating the armour, but he and his crew came through unscathed. Klein writes, "the lesson of the added protection afforded by the outside cover of bedrolls and packs was well learned: a request was even made for a supply of biscuits (army mattresses) to hang on the cars to deflect [the] armour-piercing bullets."

On 23 August 1941 Lieutenant-Colonel Newton-King took over responsibility for the forward reconnaissance line from the 11th Hussars, after which Klein notes, "there followed a hard but interesting period. The war diary records daily reconnaissance work, shelling by enemy tanks, and encounters with enemy armoured cars; and lists the stream of wireless messages flashed from the forward troops to squadron and Regimental Headquarters."

To illustrate the daily routine he quotes from the daily regimental intelligence summary of 29 August 1941, compiled by Lieutenant Harry Oppenheimer, the unit intelligence officer:

A considerable enemy concentration in the Frontier Area was reported as follows:
1153 hours 8 Tanks North of B.P. 38
14 Tanks South of B.P. 38
2 Groups of 27 and 25 Tanks respectively near the X tracks at Map References 516361
10 Medium Tanks at Quaret Abu Faris
17 MET [mechanized enemy transport] at Sheferzen.
1548 hours 60 Medium Tanks (believed Italian) at Map Reference 518359 ...
'B' Squadron patrol in the Battuma area was heavily shelled and withdrawn to Madiya.

Such laconic records do not convey a true sense of what it took to garner such small but

4th Armoured Car Regiment members with their Marmon Herrington Mk3. They were part of the 7th Armour Division, the Desert Rats and were entitled to wear the red Jerboa emblem.

4th Armoured Car Regiment Marmon Herrington Mk3 crew, Klerck, White Wittenberg, Wright.

important items of information, or the tremendous heat. At high noon "the landscape blurred and shook with the heat, and mirages appeared," as Klein says, the hordes of flies, the monotonous food and the permanent shortage of water. The keynote was sleepless vigilance, night and day.

At first light the forward observation troops would move into their positions on whatever high ground was available and stay in place until after last light. The nights they spent listening hour after hour for sounds of wheeled or tracked enemy vehicles moving around – distances were too great for attacks on foot – ready to defend themselves if necessary.

At the squadron and regimental headquarters, officers and men worked through the hours of darkness dealing with the endless "bumph" any army generates: answering routine correspondence, filling in and transmitting various returns, compiling the next day's radio codes and frequencies – so that "there were not many hours left for sleep."

By way of explanation, one can quote Sandars on the general modus operandi at this time:

In static periods the armies were usually many miles apart, and our armoured cars would establish continuous patrol lines to report any enemy activity. Squadron headquarters would be positioned up to 20 miles ahead of the main body of Allied forces and would have their sabre troops in line some 10 miles further ahead still.

Sometimes these lines stretched for over fifty miles; if the ground was flat and the number of armoured cars sufficient they would observe from static positions, but if not they had to move about to cover their area, and this made them more likely to be seen and attacked by enemy aircraft.

The normal drill for keeping observation in this way was to have three troops in the line, and two back with squadron headquarters resting and maintaining; a fresh troop relieving one in the line every day.

In the advance they scouted ahead and on the flanks of the main body, and in addition to reporting any enemy sighted they often gave details of the 'going' which enabled the best route to be picked for the bulk of the force.

Owing to the weak armament and lack of integral infantry and artillery of our armoured car regiments, for most of the campaign they were seldom able to bounce the enemy out of weak positions on their own, as the German recce units did, and at least until late 1942 they had difficulties driving into the enemy's armoured car screens to see what his main body was up to. During actual battles the armoured cars hovered on the wings, following and reporting groups of enemy vehicles, and looking for opportunities to attack unescorted soft vehicles. Raiding into the rear of the enemy lines was also an important part of their role.

This trying routine meant that 4 South African Armoured Car Regiment had been thoroughly salted by the time Rommel made his next move. For the past two months the tireless screen of British and South African armoured cars had prevented any German ground reconnaissance east of the Sallum–Sidi Omar Line and its southern flank, and he had come to suspect an Allied build-up along the border. So he launched a reconnaissance in force which was tasked to break through the observation line and upset any such activity behind it.

It just so happened that Newton-King and his men of 4 South African Armoured Car Regiment, with a battery of the Royal Horse Artillery in support, were deployed across the axis of the German thrust in a 7½km-long arc extending from the coastal escarpment to the vicinity of Fort Maddalena in the south.

On the night of 12 September 1941 they received early warning that the situation was about to change: information processed from radio intercepts indicated that a forward movement of the enemy was likely within the next 48 hours – a demonstration in force, perhaps, possibly to cover another assault on Tobruk.

Next morning 4 South African Armoured Car Regiment's squadrons were warned of what might happen. Preparations for a withdrawal were put in hand, and all sub-units went on standby. Nothing happened during that day, but after dark the watchers reported hearing enemy vehicle movement and seeing frequent flares.

At 0100 on the 14th, B Squadron, which was stationed on the right arm of the arc, reported sighting the first actual enemy concentration. At 0300 it spotted enemy tanks moving forward and alerted the Royal Horse Artillery Battery. Then at first light contact was made and Reeves-Moore started to withdraw as per plan.

Soon after dawn both B Squadron and A Squadron, which were in the centre of the arc, reported the rapid approach of tanks. They did not know it then, but the tanks belonged to three columns of the Deutsches Afrikakorps' 21 Panzer Division, with Rommel himself directing a detailed encircling manoeuvre he had prepared with which he hoped to cut off any substantial British force he might encounter.

B Squadron started falling back, followed at 0648 by A Squadron. A few minutes later, at 0655, the Deutsches Afrikakorps force was clearly visible, and B Squadron reported that there were 40 tanks near Alam El Arad which were moving southeast at speed. At the same time, 40 mechanized transport vehicles were reported near El Rabata, moving south toward Fort Maddalena.

4 South African Armoured Car Regiment continued to fall back, reporting the enemy's movements and strength. At 0900 Newton-King's headquarters section came under fire from German tanks which were heading south, only a little over a kilometre away. His car chose this perilous moment to break down; he and his crew set it alight, climbed on to a passing Royal Horse Artillery gun tractor and got away, but it took half an hour for him to find another car and re-establish his forward radio link.

A little later the headquarters orderly-room lorry broke down as well – a much more serious loss this time, because the Germans captured it and its three occupants, as well as a variety of important documents and cipher material.

But the withdrawal plans functioned smoothly. Screened by the armoured cars, British columns in the frontier area withdrew behind minefields that had been laid at outposts named North Point and Playground, and dug in. Having spent all day shadowing the German tanks, 4 South African Armoured Car Regiment positioned itself at nightfall along a line running more or less north and south through Bir Thalata, where the centre and right squadrons listened to the ominous sound of unseen vehicles.

At first light on 15 September 1941 the cars began probing forward to divine the enemy intentions. They found nothing. Rommel had turned back; he had come under heavy aerial attack and firm resistance from the defensive positions without finding any worthwhile British forces to cut off.

4th Armoured Car Regiment Marmon Herrington Mk 3, named *Jakhals* II.

4th Armoured Car Regiment Marmon Herrington Mk 3 named *Rooikat* II.

The squadrons began to return discreetly to their earlier observation line, but the Deutsches Afrikakorps had not left altogether, and at 1815 one of the right-hand squadron's patrols came speeding back, chased by shells from 20 tanks it had encountered near Alem el Arad and which were now hot on its heels.

The pursuit continued until the tanks came under fire from British artillery located at Ilwet, after which the Germans circled away to the south and finally withdrew to the northwest along the escarpment after several other British gun positions also started shelling them.

At dusk it was still not known whether these tanks had actually withdrawn or were simply lying in wait, so the armoured cars were pulled back to spend the night in areas which were known to be in full view while a general lack of clarity about the situation and the possibility that other tanks might have moved in behind the normal observation line (which, it was later confirmed, was actually the case) proceeded.

That night the cars in the centre of 4 South African Armoured Car Regiment's line heard more sounds of tracks, and British troops on the extreme left were attacked by two lorry-loads of German infantry, who withdrew without inflicting any casualties after much firing had taken place.

That was the end of Rommel's probe, and at first light next morning the forward cars were back in their old positions on the observation line. 4 South African Armoured Car Regiment had survived its first contact of the desert war almost unscathed. It had lost the three orderly-room clerks and the two vehicles, but in the process its officers and men had gained valuable experience in the new style of desert warfare.

By the end of October 1941 almost all of the South African Tank Corps' stragglers were in Egypt, and a number of changes had taken place in the command appointments as it prepared itself for the battles that lay ahead – not only by training but also by some small-scale operational deployments.

Most of 1 South African Light Tank Company, having finally said goodbye to Abyssinia after the surrender of Jimma, had left from Massawa on 16 August 1941, and on arrival had been absorbed into 3 South African Reconnaissance Battalion. So had Major Jenkins's Addis Ababa detachment of motorcyclists, which had departed on 27 August 1941 with the praises of the British military administrators ringing in their ears.

The British sub-area commander stated in a letter to Jenkins that all kinds of duties he had given the detachment in connection with the maintenance of law and order in the town had been cheerfully and effectively carried out. The improvement in security was, he considered, very largely due to the firm and efficient way in which the company had dealt with the many disturbances which had occurred.

The commissioner of the new Ethiopian police, in turn, wrote that the detachment's arrival had been an immense relief to him; they had done everything possible to help, and had given him the opportunity to start building up the police force.

By early September 1941 the detachment was in Egypt and joining the rest of its company in the ranks of 3 South African Reconnaissance Battalion, with Major Jenkins becoming the unit's second-in-command (and later its commanding officer), while Major Stander was posted back to the Union after his 2 South African Motorcycle Company's absorption.

The surplus battle-experienced officers, resulting from the reorganization, now made it possible to feed some of the expertise back into the system. With the absorption of 1 South African Armoured Car Company Major Harry Klein was made the Armoured Fighting Vehicle staff officer in Durban, his second-in-command, Captain E. H. Torr, taking his place as company commander.

Major C. G. Walker of 2 South African Armoured Car Company handed over to Captain C. A. H. Heard before returning to the Union (he later commanded 2 Armoured Car Battalion). Major Sid Gwillam of 3 South African Armoured Car Regiment remained in the Middle East but was transferred to divisional staff duties, while his second-in-command, Major L. S. Steyn, was posted back to the Armoured Fighting Vehicle Training Centre as an instructor.

Major G. K. Roodt had to relinquish command of 3 South African Reconnaissance Battalion in late October 1941 because of ill health and handed over on the 24th to Lieutenant-Colonel J. P. A. Furstenburg, but his expertise was not lost, because after he had recovered he took Furstenburg's place as commanding officer of the Armoured Fighting Vehicle Training Centre.

In between everything else, several units of the South African Tank Corps took to the field in various places. 3 South African Reconnaissance Battalion ran patrols in the vicinity of Siwa Oasis in early August, even though it was not yet fully equipped for the desert and was still awaiting the arrival of 1 South African Armoured Car Company and 1 and 2 South African Motorcycle Companies to bring it up to strength, and later that month Major C. A. C. Saunders added to his East African know-how by commanding the Melfa Group.

This was a small all-arms force based on 3 South African Reconnaissance Battalion's headquarters reconnaissance group and operating from Melfa, near the Jarabub Oasis, which was on detached duty along the southern end of the observation line. The Melfa Group did not see much action, but accumulated valuable experience in desert navigation and radio communication.

Saunders' men also got their first real taste – in more than one sense of the word – of the severe discomfort they could look forward to: "A maliciously persistent and irritating type of midge aggravated the desert sores prevalent among the men," Klein writes, "and this, together with the peculiar properties of the water, which contained a mineral giving it the taste and effect of Epsom salts, did much to undermine their health and morale."

6 South African Armoured Car Regiment went through the same preparation process as the other units – training exercises at Almiriya, west of Alexandria, and the despatch of officers to the forward area for sojourns with the 11th Hussars, while nightly raids on Alexandria by the Italian Air Force "provided speculative talking points on what lay ahead in the desolate reaches to the west."

Then on 12 October 1941 6 South African Armoured Car Regiment got its turn to sample the dubious delights of Melfa when Lieutenant-Colonel Short was ordered to move his regimental headquarters and one squadron there, under command of Oasis Group for operations against the enemy lines of communication in the up-coming operations.

October 1941 saw 4 South African Armoured Car Regiment on the receiving end of serious

4th Armoured Car Regiment officers.

4th Armoured Car Regiment other ranks.

4th Armoured Car Regiment officers.

4th Armoured Car Regiment other ranks.

Luftwaffe strafing attacks for the first time – but not the last. At 1410 on the 9th, No. 2 Troop of B Squadron under Lieutenant Billy Klerk (three standard Marmon-Herringtons and one with a scrounged French Hotchkiss gun in place of its turret) were on duty in the observation line when nine Me 109 fighters appeared out of the blue and began strafing them.

Klerk immediately dispersed his troop into the standard diamond formation with 400m between each car, and to reduce the possibility of losses ordered his crews to bail out and take cover except for one anti-aircraft gunner in each car, although he and his radio operator stayed in theirs. Then followed 10 hectic minutes as the Me 109s attacked in successive waves of three, each wave targeting one particular car from different angles, then gaining height and coming in again.

The gunners stayed in action throughout the attack, and although the fighters jinked as they came in, they managed to shoot one down. In one car the Vickers jammed and the gunner, Corporal W. C. Fouché, was wounded in the head. In spite of this Fouché jumped out with his Bren gun, took cover and continued firing at the aircraft despite of being targeted by the enemy pilots (he was later decorated with the Military Medal).

By the time the Me 109s left the cars were pock marked by hits and between them had been holed in 15 places; in addition to Fouché, Klerk had been wounded in the knee, while Trooper T. D. Wright had been hit three times in the back and another trooper named Schapps in the face.

A little over a week later, on 21 October 1941, five Me 109s attacked C Squadron's No. 1 Troop with armour-piercing and high-explosive ammunition, hitting the cars 74 times during the five-minute attack and fatally wounding Trooper M. G. Visser.

But far greater battles lay immediately ahead. By now the Western Desert Force of Wavell's day had been reorganized, strengthened and rechristened the Eighth Army, a name which was to become famous, and in Cairo Auchinleck was planning an offensive which is remembered to this day as a landmark in the desert war: Operation Crusader. The South African armoured cars would be in it from the beginning. By the end they would have gained a reputation which would never be tarnished.

Auchinleck's field commander, General Sir Alan Cunningham, disposed over two army corps, made up of seven divisions – by far the largest Allied force seen so far – and more than 600 tanks, not counting the 126 at Tobruk. He had more than 600 serviceable British and Commonwealth combat aircraft on call, with direct support to the ground forces being exercised by Air Headquarters Western Desert, while at that stage the Axis air forces comprised only about 120 German and 200 Italian aircraft.

4th Armoured Car Regiment troopers on a training device.

The British XXX Corps under Lieutenant-General Willoughby Norrie was made up of 7 Armoured Division (Major-General William Gott), Major-General George Brink's veteran bush fighters of 1 South African Division, just arrived from East Africa and still short of 2 South African Brigade and the independent 22 Guards Brigade. XIII Corps, commanded by Lieutenant-General A. R. Godwin-Austen, consisted of 4 Indian Infantry Division (Major-General Frank Messervy), the newly arrived 2 New Zealand Division under the Major-General Bernard Freyberg VC and 1 Army Tank Brigade. In reserve Cunningham had 2 South African Division.

Out of sight (although definitely not out of mind) was Tobruk, which also formed part of the Eighth Army and whose garrison was a potent one. Major-General Leslie Morshead's 9 Australian Division which had held it so stoutly had now been replaced by 32 Army Tank Brigade, 70 British Infantry Division under Major-General Ronald Scobie, who was also the fortress commander, and the Polish Carpathian Brigade.

Opposing the Eighth Army was what was now called Panzergruppe Afrika under General Rommel, an equally formidable German–Italian force. Panzergruppe Afrika consisted of the Deutsches Afrikakorps under Lieutenant-General Ludwig Crüwell, 15 Panzer Division and 21 Panzer Division with a total of 260 tanks between them, a special-purpose composite formation which would later gain fame under its new name, 90 Light Division and the Italian 55 (Savona) Infantry Division.

Rommel also had XI Italian Army Corps under General Enea Navarini, comprising 17 (Pavia) Infantry Division, 102 (Bresia) Infantry Division, 102 (Trento) Motorized Infantry Division and 25 (Bologna) Infantry Division. In addition, the Italian high command in Libya retained direct control over another large formation, 10 Motorized Corps, consisting of the efficient 132 (Ariete) Armoured Division and 101 (Trieste) Motorized Division.

But the equipment figures were misleading. Of Cunningham's 600-plus tanks, only 339 were cruisers, fast tanks meant primarily for fighting other tanks. Of these, 210 were the new A15 Crusaders (which in fact were so new that they often suffered teething troubles) and the others the older 1938-vintage A10 cruisers and the newer A13s, which were faster than the A10s but had only half their thickness in armour.

Another 210 were infantry tanks, mainly the Matilda Mark II, which was heavily armoured but very slow (about 25kph on roads and 14kph across country) and, like all the other British tanks, mounted the inadequate 40mm 2-pdr gun, which apart from a lack of penetrative power had the serious drawback of not possessing high explosive shells in addition to its solid armour-piercing shot.

This severely restricted the number of ways in which a 2-pdr tank could be used on the battlefield. The gun was all but useless against infantry, and to knock out an enemy anti-tank gun required a direct hit, whereas a near-miss with a high explosive shell would have been enough to kill or incapacitate the gunners.

A new addition were 173 of the small, nippy but under-gunned American M3 Stuart, weighing 14.7 tons and crewed by four men: the driver, commander, gunner and co-driver.

Marmon Herrington Mk2 used for Anti-Aircraft purposes in Libya.

Marmon Herrington Mk 3 crew busy with a tyre change in North Africa.

It was powered by a 190kW 7-cylinder radial engine that gave it a high road speed of 58kph, and a range of 120km.

The main armament was a 53-calibre 37mm gun that could fire armour-piercing capped and high explosive ammunition; early versions also mounted no less than five .30-calibre Browning machine guns – one co-axial with the 37mm gun, one on top of the turret on an anti-aircraft mounting, a third in a ball mount in the right bow, and the other two in right and left hull sponsons.

The Stuarts had some significant weaknesses. The two-man turret crew was one; another was that it was fuel-thirsty, so that its maximum range was only 120km – a serious problem in highly mobile desert battles in which units often outran their supply echelons or lost contact with them and then ran the risk of being stranded when they ran dry.

The 37mm gun with its variety of ammunition types was more versatile than the 2-pdr, but also lacked penetration of the Germans' tank armour, which had been growing thicker ever since the Polish campaign of 1939.

On the other hand, crews liked its speed and its mechanical reliability when compared to the British cruiser tanks, especially the Crusader, and almost immediately the Eighth Army dubbed it the 'Honey'.

In his book *Brazen Chariots*, R. J. 'Bob' Crisp, a renowned pre-war South African Springbok cricketer who served in 3 Royal Tank Regiment, claimed credit for the name on behalf of his driver. Crisp had just returned to Egypt from the abortive campaign in Greece and Crete at this time, and in his book has left a graphic description of his regiment's introduction to the diminutive Stuart at Heliopolis, outside Cairo:

[In Greece] we had been equipped with ancient A10s and A13s, and even some A9s dragged out of various war museums and exhibitions. They were ponderous square things, like mobile pre-fabricated houses and just about as flimsy. By far their worst failing was their complete inability to move more than a mile or two in any sort of heavy going without breaking a track, or shedding one on a sharp turn.

Of the 60-odd tanks 3 Royal Tank Regiment had taken to Greece at the beginning of the year, not half a dozen were casualties of direct enemy action. All the others had been abandoned with broken tracks or other mechanical breakdowns. They littered the passes and defiles of Macedonia and Thessaly, stripped of their machine guns, but otherwise intact. They were of no help to the enemy; no other army would have contemplated using them …

We regarded the advent of our new tanks with a good deal more vital interest than a newly married couple inspecting their first home. We were also fascinated by the group of American army technicians who came with them.

The Stuart was a strange looking contraption, straight from Texas, tall in the saddle and with the Western flavour accentuated by a couple of Browning machine guns and the rangy Texans. The main armament was similar to the peashooter that all British tanks carried at that time, but the frontal armour was much thicker than in our own light tanks and cruisers.

The really intriguing things about the M3 were its engine and the tracks. Drivers gasped in astonishment when the back covers were lifted off... it was simply an aeroplane engine stuck in a tank, with radial cylinders and a fan that looked like a propeller.

Fuel was to present a new problem to the supply services, as the engine ran efficiently only on high octane aviation spirit. But this was not our problem, and the consensus of opinion was that anything that was likely to assist in a fast take off was probably a good thing.

After the engines had received their share of comment, we gave our undivided attention to the tracks. There had never been anything like them in the British army. Each track link was mounted in solid rubber blocks on which the vehicle moved. After one look we wondered why the hell British tank designers had never thought of it.

As soon as he could manage it, Crisp took one of the Stuarts into the desert for field testing and was even more impressed:

We tested her for speed first, and found that on good going we could get up to 40mph. It was a comforting thought, in the circumstances, to know that the German Marks III and IV could manage only 20 or so. Then I told my driver, Whaley, to make a few fast turns, and waited with some foreboding for the inevitable bang, clatter and swerving halt that meant a broken track. Nothing happened. It was wonderful. That tank handled like a well-trained cow-pony.

"Let's see just what it will take," I said down the intercom. "Try and shed one of these tracks."

Whaley put her through a variety of turns and manoeuvres that made the sandy floor of the desert look like an ice-rink after a hockey match, spurting up great fountains of sand and dust behind the tracks.

"That'll do," I shouted to the driver at last. "We're beginning to wear out the desert."

Back at the camp the CO and a small crowd were waiting for us. We climbed out, all grinning happily.

"Well, Whaley," I asked my driver, "what do you think of it?"

He, plainly under the influence of the nearby Texan, beamed and said simply: "It's a honey, sir."

From that moment they were never known as anything else.

Opposing the Eighth Army's motley and under-gunned array of old and new armour were 379 Panzer Mark III and IV cruiser tanks with 42-calibre 50mm and 24-calibre 75mm guns respectively, the best fighting tanks produced in the war up to that time, as well as Panzer Mark I and II light tanks. There were also 154 Italian cruiser tanks, almost all the Carro Armato M13/40 with its 32-calibre 47mm gun.

This is not to mention the fact that the most potent British anti-tank gun was once again the 2-pdr, whereas the Germans' efficient 37mm gun was backed up by the long-reaching 88mm anti-aircraft gun, deployed in an anti-tank role.

The figures for air support are also misleading without the benefit of analysis. Cunningham's aircraft operated out of Egypt and Malta, meaning that it took some time for them to reach the battle area, whereas Rommel could draw on a total pool of 750 serviceable combat aircraft based in Tripolitania, Sicily, Sardinia, Greece and Crete.

An invisible but definite advantage on the German side was that on the whole Rommel's armoured division commanders had a better grounding in tank (and anti-tank) warfare than their British equivalents, although all of the latter had had distinguished earlier careers.

Cunningham had spent most of his career as a field and anti-aircraft artilleryman, and although he had conducted a successful campaign in Abyssinia it had borne no resemblance to a heavily armoured mobile conflict. Gott was an infantryman who had been a lieutenant-

Mamon Herrington Mk 3 upgunned with an Italian 47mm gun.

Marmon Herrington Mk2s and 3s cover a mountain pass in North Africa.

colonel and battalion commander as recently as late 1939, then served briefly in staff posts; his only hands-on experience of armour before his posting as general officer commanding 7 Armoured Division came from a short period as commander of a composite support group.

Norrie was a former horse cavalryman who had commanded a light tank brigade before and at the start of the war, but not in action, served briefly as inspector royal armoured corps and was then sent to Egypt in command of an armoured division, but before seeing action he had been catapulted unexpectedly into command of XXX Corps when the designated commander, the brilliant armoured-expert Major-General Vyvyan Pope, died in an air crash in September 1941.

In Bob Crisp's opinion, "probably the best handler of armour in the desert at the time" was Brigadier Alec Gatehouse, commanding 4 Armoured Brigade, "who could be described as a tank officer as distinct from a cavalry officer."

Rommel had constructed a strong defensive line running from Sallum to Fort Capuzzo and then up to the port of Bardia, about 55km east of Tobruk, which was manned by elements of 21 Panzer Division and 55 Infantry Division; the rest of his manoeuvre forces were lying up in the vicinity of Tobruk, which he intended to attack again on 24 November 1941 when his supply situation had eased.

But Auchinleck had no intention of sticking his head into Rommel's meat-grinder, and obviously judged that Rommel did not think he would either. Therefore any attack would take place inland. The question was where and when. Auchinleck mounted an elaborate deception plan to convince Rommel that he would not be able to move until early December, and that when he finally did so he would cross the border as far south as possible, near Jarabub Oasis on the fringe of the Sand Sea, and then carry out a wide out-flanking advance toward Tobruk.

It was so convincing that when Crusader's wheels started rolling on the night of 17 November 1941 Rommel was away on a visit to Germany, secure in the belief that there was no immediate threat from the British, with the possible exception of a reconnaissance in force which could easily be beaten off.

Actually the Eighth Army's plans were quite different. Firstly, of course, it would move almost two months earlier than Rommel had been led to believe; secondly, it would strike across the border at a point much closer to the coast than Jarabub.

The intention was to leave its base west of Mersa Matruh during the night of 17 November 1941 and cross the border near Fort Maddalena, about 80km south of Sidi Omar and 240km north of Jarabub. Then in the early hours of 18 November 1941, Cunningham would start the actual advance to contact.

Norrie's XXX Corps would head northwest, so that 7 Armoured Division (minus 4

Armoured Brigade) could attack and destroy the Axis armour in the vicinity of Tobruk, with 1 South African Division covering Norrie's left flank against any attempt at encirclement by the wily Rommel.

On Gott's right, meanwhile, Godwin-Austen's XIII Corps would wheel around and strike north to capture Bardia and threaten the rear of the Axis defence line running eastward from Sidi Omar to the coast at Halfaya. Although XIII Corps was lightly armoured, it would have 4 Armoured Brigade attached and Norrie's attack would shield it from a heavy reaction by the Axis tanks. Then, when Norrie got close enough to Tobruk, Scobie's 70 Division would break out and join hands with him.

The keys to the operation's success were the early destruction of the Axis armour by 7 Armoured Division, as well as two days of intensive air raids by the Desert Air Force to disrupt the Axis airfields and destroy as many of their aircraft on the ground as possible, thus protecting XIII and XXX Corps from the Luftwaffe and Regia Aeronautica. But as it transpired, neither of these keys was as easy to turn in the Axis lock as Auchinleck hoped.

It would appear that the British under estimated the Axis tank strength. Auchinleck had just one armoured division – weakened by one third because of the detachment of 4 Armoured Brigade to XIII Corps – and a very under-strength independent tank brigade, while the Germans had two armoured divisions and the Italians one. The battle plan also had one serious flaw: Cunningham did not concentrate his armour. And on top of it all, the weather would ally itself with Rommel.

The South Africans did not know it yet, but they were to play an integral part in Auchinleck's deception plan, which was the responsibility of Brigadier D. W. Reid of 29 Indian Infantry Brigade, commander of the Oasis Group.

In the earlier planning stages of Crusader there was to have been a strong, sweeping attack on Rommel's southern flank from the oases of Jarabub, Jalo and Aujila, located on the fringes of the awe-inspiring Libyan Sand Sea, while the main body of the Eighth Army crossed the border approximately at its centre point. The aim was to disrupt Rommel's southern lines of communication and persuade him that the British were invading Libya from the extreme south as well.

Subsequently, however, this was drastically reduced to a feint attack by Reid's Oasis group, for the purpose of which he was provided with two battalions of dummy tanks and an armoured car contingent consisting of the headquarters and two squadrons of Lieutenant-Colonel P. H. Grobbelaar's 7 South African Reconnaissance Battalion and the headquarters and B Squadron of Lieutenant-Colonel V. C. G. O'B Short's 6 South African Armoured Car Regiment.

For support he was allocated one battery of 2 South African Field Regiment, one battery of 73 Anti-Tank Regiment Royal Artillery and a battery of 6 Light Anti-Aircraft Regiment Royal Artillery.

In mid-October 1941 Reid's forces had started to gather at Melfa when Short was told to move his headquarters and two squadrons there for attachment to 29 Indian Brigade. This done, 6 South African Armoured Car Regiment settled down to routine patrols, completely unaware of why they had been sent down south.

Grobbelaar's entry into the scheme was much more dramatic. As October neared its end he was summoned by Major-General I. P. de Villiers, general officer commanding 2 South African Division, and informed that his headquarters and two squadrons were on standby to take part in a mission so secret that he could not be told what it entailed.

Grobbelaar made some discreet enquiries at Eighth Army headquarters but failed to discover any clues except that he would later be joined by a squadron of Royal Air Force armoured cars; his mission would entail covering long distances in arduous conditions and that he would have just one week of special desert training south of the Qattara Depression.

Marmon Herrington Mk2 bogged down in sand.

Members of Regiment President Steyn, unfortunately only their first names are known: Fish, Percy, Tim, James and Gordon.

Time was of the essence. In that week Grobbelaar also had to have his 49 armoured cars modified for desert warfare. Technicians from all the workshops in 2 South African Division were inspanned for a concentrated effort to fit anti-aircraft mountings and carry out other modifications. With most of these completed, Grobbelaar headed for Melfa, taking a short-cut across the eastern tip of the supposedly impassable Qattara Depression.

Grobbelaar spent almost three weeks at Melfa, gaining valuable desert experience while escorting supply columns engaged in preparing a new airfield for the coming offensive, Landing Ground 125, which was located about 150km northeast of Jarabub and halfway to Agedabia. The whole enterprise was conducted with the utmost secrecy: the supply columns did not move between early morning and late afternoon, and between times all vehicles were widely dispersed and camouflaged to avoid detection from the air.

But Grobbelaar still did not know what Reid's objectives were, or even when D-Day would be. It was not until 12 November 1941, when Grobbelaar was told to protect LG125 with the help of the Royal Air Force armoured cars, that he received some vague hints about what would be expected of him:

> As D-Day, 17 November, approached, I was told our task would be a raid on either a road, on an aerodrome, a dump, or a garrison or a post, on a supply route or a harbour area – in an area which just about included the whole desert. The eastern boundary was a north–south grid line near Tobruk. The western boundary was a north–south grid line through Mekili [an airfield northwest of LG125]. The southern boundary was an east–west grid line through LG125.
> On D minus two our objective would be given to us; on D minus one we would carry out the raid, which would be at dusk. During the night we would have to break from the objective, and move sufficiently far from it not to impede bombing operations the following morning.

But Grobbelaar still did not know exactly what or where his objective was: that vital information, he was told, would be delivered by an aircraft on D minus two. This was bad enough, since it left him with very little time for planning, but it was made even worse when the aircraft was kept away by a sandstorm which also prevented radio communication.

"Only on D minus one, at 0755 hours, did the aircraft arrive with instructions as to our objective; of which we had the choice of two – Mekili or Bir Hakeim," he later reported. "The latter was reported to be strongly covered to the south and east by units of the Italian Ariete Division and had to be approached from the northwest. Mekili was a landing ground and could be tackled by a straight approach. Because of the little time allowed for the operation I chose Mekili."

Success was not guaranteed, because Mekili was more than 200km away and, thanks to the non-arrival of the aircraft, the raid would be starting out a day late. Grobbelaar nevertheless felt it was worth trying, although he knew that he would be cutting things very fine indeed.

He would have to reach Mekili by dusk on the same day he left LG125 (17 November 1941), attack the airfield during the night and be away before dawn on the 18th to leave the way clear for the Royal Air Force. If the going was not too bad, he calculated, it would be just possible to reach Mekili by dusk. In addition, he would have to proceed under strict radio silence until contact had been made.

He could do nothing about the radio silence, but because speed was now the crucial factor he decided to leave his Royal Air Force Rolls-Royces behind:

> … because they were very old military types and not very mobile from a desert-going point of view.
> We left LG125 and travelled at our best speed, with visual communications. The going was difficult in parts, but we made good progress until between 1500 and 1600 hours, when the clouds started to form and we could not run on the sun-compass. This slowed us down no end, as we had to keep on stopping to check our position with the oil compass. Stopping the cars in soft sand and getting them going again led to further delay. It became obvious we could not get to Mekili before dark.
> Just as it was getting dark we came to a dump of 44-gallon drums in the Tengeder area, 40 miles south of Mekili. It was obviously a harbour area, but there was nobody there. Some armoured cars were detailed to fire into the drums. We decided that notwithstanding the orders about a dusk attack we would make Mekili that night.
> But now the going worsened dramatically, and springs began to break as the big cars bumped over one rocky outcrop after another. Eventually his force was so diminished that he could see no choice except to call the raid off, much to everybody's disappointment.

Now Grobbelaar faced another problem: How to call his cars to him without using his radio. He had to settle for firing a coded signal with Verey flares:

> [The flares] I considered … must have given the show away – we had not been detected until then – and as I had been told to be clear of Mekili by dawn, I decided to switch my line. The men were most disappointed by the tame conclusion of their raid, and we withdrew south of Tengeda, halfway back to LG125, where I had left some supply vehicles. We refuelled and had a quick bite, and I decided to go for Bir Hakeim, army orders or not. We were all very keen to make contact with the enemy.
> We moved off, crossed the upper reaches of the Wadi el Mra at about the zero grid line, and found the going not difficult. We then planned to hit the southern outpost of the Ariete Division from the west; there was a good chance of giving them a bit of a scare.
> At about 1500 hours we did spot some vehicles to the east and went flat out to contact them, but they did not stay. They began to move east and all we saw were plumes of dust, and we were unable to overtake them. About an hour before sunset I had to call the chase off, for maintenance and refuelling.
> We stood to in laager, but the enemy did not contact us, though all around us we could see their Verey lights. Nothing developed and, as I had to join Brigadier Reid at LG125 next day, an hour before dawn we switched direction and made for the LG.

It was a disappointing end to what had promised to be an episode of high adventure. On the other hand, Grobbelaar and his men had gained valuable hands-on experience of long-range raiding which would stand them in good stead later on.

But his immediate priority was to get back to Jarabub, where Brigadier Reid was standing by to attack Jalo oasis, the first of the diversionary raids in the south which were meant to distract Rommel from events on his doorstep. His Oasis Group with its attached armoured

South African troops in Marmon Herrington Mk 2s and Mk3s in Maddalena, Western Desert.

South African troops in Marmon Herrington Mk2 in Derna, Libya.

cars and guns had now been codenamed "E Force," and much would be heard of it in the next few weeks. There seems to have been a certain light heartedness about this operation. In *The Sidi Rezegh Battles* Agar-Hamilton and Turner record:

> The whole atmosphere in which E Force moved and had its being was charged with a happy irresponsibility. Before he took over, Brigadier Reid had been told that his task, in addition to providing protection for a projected chain of airfields between Jarabub and Agedabia, would include the making of plans for the capture of Jalo, but no definite order to move against the place ever reached him.

On 16 November – two days before the opening of the offensive – Major Towsey flew down to Jarabub as liaison officer from the Eighth Army. "I asked him," says Brigadier Reid, "what my actual task was to be, and he said: "Oh! They all reckon you are going for Jalo." And so for Jalo we went!

One small element of the South African Tank Corps was to miss out on their comrades' first great Western Desert battle so far: Captain G. A. Elliott, lieutenants J. L. Tucker, D. T. Kenyon, L. A. Larson and J. H. Gage, and 38 non-commissioned officers and men, who it will be remembered, had been dispatched southward by General Wetherall on a fruitless venture and were still marooned at Gilgil long after the rest of the corps had left for the Middle East.

But late in September 1941 this idyll had been brought to an abrupt halt. As Klein tells it, the tankers were placidly enjoying breakfast when "the quiet tenor of the early morning was shattered" by a signal from the higher headquarters.

One last battle remained to be fought in Abyssinia. In the formidable mountains north of Lake Tana, 400km as the crow flies from Addis Ababa – General Nasi, acknowledged as the best Italian commander in East Africa – was making a last stand in the ancient fortresses of Gondar, Wolchefit, Chelga, Amba Giorgis and Gorgora with the puny remnants of his country's East African army.

The Italians had gained a short breathing space after Jimma when Allied operations had been postponed until the end of the rainy season. Now the dry weather had arrived, and British forces closed in from the Sudan, Eritrea and Dessie, near Amba Alagi.

The overall commander of the operation was C. C. Fowkes, now promoted to major-general and appointed general officer commanding 12 African Division, which was responsible for the northern part of the remaining enemy area, and consequently for the operations against Gondar.

In all haste the Light Armoured Detachment made its preparations, and on 1 October 1941 sailed from Mombasa with three aged light tanks (the newest of which was seven years old), four Bren carriers, four light aid detachment workshop sections, portées for all the tracked vehicles and a few 3-ton lorries for kit and equipment.

Eighteen days later the detachment arrived at Massawa, scooped up another six South African Tank Corps men who had been left behind when 1 Light Tank Company had sailed for the Middle East and climbed the meandering mountain road to Asmara. Three days were spent there servicing the distinctly decrepit portées, and on 22 October 1941 Elliott's force headed for Dessie.

Just before they got to Dessie, however, they were diverted to Amba Giorgis, south of Lake Tana, where 12 African Division was lying up after capturing the Wolchefit Pass and was preparing to attack the Italian stronghold at Kulkaber, which guarded the southern approaches to the main objective of Gondar.

The detachment reached Amba Giorgis on the evening of 1 November 1941, after a long struggle with bad road conditions and one transport breakdown after another; Elliott was tasked to support 25 and 26 East African Brigades, which were to capture Kulkaber and then advance on Gondar.

Early on 7 November 1941 the detachment set out to reconnoitre the country ahead: A belt of high mountains, deep kloofs and dense grass and bush which was totally unsuited to tank operations. South African sappers, however, found a ruinous disused track that could be cleared enough for the tanks and Bren carriers to use it, although not the wheeled vehicles. But only just – it took them three days to cover a mere 8km, and then at the cost of unending toil and a prodigal expenditure of petrol.

Then they were through the mountains and on the plains, halfway to Kulkaber. After three days of reconnoitring and servicing the sorely tested tanks and carriers, Elliott's men linked up with 1/6 King's African Rifles and attacked Kulkaber from the west in the face of a fierce defence, with the Italians inflicting heavy casualties on the infantry and shelling the light tanks under Lieutenant Kenyon when they burst into view.

Kenyon and his tanks managed to get through the artillery barrage unscathed and took the first objective by 0730, then swung around to the east of Ferkaber Hill to deal with heavy machine-gun and mortar fire which had pinned down 1/6 King's African Rifles. Kenyon charged in and silenced the opposition with the loss of one man wounded.

The tanks now had to withdraw to refuel and take on more ammunition at the King's African Rifles' battalion headquarters, after which they returned to the fighting and gave further fire support to various infantry groups. One of these was a large band of Shifta whom Lieutenant Jack Gage found wandering aimlessly about the battlefield without a clear idea of what to do.

Gage promptly organized them into some sort of coherent force and led them in an attack on a series of Italian machine gun posts, his Vickers guns blazing. This suited the Shifta very well and they captured one position after another, making prisoners of the local area commander and hundreds of soldiers.

While Gage and his *ad hoc* Shifta army were thus engaged, Captain Elliott and Lieutenant Larson, each commanding a sub-section of two Bren carriers, were also providing fire support for another part of the infantry attack under the most adverse conditions, "through 12-foot-high grass and scrub, dodging boulders and crashing through concealed dongas," as Klein relates. By 0930, however, they and the infantry had taken the first objective.

This done, the carriers dealt with some of the more isolated machine gun positions and then made use of the broken terrain to manouvre themselves, completely unseen, into dead ground from where their machine guns could rake the last of the Italian defensive lines. This unpleasant surprise unsettled the Italians, who then succumbed to an attack by 2/4 King's African Rifles, and resistance at Kulkaber ended.

South African troops in Marmon Herrington Mk2s liaise with locals in Derna, Libya.

SAAC Radio operator in MaHe as used in North Africa.

It was the first time that Bren carriers had ever been in action with the South African Tank Corps, and they had shown what they could do if properly handled, although if Klein is to be believed, they mounted some unauthorized armament in addition to their light machine gun.

Between them, he says, they fired a total of 5,000 .303-calibre rounds, 3,000 rounds of (Italian) Breda ammunition and 35 anti-tank rounds, presumably from Boys rifles. Miraculously the thinly armoured, open-topped carriers suffered no crew casualties despite of having been repeatedly hit by Italian fire.

The Light Armoured Detachment spent the night guarding about 1,500 Italian prisoners, and in the next two days reconnoitred ahead for the attack on the next objective, Tadda Hill, a needless precaution because it was evacuated before a shot was fired.

But there was no time for the detachment to rest on its laurels. Gondar had to be taken and promised to be a difficult objective. This meant extensive reconnaissance of all types, the lion's share of which fell on the Bren carriers; the ground conditions were too bad for Fowkes' armoured cars to operate.

"The Bren carriers were on the road day after day under the most difficult and trying conditions," Klein writes. "Not only did the crews spend most of their days in their vehicles, but a good many of their nights as well in keeping them in fighting trim.

"The Light Aid Detachment mechanics performed great service. Often Staff Sergeant Lawrence and his workshop lorry would move forward with a reconnaissance party to be close at hand in case of a breakdown. Every evening the workshops were hard at work, welding, repairing and tuning up engines."

The final key to the capture of Gondar was the fort at Azozo, just to its south. Ground conditions were so bad that even the light tanks and carriers could not range ahead as freely as they would have liked, but nevertheless Captain Elliott's men joined C Company of 2/4 King's African Rifles to form the vanguard of the advance on Azozo on 27 November 1941. Azozo fell without a fight, and now only Gondar lay ahead.

But the end had come for the Italian army in East Africa, and General Nasi knew that further resistance would be wasteful and futile. That same afternoon he surrendered unconditionally to a squadron of the Kenya Armoured Car Regiment.

The final shot of the campaign had now definitely been fired, and Elliott's Light Armoured Detachment was ordered back to Massawa, from where they left for the Middle East on 26 December 1941. The light tanks had travelled a long road, both figuratively and literally. They had been the very first element of the South African Tank Corps to be deployed in East Africa, and they were the last to leave, having been in action to the very end.

In the first week in October Bob Crisp and the rest of 3 Royal Tank Regiment moved into the desert west of Cairo for battle practice with live ammunition, and he took advantage of an inter-troop and inter-squadron competition to test a theory he had been developing:

> I had an idea that I wanted to try out. It was inspired by the fact that enemy anti-tank weapons, especially the newly introduced 88mm gun that had played havoc with our tanks in the ill-fated Battleaxe show, could knock us out at 3,000 yards, whereas the maximum effective range of our 37mm and 2-pdr guns was reckoned to be about 1,200 (this turned out to be wildly optimistic). The result, in simple arithmetic, was that we would have to be within range of their tanks and guns for 1,800 yards before we could hope to get close enough to do any damage. Eighteen hundred yards, in those circumstances, is a long way …
>
> My mind was occupied with two problems: how to get near enough to the enemy, and how to live long enough to get there. Obviously, armour-plating was not enough protection. There were alarming stories going about of what the 88s could do to the massive turrets of the I-tanks, hitherto considered almost impenetrable. The only answer lay in mobility, and pretty fast mobility at that.
>
> At the same time I completely discounted the possibility of shooting accurately from a moving tank, which was what we had all been taught to do when it was not possible to take up a hull-down position. So I worked out a system in my troop whereby, after the target had been indicated, a more or less automatic procedure followed if the circumstances were favourable.
>
> The objective was to get close enough to the enemy tank to be able to destroy it. The first order, then, was: "Driver, advance; flat out." The gunner would do his best to keep the cross-wires of his telescopic sight on the target all the time we were moving.
>
> The next order, heard by gunner, driver and loader, would be: "Driver, halt." As soon as the tank stopped and he was on target, the gunner would fire without further command from me. The sound of the shot was the signal for the driver to let in his clutch and be off again. From stop to start it took about four seconds. All I did was to control the movement and direction of the tank. The battle practice convinced me that I was right, and that in tanks that were outgunned and out armoured, mobility was an essential element in survival. Needless to say, by "mobility" I did not mean speed in the wrong direction.
>
> I did not win any competitions, but I had established to my own satisfaction that I could get within the effective range of my own gun without the use of concealment and in a fairly aggressive manner. I put myself in the place of a man in the target, and thought it would be very disconcerting to have four tanks thundering down on top of you, all firing accurately and none of them in one position long enough to be aimed at.
>
> I was hopeful that by using these tactics whenever the ground permitted, I would very much lessen the chances of being hit. It was not a substitute for the best battle position, which was hull-down upon ground of your own choosing, but I was quite certain that an over-emphasis on the hull-down position in what was going to be a war of considerable movement was not a good thing. It tended to induce in tank commanders a hull-down mind, which was quite likely to develop into a turret-down mind.

During Operation Crusader Crisp practised what he preached. Time after time he took the fight to the enemy, and personally knocked out between 35 and 40 German tanks before his luck ran out and he suffered a near-mortal head wound from a direct hit near the end of the operation. He awarded a Distinguished Service Order, a Military Cross and four mentions in dispatches; according to one source, the hot-tempered, highly individualistic Crisp might have gained more decorations, but for his continual clashes with authority.

23

Operation Crusader: test of fire

On the moonless, bitterly cold night of 17 November 1941 Cunningham's force set off westward, its progress slowed by rainfall so heavy that parts of the desert were actually flooded. Movement was made even more difficult because of the broken terrain and the fact that units had only a limited amount of training in night manoeuvre. The rain was to have an even more catastrophic consequence: all of the Desert Air Force's raids which were so vital to Cunningham's plans would have to be cancelled.

South African Tank Corps units were distributed throughout the Allied force. Furstenburg's 3 South African Reconnaissance Battalion marched with its old comrades of 1 South African Division; 4 South African Armoured Car Regiment under Newton-King was with 7 Armoured Division alongside its colleagues, the 11th Hussars and the King's Dragoon Guards; 6 South African Armoured Car Regiment Headquarters and one of its squadrons were attached to the Oasis group in the south, along with 7 South African Reconnaissance Battalion's headquarters and two squadrons. The other elements of 6 South African Armoured Car Regiment and 7 South African Reconnaissance Battalion were in reserve *pro tem* east of the frontier wire with 2 South African Division.

It was a momentous time for both the South African and British armoured cars, "the ubiquitous ground eyes of the Army … [as they] forged ahead of the tanks, infantry and guns into the storm of the conflict ahead," Klein writes. Meticulous navigation was needed to find the gaps in the border wire in darkness that was relieved only by sheets of lightning, the warning sign that rain was on the way. One headquarters car had to be abandoned when it was seriously damaged in a collision, but by midnight Newton-King's headquarters was on Libyan soil.

When all of the Allied force was over the border it stood fast for a few hours, then refuelled from pre-positioned dumps, and early in the morning resumed the advance. As per schedule Gott swung 7 Armoured Division around to the north and set off in the direction of Tobruk in line abreast – 4 Armoured Brigade and the King's Dragoon Guards on its right, 7 Armoured Brigade with 4 South African Armoured Car Regiment in the centre and 22 Armoured Brigade with the 11th Hussars on its left.

The armoured car regiments fanned out into a line 60km wide as they roamed out ahead of the main force, intent on working their way through the Axis reconnaissance screen, keeping watch for enemy movement on 7 Armoured Division's central sector and finding out where Rommel's main force and its flanks were.

For several hours the Division moved forward unhindered, although a cold, overcast sky with low clouds promised more rain. They made good time because here, about 120km south of the coast, they were on the wide plain of the coastal escarpment, whose terrain was broken but without any natural obstacles.

The first visual contact with the enemy did not come until 0930. Then, as 4 South African Armoured Car Regiment's A and B squadrons neared the Trigh el Abd, the road running eastward from midway between Fort Maddalena and Sallum, they reported back that three armoured cars had been seen moving northeast. Forty-five minutes later they sighted a

50-vehicle column led by eight armoured cars in the vicinity of Gabr Saleh, which lay just north of where the road to Bardia crossed the Trigh el Abd.

To the armoured cars it looked at first like a routine convoy of some sort, but the "routine convoy" was actually a small but heavily armed element of the Deutsches Afrikakorps' 33 Reconnaissance Unit. They discovered their mistake at 1100, when six enemy armoured cars attacked B Squadron's left flank near the crossroads. The armoured cars did not press home the attack, however, and after 20 minutes moved off, although the squadron reported that it had spotted two Axis tanks "swanning around" in the area.

No more was seen of the tanks, but between 1145 and 1230 4 South African Armoured Car Regiment and Axis armoured cars exchanged fire several times. Although neither side suffered any damage during these skirmishes, it was clear the Germans did not intend to let the armoured cars get closer to the main concentration of their forces, and that without support the cars would not be able to reconnoitre past the general line of the Trigh el Abd.

The support arrived at 1230, when a detachment of Gott's tanks advanced through 4 South African Armoured Car Regiment's screen and headed straight for Sidi Rezegh, less than 45km to the northwest ... a mere speck on the map which appeared there only because of a Muslim holy man's small tomb, which stood on a low rise above a gently sloping valley. It was a name that would soon forever be burnt into the memories of the desert soldiers after the most savage fighting of the entire operation.

The tanks' advance was not contested by the Axis forces, which fell back to the northeast, but the skirmishes meant that the right of Gott's line was delayed because A Squadron 4 South African Armoured Car Regiment could not carry out its forward reconnaissance as it was supposed to have done after the Trigh el Abd had been crossed. 7 Armoured Brigade and its other armoured cars kept moving, however, and reached the first-day objective a few kilometres northwest of Gabr Saleh without difficulty.

In the process it captured one of Rommel's eight-wheeled armoured cars, which had, Klein writes, "aroused tremendous interest and excitement in armoured fighting vehicle circles, but on close inspection the much-respected mammoth German armoured car, with its 20mm gun, which far out-punched the official armament of the Marmon-Herringtons, was found to be a less formidable weapon than had been imagined, and the myth of its invincibility was exploded."

1 South African Division, tasked with covering XXX Corps' western flank, crossed the Wire on a six-mile front about 50km from Fort Maddalena with Furstenburg's 3 South African Reconnaissance Battalion leading the way, and reached its first stop that evening without encountering any opposition. Its two brigades set up defensive perimeters, 1 South African Brigade (having covered 135km) at El Cuasc, and 5 South African Brigade, 30km to the north of it, at Bir el Duadar. 5 South African Brigade was now very short of fuel, which was to have an important effect on the next day's fighting.

Far away to the south, while XXX and XIII corps advanced into enemy territory, Brigadier Reid rolled out of Jarabub at the head of E Force for the first diversionary attack on Jalo Oasis. Led by Lieutenant-Colonel Short with 6 South African Armoured Car Regiment Regimental Headquarters and his B Squadron; E Force headed northwestward toward LG125 and then Jalo.

The going was not too bad for that part of the world, and by nightfall E Force had covered about 60km; in London the British Broadcasting Corporation made a carefully guarded announcement about Reid's departure from Jalo and the direction in which he was going. As it turned out the Germans were not distracted by the news, as had been hoped, although the timing of the Eighth Army's main attack had definitely caught them unaware. Next day Reid reached LG125 and kept going, leaving word for Grobbelaar to catch up.

The initial Axis reaction had been slow because its higher commanders had believed that the British were busy with a mere reconnaissance in force and refused either to be drawn from the main positions or to change the plans for an all-out assault on Tobruk they had scheduled. But on the second day it was clear that this was actually a full-on offensive and General Ludwig Crüwell immediately moved 21 Panzer Division forward from Gambut, southeast of Tobruk, and 15 Panzer Division toward Sidi Azeiz, northwest of Fort Capuzzo.

Cunningham's plan for 19 November 1941 envisaged 7 Support Group joining hands with 7 Armoured Brigade for a joint advance to Sidi Rezegh, while 1 South African Division advanced to Bir el Gubi, about 35km west of Gabr Saleh, which was located on the track that led to El Adem and eventually Tobruk. There it was to hold one of its two brigades in readiness to close in on Sidi Rezegh as well. 22 Armoured Brigade would operate north of Bir el Gubi, while 4 Armoured Brigade would remain on standby at Gabr Saleh.

On 19 November 1941 4 South African Armoured Car Regiment's squadrons fanned out into a wide screen ahead of 7 Armoured Brigade, maintaining contact with the Axis forces, which were still falling back as the British advanced. It was a laborious business; the clouds had not lied and heavy rain made the going difficult, to the point where the desert was such a morass in some places that armoured cars, guns and transport vehicles were bogging down.

A Squadron was the first of the armoured car sub-units to fall victim to the mud when its left-hand troops got stuck. While it was struggling to dig them out, B and C squadrons ranged far ahead, despite of going that was so bad that in one particularly awful patch near Bir el Reghem Reeves-Moore's men found 20 German lorries, an ambulance, four staff cars and an armoured car so completely bogged down that their owners had abandoned them.

Somehow the two squadrons managed to keep going, sending back a stream of information about enemy concentrations and movements, although B Squadron's right-hand cars were strafed by a Me 110s without suffering any damage and C Squadron had to fall back temporarily when it was fired on by enemy tanks.

Early in the afternoon A Squadron was sent off to join 4 Armoured Brigade, but B and C Squadrons made steady progress with the tanks close behind. At 1348 B Squadron's leading elements were able to report that they had reached the escarpment and were looking down on Sidi Rezegh, where there was a large enemy camp with a number of tanks and staff cars, next to a landing ground with 15 aircraft parked on it.

The lightly armed cars could do nothing but keep an eye on the landing ground. But not for long. At 1400 7 Armoured Brigade Headquarters told B and C squadrons to reconnoitre more widely in the Sidi Rezegh area. Twenty minutes after that C Squadron reported that a strong enemy column which included 100 tanks was moving southeast, while B Squadron saw five more aircraft touch down on the landing ground.

At 1630 A Squadron radioed that it had not been able to contact 4 Armoured Brigade and that a battle was in progress in its vicinity; it did not know it yet, but Crüwell's and Cunningham's tanks had now come to blows for the first time. Just then the enemy started to evacuate from Sidi Rezegh, hastened on their way by 6 Royal Tank Regiment, which had appeared from the south and now dashed down the escarpment with the South African armoured cars to attack the landing ground.

4 South African Armoured Car Regiment's war diary only stated: "At 1630 hours B Squadron's centre shot up some 'planes on the landing-ground at 417403. Ten men succeeded in getting away in two lorries."

It was in fact a great deal more exciting than that. J. A. I. Agar-Hamilton writes in *The Sidi Rezegh Battles* that "for once the armoured cars enjoyed the exhilarating experience of a 'charge', using their machine guns on that most vulnerable of targets – aircraft in process of taking off.

"Some enemy aircraft stopped suddenly in mid-career across the airfield: some blazed up and dissolved in black smoke, but there were others which turned the tables by flying low and shooting up the attackers." The tanks then ran over all the grounded aircraft just to make sure that they were out of action."

After this satisfactory encounter the armoured cars moved westward toward the track between El Gubi and El Adem where the Italian Pavia Division fired on them scoreing a hit on one car. Some cars ranged far enough forward to observe movement on the Trigh Capuzzo road, which ran west–east from the fort through El Adem, but night was coming on and at dusk 4 South African Armoured Car Regiment holed up southwest of Sidi Rezegh.

While 4 South African Armoured Car Regiment had been engaged in the centre on the morning of 19 November 1941, 22 Armoured Brigade and the 11th Hussars had reached Bir el Gubi, There they had run into the Italians' crack Ariete Division, which put up a stiff resistance and inflicted considerable casualties. On the British right flank 4 Armoured Brigade came into contact that evening with a force of 60 tanks from 21 Panzer Division, supported by 88mm gun batteries and anti-tank units, and a hot engagement followed.

Next day [20 November] fighting took place at several different locations. On the British left, 22 Armoured Brigade and the Ariete Division came to blows again at El Gubi, while at Sidi Rezegh 7 Armoured Brigade beat off an infantry attack by the German 90 Light Division and the Italian Bologna Division. On the right flank, 4 Armoured Brigade's light Stuart tanks fought it out once more with 21 Panzer Division, making maximum use of their speed and agility to counter the Germans tanks' heavier guns.

This worked, but only to an extent because the Stuarts had to forge their way through the German tank guns' fire, not to mention that of the 88mm guns, for a considerable distance before their 37mm guns could become effective. It was a weakness that was to operate to their extreme detriment in the next four days.

At this stage 15 Panzer Division was well on the way to Sidi Azeiz, where there was no one to fight, but then 4 Armoured Brigade began picking up information that the Germans intended linking up their two armoured divisions. This was what Cunningham had hoped for, since it would provide his armoured force with one target on which to focus.

But there was a near-fatal weakness in his planning: instead of 7 Armoured Division being concentrated in one compact assault force with which to smash into the German armour, it was now dispersed into three different penny packets. 4 Armoured Brigade was with Godwin-Austen's XIII Corps in the east, 22 Armoured Brigade was trading shots with the Ariete Division to the west and 7 Armoured Brigade was to the north around Sidi Rezegh.

To remedy this he disengaged 22 Armoured Brigade and sent it eastward to link up with 4 Armoured Brigade, which by now had suffered heavy losses, leaving Brink's 1 South African Division infantry and artillery to keep the Ariete Division from intervening in the rest of the fighting.

22 Armoured Brigade could not make the link up before dusk, however, and by that time 4 Armoured Brigade was at the tailend of yet another fierce battle, this time with 15 Panzer Division, 21 Panzer Division having withdrawn *pro tem* to replenish its fuel and ammunition. The day was too far gone for a decisive action, but when the two forces broke contact 4 Armoured Brigade had lost about 40 of its tanks, reducing its total original force of 164 by more than a quarter.

That night Rommel ordered all his tanks northwest toward Sidi Rezegh, while in Tobruk General Scobie made ready to start his break out in the morning. The plan was that Scobie and 70 Division would sally forth and cut the Via Balbia, the coastal road along which the main German line of communication ran. At the same time 7 Armoured Division, having taken Sidi Rezegh, would link up with Scobie and destroy the Axis positions around Tobruk.

While this was happening, and the German armour was otherwise engaged, 2 New Zealand Division from XIII Corps would advance northeast for about 45km to the vicinity of Sidi Azeiz on the escarpment above Bardia. By way of reinforcement for the thrust toward Tobruk,

4th Armoured Car Regiment Marmon Herrington Mk2, *Jakhals* II.

Marmon Herrington Mk 2 at the occupation of Derna airport North Africa.

General Norrie detached 5 South African Infantry Brigade, leaving General Brink at Bir el Gubi with only Pienaar's 1 South African Brigade to keep the Ariete Division pinned down. Brink acquiesced with reluctance; he had been promised that 1 South African Division would be kept together as a cohesive fighting formation and used in the breakout from Tobruk.

3 South African Reconnaissance Battalion's No. 3 Company (Major Crowther) screened 1 South African Brigade on the advance to Bir el Gubi – No. 1 Platoon forward, No. 2 Platoon on the right flank and No. 3 Platoon on the left. The advance was fairly uneventful and met with no hostile action, apart from occasional strafing attacks on the division, until they neared Bir el Gubi at 0825 and came under such heavy artillery fire that the armoured cars were compelled to halt, out of range. Brigadier Pienaar then also halted and deployed his brigade south of Bir el Gubi, but nothing more happened that day, except for intermittent shelling while the armoured cars provided reconnaissance screens forward of the infantry battalions.

Klein comments acidly:

On 20 November ... the British command considered that the armoured battle, which was the key feature of the master plan, was imminent. It was now evident that the British commanders in the field were so confident of the outcome of the armoured battle – based on incorrect assessment of the tank fighting to date and an over-optimistic appreciation of the strength of the British armour – that a major change was made in the original plan, in that the South African infantry were to be committed to action and the planned sortie from Tobruk was to be undertaken on 21 November – before the tank battle had been decided.

The 5th South African Infantry Brigade was to reach Sidi Rezegh (from Bir el Gubi) at 0700 hours on the 21st, to cooperate with the 7th Armoured Division's Support Group; and the 1st South African Infantry Brigade was to mask the Italians at Bir el Gubi. This was a marked change from the original plan, in which the whole 1st South African Division was to cooperate with the sortie from Tobruk after the enemy's armour had been decisively engaged.

For 3 South African Reconnaissance Battalion "the time of testing had arrived, going into battle for the first time in the Western Desert," as Klein notes. The major concerns of the battalion's No. 1 Company (Captain E. H. Torr), which was attached to 5 South African Brigade, were aerial attacks and a serious fuel shortage.

While screening the Brigade on the approach to El Cuasc on 19 November 1941, No. 1 Company had been machine gunned by Me 109s and bombarded by Ju 87 Stuka dive-bombers, a frightening but not expensive experience in terms of damage done: several cars were hit and kit and bedding rolls attached outside were perforated but as Klein writes, "the protection provided by kit hanging on the outside of cars was again established on this and subsequent occasions."

Much more worrying was the fuel shortage. On 20 November 1941, with the Brigade still southeast of Bir el Gubi at Bir Duedar, Torr's cars were down to an average of 13km of petrol each. Torr derived little comfort from repeated assurances by brigade headquarters that the arrival of a petrol convoy was imminent, and he pointed out several times that a brigade march of 30km meant at least 75km worth of screening and reconnoitring by the armoured cars.

At an order group that afternoon before the move to Sidi Rezegh, Brigadier Armstrong asked Torr if his cars could throw out a screen of 22km in front and to the left of the brigade. Torr said he could, provided he was given 1,800-litres of petrol. Armstrong's reply showed 5 Brigade's truly parlous situation: what petrol he had, he said, he needed for his infantry battalions; he had only 105km's worth for the entire brigade. Units which were running short would have to remain where they were and wait for the petrol convoy to come up.

The only solution was to siphon petrol out of No. 2 and No. 3 platoons, so that No. 1 Platoon (Captain Guy de Marillac) would be able to provide some sort of screen. With this scanty reconnaissance resource the brigade moved out of Bir el Duadar at 1600, hounded on its way by no less than three air attacks which brought a number of casualties. The brigade halted for the night 3km beyond the Trighh el Abd, still at least 18km from its destination, but De Marillac's travails were not yet over.

That night he was set out with a section of his cars to escort the brigade's intelligence officer to 22 Armoured Brigade with a message for its commander from Brigadier Armstrong. 22 Armoured Brigade was believed to be somewhere just south of the Trigh Capuzzo, but a nerve-wracking search failed to find it. Eventually the cars ended up at 7 Armoured Brigade Headquarters, where De Marillac was informed that 22 Brigade was actually still somewhere near Bir el Gubi. As a result of the next day's tank battles De Marillac was cut off from 5 South African Brigade, leaving it with only his remaining two sections of cars to screen ahead of its advance

On 20 November 1941 Newton-King's 4 South African Armoured Car Regiment was deeply involved in the Sidi Rezegh fighting. Klein writes:

While the 3rd South African Reconnaissance Battalion was finding its feet in the desert battle, 4 South African Armoured Car Regiment was heavily committed in the mêleé of confused fighting of the tank battles, which for four days from 20 November raged between Sidi Rezegh and Tobruk.
During these four decisive days the fighting was the fiercest yet seen in the desert. Around Sidi Rezegh airfield in particular the action was unbelievably confused, and the rapid changes in the situation, the smoke and dust, the sudden appearance of tanks, first from one direction and then from another, made great demands on regimental commanders.
That they did not fail is borne out by the ultimate results of the Crusader offensive and by the records of gallantry contained in regimental histories. It was the higher command that faltered at times, varying plans and decisions and making the cardinal error of dispersal of force.
Because of the fluidity of the battle and the 'fog of war' that descended on the wide-flung battleground, the British high command was not always in the picture regarding the extent of its tank losses, and plans previously designed to capitalize on a great British armoured victory were implemented in advance of the scoring of that victory, with disastrous and near-fatal results.

Klein quotes extracts from 4 South African Armoured Car Regiment's war diary:

... from the armoured car point of view the fluctuations, confusion and gallantry of the battles around Sidi Rezegh are best revealed in (a) stark simplicity.

A Marmon Herrington Mk 2 observe a destroyed German Ju52s at Derna Airfield, Libya.

MaHe Mk3 bogged down in sand, North Africa.

Nov 20: At about 0400 hours much movement was heard from West to East approximately along the 400 grid line. Men could be heard speaking German. Subsequently the sound of both tracked and wheeled vehicles could be heard from area 425409. German words of command were heard.

At 0630 hours Regimental Headquarters, which had just started to move north in order to get closer to Brigade Headquarters, found itself in the path of a dawn attack by the enemy infantry with anti-tank guns. Regimental Headquarters joined in a general scurry for a short distance East, speeded on its way by a fine display of tracer fire from machine guns and anti-tank guns.

At 0800 200 Germans launched yet another attack, supported by heavy artillery fire, but were repulsed by two batteries of 4 Royal Horse Artillery which was attached to 7 Armoured Brigade. 4 South African Armoured Car Regiment's contribution to this attack was in rather unexpected form. According to the diary:

Regimental Headquarters had (rather rashly perhaps) parked next to a battery of 25-pdrs, which were severely shelling the enemy position on the Sidi Rezegh ridge to the northwest. This idyllic state of affairs came to an end at 0830 hours when the enemy artillery got the range of these guns (and incidentally of Regimental Headquarters) with unpleasant accuracy.

A rapid move of a few hundred yards became necessary, and such was the urgency of the case that Regimental Headquarters' tea and sausages, which had just then been prepared, were left to waste their sweetness on the desert air.

The 25-pdrs were forced to pull out also, but not so fast but that a gunner (evidently a man of unusual presence of mind) contrived to carry off Regimental Headquarters' breakfast with him. He undoubtedly deserved the tea and sausages, but he might perhaps have left (or anyhow returned) the plates and mugs.

At 0900 hours C Squadron were at Bir el Haleizin [right] and just East of Bir er Reghem [left]. The right-hand patrol was having some sport shooting at motorcyclists. They knocked out one motorcycle but the rider got away. At 0945 hours Lieutenant A van Niekerk, commanding C Squadron's right patrol, engaged some enemy vehicles, and opened what was to be, before the end, a most impressive score, by knocking out 11 lorries, 2 staff cars and 2 motor-cycles, and taking 13 prisoners.

During the morning of 20 November the armoured cars had a break from their normal role for a while. B Squadron was tasked to carry out what was called a policy of aggravation to unsettle the enemy without exposing itself too much to his artillery. Reeves-Moore did this by venturing out westward and shooting up some Axis infantry who were busy digging in on the high ground at Point 178, just south of Sidi Rezegh. One patrol reached Hagfet en Nezha, south of El Adem and just west of the Bir el Gubi–El Adem road, more than 18km from Sidi Rezegh, where it drew fire from the Pavia Division.

Meanwhile C Squadron's right wing was pinned down in front of Bir el Haleizin, southeast of Sidi Rezegh, so it was told to stay in place while the squadron's left pushed on northward toward Point 175 on the high ground, east of Sidi Rezegh. The left wing duly moved forward until it reached Point 175: a strong position protected by deep wadis, or gulleys, and defensive works.

The C Squadron cars saw their first taste of action when they came up against a line of trenches defending Carmuset en Nbeidat, on Point 175's southeastern flank, with field artillery protecting the centre and lighter anti-tank guns on either side. The centre patrol worked its way around to a position from which it could enfilade the trenches and hosed them with machine-gun fire, causing a number of casualties before the anti-tank guns forced the cars to pull back.

These activities by 4 South African Armoured Car Regiment were mere pin-pricks that did not have any decisive effect because the cars had no infantry with them to take and hold ground, although they doubtlessly helped to spread alarm and despondency.

At 1630 4 South African Armoured Car Regiment Regimental Headquarters was attacked by 15 Stuka dive-bombers 7km south of Sidi Rezegh. According to the war diary "there was much sound, smoke and fury but no casualties, though minor damage was done to a wireless van and to the Technical Officer's truck. The twin coaxially-mounted Brens in Major Anderson's armoured car were seen in action for the first time and certainly made a fine encouraging noise."

In the south, Grobbelaar caught up with E Force on 20 November 1941 as it forged its way around the northern outskirts of the Great Sand Sea, making good progress over acceptable going. To Brigadier Reid's gratification it was overflown around noon by an Italian reconnaissance aircraft. According to Agar-Hamilton and Turner, this was:

> ... much to the satisfaction of the column commander, since there are few things more depressing than the ignoring of one's carefully elaborated deceit, and Brigadier Reid had disposed his force with 4-mile gaps between advance guard, main body and rearguard, in order to give the impression that it was a good deal stronger than the reality. Next day Panzergruppe Intelligence records 'English motorized spearheads ... moving toward Benghazi'.
>
> Once again the planners had been justified by the event, and E Force achieved precisely the impression that it was intended to produce. The Panzergruppe records that the 'advance was evidently aimed at the rearward communications of the Army in the area Benghazi-Agedabia'. At that time there were only two weak Italian battalions in Benghazi to hold the neighbourhood as well as the harbour, both of paramount importance for the supply services ... The Luftwaffe was requested to subject this enemy to continuous attacks from the air.
>
> But although Rommel had been fooled into believing that no large-scale British attack would take place until late December 1941, he was too old a hand to be drawn into diverting troops and tanks to the far south, and so as Klein says, "he left E Force to fight its own little war against the Italian garrisons at Aujila and Jalo."
>
> By the time E Force halted for the night of 20 November 1941 it had covered about 450km, leaving it with a final southward advance of about 125km to Jalo. Now Reid drew up his final plans for the attack, which would be carried out by three columns. A Force – troops and a squadron of armoured cars commanded by Short – would capture Aujila, about 30km northwest of Jalo to block the retreat of its garrison. A second column under Grobbelaar, comprising armoured cars, C Company of the 3/2 Punjabis, detachments of 40mm Bofors guns and royal engineers, plus one 3-inch mortar, would make a demonstration in force from the north, while E Force's main body and one squadron of armoured cars, under himself, would assault Jalo from the west. "At the evening order group," Grobbelaar recalled, "the Brigadier warned us against air attacks the next day, though no recce aircraft had yet been over us. Yet Rome Radio, in a news broadcast, had reported our presence."

On 21 November 1941 General Scobie duly broke out of Tobruk. Rommel had under estimated 70 Division's personnel and armoured strength, and was unpleasantly surprised by the scope and vigour of Scobie's sally – a three-pronged tank and infantry attack that overran a series of strong points leading to Ed Duda, east of El Adem. By mid-afternoon Scobie's men had taken heavy casualties but were about 5½km down the main road to Ed Duda.

But there was no sign of 7 Armoured Division, which had run into serious trouble. Gott had been scheduled to start his advance on Tobruk at 0830 that morning, but at 0745 his patrols reported that an enemy force with about 200 tanks had arrived from the southeast. Gott had no option but to send 7 Armoured Brigade and a battery of field artillery to fight off this unexpected threat, leaving 7 Support Group's four infantry companies and artillery to carry on toward Tobruk on their own, deprived both of their promised armour and of Brigadier Armstrong's fuel-crippled 5 South African Brigade, which had got no further than Bir el Haiad, about 18km southwest of Sidi Rezegh and roughly halfway between Bir el Gubi and El Adem.

As a result 7 Support Group could not get near to joining hands with 70 Division's forward elements. Back at Sidi Rezegh, meanwhile, all hope Scobie might have had of getting his promised armour support vanished when 7 Armoured Brigade took such a hammering that by nightfall it had only 28 functioning tanks left out of its original 160 and was having to hold off the Germans with the aid of 7 Support Group's artillery.

5 South African Brigade dug in at Bir Haiad, its position distinctly perilous because the German armour now blocked the way to Sidi Rezegh, although by that evening 4 Armoured Brigade had got to 12km southeast of Sidi Rezegh, while 22 Armoured Brigade was in action against German armour near Bir el Haiad.

While all this was happening, Captain Torr was fretting impatiently at Bir Duedar, waiting for the truant petrol convey to arrive. He finally decided to use his initiative, and at dawn on 21 September 1941 made contact with a 22 Armoured Brigade petrol convoy, whose commander heeded his pleas and gave him six hundred litres, enough for his company headquarters and remaining two platoons to set off after 5 South African Brigade.

They had gone barely 10km when they sighted a large transport column speeding southeastward, away from Bir el Gubi. Torr flagged it down and discovered it was a 7 Armoured Division replenishment convoy which told of a hair-raising experience: south of Sidi Rezegh it had been shot at by German armour and chased to El Adem, then southeast past Bir el Gubi where it encountered another inhostile reception (from elements of the Ariete Division).

Torr knew that a few kilometres away to his right was 7 Armoured Brigade Headquarters, and the column commander decided to make for it. Torr offered to screen the convoy on the journey there because it was very near his own axis of advance. The offer was accepted, but just as he was about to move off 1 South African Division came on the air and ordered him to stay where he was until further notice. That was the end of Torr's venture, and the cars did not move again for the rest of the day.

Brigadier Reid's warning about air attacks came true three hours after Short's force set off for Aujila at 0745 on 21 November 1941. The first target was Grobbelaar, who had a near-miraculous escape: "When travelling between the main body and the maintenance party (the latter had more vehicles than the fighting troops), just as I had crossed the Wadi el Hamin, my staff car was attacked by [an] Me 110. Four of us were in the car, and 19 bullets went through it. But we all escaped, save for scratches. A wheel was punctured, and the wireless set destroyed."

It was the start of continuous air attacks that went on throughout the next few days. An entry in 7 South African Reconnaissance Battalion's war diary by the intelligence officer, Lieutenant F. C. van N. Fourie, reflects the respect the unit gained for Reid's Indian soldiers:

[We] replied with the few anti-aircraft guns at [our] disposal and with all available small arms fire. We saw Indians in action for the first time. Squatting in the open – which always seems so much more open and vulnerable when one is under fire – they fired with their Bren guns at the attacking aircraft. When directly attacked they would huddle up over their guns, to re-open fire immediately the plane had passed overhead.

When on the move we in the armoured cars were grateful to them for their ability to detect approaching aircraft and, when near their vehicles, we left air observation entirely to them. It was merely necessary to watch them and prepare for action as soon as they stopped and dispersed.

At 1400 Colonel Short's column reached Bu Etla, about halfway to Aujila, having survived another strafing attack that fortunately had done little damage and inflicted no loss except for one wounded trooper. About 7½km behind Short came E Force's main body. Progress was slow: the alleged road was actually no more than a camel path meandering through deep sand, and two huge wadis that were more than 25m high had to be crossed. At 1430 Brigadier Reid halted the main body at Bu Etla and called it a day, although he sent Short on for another 30km to the west in preparation for an attack in the morning.

The 6 South African Armoured Car Regiment war diary states: "Country very bad – sand and scrub. Force A completes only 15 miles before dark. Certain troops fail to arrive – 4 Troop, Lieut. Gordon; 8 cwt. and workshop; 8 cwt. wireless truck; two 3-tonners; 2 medical 8 cwt; 3/2 Punjabis; one 3-tonner; A/Tk guns – one section (2 guns)."

Halfway between Bir Duedar and Sidi Rezegh 5 South African Brigade shivered through the bitterly cold night of 21 November 1941, hearing and seeing the sights and sounds of distant battle to the north. The thud of heavy artillery, innumerable gun-flashes, bursts of tracer illuminating the horizon and the rumbling of tanks and vehicles could be heard.

One of those shivering in the dry desert cold was General Gott, who spent the night at the brigade headquarters. General Cunningham was keen to see 5 South African Brigade join hands with Scobie's sortie from Tobruk as soon as possible, he said, and warned Brigadier Armstrong to stand by to advance at 0930 next morning, by which time he expected to have a clearer idea of what had happened in the day's tank battles.

But clarity would be in short supply in the next day or so because Rommel was now ready for his next moves: interdicting the Tobruk breakout and destroying the British armour at Sidi Rezegh. To this end he had used the night of 21/22 November 1941 to divide his armoured force in two. 21 Panzer Division and 90 Light Division took up a position between Sidi Rezegh and Tobruk, while 15 Panzer Division was moved 22km eastward to Gasr el Arid for a battle of manoeuvre which Crüwell planned against XIII Corps.

21 Panzer Division had been considerably worn down by this time as a result of the recent fighting, so that it had significantly fewer tanks than the British. XXX Corps might well have been able to break through 21 Panzer Division, brush 90 Light Division aside and link up with Scobie, but Gott was painfully aware of the fact that 7 Armoured Division had just 200 tanks left and did not take advantage of the opportunity. And so Rommel moved first.

24

War in the north and south

At 1030 on 22 November 5 South African Brigade finally set off, its objective a low rise just south of Sidi Rezegh nicknamed Point 178, it was occupied by a German infantry regiment and was scheduled to be assaulted by Lieutenant-Colonel W. H. Kirby's 3 Transvaal Scottish. Captain Torr and his cars had now managed to catch up with Brigadier Armstrong and he deployed No. 1 Platoon as an advance screen, No. 3 Platoon on the brigade's right flank and No. 2 Platoon to the left.

Armstrong's advance was unopposed until the Brigade was close to Point 178, a little before 1400. Then the armoured cars attracted machine-gun fire from a position 3,000m west of the objective. When Armstrong halted the brigade to deploy into battle order Torr drove up to the head of the column and unexpectedly found himself cast in a unusual role, that of good samaritan.

Unbeknown to him, the chief engineers of XIII Corps and the Eighth Army, two brigadiers named Clifton and Kisch, and a Major Wadeson of the corps engineer staff, had been travelling in Clifton's staff car when it had been hit by heavy machine-gun fire from a wadi about 1½km northwest of the column's front elements. Wadeson had managed to get away and reach the brigade column, but there was no sign of the two brigadiers. Could Torr assist in finding them?

Torr sent Wadeson off with Lieutenant R. D. Meeser and three cars from No. 2 Platoon. It turned out to be a hairy experience. When the section found the shot-up staff car it came under heavy artillery and machine-gun fire from the wadi, with a stationary tank also lending a hand. The cars fired back at the tank with their Boys rifles and machine guns, but it hit Meeser's car three times and badly wounded his radio operator. Since there was no sign of the missing brigadiers, Meeser turned away to head back to the brigade column.

Just then another car under Staff Sergeant T. Griffin of No. 1 Platoon arrived with a warning from Captain De Marillac of enemy artillery near the wadi. He had barely arrived however, when an enemy shell scored a direct hit on his car, killing the driver and badly wounding Griffin (he and his two other crew members were taken prisoner).

When Torr reported to the brigade commander on this unsuccessful sortie, Armstrong told him to pass on Meeser's painfully gleaned information to Colonel Kirby, whose regiment was just then deploying for the attack on Point 178. Kirby, in turn, told Torr to speak to his artillery commander and also the commander of his C Company on the left flank, and asked that he send a section of cars over to the regiment's right flank to brief it as well.

While Torr was thus engaged, the missing brigadiers turned up at the brigade headquarters, Clifton having been picked up, as he put it "by the most perfect armoured car in the world, manned by a crew of Springbok angels" after lying doggo in the sparse vegetation for two hours.

Hard fighting ensued when 3 Transvaal Scottish went into the attack in the face of intense enemy machine-gun fire, Meeser's cars preceding the left flank's advance. When the cars came under fire from field artillery and machine guns, Meeser called back the location of the machine gun positions to 3 Transvaal Scottish mortar platoon, and with him spotting for them the mortars were able to knock out a number of them.

It was dangerous work, and after about 45 minutes Meeser was hit and wounded. He and his cars were replaced by a section from No. 3 Platoon under Lieutenant W. H. Penny, but so much fire was now being brought down on the cars, to the detriment of the accompanying infantry, that Kirby ordered them back to avoid further casualties to his men. The advance continued, but despite of their best efforts the Scottish could not prevail.

Early that afternoon, while Kirby's men were struggling to get to grips with the defenders of Point 178, Rommel made his move. He launched 21 Panzer Division at Sidi Rezegh and captured the airfield. Desperate fighting ensued and now the Germans' expertise at combined-tactical operations was demonstrated. In spite of its reduced tank force 21 Panzer Division compelled 7 Armoured Division to withdraw after losing 50 more tanks, mainly from 22 Armoured Brigade.

Throughout the day 4 South African Armoured Car Regiment's cars were in the thick of the fighting around Sidi Rezegh, and its war diary entries – always laconic yet starkly dramatic and sometimes leavened by a touch of humour – bear testimony to the deadly ebb and flow of the battle, with all its confusion, disasters and triumphs. One such excerpt reads:

> At 1030 hours 150 vehicles were observed stationary at 443392 and in front of them a further 16 vehicles, of which some were towing guns, were seen moving west. Ten minutes later these 16 stopped and the guns were prepared for action. Meanwhile the column of 150 had been moving SW.
> A C Squadron patrol engaged 15 vehicles in the rear of this column and undoubtedly did considerable damage to material and personnel; however an A/T gun was with this enemy group, and opening up at short range it holed the Troop-leader's car 3 times.
> Meanwhile another C Squadron patrol came across 40 harmless-looking enemy vehicles (half the drivers were out of their vehicles) and engaged them. But the enemy suddenly produced 4 tanks (out of a hat it seems) and our Troop withdrew in haste and under fire from this disappointing offensive.

4 South African Armoured Car Regiment did not come through unscathed. A heavy blow was the capture of Captain Rohr, the technical officer, and his entire staff of mechanics and technicians who were so vitally important for keeping the cars running. Rohr had been in command of the regiment's rear headquarters and, as Klein writes, had been "hovering uncomfortably on the fringe of the tank battle and [keeping] out of trouble," because his group needed to stay near to 7 Armoured Brigade Headquarters.

Then, just before noon, he was ordered to join 7 Support Group's B echelon. Obediently Rohr and the rear headquarters' group moved away from the main scene of the fighting and then turned south to look for the echelon. It was not a good move, as 4 South African Armoured Car Regiment's war diary records: "This proved unfortunately an example of the well-known 'frying pan to fire' sequence, in that he ran into enemy light tanks and armoured cars scouting from Bir el Gubi, and he was finally surrounded by 7 Italian tanks."

It was at this moment that Staff Sergeant H. J. Lawrence, the regimental intelligence sergeant, in the wireless van sent his *cri de coeur* over the air and asked for instructions. These, from regimental headquarters, were: "look for the widest gap between tanks and go like hell. Try for a general southerly direction."

Lawrence did just that. The radio van and an ambulance fled with the tanks in hot pursuit, Lawrence tearing up all his secret documents into small pieces and broadcasting them over the desert as his van and the ambulance bumped along. After 15km of this impromptu paper chase his pursuers gave up and the two vehicles ultimately reached 1 South African Division south of Bir el Gubi. But Captain Rohr, his technical staff and their recovery vehicle had all

A crew tent set up on the side of a Marmon Herrington Mk 3 U40654, with the Vickers gun protruding from the top.

An armoured wireless transmission car with a Lewis MG in the Western Desert.

been 'put in the bag' (Lawrence was decorated with the Military Medal for his courage and perseverance).

In the south, Colonel Short's column set off for Aujila at 0700, the vehicles fighting their way through thick sand that caused further in roads into E Force's dangerously depleted stock of petrol. Then, when they reached Aujila after four arduous hours, they found that the maps were incorrect, the track ran down west of the oasis and not between it and what Short later described as a "typical Beau Geste fort" with a ramp leading up to it.

To deal with this unexpected contingency Short ordered an encircling movement: No. 2 and No. 5 troops of B Squadron approached the fort from the eastern side, while No. 4 Troop (minus one car which had bogged down to its axles) and a platoon of the Punjabis moved around the north along the ramp to the fort and an adjacent blockhouse. In the meantime Short's main body rounded the southern fringes of the oasis, fighting their way through such thick sand that vehicle after vehicle got hopelessly stuck.

At noon No. 3 Troop radioed that it had cut the Aujila–Agedabia road, but No. 1 Troop sent a message to say that it had run out of petrol about 3km west of the oasis. No. 2 and No. 5 troops were now closing in on the fort, and 6 South African Armoured Car Regiment started taking casualties. A burst of 20mm anti-tank fire riddled the car of Lieutenant A. J. Kelly of No. 5 Troop, killing him and two of his crew; although mortally wounded, the fourth man, Corporal A. C. D. Robson, managed to warn off an accompanying car (Robson died during the night). Anti-tank fire hit another car but did not disable it.

Within less than half an hour Short and the main body had advanced up to the fort and taken the surrender of the garrison – one officer and 38 Bersaglieri, along with two 20mm anti-tank guns and six Breda light machine guns. At Jalo, some of the prisoners said under interrogation, there were 700 men, two 75mm field pieces and many anti-tank guns.

Short now stood fast because he had too little fuel to continue and waited for the main body of E Force to come up and replenish his vehicles. But when Brigadier Reid arrived with his advance elements at 1500 he told Short that E Force was in little better shape, with only 45 litres per vehicle left. The advance would have to be halted until more petrol came up from the rear.

In fact it would have had to halt in any case; the very bad going had turned E Force from a coherent fighting formation into a mass of stragglers. 4 South African Field Battery had got so hung up that its elements were spread out over many kilometres, while most of the main body had been misled by faulty navigation and had run into very soft sand and scrub.

Reid and Short settled down to wait, chafing at the delay, while relays of Italian aircraft strafed them (Short's command car was holed 12 times, although without injury to its occupants). The last of the main body's stragglers did not reach Aujila until 1600, while elements of 4 Field Battery kept arriving for another hour, and the last of Short's stragglers came in only at 1900.

Meanwhile Grobbelaar was still struggling south from Bu Etla to Jikheira. "The going was very heavy," he reported, "hummock and sand; constant sand-channel work. It took us until 1600 hours to do 10 miles. All day there was enemy air strafing. Fortunately the enemy aircraft preferred soft-skinned vehicles and gave the armoured car crews some respite."

Near sunset Grobbelaar reached the outskirts of Jikheira, where friendly Sanusi tribesmen warned the leading armoured cars that it was being held by the Italians. Grobbelaar was in no condition for any decisive action since most of his force was strung out for several kilometres behind him, so he called a halt and sent two three-car sections forward to reconnoitre.

The Italians had some well-camouflaged 47mm anti-tank guns, which held their fire while the cars advanced to very close range and bogged down in the sand. Then, as the crews started digging them out and laying down the sand-channels, the defenders let rip. Since the crews were dismounted they could crawl to safety, but had to abandon three of the cars. While more stragglers arrived, Grobbelaar sent out a platoon of the Punjabis to determine the strength of the garrison, and during the night dispatched a salvage party to recover the abandoned cars' Vickers guns.

He was in a hurry now because his schedule called for him to be further south at Gur el Dib by noon next day. He prepared to attack at first light with everything he had on hand, namely the Punjabi company, his lone mortar and the guns salvaged from the abandoned armoured cars; his only heavier ordnance, his two Bofors anti-aircraft guns, were still battling with the sand somewhere to the rear. This inconsiderable supporting fire would be controlled and coordinated by means of flags and Verey flares, the only available means of communication.

By midday it was clear to the South Africans in the north that things were not going as well as had been hoped, although 4 South African Armoured Car Regiment was heartened at 1350 by a message from the higher headquarters stating that 22 Armoured Brigade was advancing on Point 175. Surely the brigade would bring about the annihilation of Rommel's forces? No one knew just how bad the larger situation was.

During this stage of the battle two C Squadron patrols under lieutenants R. E. Cole-Bowen and D. W. Waddingham used their wits to strike a blow of their own against the Axis forces. The patrols ventured out about 3km apart to investigate an enemy column they had spotted, passing a squadron of British cruiser tanks ensconced hull-down behind a ridge about midway between them.

Braving heavy shell fire, Cole-Bowen and Waddington closed in about 1,000m apart to count the number of enemy tanks in the column. Then a group of 25 panzers broke away from the main body and came straight at them. Dodging shells from the tanks, the two lieutenants indulged in some skilful manoeuvring, using themselves as live bait to draw the German tanks in under the guns of the British cruisers concealed behind the ridgeline. It worked: the cruisers knocked out five German tanks and scored direct hits on six more without any loss to themselves.

West of Point 178, meanwhile, Sergeant E. Camacho took time off from escorting General Norrie's battle headquarters to attack a strong infantry position on some high ground, overran it despite of anti-tank fire that holed his car in seven places, and took 25 prisoners, as well as a swastika battle flag which a suitably impressed General Norrie, who had watched the whole thing, then autographed as a mark of his appreciation. (Camacho later received more concrete evidence of official gratitude by being decorated with the Military Medal.)

By mid-afternoon the tank battle resumed, and another passage in 4 South African Armoured Car Regiment's war diary reads:

> At 1500hrs activity restarted in the area of the morning's tank battle and at 1510hrs the enemy was seen to be debussing and massing infantry, estimated at two battalions, behind his tanks in the area 433400 (about two miles east of Point 178).
> At 1525hrs the enemy put down a smoke-screen behind which the enemy infantry presumably attacked from east to west along the Sidi Rezegh ridge. Nothing further could be seen by us, however, owing to the fact that at 1545hrs a new grand-scale tank battle started.

Newton-King's regimental headquarters "found themselves, as usual, on the fringe of the tank battle," according to the war diary, "and were forced to beat a hasty retreat to the west with shells bursting very close indeed. As they moved west they came under small-arms fire from infantry dug in on the ridge immediately to the north." The two cars of the headquarters' group fired back, and opened up on an enemy armoured car before going on their way. Then, at last, the diary records:

> 22nd Armoured Brigade appeared from the west, and at 1650 hours were sweeping in majestic waves past Regimental Headquarters as they moved into battle. It was a fine array, and at the time it seemed to us that within the next half-hour General Rommel's final defeat would be accomplished. As darkness fell, pierced by the innumerable tracers of the continuing tank battle, we vainly imagined that during the next few days we should be helping to collect the spoils of Victory.

At Bir el Gubi all remained quiet that day. While Pienaar awaited new orders, two sections of No. 3 Platoon patrolled 32km northwest toward Bir Hakeim – soon to be the scene of a famous stand by the French Foreign Legion – spotted some enemy transport and came across a crashed Royal Air Force aircraft, whose pilot they buried (they found another crashed aircraft next day, and brought back the pilot, who had survived).

Major Crowther received some welcome reinforcements when Captain C. A. H. Heard's No. 2 Company, which had been placed in the divisional reserve and tasked with reconnoitring to the south and west of 1 South African Division's area of responsibility, was released and ordered to rejoin 1 South African Brigade; 3 South African Reconnaissance Battalion's Lieutenant-Colonel Furstenburg and his headquarters' group, which had been in support of No. 2 Company, were ordered to report to 1 South African Brigade's advanced headquarters at Bir Duedar.

Elsewhere though the action came thick and fast. At Tobruk General Scobie ordered the break-out force to consolidate its gains and widen out the corridor it had created for the link up with 7 Armoured Division that he still hoped could be effected. After an infantry and tank assault on an Axis strongpoint nicknamed 'Tiger' he had a gap 7,000m wide between himself and Ed Duda.

But if any hope of an intervention by 7 Armoured Division had still existed, it was now completely gone. Throughout 22 November the fighting raged around Sidi Rezegh. An attempt to recapture the airfield failed, and Rommel's counter-offensive began to gain momentum. A badly battered 7 Armoured Brigade withdrew with only four tanks still running out of its original 150. In just four days the Eighth Army had lost a staggering 530 tanks and the Axis forces only about 100.

A strong tank and infantry thrust by Scobie in the direction of Bel Hamed, southeast of Ed Duda, the aim of which was to reach out toward Sidi Rezegh, drove back the Italians manning the siege line at first, but was eventually thwarted when the Pavia Division counter-attacked.

XIII Corps was not idle during this time. While tank battles raged to the west, 22 November saw 5 New Zealand Brigade advance northeastward to the main Sallum–Bardia highway and capture Fort Capuzzo, but it failed to take Bir Girba, south of the fort, where the Savona Division was headquartered. Radio Rome's version of what happened was thus: "… fierce attacks launched by three enemy divisions against positions held by the Savona Division have been smashed by the iron-like resistance of our troops. The attackers suffered further bloody losses and failed to achieve any success. More than 20 tanks were destroyed and many others were hit."

South of Bir Girba 7 Indian Brigade overcame extremely stiff resistance from soldiers of the Savona Division to capture the border post of Sidi Omar and most of the Axis positions around the nearby Libyan outpost of the same name – the westernmost of Axis strong points – but then had to stop because so many of its attached tanks had been damaged or destroyed that further action would have been foolhardy until the losses had been made good.

As the morning hours of 22 November dragged by, General George Brink became more and more concerned about his two brigades. Pienaar's 1 South African Brigade was marooned at Bir el Gubi without any sort of tank support. Armstrong's 5 South African Brigade, equally tankless, was south of Sidi Rezegh, from where little was being received except contradictory accounts of British and German tank losses.

Then at 1440 Brink was informed by XXX Corps that 22 Armoured Brigade had taken considerable damage to its tanks and artillery, and was told to move his headquarters and 1 South African Brigade to Sidi Rezegh where 5 South African Brigade would revert to his command. The signal said that it was "essential you move quickly and before dark," which was manifestly impossible, since Pienaar's brigade was sprawled out at Bir el Gubi. Brink therefore advised Norrie that he would not be able to move until late in the afternoon at the earliest.

By sunset on 22 September 3 Transvaal Scottish were pinned down, unable to move, with Colonel Kirby mortally wounded and his second-in-command dead. Under cover of darkness the battalion withdrew. Armstrong moved 5 South African Brigade about 3km to the southeast of Point 178 and halted for the night.

4 South African Armoured Car Regiment's war diary entry for 22 November starts with the simple statement: "It was immediately clear that the enemy was very far from being annihilated. Rather it was a large part of our own armoured force that had suffered that fate."

It was no more than the truth. And the diarist could have had no inkling that, no matter how bad the day's news had been, a staggering blow lay just around the corner.

25

South African disaster – and triumph

At first light on 23 November 1941 1 South African Brigade set off for Sidi Rezegh, followed by the divisional tactical headquarters and the divisional troops. But after some distance had been covered Pienaar came up against a strong Axis force with between 60 and 80 tanks. Brink personally reconnoitred, noted the enemy armour strength and advised Pienaar to halt and dig in, in case of a possible tank attack.

Frustrated in his attempt to join hands with 5 South African Brigade, unable to move forward because of his lack of heavy armour, Brink set out soon after dawn with his tactical headquarters and Colonel Furstenburg's 3 South African Reconnaissance Battalion headquarters to try to contact General Gott, who was still at 5 South African Brigade Headquarters, and get Armstrong pulled out of his vulnerable situation. It proved to be a hazardous undertaking.

At various times during the morning Brink's group encountered German tanks sweeping down southeastward from Sidi Rezegh, it was shelled several times and came close to being overrun. But he could not make contact with Gott or reach 5 South African Brigade. And so Brigadier Armstrong, lacking any protective armour, short not only of fuel but also of artillery ammunition, was effectively left to his fate without hope of reprieve.

5 New Zealand Brigade renewed its advance down the main road from Fort Capuzzo toward Sallum and isolated the Axis defensive strongholds along the Sidi Omar–Sallum–Halfaya Line from their supply route to Bardia. Meanwhile, 6 New Zealand Brigade Group had also been thrown into the Sidi Rezegh fighting by being ordered to leave Bir el Hariga on 2 New Zealand Division's left flank and head northwestward along the Trigh Capuzzo to come to the aid of the battered 7 Armoured Division.

At first light the brigade had a stroke of luck when it arrived at Bir el Chleta, about 22km east of Sidi Rezegh, and found that it had unexpectedly run into the *Deutsches Afrikakorps* headquarters. The New Zealanders wasted no time in jumping the surprised Germans. After a brisk fight the headquarters was in ruins and most of its staff in the bag, except General Crüwell who happened to be elsewhere at the time. Apart from the disruption this lucky find caused, it meant that neither of Crüwell's panzer divisions received any supplies that day.

5 New Zealand Brigade was followed later in the day by 4 New Zealand Brigade Group, which had been ordered to proceed northwestward to harass the Axis forces around Tobruk, while 5 New Zealand Brigade made sure that Bardia remained cut off from the Sallum–Halfaya defence line.

But Rommel had other plans that did not immediately involve the coastal defence line. 7 Armoured Division had sustained such heavy tank losses that its ability to influence events was at a low ebb; ever one to seize any opportunity that presented itself, he now decided to cut off and destroy what remained of Norrie's XXX Corps – 7 Armoured Division's remaining tanks, 5 South African Brigade and the forward elements of 6 New Zealand Brigade – with one great blow.

To this end he drove at the Sidi Rezegh pocket with both his panzer divisions and the *Ariete* Division – after his triumph at Sidi Rezegh the Italian supreme command had put the Italian

X Mobile Corps, including the Ariete Armoured and the Trieste Motorized divisions, under his direct command – on the morning of 23 November, a cold, soggy Sunday made even more miserable by an icy wind and intermittent showers of rain.

His first objective was 5 South African Brigade, to which the Axis attack came as a total surprise – except for its armoured cars. As Klein writes:

> Weary and confused by the battle of the previous day, the British formations in the vicinity of Sidi Rezegh initially seemed to have little idea of what was required of them. Commenting on the situation, the War Diary of the 4th South African Armoured Car Regiment notes that 'the fog of battle was dense, and in consequence the idea of a definitely prescribed line of observation largely lost its significance. There was also a certain amount of overlapping with other Regiments.'

[In 1962 Lieutenant-Colonel Newton-King gave it as his opinion in correspondence with Klein that the disorganization was really due to the bad use of the armoured car regiments at the disposal of 7 Armoured Division, and "had their rear wireless links been on the same frequency, all would have been clear".]

This fog of battle seemed to encompass the minds of higher formation commanders as well. At 0750 hours Lieutenant van Niekerk of the 4th South African Armoured Car Regiment reported a strong enemy column, including 100 tanks, two miles (3km) south of Abiar en Nbeidat, and stated that his troop had come under heavy shell-fire from these tanks.

When this information was passed to higher authority, however, a strong disinclination to accept the accuracy of the report was evinced and it was suggested that the alleged column did not exist at all, or if it did it was friendly. Ample evidence that the column was real and not friendly was provided shortly afterward when the formation, which proved to be the 15 Panzer Division, wheeled due west and subsequently crashed through the tailend of 5 South African Brigade's B Echelon, scattering vehicles like chaff before a high wind.

The brigade headquarters seems to have been unaware of the attack until around 0845, when the brigade major, Major D. H. Ollemans, informed Torr that "something is happening in the rear of the brigade position," and asked that the armoured cars go and investigate. Newton-King sent his regimental liaison officer, Captain G. G. Brown to 5 South African Brigade Headquarters to give Brigadier Armstrong the latest information and to warn him of the danger from the southwest. Likewise, urgent reports from 3 South African Reconnaissance Battalion armoured cars in the south stressed an impending German attack from this direction. At this stage General Gott was still at the brigade headquarters and Klein says:

> that [he] was aware of the seriousness of the situation is evinced by the fact that before he left 5th South African Brigade Headquarters at about 1400 hours, he warned the Brigade staff of the danger from the southwest; but the 5th Brigade Report says that 'Comd 7 Armd Div... assured the Bde Comd that with the guns available on that sector our tanks would be able to take care of the enemy'.
>
> It would appear that at this stage, there was in the minds of the 5th Brigade staff a conflict in appreciation of the direction from which the impending attack could be expected. The 3rd Transvaal Scottish reported at 1445 hours that a very strong infantry attack, covered by heavy machine-gun fire, was being launched against their front and that tanks appeared to be approaching from the northwest.

This attack in the northwest corner, which subsequently was presumed to be a feint, drew the 22nd Armoured Brigade to that area, so that when the main German attack was thrown in from the southwest it was opposed by only the 5th South African Brigade artillery, which was then running short of ammunition.

Yet, when he left the South African perimeter and drove to the headquarters of C Squadron 4 South African Armoured Car Regiment, which lay northeast of the 5 Brigade, Major-General Gott was critical of the defensive layout of the brigade. This criticism is difficult to understand in light of the tank attack in the northwest and the fact that General Gott himself was largely responsible for the 5th South African Brigade dispositions.

Agar-Hamilton quotes Major Vic Larmuth, commander of C Squadron 4 South African Armoured Car Regiment, to the effect that while Gott was at his headquarters news came through from the South African armoured cars south of 5 South African Brigade that a German column had "formed up almost in line abreast and facing north."

But "when I asked Gott about this … he said he knew all about it. He said the enemy force there would be tackled 'later on' if it wasn't too late. He said distinctly to me that 'your South African Brigade seems stuck down with gum – they won't move and they won't turn their artillery round and they are not dug in – I am sorry for them'. This rather shocked me, and Gott said that he could not get them to move round and it was too late to dig. He said he couldn't understand them at all."

Worse was to come. At 1400, No. 3 Platoon of 3 South African Reconnaissance Battalion's No. 1 Company reported that 60 enemy tanks were massing three to five kilometres southwest of the brigade. Lieutenant Penny was so perturbed by the fact that the brigade's artillery was not dispersing the tanks that he reported in person to Brigadier Armstrong. He was still on the line to Armstrong when his radio operator handed him a message saying that the tanks had started to move closer. Penny immediately got his platoon in motion and, says Klein, "continued to relay information to the last."

In fairness to Brigadier Armstrong and his brigade headquarters staff, Klein writes, "it should be recorded that artillery ammunition was in very short supply and that conflicting reports of enemy attacks from the north and south kept the staff guessing until the last moment, when the real attack was thrown in. Also, Brigadier Armstrong expected the imminent arrival of 1 South African Infantry Brigade (Brigadier Pienaar) from the southwest to bolster his exposed position.

In a post-war comment on the situation, in the light of the armoured car reports of the danger from the southwest, Colonel D. H. Ollemans told Klein that the reports had not been disregarded, but that because of the uncertainty of the general situation the brigade command "reacted slowly."

At 1500 the armoured cars reported that 50 to 60 enemy tanks were moving forward toward the sector of the Brigade position, approaching to within 1,500m without so much as a shot being fired by the artillery. A desperate Lieutenant Penny not only radioed this information to the headquarters but sent his second-in-command back to make sure the urgency of his report was understood.

4 South African Armoured Car Regiment's war diary graphically recounts what happened next:

> At 1505 hours the enemy started to move his tanks north toward the 5th Brigade. In front were 25 tanks in line abreast and behind them embussed infantry and 8 large guns with tractors. The remainder of the tanks and B Echelon vehicles were well in the rear.
>
> *Our Regimental Headquarters now moved through the South African camp and took up a position on a ridge about 1 500 yards to the east, from where to report the battle. Shells were already falling in the camp, but there had been a certain amount of shelling all day...*
>
> *At 1530 hours the enemy tanks were rapidly moving in to attack. Our infantry were lying in shallow slit trenches, which did not appear to be laid out according to any plan. Almost all our artillery was facing north and for the most part the closely concentrated Brigade transport was between the guns and the enemy...*

It was the beginning of the end for Armstrong's brigade, and in *Pienaar of Alamein* A. M. Pollock provides a vivid description of its final death-throes:

> Lines of enemy shells symmetrically pitting the sands marked the approach of the Germans. So the attack was coming from the south -- or was it not? Yes, yonder they came, but the South African gunners were ready. Like a wave meeting a breakwater, the rows of tanks stopped short. They were drawing off and the British tanks were after them, mixing in the scrum.
> Suddenly a cloud of dust went up and out of it whirled a vehicle, a friendly armoured car. What news did it bring?
> Rommel was almost in sight. Eighty German tanks, 500 trucks, another 500 motor vehicles with supplies were roaring nearer. The sun was near the zenith when a bombardment began from the north, directed at the camp of the 5th Brigade, which was almost more than flesh could stand.

At 1330 the drumming of the shell fire was described as "intense" and an hour and a quarter later a group of Transvaalers turned to face waves of German infantry coming from the north and the northeast. As they did so, and as British tanks and South African guns fended off the assault, a lull gradually set in, so that the artillery proudly reported: Situation in hand.

Almost as they spoke the culminating attack in the Battle of Sidi Rezegh fell upon them like a flail. Moving 10 deep and seven abreast a Panzer spearhead avalanched upon the camp. The tanks smashed through as though they formed one single monstrous body, crushing and destroying the supply convoys, the field fortifications, the guns themselves.

Not a round of ammunition was left. Brigadier Armstrong, moving forward in a tank, was a prisoner ... It was one of the blackest days in South African military history.

"The 5th South African Infantry Brigade suffered 3,394 casualties – mostly prisoners – and ceased to exist as a fighting formation," Klein writes. "The Germans, however, did not escape lightly: at least 60 (possibly 70) tanks were destroyed or damaged, and the loss of officers and non-commissioned officers was very high. Although the German victory at Sidi Rezegh cannot be denied, Rommel's eventual defeat in the next 14 days can be attributed in certain measure to the heavy tank losses suffered at the hands of the men of the 5th South African Infantry Brigade in their valiant stand."

All things considered, 3 Reconnaissance Battalion's No. 1 Company under Captain Torr did not suffer too heavily in the defeat, and in fact was the only unit to survive the destruction of 5 South African Brigade more or less intact. The company had given way before the advancing German tanks. Two cars were disabled and abandoned, but 23 others and two light workshop detachments rendezvoused to the north; four other cars which had been cut off moved southeast and eventually reached 1 South African Brigade. With the battle irretrievably lost, the cars went eastward for about 7½km and sought refuge with 6 New Zealand Brigade, where they spent the night, then joined Brigadier Jock Campbell's 7 Armoured Division Support Group.

Here Klein writes the epitaph of Armstrong's 5 South African Brigade:

> From the armoured car point of view the loss of the 5th South African Infantry Brigade at Sidi Rezegh will long remain a sore talking-point. It was contended by the 4th South African Armoured Car Regiment and by the 3rd South African Recce Battalion that if more attention had been paid by the Brigade command to information relayed by armoured car reconnaissance from both regiments, the Brigade would have been in a better position to have withstood the German tank attack which overran it in the mid-afternoon of 23 November 1941.
> However, deeply as the armoured car commanders felt about the disaster, they were not fully aware, at the time, of the overall strategy of the battle, directed on the British side by Major-

General Gott, commanding the 7th Armoured Division, and of the conflicting pressures to which Brigadier B F Armstrong, commanding the 5th South African Brigade, was subjected during the critical moments of the German assault.

The sortie from Tobruk was ordered under way prematurely; the South African infantry were committed before the defeat of the enemy armour; and a proud brigade – the 5th South African Infantry – perished at Sidi Rezegh. On that sad day of 23 November 1941, the 5th South African Infantry Brigade ... was destroyed against the run of the plan previously accepted by Major-General George Brink – that his infantry would not be committed until the tank battles had been decided ...

In the calm light of history, with the din and turmoil of the conflict far removed, it is clear in the mature judgment of time that the first Sidi Rezegh battle and 5 South African Infantry Brigade were lost in advance of the actual battle itself. Firstly, the dispersal of the full striking power of the 7th Armoured Division, fell piecemeal to the superior armament of the German panzer divisions and secondly because of the splitting of the concentrated force of 1 South African Division, contrary to the original Crusader plan, and the commitment and exposure of the 5th South African Brigade at Sidi Rezegh in advance of the successful conclusion, from the British angle, of the tank battle on which was hinged the whole strategy of the Crusader operation.

Immediately after the destruction of 5 South African Brigade General Cunningham sent a personal message to General Brink: "I want to say how sorry I am about the 5th South African Brigade. I have heard many stories first-hand of the gallantry shown by them and the magnificent manner in which they fought. Their doings will make a page of history – I am sure the battle will prove a keystone of our success to come." No doubt this was cold consolation for a grieving General Brink, who had to stand by helplessly while a brigade he had nurtured and then led to victory in Abyssinia was destroyed in one dreadful afternoon.

In the south, Grobbelaar's first-light attack on Jikheira commenced, with the Punjabis in place to the north and west, waiting for the mortar and machine guns to soften up the Italians before charging in. But things started to go wrong almost immediately when the mortar, having fired two ranging shots, broke down beyond hope of immediate repair.

The Vickers guns took over and hammered the Italian positions to good effect, but ignored the Punjabi company commander's Verey light, the signal to stop so that the attack could go in – the Verey lights were invisible against the sun rising immediately behind the infantry company headquarters.

"Enemy fire was intense," Grobbelaar records. "47mm HE; 20mms; Bredas and small machine guns, and rifles. The attack was completely stalled. We were at our wits' end, when up rolled (the) two Bofors under Lieut. Jackson, Royal Artillery ... Jackson immediately summed up the situation. He rushed up close to the enemy and opened fire. With his first tray he knocked out one of the 47mm guns. After a few more trays the enemy ran up the white flag."

By 1100 it was all over. Two officers and 50 other ranks were made prisoner and Grobbelaar laid hands on two 47mm guns, four of 20mm calibre and a variety of machine guns. Grobbelaar set off again without delay, the armoured cars patrolling on the column's south and west. But at day's end he was at a standstill again, this time because he did not have enough fuel to reach Jalo in time for Reid's attack.

Fuel supplies eventually reached Grobbelaar and he managed to catch up with the main body in time for the attack. Reid intended to carry out a night march from Aujila and then assault the fort at Jalo at dawn of the 24th with his main body, while Grobbelaar carried out a diversionary attack from the north. It was agreed that the armoured cars' main role would be to provide covering fire for the infantry, since the thick sand around the fort would not allow them to use their mobility.

After a deeply disappointing and frustrating day General Brink and his headquarters put up for the night east of the 1 South African Brigade area. "It was a particularly unhappy evening," Klein writes. "Enemy flares were seen to the north and east of the 1st Brigade's position. Very few men slept in the prevailing tension and uneasiness. Added to the rumble of distant gunfire was the noise of tanks clanking and thundering through the darkness. Friend or foe? It was difficult to know in the confusion.

"Throughout the night survivors from the 5th South African Brigade drifted in to advance divisional headquarters, some telling clear, others disjointed, stories of the South African disaster. All were however alike in one respect – almost every man was truly convinced that he was the sole survivor of the ill-fated brigade. It was a sombre gathering that assembled that night in the dimly lit command vehicle to hear confirmation from Major-General Brink of the loss of the 5th Brigade."

1 South African Division – effectively consisting of no more than Pienaar's brigade and the divisional reserve – was now on its own, just as much as 5 South African Brigade had been. Brink issued his orders: at first light Pienaar must dig in 6km to the east at Taib el Esem.

From a defensive point of view it was as unpromising a place as Sidi Rezegh. There was a well on a slightly elevated feature, but "everything else was just about as flat and barren as a highveld cricket ground," according to *Pienaar of Alamein* by Eric Rosenthal. "The locality lay south of the land of camel humps, with their little tufts of vegetation. It was just plain desert – a place where Nature herself had first applied the scorched-earth policy."

But here Dan Pienaar, his infantry, gunners and armoured cars, would make history.

While 1 South African Brigade dug in at Taieb el Esem on the 24th and Furstenburg's headquarters' cars roamed around, sending back a stream of reports on enemy movement, Rommel set off on the next phase of his struggle against the Eighth Army.

He had dealt with the Allied forces at Sidi Rezegh, and there was now no immediate threat of Tobruk being relieved, so he decided to maintain the momentum he had generated and destroy all the Allied forces west of the Wire, the Libyan–Egyptian border. Then he would surround and destroy the substantial Allied forces which he believed were besieging his border strongholds. That done, the Eighth Army would be finished.

It was a bold decision, since the Deutsches Afrikakorps had only about 40 tanks ready for action at that stage, but Rommel never lacked for boldness, and so the two panzer divisions and the Ariete Division headed off in the direction of Sidi Omar as fast as they could, turning confusion into chaos as they went. Numbers of Allied units were destroyed, XXX Corps was split in two and XIII Corps came close to being cut off from any prospect of retreat. The Matruh Stakes, as some horse-racing fan dubbed the eastward rush by parts of the Eighth Army, was now well under way.

But Rommel had made two mistakes. There were no large Allied forces tied down around the border strongholds, as he believed, and although the popular conception of the Matruh Stakes is of a lemming-like scramble by the entire Eighth Army, this was not so. Most of the Allied elements his armoured divisions chewed up were rear-echelon support units, air force ground units and the like; the disciplined British, South African, Indian, Polish and New Zealand combat units and formations mostly stood firm and were ready to fight on.

He might have been better served, some historians have pointed out, if he had concentrated instead on destroying the Eighth Army's main supply dumps and the Desert Air Force's principal landing grounds, and he would later pay for not knocking out the Allies' aerial capability when the opportunity presented itself.

With the battle area now in total chaos, the role of the South African armoured cars, Klein writes: "… assumed increasing importance in keeping track of the fluid operations which now spread from the Tobruk–Sidi Rezegh area back to the Frontier Wire … It was then, when the battle was most fluid and other channels of communication had temporarily broken down, that the armoured cars rose to some of their greatest heights of reconnaissance service in the desert battles." Based on the 1st South African Infantry Brigade, No. 2 and No. 3 companies of 3 South African Recce Battalion, and battalion headquarters (with Major-General Brink's battle headquarters) maintained contact with hard-striking enemy columns on all fronts throughout the difficult days that followed.

Dan Pienaar deployed his scanty forces, all the time acutely aware of the German advance flowing past his rear and the likelihood of imminent attack. There was nothing neat or "by the book" about his dispositions; he was too old and cunning a fighter for such nonsense. To the north lay the Carbineers, to the west the Dukes. The east was held by the Transvaal Scottish.

Pienaar's beloved 25-pdr field guns, Dan's pianos, as his soldiers fondly called them, were deployed so that they could fire on an enemy attack from any direction, because he knew very well that if the Germans were repulsed at one point of the perimeter they would try somewhere else until they found a weak spot. At several strategic points were what he called "hard-hitting packets" – groups of his own devising that packed a considerable punch.

But his guns were short of ammunition, and one of his staff officers, Captain A. P. G. van den Heever, volunteered to creep out through a narrow gap in the surrounding enemy forces and see if he could locate some more. Pienaar gave permission, and at 1745 van den Heever drove off into the fading light. After that nothing more was seen or heard of him.

During all this time 3 South African Reconnaissance Battalion's No. 2 and No. 3 companies under Major R. D. Jenkins were engaged in a variety of life-threatening activities. One of their exploits involved an attempt by Captain E. K. Hutchings of No. 2 Company to recover a 3-tonner loaded with 25-pdr artillery ammunition that had been abandoned a few kilometres north of the brigade position. When he got there Hutchings was jumped by a column of about 50 enemy tanks, which sped down toward him from the northwest.

Hutchings made himself scarce and radioed a warning to Captain C. A. H. Heard at his company headquarters, which was a few kilometres southeast of him. Heard set off back to the brigade with all due dispatch, followed by half the enemy tank force. At times he reached a speed of more than 50kph – no mean feat in that terrain – but could not shake off the tanks or increase the distance between him and them, and they did not give up until Heard was within range of the brigade artillery. Hutchings, meanwhile, swung eastward and finally made contact with his regimental headquarters.

Elsewhere, No. 3 Company and Major Jenkins' section of the battalion headquarters were also having trouble with intruding Axis tanks. At noon Jenkins was on the way from the brigade to link up with Furstenburg at the divisional tactical headquarters a few kilometres to the east when Major Crowther, with No. 1 and No. 2 platoons of No. 3 Company under command, crossed the route of a large German tank column. Just then Crowther's car broke down. The No. 2 Platoon commander, who had been standing by, picked them up, fled with the tanks only a few hundred metres behind and got clean away.

The tanks then fell on 3 South African Reconnaissance Battalion headquarters, which was temporarily immobilized because the armoured car carrying the rear radio link was minus both its rear wheels, which had been taken off to repair punctures. The tanks came on at such speed that there was nothing to do but destroy the radio and abandon the car. Then there followed a high-speed (for the desert) chase of more than 13km before Jenkins could pull his headquarters together, take 20 cars of No. 3 Company under command and turn northwest again.

Skirting the right flank of the enemy advance (which was one of Rommel's columns striking at the Wire) Major Jenkins' armoured cars were making good time toward 1 South African Brigade when their progress was impeded by fire from a disabled German tank. Jenkins tried to get some of his cars around to the tank's blind side and destroy it; but there was nothing wrong with its turret and it beat off the cars on all sides. Some 4 South African Armoured Car

Regiment cars then arrived with two anti-tank guns, but they had as little success as Jenkins, and eventually the tank was left to its own devices.

Now far from home, Jenkins' group spent the night with some guns of 7 Medium Regiment Royal Artillery, and at first light next morning he headed back to 1 South African Brigade with the British gunners in tow. Once there he assumed temporary command of all the 3 South African Reconnaissance Battalion sub-units in the absence of Furstenburg at 1 South African Division Headquarters.

Marmon Herrington Mk 3 under shell fire in North Africa.

Now, for the first time, 3 South African Reconnaissance Battalion was concentrated as a unit instead of having elements scattered all over the desert; its only absentees being No. 1 Company, which was still attached to 7 Armoured Division Support Group under Brigadier Jock Campbell, and No. 3 Platoon of No. 1 Company, attached to XXX Corps.

1 South African Brigade's situation was serious. It was not only short of artillery ammunition but had enough petrol for only about 45km of movement. This meant that Jenkins' crews, as they ranged around the Brigade position, anxiously watched their fuel gauges and snapped up any unconsidered trifles they encountered: "patrols kept going this day." 3 South African Reconnaissance Battalion's war diary for the following day commented, "on petrol drained from derelict tanks and on one abandoned truckload brought in by Lieutenant [F. H.] Lawlor."

4 South African Armoured Car Regiment – now including A Squadron, which had been recalled and had just reported in – spent the anxious day of 24 November creating as much mayhem as possible, starting at first light just north of Bir Berraneb. The regiment had earlier been ordered to go into reserve for a short rest, but this was clearly not an option at a time when, as Klein notes, "the desert was a welter of fleeing Eighth Army B Echelon transport and swiftly moving enemy columns."

According to the 4 South African Armoured Car Regiment war diary: "At 1030 hours 16 medium and 40 light tanks were reported in the offing and a further 35 tanks and 500 other vehicles at 41039°. At 1140 hours an unknown number of enemy tanks were reported being engaged by our Honey tanks north of Regimental Headquarters. A moment later a euphemistic message was received – "The battle is moving rapidly south.

"An immediate move south by regimental headquarters became necessary. The German column was now in sight, in pursuit of our Honeys, while from the west enemy light elements rapidly approached and were engaged by regimental headquarters, firing between and over the heads of a welter of fleeing B Echelon vehicles."

A little later the cars spotted another column – a very large one this time, just due west of the previous one. They suspected it was the main enemy force, and an idea of what Rommel was up to dawned on them. 4 South African Armoured Car Regiment now became more aggressive than before, carrying out a number of successful attacks on the Axis forces' soft-skinned transport and other support vehicles, even though the Germans protected their echelon vehicles with tanks in most cases.

It was in this spirit that 4 South African Armoured Car Regiment organized some extra firepower for itself by press-ganging a British Crusader it found, in good shape but out of petrol. Newton-King struck a deal with the tank's crew, whose sleek lines immediately earned it the nickname the Cat: the armoured cars would fuel it up, on condition that the cruiser helped them with their assault on the Axis echelon convoys.

Marmon Herrington Mk 3 used by C Squadron, Kings Dragoon Guards.

Post delivered by motorcycle U99326 to Marmon Herrington Mk 2 'Peggy', North Africa.

This was done, and at 1525 4 South African Armoured Car Regimental Headquarters and the Cat set off northward toward the enemy column it had sighted earlier. En route they encountered Lieutenant-Colonel Furstenburg of 3 South African Reconnaissance Battalion, who instantly coveted the new addition, but, as the war diary says, "a disingenuous attempt on his part to make off with our 'Cat' was defeated." Newton-King could now proceed with his plan, which was for the cars to sneak up to a designated enemy victim tank and then show themselves. This would attract the victim within range of the Crusader, which would then brew it up.

To their disappointment this ingenious scheme failed: "Unfortunately the greater range of the German tank guns defeated our 'Cat'," according to the 4 South African Armoured Car Regiment war diary, "but Regimental Headquarters' part of attracting the Germans' attention was uncomfortably successful."

In the south, Brigadier Reid's night march on Jalo started at 0315 on 24 November and reached the objective just after first light, but due to a miscalculation the infantry debussed too early, so that they had to struggle across 6km of dunes to get within fighting distance.

Short's armoured cars, meanwhile, crept up to the outskirts of the oasis in the murk of dawn and immediately did some damage to the enemy when Lieutenant J. A. Hill of No. 1 Troop spotted an aircraft on the airstrip and sent it up in flames with a burst from his Vickers; a machine gun then fired back at him and he knocked it out as well, but had to withdraw when the Italian anti-tank guns started shooting at him.

No. 4 Troop under Lieutenant N. W. Gordon went into the oasis with the left flank of the infantry, but as Reid had anticipated, the thick sand proved to be the cars' nemesis and they bogged down. The Italians were fighting with spirit, and long, accurate bursts from their machine guns pinned down the Punjabis in the dunes throughout the morning, despite return-fire from the armoured cars, as well as from Grobbelaar's column when he arrived from Jikheira.

At sunset the Punjabis went in again with bayonets fixed, with Short's and Grobbelaar's armoured cars providing as much supporting fire as possible, both to distract the Italians and suppress their artillery pieces and machine guns. This time there was no stopping the Indians, and one by one the Italian strong points were taken.

Then, Klein writes, "amid the hubbub of battle the Punjabis burst into the village and took the fort. To Brigadier Reid was left the satisfaction of personally forcing the surrender of the Italian commander at pistol-point. The rest of the oasis was soon cleared, and Indian infantry patrols spent the rest of the night combing the immediate area around Jalo, bringing in many prisoners."

Late on the afternoon of the 24th General Brink summoned Pienaar to rendezvous with him about 9km away for new orders. They had barely got to the orders when about 60 Axis tanks and their supporting infantry and artillery appeared from the north, fired at them and then headed in the direction of 1 South African Brigade. Brink hurried off back to his tactical headquarters and Pienaar left with equal speed for his own, with enemy shells chasing his staff car all the way.

"The enemy tanks … swung their turrets around to take pot-shots at him," writes Eric Rosenthal. "Now in front of the car, now behind it, the shells dropped closer and closer, but they always just missed him. Then they thinned out and he knew that – if the compass was right – he must be getting near the First Brigade Camp at Taieb el Essem …

"Anxious faces were to be seen in the trenches and behind the natural and artificial ramparts. The men knew that their commander was somewhere out in the desert, most probably in the direction whence the increasing thunder of a bombardment now reverberated.

'Is Dan back?' they called to the sergeants in anxious voices.

"Someone pointed at a grimy old staff car creaking up the rise.

"A delighted cry went up.

"Cool as a cucumber and looking as though he had not a care in the world, Pienaar sat down to talk to his officers.

"We're going to stop them," he said, "Rommel and everybody else – right here."

"A member of his staff noticed that he was bleeding. "Oh, I just stopped one," he casually remarked, and only after a good deal of delay could he find time to have the wound dressed. "He waited impatiently at the dressing-station and then hurried back to his headquarters van."

The brigade had been busy during his absence, deploying and digging in as he had ordered, having brushed off several probing attacks. The Carbineers, the Dukes and some elements of Regiment President Steyn were already in position. The Transvaal Scottish, which had been the rearguard in the move to Taieb el Essem, was about to do the same. Most of the artillery was in position and dug in.

Now, as shells dropped on his brigade, Pienaar considered his position. If he had been isolated before, he was doubly so now, and it was clear that a mass attack could be expected at any time. He spent an hour pacing up and down in the deepening dusk, accompanied only by his brigade major, sunk in agonizing thought. Then he called his staff officers and unit commanders to an orders group, briefed them and then uttered the hardest command of all: "My orders to you are to fight to the last man and the last round."

Pienaar spent the night in sleepless vigil, while the drone and rumble of nearby enemy movement disturbed the night and signal flares soared into the dark sky. By now he had acquired some modest but welcome unsolicited assets in the form of three Crusader tanks, all more or less damaged in the fighting, towing two others. Their crews were still ready to fight, however, and he promptly fitted them into his defence plan as well.

But he was still desperately short of artillery ammunition. Then at 0430 Captain van den Heever returned from his quest with eight 3-tonners, loaded with enough shells to feed the 25-pdrs for a full day's heavy fighting.

The attack Pienaar had anticipated – by strong elements of 21 Panzer Division and the Ariete Division – began at precisely 0700, with a storm of shells that battered every corner of the brigade's perimeter. Pienaar's gunners fired back, Heard's armoured cars feeding them with reports of the enemy movement so that the brigade's shells stayed on target as the Axis infantry and tanks formed up for the attack opposite 1 Transvaal Scottish's positions.

B Squadron 4 South African Armoured Car Regiment tracked the Ariete Division's movements, while C Squadron scouted along the Wire between the Libyan side of Bir Sheferzen southward to El Beida, and the regimental headquarters joined 7 Armoured Division Headquarters at Agheret Sciueia, about 37km southeast of Taieb el Esem.

At 0800 the Axis force attacked. Firing at every target in sight, about 60 tanks, mainly

Panzer Mark IIIs and Mark IVs, rumbled toward the South African positions, with infantry and mortar teams close behind to exploit the anticipated breakthrough. But the fast, accurate shooting of Pienaar's gunners and mortar men stopped them, and as the attackers hesitated, two of the damaged Crusaders charged out through the gun lines and knocked out four of the German tanks.

At 0900 the attackers broke off and joined another group of about 60 tanks and their attached infantry that had been massing a little more than 2km away to the north, facing the Carbineers.

"The crash of battle filled the air and for a moment it seemed that the tanks must sweep all before them," writes Pollock, quoting an eyewitness account. "But the Carbineers had dug in well. Like the Transvaal Scottish, they fought back with coolness, self-reliance and grim determination, and again the gunners and mortar crews backed up the infantry magnificently.

"The Carbineers' ordeal lasted 90 minutes and then, suddenly and almost miraculously, they and the gunners realized that they were taking the advantage, and the Germans began to disengage through the smoke and swirling dust.

"During this action Dan Pienaar was in a slit trench with his brigade major and was hit in the back by a shell splinter. Fortunately he was thickly clad and this saved any penetration; he only suffered a nasty bruise on the left shoulder blade …"

By now the German losses were giving new urgency to their actions. Two full-scale attacks had been beaten off. Unless that elusive weak spot could be found in the next attempt the day was lost. And lost it was, for as the Germans formed up again, still under heavy fire, for an attack from the west against the positions held by the Duke of Edinburgh's Own Rifles, Brigadier Pienaar received a visitor – a very welcome visitor.

The swashbuckling Brigadier Alec Gatehouse, now commander of 7 Support Group. Gatehouse had been engaged in another action a few kilometres away when he'd heard of the fighting at Taieb el Esem and had come to help with 38 of his Stuart tanks. The Germans had sent up a smokescreen to disguise their intentions, but Heard's armoured cars had outflanked them and reported back.

As a result the Germans were just moving into the attack when Gatehouse and his little Stuarts charged into them from the side and threw them into disarray. It was a daring move, given the fact that Gatehouse's Honeys were no match for the Panzer Mark IIIs and Mark IVs, but it worked. The Germans abandoned the attack and withdrew behind their smokescreen.

The German artillery kept pounding 1 South African Brigade until dusk, but the battle for Taieb el Esem had ended with Gatehouse's charge. 1 South African Brigade had lived to fight another day.

"For a long time Taieb el Esem remained the forgotten battle of the Western Desert," Pollock writes, "for there were no war correspondents present to tell the world of this gallant stand … It was not a victory in the sense that ground had been gained, but it was a victory because it revealed for the first time that infantry and guns, properly handled and disposed, were a match for the dreaded German panzers …

"While the battle raged at Taieb el Essem the Eighth Army was given a chance to regroup for the thrust which eventually relieved the Tobruk garrison and took the Allies well beyond Benghazi in January 1942. Had the Brigade not held fast or if it had been wiped out, there is no knowing where the Germans would have stopped."

3 South African Reconnaissance Battalion's war diary inscription for the day was as laconic as always:

Patrols sent out. Heavy enemy shelling on camp during entire day. Two determined tank attacks broken up, gunners on occasion engaging over open sights – ranges of 800-1,100 yards. In the afternoon a tank brigade arrived … Situation healthier.

Enemy tanks reported by armoured car patrols NE, north, NW and west. Patrols under fire all day and occasionally pursued by tanks. At approx. 1500 hours a further 44 tanks reported massing in the west; supported by strong infantry forces. Withdrew (3 South African Recce Battalion) from unhealthy position after dark in SSE direction.
Many anxious moments; column stopped on one occasion for 15 minutes to allow suspected tank column to pass in NNW direction. Five Humber armoured cars now attached to us, and one A15 [Crusader] tank.

While elements of 21 Panzer Division and the Ariete Division were involved at Taieb el Esem, 15 Panzer Division advanced on Sidi Azeiz, only to discover that it was not under siege, as Rommel had supposed. The Desert Air Force was now harassing 15 Panzer Division unmercifully, and by the evening of 25 November the Division had lost all but 53 of its tanks, virtually the only ones the Deutsches Afrikakorps still had running.

A strong element of 21 Panzer Division, 5 Panzer Regiment, also suffered badly when it attacked 7 Indian Brigade at Sidi Omar. Firing over open sights at ranges as short as 500m, the brigade's 25-pdr guns twice drove them back, inflicting such losses that the German regiment had been virtually destroyed by nightfall. Licking its wounds, the remainder of 21 Panzer Division headed roughly northeast in the direction of Halfaya.

Lieutenant C. D. F. Osmond, commanding No. 2 Platoon of 3 South African Reconnaissance Battalion's No. 2 Company, had another task for 25 November that should have used up only a few hours. He was ordered to take four other armoured cars and try to find 2 New Zealand Division, which the brigade believed was somewhere to the north-northeast of Bir el Gubi. It was appreciated that by the time Osmond managed to do this he would be out of radio contact, so he would have to bring back the news himself.

Osmond set off, and after about an hour he was on the outer edge of the radios' reach. When he was about 15km out he sent a radio message that he had spotted a large force to his front, and that was the last the brigade heard from him. But Osmond and his men had not been killed or captured; they had simply embarked on what Klein rightly describes as "a series of hectic adventures," which started almost immediately after his last message reached Taieb el Esem.

"I was cut off by a strong column of the enemy, moving southwest and south," Osmond reported much later. "Contacted New Zealanders at 1200 hours and tried to break through the enemy column. I failed to find an opening so went north again where we ran into another enemy column. We ran from them and reported their position to the 22nd Armoured Brigade, who knocked out five tanks, two armoured cars and a lot of transport." But this was just the beginning of Osmond's adventures.

With Jalo taken, Short spent 25 November clearing the El Libba sector to the northeast of the oasis with three headquarters armoured cars, two cars of No. 3 Troop under Lieutenant Holmes-a-Court and a backup infantry element of sorts consisting of 13 officers and men, among them seven mechanics. Short's instructions to his armoured car crews was that if their cars bogged down they were to dismount and attack the enemy "with whatever weapons the individuals can use best."

Short then proceeded to show what leading from the front meant when his car was the first one to get stuck. True to his instructions, he jumped out with a rifle and led his crew in an attack on the nearest enemy presence to hand, a strongpoint from which the Italians were firing with 20mm guns and machine guns. An officer and three mechanics from the Light Aid Detachment lorry then joined him, and with this "peculiar little force" (in Brigadier Reid's words) Short captured the strongpoint.

Now reinforced by two officers, two corporals and a trooper, Short took the remaining Italian positions at bayonet-point, while the three surviving cars moved around, supporting him with Vickers fire at point-blank range. The Italians resisted stoutly and knocked out one of the cars, killing one crew member and wounding two others, but after four hours the action was over, with two Italians dead and 27 taken prisoner.

A Squadron (Major C. W. O. Henderson) of Short's 6 South African Armoured Car Regiment had its first taste of action on 25 November, after the start of Rommel's dash toward the Wire. When Rommel's thrust eastward started on 24 November, Henderson's squadron had been east of the Wire at Ruweibit el Warani, south of the Halfaya Pass, in the company of armoured cars of 4 Indian Division's Central India Horse. Now on 25 November it witnessed unparalleled scenes of confusion as the starting shots of the Matruh Stakes were fired. The war diary for that day reads: "Reports were received that the enemy force was closing in, and the order to withdraw was given. The whole of the front seemed to be thrown into confusion. Small parties of vehicles were wandering around aimlessly until directed by Squadron Headquarters to report to formation collecting points. Convoy after convoy was encountered on our way south, indicating some confusion in the northwest sector."

The squadron was not directly in front of the main German thrust toward the Egyptian frontier, but fighting was in progress on such a large scale that in its first clash No. 1 Troop lost two of its cars and crew, while No. 2 Troop lost one.

In one incident on 25 November a Sergeant Whittaker rescued the four-man crew of a British tank that was under heavy enemy artillery fire without suffering any damage or injuries. But that same day No. 3 Troop lost a trooper named Rowbotham in an incident of a type that was to happen again and again as the campaign went on and each side started using vehicles of the other side that it had captured, without any clear system of identification.

The squadron war diary reads: "It seemed that there was some uncertainty as to whether certain vehicles were British or not, as they were just visible over the brow of a hill. Trooper Rowbotham volunteered to walk up to the vehicles to establish their identity. Rowbotham was seen to be stopped near the convoy and then he put up his hands in surrender."

Brigadier Reid's Jalo operation had been a success by any standards despite of the scanty resources at his disposal, with a total of 670 prisoners and a considerable amount of weapons and equipment, and his achievement was duly recognized by General Ritchie in a signal on 27 November stating: "Well done. Press on to Agedabia."

Reid was now positioned to carry out Auchinleck's instruction to Ritchie a few days earlier that E Force must attack enemy lines of supply in western Cyrenaica: "Direct Oasis Force at the earliest possible moment against the coast road to stop all traffic on it and if possible capture Jedbaya or Benina, neither of which is strongly held apparently."

However, the plan was dead in the water because the operations against Jalo had left E Force practically without petrol. Reid had believed that he would be able to lay hands on a large stock of fuel at the oasis, but there turned out to be very little to hand; with the armoured cars averaging only two or three miles to the gallon, E Force simply could not immediately carry on northward.

"The possibility of further offensive action," as Klein says, "was out of the question until the supply position had been placed on a different level of importance. This was not possible because of the desperate fluctuations of the main Crusader battle in the north, and Brigadier Reid's force was virtually immobilized at Jalo without fuel: a particularly unfortunate circumstance at a period when fast raiding columns on Rommel's lines of communication would have had strong psychological and material effects on the course of the main battle."

Just how desperate E Force's situation was can be seen from Grobbelaar's remark that his column was "left in a very poor state... in supplies and fuel we were desperately low... motor transport and armoured car movement had to be restricted to the bare minimum and troops were placed on half rations." To fuel the convoy Reid now sent back to LG125 to fetch further supplies, Grobbelaar had to "collect odd gallons of petrol from the armoured cars."

The fuel shortage compelled E Force to concentrate on local patrolling and reconnaissance, "which had fair value," as Klein writes, "but was not the advance in full strength which Eighth Army required. By the time an advance was possible, the opportunity of seriously disrupting the Axis communications had passed."

During the next few weeks, therefore, the most that could be achieved was to send out light reconnaissance patrols from Jalo, which, according to Reid, were "of the utmost value," with each bringing back valuable information and also several prisoners to be interrogated. One of the most successful ventures was led by Lieutenant M. M. Smuts of 7 South African Reconnaissance Battalion. Grobbelaar's description of Smuts' exploit in his personal account is: "Smuts' little force consisted of a troop of armoured cars and a detachment of infantry commanded by an Indian non-commissioned officer called Lulerai. They had a very exciting experience. At Sahabi they came across a German light armoured car, but failed to capture it. They left Jalo in the direction Gasr es Sahabi on the afternoon of 5th December.

"Moving on toward Giof el Matar, they found the fort occupied and decided to ambush whoever approached or left it. Early one morning they surprised and captured an approaching lorry with five occupants, all Italians, and thereupon made a good break back to Jalo. The party delivered their prisoners at the oasis on the afternoon of 9th December."

In addition to the shortage of fuel, Reid was concerned about his stock of rations: "We had retained the services of six Italian bakers and cooks and we were able to have fresh bread once every two days. In order, however, to ensure that I would be able at any time to push out detachments or patrols for any length of time up to five days, it was essential that we hold a reserve of rations, and from the time that we left Jarabub the whole E Force was on half rations, and remained so until January."

An extension of the mutual respect and affection that existed between the South Africans and the rest of E Force can be found in the fact that the 7 South African Reconnaissance Battalion men now voluntarily made the sort of sacrifice that only a soldier who has been hungry in the field can fully appreciate. The South African ration-scale was better than the British one, but they decided that they would adhere to the same scale as the British and Indians.

"This meant," as Klein says, "they received 25 cigarettes a week instead of 50 and had to do without their special ration of sugar, coffee and mealie meal. This they were glad to do, Lieutenant-Colonel Grobbelaar remarked, 'as we did not wish to have *more* than our comrades in arms from other countries. In privation good soldiers share and share alike, and this was an example of the cooperative spirit shown by the South African forces in their contacts with the various Commonwealth and foreign forces who made up the conglomerate of the Eighth Army'."

26

The tide begins to turn

On 26 November 1941 Captain Torr's No. 1 Company arrived back at 1 South African Brigade, having been recalled from its sojourn with 7 Armoured Division Support Group (and departing with Campbell's regrets and appreciation for its work). Major Jenkins now had the entire reconnaissance battalion in one place, minus the platoon of No. 3 Company attached to XXX Corps Headquarters.

Pienaar's successful action at Taieb el Esem notwithstanding, he was not happy about his brigade's exposed position. While 4 South African Armoured Car Regiment continued taking the war to the enemy in addition to its scouting tasks up and down the Wire (that day, for example, it captured three lorries and 16 prisoners), he set about moving 22km to the south, screened by No. 2 Company's armoured cars.

But in fact the turning point of Operation Crusader had been reached, starting right at the top. Auchinleck had spent three days at Cunningham's headquarters during the worst of the fighting, and had no intention of following his suggestion that the Eighth Army halt the offensive and withdraw. On 25 November he had given Cunningham written orders that said, among other things: "There is only one order, Attack and Pursue." Now, having returned to Cairo, Auchinleck consulted with London and relieved Cunningham of command.

Cunningham's replacement was his deputy, Major-General (now Lieutenant-General) Neil Ritchie. A highly decorated infantryman and Great War veteran, Ritchie was junior in his post and rank and had never commanded an armoured formation in the field. However, he shared Auchinleck's fierce determination to knock Rommel, and keep knocking him, regardless of the cost, until he had been chased back to the far west of Libya. Ritchie's was meant to be a temporary appointment, but in the end he occupied it for six months.

It was not an impossible dream. On the ground Rommel was now in a far weaker position than it might have appeared to the Eighth Army's field troops. A victim of his own initial successes, his lines of communication were long, his flanks were exposed and supplying his far-flung combat elements was very difficult; his main dumps were along the coast between Bardia and Tobruk, where 4 and 6 New Zealand Brigades kept a vigil on enemy movement.

26 November 1941 saw General Scobie launch a successful attack on the Ed Duda ridge outside Tobruk, while to the east 15 Panzer Division under Major-General Walter Neumann-Silkow managed to reach Bardia around midday by going around Sidi Azeiz, where 5 New Zealand Brigade Headquarters was located, along with some infantry, the New Zealand armoured cars and elements of the divisional field artillery, anti-tank guns, anti-aircraft guns and machine gun units.

Meanwhile Major-General Johann von Ravenstein's gravely thinned-out 21 Panzer Division attacked northwestward from Halfaya, also heading for Bardia by way of Fort Capuzzo. It was so weakened, however, that Rommel ordered the Ariete Division – which at this stage was approaching Bir Ghirba, 24km northeast of Sidi Omar – to head for Fort Capuzzo as well to take out any hostile forces and link up with von Ravenstein. By way of further support he ordered 15 Panzer Division's 115 Infantry Regiment (itself badly under strength) to advance southeastward from Bardia to Fort Capuzzo with some attached artillery.

At dusk the 15 Panzer Division column attacked the two infantry battalions of 5 New Zealand Brigade that lay between Fort Capuzzo and Sallum. The fighting went on into the night but despite strong resistance, 115 Infantry Regiment had advanced to within 700m of Fort Capuzzo, it was suddenly ordered to disengage and advance on Upper Sallum to join hands with the remains of 21 Panzer Division, which was now approaching from the south.

In the pre-dawn hours of 27 November, with Scobie having made contact at long last with the advance elements of 4 New Zealand Brigade at Ed Duda, Rommel met at Bardia with Neumann-Silkow and von Ravenstein to discuss what was now becoming a very delicate situation.

On the one hand, Scobie's 70 Division and 2 New Zealand Division had joined hands and gained the initiative on the Tobruk front and needed to be attended to. On the other hand, it was still necessary to deal with the Allied forces which, Rommel remained convinced, were besieging several of his strongholds west of the Wire.

The final decision was that 21 Panzer Division must head for Tobruk because it was now so weakened that it was not capable of making a significant impact west of the Wire. 15 Panzer Division, meanwhile, would spread itself out on a broad front for attacks between Fort Capuzzo and Sidi Omar, starting with the capture of the New Zealand stronghold at Sidi Azeiz, which was believed to accommodate a major British supply dump. Neumann-Silkow, it appears, felt that his task had little chance of success and instead decided to capture Sidi Azeiz and then head for Tobruk.

The two divisions set off as soon as possible. Later that morning 15 Panzer Division overran the New Zealanders at Sidi Azeiz after an attack in overwhelming strength that was fiercely resisted by its occupants. The divisional armoured cars managed to escape, but everything else fell into German hands, including 5 New Zealand Brigade's commander, Brigadier James Hargest, and about 700 officers and men.

Neumann-Silkow then made for Tobruk, but at Bir el Chleta – where the New Zealanders had shot up the Deutsches Afrikakorps headquarters a few days earlier – he found 22 Armoured Brigade, which was now down to less than 50 tanks and had been organized into a composite regiment.

This immediately developed into a full-scale battle, with 15 Panzer Division on the losing end by mid-afternoon. 22 Armoured Brigade blocked Neumann-Silkow's progress toward to Tobruk, not without considerable difficulty. His rear echelons were being mauled by Gatehouse's 4 Armoured Brigade and its 70 remaining light tanks, which had carried out a wild 32km cross-country dash from the northwest and fallen on his left flank. In addition, Allied aircraft were inflicting great damage on the Germans.

At nightfall the British tanks disengaged to restock on fuel and ammunition, but for some reason moved south for this purpose, leaving Neumann-Silkow in a position to take the gap toward Tobruk, which he did. This decision by the British armour, which remains inexplicable, meant that 2 New Zealand Division was now under threat.

4 New Zealand Brigade was fighting hard to hold the southeastern end of Scobie's corridor to Tobruk, and 6 New Zealand Brigade had finally cleared the Sidi Rezegh escarpment at great cost to itself, but now it was under attack by elements of the Deutsches Afrikakorps and the Trieste, Bologna and Pavia Divisions, which were determined to recapture the high ground north of the airfield, overlooking the road to Tobruk.

While 15 Panzer Division was fighting it out at Bir el Chleta, von Ravenstein and 21 Panzer Division were not making much headway in the advance to Tobruk. At Bir el Menastir, a mere 15km or so west of Bardia, the division ran into a battalion of 5 New Zealand Brigade, and the two formations spent most of the day exchanging fire without either side achieving any conclusive result. Eventually von Ravenstein broke contact to take the long way around, via Sidi Azeiz, which meant losing an extra precious day of movement before reaching Tobruk.

All in all, the Eighth Army's situation had improved by the time Rommel met with Crüwell

Marmon Herrington Mk 3 'Dairy' in North Africa.

Marmon Herrington Mk 3 in North Africa.

on the night of 27 November to discuss the next day's moves. Norrie's XXX Corps had managed to bring some order to the chaos caused by Rommel's breakthrough, Scobie and the New Zealanders had joined hands and the Desert Air Force was still fully functional and inflicting great damage. The remaining Allied infantry brigades were intact, if slightly battered: 7 Armoured Division was still functioning, albeit on a much smaller scale, and from Ritchie downward the Eighth Army's fighting spirit remained strong.

Rommel's immediate priority remained the cutting of Scobie's corridor to Tobruk and the destruction of 70 Division and 2 New Zealand Division, although a worried Crüwell felt that top priority should be given to dealing with the threat from the south posed by 7 Armoured Division. But Rommel's prioritization prevailed, and Neumann-Silkow's 15 Panzer Division spent most of 28 November successfully fighting 4 and 22 Armoured Brigades.

In spite of being outnumbered two to one in tank strength and plagued by such serious replenishment problems that at times his vehicles literally ran out of fuel, Neumann-Silkow eventually managed to drive the two British brigades southward, and then resumed his advance on Tobruk.

Meanwhile the battle for control of the Tobruk corridor itself continued throughout the day, made more difficult for the Allies because for one reason or another 70 Division and 2 New Zealand Division had not been able to establish a firm communications link.

That night Rommel and Crüwell revised their plans for the capture of Tobruk. Crüwell favoured advancing directly on the port, while Rommel – mindful of the fact that the various head-on attacks he had sent at Tobruk during the siege had all failed – settled instead for a pincer movement. 15 Panzer Division would move south past Sidi Rezegh and then west and attack southeastward toward the Tobruk corridor; what was left of 21 Panzer Division would move up to 15 Panzer Division's right to form the eastern jaw of the pincer. Between them they would cut through the corridor and destroy its defenders.

On the morning of 29 November 15 Panzer Division set off along its planned route, but the rump of 21 Panzer Division was slow off the mark because of an unexpected disaster: von Ravenstein had been captured while out on a personal reconnaissance. Disaster also befell 2 New Zealand Division's 21 New Zealand Battalion, which had earlier occupied Point 175 – the scene of the earlier attack by 3 Transvaal Scottish – but were now overrun by a large element of the Ariete Division, supported by artillery and tanks; which according to Lieutenant-Colonel Howard Kippenberger, later general officer commanding 2 New Zealand Division, "rolled straight over our infantry".

The New Zealanders were taken by surprise because at first they thought the Ariete force was actually part of 1 South African Brigade, but Pienaar could not advance because he could not move over open ground without support from 4 and 22 Armoured Brigades, and that support was not forthcoming. It left the New Zealanders with a lasting grudge against him because it was felt that he had let them down, but in the circumstances an advance without substantial armoured support would have been suicidal.

15 Panzer Division completed its hook around Sidi Rezegh, attacked from the southwest as scheduled and eventually fought its way through to Ed Duda, but by nightfall had not been able to beat down the British defences. Then 4 Royal Tank Regiment and supporting Australian infantry counter-attacked and regained the lost ground. 15 Panzer Division fell back about 1,000m and dug in. That evening 1 South African Brigade was temporarily placed under command of 2 New Zealand Division and ordered northward to recapture Point 175.

Back in Cairo, General Ritchie was well aware from his intelligence department's radio intercepts that 15 and 21 Panzer divisions were in bad shape. He ordered 7 Armoured Division to keep applying pressure. But Rommel was far from defeated. He pulled 15 Panzer Division and its 40 or so remaining tanks another 8km to the south, then next day attacked northeastward, his intention being to pass between Sidi Rezegh and Belhamed – both held by the New Zealanders – and then emerge east of Ed Duda.

6 New Zealand Brigade was in his way at the western end of the Sidi Rezegh sector, and by mid-afternoon was suffering the consequences; the depleted 24 New Zealand Battalion was overrun, then two companies of 26 New Zealand Battalion, but an attack by the Ariete Division from Point 175 on the eastern flank of the position was beaten off by 25 New Zealand Battalion.

Rommel's thrust spilled over into 1 December with an armour and infantry attack on Belhamed, preceded by an intense artillery barrage at 0615 which resulted in the virtual destruction of 20 New Zealand Battalion. 4 Armoured Brigade arrived during this action, but due to its staff misunderstanding their orders – they thought they had been sent to cover the withdrawal of what was left of 6 New Zealand Brigade – it did not intervene, although their tanks outnumbered those of the Germans.

Lieutenant Osmond's pilgrims were heavily involved in all these momentous happenings, lending a hand wherever they were needed and if necessary keeping their cars running without the benefit of workshops. On 26 November they had "spent the day working with 11th Hussars, who had one squadron attached to the 22nd Armoured Brigade," according to Osmond's later report, and on 27 November had moved due east for 35km and stationed themselves at a road junction on the Trigh Capuzzo, passing back information to XIII Corps.

On 28 November XIII Corps "sent us out to recce a suspected enemy column to their south – their suspicions were not exaggerated, and [XIII] Corps made a night move up the Trigh Capuzzo to the New Zealanders. They refused to help us (three cars were broken down) beyond suggesting abandoning the cars."

Osmond and his men had no intention of doing this, so on 29 November he made a plan in true South African fashion: "We repaired [the] cars by taking spring clamps from derelicts and by blocking and lashing springs. We had the cars ready by 0930 hours and were just moving when [an] enemy column came into sight moving on our line of march up the Trigh Capuzzo. Five light tanks closed in on us [and] opened fire, but fell back when we split up.

"We kept the column in sight for 25 miles until we rejoined [XIII] Corps. That afternoon we spotted for the artillery in the action between the enemy column and the troops who had been called in to support [XIII] Corps."

A Squadron 6 South African Armoured Car Regiment, still in position south of Halfaya Pass on temporary attachment to 7 Indian Infantry Brigade, came close to losing No. 5 Troop when it was surrounded by enemy tanks. The tanks did not fire, and the troop reported this to the squadron headquarters, saying it appeared that the enemy was short of ammunition. Apparently it guessed right, because it made its escape without a shot being fired at the cars.

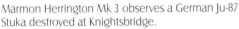

Marmon Herrington Mk 3 observes a German Ju-87 Stuka destroyed at Knightsbridge.

South African Marmon Herrington Mk 3 crew look out over the Mediterranean Sea.

It was a bloodless if nerve-wracking introduction to the battlefield, but when A Squadron was attached to 2 South African Division after 4 December 1941 it would see much action when it took part in the capture of the German strong points at the Halfaya Pass.

The new offensive spirit brought about by General Ritchie's accession to command of the Eighth Army led to the South African armoured car units undertaking an aggressive role as raiders that was more to their liking than the vital, but essentially passive, observation duties they had been performing for the most part. On 29 November Newton-King's 4 South African Armoured Car Regiment was taken off its observation role and tasked to go in behind the enemy front to disrupt the Axis lines of communication in four different places.

A and B squadrons were to attack traffic along the road west of Tobruk, A Squadron between Gazala and Acroma, and B Squadron more to the west, between Gazala and Tmimi; C Squadron and the Regimental Headquarters were ordered to move northward from Got el Aslagh and try to attack traffic on the road between Acroma and El Adem, with the headquarters squadron arranging for replenishment from Bir Belchonfus, south of El Gubi.

Newton-King had just 16 hours to prepare before his scheduled departure from Bir er Reghem on 30 November 1941. The time passed quickly as he and his staff struggled to do what was necessary. Patrols were called in, some from many kilometres away. Cars were refuelled, ammunition was replenished, rations were issued and the necessary maintenance carried out. Fresh maps were drawn and marked, while signallers tuned into a special radio frequency and familiarized themselves with new codes.

It was to be a bare-bones operation, without any tanks or artillery, although air support was promised. Newton-King asked General Gott to give him a free hand instead of restricting 4 South African Armoured Car Regiment to a defined area, but Gott, who looked "very tired and despondent" and pessimistic about the expedition, said he could not change the instructions he had received.

At 1100, 4 South African Armoured Car Regiment moved off westward. To their dismay the Regimental Headquarters and B and C squadrons were attacked soon after setting off by a large number of Stukas returning from a bombing raid. The Stukas had used up their bombs but machine-gunned B Squadron and knocked out one of its echelon lorries. Two Stukas, damaged earlier by Allied anti-aircraft fire, force-landed near the line of march of Regimental Headquarters and C Squadron. The squadrons destroyed both and captured an Italian pilot, but mechanical problems halted the advance for two hours before they had even left the vicinity of Belchonfus.

Newton-King knew very well that the enemy aircraft could hardly fail to report the presence of an outward-bound armoured car regiment and decided to move mostly by night, marching north to the Trigh el Abd and then proceeding along it, in the hope, as the war diary says, of "firstly of finding better going, and secondly of bumping and attacking an unsuspecting leaguer, and so spreading alarm and despondency among the enemy". But "neither of these hopes was realized".

4 South African Armoured Car Regiment had intruded on an area where the Italians were busy setting up a fall-back defence line, covered by a substantial force of infantry and artillery which clearly had no intention of simply rolling over, as it discovered when it reached the Trigh Bir Hacheim after some very heavy going. In the vicinity of Bir Harmat (where, so it was later discovered, there was a number of supply dumps) the cars came under heavy fire, an indication that their cover, such as it was, had now been thoroughly blown.

In the end Newton-King could not carry out his mission. Two troops of C Squadron reached the Trigh Capuzzo but found no signs of life, although the squadron did manage to capture an Italian lorry and its four occupants, but B Squadron could not reach the Gazala–Tmimi road in time. An A Squadron troop got to the lip of the escarpment above Gazala and reported seeing 17 aircraft on one of the airfields there. C Squadron's headquarters troop ran into and promptly attacked an enemy position it chanced upon, but broke away when two camouflaged and hitherto unnoticed anti-tank guns opened fire and disabled the troop's Breda car before concentrating their fire on it.

Sergeant J. M. Haswell, the troop sergeant, immediately turned back despite of the intense fire, stopped at the Breda car, pulled out the only surviving crew member who was badly wounded, and carried him off to safety. Haswell came through this short but intense action unscathed, although his car was hit repeatedly (he was later decorated with the Distinguished Conduct Medal and his driver, Trooper G. J. Warburton, with the Military Medal).

The distinct danger of air attacks – given that they were close to the Gazala airfields and far from friendly support – which had been on Newton-King's mind from the very beginning, now proved correct. The cars were thoroughly strafed by Me 110 fighter-bombers against which, of course, they had no defence.

The story is best told by 4 South African Armoured Car Regiment's war diary:

> In the early afternoon, enemy reconnaissance planes started methodically to quarter the ground, searching for us, and it was plain that our fears of air attack were going to be realized. It was A Squadron (Major R. Whitley) who were unlucky. At about 1660 hours they were attacked unremittingly for half an hour by eight Me 110s.
> Plainly, with the position known to the enemy, the Regiment could not maintain themselves in the face of concentrated air attack, without any fighter support or anti-aircraft guns on our side. After consultation with 7th Armoured Division, it was decided to withdraw.

A Squadron's trial was, however, not yet over. After the first attack, a recce plane had looked carefully from 'mast' height at the dispositions of Regimental Headquarters and C Squadron, and it seemed certain that their turn had come. But when the Me 110s returned it was again A Squadron just pulling out of their position who were attacked and machine-gunned for another half an hour.

They lost three armoured cars, all their thin-skinned vehicles, and suffered serious casualties in killed and wounded. Great bravery was shown by A Squadron personnel in these attacks: Lieutenant H. W. A. Cheales was awarded the Military Cross and Lance-Corporal N. A. Nicholl the Military Medal for their outstanding conduct.

It had been a harrowing and costly operation that had not achieved its main purpose of cutting Rommel's coastal route, because no way down the escarpment could be found. But it was far from being a total loss. 4 South African Armoured Car Regiment had managed to capture many enemy supply vehicles (Newton-King himself arrived back at base with no less

South African Marmon Herrington Mk 3 upgunned with a British 2-Pdr anti-tank gun.

South African troops, in front of a Marmon Herrington Mk3, enjoying chicken in the streets of Cairo.

than 11 lorries as well as some prisoners, and had certainly created a considerable amount of alarm and despondency in the enemy ranks. The measure of what the regiment achieved can be gauged from 7 Armoured Division's history:

A special task was given to the 4th South African Armoured Car Regiment under Lieutenant-Colonel D. S. Newton-King. This was to raid the Gazala–Acroma area and to prevent the supply of petrol to the enemy. They returned from their raid on December 2nd having destroyed much petrol and many vehicles and having had a widespread effect on the enemy's morale. Unfortunately, however, they had suffered many casualties from heavy and sustained air attacks, but the destruction they caused was to affect Rommel's plans in a few days' time.

"The experiences of the South African armoured cars with E Force, and the partial success of the 4th Regiment's raid, emphasized the limited offensive value of the Marmon-Herrington armoured cars, with their light armour-plating and armament, against well-equipped opponents," Klein writes.

"Though disappointed many times by the comparatively passive reconnaissance role for which they were cast by virtue of the limitations of their armoured cars, South African Tank Corps personnel, and their comrades of the out-gunned British tank regiments in the Western Desert, proved by their initiative and courage that it was the man and not the vehicle that in the end decided the fate of the Crusader battle."

What remained of 2 New Zealand Division was now concentrated near Zaafran, 8km east of Belhamed. It was at the end of its tether, and during the morning of 1 December General Freyberg signalled Eighth Army headquarters that without 1 South African Brigade (which was, of course, still unable to move because of its lack of armoured support) his position at the lower end of the Tobruk corridor was untenable; he was therefore planning to withdraw.

Freyberg intended to start moving out at 1730, but at 1630 15 Panzer Division, newly replenished, attacked again. The New Zealanders formed up on time and at 1845 set off, covered by tanks and artillery that had been sent to support them. They arrived safely at XXX Corps – just 3,500 men and 700 vehicles – having conducted a disciplined fighting withdrawal, that most difficult of manoeuvres.

It was a defeat by any standards, yet within it lay the seeds of victory for the Allies. "The New Zealanders had suffered heavy losses, as had the British 7th and 70th Divisions," Klein writes, "but determined resistance by the Eighth Army made Rommel's situation impossible, and his losses had been such as to force him to the conclusion that he could no longer carry on the investment of Tobruk."

Both sides in the long battle were now near to exhaustion yet far from willing to give up. "The desert was covered with abandoned vehicles which both sides were striving to collect and repair," Klein writes, "while supply columns were feverishly endeavouring to bring forward materials of all sorts to build up again the reserves without which the battle could not be continued. The task of the armoured car regiments had become more intricate, for by now identification of men and vehicles was difficult because uniforms and vehicles had all assumed a dull desert colour, and the difference between enemy and friendly forces was not easily seen."

The very next day Rommel made another foray to the west to liberate his border strongholds, sending two improvised battalion groups named Geissler and Knabe to open the Bardia–Capuzzo–Sallum route. They achieved nothing. On 3 December 1941 elements of 5 New Zealand Brigade decisively defeated the Geissler Group on the Bardia road near Menastir, and to the south the Knabe Group encountered an Allied composite group called 'Goldforce' while advancing along the Trighh Capuzzo and withdrew after an artillery duel.

For the next few days General Ritchie took what advantage he could of the Axis withdrawal from the Tobruk perimeter. For 3 South African Reconnaissance Battalion, operating from 1 South African Brigade at Taieb el Esem, this meant that, in addition to normal patrol and reconnaissance duties with Pienaar's infantry battalions, it could also turn its hand to active raiding.

In pursuance of his plan to drive the Axis forces away to the west of Tobruk, Ritchie directed Pienaar to send out small columns to harass the enemy in the El Adem–Acroma area, using "mosquito tactics with a view to causing apprehension in the rear areas," which he considered was "of the greatest importance to the general plan".

Pienaar was happy to oblige, as was 3 South African Reconnaissance Battalion, which had long yearned for a more aggressive role. Drawing on his East African experience, he put together small columns whose emphasis was on mobility and firepower to carry out what soldiers of the Vietnam generation were to dub 'shoot and scoot' tactics.

The mosquito columns soon showed what they were capable of. On 3 December 1941, for example, while Rommel's Geissler and Knabe groups were trying to open up the Bardia–Capuzzo–Sallum route, a mosquito column commanded by Captain D. S. Botha of 7 Field Regiment South African Artillery left Taieb el Esem on a typical long-distance raid. The column – consisting of seven cars from 3 South African Reconnaissance Battalion, two 25-pdr field pieces and two 2-pdr anti-tank guns – headed northwestward for about 45km, and then joined hands with a squadron from the King's Dragoon Guards, to fall on a large Axis dump near Point 182.

By the time some Italian tanks managed to drive them away, they had destroyed thousands of litres of petrol and diesel, blown up large amounts of ammunition and knocked out about 60 lorries laden with rations, at no cost to themselves. General Norrie, needless to say, was much taken by this bold little action and offered his personal congratulations.

Not all mosquito patrols were this successful, though – on 5 December 1941 another column, involving Lieutenants A. W. Thompson and P. Hugo with eight cars, wisely decided to turn back when it ran up against an enemy column with tanks and artillery – and German and Italian air attacks were now a constant menace.

On the other hand, on 4 December 1941, Lieutenant W. J. Whiteley, commanding No. 3 Troop of C Squadron 6 South African Armoured Car Regiment – which was then attached to the King's Dragoon Guards for operations north of Bir el Gubi – happened on an Italian convoy of lorries whose drivers were engaged in digging themselves in. Whiteley was "instructed to give the drivers a go" as the squadron war diary has it, and he obliged to great effect, destroying 20 of the Italian vehicles for the loss of one armoured car but with no casualties.

South African troops in Marmon Herrington Mk 2s and
Mk 3s in Benghazi, Libya.

South African troops with their Marmon Herrington
Mk 2 turret replaced by an Italian Breda 47mm gun.

While Whiteley was destroying the Italian convoy, larger events were taking place along the coast, where Rommel was engaged in one last attempt to open up the Bardia–Capuzzo–Sallum lifeline, this time with the remains of 15 Panzer Division and the Italian Mobile Corps. The foray caused something of a flap at Eighth Army headquarters , but the formation got no further than Gasr el Arid, about 40km east of Belhamed.

There he called it off, because it was now plain that Tobruk was anything but subdued. Instead he launched another attack on Ed Duda, but it, too, was beaten off by 70 Division's 14 Infantry Brigade.

Rommel's most immediate preoccupation at this stage was Norrie's XXX Corps, which had got its second wind after being reinforced by three brigades from Ritchie's reserve and now represented a renewed threat – in fact 11 Indian Brigade was already involved in a fierce clash with two battalions of the Italian 136 Giovanni Fascisti (Young Fascist) Regiment of the Ariete Division, which was holding a hilltop strongpoint near Bir el Gubi codenamed Point 174.

This action was part of a foiled attempt by Ritchie to cut Rommel off by a thrust from Bir el Gubi toward Acroma which ran aground on the stubborn defence of Point 174, whose garrison not only refused to crumble under 11 Indian Brigade's attacks but gave as good as it got. The fighting was observed by No. 2 Platoon of 3 South African Reconnaissance Battalion's No. 3 Company, which was lying up well to the west; but C Squadron of 6 South African Armoured Car Regiment under Major P. E. Ferguson, which was under command of the King's Dragoon Guards, was intimately involved in the Bir el Gubi fighting, and on 6 December 1941 had a car knocked out by artillery fire during a reconnaissance patrol toward Bir Hakeim.

Although Rommel's rescue attempts had failed, they had benefited the defenders of Point 174 because they prompted Eighth Army headquarters to order Norrie's 4 Armoured Brigade with its 126 tanks to the southeast, so that when General Crüwell took the Deutsches Afrikakorps with its remaining 49 functional tanks to relieve the Young Fascists on 5 December 1941 he was able to inflict such heavy losses on 11 Indian Brigade that it had to be withdrawn and replaced by 22 Guards Brigade.

Crüwell might have done even more damage had he not then withdrawn to the west, unaware that in fact 4 Armoured Brigade was not in the vicinity but more than 30km away. Next day Crüwell had another opportunity to finish off the Indians, because 4 Armoured Brigade still had not made a move to support the Guards, but he waited too long to strike a conclusive heavy blow and, on 7 December 1941, 4 Armoured Brigade finally arrived at Point 174 to assist 22 Guards Brigade.

That day 4 Armoured Brigade fought another action against 15 Panzer Division and knocked out 11 more of its tanks. Rommel's supply problems had become so serious now that they threatened to bring him to a standstill altogether, and he knew he could expect no improvement before the end of the month. He thereupon did the only logical thing: he abandoned attempts to relieve his frontier garrisons, evacuated his positions around Tobruk and set in motion a withdrawal all the way westward to the Gazala Line that Italian support units had been preparing in the interim.

By now it was clear to all concerned that Rommel had given up on Tobruk altogether and was moving his forces westward, but there was little the Eighth Army could do about it. Ritchie simply did not have the strength to outflank him, and "his retreat … was well conducted and never became a rout," Klein writes. "The German armour was handled with skill, generally behind a screen of anti-tank guns which the British armour could not penetrate. The skill of the German withdrawal likewise did not permit of any major raiding liberties being undertaken by the armoured cars."

4 South African Armoured Car Regiment was not involved in any of this. It had taken so much punishment that in the first days of December 1941 it was withdrawn from 7 Armoured Division for refitting; its departure was marked by a singular honour: the right to wear the Division's jealously cherished 'Desert Rat' arm-flash. The first element to leave, on 2 December 1941, was A Squadron, which had suffered particularly heavily during the Gazala raid. Within a week the other squadrons followed, and the regiment spent 14 days at El Adem resting and overhauling their battered armoured cars. The appropriate entry in the war diary reads:

> This was the end of the Regiment's part in the offensive, a part to which they look back with reasonable pride. Their primary duty of observation was carried throughout to the satisfaction of Corps and Divisional Commanders, who both congratulated the Regiment on their showing. The Regiment also received an unsolicited and much appreciated testimonial from the Officer Commanding the 21st Panzer Division, General von Ravenstein, captured by the New Zealanders, who attributed largely to the Regiment the failure of his reconnaissance in force of 14/15 September.
>
> In addition to its role of reconnaissance the Regiment initiated, at the time of Rommel's move back to the Frontier, an aggressive policy, the success of which may be judged by the fact that the three fighting squadrons between them took their own numbers again of German and Italian prisoners.
>
> Little mention has been made in this Diary of the part played by Headquarters Squadron. This is not because that part was not of the first importance. It is rather that the work was done with such regular efficiency that there is little to say about it, and this despite of the fact that our B Echelon was the object of very heavy air attacks. One serious and unavoidable loss was sustained, the capture by the enemy of A Squadron Echelon. Otherwise supplies reached the Regiment in the forward area with unfailing regularity, despite conditions of the greatest possible difficulty.
>
> The Commanding Officer [Lieutenant-Colonel D. S. Newton-King] has been awarded the Distinguished Service Order for his handling of the Regiment during this period, a distinction which is felt to be not only richly deserved on personal grounds, but also a highly valued honour to the whole Regiment.
>
> The Regiment's work was obviously not done without loss. During the period covered by this Diary the Regiment sustained a total of 58 casualties: 8 killed, 18 seriously wounded, 6 slightly wounded and 26 taken prisoner or missing.

Rommel moved quickly, as always, and by 8 December 1941, was moving into the Gazala Line. At the coast he placed the Italian X Corps, and the Italian XXI Corps further inland. The southern end was held by the Italian Mobile Corps, with the Deutsches Afrikakorps behind it to act as a counter-attack force.

Upgunned Marmon Herrington Mk 2, North Africa.

Upgunned Marmon Herrington Mk 2 with the 47mm Italian Breda gun, North Africa.

Around 10 December 1941 Brigadier Reid flew up to Eighth Army headquarters for further orders and was told to cooperate with 'Bencol' (consisting of 22 Guards Brigade under Brigadier Marriott and the 11th Hussars), which was tasked to cut across the desert and disrupt Rommel's retirement from Gazala in the vicinity of Antelat–Agedabia. E Force would join hands with Bencol in this area. But there was a lack of logistic vehicles, so Bencol would not be able to set off for Agedabia until 20 December 1941; E Force would link up with it on the 22nd.

Brigadier Reid decided to establish his operational base at Giof el Matar, about 200km northwest of Jalo:

> My problem would be water and I decided that for a base of operations I must base myself on Giof el Matar where water existed. At Sahabi on the Agedabia track no water existed, and at El Haseiat the well had been destroyed. Giof el Matar incidentally was well known later as 'WWWP' (well with wind pump).
>
> During our recces it had been discovered that it was possible to move up by a concealed route of reasonable 'going' due north from Sahabi to WWWP. A reconnaissance some four days before we were due to move bumped into German patrols in the Sahabi area.
>
> It was therefore possible that we might find the garrison at Giof el Matar either reinforced or taken over by the Germans. Agedabia was known to be held strongly and in addition there were reckoned to be between 30 and 50 aeroplanes on the airfield there.

Major Ferguson's C Squadron 6 South African Armoured Car Regiment was the only South African unit other than 3 South African Reconnaissance Battalion to participate in the chase after Rommel's forces as they withdrew to the Gazala Line, and it smelled plenty of powder in the process as its patrols and those of the King's Dragoon Guards roamed around between Bir el Gubi and Bir Hakeim on 8 and 9 December 1941.

On 10 December 1941 the King's Dragoon Guards was relieved by the Royal Dragoons and attached to 22 Guards Brigade, which was then in reserve and protecting the lines of communication. This was a welcome respite for the King's Dragoon Guards after three weeks of continuous operations, but just two days later they were back in action when they ran into enemy armoured patrols that were too strong to deal with. On 14 December 1941 the King's Dragoon Guards came under command of 7 Armoured Support Group and spent the next few days patrolling along the Gazala Line west of Rotonda Mteifel.

Tobruk had finally been relieved after 19 days of fighting. But Operation Crusader was not over yet …

27

Push to Benghazi

While the King's Dragoon Guards and C Squadron 4 South African Armoured Car Regiment prowled up and down around Rotonda Mteifel, General Ritchie launched a strong assault on the Gazala Line after pulling the Eighth Army back into some sort of fighting shape. 7 Armoured Division had now been transferred to XIII Corps, as well as 4 Indian Infantry Division and 5 New Zealand Infantry Brigade, while XXX Corps had been given 2 South African Division and directed to besiege the remaining Axis border strongholds.

On 13 December 1941 the Eighth Army hit the Gazala Line, 5 New Zealand Brigade attacking over a 12km front and 5 Indian Brigade hitting Alem Hamza from the flank, with 1 Battalion The Royal East Kent Regiment (The Buffs) assaulting a strongpoint to the west nicknamed Point 204.

The Buffs took Point 204 but found themselves in a salient and therefore vulnerable to counter-attack when the Italian Trieste Division beat off 5 Indian Brigade at Alem Hamza. Ritchie's response was to order 7 Indian Brigade, which was on 5 Indian Brigade's left, to send reinforcements in the shape of 4/11 Sikh Regiment, with a contingent of 25-pdrs from 25 Field Regiment Royal Artillery.

Rommel considered Point 204 a key position, and about 9km from its destination the 7 Indian Brigade reinforcement column ran into a potent Deutsches Afrikakorps force that was headed there as well.

"The opposition was even stronger than it looked," according to New Zealand historian W. E. Murphy. "Once again Afrika Korps had been able to concentrate without hindrance by the British armour and was now counter-attacking with the 51 tanks of 5 and 8 Panzer Regiments [and] their usual accompaniment of '88s' and other anti-tank guns, 2 Machine Gun Battalion following closely to their left rear, and 8 Machine Gun Battalion as well as the artillery firing in support – a formidable threat indeed."

A hard-fought, mainly armoured action ensued, in the course of which assistance came from 15 Valentine cruiser tanks of 8 Royal Tank Regiment which appeared from the left flank, 25-pdrs from 8 Field Regiment Royal Artillery which came into action a mile to the east, and anti-tank and Bofors guns. The outnumbered Allied force managed to halt the counter-attack and destroy or disable 15 German tanks, although at heavy cost to 25 Field Regiment and 8 Royal Tank Regiment. 7 Armoured Division was nowhere near, which Murphy finds intriguing in view of an instruction General Godwin-Austen had sent Gott that very day:

"Early destruction enemy's armour is imperative," Godwin-Austen signalled to Gott at 1020 on the 13th and that "we may miss great opportunity for destruction of his [the enemy's] armour," he added, unless 4 Armoured Brigade was moved to a central position, ready to strike round either flank.

Early next morning Gott replied that he was moving his armour to the northwest and thought this would "affect enemy on 4 Ind Div front" at about 1600. This was a slower tempo of operations than Godwin-Austen required and he urged Gott to get the armour into "immediate readiness to attack". Later in the morning the two met and agreed on a left hook by 4 Armoured Brigade toward Tmimi to threaten the rear of the Gazala Line and "bring enemy to action" not later than 1100 on 15 December.

But the action against 25 Field Regiment on the 13th deserved close study. It showed that the Germans had not lost the art of concentrating all arms in support of panzer counter-thrusts and were still able to strike back hard, as 7 Indian Brigade had twice found out and 5 Indian Brigade was soon to learn the same lesson.

A remarkable change had meanwhile taken place in the minds of Gott, Gatehouse, and other senior armoured commanders, unperceived by their superiors. The main objective was still to seek out and destroy the enemy armour, but these commanders had given up hope of achieving this by direct means, though they now knew they outnumbered the enemy in tanks by at least two to one.

"In every action the enemy showed his skill in effecting cooperation between tanks and field and anti-tank artillery," Gott wrote shortly afterward. "No attack by our more lightly armoured tanks was possible," he added, "except by making a very wide detour and coming in on his soft-skinned vehicles."

Godwin-Austen's earnest efforts to bring the British armour into the main battle were therefore wasted and any serious infantry threat to the Gazala Line would run a grave risk of overwhelming panzer counter-attack. Fortunately Rommel's estimate of the potentialities of the British armour was higher than that of both Gott and Crüwell.

The following day the Polish Independent Brigade was brought in to augment 5 New Zealand Brigade, and at 0300 on 15 December 1941 the two brigades hurled themselves at the Gazala Line, surprising the defenders but without achieving a breakthrough. At Alem Hamza 5 Indian Brigade similarly was beaten off, although at Point 204 The Buffs, supported by a motley collection of infantry tanks, armoured cars, field artillery, anti-tank guns and sappers, easily repulsed an attack by about a dozen tanks from the now seriously depleted Ariete Armoured Division.

But later in the same day the Germans attacked again, this time in overwhelming strength, and finally overran Point 204. The majority of officers and men of The Buffs were killed or made prisoner, but 5 Indian Brigade at Alem Hamza was spared the Deutsches Afrikakorps' attentions because the Germans had lost so heavily that they were unable to exploit their success.

Pienaar's 1 South African Brigade had started moving back to Mersa Matruh on 13 December 1941 for reorganization, leaving C Squadron 6 South African Armoured Car Regiment, which was still attached to the King's Dragoon Guards, as the only South African armoured cars in the Western Desert. But Rommel's resurgence at Point 204 changed everything, and Pienaar got no further than the Libyan side of the Bir Sheferzen border crossing.

There, on the 14th, he was abruptly ordered to move back to the west again and go into army reserve southwest of El Adem. These orders were then amended and the Brigade was sent first to a position a few kilometres southwest of Acroma and later to another about 20km south of Gazala, near Alem Hamza.

But the threat from Rommel was now over for the time being. Concerned about the possibility of a flanking attack by 7 Armoured Division, he ordered the immediate evacuation of the Gazala Line; it began that same night, with the Brescia Division as the rearguard. Both Crüwell and his Italian generals objected strongly to the evacuation, but subsequent events proved Rommel right.

With only eight German and about 30 Italian tanks in running order, he was in no position to take on 7 Armoured Division, whose functional tanks outnumbered his by a large enough margin to rob him of much of the advantage of his superior tanks and anti-tank guns. In addition, as Murphy says, "though such a long retreat was a difficult operation, every mile on the way back would ease Axis supply problems and increase those of the British, thus tipping the scales another degree in Rommel's favour."

It would also, of course, buy him time to rebuild his all-important armoured force. His workshops would be able to repair large numbers of damaged tanks which had been recovered, and, as Murphy points out: "[Although] two companies of German tanks and a battalion of Italian tanks had been sunk on their way to Libya on the 13th … two more panzer companies were at sea, one bound for Tripoli and the other for Benghazi, and they both arrived on the 19th.

"They were badly needed, for Eighth Army had another armoured brigade at hand [the reconstituted 22 Armoured Brigade] with which to relieve 4 Armoured Brigade as soon as the situation allowed, and another armoured division [the 1st] would soon take over from 7 Armoured Division." The evacuation might well have been even more difficult if the British armour had reacted more swiftly, Murphy says:

> Godwin-Austen had signalled to both Gott and Gatehouse at 7.50 p.m. on 14 December that the British armour would next day have "such a chance of destroying enemy forces as seldom arises in war." His orders were therefore simple: "Smash them relentlessly."
> By 3 p.m. on the 15th, 4 Armoured Brigade reached Bir Halegh el-Eleba, southwest of Tmimi, and was thus admirably placed for this purpose. The Royals and B Squadron of 3 Royal Tanks moved northward and engaged enemy who soon withdrew; but the rest of the Brigade halted. Godwin-Austen pressed again for early action against the rear of the enemy facing 4 Indian Division, which was "hard pressed", but Gott objected to any immediate attack on administrative grounds, though he agreed that the Brigade should attack at the earliest possible hour next day. Again at 6.50 p.m. Godwin-Austen urged Gott, "if humanly possible," to cut the enemy's [line of communication] near Tmimi early on the 16th. Gott replied with some unrecorded objection which Godwin-Austen acknowledged but refused to accept, insisting that his wishes remained and pointing out that "any aggressive action even if only local will materially affect situation which is now reaching climax".
> But Gott had already thrown a spanner in the works by authorizing 4 Armoured Brigade to move south early next day, away from the enemy. The B Echelons had been held up by bad going and the Brigade would "facilitate replenishment" by going back to meet its supply lorries.
> The panzer troops could have told Gott that running out of petrol on the battlefield need not be so disastrous as he feared; they had done it several times already without dire consequences. There was, moreover, no shortage of ammunition, for most of the 85 to 95 tanks had done little or no fighting for some days …

In the afternoon 15 Panzer, moving west, was able to pass by 4 Armoured's rear and block any return move to the north. While the mere presence of the British armour had tipped Rommel's hand to withdraw from Gazala, the opportunity to gain a decisive victory had been missed.

On the 16th Gatehouse turned about and headed southward; but before doing so he despatched two detachments to raid the enemy's rear. C Squadron 3 Royal Tanks, with a squadron of armoured cars and a troop of anti-tank guns, made an extremely bold thrust at the Battle headquarters of Afrikakorps near Bir Temrad, causing much confusion and alarm, and another armoured car squadron raided Tmimi.

Had the whole brigade acted in like manner (and in the afternoon of the 15th rather than the morning of the 16th) Crusader might well have been brought to a victorious conclusion in a matter of hours. The 18 miles that 4 Armoured Brigade moved in the morning, had they been to the north instead of the south, would have put it within a mile or two of Tmimi. Godwin-Austen's vision was correct; but its fulfilment was denied by this southward move, which nullified all hope of decisive action.

Rommel spent the next ten days withdrawing to a line between Agedabia and El Haseia, keeping his supply lines open. As they shortened and he began to receive imports of new equipment at El Agheila his armoured force began to grow again.

Patrols of C Squadron 6 South African Armoured Car Regiment had some brushes with enemy detachments during this period. On 17 December 1941, when it was discovered that Rommel was withdrawing from the Gazala Line, C Squadron joined 'Wilson Column' – one of two drawn from 3 Coldstream Guards and 9 Rifle Brigade respectively and attached to the King's Dragoon Guards – which was proceeding to Mekili.

According to the King's Dragoon Guards history "patrols reached the vicinity of Mekili on 18 December 1941, reporting huge enemy columns moving to the west." C Squadron's war diary noted that a concentration of 3,000 to 4,000 enemy vehicles were engaged by Wilson Column, and from then on the concentration "appeared to filter out all the time from Mekili".

The going seems to have been very rough, because only six out of 21 cars reached Mekili with Wilson Column, although with one exception all were later recovered. This was obviously the tail-end of Rommel's forces, because next morning Mekili was clear of the enemy.

On 18 December 1941 3 South African Reconnaissance Battalion's No. 1 and No. 2 companies were detached to 5 Indian Brigade, which had been tasked with a cross-country advance to cut off enemy forces retreating from the port of Derna. This was a fighting withdrawal and not a rout, as they soon discovered, and both companies took a shelling, No. 2 Company from the Axis 6-inch guns at Tmimi.

On 19 December 1941 No. 1 Company – 20 cars in all – under Captain Guy de Marillac escorted 4/6 Punjab Rifles in a cross-country dash to cut off enemy movement on the Derna–Lamluda–Barce road near the coast. De Marillac and his colleagues fought their way over very bad terrain, only to make a mediocre haul – three German staff cars and a motorcycle, yielding a total of nine prisoners. From there the cars headed for the Lamluda crossroads a few kilometres further west and were passed on to 3/1 Punjab Rifles for the next day's attack on the town of Giovanni Berta (today's Al Qubah), and this was another story altogether.

While No. 1 Company was involved at Giovanni Berta, No. 2 Company under Captain E. K. Hutchings had been sitting astride the coast road to protect 5 Indian Brigade's flank from interference from Tmimi, and on 19 December 1941 took part in the capture of Derna with its twin airfields, undoubtedly the most spectacular action involving the South African armoured cars in the war so far.

Hutchings's men, 4/11 Sikh Regiment and a contingent of Bren carriers advanced through a defile north of Martuba, halfway between Tmimi and Derna, and came out on to the Via Balbia, the main coast road, near where it passed between Derna's two airfields and went to the edge of the escarpment. What happened then is best described in an anonymous eyewitness account from the Sikhs:

Five miles away aeroplanes could be seen landing and taking off constantly. The road itself was choked with transport. Two companies of the Sikhs were deployed to block the road against forces retreating from the east, while Bren carriers and the remainder of the battalion scrambled down on to the plain. Then the carriers and armoured cars led the charge.

The enemy columns were completely unprepared as the carriers and lorried infantry swept down upon them, shooting them up in Wild West fashion. Three hundred prisoners, five 88mm guns and many vehicles were captured. Such transport as escaped stampeded down the road toward the brink of the cliffs above Derna.

The carriers poured onto the airfields, and riddled planes, large and small. Transport planes, bombers, fighters, gliders, all were destroyed or captured in the wild scrimmage.

While this was happening a number of Ju 52 troop carriers appeared and came in to land, only to be shot up as soon as their wheels hit the ground. No. 2 Company's cars had led the charge on to the airfield, and a vivid account by a sergeant who participated was later distributed by the South African Press Association:

> Our guns were shelling the tarred road past the 'drome and enemy troop concentrations on the right side of it when, fairly late in the afternoon, we came over a ridge and made for the west corner of the landing-ground.
>
> I was in the turret of the leading car. Suddenly I saw a number of bombers [actually troop transports] in the air approaching the landing-ground. At first I thought they were our own, but I grabbed my binoculars and saw the black German crosses on them. I gave orders that nobody was to open fire.
>
> We kept quiet, despite our natural impatience, until all of them – there were 11 or 12 – had landed. As soon as the last had got down we opened fire with our machine guns and charged the aerodrome with 11 armoured cars.
>
> Several of the bombers went up in flames immediately. Two of them took off. One of them was limping badly and must have crashed soon afterward, for it had been badly hit. Pilots leaped out of some of the blazing planes. Some of them raced to the road, where enemy transports were standing, and others ran for the hangars. We shot down some of them as they ran. Others died in their planes.
>
> Some of the pilots reached for their machine guns and opened up at us, and things got pretty hectic. The enemy started to shell us from farther down the tarred road. They concentrated on the troops on our right flank [the Sikhs] who were mopping up lots of prisoners. On the left flank the enemy also opened up with machine-gun fire and began to shell us as well. Hot exchanges went on for some time.
>
> [The Sikh] infantry … who came charging along behind us and on our flank, gave the most amazing display of aggressive courage I have ever seen. They charged one Ju with fixed bayonets, firing as they charged. They just failed to reach the plane before it staggered off the ground, but they brought it down with rifle and Bren gun fire.
>
> As the sun went down a mass of planes was still burning fiercely on the aerodrome. They looked like bonfires. We had got nine Junkers 52s, transport planes. We pulled back a short distance from the aerodrome and camped for the night.

What made the attack even more remarkable was that a South African Broadcasting Corporation team under the well-known radio personality Bruce Anderson had actually gone along on the raid and broadcast an account of the action from the airfield itself – a commonplace today in the era of 'real-time coverage', but not in 1942.

To add to the drama, Captain Hutchings shot down a Ju 88 while Anderson was recording his news, and another aircraft bombed the top of the pass but was damaged by the guns of No. 2 Company's rear party; Anderson recorded this episode as well. For hundreds of thousands of listeners at home in South Africa the war – and the armoured cars' part in it – was suddenly on their doorstep.

After the capture of Giovanni Berta, No. 1 Company was recalled into army reserve with 1 South African Brigade and replaced at 5 Indian Brigade by No. 3 Company. The newcomers patrolled to the vicinity of Cirene and Barce without any hostile contact except one bombing attack by a Ju 88, and together with the Central India Horse's armoured cars ranged forward for more than 100km, clearing various villages.

Far south of the dramatic capture of Derna, Brigadier Reid prepared for the advance to Giof el Matar by sending off 6 South African Armoured Car Regiment's Lieutenant-Colonel Short from Jalo with E Force's advance element, 'Shortcol' – comprising his headquarters and B Squadron, B Company 3/2 Punjabis, anti-tank and anti-aircraft sections, one 25-pdr of 2 South African Field Regiment and a detachment of sappers – 24 hours ahead of the main body.

Short's orders were to secure Sahabi, find out whether Haseiat was occupied and capture Giof el Matar by the evening of 21 December 1941. The route for E Force's main body under

Brigadier Reid would depend on what sort of enemy presence Short encountered. Reid would head straight for Ain en Naga on the Wadi Faregh; his route from there would be decided on when Short had apprised him of what lay ahead.

From Sahabi he could move due north to Giof el Matar on the concealed route his earlier reconnaissance patrols had uncovered, but if Short found a substantial enemy presence in the Haseiat-Giof el Matar area, the E Force main body would cross the Wadi Faregh at Ain en Naga and then advance northeastward to attack and capture both Haseiat and Giof el Matar.

The Axis airfield at Agedabia was an obvious danger to E Force, and Reid enlisted the help of that perennial thorn in the Axis flesh, the Long Range Desert Group, to insert a small raiding party consisting of an officer and three other ranks of the Gordon Highlanders, which would try to destroy some or all of the aircraft on the ground. As an additional precaution Reid detailed a small column, commanded by Captain M. Flint of 7 South African Reconnaissance Battalion and consisting of A Squadron 7 South African Reconnaissance Battalion, minus one troop, C Company 3/2 Punjabis and a section of anti-aircraft guns, to make sure that there was no enemy presence east of Giof el Matar.

At 1415 on 19 December 1941 Short's column left Jalo without any regrets, since it was a far cry from the traditional romantic depiction of a desert oasis. They covered about 75km, halted for the night and then set out again early next morning. About 15km west of Sahabi Short halted while an advance party scouted ahead; it turned out to be unoccupied by any Axis presence, and Short continued on to Dartet Ben Zebla. When he got there just after 1500 a local Arab told Short that at Haseiat there was an enemy force about 100 strong; Short decided to stop for the night near Dartet Ben Zebla and attack Haseiat through the Wadi Feragh next morning (21 December 1941).

Brigadier Reid, meanwhile, had left Jalo with the main body that morning, but by nightfall he had yet to receive any information from Shortcol, which he put down to the armoured cars' temperamental Western Electric radio sets. He therefore gave instructions that a patrol was to move out at first light next morning to see whether Sahabi was occupied and try to deduce from vehicle tracks whether Shortcol had headed toward Haseiat or Giof el Matar.

Meanwhile Reid and his main body would move to Ain en Naga in the Wadi Faregh, and within two hours of first light on 21 December 1941 hide in ground cover which previous scouting had spotted. From there he would advance northeastward up the road to Giof el Matar.

In the coastal area, 7 Armoured Support Group was ordered on 20 December 1941 to follow up on the retiring Axis forces with all possible speed. But the enemy bird had flown, and the King's Dragoon Guards with C Squadron 6 South African Armoured Car Regiment battled its way over very bad going as far as El Charruba without encountering any significant enemy opposition except for heavy Stuka raids that destroyed a number of vehicles and inflicted some wounds, but no fatalities.

Next day the King's Dragoon Guards reverted to 7 Armoured Division command again, its A Squadron being tasked to protect the route between Charruba and Got Derva, 25km to the east, while B Squadron was to protect the divisional battle headquarters. C Squadron 6 South African Armoured Car Regiment was given the mundane job of escorting the 186 Italian prisoners taken at Charruba back to a collecting point.

In the south, meanwhile, Short set out early on the morning of 21 December 1941, reached the Wadi Faregh at 0830 and was pleasantly surprised to find no enemy presence at Haseiat. He carried on toward the northeast and by 1430 was about 5km to the northwest of the little Italian fort at Giof el Matar. There he sent a reconnaissance group to lurk behind the rim of a depression west of the fort and a troop of armoured cars supported by a troop of anti-tank guns to watch the Agedabia road about 7km to the west.

This done, he divided his miniature assault force into two detachments and went straight into the attack. One, a troop of armoured cars and a platoon of infantry, supported by an anti-aircraft gun and a captured Breda machine gun, was tasked to advance along a ridge overlooking the fort; the other – a troop of armoured cars and a platoon of infantry with another Breda – would head straight for the fort from the west after Short's solitary 25-pdr had opened the proceedings at 1545 by shelling it.

The ensuing action was an inconsiderable one that lasted no more than ten minutes. At zero hour the 25-pdr fired six shots and the fort's garrison surrendered – understandably, since it consisted of only 11 Italians and three Libyans.

Short tucked away his column in a nearby wadi and, since his signallers still could not make contact with the main body, sent back a liaison officer to find Brigadier Reid. But the attempt to make contact did not succeed, so that by nightfall Reid, who was now about 7km north of Ain en Naga, had still heard nothing, although a patrol he had sent out came back to report that both Sahabi and Haseitat were unoccupied.

Along the coast, the race was now on to see which of the Allied forward elements would be the first to reach Benghazi. On 22 December 1941 the 12th Lancers and 11th Hussars set off from Charruba toward the Benghazi–Agedabia road through Sceleidima and Antelat respectively, and the King's Dragoon Guards was ordered to leave the following morning for Benghazi, 120km away.

Just before first light on 22 December 1941 E Force's main body left for Giof el Matar, and almost immediately made contact with Lieutenant Fraser and his Long Range Desert Group raiders, who were the bearers of magnificent tidings. Brigadier Reid describes the meeting as follows:

> At first light there was a certain amount of excitement amongst the forward troops and recognition signals by Verey light were fired. I drove forward to see what was the matter and met Fraser of the Gordons patrol whom I eagerly asked how he had got on. He said, "Very sorry, Sir; had to leave two aircraft on the ground as I ran out of explosive, but we destroyed 36." This was indeed a wonderful achievement by one officer and three men. Incidentally, we heard later that Rommel had been in Agedabia that night. He must have had a bit of a headache.

"Much cheered and relieved," Reid set E Force in motion again and ordered Lieutenant M. M. Smuts of 7 South African Reconnaissance Battalion to head at maximum speed for Giof el Matar, where, he was convinced, Short had already taken occupation. This was confirmed by a signal from Smuts, and at noon E Force arrived at Giof el Matar and took up defensive positions. Later that afternoon two enemy aircraft – no doubt the survivors of the Long Range Desert Group raid – came in very low and destroyed three Punjabi lorries. Apart from that, however, there was no enemy reaction.

Reid's first priority was to join hands with Bencol, and as soon as he arrived he gave Short two extra 25-pdrs and sent him off with orders to establish a base in the vicinity of Bir el Giocch and contact Brigadier Marriott somewhere in the Antelat area. At 1330 Short moved off, and at 1500 sent Lieutenant N. W. Gordon ahead with two armoured cars to get to Antelat as soon as possible with a message for Brigadier Marriott.

When Short's main body reached the secondary Antelat–Ajedabia track two hours later he decided to have the regimental headquarters stand fast, along with one and a half infantry platoons, the Breda troop, the B Echelon transport vehicles and one of the 25-pdrs, with the rest going on for another 6km to cut the main Antelat–Ajedabia road at Bir by Fettah. This they did at 1730, but there was no sign of Bencol or any indication of where it might be.

On the morning of 23 December 1941 the King's Dragoon Guards and C Squadron 6 South African Armoured Car Regiment set off for Benghazi, A Squadron leading the way. On reaching El Abiar, the squadron reported that the town was clear of all enemy personnel except the wounded in the hospital, but the god of battles was not with the King's Dragoon Guards that day, because from there on it ran into a series of morasses caused by the heavy rains of the past few days.

En route the King's Dragoon Guards regimental headquarters and A Squadron passed a thoroughly bogged-down and abandoned South African armoured car that had been captured and pressed into Axis service. They decided it was beyond hope of salvage, removed various detachable parts for spares and kept going. Major Ferguson's C Squadron 6 South African Armoured Car Regiment took a less gloomy view, dug the liberated car out of the bog in which it was residing and replaced what was necessary.

"That night," the King's Dragoon Guards history records admiringly, "they reported one extra armoured car on the road, having recovered and re-equipped this abandoned car with their usual resourcefulness." The squadron war diary's entry indicates that Ferguson's men did not regard their salvage operation as anything exceptional: "An abandoned A/car picked up by Sqn."

Brigadier Reid soon discovered why Bencol had not appeared. In a nutshell, their scheduled rendezvous had been overtaken by events. On the morning of 23 December 1941 E Force heard extremely heavy artillery fire coming from the north. Reid sent out patrols to reconnoitre toward Antelat. The hours passed. Then at 1530 Lieutenant Gordon's patrol rejoined Short at Bir bu Fettah to report that a large tank battle – "about 60 tanks each side," as he put it – had been in progress at Antelat ever since about 0900, and that now the British were withdrawing toward Saunnu.

What had happened, he explained, was that 22 Guards Brigade and 3 Royal Tank Regiment had been attacked in the Antelat area and forced to retreat by an Axis force with about 30 tanks that had been waiting at Beda Fomm to cover the retreat of the Panzergruppe's main body down the coastal road.

7 Support Group, which was mauling a small enemy force west of Sceleidima at the time, had been ordered to break contact and aid the Guards and Royal Tank Regiment. When it arrived the enemy tanks withdrew southwestward, but the initial attack at Antelat had kept open the coastal route long enough for a considerable part of Panzergruppe Afrika to escape to the south.

As a result of the mud A Squadron did not reach Benghazi until the morning of 24 December 1941, arriving from the east neck-and-neck with a patrol of the Royal Dragoons coming up from the south. C Squadron 6 South African Armoured Car Regiment reached the outskirts at 1630 and laagered there for the night. Not a single shot was fired by any of the squadrons: Benghazi was a ghost town, abandoned by all Axis troops and most of its civilian population

By the time the King's Dragoon Guards and Royals occupied Benghazi, No. 3 Platoon and the Central India Horse had liberated Barce farther to the east, although not without some loss: on the 22nd the South African armoured cars were scouting ahead of the Central India Horse when the four cars ran into an enemy rearguard on a blind corner of the main escarpment's road, about 12km from Barce. An enemy anti-tank gunner managed to get off a shot that hit the leading car's turret and killed the commander, although the driver brought the car safely away.

This was the only significant contact, however, and the force maintained contact with the withdrawing enemy, although thanks to delays caused by mines and roadblocks the South Africans did not enter Barce until 1500 on 23 December 1941, with the main body arriving half an hour later. According to the Central India Horse's report:

The town was undefended and the Mayor surrendered his keys with obvious relief. The extensive Italian settlements to the north and west were in a state of siege, with Arab bands looting and murdering. The town was immediately placed under martial law and a curfew imposed. The

Italian police were allowed to keep their arms. Detachments were pushed out north, west and south to round up stragglers, take possession of dumps, and restore order.

No. 3 Platoon was told to carry on to Tocra, on the coast due west of Barce. It left at 4 p.m. and passed through the little settler town of Barraca, but turned back after 6km when it came up against a roadblock. Scenes of chaos greeted it when it got back to Barraca: "The Italian civilians there [were] in a sorry plight … The Arabs were plundering and killing indiscriminately." The platoon commander "then took his car out with the Chief of Police, and during an exchange of shots some 12 Arabs were killed. The cars stood by all night but nothing untoward occurred."

It would not be the last time that the South Africans and British found themselves thrown willy-nilly into internal security duties. The Italian boot had rested heavily and never comfortably on the collective Libyan neck, and now it was payback time.

While No. 3 Platoon (of 3 South African Reconnaissance Battalion's No. 1 Company) was pacifying Barraca, the company headquarters and No. 2 Platoon were 13km southwest of Luigi Razza, repairing a roadblock demolition that had proved impossible to bypass. It took so long to get through that when they finally managed to carry on they had to laager for the night about 5km down the road.

Next day, the 24th, No. 3 Platoon set off for Tocra again, encountered some delays there and then made good time along the Via Balbia. It arrived at Benghazi at 1730, on the heels of the King's Dragoon Guards, the Royals and its fellow Springboks of 6 South African Armoured Car Regiment's C Squadron. The platoon bedded down for the night about 5km outside the town and eventually made contact with advance elements of 5 Brigade.

No. 2 Platoon and No. 3 Company Headquarters also covered a considerable distance on the 24th. They started off along the Via Balbia from their camping spot approximately 18km southwest of Luigi Razza, dropping off the A Echelon and a section of cars at D'Annunzio to protect the civilian population, and lost two signallers killed when a Ju 88 bombed the village.

The rest entered Barce about 1600 and were told that No. 3 Platoon was approaching Benghazi. The company commander was then given command of a squadron of the Central India Horse and was ordered to keep moving. He did just that and the long day's travel ended at Driana, after covering the last 30km in the dark.

On 24 December 1941 Brigadier Reid travelled to Saunnu to look for Brigadier Marriott, but found only 22 Armoured Brigade, which had just arrived from Mekili. Before heading westward in search of Bencol he briefed the Officer Commanding Royal Dragoons about the going around Marada, about 100km south of El Agheila, where a squadron of the Royals was scheduled to patrol. Then he left, and met up first with the 11th Hussars and then 22 Guards Brigade. By now it was near evening, so he spent the night with Brigadier Marriott, who had been tasked to probe toward Agedabia next day.

While Brigadier Reid was chasing after Bencol, Lieutenant-Colonel Short was heavily involved south of Agedabia. At 0845 Short's gunners fired at an enemy lorry coming down the road from Agedabia, and although the vehicle managed to escape, two Germans from an artillery regiment jumped out and were taken prisoner by a Punjabi motorized section. Then at 0910 a Captain Millman of the Punjabis, with two platoons of infantry and two anti-tank guns, joined forces with Short.

Short pondered the confused situation in which he found himself and decided to concentrate his entire force about 3km east of Bir bu Fettah. He had barely done so when, at 1045, he received a signal from E Force ordering him to form two groups and attack enemy traffic on the main Benghazi–Agedabia road.

Under Major E. G. Fricker of 6 South African Armoured Car Regiment he placed two troops of armoured cars, an infantry company, a section of anti-tank guns, a 25-pdr and a Breda troop, with Short himself taking command of the other detachment – Squadron

Headquarters B Squadron and two troops of cars, an infantry company, a section of anti-tank guns, a section of anti-aircraft guns and the remaining two 25-pdrs. The battle plan was quite straightforward: Short would attack the road at Sidi Frag and Fricker would do the same at Bu Ferrara.

Fricker moved off at 1430, followed ten minutes later by Short. Fricker drew first blood, reporting at 1615 that his group had dispersed 12 enemy vehicles near the road and captured one containing five Germans. Just over half an hour later Short reached the Sidi Frag area and swiftly proceeded to create havoc among a transport column with his artillery and machine guns: according to Gunner R. V. Davis of 2 South African Field Regiment, "the armoured cars cruised up and down, firing their Boys anti-tank rifles into the engines of the transport which had been abandoned at the first shots from our men."

Having totally destroyed five vehicles, knocked out another 15 and captured one in running order with five Germans on board, Short's men set about cutting down the telegraph poles along the road. Then at 1745 enemy shells started bursting around them. The two 25-pdrs fired back "at so short a range," according to Davis, "that the signallers were ordered to use their rifles".

With night falling, Short withdrew "into the darkness, followed by parting gifts in the way of shells from 75s and heavy Breda" and laagered about 9km to the east. His column had suffered no casualties or damage, and according to his lookouts traffic did not resume until between 2100 and 2200.

On Christmas morning No. 3 Company was, according to the company report, reunited in Benghazi:

> Early on the morning of 25 December within the gates of Benghazi the Platoon Commander No. 2 Platoon made contact with No. 3 Platoon and shortly afterward Company Headquarters arrived with attached Central India Horse squadron.
> Immediately on entry, the Company Commander contacted the Chief of Police and acting Mayor informing him that British forces were now in command of Benghazi, and advised him to muster immediately all available Police, numbering 23, to maintain order in the town, where the Arabs now held sway. He also expressed his desire that the life of the town should be restored to normal at the earliest opportunity.
> When all steps to ensure law and order had been taken, and armoured cars had occupied key positions, a Major of the King's Dragoon Guards arrived, and as he was the senior officer present, any further measures that might have proved necessary were then left to him.

That day General Gott, the General Officer Commanding 7 Armoured Division, paid a visit and appointed the Officer Commanding King's Dragoon Guards as officer in charge of Benghazi, pending arrival of the infantry. The King's Dragoon Guards then, according to its history, got down to such pursuits as "dealing with looting Arabs, excitable Italian police, and war correspondents who wanted 'action' photographs, and a number of 'comic opera situations' resulted".

Major Ferguson's C Squadron 6 South African Armoured Car Regiment seems to have had an altogether quieter Christmas, the squadron war diary reporting simply that "at first light Sqn moved into Benghazi … Patrolling of important points was carried out throughout the day. No Xmas pudding. C Squadron had the opportunity of broadcasting to the Union, of which 12 availed themselves. At 1800 hrs Sqn Headquarters withdrew to outskirts leaving patrols in position".

Major Fricker spent the morning hours of Christmas Day engaged in a somewhat farcical but nevertheless welcome encounter. He was on his way back to Bir bu Fettah when around 1000 his detachment spotted a large number of armoured cars, and, he surmised (correctly), tanks as well, coming down from the north. What happened then is described by Gunner Davis:

> ... we moved back from the road a little way. An overwhelming armoured force poured over the ridge toward us. If they were enemy, we knew our time was short, so we speedily opened a tin of prunes we had been keeping for Xmas dinner and shovelled them down as fast as we could. Our gun fired a warning shot at them. Those armoured vehicles in front of us stopped, while the flanks kept going in an encircling movement. An armoured car commander came in to report that he thought they were ours. "Think be damned," said the column commander. "Go out and make certain – or draw fire."
>
> They were the advance guard of our main forces. Our one shell had burst near a tank. The tank crew told the gunners that that was one they owed them. They also told us that we, on our one- and two-gun patrols, were like little children wandering round in a bull-pen. We explained that it wasn't our idea of fun either.

The newcomers turned out to be the 11th Hussars, who, with artillery and tanks in support, were probing toward Agedabia. Short threw in his lot with them for the day and the advance continued, the South Africans providing a troop of cars as a right flank guard, with the rest of Shortcol on the left flank.

The only action they saw, however, was at 1100, when the column halted 12km north of Agedabia while the British artillery bombarded enemy gun positions. With night approaching, Short returned to Bir bu Fettah, where he stayed until the next afternoon and was then ordered back to Giof el Matar. By 2100 Shortcol was back with the rest of E Force.

While Short and Major Fricker were busy north of Agedabia, other small E Force raiding columns were engaged in harrying enemy traffic using the road between Agedabia and Mersa Brega. These activities appear not to have been extensively documented, but according to Brigadier Reid, a Lieutenant Holden of 3/2 Punjabis and Lieutenant Smuts of 7 South African Reconnaissance Battalion "had a most successful half-hour shoot on a debussed battalion of German infantry, some 15 miles south of Agedabia – this until four or five tanks started ferreting about looking for them, when they beat a wise and cautious retreat".

7 South African Reconnaissance Battalion's war diary, in the usual laconic fashion, noted only that on 24 December 1941 Smuts and Lieutenant W. J. Vos set off "to shell and otherwise harass enemy concentrations near and south of Agedabia" and on 26 December 1941 returned, "having had a successful shoot and captured two POW".

On Boxing Day 4 Indian Division took over Benghazi from the King's Dragoon Guards, which then left for Ghemines, 60km to the south. Troops of 4 Indian Division relieved C Squadron's patrols at 1630, and they were recalled to the squadron headquarters to be sent off at 1800 on a moonlight march to a night-laager just outside Ghemines.

Next morning C Squadron caught up with the King's Dragoon Guards at El Gbeirat, 15km southeast of Ghemines. The regiment then went eastward to Sceleidima, retrieved its B Echelon and B Squadron (which had been attached to Gott's headquarters since 22 December 1941) and finally laagered for the night at Bir bu Ghezzaha, between Sceleidima and Msus. The King's Dragoon Guards now came under command of 7 Armoured Support Group, which was guarding food and fuel dumps that were being established at Msus in anticipation of the advance on Rommel.

No. 3 Company spent the next few days at Benghazi, carrying out routine patrols and various other duties; one section was sent to Driana to try to locate enemy supply dumps, and in the Benghazi area itself the cars guarded aerodromes and dumps of petrol, rations and other supplies, while the company headquarters maintained a round-the-clock radio watch with 7 Indian Brigade Headquarters. On 27 December 1941 a section was sent to Soluk and

Msus to contact Brigadier Jock Campbell of 7 Armoured Support Group and liaise between him and 4 Indian Division.

The South African armoured cars still west of the Wire were scheduled to be withdrawn at the end of the month for sorely needed rest, refitting and reinforcement, but a good deal of unfinished business remained to be done in the aftermath of Operation Crusader. The German-Italian strongholds along the Wire, which were now completely isolated without hope of relief but not necessarily bereft of fighting spirit, had to be reduced, and Rommel had not run entirely out of steam by any means.

On 27 December 1941 elements of the partly revived Deutsches Afrikakorps clashed with the Eighth Army's forward formations – 22 Guards Brigade and 22 Armoured Brigade – at El Haseia, near Agedabia and less than 100km from Msus. A three-day battle ensued that cost the British 50 tanks and forced the two brigades to withdraw, giving Rommel some more time in which to fall back even further to a better defence line extending inland from El Agheila, 120km to the northwest.

At Msus 7 Armoured Support Group formed two columns, 'Wilson' and 'Currie', and sent them out toward Agedabia. Screening Wilson Column were A Squadron King's Dragoon Guards, joined by C Squadron 6 South African Armoured Car Regiment, while B Squadron King's Dragoon Guards was attached to Currie Column.

On 28 December 1941 Regimental Headquarters 3 South African Reconnaissance Battalion and No. 2 Company – which had been kicking their heels at Giovanni Berta since the 22nd – were abruptly ordered back to 1 South African Brigade. On the 29th No. 3 Company at Benghazi was ordered back as well, but when it arrived at Giovanni Berta on New Year's Day it was summarily recalled to Barce, where it was to stay until 4 January.

On 2 January 1942, Major-General I. P. de Villiers' 2 South African Division took Bardia with its valuable water sources and garrison of more than 8,000 Germans and Italians, in the process liberating 1,150 prisoners of war, including 650 New Zealanders; among the attackers was an element of 7 South African Reconnaissance Battalion under Major P. J. Jacobs which had been attached to the division. Next on the list were Sallum and Halfaya, where 'Tiger' Jacobs and his men would also be involved.

In the meantime the Allied armoured cars kept a vigilant eye on the Axis forces in and east of Agedabia. C Squadron 6 South African Armoured Car Regiment stayed with Wilson Column for most of the week, ranging far and wide in the vicinity of Belandah and El Haseiat. On 3 January 1942 they were shelled on three separate occasions by the Axis artillery, and on 4 January (C Squadron's "45th day of push and the 52nd without post," as the war diary noted) they and the rest of Wilson Column were dive-bombed three times northeast of El Haseiat.

On 6 January the weather was particularly foul, not only bitterly cold but featuring a fierce sandstorm, and Rommel made use of it to withdraw the last of his forces without being noticed. When it became known next day that Agedabia, Belandah and Haseiat were free of the enemy, the columns resumed their raiding to the west.

3 South African Reconnaissance Battalion was pulled out on 7 January 1942 and sent to Tobruk for refitting, but C Squadron 6 South African Armoured Car Regiment's task was not quite finished yet. On 8 January a column under a Major Rydon – B Squadron King's Dragoon Guards, two troops of 6 South African Armoured Car Regiment's C Squadron, some 25-pdrs of 2 Royal Horse Artillery and anti-tank guns of the Northumberland Hussars – set out to harass the remaining Axis elements in the Maaten Bettafal area, about 90km west of El Haseiat along the Wadi Faregh, where the Royal Air Force had reported seeing enemy vehicles. The King's Dragoon Guards' A Squadron remained behind to monitor enemy patrols west of Gtafia.

Rydon Column found no enemy presence at Maaten Bettafal (the vehicles reported by the Royal Air Force "were probably camels" according to a rather acid entry in the King's

Dragoon Guards history, "for the number of bushes and camels reported during the desert campaign as enemy armoured vehicles was legion") but on 9 January its 'tail' ran into disaster when it hit a minefield in the Wadi Faregh.

Several echelon vehicles were blown up, among them a South African Light Aid Detachment workshop lorry, and to add to the confusion a German armoured car patrol appeared and opened fire, mortally wounding one King's Dragoon Guards lieutenant named Hall and capturing another lieutenant and 11 other ranks; the three South African occupants of the Light Aid Detachment lorry were also taken prisoner, although one later contrived to escape.

Severe sandstorms during the next two days made it almost impossible for Rydon Column's patrols to observe any enemy movement, although they had a few skirmishes with their Axis equivalents. On 12 January 1942, the day Sallum fell to 2 South African Division after a short but hotly waged struggle, Currie Column arrived at Maaten Bettafal to reinforce Rydon Column, and between them they carried out a minor operation that achieved very little, their only reward being several attacks by the resurgent Luftwaffe that day and the next.

C Squadron's long and friendly attachment to the King's Dragoon Guards had now come to an end after three hectic months; their armoured cars so worn out by this time that although they patrolled actively, they had to do so in borrowed British cars. On 13 January 1942 A Squadron King's Dragoon Guards came up from Msus to relieve Rydon Column, and the South Africans took their leave.

"We were sorry to see them go," the King's Dragoon Guards history says, "but as their armoured cars were beginning to crack up and they could muster only two troops, it was better that they should be withdrawn."

C Squadron limped back to Giof el Matar to join the rest of 6 South African Armoured Car Regiment, and on 14 January 1942 Short and his men said goodbye to Brigadier Reid and E Force, then set out on the long trek back to the base workshops at Amiriya in Egypt "after a series of tasks in the southern deserts," as Klein says, "as exciting as could come the way of any armoured car unit".

Now Grobbelaar's 7 South African Reconnaissance Battalion with E Force was the only South African armoured unit left in the line "and except for frequent air attacks our stand was a good one," Grobbelaar later recalled. "Daily our commander sent out Jock Columns to the west and south, and though we had no great hitting power we certainly harassed the enemy flank in no small degree."

Here, too, there had grown a spirit of respect and affection between the British and South Africans, and Grobbelaar recalls: "I must pay tribute to the most unselfish way in which Brigadier Reid commanded his force. He always gave Lieutenant-Colonel Short and myself opportunity to command a mixed column, and I am grateful today that my battle inoculation occurred under his command and direction."

On 17 January 1942, three days after Short's departure from E Force, the heavily fortified Axis stronghold at Halfaya with its 5,000 defenders fell to 2 South African Division. Though surrounded, cut off from any replenishment by sea and very short of food and water, the garrison had held out stubbornly despite heavy artillery and aerial bombardment until hunger and thirst compelled its surrender as well.

Operation Crusader and its aftermath were over at last. It had been a gory and often heart-breaking business – especially for the South Africans and New Zealanders – and had failed to demolish the German armour. However, between them Auchinleck and Ritchie had beaten back the threat to Egypt and the all-important Suez Canal – if only for the time being. Now another uneasy lull fell over the Western Desert as both armies regrouped, reorganized, rebuilt their tank forces and started planning for a summer offensive. But the lull would not last for long.

28

Rommel strikes again

Rommel struck first. He had started planning a counter-attack as soon as 55 new Mark III tanks and fresh supplies arrived on 5 January 1942, and on 21 January 1942 he sent out an armoured reconnaissance in force that caught the Allied forces at a moment of maximum weakness when they were in no shape to conduct a coherent defence.

Lying right in the path of Rommel's advance was a second tank formation the British had imported, 1 Armoured Division under Major-General F. W. Messervy (former General Officer Commanding 4 Indian Division), but it was new to the desert, and its commander had no previous experience of handling armour – nor, thanks to Rommel's timing, would he have an opportunity for gaining any in the short term except in the most painful way.

Messervy had made the well-nigh fatal mistake of sending back all his experienced armoured car units for refitting in preparation for the planned attack on El Agheila, so that he was caught by surprise, and in addition the battle-wise Desert Rats were in army reserve and therefore out of immediate reach. The result was that the panzers routed 1 Armoured Division.

Rommel's onslaught came at an awkward time for 7 South African Reconnaissance Battalion, which was now scheduled to withdraw to Tobruk for refitting but had not yet left Brigadier Reid's E Force. To make matters even worse, Grobbelaar was ill, and since no enemy attack was anticipated in the near future he had left for treatment at 2 South African Division at Sallum.

In his place he left his senior squadron commander, Captain M. R. Flint, in charge of taking 3 South African Reconnaissance Battalion's Regimental Headquarters and two forward squadrons to Tobruk. In the event Flint would be in command for considerably longer than expected, because it turned out that Grobbelaar was, in fact, so ill that he was sent on to a base hospital in Cairo and later evacuated to South Africa.

An unsuspecting Flint had just received a warning order for the trek back to Tobruk when the panzers rolled over the Allied line on 21 January 1942. Needless to say, Rommel's thrust changed everything, and for the next few days 7 South African Reconnaissance Battalion was exceedingly busy. On 23 January 1942 the unit made contact with forward German units at Maaten el Grara and had a car and its crew knocked out by artillery fire, while early on the morning of 24 January it came close to being cut off by a swift enveloping movement and lost another car to German shelling, although the crew was saved.

Flint found a gap in the northeastern Axis flank and managed to break out with his armoured cars and some elements of E Force, while Lieutenant M. M. Smuts got away to the south with some of E Force's B Echelon. Smuts's report of what happened paints a vivid word-picture of the confusion and panic resulting from Rommel's attack:

On the morning of 24th January E Force was 10 miles south of Saunnu. My troop was advanced guard to the B Echelon. When the enemy opened fire with artillery on the Echelon I was ordered to proceed six miles east and endeavour to break through. On going east we struck about 16 enemy guns which immediately opened fire on us. Wireless instructions were then received to follow Captain Flint.

As all the B Echelon were moving southeast we endeavoured to find Captain Flint. Before reaching the head of the Echelon enemy tanks appeared to the right flank and rear, causing general disorder. We followed the bulk of the B Echelon fleeing south and managed to catch up and stop 45 vehicles at Matar. We then found that Captain Flint had not led these vehicles out. Lieutenant Manning and I then tried to reorganize and decide what action to take. For some unknown reason the B Echelon started running again, heading due south. We followed in our armoured cars endeavouring to stop the lorries, but we only caught up with them when they reached the salt marshes in the Sahabi area, where a lot of vehicles were badly bogged and others abandoned by Indian troops.

After a great deal of trouble and delay we managed to get the situation under control, and sufficient vehicles through the marshes to accommodate all the personnel. Not knowing the position of our own troops and that of the enemy, we decided to make for Gazala which we struck after a lot of trouble due to the poor condition of our armoured cars and other vehicles.

We reached the main road on the early morning of 27th January and headed for Tobruk, arriving there the same day, and brought through 8 Armoured Cars, 15 B Echelon vehicles, 156 Indian troops and 95 other troops … It is regretted that we had to abandon five armoured cars and two lorries after leaving Sahabi salt marshes due to serious breakdowns caused by the generally poor condition of our vehicles.

C Company 7 South African Reconnaissance Battalion under Captain 'Shorty' van der Merwe had an equally hectic time when it was ordered to Derna to support 4 Indian Division in covering the Eighth Army's withdrawal along the coast. It was surrounded while providing rearguard cover to Royal Engineers demolishing the Derna passes, but managed to make a night-time escape. At Tmimi Van der Merwe was surrounded a second time, but escaped once more by means of a night break-out which cost him one of his cars.

Lieutenant J. J. (Jan) Wahl had the well-nigh unbelievable (and surely unique) experience of being shelled by a U-boat while he was heading down the escarpment road from Derna to Tmimi; as Klein notes dryly, "it took him some time to convince his Commanding Officer of the authenticity of this occurrence." (Lieutenant Wahl eventually finished his army career with the rank of commandant (lieutenant-colonel) as Officer Commanding 1 Special Service Battalion.)

When Rommel attacked on 21 January 1942 4 South African Armoured Car Regiment was at El Adem, five days into what was supposed to be a fortnight's refit for its very well-worn vehicles; Lieutenant-Colonel Newton-King's first intimation of what was happening was an urgent signal from Eighth Army headquarters, ordering the regiment to report immediately to 1 Armoured Division Headquarters at Msus, about 270km to the west.

This was clearly wishful thinking, since B Squadron's refit was only partly complete and work had not even started on the others. Newton-King hurried to the Eighth Army's rear headquarters about 15km away to find out more. Nobody there would tell him what was happening. The situation had obviously gone radically wrong, however, and he was told that 4 South African Armoured Car Regiment must obey the recall signal as soon as possible. Newton-King went back to El Adem and got busy. Within 12 hours B Squadron was on the way to Msus with a petrol and ammunition echelon. A Squadron and the Regimental Headquarters with their own echelon left within 24 hours, while C Squadron and the Headquarters Squadron and their echelon were on their way after another 12 hours.

B Squadron waded through a torrent of eastbound transport vehicles whose panicky occupants regaled it with tales of the unstoppable panzers and finally arrived at Msus, to find it in possession not of 1 Armoured Division Headquarters but Panzer Mark III tanks. The squadron immediately deployed along the breadth of the German advance elements to observe its movements and composition, so that when Newton-King was within radio range it could give him some indication of what they were facing, although not of what had happened to Messervy's headquarters.

7 Field Regiment Marmon Herrington Mk 3, North Africa.

After the Gazala Gallop.

Newton-King had 1 Armoured Division Headquarters' radio frequency and tried to make contact, but without success, then or later. He decided to take B and C squadrons southward in the direction of Agedabia and Antelat, although this would mean that they would be temporarily cut off from their echelons, which would have to remain on the Tengeder–Msus road.

To this end Major Vic Larmuth's C Squadron and the regimental B Echelon sneaked undetected through the German right wing after dark – Larmuth's navigation being unwittingly assisted by the Axis forces, which maintained tight communications security but tended to have fires and show lights at night – to lie up north of the observation line.

Newton-King finally managed to establish contact with 1 Armoured Division Headquarters, which was located about 30km to the north, and went to report to Messervy in person. There he found a dismaying situation: the only knowledge the disheartened divisional staff had about German movements was what 4 South African Armoured Car Regiment had been able to send back.

Next day the 4 South African Armoured Car Regiment men – experts by now at laying hands on other people's property – achieved something of a coup when they found no less than 13 undamaged Crusader tanks which had been abandoned by 1 Armoured Division. Instead of leaving them behind Newton-King replenished their petrol, put in his own drivers and took the tanks back to 1 Armoured Division Headquarters.

4 South African Armoured Car Regiment spent the next few days screening for 1 Armoured Division, which provided the rearguard for the Eighth Army's retreat to Mekili once Messervy had pulled it back into some sort of battleworthy shape. The South Africans ended up at the Gazala Line after what Newton-King later described as "our finest week of action".

On 3 February 1942 Captain Flint's detachment was ordered back to 2 South African Division at Sallum, minus a Vickers machine-gun section under Lieutenant Wahl, which Brigadier Reid retained for a further three days as a protective element for his headquarters. From there they moved on to Sidi Barrani, abandoning three armoured cars that gave up the ghost along the way.

The remaining vehicles were in little better shape: "Those vehicles which withstood the return journey – armoured cars and transport lorries – were in a sorry state of disrepair after their gruelling adventures with E Force," Klein says, "and were virtually fit only for the scrap-heap."

Rommel's incursion lasted less than a fortnight. In that time he had knocked out more than 100 British tanks and other heavy equipment, recaptured Benghazi and then Tmimi, then pushed the Allies back to the Gazala Line. Once more an uneasy lull descended over the

Western Desert which was to last for three months, which both sides used to build themselves up for battles yet unfought.

The British spent their time digging in along the Gazala Line and initiating 1 Armoured Division into desert warfare, preparatory to attacking the Axis forces. Rommel, on the other hand, had no intention of waiting for his opponents to attack him; his intention was to unleash a classic blitzkrieg-style push that would outflank the highly fortified British positions in the Gazala area, then destroy them from behind.

Intensive German and Italian air attacks in the Mediterranean had partly neutralized the island of Malta's airfields, so that for the first time there was air parity. This made sea-convoying extremely costly for the British, and as a result Rommel's constantly nagging problem of obtaining enough supplies had improved dramatically.

Rommel's plans flew in the face of the truism that attackers should outnumber defenders by three to one; in most respects his version of the time-hallowed ratio was just the reverse. Against about 900 British tanks – some 200 of them the new American-made General Grant with its side-mounted 31-calibre 75mm M2 gun – he had about 600 in total. Of his 320 German tanks, only about 270 were the excellent Panzer Mark III with its 50mm gun, the others being the obsolescent Mark II, with its thinner armour and 37mm main armament. His 240 Italian tanks were the equally obsolescent Carro Armato M13/40s. In addition he had far fewer field artillery pieces, and many of his infantry units were understrength after the severe losses they had suffered both during Operation Crusader and his thrust in January 1942.

What he did have, though, was his lethal 88mm anti-tank guns, although not as many as he needed, and the air parity that would counter and reduce the incessant attacks by the Royal Air Force and South African Air Force. He had one other advantage: he was a dedicated tank general, and there was something ironical about the fact that his principal opponent had been and still was 7 Armoured Division, the creation of Percy Hobart, whose revolutionary teachings had been so carefully absorbed by the Germans while largely ignored by his own colleagues and superiors.

Rommel also had a secret weapon that, it is believed, was at least partly responsible for what seemed an uncanny gift on his part for divining Allied intentions: a very efficient radio interception section. It not only broke the rather unsophisticated code used by an American liaison officer at Eighth Army headquarters, Colonel Bonar Fellars, for his communications with Washington DC, but monitored inter-unit radio communications between British units, much of which was *en clair* and provided a great deal of useful intelligence.

On the other hand, the Allies had broken the code used by the top-secret German Enigma machine, which enabled their air and sea forces to intercept and sink many shipments of arms and supplies destined for Rommel. The Germans' interception section operated up to the First Battle of El Alamein, many months later, but thanks to extreme British security precautions they never did discover that the Enigma code had been broken.

During the lull Auchinleck concentrated on improving and expanding the Gazala Line. By May 1942 it ran from Gazala on the sea to Bir Hakeim, 60km to the southeast. Some 45km east of it was Tobruk, the Eighth Army's main base and its forward administrative hub. The Gazala Line consisted of a string of 'boxes' – heavily fortified strongpoints, each large enough to be held by one brigade plus supporting arms such as artillery. Between the boxes were hundreds of thousands of mines and deep belts of barbed wire.

In the north the line was held by the divisional troops and two brigades of 1 South African Division, now commanded by Major-General Dan Pienaar after General Brink had suffered a serious accidental back injury and been medically evacuated to South Africa for treatment. Pienaar's Abyssinian veterans of 1 South African Brigade were now under Brigadier J. P. A. Furstenburg, and 2 South African Brigade was commanded by Brigadier W. H. E. Poole, under whose chairmanship the Mark I reconnaissance car prototype had been tested and approved.

Immediately south of 1 South African Division, 50 British Division (Major-General W. R. Ramsden) held responsibility down to Sidi Muftah. About 30km south of 50 Division was 1 Free French Brigade under Major-General Marie Pierre Koenig at the desert outpost of Bir Hakeim – "a simple crossroads in the middle of an arid desert, a naked and rocky place swept by sand and winds," as one French general described it.

Tobruk and the region between it and Gazala was the responsibility of 2 South African Division, which also had 9 Indian Brigade under command. The General Officer Commanding 2 South African Division was now Major-General H. B. Klopper, who had replaced Major-General I. P. de Villiers on 14 May 1942. Klopper's 6 South African Brigade was tasked with the defence of the coastline between Gazala and Tobruk, while 4 South African Brigade and 9 Indian Brigade garrisoned Tobruk itself.

Tobruk was not what it had been during the glory days of the siege and break-out. Eighth Army policy was that if there had to be a withdrawal from the Gazala Line no attempt would be made to hold it. As a result almost all of its extensive minefields and barbed-wire entanglements had been lifted for re-use in the Gazala fortifications, and its tank-trap had been allowed to blow closed to such an extent that it was now little more than a depression in the sand.

Before his evacuation in March 1942 General George Brink clearly did not trust the Eighth Army high command to adhere to this undertaking, and was haunted by the possibility of his division being trapped in Tobruk if there were a retreat from Gazala, and either wiped out or forced to surrender. As early as February 1942, just after the end of Rommel's thrust from El Agheila, he had raised the matter very pointedly in a discussion with Ritchie and Gott, as he recalled to Klein in 1962, two decades later:

I can say quite definitely that, when the possibility of a withdrawal from the Gazala Line was discussed during February 1942, Lieutenant-General Ritchie told me in the presence of Lieutenant-General Gott that in such an eventuality Tobruk would not be held as the Royal Navy had indicated that it could not be supported administratively and the Royal Air Force had indicated that it would not be able to give the invested forces air support.

I raised the matter of the re-occupation of Tobruk at the time of the discussion, and told both Ritchie and Gott that in the event of a decision being taken to hold Tobruk I hoped my division … would not be detailed for the task as it was my confirmed opinion that it would not be possible to hold the Fortress successfully, particularly if it had to be done at short notice.

I told both the generals that I had made a reconnaissance of the [Tobruk] defences on my way forward to the Gazala Line early in February, and had found them to be in a very bad state. I also informed them that my division had removed about three-quarters of a million land-mines – with Eighth Army approval – from the Tobruk perimeter and laid them in front of the Gazala defensive line.

During this talk I had with Ritchie and Gott I made it quite clear to them that, should I be ordered to occupy Tobruk, I would lodge a protest as I was not prepared to sacrifice my division. General Ritchie then said that it had been decided at top level that Tobruk would not be held, but that in the event of a withdrawal I would have to detail a strong rear-guard to carry out demolitions in the Tobruk area and that this party would probably have to be sacrificed. I conceded that such a duty would, as a matter of course, be the duty of the 1st South African Division.

When I handed over the Division to Brigadier Pienaar, prior to my departure for medical treatment in Cairo, I gave him the gist of my conversation with Ritchie and Gott, and asked him not to allow himself to be trapped in Tobruk. I warned him that he would lose the Division and South Africa would blame him. He assured me that he would heed my warning.

When I returned to the Union for medical treatment I told General Smuts that I feared that, notwithstanding assurances to the contrary, Tobruk would not be held in the event of a withdrawal

from the Gazala Line. I told him what my fears were; also that I had told Ritchie and Gott that I
would lodge a strong protest if I were ordered to hold Tobruk.
The 1st South African Division was able to get away [from Gazala] because it had the transport.
I consistently refused to allow Corps and Army to take away any of my divisional transport.

Brink, the master of encirclement and flanking attacks in Abyssinia, was also concerned
about the static nature of the Gazala Line and forecast with complete accuracy that Rommel
would try to outflank it by hooking around south of Bir Hakeim and then striking north
toward the coast. No notice was taken of this warning, or of similar ones from other field
commanders.

Klein quotes from Colonel Newton-King's personal notes, which state that Messervy had
told him that logistically it was quite impossible for Rommel to sweep around Bir Hakeim
from the south, and "General Messervy only reluctantly gave me permission to withdraw that
way myself instead of through our minefields. He consistently overlooked the risks Rommel
was prepared to accept as regards petrol supply". The Maginot mentality, it was clear, was
alive and well in the Eighth Army's upper command levels.

Between February and May 1942, while Rommel and Auchinleck prepared for their next
round of fighting, the South African armoured cars were kept very busy with long-range
reconnaissance, sometimes of a distinctly hazardous nature.

4 South African Armoured Car Regiment, once more under command of 7 Armoured
Division's 4 Armoured Brigade, joined the King's Dragoon Guards and 12th Lancers at the
southern end of the Gazala Line. 3 South African Reconnaissance Battalion – temporarily
under command of Lieutenant-Colonel Sid Gwillam, who had been recalled to replace
Furstenburg on the latter's promotion – was back with 1 South African Division in the
northern sector, and 6 South African Armoured Car Regiment (minus one squadron at
Jarabub Oasis) was attached to 50 Division in the centre of the Gazala Line.

7 South African Reconnaissance Battalion was in the Tobruk area with 2 South African
Division, temporarily commanded by Lieutenant-Colonel G. K. Roodt, who had been
hurriedly flown up from South Africa to replace the ailing Lieutenant-Colonel Grobbelaar
on 30 March.

"Threading their way through minefields and strung-out enemy positions, the armoured
cars kept close watch on the enemy's movements and build-up for the renewal of the battle,"
Klein writes, "[making] long trips into the desert way ahead of the Gazala Line itself around
the enemy's southern flank, and into his rear areas as well.

"Theirs was a serious duty under exacting conditions. At times the 4th South African
Armoured Car Regiment's patrols were 70 miles ahead of the 7th Armoured Division. During
this time of watching and waiting, the 4th Regiment in the extreme south maintained a
wireless link with the 3rd South African Reconnaissance Battalion in the extreme north. This
link functioned until the Gazala defences crumbled."

While at Rotonda Segnali with 4 Armoured Brigade, Klein writes, "the 4th Regiment
struck up a firm friendship with the Free French Brigade at Bir Hakeim. Daily Major-General
Koenig sent out one of his battalions to work with the South African armoured cars and to
gain experience of desert conditions."

"The 13th Battalion, French Foreign Legion, under the Georgian Colonel Amilakvari,
became particularly friendly with us," Lieutenant-Colonel Newton-King later recalled to
Klein, "and their many Flemings exchanged tall stories with our Afrikaners, each in his own
language. We kept in contact with them until the sad day of the evacuation of Bir Hakeim, at
which we assisted, taking many of them away in our cars."

4 South African Armoured Car Regiment's Regimental Sergeant-Major Goode was
Koenig's liaison officer at Bir Hakeim, maintaining a radio link to his unit that functioned

Marmon Herrington Mk 3 and crew.

The Marmon Herrington Mk 3 "Moon" and its crew at Gazala 1942.

until Bir Hakeim was evacuated, and kept both Koenig and Messervy (who now commanded 7 Armoured Division) up to date on an hourly basis of events in both north and south when battle was rejoined near the end of May. Sometimes Lieutenant-Colonel Short of 6 South African Armoured Car Regiment joined in as well on the radio network that linked 4 South African Armoured Car Regiment with 3 South African Reconnaissance Battalion, the Free French and 7 Armoured Division.

Klein quotes from General Brink's personal war diary to illustrate episodes in the armoured car activities during the occupation of the Gazala Line:

12th February 1942: Our armoured car patrols very active and report that, fitted with captured 47/32 and 37mm guns, they can take more aggressive action than when armed as per establishment. The enemy 8-wheeled armoured car now not as aggressive and the recce position in general more satisfactory.

13th February 1942: Informed General Gott that a going and topographical map compiled by 3rd South African Recce Battalion.

14th February 1942: Reports by 3rd South African Recce Battalion to the effect that enemy advancing in three columns on 98, 94 and 88 grids. Armoured cars withdrew and also Polish SP [strongpoint] at Gabr er Regem. Polish SP later re-established.

15th February 1942: Congratulatory signal from Army Commander commending 3rd South African Recce Battalion and 4th South African Armoured Car Regiment on excellent reconnaissance and accuracy of reports and information. This was well-deserved praise.

26th February 1942: Army Commander, Lieutenant-General Ritchie, and Corps Commander, Major-General Gott, arrived at my headquarters to inspect the area held by the Division. On arrival they inspected the armoured cars of 3rd South African Recce Battalion fitted with captured enemy guns. These guns and the remarks of the crews impressed both very favourably.

1st March 1942: Our armoured cars (3rd South African Recce Battalion) and 50th Division patrol penetrated as far as Halegh el Eleba.

While the other armoured car units were roaming the desert, Lieutenant-Colonel Roodt at Tobruk was very busy trying to define 7 South African Reconnaissance Battalion's current and future roles, about which there seemed to be a certain lack of clarity.

On his arrival he found that the 7 South African Reconnaissance Battalion cars, instead of being used in the mobile role for which they were intended, were holding one sector of the defence lines as a type of machine gun battalion, although soon afterward A Company (Captain P. D. Anderson) took over reconnaissance duties in the Gazala Line from No. 1 Company of 3 South African Reconnaissance Battalion, and 7 South African Reconnaissance

Battalion's remaining handful of cars was employed on mobile patrols within the Tobruk Fortress area.

In April 1942, however, the battalion was brought up to full regimental strength with 58 cars as the Eighth Army began to get itself into shape for the coming offensive against Rommel. Roodt was allocated a reasonable amount of soft-skinned transport vehicles, but radio equipment was at a premium and there were many new and untried faces among his officers and men.

Having carried out the necessary reorganization, Roodt set up patrol lines for the entire Tobruk perimeter, meanwhile maintaining contact with other reconnaissance units in the Gazala Line and around Bir Hakeim and Bir el Gubi.

It was a time in which "confusion … reigned in the Tobruk area of operations … with units changing position daily and supply columns moving to and fro at bewildering frequency – and at times to no discernible plan," Klein writes, and 7 South African Reconnaissance Battalion made itself useful in a number of ways:

> 7th South African Recce Battalion patrols, roaming far afield, kept a day-to-day 'location map', which Major-General Klopper described as extremely useful and for which the unit was commended by Lieutenant-General Gott. The battalion prepared a very comprehensive 'going' map, locating the multitude of minefields, charted and uncharted, often located only after one of its vehicles had been blown up. During this phase Captain J. G. Gilchrist's squadron was 'blown up' repeatedly and attacked [by Stukas] every day.

The battalion also provided detachments as reconnaissance patrols for the number of mobile columns which were then operating between Tobruk and the Gazala Line southward, such as 'Tonycol', 'Ogcol' and others. During efforts to locate temporarily missing or vanished units, for which task there was a continuous demand from Army Headquarters, patrols from the battalion often had to bypass enemy units: such was the chequered pattern of friend and foe in this congested arena that patrols were often fired upon without knowing whether by friend or foe.

With enemy columns now moving boldly between the Gazala Line and the Tobruk perimeter, skirmishes took place, Klein notes "with monotonous regularity". On one occasion Lieutenant Wahl (of U-boat fame) carried out a spectacularly bold rescue when one of his cars stood on a mine. He dashed past a group of German tanks, picked up the disabled car's crew and then slid through a gap between two German tanks, chased by heavy and accurate shellfire (he was later decorated with the Military Cross for gallantry).

Meanwhile A Squadron under Captain J. G. Gilchrist had been given a mammoth task. The higher command believed that there was a possibility of enemy paratroops being dropped somewhere in the coastal strip, where the important Mrassas water-point was located. Gilchrist was tasked to patrol this vast area at almost all hours of the day and night, fighting an endless battle with extremely bad going that exacted a heavy toll in broken springs. It became, as Klein writes, "a supreme endurance test for men and machines in the effort to keep going, round the clock, twenty-four hours a day."

One 7 Reconnaissance Battalion trooper even swam hundreds of metres out to sea one day, "watched by the entire Regimental Headquarters personnel, which did not include a swimmer capable of doing more than a score of yards," to rescue an enemy fighter pilot who had baled out after being shot down in a dogfight over the headquarters (the rescue was a success, but the pilot died on the way to shore).

A most unfortunate casualty at this time was Honkey the mascot, which had survived several *ad hoc* excursions into minefields and numerous air attacks (some of the battalion's attached troops firmly believed that she had magic that guaranteed immunity against Stukas) to grow from a cute little piglet into a fine figure of a porker, experienced in the ways of war. Some officers claimed, Klein writes, "that she could distinguish the purr of the 3-tonner on which she was accustomed to travel from that of hundreds of other vehicles. She certainly knew the sound of the hooter. As soon as the engine was started up or the hooter sounded, Honkey would come squealing and running from wherever she was rooting – more from habit than in expectation – to the platform at the rear of the 3-tonner, to be hoisted on board by the two Pioneers who were her honorary keepers. [But] a Royal Army Service Corps company in transit … allegedly found Honkey straying, and caused her to end in the way destined for pigs."

Roodt could never obtain a clear decision about what 7 South African Reconnaissance Battalion's role would be if Tobruk were to be laid under siege again. The divisional staff believed that the unit could most profitably be used within the fortress perimeter, while Roodt was of the opinion that it would be more useful in a mobile role outside the perimeter. As it turned out, he would not have the opportunity to test his theory, although the lull in the desert fighting was almost over.

"That the work of the armoured cars was well done during the static time of waiting was proved by events at the time of action," Klein writes. "That time came on the afternoon of 26 May, when the 4th South African Armoured Car Regiment was operating on a wide front some 70 to 100 miles to the west of Segnali and Tengeder."

29

The Gazala Gallop

On 26 May 1942, presumably to General Messervy's surprise, Rommel did exactly what Brink and others had predicted. His Italian infantrymen, backed by tanks, attacked the Gazala Line's fortifications head on, but this was actually a diversionary assault. At the same time Rommel's main assault force – a horde of infantry troop carriers, tanks and guns – outflanked the southern extremity of the line, then attacked directly northward with the aim of destroying the Eighth Army's rear and fighting through to the coast. This would give Rommel access to the Via Balbia and allow easier reinforcement and supply by sea.

In the south, patrols from Newton-King's 4 South African Armoured Car Regiment began reporting considerable enemy activity during the morning of 26 May 1942, but gusty sandstorms and poor visibility made it difficult to define the nature of what was going on ("we now know the 'sandstorms' to have been caused by lorry-mounted aircraft propellers ordered by Rommel to deceive on the line of advance," according to Newton-King's personal notes).

Conditions improved as the morning wore on, and the cars began to send back more detailed information. At 1530 the patrols were feeding 7 Motor Brigade with reports of what turned out to be the start of the Axis advance; by early evening tank and artillery movement to the southeast could be seen and heard, and "it was clear," Klein writes, "that something big was afoot." From 2237, according to the 4 South African Armoured Car Regiment war diary, "the change of direction round Bir Hakeim was continually reported".

B and C squadrons were so determined to ferret out the most detailed possible information that they crept up to perilously close quarters – so close that in one case a German motorcyclist and a group of armoured cars were allowed to come right up to their troops without recognizing their enemies. The stream of messages from the armoured cars continued throughout the night of 26/27 May 1942.

The Southern Rhodesian anti-tank gunners in the Retma Box picked up the first message that German tanks were approaching and "from then on until daylight," according to their history, "Headquarters of the 4th South African Armoured Cars kept up a fascinating running commentary of the enemy movements. The darkness and the stillness gave an eerie feeling of apprehension."

The defenders felt the full fury of Rommel's attack on 27 May 1942 as his tanks rumbled north, overrunning the 7 Motor Brigade position and 7 Armoured Division Headquarters. But he did not have it all his own way; his attempt at encirclement was foiled by a fierce running battle with 7 Armoured Division that lasted all day and caused heavy losses to both sides.

In the process 4 South African Armoured Car Regiment not only kept up its normal observation and reconnaissance duties but captured a number of German vehicles, some of them unknown in Libya up to that time. In one case it bagged a German signal van with three occupants, a staff car and two lorries which netted 22 more prisoners, and also one of the first, if not the first, of a new type of vehicle called the 'Kettenkrad' that had a small tracked body mated to the front half of a motorcycle. The two men on the Kettenkrad joined the other prisoners.

B Squadron 4 South African Armoured Car Regiment made an even more surprising capture. The squadron was engaged in keeping an eye on a German panzer regiment which had run short of fuel and halted when it spotted a tank heading in its direction, and alerted Major Larmuth's C Squadron, which was then in reserve. Larmuth reported back to B Squadron headquarters and it despatched Lieutenant Billy Klerk and his troop to deal with the intruder.

Under Larmuth's direction Klerk pursued the tank northwestward for two and a half hours in what Agar Hamilton and Turner later described as an "exhilarating chase" that reached speeds of up to 50kph at times. When Klerk finally closed in on the tank he noticed that its gun was forward-facing and not capable of all-round traversing, so he placed his cars behind and on either side of it, then put the gun out of action with an accurately aimed 2-pdr armour-piercing shot that hit the protective mantlet. At this stage the tank ran out of fuel and the crew surrendered.

What Klerck and his men had actually captured was not a tank but one of Rommel's new weapons, the StuG self-propelled assault and anti-tank gun, consisting of a Panzer Mark III hull on which was mounted a potent 75mm artillery piece – the first to be captured in Libya. Elsewhere the South African armoured cars also seized two other unfamiliar vehicles – SdKfz252 half-track personnel carriers – as well as a lorry and a staff car, taking eight Germans prisoner and freeing two British officers and 20 other ranks.

In the centre and northern sectors of the Gazala Line, meanwhile, 6 South African Armoured Car Regiment and 3 South African Reconnaissance Battalion were staying in close contact with the Axis patrols forward of their formations: 3 South African Reconnaissance Battalion's patrols, for example, covered the entire 1 South African Division front and part of 50 Division's as well, their task made harder by the fact that each also had a detachment serving with 32 Army Tank Brigade.

On 28 May 1942 Rommel renewed his attack, concentrating this time on outflanking and destroying separate components of the British armour (which once again had been penny-packeted along the line instead of being held together in a solid mass). Fierce British counter-attacks did so much damage to his forces that for the moment he delayed his coastward thrust while he set to work pulling his battered armoured forces together for a new attack, this time west of the Knightsbridge Box, in the area which became known as the Cauldron.

Meanwhile 4 South African Armoured Car Regiment fell back east of Rommel's flank and set up an observation line to the west of Bir el Gubi, making use of whatever opportunity for mischief presented itself; on the 29th Lieutenant Klerk also found himself playing the role of liberator when he came across an enemy field-dressing station and left with 30 British casualties the Germans had been treating.

By 30 May 1942 elements of the Italian X Corps had cleared a path through the Allied minefields, and Rommel attacked eastward to link up with them and establish a supply line. At this stage the Eighth Army was contemplating a counter-offensive, and 4 South African Armoured Car Regiment and the King's Dragoon Guards (under command of 7 Motor Brigade) were ordered up by way of a route that would take them around the minefields south of Bir Hakeim and the Axis concentrations. They set off in the early hours of 1 June and circuited Bir Hakeim at first light, C Squadron on the right, A Squadron on the left and B Squadron in reserve, with the King's Dragoon Guards also on their left.

The advance proceeded west through enemy derelicts: two tanks among these were destroyed by the engineers attached to the 4th Regiment. Klein writes, "Permission was asked for the regiment to turn north against the enemy's lines of communication, but was refused. Instead, the 4th Regiment took up an observation line facing north and carried out local raids against enemy transport."

The day's bag of prisoners included four Italian officers, one German warrant-officer and forty-four other ranks. Apart from air strafing, which caused little damage except to tyres, the regiment emerged unscathed from a fairly exciting day. The King's Dragoon Guards reported Rotonda Segnali had been evacuated, and the indications pointed to a German reverse. This impression was dispelled the next day when enemy tank columns were reported to be moving on Bir Hakeim.

The reports were correct. On 2 June 1942 90 Light Division and the Trieste Division surrounded General Koenig's brigade at Bir Hakeim, whose garrison had already beaten off a determined attack by the Ariete Division; although heavily outnumbered and out-gunned, the French refused to surrender and the first of nine days of almost continual fighting followed.

Although the French would not give in, Bir Hakeim was now in no position to influence events farther to the north, and Rommel launched another attack toward the coast, using the defence line's minefields – painstakingly laid to keep him out – to protect his left flank. It succeeded and he pushed the Eighth Army back.

Given the general confusion, Newton-King took the precaution of moving his Headquarters Squadron (Major G. K. Lindsay) and the Echelon to a safer location to the east, which, as it transpired, was not so safe after all. Lindsay – and a C Squadron car commanded by a corporal named Brookes, of whom more later – moved off amid a bad dust storm which reduced visibility almost to zero. Then reports started coming in, indicating that the Axis forces were infiltrating south and west of Bir Hakeim. These reports, the war diary says, caused "considerable alarm and confusion and even Regimental Headquarters came under shell-fire from friends".

But worse was to come. Early that afternoon Lindsay radioed to report that he was completely surrounded. After that nothing further was heard from the Headquarters Squadron until 1538 when C Squadron reported that Corporal Brookes and a small party had managed to slip through the German net, but that the rest of Headquarters Squadron had been taken prisoner.

Its blood now well and truly up, 4 South African Armoured Car Regiment asked to be relieved of its reconnaissance duties "so as to go and fight it out with those people who had captured our Echelon," as the war diary puts it. The request was turned down, no doubt wisely. Then 4 South African Armoured Car Regiment asked for permission to move north to the coast at Derna by way of the Martuba airfield (which was now occupied by the Axis) and there cut Rommel's communications. This request, too, was turned down.

The only lightness in this hour of rage and despair was the capture of three Axis lorries containing 58 captured British soldiers, which was later vividly described by a South African Press Association correspondent who was in the forward area at the time:

One of the most remarkable rescues of prisoners of war made in the desert was described to me today by a sergeant from Ilford, Essex, who, with a number of men, was captured by the Germans a few days ago.

They were being rushed in trucks to Derna and were driving in an enemy convoy when, in the late afternoon, 20 miles inside enemy territory, a patrol of South African armoured cars suddenly appeared, shelled the convoy and split it, enabling the British prisoners to escape and take their German guards with them, as well as several lightly wounded German soldiers.

"We were bumping along the desert track late in the afternoon," said the sergeant. "Suddenly shells started exploding among the convoy vehicles. The enemy split immediately, and the Germans went into a panic. Then, from round a small hill, we saw several South African armoured cars appear, firing as they came.

"We jumped from our trucks, overpowering the German guards, and put them back on the lorries, which we drove away as fast as possible. My little party of four men brought in six Germans as prisoners."

Meanwhile Rommel was well into his second attack, which was to prove a decisive one. 21

Panzer Division struck north, its objective Acroma in the rear of the Gazala Line, about 37km north-northwest of Tobruk. West of the Cauldron, 150 British Infantry Brigade was overrun and destroyed. The British armour – "out-generalled and out-gunned," Klein comments – was defeated in a series of savagely fought actions in the Cauldron.

Major Roy Farran, a highly decorated armoured and later Special Forces soldier who was present at the time, later savagely criticized the Eighth Army's direction at the Cauldron in his classic 1948 war memoir *Winged Dagger*:

Rommel's army was penned into a pocket in the minefield, which came to be known as 'the Cauldron'. Then began certain miscalculations by the Generals, which turned victory into defeat. I do not know what other facts have come to light, but no soldier who fought in that battle can ever excuse those high-ranking officers, who at the time were damned but have since been resurrected.

Perhaps the term 'Cauldron' led to a misconception of the true situation from the start. The Germans were at first receiving their supplies through a narrow channel in the minefields. All the weight of the Royal Air Force was turned on to this gap and the 150th Brigade of the 50th Northumbrian Division was put in as a 'cork to stop the bottle'. Quite naturally, they were crushed from both sides.

The trouble was that certain people mistook what was obviously a widening bridgehead for a watertight trap. Instead of cutting off the Germans by a powerful outflanking movement south of Bir Hacheim, which would have been the normal desert technique, they were reluctant to expose Tobruk by moving our armour. This meant that we had partly lost the initiative which was ours by right of battle.

Then we proceeded to launch the sort of attack which has brought disaster to British arms throughout history. We began a frontal attack on the Germans' strongest defences in the 'Cauldron'. If the attack had gone in immediately it might have been successful, but instead there was a fatal delay of three days while we made our intention painfully obvious ...

Although the troops fought bravely under the direct command of General Messervy (who himself went up to the front), they recoiled in disorder from the strength of the German positions around Got Aslagh. Tanks foundered on their old enemy, the concealed anti-tank gun. By the second day it was obvious that the attack had failed.

Then began a period (I forget how long, but it must have been nearly a week) of errors being heaped upon errors. Bir Hacheim had quite plainly become the key to the battle. It was some way south of the 'Cauldron' and was the southern extremity of the minefield. Rommel was not prepared to advance so long as this stronghold remained to menace his flank.

He launched the whole of his weight against the gallant garrison, while the major part of the Eighth Army concerned itself with small skirmishes around the 'Cauldron'. The French pleaded for help, but all they received was the assistance of harassing columns from the 7th Motor Brigade, who had already demonstrated how easy it would have been to cut off Rommel by their shelling of German transport west of the gap. One or two other stupid little columns (aptly named after fish) were formed by the Indians, but they only contributed to the further frittering away of our strength.

While the fighting raged in the Cauldron the armoured cars of 6 South African Armoured Car Regiment and 3 South African Reconnaissance Battalion inflicted as much damage as they could on enemy positions and supply columns. On 5 June A Squadron 6 South African Armoured Car Regiment under Captain Gallimore destroyed five enemy vehicles and took a number of prisoners. Next day Lieutenant H. P. Williams's troop not only captured and destroyed five enemy vehicles but actually shot down a ground-strafing Me 109F, and Gallimore captured another five vehicles.

On 9 June 1942 Gallimore and Williams, with five armoured cars of their regiment and a detachment from 3 South African Reconnaissance Battalion's No. 2 Company, supported an attack by five tanks and two platoons of infantry against an Italian strongpoint. The tanks overran the position in the face of shell-fire that destroyed one of 3 South African Reconnaissance Battalion's cars and killed Trooper A. D. Brown; according to the 6 South African Armoured Car Regiment war diary the cars' crews were so hell-bent on being in at the kill that they dismounted and went in with the infantry. A total of 25 officers and 340 other ranks were taken prisoner.

At Bir Hakeim the end came on 11 June 1942 – but in France, where its defence rightly remains a treasured memory to this day – it is seen as a victory rather than a defeat. General Koenig and his men fought on until their food, water and ammunition were all but finished. With death or surrender inevitable, they then carried out a night withdrawal and got clean away.

Koenig had lost 99 men killed or wounded during the siege, and 814 taken prisoner, while another 42 died and 210 were wounded during the withdrawal, a heavy toll for the comparatively small Free French forces. But Koenig and most of his legionnaires had lived to fight another day, and the siege had cost the Axis 3,300 dead and wounded, 51 tanks destroyed and a fortnight of lost time which helped to save the Eighth Army from annihilation (Hitler ordered that the French prisoners of war be executed, an edict that Rommel simply ignored).

After the fall of Bir Hakeim, Farran writes, "Rommel immediately swung into the outflanking attacks which were to beat us back to Cairo. There was no 'black day' in which the battle was lost by a fluke. Every day was a black day from this moment onward, because the Generals had lost control of the battle."

All this time some of 3 South African Reconnaissance Battalion's armoured cars were supporting 1 South African Division's infantry patrols against the enemy on their front, while detachments were protecting the division's rear in cooperation with 7 South African Reconnaissance Battalion's patrols west of Tobruk.

"Particularly trying and dangerous," Klein writes, "were the patrols to the west of the 1st South African Division, which were made through gaps in the minefields into the enemy's forward defended localities. For, as soon as the armoured cars and infantry made their appearance, enemy shell-fire was brought to bear on them, with serious losses in men and vehicles.

"It was a dangerous and critical time, with the enemy armour striking behind the Gazala Line, but none expected the cold douche of defeat and withdrawal that followed Rommel's reduction of Bir Hakeim and the defeat of the British armour in the Cauldron."

On 12 June 1942, while the tank battles raged on the Gazala front, Colonel Roodt handed over command of 7 South African Reconnaissance Battalion to a newly promoted Lieutenant-Colonel G. N. Nauhaus and left for South Africa to take up an appointment as GSO1 to General Brink, who had been made General Officer Commanding Inland Area Command – a strangely timed appointment, given the prevailing circumstances, although Nauhaus proved to be a worthy successor.

Nauhaus attended a conference at 2 South African Division Headquarters on the first day of his command, the subject being planning for the siege that was now obviously on the cards, and discovered that specific tasks for his unit were still unclear. Klein writes:

Seeing no realistic role for his armoured cars in the Fortress, Lieutenant-Colonel Nauhaus inquired where he had to go and under whom he would have to operate. He was informed that he had to stay in Tobruk and that adequate work would be found for the battalion. Not satisfied with the thinking of Fortress Command, [he] pressed for a specific task as he could not visualize a reconnaissance role for the armoured cars in the Fortress area.

Brigadier [A. C.] Willison of the 32nd Army Tank Brigade said he could not use armoured cars in a tank battle and pressed for the retention of the battalion within the Fortress. A compromise suggestion, to leave only one company in Tobruk, was rejected with the aside: "Do you also want to leave the Division in the lurch?"

With Bir Hakeim finally out of the way, Rommel was free to throw all his forces into a resumption of his original drive to capture Acroma, El Adem and Tobruk, trapping and destroying 1 South African Division and 50 British Division along the way.

General Ritchie was now worried by this very real danger, and on the 13th, after the fall of the Knightsbridge Box, he ordered the two divisions to vacate their positions. 50 Division should break out southward via Bir Hakeim, while 1 South African Division was to withdraw along the coast road to Tobruk – by far the more dangerous route, given Rommel's determination to reach the Via Balbia.

Rommel, meanwhile, had ordered 15 and 21 Panzer divisions northward to cut the coast road, thus trapping the South Africans, Harry Klein's trenchant description of how Dan Pienaar extricated his division remains the best:

The escape of the 1st South African Division and the 50th British Division from Gazala was a near thing. In both, all reserves of food, water, fuel and non-essential stores were silently destroyed and made useless during the morning of 14 June, and the South African division started thinning out early in the day. The enemy air forces, German and Italian, soon got on to the withdrawal, and there were repeated Stuka dive-bombing and fighter strafing attacks which, however, caused comparatively few casualties.

Three passes along the escarpment were available for the withdrawal, and the 29-mile stretch of the Via Balbia, the coast road to Tobruk, was defended against German attack from the south by detachments from the 1st South African Division, the 1st Worcestershire Regiment, the 2nd South African Division and what were left of the British tank formations.

Armoured cars of the 3rd South African Recce Battalion were detailed to protect the rearguards of the three South African brigades, and the somewhat dubious distinction of providing the rearguard to the divisional rearguard fell to Major Torr and No. 1 Company. The rearguard of the Division was made up of detachments from the three brigades, each consisting of a composite company of infantry, with field, anti-tank and anti-aircraft guns; the whole rearguard was commanded by Brigadier C. L. de W. du Toit.

No. 3 Company of the 3rd Recce Battalion lay on patrol between Elwet et Tamar and Acroma, in the vital area where Rommel threw in his panzer attack against the Via Balbia The story of how the coast road was kept open for the withdrawal from Gazala by the inspired defenders, South African and British, of William's Post, Best Post, Point 187, Point 208, Commonwealth Keep and Acroma Keep, is one of the great legends of the desert war.

That the road was kept open and the German panzers held at bay in a day of bitter and exhausting fighting accounted for the safe withdrawal of the bulk of the South African division. During all of that critical day of 14 June, 3rd South African Recce Battalion armoured cars kept track of the enemy and defended the rearguards, at most times under artillery and anti-tank fire, sustaining heavy Stuka raids and machine-gun and shell-fire from enemy tanks.

Before nightfall, when the withdrawal was well under way, the enemy all but broke through the defence posts south of the coast road, but at 2030 the attack was held and the enemy brought to a standstill.

1 South African Division's main body passed safely through Tobruk on 15 June, "mainly because of the inertia of the Germans," Klein writes, "who, exhausted after the heavy fighting of the previous day, failed to move early enough on the 15th," but a battalion of German infantry with tank support drove a small protective detachment of 2 South African Division out of its positions at El Mrassas and cut the main road before most of the rearguard had passed.

1 South African Brigade's rearguard detachment and 3 South African Reconnaissance

Battalion's No. 2 Company fought their way through a gap in the Mrassas minefield and managed to reach Tobruk, but the 2 and 3 South African brigade detachments were marooned on the wrong side of the Germans, along with 3 South African Reconnaissance Battalion's No. 1 Company, some 50 Division units and 6 South African Armoured Car Regiment's C Squadron under Major P. E. Ferguson, which had not been able to break out to the south.

A chaotic situation soon developed. Traffic piled up as the two brigade rearguards found themselves between a rock and a hard place. In front of them the Germans blocked the road; behind them more Germans were pushing forward. At the tail-end of the rearguard, No. 1 Company's cars were fighting the Germans with great spirit, so much so that they actually took 17 prisoners. But, as Klein writes, the situation of the two rearguard detachments "looked extremely unhealthy".

That afternoon Lieutenant-Colonel J. E. S. Percy of 9 Durham Light Infantry, one of the 50 Division units that had attached themselves to 1 South African Division, broke through the Germans in company with a scratch force of armoured cars, including 6 South African Armoured Car Regiment's C Squadron and elements of No. 1 Company.

Three troops of C Squadron cars under Captain C. N. Saville joined hands with infantry and Bren carriers of the Durham Light Infantry, and crashed through a company of German infantry defending a wadi, while the guns engaged enemy tanks as well as a captured British 25-pdr. Meanwhile the main body of Percy's break-out column, with the rest of C Squadron's armoured cars, became involved in a spirited hour-long exchange of fire with six enemy tanks before emerging outside the German lines.

In his report on the action Major Ferguson wrote that "many of our infantry were forced into the sea and walked in the water to avoid enemy fire. One of my patrols, seeing some Arab women outside their huts, put a burst of Bren fire through the huts and out came about thirty German infantry, who were all killed except three. We moved along the coast and eventually reached a point about four miles west of Tobruk where we re-assembled and continued on our way."

All of 3 South African Reconnaissance Battalion except No. 1 Company braved enemy artillery and tank fire to get away scot-free, and in the course of the afternoon part of No. 1 Company under Lieutenant R. D. Meeser also arrived after escaping through a curtain of shell-fire from enemy tanks less than 1,000m away. But Major E. H. Torr, the company commander, decided to stand by the 3 South African Brigade detachment commander who believed that it would be better not to try to push through the mass of derelict transport vehicles along the road, but to disperse and slip through to safety after dark.

The pursuing Germans arrived before nightfall, however, and the two brigade rearguards had no option except to surrender. With them into captivity went Major Torr, Captain Guy de Marillac, a Lieutenant Ferguson and 25 other ranks, as well as seven cars.

With Rommel's forces focused on the coastal route, 50 British Division managed to break through virtually without loss. The General Officer Commanding 50 Division, Major-General W. R. Ramsden, decided to head directly westward, smash through the Italian lines and then head toward the southwest.

For this purpose he split the Division into two groups, one under Brigadier L. B. Nicholls of 151 Infantry Brigade, with 6 South African Armoured Car Regiment's A Squadron attached; the other under Brigadier L. L. Hassell of 69 Infantry Brigade, with C Squadron 6 South African Armoured Car Regiment. Each group would consist of self-contained columns, with one infantry battalion with the appropriate supporting arms tasked to carve a gap through the Italian defences, then keep it open while the columns passed through.

At the rear would be 50 Division Headquarters, with Regimental Headquarters 6 South African Armoured Car Regiment attached. Absent from the 6 South African Armoured Car Regiment line-up was B Squadron, which was still on attachment to the King's Dragoon

Guards with 7 Armoured Division.

Having completed its preparations with the serendipitous aid of a dust storm in the afternoon, the groups assaulted the Italian lines at full steam. 5 East Yorkshire Regiment and 8 Durham Light Infantry smashed open the gaps as planned, and the columns burst through the enemy positions into the open desert with virtually no losses.

In the process Lieutenant-Colonel Short, who was travelling with 50 Division Headquarters, found himself in a new role: mine-detector. The divisional headquarters column had halted, so Short drove up to its head. Here he dismounted and went forward on foot, to find that the two leading vehicles had been blown up. As he reported it later:

> I looked ahead of the blown-up vehicles and saw the ground was darker in circular patches, and on putting my arm down one of these holes I found a mine. I went back down the column and called for an officer. A Captain Kirby answered, and we both went back to the front of the column with two privates and located mines by feeling with our hands.
> I left Captain Kirby to carry on while I got the column on the move again. Two vehicles blew up while I was guiding them, but I succeeded in getting the rest going and rejoined my own car. We passed an enemy leaguer about 15 miles west-northwest of Hakeim, and just before we were due to turn east met a column under Lieutenant-Colonel Baltiscombe, to whom we attached ourselves and came through to Maddalena without further incident of note.

Against all odds, the last two Allied divisions west of Tobruk had extricated themselves by a combination of good fortune, German exhaustion, skill and determination; all that remained now was Tobruk, where Major-General Hendrik Klopper's 2 South African Division awaited an inevitable onslaught with 4 and 6 South African brigades, little field, anti-tank or anti-aircraft artillery and three battered and much-weakened British groups – 32 Army Tank Brigade, 201 Guards Brigade and 11 Indian Brigade, about 33,000 men in all. It was a paltry force with which to defend an indefensible position against the full force of Rommel's Panzer Group Africa.

30

Retreat to the east

Having set up a temporary regimental headquarters at Fort Maddalena, Lieutenant-Colonel Short ordered all his soft-skinned vehicles and non-combat personnel to report to 50 Division headquarters at Thalata, then sent his armoured cars out into the desert to look for stragglers; Captain Gallimore, with seven cars under command, did not report back to Thalata for five days. Meanwhile Short counted the cost of 6 South African Armoured Car Regiment's successful breakout: one man killed, 14 wounded and 43 missing out of a total of 380 all ranks and 12 out of 40 armoured cars lost to enemy action and mechanical failure, as well as 34 of his 68 transport vehicles.

The last stragglers from 3 South African Reconnaissance Battalion's No. 1 Company under Lieutenant Meeser crept into Tobruk and joined the rest of the unit there. Then 3 South African Reconnaissance Battalion headed east to the Wire, where all its battleworthy cars – a total of just 11 – paused to carry out temporary patrol duties while the others started limping back to the base workshops at Amiriya, with the 11 more or less serviceable ones scheduled to rejoin them along the way.

Far to the southwest, Newton-King's 4 South African Armoured Car Regiment lay up at Bir el Gubi. It had not been part of the fighting retreat from the Gazala Line and subsequent breakout, but was now preparing for a general withdrawal, its tasking being to provide the rearguard on the left and southern sectors. By now it had lost 12 out of 64 cars, mainly through air attacks (although within three days it would lose another, the first to fall victim to shell-fire since the regiment's arrival in the desert) and failed steering-boxes; its cars were showing the effects of months of operations over mostly bad terrain.

Up to mid-June of 1942 it was a given that Tobruk must not be allowed to fall under siege again under any circumstances, and when he gave permission to General Ritchie to withdraw from the Gazala Line, General Auchinleck made it clear that a new defensive line was to be established that ran from Tobruk westward to Acroma and then to the south past El Adem.

On the 16th, however, in light of Rommel's seemingly unstoppable advance and the disarray into which the Eighth Army had been plunged, Auchinleck wavered and let it be known that while he was prepared to accept Tobruk's temporary isolation, it must not be exposed to a full-scale, unhindered assault.

In London, however, Prime Minister Winston Churchill was adamant that it had to be held at all costs, while Lieutenant-General Gott who, as General Officer Commanding XIII Corps was responsible for Tobruk, openly believed that an investment of the port was inevitable and tried to prepare for it.

"It was General Rommel in the end," Klein writes

who decreed the fate of Tobruk, by his smashing victories on 16 June at El Adem and on the 17th, when his panzers defeated the 4th Armoured Brigade at Sidi Rezegh. Tobruk was then, contrary to the Commander-in-Chief's intention, isolated and besieged.
In the welter of indecision regarding the ultimate role the forces under his command were to play, whether as a static garrison or a mobile force ready to break out if necessary, Major-General

Klopper, commanding the 2nd South African Division (under whose command the Fortress of Tobruk, had been placed), took his unenviable place in history.

He had under command in the Fortress a very mixed force of roughly 33,000 men, comprising the 4th and 6th South African Infantry Brigades, the 7th South African Recce Battalion, and the weakened and battle-weary British formations – the 32nd Army Tank Brigade, 201st Guards Brigade and 11th Indian Brigade. He had minimum requirements of field artillery, anti-tank and anti-aircraft guns.

Although he expressed his confidence in the outcome of the battle, Major-General Klopper little knew at the time of the tremendous disadvantages under which he laboured while preparing to meet the German onslaught – with the Eighth Army being forced back toward the Egyptian frontier and his command cut off from possible reinforcement or relief. With the Eighth Army out of the way, the victorious Panzer Army turned west for the achievement of Rommel's long-cherished desire – the capture of Tobruk.

Klopper was a very junior general, having put up his 'knife and fork' only a month earlier, but he was an experienced and competent officer who had been Major-General de Villiers' GSO1 and had earned a Distinguished Service Order as a brigade commander. Brigadier Scrubbs Hartshorn, never one to mince his words if he felt the need to criticize, saw him at work in December 1941, and "as I sat with him listening to him coping with the stream of queries that poured in from units and individuals, I formed a very high opinion indeed of his firm grasp of military realities in what was to be a difficult operation".

He needed every bit of his experience and competence when Ritchie and Gott visited him on 16 May 1942 to give him the bad news, just two days after he had taken over 2 South African Division. The overall situation had changed, they said. They were afraid that Rommel would beat them to the punch before they could launch a counter-offensive. Therefore Klopper was to protect the Tobruk area and also plan for defending the coast between Gazala and Tobruk against a possible enemy landing.

What it meant, in fact, Hartshorn writes in *Avenge Tobruk*

was that Tobruk was once again to be turned into a defensive position, a complete reversal of all the planning and thinking that had gone before.

An immense task devolved upon General Klopper. His 2nd South African Division at that time comprised the 6th Brigade, which was scattered over a distance of 40 miles between Gazala and Tobruk; the 4th Brigade inside Tobruk; one artillery regiment only – the other two had been lent the previous January to the 1st Division – the 7th Reconnaissance Regiment, together with engineers and supply units.

The 3rd Brigade had been transferred to the 1st South African Division at Gazala. In Tobruk, too, were British administrative troops in the harbour area and British anti-aircraft units – a hotchpotch of fighting units which required an immense amount of sorting out if they were to become anything approaching an organized fighting force ready for battle.

A further factor was that the 2nd South African Division for the past two months had, for reasons best known to the higher command, devoted all their energies to digging defence positions, doing patrol work and other varying and multiple duties in the country between Gazala and Tobruk.

However, the troops set to work with a will to restore as quickly and efficiently as possible the defensive strength of Tobruk, which so shortly before had been happily dissipated on the orders of the High Command … General Klopper set vigorously about the task of redeploying the forces under his command in the light of his new orders.

Klopper moved 6 South African Brigade's headquarters back to Tobruk and tasked the brigade to guard the 60km of coastline between Tobruk and Gazala, although his shortage of support weapons meant that the coastal infantry defences were no more than infantry posts supported by machine guns and light anti-aircraft guns. In addition, 6 South African Brigade machine guns had also to man the defensive position at Acroma.

Klopper's only armoured asset, Brigadier Willison's 32 Army Tank Brigade, was actually a battle-worn and badly understrength composite unit of only 58 Matilda II infantry tanks and Valentine cruisers that he had managed to scrounge from a reluctant Ritchie. Cobbled together from survivors of the wrecked 1 Army Tank Brigade's units, they were not only outclassed by the German armour but more than half arrived so badly damaged that the South African workshops had to spend three days of round-the-clock effort getting them battleworthy again.

Klopper formed the emaciated brigade into two mobile columns he called 'Seacol' and 'Stopcol', and strengthened a position called Point 209, which he manned with a mixture of South African and British troops; with no artillerymen – or artillery – to spare, most of the guns in his strongpoints were captured Italian weapons crewed by infantrymen whose only training as gunners was strictly of the on-the-job variety.

Hartshorn writes: "This, then, was the defensive organization which General Klopper built up from his attenuated 2nd South African Division to face the eventualities which, day by day, became ominously clear. Tobruk was now the target of intensive bombing – the German aircraft flying in from the sea in wave after wave to drop their bombs. On one night alone they launched 121 air attacks on Tobruk and the anti-aircraft defences fired no fewer than 30,000 rounds of ammunition. Armoured car patrols also brought confirmation that something big was afoot. They reported seeing large concentrations of enemy armour moving in a southerly direction."

"We in Tobruk," Klopper told Hartshorn in 1960, "were under no illusions that grave developments were imminent. But my men were in good heart and we awaited the future in the confident knowledge that when Rommel came he would get a hot reception."

"On 13 June 1942, Klopper's task became even more onerous," Hartshorn continues,

General Klopper was directing the laying of a minefield between Tobruk and Acroma so that elements of the British Armoured Division could seek shelter behind it, when he was called to the Corps Commander. General Gott told him that the Supreme Command had decided to withdraw from Gazala and to form a new line – Tobruk–El Adem-Bir el Gubi. The Eighth Army's armoured units would regroup behind the line, he said.

To General Klopper the news came like a bombshell. It was a total reversal of the previous plan by which, in the event of withdrawal, the 2nd South African Division would fall back to Halfaya to form a checkpoint. Now, General Klopper was being told, two Divisions in Gazala could not withdraw successfully unless they had the protection of Tobruk and its surrounding fortresses. The Tobruk Fortress, he was told, would protect the desert flank with columns while the surrounding strongholds would fall back on the main Tobruk stronghold the next morning. The 1st South African Division would go back as far as the Egyptian border and would send out columns from there to form the left flank at Bir el Gubi.

On the night of Sunday, June 14, and Monday, the 1st South African Division and part of the 50th Division were successfully withdrawn. General Klopper recalls that Dan [Pienaar] and his staff "came through my headquarters, drank up everything we had, and took off." Conversation, naturally, was on the grim situation confronting them, in particular the position of Tobruk under the new orders. Dan, General Klopper remembers, was painfully blunt. "Kloppie," he said, in Afrikaans, "you've had it."

In its final form Tobruk's 30km-long outer perimeter line was approximately a lopsided hollow square with the coastline forming the open end. 6 South African Brigade was deployed along the western flank of the outermost defences, with the road to Derna running through the middle of its position. The southwestern aspect was held by 4 South African Brigade and the two fighting columns loaned by 1 South African Division, Beer Group and Blake Group, as well as the Kaffrarian Rifles.

Blake Group is of specific interest to this narrative because it was drawn from the Imperial Light Horse, a 'parent' unit of 6 South African Armoured Car Regiment, and one which was to have a close association with South African armour later in the war.

On the southeastern corner were 2 Cameron Highlanders and 2/5 Mahratta Regiment. From the Mahrattas to the coastline lay 2/7 Ghurkha Rifles. The inner perimeter was manned by the much-diminished 201 Guards Brigade, facing approximately south with its headquarters at 'King's Cross', the junction of the road from Bardia in the east, in positions that would allow it to be used as a counter-attack force.

At the intersection between 4 and 6 South African brigades was a minefield, and another covering the south-southeasterly side of 11 Indian Brigade, leaving three wide gaps in the outer defences. The Allies' Desert Air Force, too, had had to pull its landing grounds so far back that Klopper had no protection against the Luftwaffe and Regia Aeronautica, which was now operating from the El Adem airfield, less than 30km away.

In the next few days Tobruk would receive a few extra bits and pieces, *inter alia* a battery of medium artillery, but as far as support was concerned Klopper's cupboard resembled Mother Hubbard's. The only thing he was not short of was food, water and fuel.

Time was fast running out for Tobruk. The first signs came early in the morning of 18 June 1942, when Nauhaus' B and C companies reported that the fortress was now completely surrounded. On 19 June 88mm guns on the road to Derna fired on a 7 South African Reconnaissance Battalion patrol, knocking one car out. On the eastern sector another patrol fired on German reconnaissance troops and dispersed them.

After this there is a day-long gap in 7 South African Reconnaissance Battalion's records, because all of its documents perished during the fall of Tobruk; the only partial record that is known to exist of what happened to it, from the 20th onward, was compiled two decades later by Harry Klein from the memories of Nauhaus and Roodt, augmented by a few printed references.

Hartshorn says that on the afternoon of 19 June 1942 Ritchie warned Klopper that he could expect an attack next day. Klopper believed (correctly) that the attack would almost certainly come from the east and south, and sent out strong armoured car patrols along the Bardia road. At about 0400 one of the patrols reported to him that although it had not made contact with the enemy, it had heard sounds of great armoured activity during the night. Klopper now made his final preparations to withstand the inevitable assault. "There was an ominous calm over Tobruk on the night of June 19. In the distance guns were firing, but that was the only prelude to the hell that was about to break forth. Tobruk stood tense and ready. At first light the blow fell. One hundred and eleven Stukas thundered over the eastern flank between the Bardia and El Adem roads, shells began raining on the stronghold from all sides."

At 0800 Rommel attacked the eastern sector of the perimeter in great force. Within an hour his forces had smashed through the line and were nearly 3km inside despite stubborn and often heroic resistance by the infantry in the various strongpoints, while the British Matildas and Valentines were "being systematically blown to pieces by German Mark IV tanks."

Klein quotes Nauhaus as saying: "At about 1000 hours on the 20th, A Company came under direct tank fire and was given permission to withdraw down the escarpment. Two hours later the battalion received orders to stop the enemy infantry who were following behind their tanks. This was an impossible task as the tanks were certainly not going to allow the armoured cars to interfere with their advance, seeing that they had already effectively dealt with the tanks of the 32nd Army Tank Brigade. The 7th South African Reconnaissance Battalion companies thereupon formed a screen and slowly withdrew to the harbour and the 6th South African Brigade area, setting alight abandoned petrol and other dumps in passing."

By the afternoon of 20 June 1942, the Germans had penetrated so far that they were only about 1,000m from Klopper's headquarters; by this time, *Crisis in the Desert* states, "the only opposition [to the oncoming tanks] came from a few armoured cars which were falling back from King's Cross."

In his book *Tobruk* Anthony Heckstall-Smith, a veteran of the battle, recounts:

By the early afternoon, news from the front was still vague. But air attacks were more or less continual … Everywhere one looked … there were signs in plenty that Tobruk as a fortress was falling apart. On the flat Salaro Plain [in the centre of Tobruk, near Klopper's main headquarters], where were the two little airfields, the NAAFI was burning furiously, and the German tanks wandered about unhindered shooting up the mass of trucks – 700 of them …

They had never been dispersed or camouflaged, and now the German tank commanders were having a high time making a glorious bonfire of them. Other enemy tanks and armoured cars were calmly refuelling at our petrol dumps, before moving on at leisure to knock out the few remaining batteries of Bofors.

But the Germans, as they admitted afterward, did not have it all their own way. They never knew, they said, when these little isolated pockets of men and guns would not decide to resist to the last round of ammunition.

For example, there were those 3.7s near the junction of the Derna–Pilastrino road [southeast of Klopper's headquarters]. Their crews did not receive the warning that the German tanks were upon them until it was too late to remove the blast-walls around the emplacements to enable them to depress their guns. So they just blew away those emplacements. Their crews were magnificent. They kept on blazing away at the tanks until every man of them was either killed or wounded, destroying four tanks and putting several others out of action. This heroic battle was spotted by some South African armoured cars from across the road, but when they tried to interfere the Germans just blew them to bits …

"Late that afternoon," Klein writes, "Klopper told Nauhaus that he could attempt a break-out if he wished, and take a battery of artillery with him. Nauhaus was willing, and scheduled an order group to plan it." But by early afternoon the situation was so desperate, Hartshorn says, that Klopper

resorted to last-ditch fighting with everyone who could be spared facing the oncoming Germans with what weapons they could lay their hands on.

The Germans came inexorably on. One pincer came down the ridges into Tobruk town and the harbour, and the other advanced in the direction of Pilastrino and Divisional Headquarters. General Klopper worried about four ammunition ships which had arrived in the harbour early that morning and gave orders they were to set sail immediately.

At 3 p.m. General Klopper was informed that hardly any British armour remained. The Guards headquarters had surrendered. An hour later the Commander of the 11th Indian Brigade arrived on foot to say that almost all his vehicles had been destroyed and he had no supplies left … General Klopper … was able to observe the German armour advancing on the harbour, and noted, with satisfaction, the blowing up of the harbour installations.

German armour was now firing on General Klopper's little rear headquarters. He gave orders for the burning of petrol and other supplies and ordered Colonel Nauhaus, his Reconnaissance Battalion Commander, to be ready that night to lead the break-out [from] Tobruk.

But then, as Nauhaus went to make arrangements with the artillery battery, Klein writes, "[he] met up with Major-General Klopper at 6th South African Brigade Headquarters. The General Officer Commanding then told Lieutenant-Colonel Nauhaus he was cancelling his previously given permission for a break-out, as he had decided to fight it out with the enemy and the battalion would be required the next day."

"A very bewildered [7 Recce] Order Group ascertained from me that the permission to break out had been withdrawn," Nauhaus later wrote, "and that they would receive further orders for the operation planned for the next day. Alas, the only order they received next morning was to destroy equipment, and every man for himself!"

The reason for Klopper's about-turn, it seems, was because he still believed that there was a chance of rescue from the Eighth Army. According to Hartshorn:

He informed the Brigade Commanders that it was his intention to lead what was left of his Division out of Tobruk ... All documents, including the latest radio code, as well as most of the radio sets, had already been destroyed, but a signaller, using the old code, managed to communicate with Eighth Army Staff Officers. General Klopper told them he intended breaking out of Tobruk that night with what he had left of his troops.

His break-out plans, however, met with opposition from two of his Brigade Commanders who claimed they did not have sufficient transport, but General Klopper overruled them and ordered them to send out patrols to establish where the enemy would be laagering that night so that the units breaking out could avoid them.

At 11 p.m. he received orders from Eighth Army. He was told not to break out that night but to wait for the following night when columns of the Eighth Army from the south would help him. He summoned the Commanding Officers and passed on the new orders, instructing them to take up positions against the enemy until the following night. Several of his Staff Officers demurred. Resistance was no longer possible. They should break out at once, they told him.

It was a moment taut with the tension and strain of the last hours. General Klopper carefully listened to their arguments. Then he gave his decision. They would obey the Army Commander's order. They would remain until the following night. Every moment that they succeeded in delaying the enemy in Tobruk, he told them, was of vital importance to the Eighth Army ...

The Germans began a dawn attack on June 21 with armoured thrusts at two points – one aimed at the centre of the 4th Brigade and the other at 6th Brigade. General Klopper realized, with despair, that within the hour these Brigades would be annihilated. He decided swiftly and firmly. He informed the Brigade Commanders that if any chance of a breakout existed this was the last and only opportunity. Therefore all men and units who wished to escape should try and do so. He believed that anything up to 5,000 troops might get away.

He then signalled General Ritchie telling him that in order to avoid another bloodbath he had given the orders he had. General Ritchie replied that he left the matter in General Klopper's hands and that he should try and get as many men out as possible. "I wish you and your men God's blessing," his signal concluded.

Then remained the one step any fighting commander hopes he will never have to take.

In the early pre-dawn hours of 21 June, faced with the critical decision of whether to continue the hopeless battle or to surrender in order to avoid unnecessary bloodshed, Major-General Klopper pondered over his predicament. His command had given of its best in the effort to deny the enemy the Fortress of Tobruk, and by its stand had gained a valuable respite for the Eighth Army.

Trapped by the inevitability of his impossible position, Major-General Klopper made his decision: the white flag of surrender was raised at dawn.

Orders were given for all units to destroy their equipment, but those who wished to escape had been told they could keep their vehicles for this purpose. "Nearly all the guns were effectively put out of action," it is recorded *Crisis in the Desert*. "The armoured cars down by the coast were pushed over the cliffs into the sea, and equipment generally was destroyed with a grim efficiency which was in itself a measure of frustration."

It was, Klein adds, "the worst disaster that befell the South African Tank Corps and the South African forces as a whole during the entire war." Almost the whole of 2 South African Division went into captivity, including all of 7 South African Reconnaissance Battalion except two cars, and 153 officers and men of the Imperial Light Horse, among them its commanding officer, Lieutenant-Colonel E. J. R. Blake.

Reflecting on Tobruk in later years, Hartshorn says that Klopper remained convinced that he acted correctly in holding out for as long as possible. The few days Rommel spent taking Tobruk bought time for the Eighth Army to withdraw and set up the check-line that enabled it to defend El Alamein, thereby gaining even more time to prepare for the second Battle of El Alamein in October 1942 that eventually spelt the end for Panzer Group Africa.

Hartshorn might have added something else. Rommel had been counting on capturing large stocks of petrol at Tobruk, but by the time Klopper surrendered they had all gone up in smoke – Rommel's fuel shortage was another reason why the weakened Eighth Army was later able to beat off the Axis forces at the defence of El Alamein.

Rommel said all this himself at his first meeting with Klopper; according to Hartshorn:

> General Rommel … was in his staff car about three miles distant from the supply dumps in the harbour area. Rommel was standing up when General Klopper drove up. The German General was in a furious temper. "Why," he demanded of General Klopper, "did you not cease fighting last night? You have held me up."
>
> "I, too, have a duty to carry out," General Klopper reminded him.
>
> Rommel, with an angry gesture, indicated the smouldering supply dumps and shouted: "Why did you permit the water and petrol to be destroyed? Your men will suffer... they will march without water."
>
> "This," General Klopper recalls, "made me mad – it hit me on the raw."
>
> "My men are now prisoners-of-war and must be treated as such," he told Rommel. "Do as you please with me."
>
> This seemed to have a sudden calming effect on Rommel. "My officers will show you where you have to go. I have to get on with my job," he said more quietly.

Tobruk's epitaph is best given in the simple words of one line in 4 South African Armoured Car Regiment's war diary for 21 June: "An exceptionally hot day. Tobruk fell during the morning, which was an unexpected blow." Or perhaps in a bitter comment by Roy Farran six years later: "The attempt to hold Tobruk was the final error in a grossly mismanaged campaign."

31

Standing firm at El Alamein

With Tobruk in his hands at last – even though it had not provided him with the fuel he needed so desperately – Rommel continued his push eastward into Egyptian territory without encountering any immediate resistance. General Ritchie had abandoned any idea of trying to hold the border. Originally he had planned to set up a chain of heavily fortified infantry positions, with a strong armoured force held in reserve to deal with any attempts at penetrating or outflanking it, but now he had so few battle-worthy tank units left that Rommel would be able to systematically reduce the infantry positions without any hindrance from the remaining British armour.

His revised planning called for the Eighth Army to fall back about 160km eastward into Egyptian territory and make a stand at the port of Mersa Matruh. Here, too, the defensive plan called for a practically non-existent mobile armoured reserve, but there were extensive minefields between the strongpoints around the port, and Ritchie envisaged deploying his infantry in such a way that they would be able cover the minefields by fire and thereby inhibit Rommel's sappers from clearing safe lanes for the Axis armour.

Inside Mersa Matruh itself Ritchie intended to deploy 10 Indian Infantry Division, with 50 (Northumbrian) Infantry Division about 24km down the coast under command of X Corps headquarters, which had just arrived from Syria. About 32km south of X Corps, at Sidi Hamza, would be XIII Corps with 5 Indian Infantry Division, which at this stage comprised only 29 Indian Infantry Brigade and two artillery regiments.

On the escarpment, about 50km from the coast, would be 2 New Zealand Division, newly arrived in the Western Desert and lacking one of its three brigades because of transport difficulties. In the open desert to the south, near the Qattara Depression, would be 1 Armoured Division, which would take over 7 Armoured Division's 4 and 22 Armoured Brigades, although they had suffered such heavy losses that between them they could muster only three tank regiments.

On 23 June 1942, as Rommel sent his forces barrelling eastward, Lieutenant Meeser and 3 South African Reconnaissance Battalion's remaining No. 1 Company's cars finally "struggled back to Amiriya, a sorry collection, some of whose records extended to Abyssinian days; the few which were able to move under their own power towing or pushing the remainder".

South of the German line, Newton-King's 4 South African Armoured Car Regiment observed the melancholy sight of clouds of black smoke towering over Tobruk's furiously burning oil and petrol installations. Then, reinforced by four new Mark IIIA armoured cars it had just received, 4 South African Armoured Car Regiment turned to its assigned task of covering the withdrawal of 7 Motor Brigade on the Eighth Army's southern flank.

"Our patrol line was then switched to west instead of north," according to the war diary. "Our front of 24 miles was covered by A and B Squadrons, with C Squadron in reserve. Regimental Headquarters moved east to El Beida, where a gap had been made in the Wire. B Squadron on the left was strafed several times by Me 110s, which was the first indication of the German intention to turn the desert flank."

4 South African Armoured Car Regiment came under fire several times from heavy German

artillery pieces as it fell back toward El Beida behind 7 Motor Brigade, but on one occasion Lieutenant John McNally's troop turned the tables on the enemy by launching a swift pre-emptive attack and capturing a 150mm gun and its seven-man crew about 22km from the Wire. As the war diary describes the incident, "as the early morning mist lifted, the gunners and the armoured car men saw each other simultaneously, but the armoured car men beat the gunners to it."

44 Tank Repair Workshop, Alexandria, Egypt.

At 0630 on 23 June 1942 Newton-King's headquarters passed through the El Beida gap, having observed that Rommel was "moving some 3,000 vehicles, including tanks, on [Fort] Maddalena and El Rabta". The regiment kept moving eastward throughout the day and into the night – the Germans made a surprise advance by moonlight, imposing great strains on 4 South African Armoured Car Regiment's well-worn cars.

At first light on 24 June, south of Sidi Barrani, a troop under Sergeant D. W. Denman of C Squadron – who were apparently dismounted at the time – nearly became a victim of the general confusion when it met up with a turretless South African armoured car, of the type used by artillery forward observation officers, and that was flying the correct pennants. At close range, however, Denham and his six men discovered that it was in German hands, but only after its occupants had taken them prisoner.

The South Africans were not of a mind to surrender and, "having gone nearly a mile, Lance-Corporal Flanagan decided to fight it out. During the ensuing struggle Corporal Pearce, Lance-Corporal Flanagan and Trooper Piggott were knocked off the car, but the remaining four members of the troop overpowered the Germans, threw them overboard, and went back to pick up their friends. Trooper Piggott could not be found, but the remainder went back to their cars and drove off. It was discovered later that friends had picked up Trooper Piggott and captured the three Germans".

Along the coast, meanwhile, 6 South African Armoured Car Regiment was screening 59 Brigade as it moved eastward to Sidi Barrani ahead of the advancing Germans, with the war diary, as Klein writes, recording "the melancholy story of the retreat":

24.6.42. At 0600 hours informed that the Regiment is to come under command 59th Brigade. 1200 hours heavily shelled. Southern patrols withdraw, also heavily shelled. 12th Lancers take over the left sector. 1215 hours Div headquarters and Regimental headquarters move to next bound – Sidi Barrani. 1300 hours 12th Lancers withdrawing; A Squadron withdrawing; C Squadron withdrawing.

On 25 June 1942, with Rommel virtually in Mersa Matruh's backyard, the Allied battle plan changed drastically when General Auchinleck relieved Ritchie and took personal command of the Eighth Army. Concerned about a Gazala-style outflanking movement around the Mersa Matruh position, he decided rather to fight delaying actions there and at Fuka, 48km further to the east, while withdrawing to a defence line near a little railway station near the coast called El Alamein, about 110km from Mersa Matruh. There he would reorganize and mount a counter-attack.

This eleventh-hour change of plans caused some confusion among XXX Corps and XIII Corps, which had now to inflict damage on the enemy as well as ensure that they were not cut

Marmon Herrington Mk 3 U38396 named 'Glamour Wagon'prepares for a patrol.

South African troops with a Ford Truck and a Marmon Herrington Mk 3 in the Egyptian Western Desert.

off but could retreat in good order, and the inevitable result was a lack of good coordination between the two headquarters and their units.

Meanwhile 4 South African Armoured Car Regiment concentrated on retreating as best it could, enveloped by the densest possible "fog of war", taking whatever gap presented itself and living off the land as far as captured equipment was concerned. An entry in the war diary graphically describes Newton-King's situation as they toiled eastward:

25th June: Saw an enemy column northeast of our right patrols. Apparently friends on our right flank had withdrawn, which we were quite unaware of: this left an 18-mile gap in the armoured car screen. This was only one of many occasions on which we were entirely in the dark regarding the big picture of the operations as a whole, particularly those operations to our immediate right, which affected us closely.
A Squadron had a particularly quiet day, while B was most successful, capturing two 50mm anti-tank guns and two trucks carrying ammo plus 14 prisoners. One of these guns was prepared for our own use under Captain Snowden. During the capture of these guns one German propaganda officer was killed.
After one month's continuous action the regiment's bag of prisoners now totalled 186; while our losses were 87 prisoners, all from the Echelon (captured on 29th May), 1 killed, 13 wounded.

6 South African Armoured Car Regiment, minus two squadrons, was heavily involved in the evacuation of Mersa Matruh, where it arrived during the afternoon of the 26th, and spent its time reporting on the advance of 21 Panzer Division and 90 Light Division from an observation line along the escarpment about 30km southeast of the port. Of the rest of the unit, C Squadron was at Mersa Matruh as part of the fortress mobile reserve and B Squadron was with Headquarters 7 Armoured Division at Bir el Khalda, about 75km southeast of Mersa Matruh.

On the evening of 27 June 1942 the Eighth Army pulled back to Fuka after taking further losses, although 2 New Zealand Division, finding itself surrounded by 21 Panzer Division, managed to break out during the night without suffering serious damage. More confusion followed at Fuka, where some heavy losses were inflicted by Rommel. Among other things 29 Indian Infantry Brigade was destroyed, more than 6,000 Allied soldiers were taken prisoner and 40 tanks and very large amounts of supplies of various kind were captured.

Contrary to some popular impressions, the Eighth Army did not disintegrate during that hurried withdrawal to El Alamein. "It was orderly to the last, as it always had been, in spite of the fact that vehicles were crammed nose to tail on the coast road," Farran writes. "Nobody attempted to pass one another and military policemen in white gloves told units where to go as they came along. The Royal Air Force must receive great credit for staving off air attack at this time." But he adds: "Although there had been no panic in this long withdrawal, we had no confidence in our ability to stop the Germans."

On 30 June 1942 4 South African Armoured Car Regiment – still covering 7 Motor Brigade's rear – came close to disaster. Before dawn A Squadron, which had been sent about 50km forward with the workshop lorry for some repair work, reported at first light that during the night an enemy tank and transport force, estimated at 2,000, had passed by them unnoticed and was now about 30km behind the brigade.

According to Newton-King's personal notes he contacted brigade headquarters, and "on informing Brigadier Renton VC of the report, he told me they must be friendly and I informed Captain Bowden of A [Squadron] on the air accordingly. He came back with 'twelve friendly tanks now approaching rapidly. Am moving south under heavy shell-fire'. All this was some 20 miles to the rear of 7th Motor Brigade and of course our Regiment, and between us and the El Alamein line."

"The position could have been ticklish," as Major Reeves-Moore later noted, "but the situation was wholly in hand before the Germans realized who we were," and 4 South African Armoured Car Regiment continued to withdraw. A Squadron deployed in a north-facing semi-circle, while B and C Squadrons were orientated to the western flank, with the Qattara Depression's cliffs safeguarding their southern flank.

The long, hard trek eastward was now finally coming to an end. By the end of June 1942, the main body of the Eighth Army, badly battered but still full of fight, was falling back to the El Alamein boxes, where 1 South African Division was already in the line and holding the northern sector. "It had been a hard withdrawal for the South African armoured car regiments, not only because of enemy action, but particularly because of the extremely poor mechanical condition of their cars," Klein writes.

"A tribute to the quality of the achievements of the South African armoured cars in the 1942 retreat is recorded in the Rifle Brigade history. In a letter written by Major Tim Marten of the 2nd Rifle Brigade, quoted in the history, he said: 'The 11th Hussars were the oldest and most famous of the desert armoured car regiments, but we also had many links with The Royals and the 4th South African Armoured Cars. For skill and virtuosity the performance of the South Africans during the 1942 retreat was perhaps unrivalled. It never received adequate recognition.'"

At almost 70 years' remove, many modern soldiers have the vague impression that the defence of El Alamein (or the First Battle of El Alamein, as it is also known) consisted of a few defensive actions by the British, after which a lull set in that preceded the 'real' Battle of El Alamein in late October 1942, when the Allies went on the offensive for the first time. In fact any such impression is wrong. Between 1 July and 27 July 1942 the El Alamein line was the scene of almost continuous fighting, both defensive and offensive, of a ferocity that equalled or surpassed anything seen in the Western Desert up to that time, and which did not end until both sides had exhausted themselves.

With all his remaining forces back at El Alamein, Auchinleck had two immediate and interconnected tasks. The first was to stop Rommel in his tracks, then use the time thus bought to rebuild and reinforce the Eighth Army so that it would be ready for a counter-attack that would send the Axis forces reeling back to ultimate defeat. Rommel, on the other hand, was determined to maintain the momentum he had generated; if he could smash through the defence lines at El Alamein the chances were good that he would reach the Nile Delta and capture Cairo.

To achieve this he kept up a remorseless pressure in spite of his troops' fatigue, his substantial losses of earlier (at this stage he had only 55 tanks still running) and his ever-threatening shortage of water, fuel and ammunition, which was made even more difficult because he had lost so many transport vehicles that he had difficulty even bringing forward what supplies he did have. The Axis staff had originally expected a pause of six weeks after the capture of Tobruk, but as usual the imperatives of battle had made nonsense of forward planning.

Auchinleck's wisdom in falling back instead of frittering away more of his forces in a hopeless stand at Mersa Matruh cannot be doubted. El Alamein had several distinct advantages for a force in the Eighth Army's parlous situation. Although perilously close to the Nile Delta, it ensured a short line of road and rail communication, and about 15km to its south lay the stony Ruweisat Ridge, which in spite of its inconsiderable height provided good observation for many kilometres around.

Most of all, though, it had something rare in desert warfare: secure flanks which could not be turned. To the north there was the sea; a mere 55km to the south was the Qattara Depression. This meant that Rommel would not be able to take advantage of his undoubted skill at mobile armoured warfare: he would have to attack head-on, with the advantage being with the defenders.

The actual defence line, however, was almost non-existent. It consisted of three fortified boxes, only one of which – at El Alamein itself – had been partly wired and mined by Pienaar's 1 South African Division since its arrival a few days earlier. Near the centre of this largely notional line was the Bab el Qattara box, about 32km from the coast and 13km southwest of Ruweisat Ridge, which had been dug in but was not yet mined or wired. At Naq Abu Dweis, on the edge of the Qattara Depression, there was another box, but even less work had been done on it.

Meanwhile panic – 'the Flap' as wits called it – reigned at Headquarters Middle East in Cairo, with the headquarters, rear-echelon units and the British Embassy burning thousands of secret documents in case Rommel made it through to the Nile Delta. Auchinleck did not dismiss this possibility and made plans for retreating still further east while maintaining morale and retaining the support and cooperation of the Egyptians. He gave orders for parts of the Delta to be flooded and new defensive positions to be built west of Alexandria and on the route to Cairo.

But the figures favoured the British. With a mere 50km front, Auchinleck would be able to concentrate his forces – both those already in place and the reinforcements which were being shipped in, 8 Armoured Division from Britain and 9 Australian Division from Palestine. In addition, Rommel's supply lines were stretched to the limit.

Auchinleck's first priority was to make sure that Rommel did not break through the El Alamein defence line, such as it was, and to this end he used whatever resources were immediately to hand to close off the southern gap, Rommel's last opportunity for an encircling movement. At the beginning of July 1942 Pienaar's 1 South African Division held the northernmost fortified box next to the sea at El Alamein, with 2 New Zealand Division in the centre of the line, and 6 Indian Division further south in the Bab el Qattara Box area, with 7 Armoured Division also in the south. 1 Armoured Division was in reserve behind the defence line.

Rommel might well have succeeded in breaking through if he had first attacked the thinly held south, but he decided to assault the centre of the defence line in order to cut off the New Zealanders and South Africans, then deal with them in piecemeal fashion. He also underestimated both Auchinleck's willingness to take offensive action rather than sit and wait to be attacked, and the battered Eighth Army's intact fighting spirit, which had been bolstered by the arrival of 8 Armoured Division and 9 Australian Division. As a result the Axis advance was halted, although only after almost an entire month of furious fighting.

At 0300 on 1 July Rommel made his first move, sending 90 Light Division and 15 and 21 Panzer divisions to break through the defence line between El Alamein and a position at Deir el Abyad, about 35km to the southwest; this done, 90 Light Division and an Italian division were supposed to swing north and cut off the Alamein Box, which would simultaneously be attacked from the west by another Italian division. In the meantime the tanks would turn south and attack XIII Corps' rear, with the Italian XX Corps following in their wake to take out the Bab el Qattara box, with German reconnaissance units and the Italian Littorio Armoured Division protecting the Axis' right flank.

It did not work. For one thing, Rommel's intelligence was faulty. Deir el Abyad was not defended, which did not really matter, but what he did not know was that about 7½km to its east a terrain feature near the Ruweisat ridge called Deir el Shein was being turned into another defensive box by 18 Indian Infantry Brigade, which had arrived from Iraq on 28 June 1942.

Moreover, the Indians were backed by a substantial amount of firepower: 23 25-pdr guns, 16 of the new 6-pdr anti-tank guns which were replacing the ineffectual 2-pdrs, and nine of the old but heavily armoured Matilda II infantry tanks. Then again, he believed that the El Alamein Box was held only by the remnants of the British 50 Division, whereas, in fact, its occupant was the intact and comparatively fresh 1 South African Division.

These misconceptions were followed by two tactical lapses on the part of the Germans, one completely unforeseeable. 90 Light Division's navigation was faulty, so that it advanced too far to the north, came up against the South Africans' defences and ran into such heavy fire that it was unable to move. To make matters worse, 15 and 21 Panzer divisions were caught by a sandstorm and then came under a heavy air attack, so that it was broad daylight before they advanced down behind Deir el Abyad.

It was undefended, they now discovered for the first time, but then around 1000 they ran into 18 Indian Brigade at Deir el Shein, and a fierce clash erupted that went on until nightfall when the Indians were overrun, although only after inflicting heavy casualties on the Germans. 18 Indian Brigade's stubborn resistance bought time for Auchinleck to send 1 Armoured Division to Deir el Shein's aid and garrison Ruweisat Ridge with an improvised formation called Robcol, consisting of a company of infantry, a regiment of field artillery and a regiment of light anti-aircraft guns under Brigadier Robert Waller, the artillery commander of 10 Indian Infantry Division.

1 Armoured Division ran into 15 Panzer Division just south of Deir el Shein and, after another fierce action, forced it to retreat westward; in addition to its other losses, the Deutsches Afrikakorps had 18 of its precious 55 tanks knocked out. While this was happening 90 Light Division managed to get away from the Alamein Box and started moving eastward again to cut the road as per its orders, but came under such heavy artillery fire from 1 South African Division's three brigade groups that it had no option but to dig in.

Next morning Rommel renewed his offensive, but 90 Light Division still could not move, so he ordered 15 and 21 Panzer to turn north and assist 90 Light Division by swinging around the eastern end of Ruweisat Ridge, then proceed northward. On Ruweisat Ridge Waller managed to hold off the Deutsches Afrikakorps panzer divisions until more reinforcements arrived in the late afternoon in the shape of 4 Armoured Brigade and 22 Armoured Brigade.

The two brigades attacked 15 and 21 Panzer divisions respectively, while the Royal Air Force hit the German divisions with one attack after another. Though greatly depleted by the earlier fighting, the panzer divisions responded with repeated counter-attacks. All failed, however, and just before dusk they broke contact and withdrew, having lost another 11 tanks.

3 July 1942 brought yet another Axis attack on Ruweisat Ridge, led by the Italian 20 Motorized Corps. Auchinleck had discreetly reinforced the ridge during the night, however, and after making good progress along the flank of the ridge, 20 Corps' Ariete Armoured Division was stopped dead in its tracks by a combination of British armour, artillery fire and no less than 780 Royal Air Force air strikes.

Meanwhile 2 New Zealand Division was ordered northward from the Bab el Qattara Box, with 7 Motor Brigade and what was left of 5 Indian Division under command, to threaten Rommel's flank and rear. The New Zealand group's progress was slow, however, because it came under heavy fire from the Ariete Division's artillery south of Ruweisat Ridge.

But the Ariete's bolt was shot. Faced with overwhelming odds and harried by non-stop Royal Air Force strikes, the divisional commander told his units to fight their way out independently. The New Zealand group now resumed its advance northward, intending to attack the Ariete's rear and cut off its withdrawal, but its progress was soon stopped when the Italian Brescia Division at El Mrir laid down fire on it which was so intense that XIII Corps abandoned the attack. In consequence the Ariete Division was able to extricate itself, although it lost 531 dead and captured, as well as 36 artillery pieces, a number of tanks and 55 transport vehicles.

The fighting at Ruweisat Ridge was something of a turning-point in the defence of El Alamein. Rommel had thrown everything into his great gamble, and had lost. He had just 36 tanks still running, his German divisions had been worn down to little more than reinforced battalion groups and his troops were exhausted.

In addition his supply situation had deteriorated from very bad to disastrous. Shipments from Italy had been drastically curtailed, while convoys moving along the long supply routes were under fierce attack by the Desert Air Force, and mobile raiding columns operating westward from the south against his rear. At this point, Rommel decided his worn-out forces could make no further headway without resting and regrouping.

Auchinleck, on the other hand, was making full use of his short lines of communication to reorganize and rebuild the Eighth Army so that he could go on the offensive. 9 Australian Division was already deployed at the northern end of the line by 4 July 1942, 5 Indian Infantry Brigade was scheduled to take over Ruweisat Ridge from Robcol on 9 July, and 5 Indian Infantry Division had been reinforced with a fresh brigade, 161 Indian Infantry Brigade.

On 8 July 1942 he launched a two-pronged attack. XXX Corps, now commanded by Lieutenant-General W. R. Ramsden, was tasked to capture two low ridges west of El Alamein named Tel el Eisa and Tel el Makh Khad, then send raiding parties provided by 1 Armoured Division to attack Rommel's airfields at El Daba. This done, Ramsden was to send mobile combat groups southward toward Deir el Shein. At the same time XIII Corps was to stop any Axis movement northward.

In the small hours of 10 July 1942 9 Australian Division with 44 Royal Tank Regiment under command attacked Tel el Eisa, which had only rudimentary defences and was held by inexperienced soldiers of the Italian 60 Sabratha Division.

After an extremely heavy bombardment, the Division's 26 Australian Brigade stormed Tel el Eisa from the north at 0330 and captured it, routing the Sabratha Division and not only taking more than 1,500 prisoners but also – and this was Rommel's most painful loss – capturing the German signals interception unit which had reaped such a rich harvest of information for him since the beginning of Operation Crusader.

In the southeast, meanwhile, 1 South African Division with eight tanks in support easily took the lesser Axis strongpoint of Tel el Makh Khad, then dug in to cover the Australians from any Axis advance – which came later that day, when German infantry and the Italian 101 Trieste Division, with 15 Panzer Division in support, arrived to repair the damage. Attacks took place that afternoon and evening, but were beaten off by the Australians' anti-tank guns and heavy Allied artillery bombardments.

At first light on 11 July 1942, an Australian infantry battalion and tanks of 44 Royal Tank Regiment attacked Point 204 at the western end of Tel el Eisa, captured it in the early afternoon and then held on to it in spite of Axis counter-attacks that lasted until nightfall. Then a mobile column consisting of infantry and armour set off southward to attack Deir el Abyad, but was stopped by the Axis occupants of Miteirya ridge, about 8km from Tel el Eisa, and withdrew to El Alamein with more than 1,000 Italian prisoners.

Next day 21 Panzer Division and some accompanying infantry attacked the Australians once again but lost 600 dead and wounded in a failed 2½-hour action. On 13 July 1942, 21 Panzer Division struck once more, this time at both the Australians and South Africans, but were beaten off by very heavy artillery fire, although the Australians were forced to evacuate one of their positions. Still Rommel persisted in trying to reduce the Tel el Eisa salient and, on 15 July, sent in yet another attack, which also failed in the face of stubborn resistance.

On 16 July 1942 the Australians launched a counter-attack of their own, with British tanks in support, but were forced back and suffered extremely heavy casualties. Now, at last, the struggle for the salient was at an end after seven days of savage fighting that had cost the Axis forces over 3,700 captured and an estimated 2,000 dead, and deprived Rommel of his secret pipeline into British intentions through the loss of his interception unit.

But the First Battle of El Alamein was not over yet, because now Auchinleck took advantage of the Axis forces' moment of weakness by going over to the offensive again. Various German units were digging in along the coastal sector after the fighting in the Tel el Eisa salient, and Auchinleck sent 4 and 5 New Zealand Brigades and 5 Indian Brigade northwestward to attack the Italian Pavia and Brescia divisions, which were lying in front of the Ruweisat Ridge.

Auchinleck's intention was for the two New Zealand brigades to take the western end of the ridge, and 5 Indian Brigade the eastern extremity. Then 2 Armoured Brigade would pass through them and exploit toward Deir el Shein and the Miteirya Ridge, while 22 Armoured Brigade would stand by on the left, ready to protect the New Zealanders and Indians as they consolidated after capturing the ridge.

The attack started at 2300 on 14 July 1942, and by first light the New Zealand brigades had taken their objectives, while the Indians were making progress in the east. Thereafter, however, the assault developed into a hard-fought action that lasted three days and eventually involved not only the Brescia and Pavia divisions but also 15 Panzer Division's 8 Panzer Regiment, 90 Light Division and the Ariete Armoured Division.

By its end the Allies still held Ruweisat Ridge in spite of repeated attacks. The cost had been high for both sides, though. The New Zealanders had lost 1,405 men, about half of them taken prisoner, while over 2,000 Axis troops had been captured, mostly from the Brescia and Pavia divisions, and the defenders counted 24 knocked-out tanks, as well as disabled armoured cars and abandoned anti-tank guns.

To weaken the enemy pressure on the New Zealanders and Indians at Ruweisat Ridge, Auchinleck ordered the Australians to attack Miteirya Ridge, which was occupied, *inter alia*, by the Italian Trento and Trieste divisions. 24 Australian Brigade went in with 44 Royal Tank Regiment during the small hours of 17 July 1942, backed by strong fighter cover. The attack started well and 736 prisoners were taken, but strong enemy counter-attacks pushed the Australians back to their start-line after losing 300 men.

On 17 July 1942 Auchinleck launched yet another attack, this time involving 161 Indian Infantry Brigade, which was to advance past the northern aspect of Ruweisat Ridge and capture Deir el Shein, while 6 New Zealand Brigade moved forward to the El Mreir depression from south of the ridge; 2 Armoured Brigade and 23 Armoured Brigade would then sweep through the gap created by the infantry.

By now Auchinleck disposed over 173 operational tanks, while Rommel had only 89 in running order, 38 German and the rest Italian (about 100 others had been salvaged by his panzer divisions but not yet repaired), and at first the attack went well. But once again it faltered in the face of strong resistance, determined counter-attacks, minefields and complications resulting from transport difficulties and bad communications – not to mention the fact that 23 Armoured Brigade advanced along an allegedly mine-free route which was not, came to a halt and then retreated while under attack by 21 Panzer Division.

The New Zealanders lost over 900 men killed, wounded and taken prisoner at El Mreir, the Indians broke through into Deir el Shein but were forced out again, and 23 Armoured Brigade had been destroyed as a fighting formation, with 40 tanks knocked out and 47 seriously damaged. General Gott launched another attack on Deir el Shein in the early hours of 23 July 1942. The assault force lost direction and was repulsed. A third attack, this time in daylight, also failed.

In the north, the Australians remained on the attack. At 0600 on 22 July 1942 26 Australian Brigade attacked Tel el Eisa and 24 Australian Brigade with 50 Royal Tank Regiment in support assaulted Tel el Makh Khad, north of Miteirya Ridge. Tel el Eisa was taken, albeit at a heavy cost in lives, but the Tel el Makh Khad attack resulted in serious (and unnecessary) tank losses. 50 Royal Tank Regiment had not been trained in close infantry support procedures and failed to coordinate with the Australians; as a result the two components advanced independently and, thanks to the lack of infantry support, 50 Royal Tank Regiment lost 23 tanks. Why 50 Royal Tank Regiment had not been properly trained, in spite of the lessons learned from the Germans in this regard, is not known.

On 26/27 July 1942 Auchinleck made one last attempt to destroy the Axis forces in the northern sector, using XXX Corps, which had been reinforced with two of 7 Armoured Division's brigades, an infantry brigade and a light armoured brigade, an Australian infantry brigade and 1 South African Division. The aim was to break the Axis defence line south of Miteirya Ridge, gap the enemy minefields southeast of the ridge and at Deor el Dhib.

This would allow 2 Armoured Brigade and 4 Light Armoured Brigade to get through to El Wishka, southeast of Miteirya Ridge, and attack Rommel's line of communication. But this attack, too, ended in costly failure; it achieved nothing, while costing 69 Infantry Brigade about 600 killed and captured and the Australians about 400, with 13 tanks destroyed.

On 31 July 1942 Auchinleck called off any further offensive operations. Thus ended the First Battle of Alamein, which had consumed so many lives and resources without reaching a conclusive end. But Auchinleck had achieved his primary purpose of mauling the Axis forces to such an extent that the Eighth Army – all that stood between Rommel and the all-important Nile Delta – had been saved to fight another day.

Auchinleck now settled down to strengthening his defences in case of a major Axis counter-offensive, although there was no immediate likelihood of one. Rommel was short of tanks, fuel, ammunition and a variety of other necessities (which he blamed on the failure of Italian convoying, still totally unaware of the fact that the British had broken the Enigma code), as well as the collapse of the Italian formations' will to resist – though not that of the individual Italian soldier.

He did make one more attempt at a breakthrough at Alam el Halfa ridge in August, but was thrown back by British and South African forces who had been moved up when Eighth Army intelligence got wind of his intentions. After that he lay up again, rebuilding Panzer Army Africa as supplies of men, weapons and supplies reached him. Fighting would not break out again until 23 October 1942, and by that time a startling change would have come over the Eighth Army.

The South African armoured cars were intimately involved in much of the July 1942 fighting – in one case in a role far beyond their remit – although their personnel were exhausted by three months of hard campaigning and their cars were in a ruinous state after heavy punishment from the terrain and lack of full maintenance and repairs. Because of the limited extent of the front line in their sectors, 3 South African Reconnaissance Battalion and 6 South African Armoured Car Regiment temporarily changed roles to provide close support for infantry raids and positional defence, although 4 South African Armoured Car Regiment continued with normal patrol duties in the south.

3 South African Reconnaissance Battalion's effective strength was down to a composite

company of just seven cars under Lieutenant W. H. Penny, which was attached to 3 South African Brigade and suffered heavily; on 15 July 1942 Lieutenant J. H. de la Harpe, Corporal L. Stanfield and Trooper A. J. Perfect were killed, while two others were wounded. The rest of the battalion also suffered casualties, even though it was now far behind the lines.

It had gathered at Amariya to hand in its worn-out cars to 1 South African Division's base workshops for refitting, and on 3 July 1942 was preparing to move further back to Helwan for rest and reorganization when Axis aircraft raided the base, killing four of its men, Lance-Corporal G.I. van Rooyen, Trooper N. Neville, Trooper J. Jacobs and Private S. Monfalse. Grieving, the battalion then entrained for Helwan, only to be recalled to help in preparing and manning the defences of Cairo itself, where they stayed until the immediate Axis threat had died down.

Throughout the July 'flap' Short's 6 South African Armoured Car Regiment, which was now attached to 1 South African Division, was in the thick of the fighting, although its vehicles, too, were in such bad shape that elements of A, B and C squadrons were temporarily amalgamated into one while the rest of the unit was at the Ikingi base workshops to have new life breathed into its cars.

The composite squadron saw considerable action on 5 and 6 July 1942 while supporting infantry raids aimed at capturing enemy soldiers for intelligence purposes. On 5 July an 88mm shell hit Lieutenant C. W. Krige's car, wounding him and two of his crew. On 6 July two other troops (each consisting of only two cars) under Lieutenant C. A. B. Mandy and Lieutenant D. W. Shuttleworth accompanied four tanks and some troop-carrying armoured cars on another raid; two of the tanks and all the troop-carrying cars were knocked out, although Shuttleworth managed to seize a prisoner.

By 7 July 1942, however, most of 6 South African Armoured Car Regiment was back together again. C Squadron was still refitting at Ikingi, but A Squadron was with 2 South African Brigade and B Squadron and the regimental headquarters at 1 South African Division Headquarters. At this stage the Axis threat to Cairo was still so real that the war diary notes that that day Regimental Headquarters 6 South African Armoured Car Regiment received 1 South African Division Operation Order No 38, headed 'This Order Covers A Possible Operation Which It Is Hoped Will Not Be Put Into Effect', namely screening a withdrawal from El Alamein to the Nile Delta if the Axis forces managed to break through.

In the south, 4 South African Armoured Car Regiment spent the early days of July under direct command of 7 Armoured Division, maintaining a screen facing west and south between the 2 New Zealand Division's box and the foothills of the Qattara Depression, although by this stage it was down to just 32 cars, 27 of which were in such bad shape that they should actually have been under workshop repair.

A Squadron was in particular need of maintenance and repair, so on 2 July B and C squadrons were temporarily amalgamated under command of Major Reeves-Moore and sent to relieve it. That became the pattern for the rest of the month: one squadron in the line and the other in reserve, being patched up as far as possible.

On 5 July 1942 4 South African Armoured Car Regiment was placed under operational command of 5 Indian Division, an immediate result being that its cars spent the next four days constantly dodging 'friendly' shells from the Indian artillery as they moved about on the reconnaissance line – caused, according to the war diary, by the fact that "the Indians were not used to working with armoured cars". The only consolation during this trying time was the arrival of £175-worth of canteen goods, which was received with considerable joy, since the regiment had not eaten well since the Germans had captured the regimental canteen on 2 June 1942.

After four days of unintentional harassment by the Indian gunners a better arrangement was reached: 5 Indian Division moved back about 18km and detached one troop each of

25-pdrs and Bofors guns to Reeves-Moore's B Squadron, which was then in place on the observation line. This worked well on 9 July 1942, when – with 4 South African Armoured Car Regiment now under direct command of 7 Armoured Division again – the Axis forces captured the Bab el Qattara Box, about 32km from the coast.

The box had been dug in but not mined or wired, and was abandoned without significant resistance after its supply dumps had been demolished; "though this achievement was hailed by the Germans as a great success," Klein writes, "the abandonment by the British of the Qattara Box was part of General Auchinleck's over-all battle plan, and its loss did not appear to cause much upset to the 4th Regiment. Apart from recording the withdrawal on the 9th in the normal way, the war diary pays more attention to the fact that 'late in the evening Lieutenant Guy Young of A Squadron was engaged very heavily by gunners of the 5th Indian Division, who were on the left flank'."

A much greater disappointment, from 4 South African Armoured Car Regiment's point of view, was that Lieutenant Klerk returned empty-handed from the Khatatba base near Cairo, where he was supposed to have taken delivery of 40 new Mark IIIA armoured cars.

The lull toward the end of July 1942 saw the South African armoured car regiments moving out of the line at last for proper rest and refitting: 4 South African Armoured Car Regiment to Sidi Bishr near Alexandria, 6 South African Armoured Car Regiment to the Ikingi base and 3 South African Reconnaissance Battalion to Helwan.

The 4 South African Armoured Car Regiment war diary entry for 24 July says simply: "At 1000 hours our line was taken over by the 11th Hussars. Thus the Regiment was relieved after over three months in actual contact with the enemy. Perhaps the hardest three months experienced by the Regiment; certainly the longest withdrawal 'in contact'; being from south of Tobruk to the El Alamein line, a distance of 500 miles. In the afternoon we left for Amiriya to join C Squadron for a well-earned rest."

Klein writes: "It was the month that saw the blunting of the Axis thrust to the east and the return of the Eighth Army to the offensive; the month during which the South African armoured cars performed gruelling and splendid service in one of the most critical phases of the entire war in North Africa. High honours came their way ... On 19 July Lieutenant G. C. Fletcher left for Army Headquarters where he was invested with the Military Cross by the Duke of Gloucester ... the only South African at the investiture ... All told, at this stage, the 4th Regiment's awards totalled 1 Distinguished Service Order, 8 Military Crosses, 2 Distinguished Conduct Medals and 22 Military Medals. Awards to the other regiments were correspondingly high."

32

Under new management

In August 1942 Auchinleck vanished from the desert. His decision to fall back on El Alamein had proved correct, but he had made some bad mistakes – among them several unsuitable command appointments – and his relations with his subordinate commanders, both British and Commonwealth, had become strained.

Even more serious, he had lost the confidence of Churchill, who desperately needed some victories in what had been a bad year for the Allies, while Auchinleck's experiences in the First World War had given him a dislike for hastily planned and executed offensives.

The crunch came in August 1942. Passing through Cairo on the way to meet with Russian dictator Josef Stalin, Churchill and General Sir Alan Brooke, the Chief of the Imperial General Staff, removed Auchinleck both as Commander-in-Chief Middle East and as General Officer Commanding Eighth Army. It was, perhaps, not quite as brutal a dismissal as most historians have claimed. By this stage Auchinleck must have been near the end of his personal tether after shouldering the burden of two incredibly stressful appointments. Be that as it may, he was out.

Churchill offered him the new Persia and Iraq Command, which had been hived off from Middle East Command, but Auchinleck turned it down because he believed that the new dispensation was undesirable and unworkable. Instead he returned to India, although there was no immediate posting for him there.

His replacement as Commander-in-Chief Middle East was the much-respected, deeply experienced and highly decorated General Sir Harold Alexander, one of the finest British generals of the 20th century. Churchill's choice for the Eighth Army was Lieutenant-General William Gott, whose aggressive, outgoing personality – which made him very popular with his men – contrasted sharply with that of the reserved Auchinleck.

The sagacious Brooke had great doubts about the wisdom of such an appointment. While he respected Gott's abilities, he did not think he had the experience for the post, and among other things believed that he was worn out after almost two years in the desert; years later, in his memoirs, Brooke recalled that in a personal interview Gott himself said that he had "tried most of his ideas on the Boche. We want someone with new ideas and plenty of confidence in them".

Brooke personally favoured Lieutenant-General Bernard Law Montgomery – acerbic, supremely self-confident and, like Hobart, something of a heretic. So did Auchinleck, although they could hardly have been called friends. (Montgomery later wrote that when he had served briefly under Auchinleck in London in 1940 "I cannot recall that we ever agreed on anything.")

But Gott never took up his appointment: he was killed when an Me 109 shot his aircraft down on the way to Cairo. So Montgomery got the Eighth Army after all, albeit by default. Hastily summoned from England after Gott's death, he immediately set about blowing away layers of cobwebs and negativism like a one-man desert *khamsin*.

Among other things, he ruthlessly sacked staff officers who did not come up to his exacting standards of physical fitness and competency, held standing-room-only order groups to discourage long-windedness, made it plain to all ranks (personally, wherever possible) that there would be no further retreats under any circumstances whatever – "I want to impress on everyone that the bad times are over, they are finished! Our mandate from the Prime Minister is to destroy the Axis forces in North Africa … It can be done, and it will be done!" – and generally set about preparing the Eighth Army for the devastating counter-offensive against Rommel that he and Alexander were hatching.

While the powers-that-be engaged in such high-level machinations, 3 South African Reconnaissance Battalion and 4 South African Armoured Car Regiment were engrossed in reorganizing, refitting and generally recovering from their exertions in the west and south in preparation for the coming offensive, while 6 South African Armoured Car Regiment stayed in the line throughout July and August. "From the northern Kenya frontier, through the bush, deserts and mountains of Abyssinia and Italian Somaliland, through the Western Desert to the very borders of Tripolitania and back to El Alamein," as Klein writes, "the South African armoured cars had tasted the sweets of success and the bitterness of defeat. Now they were to participate in a great victory."

At Helwan 3 South African Reconnaissance Battalion underwent some fundamental changes in addition to the normal re-organizational process. Its name was changed to 3rd South African Armoured Car Regiment, which did not sit well with its members, who continued to refer to their unit as '3 Recce' except in official documents. Companies now became squadrons (although the new 3 South African Armoured Car Regiment defiantly retained numbers instead of letters for them), a green cloth backing was added to the headdress badge and the veteran Lieutenant-Colonel Gwillam departed for the Union to become Officer Commanding 8 South African Armoured Car Regiment. In his place came Major Jenkins, now promoted to lieutenant-colonel.

Both of the other two regiments also underwent a change of command. At 6 South African Armoured Car Regiment, Lieutenant-Colonel Short handed over to Major E. G. Fricker after being ordered back to the Union for an appointment in the coastal defences, while at Sidi Bishr, near Alexandria, 4 South African Armoured Car Regiment's Lieutenant-Colonel Newton-King's outstanding battle-handling during and after Operation Crusader earned him the appointment of second-in-command of the British 22 Armoured Brigade.

His place was taken by Major Reeves-Moore in the rank of lieutenant-colonel (soon after taking over he received the Military Cross, the first of several decorations he was to earn in the desert and Italy). Among various other promotions and restructuring, Captain G. Girdler-Brown took over C Squadron.

Between them, Montgomery (or 'Ginger Beer', his nickname being a reference to his famously abstemious personal habits) and Alexander ('Iceberg', the immaculate and superficially glacial Irish Guardsan) had an electrifying effect, particularly on South African senior officers like Dan Pienaar and Scrubbs Hartshorn, whose relationship with most of their British senior commanders had been rocky ever since the days of the Abyssinian campaign. Hartshorn writes tellingly of his and Pienaar's first meetings with Ginger Beer and Iceberg:

> Cautiously, I stuck my head around the door of Dan's caravan, saying, "Well, and what do you think of him?" Dan looked at me with his eyes sparkling and said, "Man, we've just had a soldier here. There's a general for us. We've never had anyone like this before – I'll follow that man – I'll follow him anywhere."
> … Dan was a new man. Gone was the tension and the curtness and in their place was the old spirit of friendliness and directness that was so typical of him in Abyssinia. A thought struck me. "I hope," I said to Dan, "you didn't use strong language with him. You know, of course, that his codename is Ginger Beer and you know why he was given it?"
> "Don't worry, man," Dan replied. "I was bloody polite. I didn't swear – I didn't even smoke. We

talked about the Bible first – he saw mine lying open here – and then we got on to other things … Man, we're all right now."

… I received a message to be at a certain map reference point to meet Ginger Beer, who was making his first visit of inspection to the army he would now command. An open staff car, filled with top brass, stopped some distance away. 1 began walking toward it and noticed a slim man vault out and make for me. Through my field glasses 1 saw that he was wearing shorts and shirt with no rank badges, no Sam Browne and he was wearing, of all things, a broad Australian felt hat. A staff wallah, I said to myself, coming to identify me. I saluted him. "Hartshorn, 1st South African Brigade, Sir."

The man smiled, greeted me with a warm handshake. "Good show, I'm Montgomery."

Lt Col Newton King, Natal Carbineers, Officer Commanding 4/6 Armoured Car Regiment.

He spent an hour with my Brigade, talking with the officers and men and asking penetrating questions which left me in no doubt as to his military alertness and intelligence.

The realization that we had, in him, a really true leader had me so engrossed in our conversation that when we got back in my truck to his staff car I found I had my arm around his shoulders and was telling him earnestly, "You've arrived just in time, Sir. You're finding an army that is recovering from being a defeated rabble … under your leadership it will become a victorious army …"

With a warm smile and, "I must be off now to spend an hour with your General," he departed for Dan's headquarters.

Hartshorn's first meeting with General Alexander was equally enlightening:

Then came the meeting with General Alexander – Iceberg … fitted him as aptly as Ginger Beer suited Montgomery. No informality here. In the staff Humber, stiffly erect and correct, stood Dan with General Alexander. As he stepped from it I knew I was in the presence of the perfect Guardee – immaculately dressed in winter uniform, medal ribbons, badges, 'brass bound' cap, riding breeches and beautifully polished field boots. He had on his Sam Browne. He was superbly correct, in fact, down even to the regulation automatic pistol …

We drove up and down the front areas and eventually we arrived at the Dukes Battalion Headquarters where Dan joined us for tea. The cold, blue eyes which had earned General Alexander his code name of Iceberg, we were soon to learn, belied a warm and human personality. I liked him immensely and wondered what Dan's reactions to him would be for, in many ways, he was the antithesis of everything Dan was, and certainly up to now Dan had shown a marked dislike for the stiff, Guardsman-type officer of which General Alexander was so typical a representative.

I determined to find out with the least possible delay. In the early dawn I went down to Dan's headquarters and found him, as usual at this time of the day, sitting on the edge of his bed in pyjamas reading the Bible.

"Come in, man," he said, "I've got something to tell you. You know the three things I hate in this world – British lords, British Generals and these bloody Guards …?"

I wondered what was coming next.

"Well, this bloke Alex – he's the fellow for us. Man, he's good. We sat here until 10 o'clock last night."

I sighed with relief. The 'players', I said to myself, were in at last.

Montgomery's initiation into desert warfare was not long in coming. Rommel knew very well that reinforcements and huge amounts of war material were heading out to Montgomery,

Marmon Herrington Mk 2 and Mk3.

Sherman Mk V, Khatatba, Egypt, 1943.

and that the only way to compensate for his own want – by now his forces had been reduced to using captured supplies and equipment – was to hit the Eighth Army hard before its build-up had been completed, thereby delaying Montgomery's counter-offensive for as long as possible.

The Germans were now heavily involved in Russia; if they achieved a quick and decisive victory over the Russians and then moved southward toward Iran and the Middle East, a large part of the troops and equipment Montgomery was accumulating at El Alamein would have to be transferred to meet this threat.

But the Germans were hung up at the tenaciously defended city of Stalingrad, and Rommel's pleas for more reinforcements which would enable him to join hands with the southward-moving forces fell on deaf ears at the Oberkommando der Wehrmacht, then and later.

Eighth Army intelligence got wind of the Axis plans in early August, however, and warned that Rommel – who had been rebuilding capacity as assiduously as the British, albeit on a smaller scale – intended to mount a great attack at the end of the month, with a force estimated at a minimum of 200 tanks and up to 75,000 infantry. The Eighth Army continued to prepare at a frantic pace, and intelligence-gathering raids were stepped up all along its front.

By 24 August 1942, 4 South African Armoured Car Regiment was deployed again, manning Mark IIIA armoured cars mounting 'liberated' 37mm and 47mm guns, as well as 17 of the new British Daimler cars which were now beginning to reach the Middle East. Two of its squadrons were placed under command of X Corps' 9 Armoured Brigade to patrol along a 36km front of the secondary defence line in the Alum Shaltut area south of Amirya.

The intelligence prediction was correct, and on 31 August 1942 Rommel sent in his two Afrikakorps armoured divisions and a grouping of armoured reconnaissance units. But his attack failed. Montgomery had set a trap south of Alam el Halfa Ridge, and "the German attack ran into a horseshoe of such concentrated and intensive artillery and anti-tank fire, reinforced by the guns of hull-down Sherman and Grant tanks, that his offensive power was totally smashed," Hartshorn writes. "It was General Montgomery's first desert action and we knew then that the Germans would never, ever, take Alexandria and Cairo."

South African infantry units were involved at Alam el Halfa, but not the armoured cars. 4 South African Armoured Car Regiment was still in place in the Alum Shaltut area, but smelt no powder because the Axis tanks could not penetrate that far, and 6 South African Armoured Car Regiment under Major Fricker was put on standby in case of an attack on 1 South African Division which did not eventuate. But both regiments' turn would come in less than two months' time.

Although Rommel had been defeated, he had not been vanquished, and he ordered his troops to dig in to stop the immediate counter-attack he expected. But no attack came;

Alexander and Montgomery did not intend merely to break through Rommel's defences but to inflict a mortal blow on his Panzer Army Africa. One reason for the back-and-forth nature of the Western Desert fighting had always been that neither side had been strong enough to fully exploit a victory and, in spite of periodical grumbling from the ever-impatient Churchill, they were determined to make sure that this did not happen again.

So another lull followed Alam el Halfa while the Eighth Army continued to stock up on troops – British, Indian, Australian and New Zealand – and tanks and transport vehicles from both Britain and the United States. Rommel, though starved of necessities because of the Germans' preoccupation with the fighting in Russia, made use of the time to prepare his defences with every means at his disposal, digging in, rolling out many kilometres of barbed wire and laying hundreds of thousands of mines, many of them captured from the Allies.

As the weeks passed he created a defensive line of a lethality hitherto unseen in the Western Desert. At the front of the line were two extra belts of mines, connected at intervals to create boxes – 'Devil's Gardens' as they were called – each of which was lightly held at the forward edge but was otherwise unoccupied and sown with anti-personnel mines and booby-traps. Behind them lay his main defensive positions, stretching back at least 2km; to make the Allied advance even more difficult, many of the minefields had fake vehicle tracks to lure unwary British tanks to destruction.

No. 2 Squadron of the newly renamed 3 Armoured Car Regiment moved up to the El Alamein Line on 1 September 1942 for patrol duties in the no man's land forward of 14 Brigade, followed within a fortnight by the rest of the unit for intensive training in combined operations with tanks and infantry – a long-standing weakness in the Eighth Army, as Operation Crusader and subsequent events had shown – and a '4th Fighting Squadron' was formed as an extra operational sub-unit.

An even greater and more painful change overtook 4 and 6 South African Armoured Car regiments at the end of the month. Both regiments were distinctly short of experienced officers and men at a time when the decisive battles of the Western Desert campaign were looming and could break out at any moment. As a result it was decided to amalgamate them.

6 South African Armoured Car Regiment's war diary closed for good on 31 August 1942 – "an uneventful day for the armoured cars," as Klein notes – and it was withdrawn from the line so that a start could be made with forming the new unit, which would be commanded by 4 South African Armoured Car Regiment's Reeves-Moore and renamed '4th/6th South African Armoured Car Regiment' in deference to the large number of 6 South African Armoured Car Regiment personnel it absorbed, a name which would soon gain the same renown as its predecessors.

Six increasingly tense weeks went by as Montgomery and Alexander crafted their immense engine of destruction until they had 220,000 battle-ready soldiers and 1,100 tanks to hurl at the Axis lines. Facing the Eighth Army were Rommel's 559 tanks and 115,000 men – vastly outnumbered and short of supplies, although highly motivated in the main and prepared to make use of all the advantages defenders traditionally enjoy over attackers.

Ironically, the architect of all the Axis preparations was not there: in September Rommel had fallen ill with jaundice and on the 23rd had been evacuated to Germany on sick leave. His temporary replacement was General Georg Stumme, another tank general, who had been hastily flown in from Russia. It was to prove a disastrous appointment, though not because of incompetence on Stumme's part.

Montgomery's edge lay not just in his numerical superiority but in the quality of his equipment. Up to this stage the Allies had had only one weapon which was better than the Germans', their superb 25-pdr artillery piece. Now all that had changed. They had Sherman tanks with 75mm guns, 6-pdr anti-tank guns and enough Spitfires and other fighter aircraft to ensure air superiority.

He envisaged a 12-day battle, taking place in three phases – the break-in, the 'dogfight' and then the final crushing blow – with great use of artillery and near-complete air superiority. Always ultra-conscious of the need for good morale, he knew that ground attacks by aircraft played a dual role, as can be seen from a quotation of his in Niall Barr's *Pendulum of War: The Three Battles of El Alamein*: "The moral effect of air action ... is very great and out of all proportion to the material damage inflicted. In the reverse direction, the sight and sound of our own air forces operating against the enemy have an equally satisfactory effect on our own troops. A combination of the two has a profound influence on the most important single factor in war – morale."

The first phase of Montgomery's attack plan envisaged an advance into Axis territory by the four infantry divisions of XXX Corps – now commanded by Lieutenant-General Oliver Leese – 9 Australian Division, 51 Highland Division, 2 New Zealand Division and 1 South African Division. Spread over a 26km front, the divisions were to overrun the forward Axis defences and advance as far as an imaginary line code-named Oxalic.

Accompanying them would be sappers who would clear safe vehicle lanes through the enemy anti-tank minefields in two places, one running southwestward through 2 New Zealand's sector toward the middle of Miteirya Ridge, the other to the west, through the sectors occupied by 9 Australian Division and 51 Highland Division, and passing 3km north of the ridge's western point. 1 South African Division would be on the left of the attack line, tasked to capture Miteiriya Ridge itself.

Once the sappers – who were equipped with a new and improved mine-detector which worked twice as fast as the older models – had cleared the lanes (each wide enough for a single-file advance), about 500 tanks from 1 and 10 Armoured divisions of Lieutenant-General Herbert Lumsden's X Corps would pour through, advance to the so-called Pierson Line and consolidate west of the infantry divisions to make sure the panzers could not intervene.

This done, they would then move forward to yet another nominal line deep inside the Axis defences, code-named Skinflint, which lay astride the tactically important Rahman track, and take on the enemy armour.

While this was happening, Lieutenant-General Brian Horrocks's XIII Corps would carry out a feint attack at the southern end of the line, with 7 Armoured Division attacking and holding down 21 Panzer Division and the Ariete Division around Jebel Kalakh, and an attached Free French brigade would secure the nearby El Taqa plateau. With 131 Infantry Brigade from 44 Infantry Division protecting Horrocks's right flank, 22 and 4 Light Armoured brigades would burst out into the open, turn north and attack the rear of designated enemy positions 8km west of Deir el Munassib.

By this stage, Montgomery had also pulled off a deception plan of Byzantine complexity to persuade Rommel that the Allied attack would take place to the south, and at a later date. In September 1942 dummy supply dumps had been set up; the Axis forces saw through this and took no action against them. The Allies then discreetly turned them into real ones. A dummy pipeline was erected, and Jeeps disguised as tanks were concentrated in the south, while Lumsden's real tanks to the north were disguised as soft-skinned transport.

Sometimes Montgomery's deception plan caused unforeseen difficulties for his underlings. "My Brigade area," Hartshorn writes, "was to be one of the greatest concentration areas for the attack from the north – a camouflage movement which necessitated the construction of thousands of dummy tanks, trucks, and guns, all of which would be removed a night or two before the battle, taken to the south end of the line and replaced with genuine material.

"We had moments of great anxiety, particularly when sudden sand storms would rip the hessian away and leave wire skeletons exposed in all their nakedness until the entire Division, rushing in all directions, succeeded in rounding up the hessian and restoring it,"

Montgomery also had a secret weapon in his arsenal – the flail tank, for opening up a safe lane through minefields – which was originally conceived by a South African armoured car officer named Major Abraham du Toit. There are at least two different versions of how this came about.

One version, narrated by Warrant Officer Dennis 'Grassy' Green, has it that early in August 1942 du Toit went to see a Major A. H. MacMillan, second-in-command of 44 Railways & Harbours Tank Workshop at Alexandria. Du Toit swore him to secrecy and then asked if he could undertake a project to build a mine-clearing tank, sketching his idea on the back of a packet of Springbok cigarettes.

MacMillan got permission to go ahead, experimented on a tank his workshop had constructed from cannibalised spare parts, and had eight Matildas mounting flails – each driven by an externally mounted Ford lorry engine with its own operator – completed in time for the battle.

Another version has it that tests du Toit carried out were so were so encouraging that he was promoted and sent to England to develop the idea, but before leaving described it to a Captain Norman Berry, a mechanical engineer who had been sent out in 1941, to evaluate the system. Later Berry served in the Eighth Army, where he experimented with the concept and handed his findings to another officer, a Major L. A. Girling, who was developing a similar flail device invented by yet another South African officer quite independently of Berry. By the summer of 1942, Girling's team had developed the Matilda Scorpion, 25 of which were ready by the time of the Battle of El Alamein.

What is in no doubt, however, is that du Toit of the armoured cars was the originator of the concept and was sent to England for further development work, because in 1948 he was granted £13,000 by the Royal Commission on Awards to Inventors for his work, while nine others, among them four South Africans, shared a further £7,000.

3 South African Armoured Car Regiment was scheduled to go in with 1 South African Division, its squadrons detached to 2 and 3 South African brigades (under brigadiers Evered Poole and R. J. Palmer), with the divisional reserve, 1 South African Brigade, to provide support for the advance and make a maximum effort to exploit whatever success was achieved. 4/6 South African Armoured Car Regiment was attached to 1 Armoured Division, and to Reeves-Moore's men, as Klein writes, "fell what was possibly the most dramatic and adventurous role given to any South African ground unit in the Western Desert – that of breaking through the front in company with their British counterpart, the Royals, to raid deep into the enemy rear."

As 23 October 1942 approached, the officers and men of the Eighth Army – some of them hardened veterans of the desert war, others newcomers to the Middle East – watched an endless stream of British and South African aircraft passing overhead, on the way to bomb and strafe the Axis airfields, convoys, airfields and defensive positions. Then on morning of 23 October they were told that the attack would start that night. A characteristically brisk and inspiring message from Montgomery was read out at unit after unit.

The night of 23 October 1942 was calm and clear, brightly lit by a full moon. At 2130, 15 Panzer Division came under a few minutes' heavy artillery fire from 24 Australian Brigade, but this was merely a diversion. Then at 2140, 882 field and medium guns spread over the entire front opened fire, "their flashes lighting up the desert sky in one of the most furious cannonades of the entire war," Klein writes. "As fast as the gunners could load, the guns roared, raining shells on enemy batteries, while the bewildered German and Italian infantrymen huddled in their slit trenches."

The shelling was not, as is sometimes thought, a random plastering of the Axis positions, but followed a carefully formulated fire-plan. For the first 20 minutes there was a general bombardment up and down the 65km front. Then at 2200 various guns were directed on to specific targets to support the infantry as they started their advance with bayonets fixed, and for the next five hours and more there would be no cessation of that monstrous sound.

For the advance Pienaar deployed 2 and 3 brigades, each leading with one battalion, the other two passing through the lead battalion at the Oxalic Line to the final objective on Miteiriya Ridge. 1 South African Brigade – reinforced by extra machine guns, anti-tank guns, 3 South African Armoured Car Regiment's armoured cars and a mobile element provided by 8 Royal Tank Regiment – was tasked with protecting his left flank. His field artillery, plus three troops loaned by X Corps, laid down a fire-plan consisting of timed concentrations which would put smoke on the intermediate and final objectives to disguise his troops' reorganization and also help units to keep direction amid the inevitable battlefield smoke, dust and general confusion.

Pienaar's South African infantrymen advanced steadily in spite of taking heavy losses, with 3 South African Armoured Car Regiment's cars moving with them to provide additional supporting fire. By 2350, the Natal Mounted Riflemen had occupied the first of XXX Corps' Oxalic Line objectives.

Elsewhere, too, all was going well and Montgomery's infantry were reaching their first objectives; but after that the Allied battle plan started going awry. Thanks to Rommel's Devil's Gardens, gapping the minefields was slow, highly dangerous work, and it was not until 0200 on 24 October 1942 that the first of Lumsden's 500-odd tanks started moving slowly forward through the lanes in single file. Now a further delay set in, because the tanks threw up so much dust as daylight dawned that visibility was reduced to zero. Movement slowed and stopped as the tanks jammed up while they groped their way forward.

Slightly to the south of Miteirya Ridge, Anderson recounts, du Toit's pioneering flail tanks went into action: "The enemy had no idea of what was coming across the minefields through the clouds and dust, exploding mines. The enemy redirected their fire at these strange objects, and some [flail] engine drivers, mainly Australians, were killed. But the tanks had helped to clear the way through the minefields, and the infantry, the tanks, the armoured cars and artillery were able to get through safely, thanks in part to a major of the armoured cars and a little drawing on a Springbok cigarette box."

The other version of the story has it that the Scorpions worked reasonably well but did not perform up to expectations – the flail system tended to break down, and so much dust was generated that air filters became clogged and caused engine break-downs or over-heating, so that most of the mine-clearing still had to be done manually. But this version confirms the alarm and despondency the noisy, dust-cloaked and generally awesome flail tanks caused among the Axis troops, so much so that several infantry units reportedly surrendered without firing a shot.

Meanwhile Horrocks had also run into trouble in the south. The Jebel Kalakh minefields were unexpectedly densely sown, so that gapping them took considerably longer than had been planned for, and the attackers came under heavy fire from the defenders, Italian and German paratroopers and a composite group. By dawn on 24 October 1942 the lanes were still incomplete, so that 22 and 4 Light Armoured brigades could not be unleashed, while 50 Infantry Division's gains further north had been limited by strong resistance from the Pavia and Brescia divisions.

Dawn on 24 October 1942 brought a panzer attack on 51 Highland Division, which it repulsed, and new orders from Montgomery. The northern lane corridor must be completed; 2 New Zealand Division must advance south from Miteirya Ridge with 10 Armoured Division in support; 9 Australian Division must develop a "crumbling" operation for that night; and in the south 7 Armoured Division should carry on trying to advance through the minefields.

The last of Pienaar's unit objectives on the Oxalic Line was overrun by the Cape Town Highlanders at 8am on 24 October 1942, by which time the armoured cars were pushing forward. They achieved little, however, because of the minefields and the heavy enemy artillery and anti-tank fire they attracted, and during the next two days they suffered significant losses.

No. 2 Squadron alone lost three cars to mines, with one man (Lieutenant P Hugo) killed and many others suffering greater or lesser wounds. Since there was no really useful role for them, the 3 South African Armoured Car Regiment cars were ordered back and put under command of XXX Corps in anticipation of the break-out from El Alamein.

At this stage the Axis forces suffered a serious and completely unforeseeable loss. General Stumme had been informed that British penetration was most likely containable, but when he went forward on a personal reconnaissance he came under fire and suffered a fatal heart attack. Major-General Wilhelm Ritter von Thoma, commander of the Deutsches Afrikakorps, temporarily took over.

By now Rommel was on his way back, having been recalled on the orders of Adolf Hitler himself, but he was returning via Rome, where he was to ask the Italian high command for more fuel and ammunition for what would now be known as the German-Italian Panzer Army, and would not reach his headquarters until that night.

The rest of the day passed without any noticeable action. The British armour was still held up along the Oxalic Line, although the Allied artillery and the Desert Air Force were mercilessly pounding the Axis positions. Then at dusk the first armoured battle took place. Tanks of 15 Panzer Division and the Littorio Division appeared out of the sun from a large depression the Allies had nicknamed 'the Kidney' and fought a short but fierce action with elements of 1 Armoured Division. By the time night fell more than half the tanks involved – over 100 – had been knocked out with no significant gains made by either side.

That night 2 New Zealand Division and 10 Armoured Division set off on their thrust southward from Miteirya Ridge. It failed, as did two other attacks, and for the next five days desperate fighting took place, with successes and failures on both sides.

The Battle of El Alamein has been told so many times that it does not need yet another account, so let it suffice to say that by 30 October, Montgomery was clearly winning the struggle. For Rommel the final straw was the loss on 1 November 1942 of two supply ships which were sunk by Allied aircraft northwest of Tobruk.

Apart from his losses in men, guns and tanks, Rommel's fuel state was now so critical that he was more and more dependent on what could be flown in from Crete, an uncertain source because Allied aircraft were carrying out one bombing raid after another on the airfields there, and the Desert Air Force was intercepting as many transport aircraft as it could (ironically, large amounts of fuel arrived at Benghazi after the German forces had started to retreat, but little of it reached the front).

Like any good commander, Rommel did not shrink from facing the facts and planning his way around his problems. On 2 November 1942 he signalled Hitler that the German-Italian Panzer Army was "so exhausted after its 10 days of battle that it [is] not capable of offering any effective opposition to the enemy's next break-through attempt …" The reply was a typical combination of rhetoric, ignorance of the situation on the ground and utter disregard for the lives of his soldiers:

It is with trusting confidence in your leadership and the courage of the German-Italian troops under your command that the German people and I are following the heroic struggle in Egypt. In the situation which you find yourself there can be no other thought but to stand fast, yield not a yard of ground and throw every gun and every man into the battle.
Considerable air force reinforcements are being sent to Commander-in-Chief South. The Duce and the Commando Supremo are also making the utmost efforts to send you the means to continue the fight. Your enemy, despite his superiority, must also be at the end of his strength. It would not be the first time in history that a strong will has triumphed over the bigger battalions. As to your troops, you can show them no other road than that to victory or death.
Adolf Hitler

The General Officer Commanding Deutsches Afrikakorps, General von Thoma, bluntly described Hitler's order as "madness". Rommel felt the same way. The Australian historian Barton Maughan quotes Rommel as saying that in his opinion the order "demanded the impossible … We were completely stunned, and for the first time in the African campaign I did not know what to do. A kind of apathy took hold of us."

But an order was an order. Rommel ordered all existing positions to be held "on instructions from the highest authority", although as a precaution he ordered the Deutsches Afrikakorps to withdraw to a position about 10km to the west during the night of 3/4 November 1942. Then he signalled Hitler to confirm that he would stand fast.

Breakout, victory and pursuit

On 31 October 1942 Colonel Newton-King, now second-in-command of 22 Armoured Brigade, had visited 4/6 South African Armoured Car Regiment and told Reeves-Moore that he would soon be undertaking the task for which he had been waiting all his life, and it was no more than the truth. Up to this stage of the battle there had been little gainful employment for the two South African armoured car regiments, but that would change dramatically in the next few days.

According to the 4/6 South African Armoured Car Regiment war diary, Reeves-Moore heard what his unit's task would be from the lips of none other than Montgomery himself:

> 1st November 1942: Our armour has inflicted heavy losses on enemy armour but the German has dug himself in – his dug-in tanks are formidable and he holds on desperately – refusing to commit his main armour to battle. Our line 'Oxalic' [first objective] is being firmly held but 'Skinflint' is not yet consolidated and a condition of 'stalemate' is threatening. Our tank losses have been heavy and it is proved beyond all doubt that tanks advancing against strongly held anti-tank positions means only the loss of those tanks.
>
> The position in a nutshell is that both sides are snookered and at a standstill – we cannot further our advance and the enemy refuses to come out and meet us. We are superior and he knows it. In the north the Australians are fighting like hell – nightly they gain ground and inflict terrific losses, but their line curves dangerously eastward.
>
> In the south we have gained little success. Something must be done to gain the initiative and press home our gains. At 1400 hours our CO is summoned to a conference with the Army Commander and meets General Lumsden and the CO of the Royals. The Army Commander [General Montgomery] is in good spirits but objects to this threat of stalemate.
>
> He says: "If our armour could break through it would be the end of the German – his losses have been terrific and he cannot face us in the open – how are we going to effect this break-through?
>
> "I'll tell you. The armoured cars will do it – they will penetrate and immediately operate behind the Germans. They will destroy every vehicle and every German they meet and the Germans will be reporting English armour [has] broken through – we will have regained the initiative and before the week is out the remnants of his army will be in full retreat with us helping him on.
>
> "On the night of the 2nd/3rd the Australians are attacking to press their line further west – our main attack will be directed on Aqqaqir – the 4th South African will move under cover of our artillery and will subsequently penetrate between 15 Panzer and 90th Light – heading for [the] area south of Daba. [The] Royals will move from the bridge-head south, southwest.
>
> "The break-through must be made before dawn – it will be the turning-point of the campaign."

"At the corps tactical headquarters later that day," Harry Klein writes, "Lumsden asked Reeves-Moore if he thought the task was reasonable and fair, to which Reeves-Moore gave an unprintable retort which was, however, "to the effect that he thought the job could be done. General Lumsden heartily appreciated the forthright reply and added his own unprintable appreciation of what General Montgomery had told him would happen if his armour did not get going".

The 4/6 South African Armoured Car Regiment war diary continues:

Marmon Herrington Mk 2 in the streets of Benghazi.

Marmon Herrington Mk3s in North Africa.

Our CO completed his recce of the area late in the afternoon and returned to his headquarters. 2nd November: Regt now under 10 Corps direct. Operation order is for two Squadrons to carry out the task – one Squadron to be held in reserve and Regimental Headquarters to remain with Corps Tac headquarters. The two Squadrons to move along Diamond track and be in position at our FDLs at 0200 hours on 3rd November.

Our CO confers with 1 Armoured Division Commander and returning to headquarters calls his Order Group. No alterations to enemy dispositions is known. A and C Squadrons were allotted to the task. B remaining in reserve. At zero hour the attack is pressed forward under cover of intense artillery barrage.

A Squadron following immediately in rear of [the] infantry and [was] followed closely by C Squadron will break away immediately barrage lifts and will move so as to pierce enemy line between 15th Panzer and 90th Light – a distance of two miles in the believed dispositions.

The attack goes favourably – a steady advance is maintained and the noise is deafening – the sky is brightly lit up by continuous gun flashes, ground flares go up everywhere and it sounds as if everything in the desert has concentrated in this area. Hell let loose. The infantry are held up, then forced slightly back. Some of our armour comes up to assist and slight progress is made – but only slight. It is getting late and dawn is not far off and we must break through.

A Squadron is ordered to move northwest and then west – C Squadron to follow closely. Their progress is good for three-quarters of a mile when they come under very heavy gun fire from 90th Light area. They move slightly SW and run head on into 15th Panzer who have moved NE toward 90th Light, while 21st Panzer have moved north to occupy 15th Panzer area.

Both Squadrons are subjected to intense fire from three sides. From Aqqaqir in the south, 90th Light in the north and 15th Panzer in the west. Our infantry are held up and dawn is breaking. The Squadrons are forced back and are subsequently ordered back. The breakthrough has been impossible and although the attack [by the New Zealanders] has been pressed home on the south slopes of Aqqaqir, the high ground in the north remains denied to us.

Fighting continues without slackening throughout the day and we retain the ground won. The CO moves his Regiment south to Square track, recces forward area and orders C and B Squadrons to stand by for second attempt, two and a half miles south of first area.

A Squadron particularly had fought well and done considerable damage. Our losses totalled three armoured cars and one ammunition truck. Trooper E. W. Brown was killed and Sergeant [D. W.] Denman and Trooper Rimmer wounded. Corps Commander sent a message to our CO during the day. "Hard luck but you'll do it yet."

On the night of 3/4 November 1942, 4/6 South African Armoured Car Regiment tried again, but once more failed to break through. Captain Girdler-Brown, who was in the lead with C Squadron, ran into an enemy minefield which was not only unmarked but covered by artillery and machine-gun fire. In the action that followed two cars fell into gun-pits and

Girdler-Brown's was blown up by a mine, leaving him so severely concussed that B Squadron took over the lead, although it was near dawn by now. But this attempt also failed and cost two more cars and a lorry.

The 4/6 South African Armoured Car Regiment men were deeply disappointed by this second failure, but not at all disheartened, and that night tried again, with Reeves-Moore personally leading A and B squadrons. By 0300 they were about 6km from their jumping-off place at Tell el Aqqaqir – a line of stone cairns – and by 0400 were ready to advance: "… the two Squadrons moved forward under the heaviest barrage we had yet experienced. Progress was good. A Squadron led the way as was instructed and at 0540 A was passing through a very heavy concentration of enemy vehicles – personnel 'standing to' and obviously taking our cars to be friendly. Progress continued and moderate quietness prevailed until 0630 hours. Both Squadrons were now in the open desert and well behind the enemy infantry and forward gun positions.

In Reeves-Moore's words, quoted by Jon Latimer is his *Alamein*, the South African armoured cars ...

the eager children of any mechanized pursuit ... scampered at dawn into the open desert beyond the mines and trenches and guns, to make their exuberant mischief amid the disintegrating enemy.

A [Squadron] reported 20 Mark II tanks who did not seem sure of our identification; we circumvented them. From then on reports started coming in of our captures and destructions, including two 88mm guns as a start.

At 1028 hours Regimental Headquarters moved through the gap with the British light armour. At 1053 hours A [Squadron] reported a bag of six trucks, one Breda [portée], two 150mm guns and two 105mm guns and 130 personnel. At 1100 hours B [Squadron] reported their bag to be five trucks, one staff car, one 150mm gun, one 105mm gun and 100 prisoners.

In the afternoon the Squadrons were ordered well west to operate in the area south of Sidi Haneish.

Montgomery's long-awaited breakthrough had been made, with Reeves-Moore and his fellow South Africans as the spearhead. If there had been any doubt about the outcome of the battle, it had now finally been removed.

By the afternoon of 4 November 1942, Rommel faced the naked facts of his predicament. Volume III of the official British publication *The Mediterranean and Middle East* quotes him: "The picture in the early afternoon of the 4th was as follows: powerful enemy armoured forces … had burst a 12-mile hole in our front, through which strong bodies of tanks were moving to the west. As a result of this, our forces in the north were threatened with encirclement by enemy formations 20 times their number in tanks …

"There were no reserves, as every available man and gun had been put into the line. So now it had come, the thing we had done everything in our power to avoid – our front broken and the fully motorized enemy streaming into our rear."

Rommel signalled Hitler, asking for permission to fall back on Fuka. There was no response and meanwhile the bad news continued to stream in. The Allies were advancing, the Ariete and Trento divisions signalled that they had been surrounded and von Thoma and members of his staff were captured by British armoured cars.

At 1730 Rommel knew he could wait no longer if the Axis forces were to live to fight another day. "Superior orders could no longer count," as he later put it. "We had to save what there was to be saved." He ordered a general retreat to Fuka, a risky – not to say personally life-threatening – decision, given the dire consequences that normally followed disobedience of a direct Führer order.

The retreat left tens of thousands of Italian soldiers to their fate – not by Rommel's choice, as is commonly believed, but because Hitler's and Mussolini's demands that he stand and

Lieutenant-Colonel Reeves Moore, Imperial Light Horse, Officer Commanding 4th Armoured Car Regiment.

South African troops in a Marmon Herron Mk 2 and Mk3 in Benghazi, Libya.

fight had forced him to deploy his Italian formations, most of which did not have their own transport, so far forward that withdrawing them at the last minute was impossible.

The Italians fought a drawn-out but hopeless rearguard action, frequently with great gallantry. The Ariete Armoured Division fought until it was destroyed, and the renowned Folgore Parachute Division to its last round. The Bologna Division tried to fight its way out on foot and surrendered only when its men were on the point of death from thirst; the commanding officer reportedly said that "we have ceased firing not because we haven't the desire but because we have spent every round" and in a last act of defiance his soldiers did not raise their hands in the traditional gesture of surrender.

That same afternoon the New Zealanders and armoured divisions started pouring through the gap after the retreating German forces: the Gazala Gallop had resumed, only now it was running in the opposite direction, and 4/6 South African Armoured Car Regiment was leading the pack. In the next few days the South African and British armoured cars tirelessly harried the retreating Germans and Italians, taking thousands of prisoners, capturing great numbers of guns and equipment and seizing large quantities of Rommel's painfully accumulated supplies.

3 South African Armoured Car Regiment also had its full share of making "exuberant mischief". As soon as the Tell el Aqqaqir gap had been opened it was ordered to break through to the south and then attack the rear and flanks of the Italians holding that sector of the Axis line.

Before first light on 4 November 1942 No. 1 Squadron moved through the New Zealand gap and soon captured some Italian prisoners, after which it captured a German gun position, destroying two 37mm anti-tank guns and taking 17 prisoners. It was then temporarily held up by other anti-tank guns, but on moving farther south made a truly impressive bag – all that remained of the Brescia Division, a total of 1,700 prisoners.

No. 2 Squadron, with No. 3 Squadron in support, attacked the remnants of the Trento Division and made an even more impressive haul: 77 officers, 1,324 other ranks, six 105mm guns, seven captured 25-pdrs, 25 20mm guns, 58 47mm guns and 117 machine guns. Further patrols in the south and west brought in a number of small parties of German and Italian stragglers.

While the armoured cars were rolling off on their great pursuit, 1 South African Division was busy with a piecemeal relief in the line of 51 Highland Division. The last of its units to move into its new positions was the Cape Town Highlanders, amid a major artillery bombardment which was supporting an attack by 5 Indian Brigade.

But when the Cape Town Highlanders and its fellow units greeted the daylight on 4 November it was to an unaccustomed sound … silence. For the first time in more than a week the air was not driven by the deep-throated bellowing of the artillery; the only sound that broke the unaccustomed silence was the distant rumbling of Allied vehicles advancing after the retreating enemy.

Meanwhile 4/6 South African Armoured Car Regiment was in full cry in the wake of the retreating Axis forces, capturing great numbers of Italian troops who had been marooned in their positions without transport. The war diary entry for 5 November 1942 gives a good indication of the general exultant spirit: "We are free of the entrenched positions and moving west through the open desert. We welcome this and our course is along the exact line of our withdrawal last June. Our troops have developed a great 'superiority complex' and they engage anything in their path – with very good effect."

While 4/6 South African Armoured Car Regiment and its fellow armoured car units enjoyed themselves on the ground, the Royal Air Force and South African Air Force, cooperating closely with the British armour, mounted constant air attacks on the Germans to prevent them from regrouping and making a stand.

The armoured cars covered ground at a phenomenal pace; Reeves-Moore with his tactical headquarters, hot on the heels of his squadrons, was sometimes 45km ahead of his own regimental headquarters. By the afternoon of 6 November 1942, less than three days after the breakout, A and C squadrons were already creating mayhem around Charing Cross (officially Mohalafa), southwest of Mersa Matruh and about 165km from El Alamein.

Here 4/6 South African Armoured Car Regiment suffered its first serious losses of the pursuit when Corporal W. P. Hittos and Trooper A. D. Mann were killed and two troopers, Levy and Smith, were wounded in a clash with the German rearguard; in the same action Sergeant G. J. Lemon was taken prisoner, but escaped and was soon back with the squadron.

The following day A and C squadrons were sent even farther west, about 65km to Fort Capuzzo on the other side of the Wire, while B Squadron was ordered to head southwest and cut the track to the distant Siwa Oasis, on the edge of the Libyan Sand Sea.

By this stage, according to the war diary, 4/6 South African Armoured Car Regiment's total catch came to 4,500 prisoners, including two generals, one colonel and two lieutenant-colonels, with staff officers of the Italian Mobile Corps, artillery pieces of various calibres and some 300 vehicles either captured or destroyed: "The two Generals, Edoar Nebbia and Arrigo Orilla, are furious at being captured by one armoured car (Lieutenant [R. L.] Downie) and decided to be annoyed with each other – in their resplendent uniforms they offer a healthy diversion."

There was nothing random or helter-skelter about the pursuit. Montgomery planned a hammer-and-anvil action involving all three of his armoured divisions. 10 Armoured Division and 2 New Zealand Division would head up the coast road toward Mersa Matruh. 7 Armoured Division and 1 Armoured Division, with the armoured cars of the Royal Dragoons, 11th Hussars and 4/6 South African Armoured Car Regiment probing well forward, would attack from the southern flank.

1 Armoured Division, at that time west of El Dada, was ordered to take a wide detour through the desert to Bir el Khalda, about 60km south-southeast of Mersa Matruh, then turn up toward the coast and cut the coastal road at the port itself. At the same time 7 Armoured Division would advance across-country to intercept the coastal road at Sidi Haneish, about 35km east-southeast of Mersa Matruh.

Unfortunately neither of the flanking attacks succeeded. At nightfall on 5 November 1942, 7 Armoured Division was still 32km from Sidi Haneish, and on the morning of 6 November ran into the remains of 21 Panzer Division and a reconnaissance group about 24km southwest

South African troops in a Marmon Herrington Mk 3 pass Sikh troops.

of its objective. This led to a running battle which lasted all day and left the Germans minus 16 tanks and a large number of guns, although they managed to avoid encirclement and escaped to Mersa Matruh in the evening.

1 Armoured Division tried to speed up its rate of advance by marching through the night of 5/6 November 1942, lost contact with its support vehicles in the darkness and at dawn on 6 November was out of fuel while still 26km from Bir el Khalda. Late that morning enough of the division's B Echelon vehicles had caught up with it and it could partly refuel two of its tank regiments so that the dash to Mersa Matruh could be resumed, but 48km southwest of the port they ran dry again.

A fuel convoy had meanwhile left El Alamein on the evening of 5 November 1942 to meet up with 1 Armoured Division's echelon vehicles, but it made heavy going of the west-bound tracks, which had been seriously chewed up by this time, and now the weather turned bad as well. At midday on 6 November heavy rain started to fall and the fuel convoy bogged down 64km from its rendezvous. The overall consequence was that both divisions had to stay put throughout 7 November.

In the meantime 10 Armoured Division, with plenty of fuel and the benefit of the relatively good coastal road, kept up its advance to Mersa Matruh; 2 New Zealand Division was heading for Sidi Haneish and 8 Armoured Brigade had moved westward and occupied the landing fields at Fuka and the escarpment.

The general confusion came to Rommel's aid at this stage, because the forward elements of the Eighth Army were now so spread out that Allied aircraft found it difficult to identify free-fire areas which were definitely occupied by the enemy (on the other hand, American heavy bombers compounded Rommel's logistic problems by raiding Tobruk, where they sank the supply ship *Etopia*, and later also attacked Benghazi, where they sank another ship and set a tanker on fire).

The overall consequence, however, was that the last of Rommel's rearguards got clean away from Mersa Matruh during the night of 7/8 November 1942 and headed for Sidi Barrani, 130km further to the west, where he intended to fight a delaying action while his main body wound its way up to the escarpment through the narrow passes above Halfaya and Sallum.

Not quite all of Montgomery's mobile force had bogged down, however. 4/6 South African Armoured Car Regiment – due, perhaps, to its veterans' experience with the Biblical-scale downpours of Abyssinia – kept up its momentum in spite of the rain and mud, so that by 8 November 1942, C Squadron was on the way to Sallum, having bypassed Fort Capuzzo. A and C squadrons were then ordered to El Adem and Tobruk. Not surprisingly, they were now feeling the effects of their headlong rush westward: "Supplies are now becoming a problem," according to the war diary. "We have not been replenished since the afternoon of the 3rd and we have covered much ground. We can reach Tobruk but no farther, and Headquarters Squadron will have to bring up supplies to our objective. Our bag has increased to 5,000 prisoners, 150 guns and 350 enemy vehicles accounted for. The Regiment moves throughout the day and is not seriously troubled from the air."

That this freedom from air attack was not to be taken for granted became clear two days later, on 10 November 1942, when the squadrons destroyed one Axis aircraft on the ground at Sidi Azeiz and put another out of action, only to be attacked by enemy aeroplanes which knocked out six of A Squadron's cars and two of C Squadron's, although without loss of life.

Reeves-Moore's men took this setback in their stride and carried on, although, according to the war diary, "it continues to rain heavily and the area of the coastal road is one continuous bog. Our armour is 'sitting' because of the state of the ground and lack of supplies."

Rommel's delaying action at Sidi Barrani was a short one. By the evening of 10 November 1942, the New Zealanders and 4 Light Armoured Brigade had reached the foot of the Halfaya Pass, while 7 Armoured Division had got going again and was swinging around from the south to capture Fort Capuzzo and Sidi Azeiz. On the morning of 11 November, 5 New Zealand Infantry Brigade charged up the pass, capturing 600 Italians.

By the evening of the 11th, the Egyptian border area was clear of an enemy presence, but all prospects of catching Rommel had gone because the main body of the pursuers west of Bardia had now well and truly outrun its supplylines. Reluctantly Montgomery ordered that, until a proper logistic flow to the larger formations was established, the pursuit must be confined to armoured cars and artillery.

4/6 South African Armoured Car Regiment was now back in the heart of the area in which so much Allied blood had been spilt only a few months earlier. On 11 November 1942, C Squadron chanced on an estimated 500 enemy transport vehicles at Bir el Gubi, moving west from Sidi Rezegh; the armoured cars gave chase, but the lorries outpaced them and managed to reach the protection of the Axis guns still at El Adem.

At 1800 that day 4/6 South African Armoured Car Regiment came under command of 4 Light Armoured Brigade, which was heading for El Adem, and at long last was replenished by its Headquarters Squadron, while A Squadron was brought up to its vehicle strength again with three troops of former 6 South African Armoured Car Regiment members which had been sent up from XXX Corps headquarters.

Reinforced and replenished, 4 Light Armoured Brigade and 4/6 South African Armoured Car Regiment dealt with a perfunctory enemy stand at El Adem, then went on to Tobruk. They arrived that evening, the first South Africans to return after the surrender of 2 South African Division, captured 12 Germans and freed a large number of black South African soldiers whom the Italians had kept there as port labourers after the surrender.

Much hard fighting still lay ahead before the Germans finally surrendered at Cape Bon in Tunisia on 12 May 1943, but the back of their effort in North Africa had been well and truly broken at El Alamein, the first great offensive against the Germans to be won since the outbreak of war. Montgomery had scored a devastating victory. Four German and eight Italian divisions had ceased to exist as fighting formations, and he had taken 30,000 prisoners, including nine generals. The Axis adventure in North Africa was over.

It had not come cheap for either side. The Allies suffered a total of about 13,500 dead, wounded, captured and missing. The Germans and Italians had lost 37,000 men – more than 30 per cent of their total strength – and by the end of it Rommel's formerly all-conquering German-Italian Panzer Army consisted of no more than about 5,000 troops, 20 tanks, 50 field artillery pieces and 20 anti-tank guns.

If the Eighth Army's main body had been able to follow up more swiftly and effectively to cut Rommel off at Fuka and later at Mersa Matruh, the desert war might well have come to

Allied parade in Cairo, two Marmon Herrington Mk 3s.   Allied parade in Cairo, a SA MaHe Mk3 can be seen.

an effective end in Libya instead of dragging on for another five months. Still, a great victory had been scored. On 10 November 1942, while the fighting west of the Wire still sputtered on, Churchill summed it up with one of his most memorable sayings: "This is not the end, it is not even the beginning of the end. But it is, perhaps, the end of the beginning."

And so it was. Every battle, campaign and war has a turning-point. In the early part of 1942 the forces of the German-Italian-Japanese Axis had appeared to be winning everywhere; by the end of the year the tide had started to flow in the opposite direction – in the arid wastes of the Western Desert, on the frozen steppes of Russia and on the wide expanses of the Pacific Ocean, where the Japanese Navy had been broken by the Americans.

As another of Churchill's memorable remarks had it: "It may almost be said: 'Before Alamein we never had a victory. After Alamein we never had a defeat.'"

4/6 South African Armoured Car Regiment did not spend much time at Tobruk. Montgomery wanted to capture Benghazi as soon as possible, to trap the garrison and prevent the port installations from being destroyed, and 4 Light Armoured Brigade set off westward along the coast road with the armoured cars screening ahead.

At the same time their old comrades of Operation Crusader days, the 11th Hussars and Royal Dragoons, leading a tank regiment from 7 Armoured Division, were also on the way to Benghazi, heading directly across the desert by way of Msus and Antelat. Once again, however, heavy rain foiled Montgomery by delaying the Allied mobile force's advance, giving Rommel time to withdraw from Benghazi in good order.

When they reached Tmimi, about 75km west of Tobruk, it appeared to 4/6 South African Armoured Car Regiment that "we ... have outrun the Army, and we are out of touch with rear formations ... the 4th Light Armoured Brigade can move no farther. Major-General Harding, commanding the 7th Armoured Division, meets our CO and greets him with 'the old firm again, they can't do without us', and he congratulates the regiment on its 'magnificent effort'. We are tired and weary, but the hunting is good and we are anxious to get going, but the 4th Light cannot move for another day."

On 17 November 1942 4/6 Reeves-Moore was ordered to find the best route to Benghazi. C Squadron took the road to Giovanni Berta, A Squadron went through Martuba and Barce, and B Squadron battled down the track to El Mekili, El Charraba and El Abiar. But once again their old friends of the 11th Hussars got there first.

There would be no further neck-and-neck races, however, because 1 South African Division's role in the desert war was over. At home the first preparations for the next phase the war, the campaign in Italy, had started. 1 South African Division would soon be sailing for home, and so 4/6 South African Armoured Car Regiment was recalled. Reeves-Moore's men said goodbye to their British comrades and headed eastward. A few days later 3 South African Armoured Car Regiment followed suit – it had been withdrawn for ten days' rest on 12 November 1942, then sent forward again to join XXX Corps in the advance to Benghazi, but while it was crossing the Wire on the 29th it, too, was recalled to rejoin 1 South African Division.

"Thus finished the desert adventures of the South African armoured car regiments," Klein writes, "with the 4th/6th farthest west of all South African fighting ground forces in pursuit of Rommel's defeated legions. Throughout the long campaign, with its vicissitudes of triumph and disaster, until victory was ultimately gained, the South African armoured car units had earned the admiration and affection of all formations with whom they served.

"With their motley collection of armoured cars, ranging from Mark II and IIIA Marmon-Herringtons to Daimlers and Humbers, some with turrets removed and 20, 37 and 47mm captured enemy guns mounted, bedecked with crews' bags, cooking utensils and any other equipment – own or enemy – to make the life of a trooper more comfortable, the regiments had been a familiar and welcome sight in the desert. Through 'Crusader', the Gazala retreat, and back west again after victory at El Alamein, the South African armoured cars had always been in the thick of the battle."

Before 1 South African Division left the Middle East. General Pienaar reviewed 3 South African Armoured Car Regiment and called it "this magnificent regiment'" It was, Klein writes, "a fitting tribute to a great regiment from one whom the 3rd Recce had always held in the highest esteem and under whom they had always considered it a privilege to serve."

But within months both Pienaar and the armoured car regiments were dead at their moment of greatest renown – Pienaar in a flying accident at Lake Kisumu on 19 December 1942, and the Tank Corps by administrative fiat early in 1943.

PART FOUR

THE MADAGASCAR INVASION

The invasion of Madagascar

While Montgomery and Rommel were trading mighty blows at El Alamein, 7 South African Brigade Group and 1 Armoured Car Commando were heavily involved in a small but important campaign which, through no fault of its own, is now little more than a footnote to the country's Second World War annals: the invasion and conquest of Madagascar between June and December of 1942.

To understand why the invasion of Madagascar was undertaken it is necessary to remember what the overall war situation was in the first half of 1942. In the West, Hitler and Mussolini between them controlled most of Europe and part of the Balkans, with the Russians still trying to hold back the German army. Britain itself was in deadly danger. In the Middle East, the Axis forces threatened the Suez Canal and much else besides. In the Far East, the Japanese were conquering one territory after another, including the Philippines; Singapore, 'the Gibraltar of the East' had fallen after an uninspiring defence.

Oswald Pirow's 1933-vintage vision of an amphibious landing (by the Japanese in this case) had become a possibility, and Vichy-ruled Madagascar would be the obvious jumping-off place. Even if they merely occupied Madagascar and did not attempt an amphibious invasion, the Japanese would still constitute a deadly threat and, at the very least, require the large-scale deployment of scarce combat troops and resources inside South Africa.

As the months marched on toward the middle of the year the threat subsided somewhat. The Japanese had suffered a catastrophic defeat at the Battle of Midway and a lesser one in the Battle of the Coral Sea which had permanently crippled (although not destroyed) their navy, the Germans had been stalled at Stalingrad and there were no signs that Madagascar was being prepared for offensive action.

On the other hand, the governor-general of the huge island, Monsieur Gilbert Annet, was an open Vichy supporter. This meant that in principle Madagascar could provide a safe haven for German and possibly Japanese submarines at the mid-point of the sea route to the Middle and Far East, which was vital to the Allied war effort.

With the effective destruction of the Italian empire in East Africa now almost complete, the British could devote some attention to Madagascar, and early in May 1942 three brigades and a commando raiding unit attacked the naval base at Diego Suarez in the extreme north, supported by the guns of a substantial naval task force that included the battleship HMS *Ramillies*, two aircraft carriers and a host of smaller vessels and troopships. Within days they had seized a substantial foothold around Diego Suarez but at a cost of seven tanks, victims of French artillery.

The invasion, it was somewhat naïvely hoped, would persuade Monsieur Annet and his fellow Vichy supporters that a more cooperative attitude toward the Allied cause would be to the benefit of all. Instead it actually strengthened the pro-Vichy attitude on Madagascar. That left only one other option: the conquest of the entire island. General Smuts strongly supported the idea, emphasizing the importance of occupying the ports of Majunga on the west coast and Tamatave in the east, and offered a complete brigade group and an armoured car unit for the venture.

The invasion force was under the ultimate authority of Lieutenant-General Sir William Platt, now General Officer Commanding East Africa Command, and led in the field by Major-General C. E. T. Smallwood. It consisted of 29 British Independent Brigade (which had taken part in the original invasion) and 22 East African Brigade (Brigadier W. A. Dimouline), with support provided by the South African Air Force and the Royal Navy's surface ships and Fleet Air Arm. The South African contribution was 7 South African Brigade Group under Brigadier G. T. Senescall, the former Officer Commanding Duke of Edinburgh's Own Rifles, and 1 Armoured Car Commando, South African Tank Corps.

It was an adequate force for the task. Madagascar was not strongly garrisoned: the Vichy French had about 7,000 men, including 2,000 Senegalese, with an estimated 20 field artillery pieces and, it was suspected, seven combat aircraft. At least a third of the garrison was reportedly made up of unreliable locally enlisted reservists of distinctly less than top quality. On the other hand, the French had the advantage of short interior lines of communication, and the invaders would have to deal with difficult terrain, since Madagascar was largely undeveloped and had few roads but a plentiful supply of mountains, rivers and thick bush.

For 1 Armoured Car Commando the invasion got off to a bad start when it arrived at Durban to board the troopship *Morton Bay*. There it was bitterly disappointed to find that due to some miscalculation by the staff there was only enough space on board for one squadron. A Squadron under Major F. W. G. Vos eventually was selected for the invasion – seven officers, a squadron sergeant-major and 103 other ranks, equipped with 20 South African Mark III armoured cars, two Mark IIs for the light aid detachments and the normal squadron B Echelon. The squadron was attached to 22 East African Brigade for the operation.

7 South African Brigade Group and the armoured cars sailed on 16 June 1942 and arrived at Diego Suarez on the 24th, "full of fight", according to the squadron war diary, and "confident that we were soon going to see action because the British forces had occupied only the northern part of the island, for only a month". Alas, it was not to be.

The French garrison made no attempt to recapture the Diego Suarez base or undertake other military action, and for the next few weeks Major Vos's men spent their time manning the defence line and patrolling all the way down to Biramanja, the southernmost British-held point. Between times they carried out tactical exercises with the King's African Rifles troops of 22 East African Brigade, striking up mutual bonds of friendship and confidence in each other and testing the effectiveness of their radio communications. The only angry shots were fired by No. 5 Troop under Lieutenant F. C. van N. Fourie, in an exchange with the Vichy forces across the river at Biramanja.

According to the squadron war diary:

This was the first experience we had of real active service conditions, and the trying 'teething period' passed off very satisfactorily. Although no one had the least inkling that we were to operate with the King's African Rifles at a future date, it was during this period that we rehearsed our part as Forward Body in all subsequent operations with the King's African Rifles ...

R/Toc was used at a range of about 23 miles on ordinary Western Electric crystal-controlled sets – probably double the distance which had been worked previously in the Union. We had no wireless mechanics and no spares, but thanks to good manipulation by the operators our communication throughout was excellent.

Then on 17 August 1942 the squadron was told out of the blue that it was to sail to Mombasa with 29 Independent Brigade for large-scale manoeuvres on the mainland. By 20 August all the armoured cars and transport vehicles had been prepared for embarkation on the transport Ocean Viking. Next morning the Ocean Viking sailed for Mombasa, the personnel following along with 29 Brigade in two other ships. It was all rather mystifying and must have seemed to some a typical army 'greatcoats on – greatcoats off' exercise, but in fact the move was all part of General Platt's invasion plan.

Platt intended to have 29 Brigade carry out a surprise night-time landing at Majunga on the west coast on 10 September 1942, with gunfire and aerial support from a naval force which included an aircraft carrier and three cruisers. It would then occupy the town and harbour. As soon as an adequate beachhead had been established, a small raiding column from 22 East African Brigade, supported by Vos's armoured cars, would advance southeastward in the general direction of the capital of Tananarive to seize two bridges about 150km and 200km from Majunga. This detachment would then be followed by the rest of the brigade.

There would also be feint attacks on the island of Nossi Bé, about 330km north of Majunga, while columns provided by 7 South African Brigade Group would advance southward to Ambanja and Voemar from the Diego Suarez area. At Majunga 29 Brigade would wait until the East Africans were on the way to Tananarive, then sail round the southern point of Madagascar to land on the east coast at Tamatave. With Tamatave taken, the brigade would head for Tananarive, about 180km to the southwest of the port.

Platt went to great lengths to make sure of springing a surprise on the French. He held large-scale manoeuvres in Kenya and set up a whispering campaign to the effect that his force was bound for India. A Squadron did not take part but spent its time offloading and servicing its vehicles, waterproofing them for an amphibious landing, sampling the local delights and (being still entirely in the dark about Platt's plans) indulging in the ancient military pastime of swapping rumours – "the men were excited at the obvious preparations for a large-scale landing," Klein writes, "and all sorts of rumours circulated regarding their destination. One strong rumour predicted a landing behind Rommel's Afrikakorps, then at El Alamein."

By 28 August 1942 their preparation was done and the vehicles, together with the armoured car and vehicle drivers, were loaded on to the transport *Gascony*. The rest of the squadron enjoyed some shore leave and then on 5 September set sail in the *Empire Trooper* – a former German troopship which had been captured and pressed into Allied service – as part of a large convoy heading for Diego Suarez. Now at last, as the troopers sweltered in the almost unbearable heat below decks, Major Vos could tell them what their task was going to be.

In detail, 22 East African Brigade would be formed into three fighting columns, each made up of one battalion and the necessary support troops. As soon as Majunga had been taken, No. 1 Group would get to shore as quickly as possible and head for the bridges over the Kamoro and Betsiboka rivers, both of which were vital to the advance because the rivers were wide and the Betsiboka was said to be unfordable. It was also very likely that they had been prepared for demolition, and Platt was so concerned about this possibility that he had asked in vain for paratroops to be dropped on them.

The group would be preceded by an advance raiding column under Major G. MacY. Dawson of 1/1 King's African Rifles, consisting of B Company 1/1 King's African Rifles, 145 Light Anti-Aircraft Battery and a detachment of engineers; once on shore they would link up with Major Vos's armoured cars and rush ahead at all speed to capture and hold the bridges while the rest of the group's personnel and vehicles were ferried to shore and followed. It was not a task to be taken lightly – Vos's men were well aware of the fact that during the landing at Diego Suarez in May, seven out of the 12 British tanks present had been knocked out by the French artillery.

Two major potential flaws in the plan were that, although Vos and Dawson would obviously have to work very closely together, they would not actually meet until they reached land, since the King's African Rifles company was coming from Diego Suarez rather than Mombasa, and that getting A Squadron ashore might take longer than expected because the crews were on one ship and the cars on another (as it turned out, however, the main problem was neither of these, but culpably careless staff work).

There was nothing to be done about it at this late stage, however, and so on 9 September

Marmon Herrington Mk 3 named 'Jeneuro' during the Madagascar invasion.

A South African Marmon Herrington Mk 3 at a road-block on Madagascar.

the East Africans' ship linked up with the Mombasa convoy off Mayotte, easternmost of the Comoros archipelago, for the only full-scale amphibious invasion in which a South African unit participated during the Second World War.

For the first time the South Africans became aware of the scope of the operation: "At a point which we were told was about 90 miles from Majunga," according to the squadron war diary, "we had a most thrilling experience, for it was here that we linked up with the whole assault fleet, which must have totalled nearly 70 ships. There were battleships, an aircraft carrier, cruisers, a monitor, destroyers, sloops, minesweepers, and a complete variety of merchantmen and troopships. All this gave one a tremendous feeling of security, though it was only then that we realized that the impending invasion was far bigger than we had ever realized."

The convoy stole southward, and at 1130 stopped engines off Majunga. 29 Brigade went ashore, encountered only minimal resistance and by 0800 had occupied the port at a cost of just 20 casualties. Now Major Vos's A Squadron was scheduled to land and meet up with Dawson and his askari, who had been waiting since 0500. But at this stage the staff's faulty planning intervened once more. Landing the A Squadron vehicles took so long that it was 1030 before the first troop, No. 4, was ready to move off – and then only because Vos had taken matters into his own hands and arranged for an extra landing craft to speed up the process.

Given the necessity for speed, Vos and Dawson decided to send off No. 4 Troop, one King's African Rifles platoon and a detachment of engineers to take the bridges, with the other troops of the advance column and then the rest of the King's African Rifles following when the remaining armoured cars were ready to move.

Dawson's contingent had barely got going, however, when its vehicles ran into a stretch of thick sand and scrub about which they had not been told, and soon were bogged down so thoroughly that digging them out by hand was not an option. There they stayed until a bulldozer had been landed. By the time it had dragged the cars out it was noon and, as Klein says, "In this amateurish fashion the invasion of the interior began."

By 1230 most of A Squadron and the rest of the askari were finally on the road as well, although it was 1430 before the squadron's administrative vehicles and the last troop of armoured cars managed to leave the beach. "It is indeed astonishing," Klein writes, "that this vital aspect of the operation should have received so little attention in staff planning ... no wonder Lieutenant-General Platt showed his grave displeasure."

Travelling at top speed, Vos's party reached the Kamoro bridge at 1600. It had not been prepared for demolition, and after a few shots had been let off at the leading car (and a

Malagasy sentry killed by the return fire), the bridge was secured. The rest of the advance column under Major Dawson arrived a little later and overtook at full speed, but now that fatal delay at the beach came into play.

Slowed down by having to negotiate various roadblocks, darkness caught the group when it was still about 9km from the Betsiboka bridge. Since it would not be able to carry on without switching on the vehicle headlights and thereby give warning of its approach, Dawson and Vos halted for the night.

At first light next morning the group set off again, only to run into more roadblocks, so that it did not arrive at the Betsiboka suspension bridge until 0600. The bridge had been sabotaged, as General Platt had feared, but the French had botched the job by merely cutting the cables, so that the central span had fallen into the river without breaking or twisting. Now it lay no more than a metre or so under water, with a steep but viable 45° slope at either end.

From the demolition, and the hummocky, thickly bushed nature of the opposite bank, it was obvious that the French intended to oppose the crossing, so Vos deployed his armoured cars to give covering fire for an attack by the King's African Rifles troops. By now the French commanders had clearly realized that the sabotage had been bungled, because at 0730 a Potez-63 fighter-bomber – one of the few Vichy aircraft to be seen at any time during the invasion – made its appearance and dropped half a dozen bombs on the bridge. All of them missed, and the askaris got down to the business of crossing the Betsiboka.

There was no reaction from the French as the King's African Rifles platoon crossed over, but as soon as the askaris reached the opposite bank they came under machine-gun and rifle fire from well-concealed positions. The armoured cars' machine guns poured bullets over the water and "we witnessed for the first time the dash and skill of the Askaris at close quarters. The enemy, although well dug in and camouflaged, were no match for the King's African Rifles, and resistance speedily cracked". The respect was mutual, and in future engagements the askari depended on the cars' guns.

The capture of the Betsiboka bridgehead was almost bloodless for the Allies: Vichy losses were ten French and Senegalese killed, four wounded and 37 taken prisoner, while the King's African Rifles suffered only six wounded. As soon as the shooting stopped, Dawson's sappers began to work furiously on making the bridge passable, and at 0700 the first armoured car was across the river.

By next morning the rest of A Squadron had followed and Dawson's column was on the road again. By nightfall the group had scaled the mountains overlooking the village of Maevatanana, which they captured after a short clash on the morning of the 13th, and carried on to Andriba, the next objective.

There were more roadblocks now, and one of them – a 39m-long bridge, the decking of which had been removed and thrown into the dry riverbed below – held up the advance guard for more than three hours while the planking was laboriously retrieved and put back in place. The terrain was changing now as the road took them up steep inclines toward the island's vast and almost uninhabited central plateau, and all through the 14th the advance guard encountered one roadblock after another.

That evening Vos lost some of his cars when orders came from Manjunga to send back one troop, and he despatched Lieutenant S. B. Grimbeek's No. 1 Troop. Now, however, the contingent gained some more teeth when the rest of 1/1 King's African Rifles and a troop of Royal Artillery field pieces arrived. The Officer Commanding 1/1 King's African Rifles, a Lieutenant-Colonel MacNab, took over from Major Dawson as commander of what was now No. 1 Group, and by nightfall the little force was 3km south of Andriba after a day spent dismantling one stone wall after another which had been built across the road.

Vos's cars made themselves useful in several ways. Their primary role was, of course, scouting and screening, so at all times a troop was ahead of the vanguard, another one with the main body and another with the rearguard – strenuous duty for the under-strength squadron. The cars also provided forward observation posts for the field gunners and handled all radio communications, with constant contact between Vos and MacNab. It worked well; transmissions were clear (all messages being sent in Afrikaans as a security precaution) and the Western Electric sets' batteries lasted long past their official life.

On 16 September 1942 the McNab group smelt its first serious powder since the fight at the Betsiboka bridge when it reached the Mamokomita river, south of Andriba. The French had demolished the bridge and blocked the approaches with trees and stones, so the King's African Rifles went in on foot with Vos providing covering fire. After some hand-to-hand fighting the Vichy force was defeated, losing 52 men, while the King's African Rifles had one officer and four askari killed and another officer and eight other ranks wounded.

The column traversed the plateau, working its way through more roadblocks, until it had crossed the Madagascan watershed and begun descending into the Marakazo river valley on 18 September 1942. The view reminded some of the South Africans of the vista from Pietermaritzburg's Town Hill, but there was no spare time to spend on admiring Madagascar's natural beauty. They pressed on, and that evening were about 7½km north of the village of Ankazobe.

From Ankazobe the advance continued on now-familiar lines – demolished bridges, some resistance at river crossings and roadblock after roadblock ("the local Malagasies were extremely helpful to both sides," Klein notes. "The French used them to make the roadblocks and damage the bridges, but when the British vanguard arrived they were always smilingly prepared to assist in remedying their own handiwork.").

On 22 September 1942 the column arrived at Mahitsy, outside the capital of Tananarive, and dealt briskly with the opposition, with the armoured cars in the van; No. 2 Troop's leading car was hit by shell-fire and temporarily disabled, but without any casualties among the crew. The way to the capital was now open, and after a brief skirmish at a village called Alakamisi, 18km from Tananarive, the local district administrative chief arrived at 1100 with a white flag and the information that envoys from the capital were ready to discuss terms of surrender.

Brigadier Dimouline and General Platt's political adviser conferred with the envoys and reached agreement as to terms, and at 1630 Major Vos led the column into Tananarive while thousands of cheering local inhabitants waved Union Jacks. In the 13 days since A Squadron's departure from Majunga the armoured cars and their King's African Rifles comrades had covered 600 frequently arduous, sporadically dangerous and constantly insect-bitten kilometres.

The South Africans, to judge by the squadron war diary, enjoyed Tananarive with its strange architecture: although the shelves of its modern stores were empty, "the overflowing native market filled the stomachs, the French girls gladdened the eyes, and the Malgache rickshaw drivers rested the legs of the triumphant warriors".

But the respite was very short. Monsieur Annet had no intention of putting up a mere token resistance and had retreated several hundred kilometres to the south with the rest of his forces, so 24 September 1942 Vos's men were told to get back on the road and head south to deal with the remainder of the Vichy forces before the rains turned all the roads into mush. Hastily they serviced their vehicles and then set off in company with 1/6 King's African Rifles, which had now relieved Colonel MacNab's battalion.

A Squadron, already short-handed because of Grimbeek's absence in Majunga, was now stretched even thinner when it was decided to send D Company 1/6 King's African Rifles off to Tamatave on the east coast, supported by one troop of armoured cars. Vos designated No. 2 Troop for the Tamatave expedition, leaving him with only his squadron headquarters and two troops until Grimbeek returned from Majunga, which did not happen until the 30th.

1/6 King's African Rifles and the armoured cars set off at dawn on 25 September 1942 and were soon back into the routine of clearing numerous roadblocks and facing the occasional skirmish in between, the first coming at dusk on 26 September, when the column reached Behenjy and the askari dealt briskly with the opposition while Vos's cars gave covering fire. Heavy rain on the 27th made it even more difficult to detour around demolished bridges, but next morning the column entered Ambatolampy, liberated four shot-down South African Air Force aircrew and some British internees, then carried on into more wooded territory. The cars struggled through numerous roadblocks – an arduous business, to judge from the war diary:

> Apart from the usual stone walls across the road, we were faced with heavy tree trunks dug in deep across the road and filled in with further tree trunks; stones were also strewn haphazardly across the road and there were the usual felled blue gums. The removal of these obstructions, especially the trees, fell to the armoured car crews and was strenuous work, especially as many men were going down with malaria and had to be evacuated to Tananarive hospital.
>
> Most cars were operating with three men and some were reduced to only two. A hand-grenade jolting from a rack caused a serious accident in one car, injuring all the crew and Trooper Opperman lost an eye.

The tedious grind continued as the last days of September faded into October, but on the afternoon of 2 October 1942 the column arrived at Antsirabe, a pleasant place which had been a health resort in better times, and for a week Vos's men had nothing to do, apart from some patrolling. The ultimate objective now was Ihosey, about 240km further south, where Monsieur Annet was holed up.

On 9 October 1942 the advance on Ihosey started. By now the railway from Tamatave, where General Platt had established his headquarters, was back in working order except for one damaged bridge, which meant a shortened line of communication. 5 King's African Rifles, to which A Squadron was now attached, covered about 45km without encountering any opposition, but around 1500 the column came under fire when it ran into its first serious ambush of the campaign: while winding its way around some large bald hills, a concealed machine gun fired several bursts into the back of the King's African Rifles signals lorry, killing two askari and wounding eight.

No further resistance was encountered until the column stopped for the night at a damaged bridge just north of the town of Ilaka. Here there was an enemy presence, and that evening some rifle shots and machine-gun bursts were fired into the squadron's bivouac area from the hills, but the King's African Rifles sent out some patrols and cleared the area. Then at 0900 the column entered Ilaka; local inhabitants warned the column that the French were sitting astride the road on the hills to the south, but that afternoon they were overrun, several Vichy soldiers being killed and 30 taken prisoner after a brief bombardment by the artillery and some attention from the armoured cars' machine guns.

So far the fighting had been desultory at best and the casualties few, but it was a different matter that afternoon when the column approached Ambositra, where the French were known to be dug in slightly to the north. A few bursts of light machine-gun fire were heard by No. 2 Troop under a Lieutenant Meyer, which was leading, but the troop took no notice, because the intention was to reach the French positions that afternoon.

The troop reached the village of Tsaratsaotra and drove in, Meyer's car second in line. The leading car went through a bend in the road, near a copse of trees, and carried on into the village, but as Meyer approached the bend a French 65mm artillery piece concealed among the trees opened fire on him, scored a direct hit and kept on firing.

The result was instant carnage. Both Meyer and his driver were wounded, four askaris riding on the car were killed and an officer and several other askari wounded. Now two machine guns, deployed on either side of the artillery piece, also started firing. Meyer's car was hit by two more shells, while one of the King's African Rifles troop carriers following Meyer's troop was destroyed and another vehicle damaged. The askaris tumbled out to take cover in the rice fields on either side of the road.

Trooper F. B. Joubert, Meyer's radio operator, took his life in his hands to get Meyer out of the wrecked armoured car and then dragged the wounded King's African Rifles officer, Second Lieutenant W. H. Williamson, to safety. But Joubert was not finished. He went back through the enemy fire to fetch the car's first-aid box, then returned a third time to relay information about the attack to Vos, in the process of which another shell struck the car and wounded him in the hand (Joubert received an immediate award of the Distinguished Conduct Medal).

Then Meyer's third armoured car opened up on the French position with its machine gun, and a British sergeant from the King's African Rifles led some askaris in an attack which silenced the French, for which he was decorated with the Military Medal.

A few days later, on 19 October 1942, the armoured cars were involved in another short but stiff fight when the column came up against strong in-depth French positions in the hills south of Ambositra. Brigadier Dimouline formulated a daring pincer attack, which called for the armoured cars and a King's African Rifles battalion to advance down the road to the French positions, with another King's African Rifles company on either flank, while the enemy positions were being bombed and shelled.

Major Vos and his three troops moved out at 0300 on 19 October in such heavy mist and drizzle that the cars had to crawl along with one man from each crew walking next to his car to give directions to the driver. In spite of this laborious approach, the cars were in position at zero hour (0435) when the artillery started a 20-minute shoot.

At 0450 the squadron started forward with Vos in the leading car. Before long they reached a small roadblock, cleared it without difficulty and carried on. But scarcely ten minutes later, at 0500, they came to a much more difficult obstacle, a bridge blocked by a stone wall. Major Vos got out to examine the block and called for some men from each car's crew to help him to clear the way. Then, as they felt their way through the murk, they were assailed by heavy machine-gun fire. The troopers dove into the ditches on either side of the road, effectively pinned down because they could not spot the locations of the machine guns in the half-dark.

Vos broke the stalemate by taking some hair-raisingly dangerous action. Having shouted to his gunners to look out for the guns' muzzle flashes, he jumped up, ran a few metres and threw himself down again before the machine gunners could get a proper bearing on him. When the fire died down he did it again and again until he had had discovered the source of the fire, then made his way back to his car. From there he directed his gunners on to the target, and their Vickers guns silenced the French weapons (he was later decorated with the Military Cross).

The armoured cars engaged other machine-gun posts and gave covering fire as the infantry went in, and a few hours later the struggle for Ambositra was over. At 0830, stunned by the British bombardment and dispirited by Brigadier Dimouline's attack, the defenders raised a white flag. It had been a remarkable victory. The Allies had taken more than 700 prisoners, two 75mm artillery pieces and many mortars and machine guns … without suffering a single noteworthy casualty.

That afternoon Major-General Smallwood and members of his staff visited A Squadron at its bivouac south of Ivato to congratulate its members on their work during the attack, but time was still of the essence, and next day the column was back to the familiar grind of forcing their way through a series of roadblocks (which now consisted of large felled trees rather than stone walls), with nothing to interrupt the monotony except occasional French shells, none of which did any damage. Just how arduous this process was can be seen from an eloquent passage in the squadron war diary:

> From here until the end of the campaign the advance was notable for the appalling number of roadblocks, which were thicker and well-prepared, and for the increased danger of snipers – machine guns, cleverly concealed, covered the main road. The country was hilly and densely wooded and suitable for obstructions of every description. Huge tree trunks were felled at close intervals, and worried us particularly when the road passed through defiles in the large forests in the area. Each tree had to be dragged away by the armoured cars.

It was tedious and heavy work as men from each troop rested only after they had worked many hours, when the next troop would take over. The cars stood up to the work very well indeed but tow-ropes became a problem, as they often snapped and were scarce. However, the advance continued. Sometimes only three or four miles were covered in 24 hours.

At 0930 on 25 October 1942 Vos's cars passed through Ambohimahasoa and kept on going. At about 1300, however, the column had to halt while the sappers repaired a small bridge, and many soldiers made use of the down-time to bathe in the stream running underneath it.

This pleasant interlude ended abruptly on a rather farcical note: according to the squadron war diary there was "a burst of fire from a machine gun. Bullets spattered the water and the river-bank. In a couple of seconds naked forms were running everywhere; many askaris were dashing about in the nude carrying their rifles. It was one of the funniest incidents of the whole campaign and we were truly 'caught with our pants down'".

These were just about the last shots fired in anger, so to speak, because the drawn-out chase was now nearing its end. On 4 November, after another ten wearisome days, Monsieur Annet finally admitted defeat and requested a ceasefire. At 1230 Ambalavao was occupied by 22 East African Brigade's advance guard, and at 1400 the end of hostilities officially took effect, "exactly eight weeks from the day," as General Platt wrote in his report of the campaign, "and 660 miles from the place of landing at Majunga."

A detachment from A Squadron escorted the French General Officer Commanding and his staff to Antsirabe and started counting the days to departure. There were not many: on 19 November 1942 Vos was ordered to hand over his cars and equipment to 22 East African Brigade and move to Diego Suarez to take ship for South Africa.

Further praise for the South Africans' efforts came on 2 December 1942, just before their departure, when Brigadier Dimouline made a special flight to Diego Suarez from his headquarters at Tamatave for an informal farewell visit to the squadron. He praised its work and said that without the armoured cars' constant presence in the forward fighting elements from Majunga to Ambalavao, it would have been impossible to maintain the speed of the advance. With his praises ringing in its collective ear, A Squadron sailed for home next day in the *Nieuw Amsterdam*, along with 7 South African Infantry Brigade, and four days later disembarked at Durban.

Let the war diary have the last word on the campaign for Madagascar:

> During the eight weeks of the campaign the armoured cars had covered roughly 900 miles and had assisted to a great extent in destroying a force of about 6,000 men. Nearly 3,500 prisoners were taken and about 16 field guns; a considerable number of machine guns, mortars and large quantities of arms and ammunition were captured.
> Though our men in the leading cars were constantly vulnerable to the danger of being ambushed by cleverly concealed guns, and to rifle and machine-gun fire when clearing roadblocks and demolitions, our field casualties were surprisingly few. It was to be expected that malaria would be a great hindrance. The number of cases, in fact, amounted to 50 percent of the personnel, of which 40 percent occurred during the period of the operation. Other casualties totalled only six. The few casualties can be attributed to the remarkable quality of the armour-plating of the

vehicles, which time and again proved to be certain protection against small-arms fire, including .303-calibre armour-piercing, and almost complete protection against point-blank fire of the famous French 75mm and 65mm field guns. It should be recorded that direct hits with High-Explosive shells did no more serious damage than to stop the cars temporarily, cause small splits in the armour and inflict minor injuries to the crews.

Mechanically, the armoured cars surpassed all expectations. Besides normal repairs and adjustments, the most serious weakness was found to be the front wheel drive mechanism, and this fault might be assessed as a very doubtful one in view of the abnormal tractor work which was demanded of the cars.

Epilogue

During one of the early project discussions about this book, one member of the Armour Association told me, "Remember one thing: the history of South African armour is mainly about the armoured car."

It was a remarkably clear-sighted statement, especially since he had made his name as a tank commander during the 1987/88 fighting. But he was right. In many countries the armoured corps mostly emerged from the existing cavalry, but South Africa has never had much of a classic cavalry tradition, simply because there has never been much call for the traditional 'arme blanche' in African warfare. So its spiritual line of descent is from the mounted infantryman or dragoon of bygone days, and in both Abyssinia and the Western Desert the South African armoured cars earned a great and well-deserved reputation doing basically what their spiritual ancestors had done.

But times and tasks began to change during the earlier campaigns of World War II, and the armoured men changed with them, although they were always hampered by the fact that they were too lightly armed, thanks to the pre-war doctrine that the armoured car's main role was scouting. It started with the more or less *ad hoc* re-arming with scrounged weapons of heavier calibre; and one wonders what would have happened if 1 South African Division had been reformed as an armoured formation, as was mooted but never followed up on.

The next step in the development of South African armour – the transition to tanks – finally came about during the Italian Campaign, of course, and the Springbok tankers covered themselves in glory, even though they were fighting in terrain which was mostly inimical for heavy armour.

But that is a story for the next volume of the SAAC history, and it is a magnificent tale which is well worth telling, because for the first time the South African armour had the tools it needed. It is a safe guess, in fact, that readers of the next volume will be enthralled not just by the exploits of the armoured soldiers there but by other astonishing Defence Force's activities – something about which comparatively little is known.

Further revelations await down the line. One is the resurrection of the armoured car, this time armed with either a 90mm gun or a 60mm mortar, and its companion of the mechanised infantry, the Ratel-90, both serving as mobile fire-support bases or tank-killers, as the occasion demanded, during the Border War; and still later the re-appearance of South Africa's main tanks on the battlefield for the first time since World War II.

At the end of the day, however, the crucial quality remained the same, in spite of the era or the weaponry: the quality of the men inside the fighting vehicle concerned rather than the vehicle itself, and the evidence is that the SAAC, like its forerunners, has proved itself equal to the challenge.

Acknowledgements

A book of this nature does not happen in isolation. A great number of people need to be acknowledged and I must apologise in advance if anybody is omitted.

First and foremost we must acknowledge the untiring efforts of Lieutenant-General Jack Dutton, the first chairman of the Association, who set a goal for the newly established Armour Association to record the history of the South African Armour, in 1993. And to Brigadier-General Schalkwyk who took over from Brigadier General Toon Slabbert as chairman and established the Heritage Committee to further this aim.

Valuable work was done in preparing the manuscript for a printer by the chairman Major-General Marius van Graan. A special word of thanks must go to the GOCs SA Army Armour Formation, Brigadier-General Chris Gildenhuys and his successor Brigadier-General André Retief for their support, input and the resources that were made available.

Special thanks to Brigadier-General Andy Anderson, the senior researcher who put together the framework of the manuscript and to H.W. Short for his untiring editing under stressful conditions

Without the help of William Marshall, superb researcher and keeper of a magnificent cache of documents and photographs, and published author in his own right, this project would certainly have been delayed even further and vastly poorer without his contribution.

It would be remiss not to thank Miss Louise Jooste of the National Documentation Centre for making available her staff and the collections of the military archive.

Brigadier-Geneneral Fido Smit made a huge contribution by sharing his knowledge and his continued motivation and support. Colonel John French lent his specialist knowledge and countless anecdotes. Appreciation goes out to all the Black Beret committee of the Heritage Project and the countless unnamed contributors.

Lastly to Willem Steenkamp for stepping into the breach at a difficult junction and producing a quality manuscript.

Lieutenant-Colonel Heinrich Janzen
Chairman Heritage Committee
South Africa, 2016

Index

Index of Persons

Aitken, Major-General A. E. 71-72
Alexander, General Sir Harold 324-326, 328
Altrock, General von 85-86
Anderson, Brigadier-General M. B. 208, 215
Anderson, Lieutenant Craig 100, 106
Annet, Monsieur Gilbert 344, 349-350, 352
Aosta, Duke Amadeo of 103-104, 111-112, 122, 124, 129, 132, 136, 179, 181, 184, 186
Armstrong, Brigadier B.F. 114, 116, 132, 139, 143, 148, 240, 243-245, 250-255
Auchinleck, General Sir Claude 210, 223-224, 227-228, 263, 265, 288, 292, 294, 306, 314, 316-321, 323-324

Badoglio, Marshal Pietro 111, 129
Balbo, Marshal Italo 102-104, 111
Belfield, Governor Sir Henry Conway 70-71
Berrangé, Colonel C. A. L. 44-45, 47
Bertillo, General 197-199
Bester, Major Jack 152-154
Beves, Colonel (later Brigadier-General) P. S. 36, 38, 40, 43, 74
Birkby, Carel 93, 164, 184
Botha, Colonel Manie 38, 73
Botha, General Louis 35-39, 41-49, 51-53, 56, 70, 105
Brink, Major-General George E. 91, 93, 116, 120, 132, 136, 139, 141, 143-145, 147, 152, 157-158, 160-161, 172, 175, 181, 211, 224, 238-239, 250-251, 255-257, 259-260, 279, 292-295, 298, 302
Brits, Colonel Coen Brits 38, 42, 45, 53, 73, 75
Brodigan, Staff Sergeant R. M. 149-151
Brown, Lieutenant C. K. 199-200
Buchanan, Brigadier F. L. A. 116, 132, 138, 143, 157-158

Campbell, Brigadier Jock 254, 258, 265, 287
Chaffee, Adna 83-84
Churchill, Sir Winston 28-29, 31, 136, 183, 195, 210, 306, 324, 328, 341
Clark, Major W.P. 114-115, 126, 130, 187, 197-198, 201, 203
Crisp, R. J. 'Bob' 225-227, 233-234
Crowther, Major 239, 249, 257
Crüwell, Lieutenant-General Ludwig 224, 237, 244, 251, 266-267, 273, 277
Cunningham, Lieutenant-General Sir Alan 122, 124, 129-130, 136, 143-144, 148, 160-162, 165-166, 171-173, 175, 179, 181, 186-187, 197, 224, 226-228, 235, 237-238, 244, 255, 265

Dawson, Lieutenant-Colonel F. S. 55, 58-59
Dawson, Major 346-348
Degaga, Haile 141-142, 152, 154-155, 160
Delaney, Captain A.E. 139-140
Deventer, Colonel Jacob 'Jaap' Louis van 31, 38, 44, 46-47, 73-77
Dickinson, Major-General D. P. 103, 144
Digby, Captain Peter 59, 101
Dimouline, Brigadier W. A. 345, 349, 351-352
Dobbs, Lieutenant-Colonel John 147, 152-155
Dunning, Lieutenant J.B. John 119, 157, 198
Durrant, Major Jimmy 137, 143, 146, 158
Elliott, Captain G.A. 231-233
Engelbrecht, Lieutenant-Colonel C. L. 147, 158, 160

Farran, Major Roy 301-302, 312, 315
Ferguson, Major P. E. 273, 275, 283, 285, 304
Fiedler, Lieutenant Paul 38, 43, 51
Flint, Captain M.R. 281, 289-291
Fourie, Lieutenant F. C. van N. 243, 345
Fowkes, Brigadier C. C. 161, 171, 178, 197-201, 209-210, 231, 233
Franke, Colonel Victor 44, 49, 52-53
Freyberg, Major-General Bernard 224, 271
Fricker, Major E.G. 284-286, 325, 327
Fuller, J. F. C. 80, 85
Furstenburg, Lieutenant-Colonel J. P. A. 116, 206, 222, 235-236, 249, 251, 256-259, 292, 294

Gaafer Pasha 54, 57, 59-60
Gage, Lieutenant Jack 231-232
Gallimore, Lieutenant L. F. 199, 209, 301, 306
Gatehouse, Brigadier Alec 227, 261, 266, 277-278
Gaulle, Charles de 84, 112
Girdler-Brown, Captain G. 252, 325, 335-336
Godwin-Austen, Major-General A. R. 114-115, 120, 122, 124-126, 130, 144, 161, 163-169, 172, 174, 181, 189, 195, 224, 228, 238, 276-278
Gordon, Lieutenant N. W. 229, 244, 259, 282-283
Gott, Brigadier (later Lieutenant-/Major General) William 'Strafer' 195, 224, 226, 228, 235-236, 243-244, 251-253, 255, 269, 276-278, 285-286, 293-296, 306-308, 321, 324
Grant, Lieutenant-Colonel R. C. 40-41
Graziani, Marshal Rodolfo 104, 111, 113-114, 116, 122, 130, 151, 155, 174-175
Grimbeek, Lieutenant S. B. 348-349
Grobbelaar, Major (later Lieutenant-Colonel) P. H. 206, 209, 228-230, 236, 242-243, 248, 255, 259, 263-264, 288-289, 294
Guderian, Heinz 84-88
Gwillam, Major S. B. Sid 117, 120, 124, 126, 144, 162-163, 166, 168, 174-175, 182, 185, 222, 294, 325

Halliwell, Lieutenant P. E. B. 165-170
Hallowes, Staff Sergeant C. W. 148, 190
Hartshorn, Brigadier E. P. 'Scrubbs' 90-91, 124, 126, 128-130, 169, 171, 178, 182-183, 307-312, 325-327, 329
Heard, Lieutenant (later Captain) C. A. H. 120, 163-164, 198-199, 201-202, 222, 249, 257, 260-261
Heever, Captain A. P. G. van den 257, 260
Hertzog, General J. B. M. 36, 90, 95
Heydebreck, Colonel Joachim von 37-38, 40-42, 44, 69
Hitler, Adolf 87-88, 94, 119, 131, 175, 302, 332-333, 336, 344
Hobart, Major-General Percy 65, 80-82, 84, 94, 111, 292, 324
Horrocks, Lieutenant-General Brian 329, 331
Hoskins, Major-General Reginald 75-76
Hoy, Colonel William 43, 45
Hugo, Lieutenant P 272, 332
Human, Lieutenant J. D. W. 150-151
Hutchings, Captain E. K. 257, 279-280

Irwin, Lieutenant (later Captain) Roy 139, 148-151, 188-189

Jackson, Air-Sergeant J. 150-151

Jenkins, Major R.D. 117, 160, 180, 221-222, 257-258, 265, 325

Kahn, Staff Sergeant A. 140-141
Kat-Ferreira, Lieutenant I. M. L. 98, 100, 106
Kenyon, Lieutenant D.T. 231-232
Kenyon, Lieutenant-Colonel A.J. 67, 113, 116, 118, 206
Kirby, Lieutenant-Colonel W. H. 148-149, 245-246, 250
Klein, Major Harry 95, 98-101, 107, 112-113, 115, 117-121, 125-126, 128-129, 132-135, 137-142, 144-156, 158-162, 164-168, 171-181, 183-191, 194-195, 198, 200, 202-203, 207, 209-210, 212, 215-219, 222, 231-233, 235-236, 239-240, 242, 246, 252-254, 256, 258-259, 262-264, 271-272, 274, 288, 290-291, 293-299, 301-304, 306, 309-311, 314, 316, 323, 325, 328, 330, 334, 342, 346-347, 349
Klerk, Lieutenant Billy 223, 299, 323
Klopper, Major-General H. B. Hendrik 293, 296, 305-312
Koenig, Major-General Marie Pierre 293-295, 300, 302
Kriegler, Lieutenant (later Lieutenant-Colonel) J.B. 88, 98

Labuschagne, Lieutenant G.J. 117, 121
Larmuth, Major Vic 253, 291, 299
Lawrence, Staff Sergeant H. J. 233, 246-247
Lettow-Vorbeck, Colonel Paul von 54, 69-74, 76-77, 92
Liddell Hart, Captain Basil 80, 84-85, 87
Lindsay, Major G.K. 80-81, 300
Looff, Commander Max 71-73
Loser, Lieutenant G.T. 117-118
Lukin, Brigadier-General Henry Timson 36-41, 44, 55, 58-61, 63, 212
Lumsden, Lieutenant-General Herbert Lumsden 329, 331, 334

MacNab, Lieutenant-Colonel 348-439
Marillac, Captain Guy de 188, 195-196, 240, 245, 279, 304
Maritz, Lieutenant-Colonel S. G. 37, 39, 41-42, 46
Marriott, Brigadier 275, 282, 284
Martel, Lieutenant-Colonel Giffard le Quesne 80, 82-83, 85
Mayne, Major-General A. G. O. M. 181, 183
McKenzie, Brigadier-General Sir Duncan 43-47
McMenamin, Lieutenant-Colonel J. G. 127, 130, 165
McMillan, Lieutenant-Colonel N.D. 136, 200
Meeser, Lieutenant R. D. 188, 196, 245, 304, 306, 313
Meinertzhagen, Captain Richard 76-77
Messervy, Major-General F. W. Frank 224, 289-291, 294-295, 298, 301
Metaxas, General Ioannis 119, 131, 155
Montgomery, Lieutenant-General Bernard Law 212, 324-332, 334, 336, 338-341, 344
Mussolini, Benito 96, 102, 104, 112, 114, 119, 129, 131, 179, 184, 336, 344

Nasi, General 231, 233
Nauhaus, Captain (later Lieutenant-Colonel) G.N. 98, 302, 309-311
Neame, Lieutenant-General Philip 155, 175
Neumann-Silkow, Major-General Walter 210, 265-267
Newton-King, Lieutenant-Colonel D. S. 209, 218, 220,

235, 240, 249, 252, 258-259, 269-271, 274, 290-291, 294, 298, 300, 306, 313-316, 325-326, 334
Niekerk, Lieutenant A van 241, 252
Norrie, Lieutenant-General Willoughby 224, 227-228, 239, 248, 250-251, 267, 272-273

O'Connor, Lieutenant-General Richard 111, 116, 122, 151, 155, 175
Ollemans, Major D. H. 252-253
Orpen, Neil 91-92, 96, 104, 107, 112, 120, 123, 127, 129-130, 134, 136-138, 144, 165, 169, 171-174, 194, 202, 208
Osmond, Lieutenant C. D. F. 262, 268
Owen Brigadier W. 120, 196

Patton, George S. 65-66, 83-84
Paulus, Lieutenant-General Friedrich 194-195
Penny, Lieutenant W.H. 139, 141, 195, 246, 253, 322
Peyton, Major-General W. E. 57-58, 60-61
Pienaar, Brigadier Dan 53, 78, 114, 120, 124, 126-127, 130, 143, 161, 164-169, 172-174, 176-178, 181-182, 184, 186, 239, 249-251, 253, 256-257, 259-261, 265, 267, 272, 277, 292-293, 303, 308, 317, 325, 331, 342
Pirow, Oswald 90-96, 107, 120, 344
Platt, Lieutenant-General Sir William 345-350, 352
Poole, Major W. H. Evered 91, 96, 98, 292, 330

Ramsden, Major-General W. R. 293, 304, 319
Ravenstein, Major-General Johann von 265-267, 274
Rees, Lieutenant E. J. W. 159, 190-193, 195
Reeves-Moore, Major (later Lieutenant-Colonel) Robert 216-218, 220, 237, 241, 316, 322-323, 325, 328, 330, 334, 336-338, 340-341
Reid, Brigadier D. W. 228-231, 236, 242-244, 247-248, 255, 259, 262-264, 275, 280-284, 286, 288-289, 291
Richards, Brigadier C. E. M. 124, 126, 133, 161, 189-190, 194-195
Riebeeck, Jan van 28, 38
Ritchie, Lieutenant-General Neil 263, 265, 267-269, 272-274, 276, 288, 293-295, 303, 306-309, 311, 313-314
Ritter, Major von 46, 49-51, 53
Rommel, General Erwin 83, 175, 179, 183, 194-195, 210, 220-221, 224, 226-228, 230, 235-236, 238, 242-244, 246, 248-249, 251, 254, 256-258, 260, 262-263, 265-268, 270-279, 282, 286-287, 289-294, 296, 298-309, 312-321, 325-329, 331-333, 336-337, 339-342, 344, 346
Roodt, Lieutenant-Colonel G.K. 116, 132, 209, 222, 294-297, 302, 309
Roux, Lieutenant-Colonel Gordon le 169-170
Ryneveld, Lieutenant-Colonel Sir Pierre van 60, 78, 88, 96

Saunders, Captain (later major) C. A. C. 147, 198, 222
Scheele, Lieutenant Alexander von 37-38, 43, 49-51
Scobie, Major-General Ronald 224, 228, 238, 243-244, 249, 265-267Villiers, Major-General I. P. de 211, 228, 287, 293, 307
Selassie, Emperor Haile 179-180
Senescall, Lieutenant-Colonel (Later Brigadier) G. T. 124-125, 345
Sheppard, Brigadier-General H. S 74, 76
Short, Lieutenant-Colonel V. C. B. O'Brian 106, 209, 222, 228, 236, 242-244, 247-248, 259, 262-263, 280-286, 288, 290, 295, 305-306, 322, 325

Skinner, Colonel P. C. B. 44, 48-50
Smallwood, Major-General C. E. T. 345, 351
Smuts, General Jan 35-36, 39, 42, 45-46, 48, 73-76, 90, 93, 95-96, 101-102, 136, 182, 293, 344
Smuts, Lieutenant M.M. 264, 282, 286, 289
Souter, Lieutenant-Colonel H. M. W. 58-60
Spee, Admiral Maximilian von 36-37, 42
Stander, Major C.L. 117, 120, 132, 155-156, 222
Stewart, Brigadier-General J. M. 71, 74
Steyn, Lieutenant (later Major) L.S. 165, 222
Stumme, General Georg 328, 332
Styles, Captain 190-193

Tanner, Lieutenant-Colonel W.E.C. 55, 57
Thackeray, Lieutenant-Colonel E. F. 55, 58-59
Thoma, Major-General Wilhelm Ritter von 332-333, 336
Thompson, Lieutenant A. W. 149-150, 160, 187, 272
Toit, Major Abraham du 330-331
Toit, Major D. S. du 107, 111, 171
Torr, Captain E. H. 188-189, 195, 222, 239-240, 243, 245, 252, 254, 265, 303-304
Tritton, William 53, 63, 66

Vos, Major F. W. G. 345-352

Wahl, Lieutenant J. J. (Jan) 290-291, 296
Walker, Major C.G. 117-118, 136-139, 158, 186, 198, 203, 222
Wallace, Major-General A. 55-57
Wavell, General Sir Archibald 103, 116, 122-124, 130, 136, 141, 143, 148, 155, 161, 171-172, 175, 183, 194-195, 210, 223
Westminster, Major the Duke of 57-58, 61, 212
Wet, Andries de 38, 42
Wetherall, Major-General H. E. de R. 120, 161-162, 172, 174, 177-178, 181-182, 197-198, 203, 209, 231
Whiteley, Lieutenant W. J. 272-273
Whitley, Major R. 218, 270
Whittall, Lieutenant-Commander W. 48, 50, 52-53, 61
Williamson, Lieutenant L. G. 147-148, 153, 155-156
Willison, Brigadier A.C. 302, 308
Willoughby, Major Sir John 73-75
Wood, Second-Lieutenant D. A. 157-158

Young, Lieutenant Guy 218, 323

Index of Places

Abyssinia 5, 20-21, 53, 77, 89, 92-94, 96, 100, 102-104, 109, 111, 113-114, 117-118, 120-123, 127-128, 133-136, 141-146, 156-157, 160-161, 166, 170-172, 174-176, 179-180, 182, 184-185, 188, 190, 195-196, 199, 203, 207-209, 211, 213, 215, 221, 226, 231, 255, 294, 325, 339
Acroma 269, 271-273, 277, 301, 303, 306, 308
Addis Ababa 5, 102, 107, 112, 115, 123, 130, 157, 160-161, 166, 172-182, 184, 186-187, 194, 197-198, 221, 231
Afmadu 129, 161-164, 182
Ain en Naga 281-282
Ajedabia 282, 286
Alam el Halfa ridge 321, 327-328
Alem Hamza 276-277
Alexandria 22, 56-57, 61, 103-104, 183, 194, 212, 214-215, 222, 314, 317, 323, 325, 327, 330

Alghe 187-189
Amba Alagi 5, 128, 179, 181-184, 186, 195, 231
Amba Giorgis 231-232
Amiriya 288, 306, 313, 323
Antelat 275, 282-283, 291, 341
Aqqaqir 334-337
Arandis 49-50
Arbo Wells 114-116, 121
Aujila 228, 242-244, 247-248, 255
Awasa (Lake) 186, 201
Awash river 177-178, 180, 198

Bab el Qattara 317-318, 323
Banno 133, 150, 152-156, 180
Barberton 20, 103, 109, 114
Barce 279-280, 283-284, 287, 341
Bardera 130, 174
Bardia 151, 227-228, 236, 238, 250-251, 265-266, 272-273, 287, 309, 340
Beda Fomm 151, 211, 283
Belhamed 268, 271, 273
Benghazi 5, 22, 122, 212, 242, 261, 273, 276, 278, 282-287, 291, 332, 335, 337, 339, 341-342
Betsiboka 346, 348-349
Bir bu Fettah 283-286
Bir Duedar 240, 243-244, 249
Bir el Augerin 60-61
Bir el Chleta 251, 266
Bir el Duadar 236, 240
Bir el Gubi 237-240, 242-243, 246, 249-250, 262, 272-273, 275, 296, 299, 306, 308, 340
Bir el Haiad 243
Bir el Haleizin 241-242
Bir el Khalda 315, 338-339
Bir er Reghem 241, 269
Bir Hacheim 270, 301
Bir Haiad 243
Bir Hakeim 229-230, 249, 273, 275, 292-296, 298-300, 302-303
Bir Halegh el-Eleba 278
Bir Sheferzen 260, 277
Bloemfontein 19, 32-33, 45
Bole 20, 177, 198-199
British El Wak 115, 124-125
British Somaliland 102-103, 112, 114-115, 123, 130, 171, 174, 197-198, 203
Brown Hut Hill 188-189
Bu Etla 244, 248
Bukoba 69, 72
Buna 134, 144

Cairo 22, 155, 175, 181, 211, 214, 223, 225, 234, 265, 268, 271, 289, 293, 302, 316-317, 322-324, 327, 341
Cape of Good Hope 27-28, 183
Cape Town 19, 31, 42-44, 55, 81, 83, 92, 106, 207-208, 331, 337-338
Carassu, Mount 183-184
Charruba 281-282
China 70, 94
Combolcia Pass 181-182
Combolcia 181-183
Cullinan 105-106, 116
Cyrenaica 56, 151, 155, 195, 263

Daba 56, 319, 334
Dalle 195, 201

Dar es Salaam 69, 71-73, 75-76
Deir el Abyad 317-319
Deir el Shein 318-321
Delville Wood 63, 167
Derna 21, 151, 195, 231, 233, 239, 241, 279-280, 290, 300, 308-310
Dessie 128, 179, 181-184, 231-232
Dida Galgalla 123, 132, 135-136, 143
Didaba river 199-200
Diredawa 176-177, 197
Djibouti 102, 112, 123, 174, 176
Doolow 166, 174
Driana 284, 286
Dukana 132, 135, 137, 143
Durban 92, 114, 116, 208, 222, 345, 352

East Africa 5, 19-21, 48, 53-54, 68-69, 71, 73, 75-77, 96, 99-100, 103, 105-107, 111-113, 116-117, 119-123, 127, 129-130, 136, 139, 144-145, 171-174, 176-181, 186, 190, 196, 198, 200, 203, 209, 211, 213, 215-216, 224, 231, 233, 344-345
Eastern Transvaal 21, 114, 215
Ed Duda 243, 249, 265-266, 268, 273
Edoar Nebbia 338
Egypt 22, 48, 54-57, 61, 94, 102-104, 111, 114, 116, 122, 133, 155, 172, 179, 181, 185, 195, 208, 210-211, 214-215, 221-222, 225-227, 288, 314, 327, 332
El Abiar 282, 341
El Adem 237-238, 242-243, 269, 272, 274, 277, 290, 303, 306, 308-309, 339-340
El Agheila 155, 175, 279, 284, 287, 289, 293
El Alamein 5, 211-212, 292, 312-320, 322-325, 327-330, 332, 338-340, 342, 344, 346
El Beida 260, 313-314
El Beru Hagia 125-127
El Cuasc 236, 239
El Daba 56, 319
El Gubi 237-240, 242-243, 246, 249-250, 262, 269, 272-273, 275, 296, 299, 306, 308, 340
El Gumu 20, 134, 137, 143-144, 147-148, 150, 152, 157, 180
El Haseia 278, 287
El Haseiat 275, 287
El Sod 157-159
El Wak 5, 115-116, 121-122, 124-132, 135, 144, 161-163
Eritrea 96, 102, 104, 114, 128, 179, 184, 211, 231
Ethiopia 104
Etosha Pan 53, 88

Falla river 194, 197
Fort Capuzzo 116, 122, 195, 210-211, 216, 227, 237-238, 240, 250-251, 265-266, 268, 270, 272-273, 338-340
Fort Maddalena 21, 211, 220, 227, 231, 235-236, 305-306, 314
French Somaliland 102, 112-113
Fuka 314-315, 336, 339-340

Gabr Saleh 236-237
Galla Sidamo 141, 152, 179, 181
Gallipoli 48
Garissa 117-118, 120, 132, 162
Gasr el Arid 244, 273
Gazala 5, 22, 269-271, 274-279, 290-296, 298-299, 301-303, 306-308, 314, 337, 342

Gelib 161-162, 167-173
Gianciaro 143, 148, 152-153, 157
Giarso 155, 187
Giof el Matar 264, 275, 280-282, 286, 288
Giumbo 161-162, 165, 167-169
Gobwen 162, 164-169
Gojjam 104, 113, 141, 179
Gold Coast, 105, 114-115, 120, 124, 126, 129, 133, 161-164, 166, 168-169, 171, 174, 186, 188-193, 195, 201
Gondar 128, 209, 231-233
Gorai 134, 143-145, 147-150, 180
Great Sand Sea, 212, 242
Greece 119, 131, 155, 179, 197, 225-226
Gundile mountains, 141, 153

Habaswein 116, 121
Hadu mountain 142, 152, 154, 160, 194
Hagadera 117, 119
Haggag es Sallum 58, 60
Halfaya 61, 122, 195, 210, 228, 251, 262-263, 265, 268-269, 287-288, 308, 339-340
Halfaya Pass 61, 122, 195, 210, 263, 268-269, 340
Haseiat 275, 280-281, 287
Helwan 322-323, 325
Hergeisa 114, 198, 203
Hobok 133-134, 138, 143-144, 148-152, 180
Homsdrift 39-40
Horn of Africa, 102-103
Hula 190, 192, 194

India 27, 55, 69, 71-75, 79, 81, 92, 102, 109, 121-122, 179, 181, 183-184, 217, 224, 228, 243, 250, 256, 259, 262-264, 268, 273, 276-280, 286-287, 289-290, 293, 305, 307, 309-310, 313, 315, 317-320, 322-323, 328, 338
Indian Ocean, 69, 71-72, 102, 121
Iraq 55, 318, 324
Italy 20-22, 27, 33-34, 54, 91-93, 96, 99, 100, 102-104, 106-107, 109, 111-117, 119, 121-130, 132, 134-138, 141-152, 154-161, 164-184, 187-194, 197, 199-203, 208-211, 213, 216, 218, 222, 224, 226-227, 229, 231-233, 238, 242, 246, 248, 251, 255, 259, 262, 264, 269-270, 272-278, 281, 283-285, 287, 292, 298-299, 302-305, 308, 317-321, 325, 330-332, 336-338, 340-341, 344
Italian El Wak 115, 124-126
Italian Somaliland 102, 115, 117, 122-123, 130, 135, 144, 160-161, 165-166, 171-172, 175, 325

Jakkalswater 45-46
Jalo 228, 230-231, 236, 242, 247, 255, 259, 262-264, 275, 280-281
Jarabub 217, 222, 227-231, 236, 264, 294
Jarabub Oasis 222, 227, 294
Jebel Kalakh 329, 331
Jijiga 130, 174-175, 198
Jikheira 248, 255, 259
Jimma 179, 181, 187, 194, 196, 209-210, 221, 231
Juba River, 20, 102, 122, 124, 130, 135, 143-144, 161-162, 164-168, 171-173, 179

Kalacha Wells 134, 136
Kalahari 42, 45
Kalkfontein 37, 39-41, 45
Karasburg 37, 39

Karibib 37, 44-45, 48, 51
Keetmanshoop 39-40, 43, 45, 47
Kenya 69-70, 96, 102-103, 106, 111-113, 115, 117,
121, 123, 130, 134, 136, 138, 144-145, 160, 162, 172,
180, 187, 198, 233, 325, 346
Keren 104, 179, 181
Khamsin Wind, 212-213, 324
Khedive 54, 61
Kilimanjaro, Mount 69-71, 74, 76
Kimberley 32, 44, 50
Kismayu 102, 122-124, 130, 135-136, 144, 160-162,
164-166, 171-172
Kondoa Irangi 75-77
Kopje 38, 41, 145
Kraaipan 19, 30-31

Liboi 117-118, 135, 163, 173
Libya 21-22, 54, 96, 102, 111, 114, 116, 122, 151, 155,
183, 214, 224-225, 228, 231, 233, 241, 265, 273, 278,
298-299, 337, 341
Lokitaung 143, 188, 196
Lüderitzbucht 36-37, 40, 42-43, 46, 56, 105

Mabungo 168, 172
Madagascar 5, 92, 207-208, 343-347, 349, 352
Magado 188-189
Maji 186, 196
Majunga 344, 346-347, 349, 352
Maktila 58, 116
Marda Pass 174-175
Margherita 168-169, 172, 186, 201
Marsabit 121, 123, 132, 134-135, 141-143, 152
Martuba 175, 279, 300, 341
Massawa 102, 128, 179, 181, 185, 195, 197, 221, 232-
233
Matruh Stakes 256, 263
Mediterranean, 22, 102, 116, 136, 183, 269, 292, 336
Mega 5, 20, 123, 134, 143, 145, 152, 155-160, 186-187,
189, 198
Menastir 266, 272
Mersa Matruh 56-58, 60, 103-104, 116, 211-212, 227,
277, 313-315, 317, 338-340
Mesopotamia 55, 79
Middle East 27, 48, 53-54, 61, 65, 94, 99, 102-103,
106, 109, 119, 122, 174-175, 179, 187, 189, 195, 197,
199, 206, 211-212, 216, 218, 222, 231-233, 317, 324,
327, 330, 336, 342, 344
Miteirya Ridge 319-321, 329, 331-332
Mitiburi 117, 119, 121
Mogadishu 102, 107, 123, 161, 166, 169-174, 178-180
Mombasa 69-71, 106, 114, 116-117, 122-123, 185, 196,
198, 232, 345-347
Mount Kilimanjaro 69-70
Mozambique 77, 102
Mrassas 296, 303-304
Msus 286-288, 290-291, 341

Nagb Medean Pass 60-61
Nairobi 69-70, 106-107, 114, 117, 128, 188-189, 194-
195
Nakop 38-39
Namibia 28-29, 34, 52, 107
Nanyuki 115, 121, 134, 160, 163, 180, 187-188, 198
Naq Abu Dweis 317
Natal 21-22, 30-31, 40, 47, 55, 125, 128, 136-138, 144,
156, 165-166, 168, 176, 186, 197-201, 203, 206-207,
326, 331
Neghelli 123, 146, 157, 159-160, 166, 174, 186, 188-
189, 195, 197, 201
New Zealand 35, 55, 109, 224, 238, 250-251, 254, 256,
262, 265-268, 271-272, 276-277, 313, 315, 317-320,
322, 328-329, 331-332, 337-340
Nile Delta 316-317, 321-322
Northern Frontier District, 113, 115, 121, 123, 132,
134
Northern Rhodesia 77, 187

Omo River, 181, 203, 209
Orange Free State, 32, 55, 96
Orange River, 28, 37

Palestine 96, 109, 317
Pforte 45-46
Point 175 242, 248, 267-268
Point 204 276-277, 319
Portugal 20, 27-28, 77, 102-103, 209
Pretoria 20, 31, 39, 42, 48, 78, 93, 98, 106, 118

Qattara Depression, 212, 228-229, 313, 316-317, 322

Ramansdrift 37, 39-41
Red Sea 102, 136
Rhodesia 44, 49, 55, 73-77, 109-110, 187, 298
Riet 45-46
Rome 104, 113, 129-131, 179, 242, 250, 332
Rotonda Mteifel 275-276
Ruweisat Ridge 317-320

Salaita Hill 73-74
Sallum 56, 58, 60-61, 116, 183, 195, 210, 212, 214,
220, 227, 235, 250-251, 266, 272-273, 287-289, 291,
339
Sand Sea, 212, 214, 217, 227-228, 242, 338
Sandfontein 39-41
Saunnu 283-284, 289
Sceleidima 282-283, 286
Sciasciamana 187, 197, 199-202
Seeheim 37, 45
Segnali 294, 297, 300
Sidi Azeiz 210, 237-238, 262, 265-266, 340
Sidi Barrani 56, 58, 60, 116, 291, 314, 339-340
Sidi Bishr 323, 325
Sidi Haneish 336, 338-339
Sidi Omar 220, 227-228, 250-251, 256, 262, 265-266
Sidi Rezegh 231, 236-246, 249-252, 254-256, 266-268,
306, 340
Singapore 90, 109, 344
Siwa oasis 58, 214, 222, 338
Soddu 187, 194-195, 201-203, 209
Sololo Hill 139-141
Somaliland 5, 102-103, 112-115, 117, 122-123, 130,
135, 144, 160-163, 165-166, 171-172, 174-175, 178,
197-198, 203, 325
Somme, 63-66
South West Africa 5, 8, 19, 29, 34-38, 41-42, 45, 48-49,
51-57, 61, 67-70, 73-74, 79, 81, 88, 93, 96, 101, 107
Sub-Saharan Africa 48, 68
Sudan 102-104, 114, 122, 128, 130, 231
Suez Canal 54, 102, 122, 288, 344
Sugarloaf Hill 137-138
Swakop River 45, 48, 51
Swakop 45, 48, 51

Swakopmund 36-37, 39, 42, 44-46, 48, 50, 105

Taieb el Esem 256, 260-262, 265, 272
Taieb el Essem 260-261
Tamatave 344, 346, 349-350, 352
Tana (Lake) 120, 122, 124, 141, 231-232
Tananarive 346, 349-350
Tanga 69-72, 76
Tanganyika 54, 69-71, 74, 76-77
Tanzania 54, 69
Tel el Eisa 319-321
Tel el Makh Khad 319, 321
Tengeder 230, 291, 297
Thalata 220, 306
Tmimi 269-270, 276, 278-279, 290-291, 341
Tobruk 91, 151, 178, 183, 194-195, 210-212, 220, 224,
    227-229, 235, 237-240, 243-244, 249, 251, 255-256,
    261, 265-267, 269, 271-275, 287, 289-290, 292-297,
    301-313, 317, 323, 332, 339-341
Trekkopjes 48-53, 57
Trigh el Abd 235-236, 270
Trigh 235-236, 238, 240, 251, 268, 270
Tripoli 34, 278
Tsumeb 37, 51
Turbi Hills, 132, 135-136, 139
Turbi 132, 135-136, 139-140
Turkana (Lake) 121, 123, 134, 186

Uaddara 145, 188-190, 192
Uganda 69-73, 96, 102, 113
Uondo 193-194
Upington 37-38, 41-42, 44-46
Usakos 45, 49, 52

Vichy France 112-114, 207, 344-345, 348-350
Voortrekkerhoogte 78, 116

Wadi Faregh 281, 287-288
Wajir 121, 123-125, 128, 130, 144, 162-164, 187
Walvis Bay 19, 40, 44-45, 51
Warmbad 39, 41
Windhoek 34, 36-37, 45, 47-48, 51, 88
Witwatersrand 39, 91
Wolchefit 231-232

Yavello 154-155
Yavelo Plain, 142, 154
Yavelo 142-143, 146, 150, 152, 154-158, 160, 187-189
Yonte 5, 165-169, 173
Ypres 73, 81

Ziway (Lake) 186, 198-199
Zonderwater 106, 114

Index of Military Formations
Allied

Indian Army 55, 81
Union Defence Force 46, 67, 78-80, 88, 90-96, 98-101,
    106-109, 114, 116, 128, 135, 144, 146

Eighth Army 217, 223-228, 231, 236, 245, 249, 256,
    258, 261, 264-267, 269, 271, 273-276, 278, 287, 290-
    294, 296, 298-302, 306-308, 311-317, 319, 321, 323-
    325, 327-328, 330, 339-340

XIII Corps 175, 224, 228, 236, 238, 244-245, 249, 256,
    268, 276, 306, 313-314, 318-319, 329
XXX Corps 224, 227-228, 236, 244, 250-251, 256,
    258, 265, 267, 271, 273, 276, 314, 319, 321, 329,
    331-332, 340, 342

1 (1st) South African Division 105, 116, 132, 135, 139,
    141, 143-145, 148, 156, 160, 172, 180-181, 185-188,
    211, 217, 224, 228, 235-239, 243, 246, 249, 255-256,
    258, 292-294, 299, 302-304, 307-309, 316-319, 321-
    322, 327, 329-330, 337, 341-342
1 Armoured Division 289-292, 313, 317-319, 329-330,
    332, 335, 338-339
1st Division 74-76
2nd Division 74-75
2 New Zealand Division 224, 238, 251, 262, 266-268,
    271, 313, 315, 317-318, 322, 329, 331-332, 338-339
2 (2nd) South African Division 211, 217, 224, 228-
    229, 235, 269, 276, 287-289, 291, 293-294, 302-303,
    305, 307-308, 311, 340
4 Indian Division 122, 224, 263, 276, 278, 286-287,
    289-290
5 Indian Division 181, 183, 313, 319, 322
6 South African Armoured Division 91, 208
7 (7th) Armoured Division (The Desert Rats) 111,
    116, 151, 183, 194-195, 210, 217-218, 224, 227-228,
    235, 238-239, 243-244, 246, 249, 251-252, 255, 260,
    267-268, 270-271, 274, 276-278, 281, 285, 289, 292,
    294-295, 298, 305, 313, 315, 317, 321-323, 329, 331,
    338, 340-341
7 Armoured Division Support Group 237, 239, 243,
    246, 254, 258, 261, 265, 275, 281, 283, 286-287
9 Australian Division 224, 317, 319, 329, 331
10 Indian Infantry Division 313, 318
10 Armoured Division 331-332, 338-339
11 African Division 105, 120, 135, 144, 161-162, 171-
    172, 174, 181, 186-187, 194, 197, 203, 209
12 (12th) African Division 105, 114, 120, 124, 130,
    135, 144, 161-162, 164, 166-167, 170-172, 174, 181,
    186-188, 190, 195, 197-198, 203, 231-232
50 Division 293-295, 299, 301, 303-306, 308, 313, 318
51 Highland Division 329, 331, 337
70 British Infantry Division 224, 228, 238, 243, 266-
    267, 271, 273

1 Army Tank Brigade 224, 308
1 Free French Brigade 293-295
1 Mounted Brigade 73-74, 206
1 (1st) South African Brigade (Pincol) 53, 55-556, 61,
    63, 65, 67, 101, 105-106, 114, 120-121, 124, 135-136,
    143-144, 160-169, 172-178, 181-183, 185, 197, 236,
    239, 249-251, 253-254, 256-258, 260-261, 265, 267-
    268, 271-272, 277, 280, 287, 292, 303, 326, 330-331
2 Armoured Brigade 320-321
2 South African Brigade 116, 132, 135-136, 138, 143,
    147, 152, 157, 159, 161-162, 185, 197, 224, 292, 322
3 Infantry Brigade 44, 48, 307
4 Armoured Brigade 227-228, 235, 237-238, 243, 266-
    268, 273-274, 276, 278, 294, 306, 313, 318
4 Light Armoured Brigade 321, 329, 331, 340-341
4 New Zealand Brigade 251, 265-266
4 South African Brigade 293, 305, 307-309, 311
5 (5th) South African Brigade 114, 116, 120, 132, 135-
    136, 143, 147-148, 155, 157, 160, 185, 236, 239-240,
    243-245, 250-256, 284

5 Indian Brigade 276-277, 279-280, 320, 338
5 New Zealand Brigade 250-251, 265-266, 272, 276-277, 340
6 (6th) South African Brigade 293, 305, 307-311
6 New Zealand Brigade 251, 254, 265-266, 268, 320
7 Armoured Brigade 235-238, 240-241, 243, 246, 249
7 Indian Brigade 250, 262, 268, 276-277, 286
7 Motor Brigade 298-299, 301, 313-314, 316, 319
7 South African Brigade 344-346, 352
7 South African Field Artillery Brigade 175-176
11 Indian Brigade 273, 305, 307, 309-310
12 Gold Coast Brigade 114-115
14 Infantry Brigade 273, 328
21 East African Brigade 161, 164, 187-189
22 (22nd) Armoured Brigade 235, 237-238, 240, 243, 246, 248-250, 252, 262, 266-268, 278, 284, 287, 313, 318, 320, 325, 329, 331, 334
22 (22nd) East African Brigade 120, 161, 163, 165, 169, 171-172, 175, 177-178, 194, 197-198, 209, 345-346, 352
22 Guards Brigade 195, 224, 240, 273, 275, 283-284, 287
23 Armoured Brigade 320-321
23 Nigerian Brigade 117, 120, 161, 171-172, 174-176, 186, 209-210
24 (24th) Gold Coast Brigade 115, 120, 124, 133, 161-164, 166, 169, 171, 174, 186, 188-189, 195, 201
24 Australian Brigade 320-321, 330
25 East African Brigade 143-144, 160, 188-189, 196, 232
26 Australian Brigade 319, 321
29 Brigade 345-347
29 Indian Infantry Brigade 228, 313, 315
32 Army Tank Brigade 224, 299, 302, 305, 307-309
69 Infantry Brigade 304, 321
161 Indian Infantry Brigade 319-320
201 Guards Brigade 305, 307, 309
East African Brigades (other) 120, 232
South African Railways and Harbours Brigades 206-207

1 Armoured Car Commando 206-207, 344-345
1 Field Force Battalion 152, 157, 186, 197, 199, 201, 208
1 Gold Coast Regiment 168, 190, 192-193
1 Rhodesia Regiment 44, 49
1 South African Infantry 55, 58-59
1/1 King's African Rifles 173, 346, 348
1/6 King's African Rifles 200-202, 232, 349
2 Field Force Battalion 116, 147, 157-158, 194, 208
2 Imperial Light Horse 43, 207
2 Regiment Botha 139-141, 143
2 South African Field Regiment 228, 280, 285
2 South African Infantry 55, 57, 60-61
3 (3rd) South African Armoured Car Reconnaissance Battalion 185, 207, 209, 216-217, 221-222, 235-236, 239-240, 249, 251-254, 257-259, 261-262, 272-273, 275, 279, 284, 287, 289, 294-295, 299, 301-304, 306, 313, 321, 323, 325, 330-332, 337, 342
3 Armoured Car Regiment 207, 328
3 Gold Coast Regiment 124, 126-127, 168, 190-191
3 Royal Tank regiment 225, 233, 278, 283
3 South African Infantry 55, 58-59
3/2 Punjabis 242, 244, 280-281, 286
4 (4th) South African Armoured Car Regiment 207, 209, 216-222, 235-238, 240-242, 246, 248-250, 252-254, 257-260, 265, 269-271, 271, 274, 276, 290-291, 294-295, 297-300, 306, 312-316, 321-323, 325, 327-328, 334
4/11 Sikh Regiment 276, 279
4/6 (4th/6th) South African Armoured Car Regiment 328, 330, 334-341
4/6 Punjab Rifles 279
5 (5th) King's African Rifles 165, 199, 209, 350
5 Armoured Car Regiment 207, 209
6 South African Armoured Car Regiment 207, 209, 217, 222, 228, 235-236, 244, 247, 263, 268, 272-273, 275, 277, 279-285, 287-288, 294-295, 299, 301-302, 304, 306, 309, 314-315, 321-323, 325-328, 330, 334-341
7 South African Armoured Car Reconnaissance Battalion 206-207, 209, 217, 228, 235, 243, 264, 281-282, 286-290, 294-297, 302, 307, 309, 311
8 Royal Tank Regiment 276, 331
9 Armoured Car Reconnaissance Battalion 207-208
9 Armoured Car Regiment 207-208
9 Armoured Commando 207-208
11th Hussars 116, 211, 214-218, 222, 235, 238, 268, 275, 282, 284, 286, 316, 323, 338, 341
12th Lancers 211, 215, 282, 294, 314
15th Sikh Regiment 55, 57
25 Field Regiment Royal Artillery 276-277
44 Royal Tank Regiment 319-320
Armoured Fighting Vehicle Regiments (various) 206-207
Cape Town Highlanders 55, 207-208, 331, 337-338
Central India Horse 263, 280, 283-285
Dorsetshire Yeomanry 55, 58-60
Duke of Edinburgh's Own Rifles (Dukes) 124, 127, 144, 165-166, 168-169, 173, 177, 182, 257, 260-261, 326, 345
Durham Light Infantry 304-305
East African Armoured Car Regiment 124, 145, 169, 172, 174, 176, 188, 190
Imperial Light Horse 40, 42-44, 47, 49-50, 206-207, 309, 312
Kimberley Regiment 44, 50
King's African Rifles 71, 74-75, 77, 135, 163-164, 166, 188-189, 196, 200-203, 210, 232-233, 345-351
King's Dragoon Guards 211, 214-216, 235, 259, 272-273, 275-277, 279, 281-288, 294, 299-300, 304
Mounted Regiments 206-207
Natal Mounted Riflemen 136-138, 156, 186, 197-201, 331
Punjabis 75, 242, 244, 247-248, 255, 259, 280-281, 284, 286
Rand Light Infantry 40, 42
Regiment President Steyn 91, 229, 260
Regiment Suidwestelike Distrikte 206-207
Regiment Westelike Provinsie 206-207
Royal Dragoons (The Royals) 214-215, 275, 278, 283-284, 316, 330, 334, 338, 341
Royal East Kent Regiment (The Buffs) 276-277
Royal Natal Carbineers 47, 125-128, 144, 165-171, 176-177, 206-207, 257, 260-261, 326
Royal Scots 55, 58
Royal Tank Regiment (other battalions) 101, 114, 116, 237, 268, 321
South African Irish 44, 147-148, 152-154, 156-157, 159
South African Mounted Riflemen 38-40, 44-45, 78, 90
Special Service Battalion 91-92, 95, 116, 207-208, 290

The Royals *see* Royal Dragoons
Transvaal Horse Artillery 39-40
Transvaal Scottish 40, 44, 50, 55, 79, 85, 101, 125-127, 139, 148-150, 159, 166-171, 175, 177, 184, 245, 250, 252, 254, 257, 260-261, 267

1 South African Field Battery 175-176, 202
1 South African Medium Battery 170, 176
4 South African Field Battery 247-248
10 Field Battery 127, 169
11 Field Battery 127, 169
Nottinghamshire Battery, Royal Horse Artillery 56-59

1 (No.1) South African Armoured Car Company 20-21, 100, 106, 117, 120, 123, 132-133, 136, 139, 141-143, 146-148, 150, 152, 155-157, 159, 161, 186-188, 190, 195-198, 209, 222
1 (No.1) South African Light Tank Company 106, 112, 114-115, 124, 126, 161-165, 168, 172, 175, 186-187, 197-198, 200, 203, 207, 209, 221, 232
1 South African Motorcycle Company 106, 117, 120, 134, 180, 207, 209, 222
No. 1 Company, 3 South African Reconnaissance Battalion 239, 253-254, 258, 265, 279-280, 284, 295, 303-304, 306, 313
2 (No.2) South African Armoured Car Company 106, 114, 116-117, 119-121, 124, 132, 135-136, 139, 146-147, 152, 157-159, 161, 163, 186, 194, 197-199, 203, 222
2 South African Motorcycle Company 106, 114, 117, 120, 132, 155-156, 160, 180, 207, 209, 222
3 South African Armoured Car Company 114, 117, 120-121, 124-126, 144, 161-167, 169, 174-175, 177, 179, 181-182, 185, 207
3 South African Motorcycle Company 106, 114
34 (Cape Town Highlanders) Armoured Car Company 207-208

Army Service Corps 73, 297
Royal Engineers 29, 31, 242, 290
Royal Flying Corps 38, 48, 76
Royal Horse Artillery 56, 81, 220, 241, 287
Royal Tank Corps 80-82, 101, 113
South African Armoured Corps 67, 92
South African Aviation Corps 38, 51, 60
South African Engineer Corps 125, 130, 165-167, 171, 209
South African Tank Corps (SATC-SATK)(*Suid-Afrikaanse Tenkkorps*) 67, 98, 100, 106, 109, 113-114, 116-117, 135, 141, 161, 187, 203, 206, 208, 215, 218, 221-222, 231-233, 235, 271, 311, 345

A Force 36, 39, 41, 44
B Force 37, 39
Bencol 275, 282-284
C Force 36, 40, 42-43
Central Force 43, 45-47
Currie Column 287-288
Dickforce 124-126
Dobbs Force 152-153, 155-157
E Force 231, 236, 242, 244, 247, 263-264, 271, 275, 280-284, 286, 288-289, 291
Eastern Force 44-45, 47

Force B 71-72
Fowcol 197-199, 201-203
Mobile Force (Egypt) 81, 94, 111
Oasis Group 217, 222, 228, 230, 235
Pinforce 124-127, 130
Rydon Column 287-288
Shortcol 280-281, 286
Southern Force 44-46
Western Frontier Force 55, 57-58, 60-61
Wilson Column 279, 287

Armoured Fighting Vehicle School 113, 206
Armoured Fighting Vehicle Training Centre 113-114, 116, 206, 222
French Foreign Legion 249, 294, 302
Imperial Service Units 55, 96, 101
Light Aid Detachments 133, 148-149, 232-233, 262, 288, 345
Light Armoured Detachment 231, 233
Long Range Desert Group 212, 281-282
Mechanical Transport Section 78, 88
Polish forces 109, 224, 256, 277, 295
Shifta 135-136, 141-142, 144, 152, 154-156, 160, 179, 181, 186, 189, 194-195, 232

Royal Air Force 94, 103, 111, 122, 171, 183, 228-230, 249, 287, 292-293, 301, 316, 318-319, 338
South African Air Force 60, 78, 88, 91-92, 94, 96, 106-107, 111, 127, 137, 142, 146, 151, 161, 164, 166, 171, 178, 186-187, 208-209, 292, 338, 345, 350
7th Desert Air Force 228, 235, 256, 262, 267, 309, 319, 332
No. 26 South Africa Squadron 74, 76
No. 40 Squadron South African Air Force 127, 137-138, 143, 146-147, 149-150, 152-153, 158

Royal Navy 29, 42, 48, 56, 60, 69, 71-72, 77, 104, 116, 136, 162, 293, 345
Royal Naval Air Service (RNAS) 29, 40-41, 45, 47-49, 51, 56-57, 71, 73, 75

Axis

Wehrmacht 87, 93, 195
Oberkommando der Wehrmacht 194, 327

German-Italian Panzer Army 332, 340
Panzer Army Africa 321, 328
Panzergruppe Afrika (Panzer Group Africa) 224, 283, 305, 312
Tenth Army 151, 155

Deutsches Afrikakorps 175, 212, 214, 220-221, 224, 236, 251, 256, 262, 266, 273-274, 276-278, 287, 318, 327, 332-333, 346
X Mobile Corps (10 Motorized Corps) 224, 251, 273-274, 299, 313, 327, 329, 331, 335, 338
XXI Corps 274

15 Panzer Division 210, 224, 237-238, 244, 252, 262, 265-268, 271, 273-274, 278, 303, 317-320, 330, 332, 334
17 (Pavia) Infantry Division 224, 238, 242, 249, 266, 320, 331
21 Colonial Division 134-135, 201
21 Italian Division 194, 203

21 Panzer Division 220, 224, 227, 237-238, 244, 246, 260, 262, 265-268, 274, 300, 303, 315, 317-318, 320, 329, 338
25 (Bologna) Infantry Division 203, 224, 238, 337
55 (Savona) Infantry Division 224, 227, 250
90 Light Division 224, 238, 244, 300, 315, 317-318, 320, 334-335
101 (Trieste) Motorized Division 173, 203, 224, 252, 266, 276, 300, 319-320
102 (Trento) Motorized Infantry Division 224, 320, 336-337
132 (Ariete) Armoured Division 224, 229-230, 238-239, 243, 251-252, 256, 260, 262, 265, 267-268, 273, 277, 300, 318-320, 329, 336-337
Brescia Division 224, 277, 319-320, 331, 337
Littorio Division 318, 332

5 Panzer Regiment 262, 276
8 Panzer Regiment 276, 320
61 Colonial Infantry Regiment 187
115 Infantry Regiment 265-266
191 Colonial Infantry Regiment 124

94th Italian Colonial Infantry 164

Banda 103, 107, 115-117, 119, 124-126, 129, 134-140, 147-150, 156, 158, 161, 163-164, 198
Blackshirts 156, 160, 177, 189-190
Free Corps 38, 42
Schutztruppe 37, 44-47, 49, 53, 69, 72, 77

Luftwaffe 179, 195, 215, 223, 228, 242, 288, 309
Regia Aeronautica (Italian Air Force) 171, 222, 228, 309

Index of General & Miscellaneous Terms

1914 Rebellion, 34, 36, 67

Abyssinian Campaign, 20, 91, 93, 99, 102, 107, 116, 133, 145, 163, 175, 183, 191, 203, 206-207, 325
Armoured Cars 5, 19-21, 29, 32, 34-35, 47-52, 54, 56-61, 63, 65, 69, 73-75, 77, 79-80, 88-89, 93-95, 99-101, 105-109, 111-113, 117-119, 121, 123, 125-128, 132-133, 135-156, 158-159, 162, 164-165, 167-171, 174-176, 178-180, 182, 187-196, 199, 201-203, 208, 210-211, 214-221, 223, 228-230, 233, 235-242, 244-246, 248, 252-253, 255-266, 270-271, 274, 277-285, 287-291, 294-295, 297-304, 306, 309-311, 313, 316, 320-323, 325, 327-328, 330-331, 334-338, 340-342, 345-353
Armoured Trains 19, 29-32, 34, 91
Askari 70, 72, 74, 76, 209, 347-351

Bab el Qattara Box 317-318, 323
Banda irregulars 103, 107, 115-117, 119, 124-126, 129, 134-140, 147-150, 156, 158, 161, 163-164, 198
Boers 19, 28-38, 43, 52, 70, 73-74, 77, 90
Boran tribe 123, 136, 141, 157

Gazala Line, 274-277, 279, 291-296, 298-299, 301-302, 306
Gharri Kifaru, rhinoceros' car 119, 139, 145, 168, 216

Ipumbu Revolt, 19, 81, 88

Lakes, Battle of the 133, 161, 175, 186, 203

Military Cross 67, 148, 151, 170, 234, 270, 296, 323, 325, 351

Operation Battleaxe 194-195, 210
Oxalic defensive line 329, 331-332, 334

Schutztruppe 37, 44-47, 49, 53, 69, 72, 77
Second Anglo-Boer War, 30, 32-35, 43, 70, 73
Shifta irregulars 135-136, 141-142, 144, 152, 154-156, 160, 179, 181, 186, 189, 194-195, 232
South West Africa Campaign, 5, 8, 34-35, 53-54, 56, 67-68, 73

Ten Year Rule 78, 89

U-boat 56, 290, 296

Vickers, Sons & Maxim Ltd 19-21, 33, 48, 50, 56, 61, 79-80, 82-84, 87-89, 95, 99, 105-106, 108-109, 112-113, 115, 118, 123, 125, 127-129, 133, 136-139, 147-148, 150, 167, 170, 178, 189, 193, 200, 208, 214-215, 217, 223, 232, 247-248, 255, 259, 263, 291, 351

War Office 32-33, 69, 80, 99, 108

Donors & Sponsors

It would have been impossible to get *The Black Beret* to this point without the financial contribution of many sponsors and donors. Chief among those were:

Mr Ben Jansen IAD
Major Roger Johnson (Ret) 2LHR
OMC Engineering
Denel.

To these members go our grateful thanks for making this book possible.